FLORIDA KEYS

LAURA MARTONE

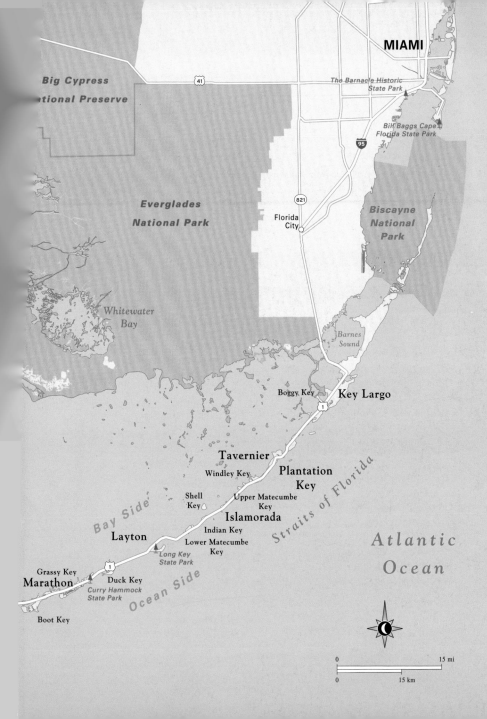

Contents

Discover the Florida Keys

Even those who have never ventured south of Disney World have probably heard of the Florida Keys. This diverse archipelago, which stretches southwest from Miami between the Atlantic Ocean and the Gulf of Mexico, is after all legendary.

With its Mardi Gras vibe, much-publicized Hemingway connection, and ongoing threat to secede from the Union, Key West is surely the most well-known island in the region. It certainly helps that this unique place offers an array of cultural and recreational diversions and nurtures a strange blend of hardy natives, eccentric artists, and wide-eyed tourists. But the Keys are more than just their southernmost city.

If you're driving from Miami or the Everglades – both vibrant areas worth a look before heading south – you'll first encounter Key Largo, the largest island in this enticing chain and a slowly burgeoning getaway town for southern Floridians. It's the kind of place where locals can dock their boats just steps from laid-back waterfront eateries, and thanks to the fascinating underwater coral reefs that extend along the eastern shore, it's also the self-proclaimed diving capital of the world.

South of Key Largo, most of the remaining Upper Keys – at least those accessible by the Overseas Highway – compose Islamorada, an area long celebrated for its bountiful sportfishing opportunities. After crossing a lengthy bridge, you'll be in the heart of the Middle Keys, a transitional

space between the natural pleasures of the north and the unabashed revelry of the south. Centered around Marathon (which, as with Islamorada,
encompasses several keys), this region offers a number of wildlife-oriented activities, from bird-watching haunts to dolphin encounters.

For even more animal sightings, venture south to the Lower Keys,
where wild creatures abound in the National Key Deer Refuge on and
around Big Pine Key. Even farther down, you'll spy mammals of a different variety – the tourists and locals who descend upon the streets of
Key West – especially from October to April, when the weather is usually
sunny and mild and offers a respite from colder places.

Of course, even those who are intimately familiar with the Florida Keys
only know a small percentage of them. The Overseas Highway (U.S. 1) – the
only drivable link to the mainland – connects less than 50 of the more than
800 islands that this unforgettable chain comprises. So, once you've seen
all that the inhabited keys have to offer, consider venturing by boat to the
more elusive ones.

Planning Your Trip

▶ WHERE TO GO

Miami and the Everglades

While some travelers head directly to Key West via boat or plane, most pass through the gateway areas of Miami and the Everglades before driving south to the Florida Keys. If you have time, consider exploring this diverse region, where you can stroll amid Miami's colorful Art Deco Historic District, soak up the sunshine on the city's stunning beaches, snorkel above the coral reefs of Biscayne National Park, take a guided canoe trip among the cypress trees of the Fakahatchee Strand Preserve State Park, and visit the critters at the Everglades Alligator Farm.

Key Largo

From the mainland, most motorists take U.S. 1, often called the Overseas Highway, to reach the Florida Keys. The first island encountered is Key Largo, the largest of this unique archipelago. Here, you'll find several

IF YOU HAVE...

- **A WEEKEND:** Experience Key West.
- **FIVE DAYS:** Add Key Largo and Islamorada.
- **ONE WEEK:** Add Marathon and Big Pine Key.
- **TEN DAYS:** Add Miami and the Everglades.

outdoor diversions, including Dolphin Cove and Dolphins Plus—sister facilities that offer a range of programs, from natural dolphin swims to Everglades ecology tours. Recreationists will especially enjoy John Pennekamp Coral Reef State Park, where you can swim alongside sandy beaches, kayak amid mangrove trees, or dive among offshore coral reefs.

relaxing at John Pennekamp Coral Reef State Park

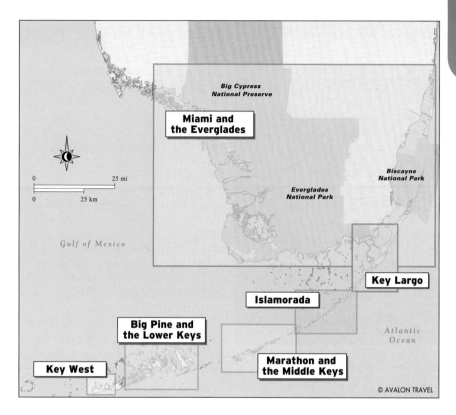

© AVALON TRAVEL

Islamorada

Southwest of Key Largo are the islands that make up Islamorada, an upscale resort area favored by anglers and scuba divers. Outdoor attractions dominate here, where you can watch sea lion shows at Theater of the Sea, feed wild tarpon at Robbie's of Islamorada, and visit four different state parks, including Indian Key Historic State Park and Lignumvitae Key Botanical State Park, both of which are only accessible via boat. Sea lovers might also appreciate the History of Diving Museum, which houses a curious collection of diving paraphernalia.

Marathon and the Middle Keys

After experiencing Islamorada, you'll pass into the Middle Keys, the heart of which is the laid-back town of Marathon. Animal lovers can swim with dolphins at the Dolphin Research Center, observe pelicans and raptors at Curry Hammock State Park and Crane Point Museum and Nature Center, or visit recovering sea turtles at the Turtle Hospital. For a quieter experience, visitors can relax on the area's lovely beaches or head south to isolated Pigeon Key, a historic base camp accessible via ferry or the Old Seven Mile Bridge.

Big Pine and the Lower Keys

Once you've crossed the Seven Mile Bridge, you'll enter the Lower Keys, perhaps the most tranquil part of this legendary archipelago. Although Bahia Honda State Park lures

Seaweed lines the shore of Bahia Honda State Park.

numerous visitors to its beaches, campgrounds, hiking trails, and warm waters, ideal for kayakers and snorkelers, you're likely to spy more wildlife in this region than fellow tourists. Among the plentiful offerings, recreationists will find wooded solitude in the National Key Deer Refuge on Big Pine Key, fishing charters on Summerland Key, and superb diving opportunities around Looe Key.

Key West

Celebrated for its breezy hotels, sunset celebrations, and festive atmosphere, especially along Duval Street, America's southernmost city will certainly keep you busy for days on end. Here, you can relax on numerous beaches, tour historic homes, visit engaging museums and nature centers, view the entire city from atop the Key West Lighthouse, or take a ferry to the Dry Tortugas. At night, you'll find no shortage of lively bars, and throughout the year, you can participate in an array of festivals and events.

▶ WHEN TO GO

You should allow at least a week for exploring southern Florida, where you could easily spend two days each in Miami, Key Largo, and Key West. Of course, where you go—and when you choose to come—will depend upon your interests.

Although southern Florida is a year-round destination, some businesses, namely restaurants in Key West, close during September. In general, summer is the least crowded time to visit, perhaps because temperatures are fairly high from June to September, when hurricane season is at its peak.

While spring and fall are comfortable in this subtropical region, winter is the high season in the Florida Keys, when the climate is much warmer than in the northern United

The Key West Lighthouse soars 86 feet into the sky.

The winning "Papa" celebrates his victory in the annual Hemingway Look-Alike Contest.

the mid-season, which, in general, includes the latter half of January, the first half of February, the latter half of April, all of May, and all of June. Hotels, inns, and resorts are often at their cheapest during the low season, which, save for holidays and festivals, is typically summer and fall, between July and early December. Although the accommodations listings in this guide reflect southern Florida's wide range in rates, be advised that every establishment has its own seasonal schedule and, therefore, its own pricing policy, so be sure to check each place in question before making travel plans.

Your activities can also determine the time of your trip. Swimmers and snorkelers might enjoy the slightly warmer waters of summer, while anglers must consider the varied fishing seasons before making plans. Blue marlin, for example, are prevalent from April to October, while king mackerel are more common from mid-November through March.

States. Late December and early January are often busy, as is the period between mid-February and mid-April, when snowbirds descend upon the Keys. Be advised that lodging rates are often higher during the peak tourist season and during major events and holiday weekends. Accommodations often cost less during

Events might sway your plans, too. From December to February, there are several noteworthy art festivals in Miami and throughout the Keys. July, meanwhile, lures visitors to Key West for Hemingway Days, and many flock to the Southernmost City for Fantasy Fest in late October.

▶ BEFORE YOU GO

Reservations might be necessary, especially for resorts and B&Bs during winter and spring. You should definitely call ahead if you're planning a trip in September, when many businesses close between seasons.

Transportation
Miami, the Everglades, and the Florida Keys constitute a fairly compact destination, especially given the fact that one main highway (U.S. 1) links much of this region. Although most visitors come by car, motorcycle, or RV,

it's possible to reach southern Florida via other forms of transportation. For instance, you can travel by train or bus to Miami, take a flight to Miami International Airport, or arrive in Key West via plane or cruise ship.

If you choose not to drive to southern Florida, your best bet would still be to rent a car and hit the road as soon as possible. After all, taxis can get expensive, and it's infinitely easier to travel the 110-mile-long Overseas Highway by car, as opposed to walking or biking.

Explore the Florida Keys

▶ THE BEST OF THE FLORIDA KEYS

First-time visitors to the Florida Keys should set aside at least a week to experience the best that these legendary islands—plus the gateway areas of Miami and the Everglades—have to offer.

Day 1

Since most travelers reach the Florida Keys by vehicle, you'll likely begin your trip in the Miami area. For a taste of the city's multicultural vibe, head to Little Havana, where you can sample authentic Cuban food and browse aromatic cigar shops. Then venture east to South Beach, where you can tour the colorful Art Deco Historic District, view impressive art and artifact collections at the Jewish Museum of Florida or the World Erotic Art Museum, and relax at the popular Lummus Park Beach.

After lunch at one of South Beach's savory cafés, head southwest to Coconut Grove and Coral Gables, both of which boast a variety of historic structures and shopping options. Savor a fine meal and perhaps stay the night at Coral Gables' 1920s-era Biltmore Hotel, where you can also play golf or enjoy a massage. If you'd rather experience Miami's nightlife, stay in one of the boutique hotels or world-class resorts in South Beach.

Day 2

Rise early and head to Bill Baggs Cape Florida State Park. Here, you can stroll along the beach, have breakfast at the

the vibrant Art Deco Historic District in Miami's South Beach

SUN AND SAND GALORE

In addition to fantastic resorts, intriguing museums, and plenty of offshore diversions, the Florida Keys boast several picturesque beaches – which, while not as famous as those in Miami's South Beach, provide rest, relaxation, and people-watching opportunities year-round.

KEY LARGO

- **Cannon Beach:** Although most visitors come to John Pennekamp Coral Reef State Park for offshore activities like snorkeling, fishing, and kayaking, this prized park, located on the ocean side of Key Largo, also offers two small manmade beaches. This one, which lies closer to the marina, provides easy access to picnic tables, a swimming area, and the remnants of an old Spanish shipwreck.

ISLAMORADA

- **Anne's Beach:** Dedicated to local environmentalist Anne Eaton, this peaceful beach on the ocean side of Lower Matecumbe Key features a shallow swimming area, several covered picnic tables, and a boardwalk that allows access to more secluded stretches of sand.

MARATHON AND THE MIDDLE KEYS

- **Long Key State Park:** Situated between Layton and Marathon, Long Key State Park contains a narrow, grass-lined beach on the ocean side of U.S. 1, not far from picnic pavilions and a canoe/kayak launching area. Only open to those staying in the state park campground, it tends to be more peaceful than the beaches farther south.

- **Curry Hammock State Park:** Little Crawl Key, one of the islands that constitute this park, features a pleasant beach and playground area that is accessible by overnight campers and day-use visitors alike. Fishing, kayaking, picnicking, and beachcombing are popular activities here.

- **Sombrero Beach:** Located in the southern part of Marathon, this beautiful beach is definitely one of the more popular ones in the Keys. Part of a public park that offers picnic pavilions and volleyball courts, this curvy, palm-lined expanse of sand is also a preferred spot for nesting turtles from April to October.

BIG PINE AND THE LOWER KEYS

- **Sandspur Beach:** Arguably the most well-favored beach in the Florida Keys, this large, sandy stretch is one of three beaches in Bahia Honda State Park, east of Big Pine Key. Breezy palm trees, turquoise waters, and white sand make this beach especially popular among photographers.

KEY WEST

- **Fort Zachary Taylor Historic State Park:** Praised by sunbathers, swimmers, snorkelers, and bird-watchers, the beach just south of Fort Zachary Taylor is surely the finest in Key West. Recently enhanced by imported sand, this beach sits at the convergence of the Gulf of Mexico and the Atlantic Ocean, where the clear, deep waters nurture living coral and tropical fish.

- **Clarence S. Higgs Memorial Beach:** At the foot of White Street lies another popular Key West beach, where, in addition to swimming and sunbathing, sun-worshipers can rent water-sports equipment or stroll amid pelicans and seagulls on the adjacent swimming pier.

- **Smathers Beach:** On warm, sunny days, crowds flock to this lengthy beach alongside Roosevelt Boulevard, an ideal place to watch the sunrise, have a picnic, play a volleyball game, or just enjoy the water.

- **Fort Jefferson Beach:** While Dry Tortugas National Park is only accessible via ferry or seaplane, this isolated beach is well worth the trip. Besides its proximity to historic Fort Jefferson, it's a terrific locale for swimming, snorkeling, and overnight camping.

Lighthouse Café, and take a guided tour of the 1825 Cape Florida Lighthouse, which provides panoramic views of Biscayne Bay.

Afterward, venture south to Biscayne National Park, where you can rent a kayak and explore Boca Chita Key, Elliott Key, and other islands. Then stop by the Everglades Alligator Farm in Florida City, which features live alligator feedings and airboat rides in the Everglades. For a more intimate tour of this subtropical wilderness, take a canoe trip through Everglades National Park, Big Cypress National Preserve, or Collier-Seminole State Park, all wonderful places to observe birds, alligators, and other native creatures.

To experience the region's heritage, head to the Miccosukee Indian Village on the Tamiami Trail or the Ah-Tah-Thi-Ki Museum on the Big Cypress Seminole Indian Reservation. After a day of sightseeing, unwind at the Miccosukee Resort & Gaming, where you'll find endless dining, entertainment, and lodging options.

Day 3

Venture south on U.S. 1 to the Florida Keys. In northern Key Largo, head to the tranquil Dagny Johnson Key Largo Hammock Botanical State Park, which lures hikers, bikers, and wildlife lovers daily. Farther south, you'll encounter John Pennekamp Coral Reef State Park, where popular activities include kayaking, snorkeling, and scuba diving.

Afterward, head to Dolphins Plus, where you can swim with dolphins and learn how to be a marine mammal trainer. Wildlife lovers will also appreciate the Florida Keys Wild Bird Center, home to rehabilitating seagulls, pelicans, and great horned owls.

Following a day of outdoor diversions, relax at one of Key Largo's many waterfront restaurants, most of which offer ideal spots to watch the sunset. Throughout Key Largo, you'll find a variety of eateries, bars, and hotels, including those at the Key Largo Resorts Marina, which also features the historic African Queen.

a watchful alligator in the Everglades

Day 4

Continue southwest to the islands of Islamorada. Here, art lovers can explore paintings and sculptures at The Rain Barrel on Plantation Key, while history buffs can learn about the ill-fated Overseas Railroad at Windley Key Fossil Reef Geological State Park. Farther southwest, it's hard to miss the enormous sign for Theater of the Sea, which offers bottomless boat rides, entertaining marine mammal shows, and the chance to swim with the resident dolphins and sea lions. On Upper Matecumbe Key, you'll find the History of Diving Museum, which houses a curious collection of diving paraphernalia.

On Lower Matecumbe Key, Robbie's of Islamorada features boat rentals, fishing charters, and an open-air market. The marina also provides boat tours of two remote islands: Indian Key Historic State Park, once the site of a lucrative cargo-salvaging business,

a fascinating exhibit at the History of Diving Museum

and Lignumvitae Key Botanical State Park, where you can tour a virgin tropical forest. While all the islands of Islamorada are worth visiting, Upper Matecumbe Key boasts most of the area's shops, spas, bars, restaurants, and accommodations.

Day 5

Just past Layton in the Middle Keys, you'll come upon Long Key State Park, a tranquil place for canoeists, anglers, hikers, and snorkelers. Farther south, you can embrace other family-friendly diversions, such as frolicking with dolphins at the Dolphin Research Center or exploring the wooded islands of Curry Hammock State Park.

Beyond Key Colony Beach lies the Florida Keys Marathon Airport, where Conch Air offers exhilarating biplane rides high above the islands and coral reefs. Back on the ground, head to gorgeous Sombrero Beach, popular with swimmers, picnickers, and volleyball enthusiasts.

If you have time, take a walking tour of the Turtle Hospital, a rescue facility on Vaca Key. Then stop by the Pigeon Key Visitor's Center, housed in a silver train car, and purchase admission to Pigeon Key, an early 20th-century base camp for bridge workers. Admission includes a ferry ride to the island, which you can also access via the Old Seven Mile Bridge.

After hours, you'll find plenty of dining and lodging options in the Middle Keys. Though most lie on Vaca Key, Marathon's lengthiest island, you may prefer more isolated places, such as Hawks Cay Resort on Duck Key.

Day 6

After crossing the Seven Mile Bridge, you'll encounter the less populated Lower Keys, where Bahia Honda State Park lures kayakers, snorkelers, anglers, and bikers daily. On Big Pine Key, you might be able to spot a tiny

ART AND ARCHITECTURE

Although southern Florida is most well known for its outdoor diversions, visitors will find plenty of impressive art collections and cultural landmarks in the region between Miami and Key West.

ART MUSEUMS AND NOTABLE GALLERIES

Miami, nicknamed the Magic City, has a thriving community of artists, designers, and collectors, so it's no surprise that it offers several fine art repositories, including the **Miami Art Museum,** which has plans to expand in the near future, and the **Museum of Contemporary Art,** which presents lectures, screenings, concerts, performances, and cutting-edge exhibits. In South Beach, you'll find the **World Erotic Art Museum,** home to the country's largest collection of erotic art, and the **Bass Museum of Art,** which contains a vast accumulation of European paintings, sculptures, and textiles from the 15th to the 20th centuries. Miami also boasts two gallery districts: the **Wynwood Arts District** in downtown Miami and the **Miami Design District** farther north.

En route to the Florida Keys, make a slight detour into the Everglades and visit the **Big Cypress Gallery,** which features the black-and-white photography of Clyde Butcher. Guided swamp walks are offered every Saturday in the fall and winter. In Key West's Old Town, the **San Carlos Institute** displays art exhibits relating to the history of Cuba and Florida's Cuban-American community, such as the photographs of poet José Martí and the portraits of Cuba's constitutional presidents. Within walking distance lies the **Key West Museum of Art and History at the Custom House,** which includes Paul Collins's portraits of famous Key West residents and Mario Sanchez's colorful wood paintings of life in Key West during the early 1900s. Another interesting stop is the flagship store of **Wyland Galleries,** where you'll see the famous muralist's marine sculptures as well as vibrant paintings of dolphins, manatees, and killer whales.

HISTORIC HOMES, HOTELS, AND LANDMARKS

For architecture fans, Miami contains a number of unique neighborhoods and structures. Perhaps most famous is the **Art Deco Historic District,** a colorful South Beach neighborhood that's listed on the National Register of Historic Places. Southwest of downtown Miami, you'll find the **Vizcaya Museum and Gardens** in Coconut Grove, once home to industrialist James Deering. In nearby Coral Gables, you can explore the historic **Biltmore Hotel,** a favorite spot for politicians and celebrities since its opening in the 1920s, and **Coral Gables Merrick House,** once home to city planner George Merrick and now an excellent example of 1920s-style architecture. Before heading south to the Florida Keys, tour the 95-foot-tall **Cape Florida Lighthouse,** rebuilt in 1846 on Key Biscayne.

South of Marathon, history buffs can visit **Pigeon Key,** a tiny coral island that's accessible via ferry or a long walk on the Old Seven Mile Bridge. Here, you can stroll among the historic buildings that once served as the base camp for bridge workers in the early 20th century.

Key West is a treasure trove of stunning architecture, from gingerbread mansions to Caribbean-style bungalows. Your first stop should be the **Ernest Hemingway Home and Museum,** built in 1851 by a marine architect and once the home of Key West's most famous resident. Across the street, the **Key West Lighthouse,** erected in 1847, provides stunning views of the city. Closer to Mallory Square is the **Audubon House and Tropical Gardens,** a gorgeous home built in the 1800s by Captain John H. Geiger, a harbor pilot and master wrecker. Not far away stands the **Harry S. Truman Little White House,** a breezy structure that once served as the command headquarters for the Key West Naval Station.

Key deer in the National Key Deer Refuge or an alligator at the freshwater Blue Hole.

While here, take a snorkeling or diving trip to the underwater coral reefs in the Looe Key National Marine Sanctuary. Then, from Sugarloaf Key, take flight with Fantasy Dan's Airplane Rides and get a bird's-eye view of the area's islands and lighthouses.

Where you choose to spend your evening depends on your budget. If you can't afford the high dining and lodging prices at the exclusive Little Palm Island Resort & Spa, consider some of the Lower Keys' more affordable options, from cottages on Big Pine Key to an RV park on Geiger Key.

Day 7

Head to Key West and survey its attractions aboard the Conch Tour Train. Then begin your self-guided tour on Duval Street in Old Town, where you can peruse art galleries, visit historic landmarks, and see colorful butterflies at the Key West Butterfly and Nature Conservatory. On nearby Whitehead Street, stroll among six-toed felines at the Ernest Hemingway Home and Museum, view the city from atop the Key West Lighthouse, and see John James Audubon's drawings at the Audubon House and Tropical Gardens.

Not far away, the impressive Mel Fisher Maritime Museum presents many of the treasures discovered in the famous *Atocha* shipwreck. Stroll to the nearby Key West Museum of Art and History at the Custom House, where you'll see portraits of famous Key West residents, and take a guided tour of the Harry S. Truman Little White House Museum. If there's time, head to Fort Zachary Taylor Historic State Park, which offers guided tours of the 19th-century fort as well as the finest beach in town.

Be sure to experience the daily Sunset Celebration at Mallory Square, and enjoy the plethora of nearby shops, bars, and restaurants. While you'll find a variety of accommodations here, from low-key campgrounds to oceanfront resorts, consider staying in Old Town, which ensures easy access to Key West's most popular activities.

Tropical gardens surround the Audubon House in Key West.

► A ROMANTIC WEEKEND IN KEY WEST

Luxury, history, and revelry combine on this whimsical island, a popular place for romantic getaways. Whether you fly or drive here, you and your sweetheart will surely have a memorable weekend in Key West. Here are a few suggestions for making the most of your time while visiting America's southernmost city.

Friday

When planning your romantic getaway, consider booking a room at one of Key West's unique hotels, such as Eden House or the Marquesa Hotel, both of which offer deluxe rooms and relaxing pool areas. For a stunning ocean view and access to a private beach, you might prefer a waterfront location like Southernmost on the Beach. No matter where you decide to stay, though, reservations are highly recommended, especially on weekends during peak season.

After checking into your hotel and freshening up, take a stroll to Mallory Square, where artists, musicians, acrobats, and tourists converge daily to pay homage to Key West's gorgeous sunsets. To avoid the crowds, head to the Westin Key West Resort & Marina, where you can watch the sunset while sipping cocktails on the Sunset Deck.

Once the sun goes down, head inland for an early dinner, perhaps at Michaels Restaurant or Café Solé, two of Key West's most intimate eateries. Afterward, you can stroll along the quiet residential streets and make your way to Duval Street, where you'll find a lot of lively bars, which are typically open late. Along this popular thoroughfare, you'll also spy plenty of curious shops and art galleries. Many of these emporiums, like Fast Buck Freddie's, close early but feature enticing window displays, ideal for browsing, while some, such as the flagship store of Wyland Galleries, are open until 9 or 10 P.M.

For a sensual, late-night dessert experience, stop by Better Than Sex on Petronia, a bordello-style lounge and restaurant that focuses exclusively on wine and decadent desserts. Featuring live jazz on most nights, this romantic, dimly lighted gem is open until 1 A.M. on weekends.

Saturday

Start the day with breakfast at Banana Cafe, a popular French-style eatery that specializes in delectable crepes. Afterward, rent a pair of bicycles from Eaton Bikes on Margaret Street (or have them delivered to you) and tour Key West at your own pace. Head to the Historic Seaport, where you'll spot private yachts and old-fashioned sailing ships alike, then to Whitehead Street, where you can visit such tranquil places as the Audubon House and Tropical Gardens and the Ernest Hemingway Home and Museum, both of which offer quiet spots to relax and gaze at the lush foliage.

sparkling, white chocolate-rimmed wine at Better Than Sex

Martin's Restaurant & Lounge features a unique brunch, with German delicacies.

If you have time, stop by the Key West Lighthouse, which lies opposite the Hemingway Home, and climb the spiral staircase for an incredible view of the verdant city below. Pedal over to Duval Street and stroll through the Key West Butterfly & Nature Conservatory, which features a glass-enclosed habitat filled with colorful birds and butterflies. Roughly eight blocks away lies Nancy Forrester's Secret Garden, yet another peaceful spot to relish nature. For lunch, circle back to the Historic Seaport, where you can enjoy fresh seafood on the breezy upper deck of the Schooner Wharf Bar.

Following lunch, you can either continue your biking tour through Key West or head to Java Cat Charters or Lazy Dog Adventure, both of which offer guided kayaking trips. Sharing a two-person kayak, you and your sweetheart can wind along mangrove creeks and get an up-close look at tropical fish, aquatic birds, and other marine wonders.

For another memorable adventure, spend the evening on a sunset cruise. Among those available, Sunset Watersports offers a tropical buffet and a variety of libations during the excursion. Couples will especially enjoy watching the sunset together and dancing on the lighted dance floor.

After the cruise, head back to your hotel for some much-deserved relaxation. Of course, if you're not yet ready to call it a night, you'll find no shortage of distractions along Duval Street, from late-night dancing at the Aqua Nightclub to clothing-optional shenanigans at the rooftop Garden of Eden.

Sunday

If you have yet to return your bicycles to Eaton Bikes, a pickup can be arranged in the morning. After checking out of the hotel, stroll to Martin's Restaurant & Lounge, a stylish German fusion restaurant on Duval, for brunch. Specialties include grilled bratwurst, seafood crepes, and eggs Benedict with lobster medallions. Following brunch, take a taxi or drive your own car to Fort Zachary Taylor Historic State Park, where you can take some time to swim in the warm waters, snorkel amid colorful coral and parrotfish, and enjoy the best beach in town, before heading back home.

▶ AN UNDERWATER JOURNEY

The ocean waters along the eastern side of the Florida Keys constitute one of the finest—and most popular—underwater diving areas in the world. Stretching the length of the 220-mile archipelago, five miles offshore, the continental United States' only living coral reef provides a thriving habitat for a wide array of fascinating marinelife, from kaleidoscopic fish to assorted coral formations, in waters that range in depth from 5 to 70 feet.

Snorkelers and scuba divers—whether amateurs or aficionados—can easily spend five days exploring the historic shipwrecks, artificial reefs, and vibrant coral formations that are now protected within the Florida Keys National Marine Sanctuary. If you, too, plan to experience these underwater delights, there's no need to bring your own snorkeling gear and diving tanks; such equipment is available throughout the Keys.

Day 1

No matter when you plan to travel to the Florida Keys, you should reserve your lodgings ahead of time. For snorkelers and scuba divers, there are three ideal places: Amy Slate's Amoray Dive Resort in Key Largo, the Looe Key Reef Resort & Dive Center on Ramrod Key, and, for an unparalleled experience, the Jules Undersea Lodge, which offers submerged accommodations in the Key Largo Undersea Park. Wherever you decide to stay, however, you'll be within relatively easy driving distance of the region's varied diving outfitters and operators.

Before checking into your hotel, make the most of the daylight hours and head to John Pennekamp Coral Reef State Park, America's first undersea park. Here, you can take diving instruction, earn PADI Open Water certification, and participate in snorkeling or scuba-diving tours amid the offshore coral reefs east of Key Largo—such as Key Largo Dry Rocks, which contains elkhorn coral and the ever-popular *Christ of the Abyss* statue.

In addition to diving classes, Key Largo–area operators like Horizon Divers, the Keys Diver & Snorkel Center, Island Ventures, and the Amoray Dive Resort also offer diving trips to the reefs and wrecks of the Key Largo National Marine Sanctuary. Such underwater sights include the *Duane* and the *Bibb*, two U.S. Coast Guard cutters used in World War II; the USS *Spiegel Grove,* a 510-foot Navy transport ship purposely sunk to create an artificial reef; and the sea caves of French Reef.

Day 2

No matter if you're staying in the Upper or Lower Keys, you should focus the

Divers examine the *Christ of the Abyss* statue near Key Largo.

ANIMAL ATTRACTION

Given the varied landscapes, typically warm climate, and bountiful fauna of southern Florida, it's probably no surprise that Miami, the Everglades, and the Florida Keys contain their share of animal attractions – from aquariums to gator parks to dolphin centers.

MIAMI TO THE EVERGLADES

In the Miami area, you'll find **Zoo Miami,** home to over 1,000 different plant species and 400 different animal species, including endangered creatures like the sable antelope and the Cuban crocodile. After a visit to the zoo, head to the **Miami Seaquarium** on Biscayne Bay, where you can watch entertaining dolphins and sea lions, observe friendly manatees, and view shark feedings.

Situated between downtown Miami and South Beach, **Jungle Island** is another fun stop for animal lovers. Here, you can see parrot shows, watch tiger and primate presentations, feed the lorikeets, and wander among the alligators in an Everglades habitat.

Of course, it's even better to venture into the real Everglades, where a dozen airboat operators guide visitors through the "river of grass" for an up-close look at alligators, turtles, birds, and other native inhabitants. Several operators even have their own alligator exhibits and shows, including **Billie Swamp Safari, Everglades Safari Park, Gator Park,** and **Everglades Alligator Farm,** home to roughly 2,000 alligators.

KEY LARGO TO ISLAMORADA

Venturing south onto Key Largo, the largest island of the Florida Keys archipelago, you'll encounter two exciting attractions: **Dolphin Cove** and **Dolphins Plus.** Together, these sister facilities present an array of year-round activities, from structured dolphin swims to trainer-for-a-day programs. For a completely different experience, take a stroll through the nonprofit **Florida Keys Wild Bird Center,** where you'll spot a slew of native species, including pelicans, common egrets, and great white herons.

Farther south, Islamorada boasts two curious animal attractions. At **Theater of the Sea,** you can swim with dolphins and sea lions, watch

Islamorada's Theater of the Sea

them frolic and paint, and take a snorkeling cruise to an offshore coral reef. Several miles down U.S. 1, you can also feed visiting schools of tarpon at **Robbie's of Islamorada.**

MARATHON TO KEY WEST

Dolphin lovers will find two delightful attractions farther south. At Hawks Cay Resort on Duck Key, the **Dolphin Connection** allows visitors to interact with dolphins from the dock or in the water. In Marathon, the **Dolphin Research Center** offers a variety of educational experiences, from brief dolphin dips to daylong research programs. Other animal diversions include the **Crane Point Museum and Nature Center,** where you can observe various bird species alongside Florida Bay, and the **Turtle Hospital,** where guests can take a guided tour of the sea turtle rehabilitation area.

On Big Pine Key, you can search for diminutive Key deer within the **National Key Deer Refuge** or look for turtles, alligators, and other elusive animals at the **Blue Hole.** Down in Key West, the **Key West Butterfly and Nature Conservatory** invites visitors to take a stroll through a vibrant, glass-enclosed habitat filled with colorful butterflies, birds, and flowering plants. In Mallory Square, the **Key West Aquarium** presents daily shark and turtle feedings, plus the chance to observe moray eels, barracuda, tarpon, and other sea creatures. Another engaging attraction is the **Florida Keys Eco-Discovery Center,** which, among other exhibits, contains a 2,500-gallon reef tank filled with living coral and tropical fish.

Tropical fish swim amid the coral reefs east of Key Largo.

second day of your trip on the waters east of Islamorada, where you'll find an assortment of shipwrecks, wall formations, and shallow coral reefs. Through the Florida Keys Dive Center, based on the northern end of Plantation Key, you can take a diving class (if you haven't already) and explore most of the nearby underwater attractions, including the Conch Wall, home to a variety of conch, barrel sponges, and rare pillar coral. Down here, you might also spy green moray eels near the Davis Reef, gorgonian coral along the Crocker Wall, and the wrecked El Infante, a Spanish galleon that sank in a 1733 hurricane. You can also explore Alligator Reef, site of the shipwrecked USS Alligator, and the Eagle, a 287-foot freighter that became an artificial reef in the mid-1980s.

Day 3

On the third day, you should venture into the waters east of the Middle Keys. Tilden's Scuba Center, located in Marathon and

open daily, provides classes, gear rentals, and Snuba diving, a patented, deep-water form of snorkeling. In addition, Tilden's offers a number of snorkeling and scuba-diving excursions, even night dives. On such tours, you're bound to see an assortment of underwater sites, including the spur-and-groove Sombrero Reef and the star, elkhorn, and brain coral of the Delta Shoals. In this area, you can also survey two historic shipwrecks: the Adelaide Baker, essentially the remains of a three-masted, iron-rigged ship, and the Thunderbolt, a 188-foot vessel intentionally sunk in the mid-1980s and now home to coral, sponges, and angelfish.

Day 4

To explore the offshore reefs and wrecks of the Lower Keys, consult the Looe Key Reef Resort & Dive Center, which offers scuba classes as well as three-hour snorkeling and diving trips to the spectacular 33-acre reef known as the Looe Key National Marine Sanctuary. Created in 1981 and named for

First-timers can easily snorkel in the waters near Key West's Fort Zachary Taylor Historic State Park.

the HMS *Looe,* which ran aground in 1744, this spur-and-groove network now abounds with parrotfish, grouper, turtles, eagle rays, and whale sharks. Given its varying depths, this reef is perfect for both inexperienced snorkelers and advanced divers.

Through the Dive Center, you can also survey the *Adolphus Busch,* an upright 210-foot

shoreline of John Pennekamp Coral Reef State Park, the country's first underwater park

freighter that was purposely sunk as an artificial diving reef and is now home to a wide assortment of marine creatures, including an enormous, legendary grouper that many divers have claimed to see. The Dive Center typically offers one wreck dive each week.

In addition, if you plan your diving excursion in mid-July, you might be able to attend the annual Underwater Music Festival, a quirky underwater concert that usually features nautically themed tunes, such as Jimmy Buffett songs and humpback whale sounds. Every year, this unique event lures hundreds of eager divers and snorkelers to the Looe Key Reef, one of the most diverse coral reefs in the world.

Day 5

On the last day of your diving adventure, head south to Key West, where you'll find an array of vibrant coral reefs and engaging shipwrecks. While first-timers can easily snorkel in the waters near Fort Zachary Taylor Historic State Park, situated on the

the *Vandenberg,* an artificial reef near Key West

southern end of the island, or Dry Tortugas National Park, which lies roughly 68 miles to the west, most of the underwater attractions in this area are only accessible with the help of professional diving charters. One such local operator, Southpoint Divers, provides gear rentals, diving classes, and guided trips to two intriguing wrecks: the 187-foot Cayman Salvage Master and the 522-foot USNS *General Hoyt S. Vandenberg,* a former World War II troop transport ship and now the foundation for an artificial reef.

Besides offering trips to these two wrecks, operators like Dive Key West, the Subtropic Dive Center, and Lost Reef Adventures feature excursions to other wrecks, such as the weather-beaten Joe's Tug, a deep-water vessel that's home to an assortment of coral formations and marine creatures. Some of these companies even provide trips to the spur-and-groove networks of Sand Key, Rock Key, and the Western Sambo Ecological Reserve. Other nearby sights include the Kedge Ledge, a patch reef that features coral-encrusted anchors from 18th-century schooners, and the Ten-Fathom Ledge, a network of caves and outcroppings that attract lobster, grouper, and sharks, among other inhabitants.

MIAMI AND THE EVERGLADES

Unless you fly into the Marathon airport, arrive in Key West by plane or cruise ship, or have access to your own boat, you'll likely reach the Keys via car or bus. Given the geography of southern Florida, you'll have to pass through at least one of three gateway towns: Miami, Homestead, or Florida City. If you're not in a hurry, you should take some time to explore Miami's vibrant neighborhoods as well as the abundant foliage and serpentine waterways that define the Everglades.

While Miami's assortment of attractions, restaurants, and activities could consume you for a week or more, time and budget might dictate a shorter stay. If so, you should definitely visit the cultural microcosms of Little Havana and Little Haiti, take a self-guided walking tour of the pastel-hued Art Deco Historic District, and soak in the ambience of infamous South Beach, a terrific place to shop for trendy apparel, dine alongside celebrities in sophisticated restaurants, and party the night away at one of numerous hip bars and dance clubs. Depending on your interests and the time of your visit, you might also catch a professional sporting event—this is, after all, the home of the Miami Dolphins, the Florida Marlins, and the Miami Heat. Of course, you're also not far from the coral reefs of Biscayne National Park, a favorite spot for snorkelers and scuba divers.

Although it would be impossible to cover all of the Everglades, you can definitely get a taste of this "river of grass" by visiting Everglades National Park—an International Biosphere Reserve, a World Heritage Site, and one of America's largest national parks. Here, you can

© DANIEL MARTONE

HIGHLIGHTS

◖ Miami-Dade Cultural Center: Centered around a pleasant courtyard area, this downtown complex invites you to browse art exhibits at the Miami Art Museum, learn about the city's pioneers at HistoryMiami, and even peruse books about the state at the Main Library (page 31).

◖ Little Havana: Home to many Cuban exiles and Cuban Americans, this predominantly Latino neighborhood, which lies west of downtown Miami, offers a plethora of cigar shops, quiet parks, authentic markets and restaurants, live music venues, art galleries, and annual events like Calle Ocho, supposedly the biggest street party in the country (page 33).

◖ Art Deco Historic District: Officially listed on the National Register of Historic Places as the Miami Beach Architectural District, this colorful South Beach neighborhood features an incredible collection of art deco-style buildings that you can experience via an assortment of guided and self-guided tours (page 34).

◖ Biltmore Hotel: Since it opened in the 1920s, the historic, oft-photographed jewel of Coral Gables has welcomed countless politicians and celebrities, and even if you choose not to stay, dine, play golf, or get a massage here, you simply have to see this architectural gem for yourself (page 38).

◖ Everglades Alligator Farm: What began as a mere airboat ride attraction in 1982 has since become southern Florida's oldest alligator farm, where, in addition to taking an airboat ride into the nearby Everglades, you can watch various animal shows and stroll amid numerous alligators, crocodiles, caimans, and native snakes (page 66).

◖ Watching Birds and Wildlife in the Everglades: Whether you explore the East Everglades Expansion Area via airboat, hike along the many trails of Everglades National Park, or simply stroll along the Big Cypress Bend Boardwalk, you're bound to encounter an array of curious birds and other wild animals, from wading great blue herons to lounging American alligators to the elusive Florida panther (page 72).

◖ Canoeing and Kayaking in the Everglades: The massive subtropical wilderness west of Miami offers a variety of interesting habitats, including sawgrass marshes, cypress swamps, and mangrove forests, all of which are ideal spots to canoe or kayak, especially if you enjoy observing or photographing wild animals in their element (page 75).

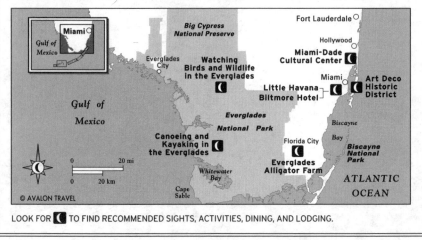

LOOK FOR ◖ TO FIND RECOMMENDED SIGHTS, ACTIVITIES, DINING, AND LODGING.

hike amid this fragile ecosystem, bike along the designated roads, or explore the marshy wonderland via kayak. Beyond the park's borders, you can even visit an alligator farm, join an airboat tour, or take a guided canoe trip through the Fakahatchee Strand Preserve State Park—all of which are experiences you'll surely never forget.

HISTORY

As evidenced by archaeological finds and the accounts of Spanish explorers in the early 1500s, the predominant tribes in this region were the Tequesta Indians, who had lived in the Biscayne Bay area near present-day Miami since at least the 1200s, and the Seminole Indians, whose ancestors had inhabited the Everglades for nearly 12,000 years. In 1513, Spanish explorer Juan Ponce de León was allegedly the first European to observe these native tribes, though there's no evidence that he actually interacted with them.

After Spain claimed the Florida territory as its own, European interactions with the native peoples increased. While the Tequesta initially welcomed the Spanish explorers who, taking refuge from a storm, arrived in Biscayne Bay in 1565, life soon changed drastically for them. A Spanish mission was established in the Miami area in 1567, and over the ensuing decades, many Indians died as a result of European diseases and various battles between the Spanish, French, and British. By the mid-1700s, in fact, most of the Tequesta Indians had either moved elsewhere or been sold into slavery by the British. Those that remained were relocated to Cuba in 1763, when Spain transferred the Florida territory to Britain. Although the Seminole were also adversely affected by the Europeans' presence, they nonetheless managed to survive in the Everglades.

By the 1780s, the United States had been formed, though Florida was once again under Spanish control. Given incidents like the First (1817–1818) and Second (1835–1842) Seminole Wars, it took some time for permanent settlements to take root, even after the Florida Territory had become part of the United States in 1821. In 1836, Fort Dallas was established

in the Miami area, where it served as a military base during the Second Seminole War.

Half a century later, however, the situation was quite different. Although some visitors felt that Miami held promise as a building site, it wasn't until Florida's Great Freeze of 1894, when all but Miami's crops were lost, that the settlement finally became a reality. Local citrus growers convinced Henry Flagler to extend his Florida East Coast Railway to Miami, and in July of 1896, it was officially incorporated as a city, with a population of only a few hundred. Soon afterward, the city experienced a real estate boom and the population grew exponentially. Three decades later, Miami was thriving culturally and financially; it was during the 1920s, in fact, that it earned its nickname, "The Magic City." Tourism also began to expand in the Everglades, largely due to the Seminole Indians, who made their living from homemade crafts and alligator-wrestling spectacles. The 1928 opening of the Tamiami Trail between Tampa and Miami, the first official road across the Everglades, also helped the region prosper.

By the 1930s, however, the Great Depression had descended upon southern Florida. Miami was now experiencing an economic decline, due to both the statewide real estate collapse and a devastating hurricane in the 1920s. As with the Florida Keys, World War II saved Miami from utter despair, especially given its location along the coast, an ideal spot in the battle against German submarines. By the 1950s, tourism became the dominant industry throughout southern Florida, and a desire for natural conservation and cultural preservation was beginning to take hold. Everglades National Park was the first such success, established in 1947 to conserve this fragile ecosystem, which had been harmed by years of water drainage, and prevent further degradation of its habitats, flora, and fauna. A decade later, the Seminole Tribe of Florida was officially formed, and the Miccosukee Tribe of Indians of Florida, which separated from the Seminoles in the 1950s, was nationally recognized in 1962.

During the 1960s, in the wake of Fidel Castro's rise to power, many Cubans emigrated to Miami, establishing their own community, known as Little Havana, and thereby increasing the city's multicultural population. In 1968, Biscayne National Monument was established north of Key Largo, eventually to become Biscayne National Park in 1980. In 1974, Big Cypress National Preserve, which had long been home to the Seminole and Miccosukee Tribes, became one of the country's first federally protected preserves.

While tourism continued to grow in the Florida Keys during the 1980s and '90s, Miami was suffering from drug wars, hurricanes, increased crime, and scandals involving Cuban refugees. Although the refurbishment and gentrification of certain neighborhoods, such as the southern portion of Little Haiti, have helped to curb some of these problems, Miami is still one of the most dangerous cities in America. Nevertheless, certain industries continue to thrive here, including tourism, international trade, and international banking, and the greater metropolitan area supports roughly 5.4 million people of various ethnic and economic backgrounds.

PLANNING YOUR TIME

Given its wide assortment of museums, historic structures, art and architectural districts, trendy restaurants and nightclubs, inviting beaches, animal attractions, shopping enclaves, and annual events, Miami could easily entertain you for a week or more. Experiencing the various habitats and wildlife-watching opportunities that abound in the Everglades will undoubtedly add a few more days to your trip. Even if you've primarily come to southern Florida to explore the Keys archipelago, try to allow yourself a little time to hit the highlights of Miami and the Everglades.

Although public transportation, taxicabs, and shuttle services are available in Miami, and several tours are offered in the Everglades, it's best to explore this sprawling region via car. The plethora of major surface streets, state highways, and federal interstates makes it fairly easy to get around, though you should be prepared for traffic jams on weekdays and holiday

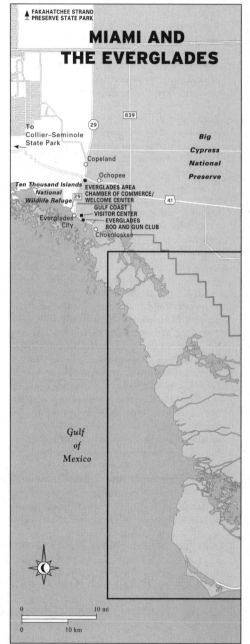

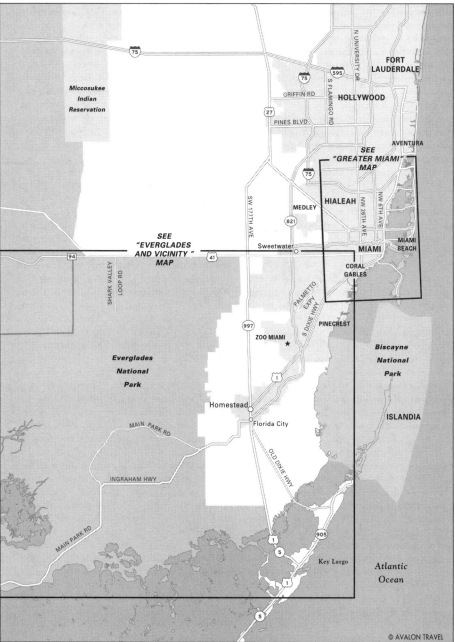

© AVALON TRAVEL

weekends. Of course, *when* you choose to pass through the gateway areas of Miami and the Everglades will probably depend on several factors, including annual events, intended activities, or your plans for the Florida Keys. Just be advised that hotel reservations are encouraged, and be prepared for pricey accommodations in the safer neighborhoods.

In addition, it helps to understand that, while the weather is fairly warm and mild in Miami and the Everglades all year long, the peak tourist season typically extends from November to April. During the hot, humid summer months, you'll often find that certain activities and establishments aren't available, such as airplane tours in the Everglades, so always call ahead when in doubt. If you plan to visit the Everglades, it's also helpful to remember the difference between the wet season (May–Oct.) and the dry season (Nov.–Apr.). In Big Cypress National Preserve and Everglades National Park, for example, hikers, bird-watchers, and wildlife enthusiasts might prefer the dry season, when there are fewer mosquitoes, more migratory birds, and an abundance of creatures in the ponds and canals; of course, there are also larger tourist crowds at this time, too. By contrast, the wet season tends to cause increased humidity, elevated temperatures, and higher water levels, which means you'll be less likely to spy alligators and wading birds, more likely to encounter mosquitoes, and yet able to enjoy the blooming flowers with fewer crowds.

As for safety, be aware that Miami can be a dangerous town, so always research an area or neighborhood before heading there. (Little Haiti, for example, is probably not a safe place for outsiders to explore at night.) Be aware of your surroundings at all times, especially when exploring non-touristed locations at night. If you want to experience the city's nightlife scene, consider heading to crowded, well-lit areas like South Beach, and keep an eye on your belongings at all times. While criminal activity is also a reality in the Everglades, the more pressing dangers involve the wildlife, so take care when exploring this vast wilderness and refrain from approaching any wild

animals, no matter how docile those lounging alligators might appear to be.

For more information about this region, consult the **Greater Miami Convention & Visitors Bureau (GMCVB)** (701 Brickell Ave., Ste. 2700, Miami, FL 33131, 305/539-3000 or 800/933-8448, www.miamiandbeaches.com) and the **Naples, Marco Island, Everglades Convention & Visitors Bureau** (2800 Horseshoe Dr., Naples, FL 34104, 239/225-1013 or 800/688-3600, www.paradisecoast.com).

ORIENTATION

As big cities go, Miami isn't too hard to traverse via car or public transportation. Several major highways and interstates, such as U.S. 1, U.S. 27, U.S. 41, I-75, and I-95, link other Floridian cities to Miami, and for the most part, all roads lead to the ocean. From downtown Miami, you can head north on I-95 or Biscayne Boulevard (U.S. 1) to reach North Miami, take U.S. 1 South or various surface streets to access Coconut Grove and Coral Gables, use I-195 or I-395 to cross Biscayne Bay toward Miami Beach, and hop on the Tamiami Trail (U.S. 41) to experience Little Havana and, farther west, the Everglades.

Of course, if you're planning to explore the Everglades, it's helpful to know how to reach the main towns. To reach Everglades City from Naples, for example, head east for 32 miles on U.S. 41, turn south on S.R. 29, and continue for roughly three miles. From downtown Miami, you can reach the same turnoff for Everglades City by taking I-95 North to FL-836 West via Exit 3A, continuing west for 10 miles, taking the NW 107th Avenue exit toward Florida's Turnpike (S.R. 985 S), merging onto the Tamiami Trail, and continuing west for 65 miles. The gateway cities to the Florida Keys, Homestead and Florida City, are also easily accessible from the Miami area. Homestead lies about 29 miles southwest of downtown Miami via I-95 South and U.S. 1, while Florida City lies roughly 34 miles southwest of downtown Miami via I-95 South, U.S. 1, FL-878 West, FL-874 South, and Florida's Turnpike (FL-821 S). Just be advised that tolls apply on certain portions of Florida's Turnpike.

Sights

DOWNTOWN MIAMI
☐ Miami-Dade Cultural Center

Centered around a pleasant courtyard area, where people often relax, eat, and read, the Miami-Dade Cultural Center (101 W. Flagler St., Miami) is essentially a complex of separate buildings that feature engrossing exhibits. The **Miami Art Museum (MAM)** (305/375-3000, www.miamiartmuseum.org, 10 A.M.–5 P.M. Tues.–Fri., noon–5 P.M. Sat.–Sun., $8 adults, $4 seniors, children under 12 and students free), for instance, houses more than 500 pieces of multicultural artwork from the 20th and 21st centuries. Founded in 1997, MAM presents the varied creations of contemporary artists like Cuban-born painter and sculptor Carlos Alfonzo, American photorealist painter Chuck Close, and American sculptor and textile artist Ann Hamilton. In the museum lobby, you'll also find a curious gift shop (305/375-1729) that features a wide selection of art books, unique jewelry, gorgeous stationery, visionary home and office furnishings, clever toys, and children's books.

Of course, this is just a tip of what awaits art lovers in the future. By 2013, the new, 120,000-square-foot facility, part of a planned 29-acre Museum Park overlooking Biscayne Bay in downtown Miami, will heighten MAM's role as a "gateway between continents and cultures." This new park, which will replace the current Bicentennial Park, will also include public gardens, sculpture installations, and the new-and-improved Miami Science Museum, which currently resides in Coconut Grove.

In addition to the current MAM, visitors to the Miami-Dade Cultural Center can peruse the various departments of the **Main Library** (305/375-2665, www.mdpls.org, 9 A.M.–6 P.M. Mon.–Wed. and Fri.–Sat., 9 A.M.–9 P.M. Thurs., free), which features a specialized Florida Department that contains an extensive collection of rare books, documents, and photographs about the Sunshine State, including Miami's history from pioneer days to the present.

Nearby, you can learn about the city's pioneers at **HistoryMiami** (305/375-1492, www.hmsf.org, 10 A.M.–5 P.M. Tues.–Fri., noon–5 P.M. Sat.–Sun., $8 adults, $7 seniors and students, $5 children 6–12, children under 6 free), which presents, in addition to a permanent exhibit called Tropical Dreams: A People's History of South Florida, several temporary displays about the region's rich history, including its seedier aspects, such as infamous Prohibition-era gangsters and the drug wars of the 1980s.

Bayfront Park

About five blocks east of the Miami-Dade Cultural Center, alongside Biscayne Bay, lies 32-acre Bayfront Park (301 N. Biscayne Blvd., Miami, 305/358-7550, www.bayfrontparkmiami.com, sunrise–sunset daily, no entrance fee though some activity and event fees apply), a well-landscaped municipal park that was created in the early 1920s and redesigned in the early 1980s by American sculptor Isamu Noguchi. Features include a sandy beach, a playground, a cascading fountain, a tropical rock garden and waterfall, and a variety of monuments and sculptures, including the Challenger Memorial, a white, metal, 100-foot pipe tower that is dedicated to the memory of the doomed Challenger astronauts. Containing two performance venues, the Bayfront Park Amphitheater and the Tina Hills Pavilion, Bayfront Park is host to numerous concerts, events, and activities, such as free yoga and self-defense classes. Several public parking lots are available in the area.

Wynwood Arts District

Given that Miami is home to a thriving community of artists, designers, and collectors, it's no surprise that you'll find several art districts here. One of the largest is the Wynwood Arts District (www.wynwood.com), which is roughly bordered by 20th Street, 6th Avenue, 36th Street, and Biscayne Boulevard. The district has well over 50 galleries, studios, and collections all within

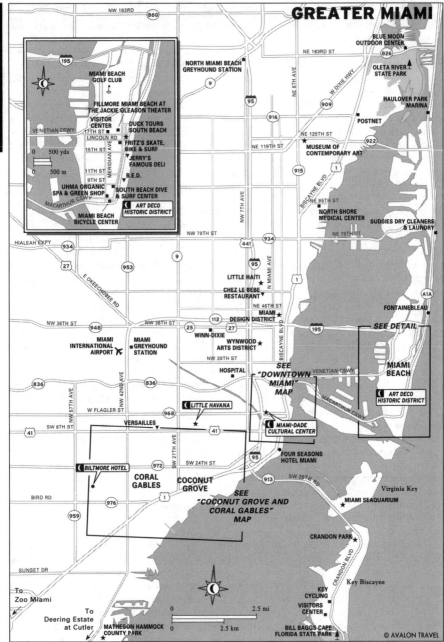

GREATER MIAMI

Inset map (upper left):

- MIAMI BEACH GOLF CLUB
- FILLMORE MIAMI BEACH AT THE JACKIE GLEASON THEATER
- VISITOR CENTER
- DUCK TOURS SOUTH BEACH
- FRITZ'S SKATE, BIKE & SURF
- JERRY'S FAMOUS DELI
- B.E.D.
- UHMA ORGANIC SPA & GREEN SHOP
- SOUTH BEACH DIVE & SURF CENTER
- MIAMI BEACH BICYCLE CENTER
- ART DECO HISTORIC DISTRICT
- 195
- VENETIAN CSWY
- 17TH ST
- LINCOLN RD
- 15TH ST
- 11TH ST
- 9TH ST
- MERIDIAN AVE
- MACARTHUR CSWY
- 0   500 yds
- 0   500 m

Main map labels:

- NW 183RD
- 860
- BLUE MOON OUTDOOR CENTER
- NE 163RD ST
- 826
- OLETA RIVER STATE PARK
- NORTH MIAMI BEACH GREYHOUND STATION
- 9
- W DIXIE HWY
- NE 6TH AVE
- 195
- 95
- 916
- 909
- HAULOVER PARK MARINA
- POSTNET
- NE 125TH ST
- 922
- MUSEUM OF CONTEMPORARY ART
- NE 119TH ST
- 915
- 1
- BISCAYNE BLVD
- NE 95TH ST
- NORTH SHORE MEDICAL CENTER
- SUDSIES DRY CLEANERS & LAUNDRY
- NE 70TH ST
- NW 79TH ST
- 934
- A1A
- FONTAINEBLEAU
- HIALEAH EXPY
- 934
- 27
- 953
- E OKEECHOBEE RD
- 9
- 441
- 95
- N MIAMI AVE
- LITTLE HAITI
- CHEZ LE BEBE RESTAURANT
- NE 46TH ST
- MIAMI DESIGN DISTRICT
- 1
- SEE DETAIL
- MIAMI BEACH
- ART DECO HISTORIC DISTRICT
- NW 36TH ST
- 948
- NW 36TH ST
- 112
- 25
- 27
- WINN-DIXIE
- 195
- MIAMI INTERNATIONAL AIRPORT
- MIAMI GREYHOUND STATION
- WYNWOOD ARTS DISTRICT
- NW 20TH ST
- HOSPITAL
- SEE "DOWNTOWN MIAMI" MAP
- VENETIAN CSWY
- 836
- 836
- NW 42ND AVE
- NW 57TH AVE
- W FLAGLER ST
- 968
- LITTLE HAVANA
- MACARTHUR CSWY
- MIAMI-DADE CULTURAL CENTER
- 41
- SW 8TH ST
- VERSAILLES
- 41
- SW 27TH AVE
- FOUR SEASONS HOTEL MIAMI
- BILTMORE HOTEL
- 972
- CORAL GABLES
- COCONUT GROVE
- SW 24TH ST
- 95
- 913
- SW 26TH RD
- Virginia Key
- MIAMI SEAQUARIUM
- BIRD RD
- 976
- 1
- SEE "COCONUT GROVE AND CORAL GABLES" MAP
- 959
- CRANDON PARK
- CRANDON BLVD
- Key Biscayne
- SUNSET DR
- To Zoo Miami
- To Deering Estate at Cutler
- MATHESON HAMMOCK COUNTY PARK
- KEY CYCLING
- VISITORS CENTER
- BILL BAGGS CAPE FLORIDA STATE PARK
- 0   2.5 mi
- 0   2.5 km

© AVALON TRAVEL

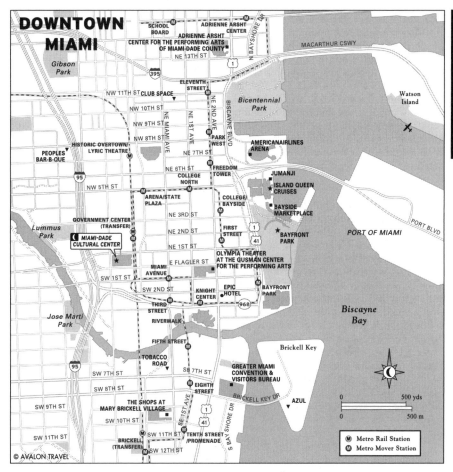

DOWNTOWN MIAMI

walking distance. Highlights include **Gallery Diet** (174 NW 23rd St., Miami, 305/571-2288, www.gallerydiet.com, 11 A.M.–5 P.M. Tues.–Sat.), which represents a small group of emerging and mid-career artists, and **Miami Art Space (MAS)** (244 NW 35th St., Miami, 305/757-6000, www.miamiartspace.com, 10 A.M.–4 P.M. Mon.–Fri.), which contains contemporary art exhibits inside and out.

◖ Little Havana

Home to many Cuban exiles and Cuban Americans since the 1960s, Little Havana

(www.littlehavana.biz) lies just west of downtown Miami. A predominantly Latino neighborhood, La Pequeña Habana offers a plethora of cigar shops, quiet parks, authentic markets and restaurants, live music venues, art galleries, and annual events like Calle Ocho, which takes place in March and is supposedly the biggest Hispanic street party in the country. To experience the unique vibe of this ethnic enclave, you should simply stroll along the major streets, such as Calle Ocho (SW 8th St., Miami) and Cuban Memorial Boulevard (SW 13th Ave., Miami), taking note of various monuments, such as a memorial plaque of Cuba, the bust of Cuban poet and revolutionary José Martí, and the black obelisk dedicated to those who perished during the Bay of Pigs Invasion. In Little Havana, you'll also encounter places like **Maximo Gomez Park** (801 SW 15th Ave., Miami, 9 A.M.–6 P.M. daily), named after a Cuban revolutionary who fought against Spanish oppression in the late 1800s. Affectionately known as Domino Park, this small meeting place is often filled with old-timers playing friendly, if competitive, rounds of chess or dominoes.

SOUTH BEACH
◖ Art Deco Historic District

East of downtown Miami lies Miami Beach, an incorporated city and part of a barrier island that's linked to the mainland by four causeways: MacArthur (U.S. 41), Venetian, Julia Tuttle (I-195), and John F. Kennedy (S.R. 934). Surely the most famous portion of this island is the southern part, known as South Beach, where you'll encounter one of the most celebrated architectural districts in southern Florida. Officially listed as the Miami Beach Architectural District on the National Register of Historic Places, the colorful Art Deco Historic District features an incredible collection of art deco–style buildings roughly bounded by Alton Road, the Collins Canal, and Ocean Drive.

The best way to experience this historic neighborhood is via walking, biking, or Segway tour, whether self-guided or otherwise. First-timers may especially appreciate the guided stroll that the **Miami Design Preservation League (MDPL)** (Ocean Auditorium, 1001 Ocean Dr., Miami Beach, 305/672-2014, www.mdpl.org) offers daily (10:30 A.M. Fri.–Wed., 6:30 P.M. Thurs., $20 adults, $15 children under 13). Departing from the Art Deco Gift Shop (305/531-3484, 9:30 A.M.–7 P.M. daily) inside the Ocean Auditorium, this 90-minute walking tour explores hotels, restaurants, and other commercial structures, providing an introduction to the art deco, Mediterranean Revival, and Miami Modern

styles found within this important district. Reservations are not required for this tour. As an alternative, MDPL features a self-guided, 90-minute tour of the area. Using a rented iPod and an accompanying map, you can learn about the district's architectural history at your own pace. This tour, which includes commentary in English, Spanish, French, or German, is available from the Art Deco Gift Shop 9:30 A.M.–5 P.M. daily.

No matter which tour you choose, you can easily reach South Beach via public bus or private vehicle. If you drive yourself, you'll find plenty of parking garages and metered street parking here; just remember to heed all residential zone parking restrictions.

Museums and Memorials

Beyond its art deco splendor, South Beach contains several curious museums and memorials. Near the southern end of the island, you'll encounter the spacious **Jewish Museum of Florida** (301 Washington Ave., Miami Beach, 305/672-5044, www.jewishmuseum.com, 10 A.M.–5 P.M. Tues.–Sun., $12 families, $6 adults, $5 seniors over 65, students, and children, children under 6 free), which includes two former synagogues, one erected in 1929 and the other in 1936. Both synagogues are listed on the National Register of Historic Places, and together, they boast an extensive collection of photographs, documents, and artifacts that illustrate the Jewish experience in the Sunshine State. Three informative films are also available: *Synagogue to Museum,* which presents Florida's Jewish history as well as the museum's history; *Jewish Settlement in Florida,* which explores four diverse Jewish families; and *L'Chaim: To Life,* which depicts Jewish traditions, including holiday cycles. Admission is free for all visitors on Saturday, though the on-site bistro and museum store are closed then. Be advised, too, that the entire museum complex is closed on Monday as well as on national and Jewish holidays.

The **Wolfsonian-Florida International University** (1001 Washington Ave., Miami Beach, 305/531-1001, www.wolfsonian.org, noon–6 P.M. Thurs. and Sat.–Tues., noon–9 P.M. Fri. mid-Sept.–Apr., noon–6 P.M. Thurs. and Sat.–Sun., noon–9 P.M. Fri. May–mid-Sept., $7 adults, $5 seniors, students, and children 6–12, children under 6 free), a wheelchair-accessible design museum in the heart of the Art Deco Historic District, houses an intriguing collection of objects from the modern era (1885–1945), all of which demonstrate how art and design influence and reflect the human experience. Admission is free after 6 P.M. on Friday.

Another repository worth visiting is the **World Erotic Art Museum (WEAM)** (1205 Washington Ave., Miami Beach, 305/532-9336 or 866/969-9326, www.weam.com, 11 A.M.–10 P.M. Mon.–Thurs., 11 A.M.–midnight Fri.–Sun., $15 adults, $14 seniors over 60, $13.50 students 18 and over), which is two blocks north of the Wolfsonian. Home to the continent's largest collection of erotic art, the 12,000-square-foot museum includes everything from Lady Godiva depictions to Indonesian and Caribbean artifacts, plus erotic chessboards, pin-up illustrations, gay photography, fetish artwork, and Picasso paintings, among other exhibits. Visitors to WEAM will encounter 20 separate rooms, all part of a fascinating yet tasteful timeline of erotica, or the "art of love." The on-site gift shop contains an array of engaging erotic books, postcards, and posters. Visitors must be 18 years or older to enter the museum.

Just south of Dade Boulevard, you'll encounter the **Holocaust Memorial** (1933–1945 Meridian Ave., Miami Beach, 305/538-1663, www.holocaustmmb.org, 9 A.M.–9 P.M. daily, free), erected to honor the six million Jews who perished during the infamous Holocaust. Constructed over a four-year period and dedicated in February 1990, the memorial features a reflecting pool; a black granite wall presenting the history of the Holocaust (1933–1945) through text, pictures, and maps; and a narrow passage highlighting the most infamous death camps. From here, visitors enter a large circular plaza paved in Jerusalem stone, surrounded by a high, black granite wall, and featuring a 42-foot-high bronze sculpture

Bass Museum of Art

composed of nearly 100 anguished figures. Of course, this engaging yet heart-wrenching tour culminates with the Memorial Wall, which contains an ever-growing list of names, representing a multitude of fallen children, parents, and grandparents from European towns.

Not far away from the Holocaust Memorial lies yet another art repository, the **Bass Museum of Art** (2121 Park Ave., Miami Beach, 305/673-7530, www.bassmuseum.org, noon–5 P.M. Wed.–Sun., $8 adults, $6 seniors, students, and children 6–17, children under 6 free), which contains an enormous selection of European, Asian, North American, Latin American, and Caribbean paintings, sculptures, textiles, and photographs from the 15th through the 21st centuries, including the work of Peter Paul Rubens and Benjamin West. There are temporary art exhibits as well as a relatively new Egyptian gallery that includes an authentic mummy and sarcophagus. Free docent tours are available, and an on-site gift shop offers a curious selection of folk art, local

jewelry, unique decorative items, educational toys, and art and photography books, plus a snack bar with free wireless Internet access.

Gardens and Beaches

Not far from the Holocaust Memorial on Meridian Avenue lies the **Miami Beach Botanical Garden** (2000 Convention Center Dr., Miami Beach, 305/673-7256, www.mbgarden.org, 9 A.M.–5 P.M. Tues.–Sun., free), a 4.5-acre greenspace that invites visitors to relax amid vibrant orchids, tropical plants, and Japanese-style foliage. For a sandier landscape, consider visiting one of the many beaches that line the ocean side of this barrier island, including **Lummus Park Beach** (305/673-7730, sunrise–sunset daily, free), the main public beach in South Beach. Lying just east of the Art Deco Historic District, this white sandy stretch extends alongside Ocean Drive between 5th and 15th Streets. Favored among teenagers, families, tourists, and celebrities alike, this often-photographed beach is popular for swimming, sunbathing, and people-watching. Amenities here include public

© GREATER MIAMI CONVENTION & VISITORS BUREAU/WWW.GMCVB.COM

a lifeguard stand in South Beach

restrooms, volleyball courts, beach chair rentals ($10 daily), umbrella rentals ($12 daily), and, of course, clear, warm ocean waters.

Watson Island

En route from South Beach to downtown Miami via the MacArthur Causeway, you'll cross Watson Island in Biscayne Bay, which has two family-friendly attractions. On one side of the road lies **Jungle Island** (1111 Parrot Jungle Trail, Miami, 305/400-7000, www.jungleisland.com, 10 A.M.–6 P.M. daily, $33 adults, $31 seniors 62 and over, $25 children 3–10, children under 3 free), where visitors can see parrot shows, view the antics of kangaroos and penguins, watch tiger and primate presentations, feed the lorikeets, and wander among the alligators in an Everglades habitat. Other activities include strolling through a lush greenhouse and relaxing on a private beach.

Meanwhile, on the opposite side of the road, the wheelchair-accessible **Miami Children's Museum (MCM)** (980 MacArthur Cswy., Miami, 305/373-5437, www.miamichildrensmuseum.org, 10 A.M.–6 P.M. daily, $15 adults and children, $12 Florida residents, children under 1 free) lures visitors with an array of interactive exhibits that allow children to operate a crane and navigate a cruise ship at the Port of Miami, play in a world music studio, steer a fire truck, explore the Everglades, peer inside a 900-gallon marine tank, and learn how to take better care of themselves and their pets. Other exhibits feature the inner workings of a bank, a supermarket, and a television studio.

COCONUT GROVE

Situated southwest of downtown Miami, Coconut Grove is a well-favored shopping and dining destination that also boasts three winning attractions. From the downtown area, the first one you'll encounter is the **Miami Science Museum** (3280 S. Miami Ave., Miami, 305/646-4200, www.miamisci.org, 10 A.M.–6 P.M. daily, $15 adults, $13 Miami-Dade County adults, $11 seniors 62 and over, students, and children 3–12, $9 Miami-Dade County seniors 62 and over, students, and children 3–12, children under 3 free), which features intriguing temporary exhibits, permanent

MODERN ART

After visiting the sights of South Beach, including the Art Deco Historic District, art lovers should take a quick detour to North Miami, where you'll find the **Museum of Contemporary Art (MOCA)** (Joan Lehman Bldg., 770 NE 125th St., 305/893-6211, www.mocanomi.org, 11 A.M.–5 P.M. Tues. and Thurs.-Sat., 1–9 P.M. Wed., noon–5 P.M. Sun., $5 adults, $3 seniors and students, children under 12 and North Miami residents free). Known worldwide for its ability to establish new trends in contemporary art, MOCA houses a permanent collection of more than 600 pieces of cutting-edge sculptures, paintings, photographs, videos, and multimedia creations from emerging and established artists, such as photographer Melanie Schiff, sculptor Dennis Oppenheim, and innovator James Turrell, whose work primarily explores the relationship between light and space.

In addition to its impressive collection, MOCA, which has plans to expand its exhibition space threefold, also presents lectures, screenings, concerts, performances, and the Knight Exhibition Series, which features mind-bending temporary installations that focus on visionaries like Anri Sala, Luis Gispert, Ceal Floyer, and Cory Arcangel. If you're in town on the last Friday of the month, be sure to stop by for Jazz at MOCA from 7 to 10 P.M., and don't forget to visit the on-site gift shop, which is open during museum hours and offers one of the city's best selections of contemporary art books, imaginative jewelry, eye-popping designs, and other unique items. Just be advised that, given its currently limited space, MOCA must typically close during the installation of a new exhibition, so always call ahead before visiting.

interactive displays like the human yoyo and the energy-capturing dance floor, and educational shows in the on-site wildlife center and planetarium.

Not far away lies the stunning **Vizcaya Museum and Gardens** (3251 S. Miami Ave., Miami, 305/250-9133, www.vizcayamuseum. org, 9:30 A.M.–4:30 P.M. daily, $15 adults, $10 seniors 62 and over, students, disabled visitors, and Miami-Dade County residents, $6 children 6–12, $5 Miami-Dade County children 6–12, children under 6 free), an expansive property that served as the winter residence of American industrialist James Deering, vice president of an agricultural equipment company, from 1916 until his death in 1925. Construction on the Italian Renaissance–style mansion, which was intended to look like a 400-year-old estate that had been occupied and renovated by several familial generations, began in 1914 and continued until 1923. During this time, more than 1,000 European and Caribbean laborers and craftsmen worked on the 180-acre complex, which included the house, the formal gardens, a farm, and several service facilities. Two hurricanes, one in 1926 and another in 1935, caused extensive damage to the house and surrounding grounds, and eventually, most of the land was sold for development. In 1952, however, Deering's heirs sold the main house and formal gardens to the county and, later, donated the estate's substantial artwork and furnishings with the condition that Vizcaya be forever used as a public museum.

Today, the house features 34 uniquely decorated rooms, with antique furnishings and art objects from the 15th through the 19th century. Although the architectural design once permitted the free flow of breezes through the open courtyard, the house now features a glass-enclosed courtyard and a climate and humidity control system that better preserves the building and contents. The gardens, meanwhile, blend elements of French and Italian Renaissance designs, including fountains, statuary, and a central pool. Listed on the National Register of Historic Places since 1970, the museum welcomes visitors on narrated or self-guided tours of the opulent house, elaborate gardens, and impressive orchidarium. Spanish-language tours are available, as are guidebooks ($3 each) in both English and Spanish. A café overlooks the historic swimming pool and serves sandwiches, salads, and desserts. A gift shop offers books, postcards, and jewelry, among other items. The facilities here are wheelchair-accessible, and the parking is free.

Farther south, alongside Biscayne Bay, **The Barnacle Historic State Park** (3485 Main Hwy., Coconut Grove, 305/442-6866, www.floridastateparks.org/thebarnacle, 9 A.M.–5 P.M. Fri.–Mon., $2 pp) preserves the former home and grounds of Ralph Middleton Munroe, a sailboat designer, civic activist, naturalist, author, and photographer who was also one of Coconut Grove's most influential pioneers. Built in 1891, the colorful, Caribbean-style house was inspired, especially throughout the interior, by sturdy, hurricane-resistant boat designs. With a lower porch and upper balcony, the building also takes advantage of the peaceful, bayside views. Although you're free to stroll through the home as well as the surrounding tropical hardwood hammock and nearby boathouse, tours are also available for an extra fee (10 A.M., 11:30 A.M., 1 P.M., and 2:30 P.M. Fri.–Mon., $3 adults, $1 children 6–12, children under 6 free) and are usually 45 minutes long. In addition, the park is open on Wednesday and Thursday for group tours, if arranged in advance. No matter the season, this park is an excellent place for picnics and bird-watching opportunities. Just remember that entrance fees must be placed in the honor box, and correct change is required.

CORAL GABLES
◖ Biltmore Hotel

Founded by George Merrick in the 1920s, the lovely community of Coral Gables is now home to the University of Miami and the historic Biltmore Hotel (1200 Anastasia Ave., Coral Gables, 305/445-1926, www.biltmore-hotel.com), which was designed in 1924 by renowned architect Leonard Schultze and developer S. Fullerton Weaver and now serves as

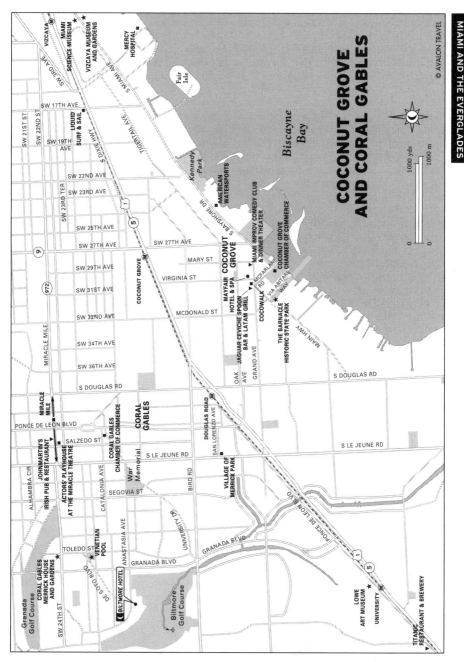

MIAMI AND THE EVERGLADES

COCONUT GROVE AND CORAL GABLES

© AVALON TRAVEL

Biscayne Bay

1000 yds
1000 m

VIZCAYA
MIAMI SCIENCE MUSEUM
VIZCAYA MUSEUM AND GARDENS
MERCY HOSPITAL
Fair Isle

SW 3RD AVE
S MIAMI AVE
TIGERTAIL AVE
S DIXIE HWY

SW 21ST ST
SW 22ND ST
SW 17TH AVE
LIQUID SURF & SAIL
SW 19TH AVE

SW 22ND AVE
SW 23RD AVE
SW 23RD TER
Kennedy Park
AMERICAN WATERSPORTS

SW 25TH AVE
SW 27TH AVE
SW 27TH AVE

S BAYSHORE DR

SW 29TH AVE
MARY ST
COCONUT GROVE
MIAMI IMPROV COMEDY CLUB & DINNER THEATER
COCONUT GROVE CHAMBER OF COMMERCE

SW 31ST AVE
VIRGINIA ST
MAYFAIR
COCONUT GROVE
HOTEL & SPA
MCFARLANE RD
COCOWALK
VIA ABITARE WAY

COCONUT GROVE

SW 32ND AVE
MCDONALD ST
JAGUAR CEVICHE SPOON BAR & LATAM GRILL
THE BARNACLE HISTORIC STATE PARK

SW 34TH AVE
OAK AVE
GRAND AVE

SW 36TH AVE

MIRACLE MILE

MAIN HWY

S DOUGLAS RD
S DOUGLAS RD

MIRACLE MILE
PONCE DE LEON BLVD
CORAL GABLES

DOUGLAS ROAD
SAN LORENZO AVE

JOHNMARTIN'S IRISH PUB & RESTAURANT
SALZEDO ST
CORAL GABLES CHAMBER OF COMMERCE
War Memorial
S LE JEUNE RD

S LE JEUNE RD

ALHAMBRA CIR
ACTORS PLAYHOUSE AT THE MIRACLE THEATRE
CATALONIA AVE
SEGOVIA ST
BIRD RD
VILLAGE OF MERRICK PARK

UNIVERSITY DR

PONCE DE LEON BLVD

TOLEDO ST
VENETIAN POOL
ANASTASIA AVE

CORAL GABLES MERRICK HOUSE AND GARDENS
DE SOTO BLVD
BILTMORE HOTEL
GRANADA BLVD
GRANADA BLVD

Granada Golf Course
SW 24TH ST
Biltmore Golf Course

LOWE ART MUSEUM
UNIVERSITY

TITANIC RESTAURANT & BREWERY

a monument to Italian, Moorish, and Spanish architectural styles. After officially opening in January of 1926, the oft-photographed jewel of Coral Gables welcomed countless movie stars, politicians, and other celebrities in its early years, including Judy Garland, Bing Crosby, President Franklin D. Roosevelt, and Al Capone. World War II altered the property's fortunes, however, and from 1942 to 1968, the Biltmore served as a military hospital. After much lobbying by Coral Gables officials and city residents, the Biltmore was acquired by the city in 1973 and remained vacant for a full decade, until an extensive, four-year restoration returned the resort to its former glory. Three years later, the hotel closed in the midst of the county's economic downturn, only to be bought and fully restored by a private corporation. In 1996, the federal government finally declared the Biltmore a National Historic Landmark, ensuring its well-deserved preservation. So, even if you choose not to stay overnight, play golf or tennis here, dine in the Palme d'Or or Fontana restaurant, or enjoy a massage in the world-class spa, you simply must see this architectural gem for yourself. Free guided tours of the Biltmore are available on Sunday at 1:30 P.M., 2:30 P.M., and 3:30 P.M.

Other Attractions

Several blocks north of the Biltmore Hotel, you can visit the **Coral Gables Merrick House and Gardens** (907 Coral Way, Coral Gables, 305/460-5361, www.coralgables.com, 1–4 P.M. Wed. and Sun., $5 adults, $3 seniors and students, $1 children 6–12, children under 6 free), once the home of city planner George Merrick and now listed in the National Register of Historic Places. Originally part of William and Sarah Gregory's 160-acre homestead, this property was acquired, sight unseen, by Reverend Solomon G. Merrick, who hoped to relocate his wife, Althea, and their children from the harsh climate of Massachusetts to the sunny Miami area. Solomon and his eldest son, George, preceded the rest of the family in order to cultivate the rocky, untamed land. By January 1900, Althea and the other children

had arrived, and the immensely hard work continued. In fact, the Merrick men were forced to enlist the help of Bahamian workers from Coconut Grove in order to replace the pine palmetto with grapefruit trees.

By 1906, however, the groves had begun to flourish, and the family had successfully expanded their small wooden cottage into a spacious, New England–style home. Despite George's college education and career goals of becoming a lawyer, his father's death in 1911 forced him to return to his family's Coral Gables Plantation, where, by the 1920s, he'd begun to envision a Mediterranean-style city with wide boulevards and lush landscaping. Eventually, George's vision became a reality when the city of Coral Gables was incorporated in 1925. Unfortunately, however, a 1926 hurricane stalled the city's momentum, and in an effort to save his new town, George lost all of his family's fortune save for the original house, where Althea continued to live with her daughter Ethel. In 1935, the house became an inn called Merrick Manor, which, following Althea's death two years later, Ethel operated until her death in 1961. By 1976, the City of Coral Gables purchased the house and restored it to its 1925 appearance. Today, as part of the admission price, visitors can take a 45-minute tour (1 P.M., 2 P.M., and 3 P.M. Wed. and Sun.) of the historic house, which contains much of the Merrick family's artwork, photographs, furniture, and personal treasures, offering an outstanding look at the early days of Coral Gables.

Of course, on particularly hot days, many tourists venture to the nearby **Venetian Pool** (2701 De Soto Blvd., Coral Gables, 305/460-5306 or 305/460-5357, www.coralgablesvenetianpool.com, 11 A.M.–7:30 P.M. Mon.–Fri., 10 A.M.–4:30 P.M. Sat.–Sun. Memorial Day–Labor Day, 11 A.M.–5:30 P.M. Tues.–Fri., 10 A.M.–4:30 P.M. Sat.–Sun. Sept.–May, $10.50 adults, $6 children 3–12, $3.75–4.75 Coral Gables residents), a tranquil coral rock lagoon designed by Coral Gables' founding father George Merrick, opened in 1923, and now listed on the National Register of Historic

Places. Encircled by brilliant bougainvillea, coconut palms, and twin observation towers, the Venetian Pool is worth a photo stop, even if you don't take a dip. Unfortunately, children under the age of three are not allowed here.

South of the Biltmore lies the University of Miami campus, where the **Lowe Art Museum** (1301 Stanford Dr., Coral Gables, 305/284-3535, www6.miami.edu/lowe, 10 A.M.–4 P.M. Tues.–Sat., noon–4 P.M. Sun., $10 adults, $5 seniors and students, University of Miami students and children under 12 free) features a wide assortment of paintings, sculptures, ceramics, photography, and glasswork, representing Greco-Roman, European, American, Asian, African, Pacific, and Latin American cultures. The museum, which is accessible via the University stop on the Metrorail, also has a metered parking lot.

The scenic **Matheson Hammock County Park** (9610 Old Cutler Rd., Miami, 305/665-5475, www.miamidade.gov, sunrise–sunset daily, $5 automobiles, $10 recreational vehicles, $12 trailers) lures visitors to Biscayne Bay, where you can enjoy a manmade pool, a breezy beach, a full-service marina and restaurant, picnic pavilions, and nature trails. Another lovely oasis is the **Fairchild Tropical Botanic Garden** (10901 Old Cutler Rd., Coral Gables, 305/667-1651, www.fairchildgarden. org, 9:30 A.M.–4:30 P.M. daily, $20 adults, $15 seniors 65 and over, $10 children 6–17, children under 6 free), an 83-acre property opened in 1938 and now nurturing an extensive collection of rare tropical plants, including palms, cycads, vines, succulents, and flowering trees.

KEY BISCAYNE

East of Coconut Grove and Coral Gables lies Key Biscayne, a barrier island in Biscayne Bay, accessible via the Rickenbacker Causeway. En route to Key Biscayne, you'll encounter Virginia Key, where the 38-acre **Miami Seaquarium** (4400 Rickenbacker Cswy., Key Biscayne, 305/361-5705, www.miamiseaquarium.com, 9:30 A.M.–6 P.M. daily, $38 adults, $36 seniors 55 or over, $28 children 3–9, $19 military personnel, children under 3 free, $8

parking) invites visitors to watch entertaining dolphins and sea lions, observe friendly manatees, and view shark feedings. There are several snack bars and gift shops throughout the park. For an extra fee, you can even interact with playful dolphins at the relatively new Dolphin Harbor. Programs here include the Dolphin Odyssey ($199 participants, $45 observers 10 and over, $36 observers 3–9, observers under 3 free), an intimate chance to touch, feed, train, and ride a dolphin; the Dolphin Encounter ($139 participants, $99 children 5–9, $45 adult observers, $36 observers 3–9, observers under 3 free), a shallow-water opportunity to touch, feed, and play with the dolphins; and the Trainer for a Day program ($495 pp). Just be advised that some programs have height and age restrictions.

On Key Biscayne, you'll encounter two lovely recreation areas. The first is **Crandon Park** (4000 Crandon Blvd., Key Biscayne, 305/361-5421, www.miamidade.gov, sunrise–sunset daily, $6 vehicles, activity fees apply), a former coconut plantation that now features a golf course, a marina, tennis courts, nature trails, kayak and cabana rentals, guided tram tours, an amusement area, and the Crandon Park Visitor and Nature Center (8 A.M.–4 P.M. daily). Visitors here can explore a variety of ecosystems, including coastal dunes, mangrove forests, tropical hardwood hammocks, and seagrass beds. Kayaking is an especially rewarding activity, as it affords you a leisurely, ecofriendly way to observe wading birds, raptors, sea turtles, and other marine creatures. Of course, many visitors come for the gorgeous two-mile beach, which offers concession stands, picnic areas, several lifeguard towers, and plenty of parking. The beach, marina, tennis center, amusement area, nature center, gardens, and cabanas are all wheelchair-accessible.

At the southern end of Key Biscayne lies **Bill Baggs Cape Florida State Park** (1200 S. Crandon Blvd., Key Biscayne, 305/361-5811, www.floridastateparks.org/capeflorida, 8 A.M.–sunset daily, $8 vehicles w/2–8 passengers, $4 motorcycles and single-occupant vehicles, $2 pedestrians, bikers, day-use boaters, and extra passengers), home to the historic 95-foot-tall **Cape Florida Lighthouse,** a whitewashed conical tower built in 1825, reconstructed in 1846, and now considered the oldest standing structure in Miami-Dade County. The photogenic lighthouse grounds, which lie at the southern tip of Key Biscayne, are open from 9 A.M. to 5 P.M. Thursday–Monday. You can watch a video presentation in the former cookhouse, view cultural displays about early island life in the lighthouse keeper's cottage, and visit the gift shop. Free guided tours of the lighthouse are offered at 10 A.M. and 1 P.M. Thursday–Monday, though it's best to call the administrative offices (305/361-8779, 8:30 A.M.–4:30 P.M. Mon.–Fri.) in advance, just in case a school group has reserved a tour. Be prepared to climb 109 steps in all, which can be a strenuous trek for some—though well worth the panoramic views, in spite of the cramped observation area. Unfortunately—and rather arbitrarily—children under 8 are not allowed to reach the top.

The park also features a 1.25-mile beach, and popular activities here consist of biking, kayaking, sunbathing, swimming, shoreline fishing, and overnight boat camping. Other amenities include picnic pavilions ($100–150 daily), bicycle rentals ($3–15 per half hour, $5–25 hourly), beach chair rentals ($7 each), beach umbrella rentals ($10 each), kayak rentals ($10–15 per half hour, $15–25 hourly), a primitive campground, and two restaurants: the **Boater's Grill** (305/361-0080, www.lighthouserestaurants.com, 9 A.M.–sunset daily, $4–42) and the **Lighthouse Café** (305/361-8487, www.lighthouserestaurants.com, 9 A.M.–sunset daily, $2–38). Although leashed pets are allowed in the park, they are not permitted on the beach or playground, near the wetlands, within the lighthouse compound, or inside the restaurants.

SOUTHERN MIAMI

Even the southern suburbs contain a few interesting attractions. Beside Biscayne Bay, for instance, the 444-acre **Deering Estate at Cutler** (16701 SW 72nd Ave., Miami, 305/235-1668, www.deeringestate.com, 10 A.M.–5 P.M. daily,

$10 adults, $5 children 4–14, children under 4 free) invites visitors to take daily nature tours of several protected habitats, including pine rocklands, tropical hardwood hammocks, salt marshes, and mangrove forests. In addition, the 1920s-era, Mediterranean Revival–style mansion, nicknamed the "Stone House," that was once the home of Charles Deering—a wealthy Chicago industrialist, environmental preservationist, dedicated philanthropist, avid art collector, and amateur artist—now boasts a fine collection of antique furniture, chandeliers, and other furnishings, plus several pieces of artwork, such as family portraits as well as paintings like *Ash Wednesday Procession in Barcelona,* one of several works that Deering commissioned from Spanish artist Ramon Casas in the early 1900s. During your tour of the house, which is incidentally listed on the National Register of Historic Places, you'll also spy some of Deering's original volumes, such as classic novels by Cervantes, Chaucer, Dickens, Kipling, and Melville, plus a two-volume 1800 edition of Henry Fielding's *The History of Tom Jones.*

For a completely different experience, head west to **Zoo Miami** (12400 SW 152nd St., Miami, 305/251-0400, www.miamimetrozoo.com, 9:30 A.M.–5:30 P.M. daily, $16 adults, $12 seniors 65 and over, military personnel, and children 3–12, children under 3 free), home to over 1,000 different plant species and 400 different animal species, including endangered creatures like the sable antelope and the Cuban crocodile. Here, visitors can stroll through a children's zoo, learn about the links between birds and dinosaurs in the American Bankers Family Aviary, explore the relatively new, 27-acre Amazon & Beyond exhibit, and take a narrated safari tram tour (11 A.M.–4 P.M., $5 pp) through the Asian or African habitat. All trams and the zoo's monorail system are wheelchair-accessible.

BOAT TOURS

If you're a first-time visitor to the Miami area, consider taking a sightseeing boat tour of the city's coastline and lovely Biscayne Bay. One such option is **Island Queen Cruises** (401 Biscayne Blvd., Miami, 305/379-5119, www.islandqueencruises.com, times vary daily, $16–55 adults, $11–45 children 4–12, children under 4 free), based out of the Bayside Marketplace and offering a variety of excursions, including party fishing cruises, dance cruises, and speedboat cruises past "Millionaire's Row."

Another option is **Duck Tours South Beach** (1661 James Ave., Miami Beach, 305/673-2217, www.ducktourssouthbeach.com, times vary daily, $32 adults, $26 seniors, $18 children), featuring 90-minute narrated tours on amphibious vehicles that lead you past famous Miami landmarks before launching into Biscayne Bay.

Entertainment and Events

NIGHTLIFE

Miami is celebrated around the world for many reasons, not the least of which is its sultry nightlife. This is a town, after all, that lures the young, wealthy, and beautiful, many of whom celebrate to excess at the city's numerous bars and dance clubs, where 24-hour liquor licenses are not unheard of. If you, too, hope to live it up in the Magic City, you surely won't run out of options any time soon.

In downtown Miami, for instance, you'll encounter **Tobacco Road** (626 S. Miami Ave., Miami, 305/374-1198, www.tobacco-road.com, 11:30 A.M.–5 A.M. daily, covers vary), which has been open since 1912 and once served as a speakeasy during Prohibition. These days, the city's oldest bar and restaurant features live jazz and blues, plus a tasty menu. For the quintessential Miami dance club experience, head north toward I-395, where **Club Space** (34 NE 11th St., Miami, 305/375-0001, www.clubspace.com, 11 P.M.–2 P.M. Thurs.–Sat., $20 cover pp), a multistory, vintage warehouse, lures countless revelers nightly. Just be forewarned that drink prices and valet parking fees are high here, and you'll likely find it easier to breach the velvet ropes if you're attractive, well dressed, and female.

In nearby Coconut Grove, the **Miami Improv Comedy Club & Dinner Theater** (3390 Mary St., Ste. 182, Miami, 305/441-8200, www.miamiimprov.com, show times and ticket prices vary) features an ever-evolving lineup of stand-up comedy routines. Meanwhile, at **JohnMartin's Irish Pub & Restaurant** (253 Miracle Mile, Coral Gables, 305/445-3777, www.johnmartins.com, 11:30 A.M.–midnight Sun.–Tues., 11:30 A.M.–2 A.M. Wed.–Sat., no cover), you can enjoy happy hour drink specials on weekdays (4–8 P.M.), karaoke on Wednesday night (9:30 P.M.–1 A.M.), live entertainment (typically classic rock music) on Friday and Saturday (9:30 P.M.–1 A.M.), and open mic night on Sunday (7–10 P.M.).

Of course, most night owls flock to neon-lit, gay-friendly South Beach, an area teeming with trendy bars, hot dance clubs, and outrageous cabaret shows. It's here that you'll find the biggest crowds, the longest lines, and the tightest door policies. In fact, if your hotel concierge can't add your name to the VIP list, your best bet is to arrive as early as possible. Some of the most exclusive, most popular South Beach clubs include—but are certainly not limited to—the **Mynt Lounge** (1921 Collins Ave., Miami Beach, 305/532-0727, www.myntlounge.com, midnight–5 A.M. Thurs.–Sat., $20 cover pp), which has hosted the likes of Paris Hilton, Jennifer Lopez, and Jamie Foxx; **Dream** (1532 Washington Ave., Miami Beach, 305/674-8018, www.dreammia.com, 10 P.M.–5 A.M. Mon.–Sat., covers vary), a sexy, spacious nightclub that features themed gatherings, like Eye Candy Saturdays; **Cameo** (1445 Washington Ave., Miami Beach, 786/235-5800, www.cameomiami.com, 11 P.M.–5 A.M. Fri.–Sat., $20–30 cover pp), an enormous dance club and celebrity magnet housed within a historic art deco–style movie theater; and **Jazid** (1342 Washington

Ave., Miami Beach, 305/673-9372, www.jazid. net, 10 P.M.–close daily, no cover Sun.–Thurs., $10 cover Fri.–Sat.), which, beyond killer drink specials, offers some of the best live funk, soul, jazz, reggae, and world music in the city.

If you're not ready to brave the nightclub crowds in South Beach, head first to the retro **Buck15** (707 Lincoln Ln., Miami Beach, 305/538-3815, www.buck15.net, 10 P.M.–5 A.M. Tues.–Sun., no cover), an underground bar and lounge situated above Miss Yip that promises no velvet ropes and features plenty of spun music, from reggae to rhythm-and-blues.

For additional nightlife ideas, consult the daily *Miami Herald* (www.miamiherald.com), the free weekly *Miami New Times* (www.miaminewtimes.com), the monthly *Ocean Drive Magazine* (www.oceandrive.com), and *South Beach Magazine* (www.southbeach-usa.com).

THE ARTS

Cultural enthusiasts will find plenty of live performances in the Miami area. In the downtown performing arts district, for example, the **Adrienne Arsht Center for the Performing Arts of Miami-Dade County** (1300 N. Biscayne Blvd., Miami, 305/949-6722, www. arshtcenter.org, show times and ticket prices vary) hosts an array of live entertainment, including intimate plays, Broadway musicals, one-act comedies and dramas, opera productions, contemporary dance performances, experimental multimedia shows, cabaret and comedy routines, family-friendly presentations, jazz and rock concerts, and even performances by the **Miami City Ballet** (305/929-7010, www.miamicityballet.org). To reach the center, you can use the Metrobus, Metrorail, or Metromover; if you plan to drive here, be prepared to pay for self-parking ($15 per vehicle) or valet parking ($20 per vehicle). Although you'll find several eateries in the downtown area, you can also enjoy a pre-show meal at Prelude, the center's on-site restaurant.

To the south, not far from Miami's Bayfront Park, is the **Olympia Theater at the Gusman Center for the Performing Arts** (174 E. Flagler St., Miami, 305/374-2444, www.

gusmancenter.org, show times and ticket prices vary). Erected in 1926 as a silent movie theater, this magnificently restored venue is now home to live performances, various screenings, and community events, including concerts hosted by the **Miami Symphony Orchestra** (305/275-5666, www.themiso.org), which performs at venues throughout the city. Other unique venues include the **Fillmore Miami Beach at the Jackie Gleason Theater** (1700 Washington Ave., Miami Beach, 305/938-2505, www.fillmoremb.com, show times and ticket prices vary), which features live concerts, comedy routines, and dance performances, and the recently restored **Actors' Playhouse at the Miracle Theatre** (280 Miracle Mile, Coral Gables, 305/444-9293, www.actorsplayhouse.org, show times and ticket prices vary), which presents mainstage performances as well as a children's theater series. To save some money, high school and college students between the ages of 13 and 22 can access various cultural events, festivals, and art exhibitions at affordable prices (typically $5 per ticket) by participating in **Culture Shock Miami** (305/375-1949, www.cultureshockmiami. com), a discounted ticketing program made possible through the **Miami-Dade County Department of Cultural Affairs** (111 NW 1st St., Ste. 625, Miami, 305/375-4634, www. miamidadearts.org).

FESTIVALS AND EVENTS
Art and Cultural Events

Like the Florida Keys, Miami honors its multifaceted culture with a wide array of annual festivals and events—too many, in fact, to list here. Given the city's passion for art, it's no wonder that many of Miami's most popular celebrations focus on architecture and other visual art disciplines. The annual **Art Deco Weekend Festival** (prices vary), for instance, lures nearly 400,000 people to South Beach in mid-January. Begun in 1976 by the Miami Design Preservation League (www.mdpl.org), this three-day event helps to cultivate an appreciation for the legendary Art Deco Historic District with an assortment of guided tours, film series, art and antiques sales, classic automobiles, live music, dance performances, and other activities.

Other area art festivals include the **Coconut Grove Arts Festival** (305/447-0401, www.coconutgroveartsfest.com, $10 pp daily), which attracts a ton of painters, photographers, jewelry makers, and glass sculptors to the Coconut Grove area for a three-day weekend in mid-February; the four-day **Art Basel Miami Beach** (www.artbasel.com, ticket prices vary), an enormous, early December show featuring an exclusive selection of more than 250 art galleries from North America, Latin America, Europe, Asia, and Africa; and the five-day **Art Miami** (520/529-1108, www.art-miami.com, one-day pass $15 adults, $10 seniors and students 12–18, children under 12 free), the city's longest-running contemporary art fair, which usually takes place in early December in the Miami Midtown Arts District.

Beyond such visual art festivals, Miami hosts several cinematic, performance, and literary events. Some of these much-anticipated happenings include the 10-day **Miami International Film Festival** (305/237-3456, www.miamifilmfestival.com, show times and ticket prices vary) in early March; the 10-day **Miami Gay & Lesbian Film Festival** (305/534-9924, www.mglff.com, show times and ticket prices vary) in late April; the **Mainly Mozart Festival** (305/444-4755, www.mainlymozart.com, $20 per concert, $100 per series), a seven-concert chamber music series in May and June; the two-week **International Ballet Fest of Miami** (305/549-7711, www.internationalballetfestival.org, show times and ticket prices vary) in late August; and the eight-day **Miami Book Fair International** (305/237-3258, www.miamibookfair.com, prices vary) in mid-November.

Heritage Festivals

In addition, residents and visitors can experience the city's intriguing cultural mosaic through such unique festivals as the two-week **Carnaval Miami** (305/644-8888, www.

carnavalmiami.com, entry fees apply), a celebration that takes place in Little Havana from late February to mid-March and features culinary and athletic competitions, live concerts, a domino tournament, and **Calle Ocho,** one of the largest Hispanic block parties in the country. Since 1976, the four-day **Miami/Bahamas Goombay Festival** (305/448-9501, www.goombayfestivalcoconutgrove.com, prices vary), which usually takes place in early June, has honored the Bahamian roots of Coconut Grove with a plethora of authentic cuisine, live Caribbean and African music, and spirited festivities, including a vibrant parade of costumed dancers and musicians. Later in the year, typically on a Saturday in mid-November, thousands of spectators gather on Virginia Key for the free-to-watch **Miami Hong Kong Dragon Boat Festival** (305/636-0902, www.miamidragon.com, entry fees apply), an energetic boat race that features several colorfully decorated, Hong Kong–style dragon boats, combining a centuries-old Chinese tradition with modern-day teamwork and aiming to share this fast-growing, international sport with the greater Miami community.

Food and Sporting Events

Of course, the year wouldn't be complete without attending one of Miami's many culinary events or athletic competitions. For die-hard gourmands, it doesn't get much better than the **Food Network South Beach Wine & Food Festival** (www.sobewineandfoodfest.com, activity times and ticket prices vary), a star-studded, four-day event in late February that showcases the talents of the world's most renowned chefs, culinary personalities, and wine producers. Sports lovers and outdoor enthusiasts, meanwhile, will appreciate such events as the five-day **Miami International Boat Show & Strictly Sail** (www.miamiboatshow.com, prices vary) in mid-February and the nine-day **Miccosukee Championship** (305/382-3930, www.miccosukeechampionship.com), a mid-October golf tournament that usually benefits local charities.

Shopping

A mosaic of cultures and a hotbed of high fashion, the Miami area is indeed a shopper's paradise, offering a wide array of outdoor malls and shopping districts, even in suburbs like Aventura, Kendall, and other surrounding communities. Here are just some of the shopping areas available to residents and visitors.

DOWNTOWN MIAMI

Even Miami's downtown area offers a few intriguing options for shoppers, including the **Bayside Marketplace** (401 Biscayne Blvd., Miami, 305/577-3344, www.baysidemarketplace.com, 10 A.M.–10 P.M. Mon.–Thurs., 10 A.M.–11 P.M. Fri.–Sat., 11 A.M.–9 P.M. Sun.). Situated alongside lovely Biscayne Bay, this popular outdoor mall features daily live entertainment, varied restaurants, and numerous shops, ranging from Brookstone to Skechers—enough to fill a few hours, if not all day. Besides bicycle, Jet Ski, electric scooter, and wheelchair rentals, other helpful on-site amenities include ATM kiosks, taxi services, foreign currency exchange, sightseeing tours, and visitor information for local attractions.

In Miami's financial district to the south, you'll encounter another classy mall, **The Shops at Mary Brickell Village** (901 S. Miami Ave., Miami, 305/381-6130, www.marybrickellvillage.com, 11 A.M.–9 P.M. Mon.–Thurs., 11 A.M.–10 P.M. Fri.–Sat., noon–6 P.M. Sun.). Featuring three packed floors and an enormous parking structure, this neighborhood mall houses a plethora of curious boutiques, eateries, and other businesses, including wine and cigar shops, a fine seafood restaurant, an Irish pub, a day spa, an LA Fitness gym, even a Publix grocery store.

LITTLE HAVANA

Known as La Pequeña Habana in Spanish, Miami's Little Havana (www.littlehavana.biz), the culturally rich neighborhood west of the city's downtown area, is home to several cigar shops, fruit and meat markets, and clothing boutiques. If you only have time for a quick visit, be sure to stop by the family-operated **Padilla Cigars Factory & Lounge** (1501 SW 8th St., Miami, 305/362-8773, www.padillacigars.com, 10 A.M.–7 P.M. Mon.–Fri., 10 A.M.–6 P.M. Sat.–Sun.), which offers a wide array of authentically fermented and matured cigars. Even if you're not a cigar aficionado, you're sure to appreciate the aroma.

SOUTH BEACH

The southern portion of Miami Beach, otherwise known as South Beach, is indeed a magnet for high fashion. In fact, you'll find an incredible array of upscale clothing emporiums, jewelry boutiques, art galleries, beauty salons, and specialty stores on **Lincoln Road** (www.lincolnroad.org), including such gems as the **9th Chakra** (1621 Alton Rd., Miami Beach, 305/538-0671, www.9thchakra.com, noon–8 P.M. daily), where you'll find incense, massage oils, crystal jewelry, and other curious gifts, and **Ghirardelli** (801 Lincoln Rd., Miami Beach, 305/532-2538, www.ghirardelli.com, 11:30 A.M.–midnight Mon.–Thurs., 11 A.M.–1 A.M. Fri.–Sat., 11 A.M.–midnight Sun.), an ice cream and chocolate shop. In addition, Lincoln Road hosts the **Outdoor Antique & Collectible Market** (www.antiquecollectiblemarket.com) on various Sundays throughout the year, while **Collins Avenue** and **Ocean Drive** offer their own share of shopping wonders, such as **Gallery Deja Vu** (1390 Ocean Dr., Miami Beach, 305/695-7355, www.gallerydejavu.com, 10 A.M.–6 P.M. daily), which offers a curious array of Faberge eggs, paintings by Mark Chagall and Salvador Dali, and sculptures made of bronze, marble, resin, and porcelain. For more information about shopping opportunities in South Beach, consult *South Beach Magazine* (www.southbeach-usa.com).

COCONUT GROVE

Situated southwest of downtown Miami, Coconut Grove is a family-friendly shopping

© GREATER MIAMI CONVENTION & VISITORS BUREAU/WWW.GMCVB.COM

Coconut Grove is a family-friendly shopping enclave.

enclave, ideal for a stroll in pleasant weather. One popular gathering place is **CocoWalk** (3015 Grand Ave., Coconut Grove, 305/444-0777, www.cocowalk.net, 10 A.M.–10 P.M. Sun.–Thurs., 10 A.M.–11 P.M. Fri.–Sat.), a Mediterranean-style, open-air complex that features several shops and restaurants, from Victoria's Secret to The Cheesecake Factory, plus late-night music venues like **Crazy Pianos** (305/567-2462, www.crazypianosmiami.com, 4 P.M.–3 A.M. daily). Other amenities include covered parking, secure bicycle racks, ATM kiosks, and 24-hour security.

CORAL GABLES

Northwest of Coconut Grove lies Coral Gables, an affluent, well-manicured village that features an array of sophisticated shopping options. One such option is the **Village of Merrick Park** (358 San Lorenzo Ave., Coral Gables, 305/529-0200, www.villageofmerrickpark. com, 10 A.M.–9 P.M. Mon.–Sat., noon–6 P.M. Sun.), a cluster of fine shops and eateries centered around a lovely urban garden. Visitors here can peruse books and music at Borders,

shoes at Cole Haan, jewelry at Tiffany & Co., cookware at Williams-Sonoma, and stylish apparel at department stores like Nordstrom and Neiman Marcus. In addition, you can visit **Equinox** (786/497-8200, www.equinox.com, 5:30 A.M.–11 P.M. Mon.–Thurs., 5:30 A.M.–10 P.M. Fri., 8 A.M.–8 P.M. Sat.–Sun.) for a range of facials, body treatments, and massage therapies and, afterward, enjoy a casual meal at the **Yard House** (305/447-9273, www.yardhouse.com, 11 A.M.–12:30 A.M. Sun.–Thurs., 11 A.M.–1:30 A.M. Fri.–Sat.), which boasts an incredible selection of draft beer.

Naturally, Coral Gables offers more than just a high-class mall experience. In the quaint downtown area, several boutiques, salons, art galleries, outdoor cafés, and convenient parking lots make up the **Miracle Mile** (www.shopcoralgables.com), which encompasses a four-block stretch between Douglas and Le Jeune Roads as well as several surrounding streets. Of the many offerings here, you'll find pricey hair-styling services, facials, and manicures at the **Avant-Garde Salon & Spa** (155 Miracle Mile, Coral Gables,

305/442-8136, www.avantgardesalonand-spa.com, 10 A.M.–7 P.M. Tues., 10 A.M.–8 P.M. Wed.–Fri., 10 A.M.–7 P.M. Sat.); classy lingerie at **Silvia's Corset Shoppe** (256 Giralda Ave., Coral Gables, 305/446-8484, www.silviascorsetshoppe.com, 10 A.M.–5:30 P.M.

Mon.–Sat.); and rare volumes at **Fifteenth Street Books** (296 Aragon Ave., Coral Gables, 305/442-2344, www.fifteenthstreetbooks.com, 11 A.M.–7 P.M. daily), which also features a spacious reading room and an adjoining antique shop.

Sports and Recreation

SPECTATOR SPORTS

Fans of spectator sports can't go wrong in Miami, where several professional teams are on display. From September to December, for instance, football fans can watch the **Miami Dolphins** (888/346-7849 or 800/745-3000, www.miamidolphins.com, game times and ticket prices vary) take on other NFL teams at the **Sun Life Stadium** (2269 Dan Marino Blvd., Miami Gardens, 305/623-6100, www.sunlifestadium.com), while from late April to early October, baseball lovers can flock to the same stadium to cheer on the **Florida Marlins** (877/627-5467, http://florida.marlins.mlb.com, game times and ticket prices vary)—until, that is, the team's new ballpark is ready for its scheduled 2012 opening. From October to April, basketball fans can catch the **Miami Heat** (786/777-4328, www.nba.com/heat, game times and ticket prices vary) at the **AmericanAirlines Arena** (601 Biscayne Blvd., Miami, 786/777-1000, www.aaarena.com), and even hockey fans will be happy in Miami, where the **Florida Panthers** (954/835-7825, http://panthers.nhl.com, game times and ticket prices vary) also play between October and April at the **BankAtlantic Center** (1 Panther Pkwy., Sunrise, 954/835-7000, www.bankatlanticcenter.com).

GOLF

While the Florida Keys offer a few public golf courses, you'll find even more options in the Miami area, including the **Biltmore Golf Course** (1200 Anastasia Ave., Coral Gables, 305/460-5364, www.biltmorehotel.com/golf.php, 7 A.M.–6 P.M. daily in winter, 7:30 A.M.–7:30 P.M. Mon.–Fri., 7 A.M.–7:30 P.M. Sat.–Sun. in summer, $50–189 pp w/cart), a well-landscaped, 18-hole course that surrounds the legendary Biltmore Hotel and features a clubhouse, bar, and restaurant. Originally created in 1925 by Scottish designer Donald Ross and restored in 2007 by architect Brian Silva, this well-favored course has lured numerous movie stars, athletes, and dignitaries over the years.

The **Miami Beach Golf Club** (2301 Alton Rd., Miami Beach, 305/532-3350, www.miamibeachgolfclub.com, 7 A.M.–sunset daily, $100–200 pp w/cart) requires proper golf attire, offers rental shoes ($20 per pair) and clubs ($60 per set), and provides an on-site restaurant. Tee times must be reserved five days in advance. The **Miccosukee Golf & Country Club** (6401 Kendale Lakes Dr., Miami, 305/382-3930, www.miccosukee.com, 6:30 A.M.–10 P.M. daily, $35–65 pp) is a picturesque course that features 27 challenging holes, a full-service golf shop, a sports bar, an Olympic-sized swimming pool, and club rentals ($40 per set).

HIKING

Although the Everglades offer more opportunities for long-distance hikers, the Miami area definitely features a few choice spots. On Key Biscayne, for instance, you'll find several scenic nature trails on the west side of **Bill Baggs Cape Florida State Park** (1200 S. Crandon Blvd., Key Biscayne, 305/361-5811, www.floridastateparks.org/capeflorida, 8 A.M.–sunset daily, $8 vehicles w/2–8 passengers, $4 motorcycles and single-occupant vehicles, $2 pedestrians, bikers, day-use boaters, and extra passengers).

MIAMI SPORTS ON SCREEN

Hot, sexy, and dangerous, Miami has long been a favorite backdrop for filmmakers and television producers. True, it's the criminal side that's most often on display – as evidenced by films like *Scarface* (1983), *The Mean Season* (1985), *Miami Blues* (1990), *Bad Boys* (1995), *Transporter 2* (2005), and *Miami Vice* (2006). While the city's vibrant nightlife scene and beautiful beach subculture also make their share of appearances, even shows on the small screen – including *Miami Vice* (1984-1990), *CSI: Miami* (2002-present), *Dexter* (2006-present), and *Burn Notice* (2007-present) – seem to focus a lot of energy on Miami's notorious criminal activities, from murder to drug trafficking. Beyond beaches, clubs, and crime, however, the Magic City is also known for its vigorous professional sports teams – a fact that two memorable, if completely different, movies have explored.

In *Ace Ventura: Pet Detective* (1994), a zany comedy written by Jack Bernstein and directed by Tom Shadyac, the story focuses on an outrageous detective (Jim Carrey) who specializes in animal-related cases – that is, reuniting owners with their lost or stolen pets. When he's hired to find the Miami Dolphins'

misplaced mascot, a bottlenose dolphin named Snowflake, hilarity and wacky adventures naturally ensue, and Ace soon finds himself tussling with a shark, facing down a transvestite, and trying to save quarterback Dan Marino from an untimely end.

Meanwhile, in *Any Given Sunday* (1999), a bold, energetic film written by John Logan and Oliver Stone and directed by Oliver Stone, the focus is again on football. Filmed at locations throughout Miami, including the Orange Bowl Stadium, this brash sports drama offers a behind-the-scenes look at the life-and-death struggles between an aging coach (Al Pacino), a quarterback legend (Dennis Quaid), an arrogant rookie (Jamie Foxx), and the young female owner (Cameron Diaz) of a fictitious Miami football team known as the Miami Sharks.

Appropriately, Dan Marino, perhaps the most famous athlete to be associated with the Magic City, has made his mark on both films. Besides co-starring in *Ace Ventura*, he also lends his spirit to *Any Given Sunday*, albeit in a not-so-obvious way. After all, the house where Jack "Cap" Rooney (Dennis Quaid's character) and his family live is actually Marino's real-life home.

You can also utilize the hiking trails at **Oleta River State Park** (3400 NE 163rd St., North Miami, 305/919-1844, www.floridastateparks.org/oletariver, 8 A.M.–sunset daily, $6 vehicles w/2–8 passengers, $4 motorcycles and single-occupant vehicles, $2 pedestrians, bikers, and extra passengers), situated at the northern end of Biscayne Bay and considered Florida's largest urban park.

BIKING AND SKATING

If you favor biking, you'll find no shortage of opportunities in the Miami area, especially in places like **Oleta River State Park** (3400 NE 163rd St., North Miami, 305/919-1844, www.floridastateparks.org/oletariver, 8 A.M.–sunset daily, $6 vehicles w/2–8 passengers, $4 motorcycles and single-occupant vehicles, $2

pedestrians, bikers, and extra passengers) at the northern end of Biscayne Bay, which has miles of off-road biking trails, ranging from novice to challenging.

Bikes can be rented from several different outfitters, including **Liquid Surf & Sail** (2484 SW 17th Ave., Miami, 305/860-0888 or 888/818-9283, www.liquidsurfandsail.com, $15 daily, $45 weekly), which offers helmets and locks with all rentals. **Miami Beach Bicycle Center** (601 5th St., Miami Beach, 305/531-4161, www.bikemiamibeach.com, 10 A.M.–7 P.M. Mon.–Sat., 10 A.M.–5 P.M. Sun., $8 hourly, $24 daily, $80 weekly) offers a variety of cruisers, hybrids, and other bikes. **Key Cycling** (328 Crandon Blvd., Ste. 121, Key Biscayne, 305/361-0061, www.keycycling.com, 10 A.M.–6 P.M. Mon., 10 A.M.–7 P.M.

Tues.–Fri., 10 A.M.–6 P.M. Sat., 10 A.M.–3 P.M. Sun., $24–40 daily, $80–200 weekly) provides mountain, road, or hybrid bikes.

In addition to biking, a popular activity here is inline skating, especially in South Beach and along Biscayne Bay. If you haven't brought your own skates, stop by **Fritz's Skate, Bike & Surf** (1620 Washington Ave., Miami Beach, 305/532-1954, www.fritzsmiamibeach.com, 10 A.M.–10 P.M. daily), which has offered the largest selection of inline skates, skateboards, and bicycles in South Beach since 1989. With a $100 refundable deposit, you can rent skates for $10 hourly, $24 daily, and $69 weekly. Protective gear is included with all skate rentals, and lessons are available. Bicycle rentals cost the same as skate rentals and include a lock and a helmet, though a $200 deposit is required.

FISHING AND BOATING

As with the rest of southern Florida, fishing and boating are both popular activities in the Miami area. If you're interested in deep-sea fishing, consider boarding the **Jumanji** (401 Biscayne Blvd., Miami, 786/486-7200, www.miabeachfishing.com, $99 hourly), a 42-foot charter boat that offers year-round opportunities to snag a variety of fish, including kingfish, tuna, marlin, wahoo, swordfish, snapper, and grouper.

Other available charter boats include the 41-foot **Old Hat** (305/773-0700, www.oldhat.com, rates vary) and the 57-foot **Spellbound** (305/785-0552, www.reeladventurecharters.com, $650 per half day, $1,250 daily), both of which are located in the Haulover Park Marina (10800 Collins Ave., Miami Beach) and both of which offer the chance to catch a variety of game fish, from amberjack to hammerhead shark.

If you'd rather bring your own boat to Miami, there's no shortage of boat ramps and marina slips. To rent a boat, head to Monty's Marina in Coconut Grove, where **American WaterSports** (2560 S. Bayshore Dr., Coconut Grove, 305/856-6559, www.americanwatersports.us, daily) offers a range of powerboats

($160–295 hourly, $480–860 per half day, $665–1,250 daily).

CANOEING AND KAYAKING

Much like the Everglades and the Florida Keys, the Miami area is surrounded by water—specifically, Biscayne Bay and, beyond that, the Atlantic Ocean. So, canoeists and kayakers will find no shortage of opportunities to explore these shimmering waters. **EcoAdventures** (4000 Crandon Blvd., Key Biscayne, 305/365-3018, www.miamidade.gov/ecoadventures), for example, offers guided trips for paddling enthusiasts, including a leisurely canoe adventure ($33 pp) along the historic Coral Gables Waterway, a kayaking excursion ($30 pp) around Key Biscayne, and a canoe tour ($25 adults, $15 children 9–14) from the **Deering Estate at Cutler** (16701 SW 72nd Ave., Miami, 305/235-1668, www.deeringestate.com, 10 A.M.–5 P.M. daily, $10 adults, $5 children 4–14, children under 4 free) to seven-acre Chicken Key.

Of course, if you'd rather venture out on your own, you can easily rent a vessel from several helpful outfitters, including **Liquid Surf & Sail** (2484 SW 17th Ave., Miami, 305/860-0888 or 888/818-9283, www.liquidsurfandsail.com), which offers sit-on-top kayak rentals ($35–45 per half day, $60–70 daily), and the **Blue Moon Outdoor Center** (3400 NE 163rd St., North Miami, 305/957-3040, www.bluemoonmiami.com, 9 A.M.–5:15 P.M. daily), which provides kayaks ($18–30 hourly, $50–90 daily) and canoes ($30 hourly, $90 daily) for rent.

DIVING AND SNORKELING

Although most diving enthusiasts head straight to Biscayne National Park or the Florida Keys National Marine Sanctuary, Miami offers helpful outfitters and operators. One such company is the **South Beach Dive and Surf Center** (850 Washington Ave., Miami Beach, 305/531-6110, www.southbeachdivers.com, 9 A.M.–7 P.M. Mon.–Sat., 9 A.M.–6 P.M. Sun.), a PADI 5 Star facility whose courses include an introduction class ($225 pp), a divemaster class ($695 pp), and a digital underwater photography class ($395 pp)—plus snorkeling ($65 pp) and diving trips ($85–120 pp) in the waters near Key Largo.

Diver's Paradise (4000 Crandon Blvd., Key Biscayne, 305/361-3483, www.keydivers. com, 10 A.M.–6 P.M. Tues.–Fri., 8 A.M.–6 P.M. Sat.–Sun.), which has been assisting area divers since 1979, features daily diving and snorkeling trips ($60 pp) to area wrecks and coral reefs as well as diving classes and equipment rentals.

SPAS AND YOGA

The Miami area features an array of rejuvenating spas, including those found at resorts like the Biltmore Hotel in Coral Gables. If you're not staying at such a resort, you'll find day spas in the vicinity, too. The **Uhma Organic Spa & Green Shop** (726 6th St., Miami Beach, 305/695-0996, www.uhmaspa.com, noon–7 P.M. Mon., 10 A.M.–7 P.M. Tues.–Sat.), for instance, provides an ecofriendly urban sanctuary, where guests can enjoy an array of facials ($100–145 pp), body scrubs and wraps ($50–120 pp), massages ($65–170 pp), water therapies ($50–55 pp), yoga treatments ($170–225 pp), and other services.

The Miami area also boasts several opportunities for yoga enthusiasts. One curious option is the Tina Hills Pavilion in **Bayfront Park** (301 N. Biscayne Blvd., Miami, 305/358-7550, www.bayfrontparkmiami.com, sunrise–sunset daily, no entrance fee), where a certified yoga instructor offers free yoga classes (6–7:15 P.M. Mon. and Wed., 9–10:15 A.M. Sat.) for beginners as well as advanced participants. All students must be at least 18 years old, and registration is based on a first-come, first-served basis. In addition, everyone must bring his or her own yoga mat, water, and towel.

Accommodations

In general, staying overnight in the Miami area can be an expensive enterprise, especially if you'd prefer to stay in a safer, more tourist-friendly neighborhood like South Beach or Coral Gables. For more information about Miami's accommodations, consult **Miami Beach 411** (1521 Alton Rd., Ste. 233, Miami Beach, FL 33139, 305/754-2206, www.miamibeach411.com).

DOWNTOWN MIAMI

While downtown Miami isn't known for the same swankiness that South Beach promises, a few premium options do exist in this part of the city. The **Four Seasons Hotel Miami** (1435 Brickell Ave., Miami, 305/358-3535, www.fourseasons.com/miami, $250–320 d), for instance, offers 221 stylish rooms and suites between the 20th and 29th floors of a 70-story tower made of glass and granite, overlooking beautiful Biscayne Bay. Besides a world-class spa and a magnificent pool, the hotel provides two amazing restaurants, a stylish lounge, and high-speed Internet access. To the north, the **EPIC Hotel** (270 Biscayne Blvd., Miami, 866/760-3742, www.epichotel.com, $224–280 d) guarantees an equally high-class experience. In addition to its 411 luxurious rooms and suites, in-house spa, amazing pools, and marina services, EPIC is also one of the few pet-friendly lodgings in downtown Miami.

SOUTH BEACH

If you're looking for a hip, youthful vibe, then South Beach is definitely the place for you. In this famous Miami Beach neighborhood, you'll find several classic options, including the **Z Ocean Hotel** (1437 Collins Ave., Miami Beach, 305/672-4554 or 877/688-4232, www.zoceanhotelsouthbeach.com, $380–440 d), which features 79 roomy suites, a private glass-bottom pool, rooftop hot tubs, and the Z Ocean Beach Club. **The Betsy** (1440 Ocean Dr., Miami Beach, 305/531-6100 or 866/792-3879, www.thebetsyhotel.com, $69–179 d), meanwhile, is a historic, landmark hotel featuring 63 rooms and suites. Located beside the beach, this intimate hotel also offers wireless Internet access, a full-range spa, two unique bars, and the BLT Steak, Laurent Tourondel's modern American steakhouse. Another winning option is the **Majestic Hotel South Beach** (660 Ocean Dr., Miami Beach, 305/455-3270, www.majesticsouthbeach.com, $130–160 d), which constitutes one of the most affordable lodgings in South Beach, despite being only steps away from this neighborhood's world-famous beach.

Farther north lies one of the most well-known hotels in Miami Beach—if not all of Miami. The **(Fontainebleau** (4441 Collins Ave., Miami Beach, 877/854-2033 or 800/548-8886, www.fontainebleau.com, $250–380 d), which featured prominently in films like *The Bellboy* (1960) and *Goldfinger* (1964), offers unparalleled luxury all year round. Following a $1 billion renovation and expansion, this enormous, oceanfront resort now offers more than 1,500 airy, well-appointed rooms and suites, seven unique restaurants, three bars and nightclubs, a stylish pool area with private cabanas, a gym that overlooks the pool, and the 40,000-square-foot Lapis Spa & Salon (305/674-4772, 8:30 A.M.–6:30 P.M. Sun.–Wed., 8:30 A.M.–7:30 P.M. Thurs.–Sat.).

COCONUT GROVE TO CORAL GABLES

Situated within an exclusive waterfront enclave of upscale restaurants, shopping, and nightlife, the stunning **Mayfair Hotel & Spa** (3000 Florida Ave., Coconut Grove, 305/441-0000 or 800/433-4555, www.mayfairhotelandspa.com, $200–240 d) contains 179 relaxing rooms and suites, most of which have private balconies and hot tubs. In addition to its convenient proximity to Miami's beaches and downtown area, the Mayfair features a 4,500-square-foot spa that provides guests with first-class massages and body treatments.

Of course, if you do plan to stay in the Miami area before heading to the Keys—even for a night—you simply must consider the **(Biltmore Hotel** (1200 Anastasia Ave.,

© GREATER MIAMI CONVENTION & VISITORS BUREAU/WWW.GMCVB.COM

Coconut Grove's Mayfair Hotel & Spa

Coral Gables, 305/445-1926 or 800/727-1926, www.biltmorehotel.com, $179–459 d), a historic, 150-acre resort that features a vibrant, Mediterranean-style structure, topped by a magnificent tower and encompassing 275 sumptuous rooms and suites. Other on-site amenities include a championship golf course, an incredible spa and fitness center, 10 tennis courts, a world-famous pool area, and several celebrated restaurants.

CAMPING

Miami may not be known for its camping options, but that doesn't mean you won't find at least one here: **Bill Baggs Cape Florida State Park** (1200 S. Crandon Blvd., Key Biscayne, 305/361-5811, www.floridastateparks.org/capeflorida, 8 A.M.–sunset daily, $8 vehicles w/2–8 passengers, $4 motorcycles and single-occupant vehicles, $2 pedestrians, bikers, day-use boaters, and extra passengers). For a daily fee ($5 adults, $1 children), large groups can stay in a primitive campground that offers a restroom, showers, barbecue grills, picnic tables, benches, tent platforms, and accessible parking. In addition, boaters can anchor overnight in No Name Harbor ($20 daily), where, during operating hours, they'll have access to restrooms, coin-operated laundry machines, a rinse shower, a picnic shelter, a free pump-out for all boats, and yummy meals at the Boater's Grill.

Food

Given the varied cultural influences in Miami, you'll find that the cuisine here ranges from Creole dishes in Miami's Little Haiti to *cubanos* (Cuban sandwiches) in Little Havana to fresh seafood and "Floribbean" cuisine throughout the city. For more information about available eateries in the Miami area, consult the **Miami DiningGuide** (http://miami.diningguide.com).

DOWNTOWN MIAMI

Just west of I-95 is an unassuming joint called **Peoples Bar-B-Que** (360 NW 8th St., Miami, 305/373-8080, www.peoplesbarbque.com, 11:30 A.M.–midnight Mon.–Fri., 11:30 A.M.–1 A.M. Sat., 1–9 P.M. Sun., $2–23), which, as the name implies, serves excellent, affordable Southern-style barbecue. Since 1962, regulars have flocked to this casual, friendly place (even when it was in a different spot) for mouthwatering fried chicken, barbecue ribs, collard greens, cornbread, and other Southern staples.

If you're looking for a fancier meal, you should head south to **Azul** (500 Brickell Key Dr., Miami, 305/913-8358, www.mandarinoriental.com, 7–11 P.M. Mon.–Sat., $18–55) at the Mandarin Oriental hotel. Enhanced by gorgeous bay views and an incredible wine list, this elegant restaurant features Chef Clay Conley's diverse blend of Asian and Mediterranean flavors, as evidenced in ever-revolving dishes like yogurt-marinated swordfish, Moroccan-inspired lamb, and "a study in tuna," an Asian-style combination of raw tuna, Maine crabmeat, tempura avocado, and Osetra caviar. Even the desserts here are multicultural delights, including Jamaican rum bread pudding with coconut sorbet and fresh pineapple, a goat cheese wonton with poached pears in a port wine reduction, and sticky rice crème brûlée with citrus saffron sauce and lemongrass sorbet. Reservations are highly recommended.

LITTLE HAVANA

In a neighborhood populated with numerous Cuban exiles and Cuban Americans, you'll find plenty of authentic delicacies, from *cafecito* (Cuban coffee without milk) and *cortadito* (Cuban coffee with steamed milk) to *cubanos,* or flattened, grilled sandwiches made with sliced ham, slow-roasted pork, Swiss cheese, and pickles, popularized by Cuban immigrants who settled in Miami in the early 1900s.

LITTLE HAITI

Just north of downtown Miami lies a curious place, the city's traditional center of Haitian Creole and Francophone culture – and the largest Haitian community outside of Haiti. Bordered by the Little River to the north, the Florida East Coast Railway to the east, I-195 to the south, and I-95 to the west, this neighborhood has long been known as La Petite Haïti, or Little Haiti. Over the years, the people of Little Haiti have fluctuated between middle and lower class, and although crime does exist here today and the residents might look at you skeptically, this unique area is definitely worth visiting – if only in the daytime. Here, you can gaze at multicolored facades, listen to snippets of Creole, visit fascinating art and voodoo shops, and, of course, enjoy spicy authentic cuisine at eateries like the long-standing **Chez Le Bebe Restaurant** (114 NE 54th St., Miami, 305/751-7639, www.chezlebebe.com, 8 A.M.-midnight Sun.-Thurs., 8 A.M.-11 P.M. Fri.-Sat., $4-12), where you'll find inexpensive delicacies like *tasso* (fried goat), *ragout* (pig feet), and *mais* (grits). While eating, you might even learn a few Creole expressions, such as *souple* (please) and *mesi* (thank you).

Not quite the ethnic enclave that Little Havana purports to be, Little Haiti has suffered culturally in recent years from the gentrification of the district itself as well as surrounding neighborhoods. In the southern part of Little Haiti, for instance, lies the trendy **Miami Design District** (www.miamidesigndistrict.net), an 18-block section featuring more than 150 art galleries, restaurants, bars, and showrooms filled with designer fashions, furnishings, lighting fixtures, kitchen and bathroom products, wall and floor materials, and fine rugs. Situated between 36th Street, Biscayne Boulevard, 46th Street, and Miami Avenue, the stylish design district, which has plans to expand, is certainly worthy of a daylong stroll, though it's obviously a world away from the heart of La Petite Haïti.

For a romantic meal, head west from downtown on U.S. 41, toward **Casa Juancho** (2436 SW 8th St., Miami, 305/642-2452, www.casajuancho.com, noon–midnight Sun.–Thurs., noon–1 A.M. Fri.–Sat., $22–30), where the Spanish-style menu includes various steaks, paella dishes, and fish and shellfish entrées, such as *salmón con vieiras al albariño*, or fresh salmon and scallops in a reduced albariño wine and saffron sauce. Live music from La Tuna Universitaria de Oviedo (7:30 and 9:30 P.M. daily) and accordionist Lino (8:30 and 10:30 P.M. daily) enhances the romantic atmosphere. Unlike other eateries in Little Havana, Casa Juancho requires dressy casual or business attire; hats, shorts, and T-shirts are not allowed, and reservations are recommended.

Farther west along U.S. 41, **(Versailles** (3555 SW 8th St., Miami, 305/445-7614, 8 A.M.–2 A.M. daily, $7–20) may sound—and even look—like a French restaurant, but it's actually one of the best Cuban/Caribbean restaurants in Miami. Given the frequent crowds here, it seems that the secret is out. Although its popularity makes parking at this restaurant rather difficult, it's a wonderful place to sample a traditional *cubano* or the fantastic garlic-roasted chicken. One tip is to take advantage of its late hours, when parking is usually less of a hassle.

SOUTH BEACH

This trendy island neighborhood offers a plethora of unique eateries, including the **Van Dyke Cafe** (846 Lincoln Rd., Miami Beach, 305/534-3600, www.thevandykecafe.com, 8 A.M.–2 A.M. daily, $5–24), which prepares inexpensive, diverse dishes like cheese blintzes and crêpes for breakfast, grilled mahimahi sandwiches for lunch, and fish and chips for dinner. After your meal, head upstairs to listen to some live jazz, blues, funk, Latino, or Afro-Caribbean music.

The fun, nostalgic **(Jerry's Famous Deli** (1450 Collins Ave., Miami Beach, 305/532-8030, www.jerrysfamousdeli.com, 24 hours

the Van Dyke Cafe in South Beach

daily, $4–30) offers well over 600 items on its impressive menu, which might make it difficult for you to decide what to eat. First established as a chain in Southern California, this casual restaurant offers almost anything you'd like, any time you want—whether you crave eggs Benedict for dinner or a Mexican pizza for breakfast.

Housed in an art deco–style dining car, the casual **11th Street Diner** (1065 Washington Ave., Miami Beach, 305/534-6373, www. eleventhstreetdiner.com, 24 hours daily, $14–55) serves traditional comfort food, from the Monte Cristo sandwich to Argentinian skirt steak—even in the wee hours. For a completely unique dining experience, walk a little farther south to ◖ **B.E.D.** (929 Washington Ave., Miami Beach, 305/532-9070, www.bedmiami. com, 8 P.M.–5 A.M. Mon.–Sat., 11 A.M.–5 P.M. Sun., $25–60), a stylish restaurant that invites you to enjoy an intimate meal from the comfort of a luxurious bed, amid diaphanous curtains and colored lighting. The menu, while not enormous, features tasty choices like the B.E.D. Surf & Turf or the Australian rack

of lamb. The cocktails and desserts are especially tasty, and although a romantic meal is certainly possible here, the place becomes a pulsating, crowded dance club after hours, complete with the ubiquitous long line out front. Even farther south, **Joe's Stone Crab** (11 Washington Ave., Miami Beach, 305/673-0365, www.joesstonecrab.com, 5–10 P.M. Mon., 11:30 A.M.–2 P.M. and 5–10 P.M. Tues.–Thurs., 11:30 A.M.–2 P.M. and 5–11 P.M. Fri.–Sat., 4–10 P.M. Sun. mid-Oct.–mid-May, 6–10 P.M. Wed.–Thurs. and Sun., 6–11 P.M. Fri.–Sat. mid-May–July, $14–55) may specialize in stone crabs and other locally caught seafood, but this popular eatery also features some amazing fried chicken—the dish most favored by former President Bill Clinton whenever he visits. Established in 1913, Joe's is actually one of the oldest restaurants in Miami.

COCONUT GROVE TO CORAL GABLES

For contemporary Latin American cuisine, head to the **Jaguar Ceviche Spoon Bar & Latam Grill** (3067 Grand Ave., Coconut Grove,

305/444-0216, www.jaguarspot.com, 11:30 A.M.–11 P.M. Mon.–Thurs., 11:30 A.M.–11:30 P.M. Fri., 11 A.M.–11:30 P.M. Sat., 11 A.M.–10 P.M. Sun., $11–30), a colorful eatery that offers a variety of ceviche, grilled meat, and seafood dishes.

If you appreciate finely crafted beer, then you simply must visit the **Titanic Restaurant & Brewery** (5813 Ponce De Leon Blvd., Coral Gables, 305/668-1742, www.titanicbrewery.

com, 11:30 A.M.–1 A.M. Sun.–Thurs., 11:30 A.M.–2 A.M. Fri.–Sat., $8–18), where you can pair a wonderful sampler tray of microbrews with any number of tasty dishes, including steamed mussels, Florida Cobb salad, crawfish and andouille bisque, shrimp wraps, or Bama burgers. The nautical decor and scrumptious desserts, from rum cake to key lime pie, only add to the fun.

Information and Services

INFORMATION
Tourism and Government Offices

For brochures, maps, and other information about Miami, stop by the **Greater Miami Convention & Visitors Bureau (GMCVB)** (701 Brickell Ave., Ste. 2700, Miami, 305/539-3000 or 800/933-8448, www.miamiandbeaches. com, 8:30 A.M.–5 P.M. Mon.–Fri.). In addition, you'll find more localized tourism bureaus, such as the **Miami Beach Visitor and Convention Authority** (777 17th St., Ste. 402A, Miami Beach, 305/673-7050, www.miamibeachvca. com, 9 A.M.–5 P.M. Mon.–Fri.), the **Miami Beach Chamber of Commerce** (1920 Meridian Ave., Miami Beach, 305/674-1300, www.miamibeach-chamber.com, 9 A.M.–6 P.M. Mon.–Fri.), the **Miami Beach Latin Chamber of Commerce** (510 Lincoln Rd., Miami Beach, 305/674-1414, www.miamibeach.org, 9 A.M.–6 P.M. Mon.–Fri.), the **Coconut Grove Chamber of Commerce** (2820 McFarlane Rd., Coconut Grove, 305/444-7270, www.coconutgrovecham-ber.com, 10 A.M.–6 P.M. Mon.–Fri.), the **Coral Gables Chamber of Commerce** (224 Catalonia Ave., Coral Gables, 305/446-1657, www.gable-schamber.org, 8:30 A.M.–5 P.M. Mon.–Thurs., 8:30 A.M.–4 P.M. Fri.), and the **Key Biscayne Chamber of Commerce and Visitors Center** (88 W. McIntyre St., Ste. 100, Key Biscayne, 305/361-5207, www.keybiscaynechamber.org, chamber 9 A.M.–5 P.M. Mon.–Fri., visitor center 24 hours daily). If you're interested in gay-related activities, accommodations, shops, bars, and restaurants, consult www.miamigaytravel.com. For

government-related issues, consult the comprehensive websites of **Miami-Dade County** (www. miamidade.gov), the **City of Miami** (www.mi-amigov.com), the **City of Miami Beach** (www. miamibeachfl.gov), and the **City of Coral Gables** (www.coralgables.com).

Media

Like any major U.S. city, Miami offers a number of helpful periodicals, including the daily **Miami Herald** (www.miamiherald.com) and the free weekly **Miami New Times** (www. miaminewtimes.com), which offers comprehensive listings of bars, restaurants, live music venues, art shows, current movies, and upcoming events. In addition, the monthly **Ocean Drive Magazine** (www.oceandrive.com) offers a look at the latest trends in fashion, beauty, art, dining, travel, and entertainment.

In Miami, you'll also have access to several radio stations, including **The Beat** (103.5 FM, www.thebeatmiami.com), which offers continuous R&B and hip-hop selections. Major television stations in town include **WFOR-TV/CBS4** (http://cbs4.com), **WSVN 7NEWS** (www.wsvn.com), and **NBC 6/WTVJ** (www.nbcmiami.com).

SERVICES

Given its large size, Miami offers plenty of necessary services for residents and travelers alike.

Money

For banking needs, stop by the **First Bank of Miami** (800/831-5763, www.firstbankmiami.

com), which offers five branches in the Miami area, including one in downtown Miami (235 SE 1st St., 305/579-4933) and another in Coral Gables (255 Aragon Ave., 305/444-4960).

Mail

For shipping, faxing, copying, and other business-related services, visit **The UPS Store** (www.theupsstore.com), which offers several locations in the Miami area, including one in downtown Miami (247 SW 8th St., 305/858-1221, 8:30 A.M.–7 P.M. Mon.–Fri., 9 A.M.–2:30 P.M. Sat.) and another in Coral Gables (1825 Ponce de Leon Blvd., 305/441-7161, 9 A.M.–6 P.M. Mon.–Fri., 10 A.M.–2 P.M. Sat.). **PostNet** (www.postnet.com) offers similar services at two area locations: one in Miami (13550 SW 120th St., Ste. 406A, 786/293-9804, 9 A.M.–6 P.M. Mon.–Fri., 10 A.M.–2 P.M. Sat.) and another in North Miami Beach (13555 Biscayne Blvd., 305/949-5898, 10 A.M.–6:30 P.M. Mon.–Fri., noon–3 P.M. Sat.). You'll also find more than two dozen **post offices** (800/275-8777, www.usps.com) in the greater metropolitan area, including one in Coconut Grove (3191 Grand Ave., 305/529-6700, 8:30 A.M.–5 P.M. Mon.–Fri., 8:30 A.M.–2 P.M. Sat.) and another in Coral Gables (251 Valencia Ave., 305/443-2532, 8:30 A.M.–6 P.M. Mon.–Fri., 8:30 A.M.–2 P.M. Sat.).

Groceries and Supplies

For groceries, fresh seafood, and other supplies, head to **Winn-Dixie** (3401 NW 18th Ave., Miami, 305/634-4492, www.winndixie.com, 7 A.M.–midnight daily), which houses an on-site pharmacy (305/634-1432, 8 A.M.–8 P.M. Mon.–Fri., 9 A.M.–6 P.M. Sat., 10 A.M.–5 P.M. Sun.). For other pharmacy needs, stop by **Walgreens** (1 E. Flagler St., Miami, 305/371-5868, www.walgreens.com, 7 A.M.–7 P.M. Mon.–Sat., 9 A.M.–5 P.M. Sun.), which also offers photo processing, fresh coffee, and baked goods. In addition, **Publix** (www.publix.com) provides plenty of grocery stores in the Miami

area, including one near Little Haiti (4870 Biscayne Blvd., Miami, 305/573-8601, 7 A.M.–11 P.M. daily).

Laundry

If you need to wash some clothes while you're in town, laundry facilities include **Sudsies Dry Cleaners & Laundry** (6786 Collins Ave., Miami Beach, 305/864-3279 or 888/898-7837, http://sudsies.com, 7 A.M.–8 P.M. Mon.–Fri., 8 A.M.–6 P.M. Sat., 9 A.M.–3 P.M. Sun.), which even offers pickup and delivery service (7 A.M.–7 P.M. Mon.–Sat.).

Internet Access

If you need to access the Internet and your hotel doesn't offer such services, head to **USA Pack and Post** (1348 Washington Ave., Miami Beach, 305/535-9660, www.usapackandpost.com, 10 A.M.–10 P.M. Mon.–Fri., 11 A.M.–10 P.M. Sat.–Sun.), where you can surf the Web, ship packages, and prepare documents.

Emergency Services

In case of an emergency that requires police, fire, or ambulance services, dial **911** from any cell or public phone. For nonemergency assistance, contact the **Miami-Dade Police Department** (9105 NW 25th St., Doral, 305/476-5423 or 305/471-1780, www.miami-dade.gov/mdpd, 8 A.M.–5 P.M. Mon.–Fri.), and for general county info, dial **311**. Also, if you need to report criminal activity, contact **Crime Stoppers** (305/471-8477).

If you're seeking medical assistance, simply consult one of several hospitals in the greater metropolitan area, including **Mercy Hospital** (3663 S. Miami Ave., Miami, 305/854-4400, www.mercymiami.org), the **University of Miami Hospital** (1400 NW 12th Ave., Miami, 305/325-5511, www.umiamihospital.com), and the **North Shore Medical Center** (1100 NW 95th St., Miami, 305/835-6000, www.north-shoremedical.com).

MIAMI AND THE EVERGLADES

Getting There and Around

GETTING THERE

By Air

To reach Miami by plane, you can fly directly into the **Miami International Airport (MIA)** (4200 NW 21st St., Miami, 305/876-7000 or 800/825-5642, www.miami-airport.com), which is located about seven miles west of downtown Miami, or opt for the **Fort Lauderdale-Hollywood International Airport (FLL)** (320 Terminal Dr., Fort Lauderdale, 866/435-9355, www.broward.org/airport), which lies roughly 25 miles north of downtown Miami. Both accommodate major air carriers, including **American Airlines** (800/433-7300, www.aa.com), **Continental Airlines** (800/523-3273, www.continental.com), **Air Canada** (888/247-2262, www.aircanada.com), and **Caribbean Airlines** (800/920-4225, www.caribbean-airlines.com). From either airport, you can rent a vehicle through such agencies as **Avis** (800/331-1212, www.avis.com), **Budget** (800/527-0700, www.budget.com), **Enterprise** (800/325-8007, www.enterprise.com), **Hertz** (800/654-3131, www.hertz.com), or **Thrifty** (800/367-2277, www.thrifty.com).

By Bus or Train

If you don't have a vehicle of your own and would prefer not to fly, you can certainly take a bus into the area. **Greyhound** (800/231-2222, www.greyhound.com) offers service to several different stations, including the **Fort Lauderdale Greyhound Station** (515 NE 3rd St., Fort Lauderdale, 954/764-6551, 5:30 A.M.–1:30 A.M. daily), the **North Miami Beach Greyhound Station** (16000 NW 7th Ave., North Miami Beach, 305/688-7277, 5 A.M.–1 A.M. daily), the **Miami Greyhound Station** (4111 NW 27th St., Miami, 305/871-1810, 24 hours daily), and the **American Service Station** (10801 Caribbean Blvd., Cutler Ridge, 305/296-9072, 8 A.M.–6 P.M. daily).

As an alternative, you can choose to travel here by train. **Amtrak** (800/872-7245, www.amtrak.com) offers service via its Silver Service/Palmetto route. The three southernmost stations include **Fort Lauderdale (FTL)** (200 SW 21 Terrace, Fort Lauderdale, 8:30 A.M.–6:15 P.M. daily), **Hollywood (HOL)** (3001 Hollywood Blvd., Hollywood, 8:30 A.M.–6:20 P.M. daily), and **Miami (MIA)** (8303 NW 37th Ave., Miami, 7 A.M.–9 P.M. daily).

Transport from Airports and Stations

If you arrive in the Miami–Fort Lauderdale area via plane, bus, or train, you can easily rent a car or hire a taxicab or shuttle service to reach your destination. From the lower arrival level at the Miami International Airport (MIA), for instance, **SuperShuttle** (305/871-2000 or 954/764-1700, www.supershuttle.com) offers one-way trips to destinations like downtown Miami ($14–16 pp), Coconut Grove ($14–17 pp), Coral Gables ($12–17 pp), South Beach ($19 pp), and Key Biscayne ($22 pp). Each additional passenger (in the same group) will run about $8–10 extra, depending on the destination. Most taxicabs, which you can also hire from the lower arrival level at MIA, will run about $22 for a one-way trip to downtown Miami, Coconut Grove, and the University of Miami in Coral Gables. A trip to South Beach will cost about $32, while a taxicab ride to Key Biscayne will cost you about $40.

From the Fort Lauderdale–Hollywood International Airport (FLL), a taxicab ride to downtown Miami or South Beach will run about $70–75. **GO Airport Shuttle** (954/561-8888 or 800/244-8252) also offers shared ride service from FLL to destinations throughout Miami, including South Beach ($24 pp), downtown Miami ($30 pp), Coconut Grove ($34.50 pp), Coral Gables ($34.50 pp), and Key Biscayne ($34.50 pp). Cabs and shuttles are typically available 24 hours daily.

As an alternative, you can also use the **Tri-Rail** (800/874-7245, www.tri-rail.com), a commuter train service operated by the **South**

Florida Regional Transportation Authority (SFRTA), which links the Fort Lauderdale and Miami airports to several other communities in southern Florida, including Hollywood and West Palm Beach.

By Car

Miami is accessible via several major roads, including I-75 from Tampa, Florida's Turnpike from Orlando, and I-95 from Jacksonville. No matter how you get here, be sure to call **511** for an up-to-the-minute traffic report.

By Boat

Given that the **Port of Miami** (1015 N. America Way, Miami, 305/347-4800, www.miamidade. gov/portofmiami) is the "cruise capital of the world," you can certainly arrive here by boat if you so choose.

GETTING AROUND
By Car

The best way to travel through Miami is via car, truck, RV, or motorcycle—all of which offer easy access to major interstates, highways, and roads.

Given the array of interstates, federal and state highways, county roads, and surface streets in the Miami area, traversing the city and its suburbs isn't too difficult a task, especially if you have a detailed map, such as the AAA Miami/Miami Beach foldout map, or access to an application like Google Maps on your cell phone. Although you can take surface streets pretty much everywhere, you'll probably save time by using major routes and highways. From downtown Miami, for instance, you can use I-95 or Biscayne Boulevard (U.S. 1) to reach North Miami, head south on U.S. 1 to access Coconut Grove and Coral Gables, and take S.R. 913 to Key Biscayne. To reach Miami Beach, you can take I-195 East and head south on S.R. A1A, and the Tamiami Trail (U.S. 41) offers relatively easy access to Little Havana and, farther west, the Everglades.

By Public Transit

Miami offers a convenient public transit

system, including the **Metrobus** (305/891-3131, www.miamidade.gov/transit, $2–2.35 per ride, transfer fees apply), which offers routes throughout southern Florida, even as far as Marathon in the Florida Keys. Each bus route has its own schedule, meaning that, while some routes, such as #3 in downtown Miami, run 24 hours daily, others have very limited timetables. For instance, as the name implies, the #500 Midnight Owl provides daily service between the Downtown Bus Terminal and the Dadeland South Station from around 12:30 A.M. to 5 A.M. daily.

As an alternative, you can travel through Miami via the light-rail system. The **Metrorail** (305/891-3131, www.miamidade.gov/transit, $2 per ride, $5 daily, $26 weekly, $100 monthly) features 22 stations, offering convenient access to stops such as the Civic Center and Coconut Grove. Of course, another option is the **Metromover** (305/891-3131, www.miamidade.gov/transit), which provides free access to a number of stations in downtown Miami, including one near Bayfront Park and another near the Adrienne Arsht Center for the Performing Arts of Miami-Dade County. For both the Metrorail and the Metromover, trains typically operate between 5 A.M. and midnight every day.

For those who need to go a bit farther, the **South Florida Regional Transportation Authority (SFRTA)** offers the **Tri-Rail** (800/874-7245, www.tri-rail.com), a commuter train service that links the Miami airport to Hollywood, Fort Lauderdale, West Palm Beach, and several spots in between. The southbound trains, which run from Mangonia Park to the Miami International Airport, operate between 4 A.M. and 10:30 P.M. on weekdays, and between 6 A.M. and 10:15 P.M. on weekends and holidays. The northbound trains, meanwhile, operate between 4:15 A.M. and 11:35 P.M. on weekdays, and between 6 A.M. and 10:15 P.M. on weekends and holidays.

By Taxi

Taxicab companies like **Flamingo Taxis**

(305/599-9999, $2.50 per pickup, $2 per mile) can help you get around Miami.

By Bike or Boat
While you can certainly traverse Miami via bicycle, the sprawling nature of this region makes it challenging for novice riders. Still, it's a lovely, ecofriendly way to experience this subtropical city. Bikes can be rented from several outfitters in the region. The **Miami Beach Bicycle Center** (601 5th St., Miami Beach, 305/531-4161, www.bikemiamibeach.com, 10 A.M.–7 P.M. Mon.–Sat., 10 A.M.–5 P.M. Sun., $8 hourly, $24 daily, $80 weekly), for

instance, offers a variety of cruisers, hybrids, and other bikes, in addition to accessories and repairs.

Of course, you can also experience the Miami coast via boat. Having your own vessel makes navigating these waters even easier, and you'll find no shortage of boat ramps and marina slips in Miami. If you'd rather rent a boat, head to Monty's Marina, where **American WaterSports** (2560 S. Bayshore Dr., Coconut Grove, 305/856-6559, www.americanwatersports.us, daily) offers a range of powerboats ($160–295 hourly, $480–860 per half day, $665–1,250 daily).

The Everglades and Vicinity

West of Miami lies a vast, legendary region of subtropical wetlands known around the world as the Everglades. Part of southern Florida's massive watershed, this ever-evolving region has been shaped over the centuries by water, fire, storms, nonnative species, even human actions. Termed the "river of grass" by writer Marjory Stoneman Douglas in the late 1940s, the Everglades comprise a complex system of interdependent ecosystems, including sawgrass marshes, cypress swamps, mangrove forests, tropical hardwood hammocks, pine rocklands, coastal prairies, tidal mud flats, sloughs and estuaries, and the marine environment of Florida Bay. Despite prolonged damage caused by activities like water drainage, this mysterious landscape and its adjacent waters are preserved, in part, by two national parks, a national preserve, a wildlife refuge, and two state parks. As amazing as this region's natural resources are, however, there are cultural gems here, too, from the Miccosukee Indian Village to the museums of Homestead.

SIGHTS
Everglades National Park
Between Miami and Naples stretches Everglades National Park (40001 S.R. 9336, Homestead, 305/242-7700, www.nps.gov/

ever, visitor center 9 A.M.–5 P.M. daily, park 24 hours daily, $10 vehicles, $5 motorcycles, pedestrians, and bikers), the largest subtropical wilderness in America and the third largest national park in the lower 48 states. Established in 1947 and since designated a World Heritage Site, an International Biosphere, and a Wetland of International Importance, this unique place protects more than 1.5 million acres and offers a plethora of outdoor diversions for recreationists, from hiking and canoeing trails to campgrounds and ample fishing opportunities. In addition, you can opt for ranger-led programs throughout the year, narrated tram tours (305/221-8455, times and rates vary) in the Shark Valley area, and boat tours (239/695-2591, times and rates vary) through the Ten Thousand Islands region. No matter where you go, though, you're bound to see an array of wildlife, including white-tailed deer, alligators, turtles, snakes, herons, egrets, and, unfortunately, mosquitoes. If you're lucky, you might even spy an endangered creature like the Florida panther, American crocodile, or West Indian manatee.

This vast park has several helpful visitor centers, all of which offer educational displays and public restrooms, among other amenities. At the **Ernest F. Coe Visitor Center**

(40001 S.R. 9336, Homestead, 305/242-7700, 9 A.M.–5 P.M. daily), the main park entrance, you'll find an art exhibit, a bookstore, and nearby walking trails. Farther west, the **Shark Valley Visitor Center** (36000 SW 8th St., Miami, 305/221-8776, 9:15 A.M.–5:15 P.M. daily) features walking trails, bicycle rentals, guided tram tours, and a nearby observation tower, while the **Gulf Coast Visitor Center** (815 Oyster Bar Ln., Everglades City, 239/695-3311, 8:30 A.M.–4:30 P.M. daily mid-Nov.–mid-Apr., 9 A.M.–4:30 P.M. daily mid-Apr.–mid-Nov.) provides boat tours and canoe rentals. The **Flamingo Visitor Center** (239/695-2945, 9 A.M.–4:30 P.M. daily), meanwhile, is the only visitor center situated deep within the park, roughly 38 miles south of the main park entrance. Here, you can procure backcountry permits; rent canoes, kayaks, and bicycles; and access campground facilities, a marina store, a public boat ramp, and several hiking and canoeing trails.

the Big Cypress Bend Boardwalk in the Everglades

© DANIEL MARTONE

Big Cypress National Preserve

North of Everglades National Park lies Big Cypress National Preserve (33100 E. Tamiami Trail, Ochopee, 239/695-2000, www.nps.gov/bicy, headquarters 8:30 A.M.–4:30 P.M. Mon.–Fri., preserve 24 hours daily, free), a 720,000-acre region that protects the freshwater ecosystem of Big Cypress Swamp, an area that helps to support the marine estuaries along Florida's southwestern coast. Home to tropical and temperate plant communities, Big Cypress nurtures a wide array of wildlife, including wild hogs, various birds, and the elusive Florida panther. Visitors here can hike along the Florida National Scenic Trail, hunt for deer and turkey in the backcountry (with the proper permits, of course), experience one of several paddling trails, or join a ranger-led nature walk (late Nov.–mid-Apr.). For reservations and other information, contact the **Oasis Visitor Center** (MM 54 U.S. 41, 239/695-1201, 9 A.M.–4:30 P.M. daily), which is situated on the north side of the Tamiami Trail (U.S. 41), halfway between Miami and Naples. Note that, while the park headquarters is closed on

weekends, the preserve is actually open to the public every day of the year.

State Parks

While you'll find even more state parks in the Florida Keys, the vast Everglades region contains two that are worth a look. Often called "the Amazon of North America," the linear swamp forest known as **Fakahatchee Strand Preserve State Park** (137 Copeland Dr., Copeland, 239/695-4593, www.floridastateparks.org/fakahatcheestrand, 8 A.M.–sunset daily, free) beckons bird-watchers and wildlife lovers. Situated along the Tamiami Trail, this lush state park lies roughly 80 miles west of Miami and immediately west of Carnestown on S.R. 29. Here, you can wander along a 2,000-foot-long boardwalk at Big Cypress Bend or take guided swamp walks and canoe trips amid bald cypress trees, royal palm groves, and colorful orchids—home to alligators, varied birds and snakes, white-tailed deer, raccoons, endangered Florida panthers, and other engaging creatures.

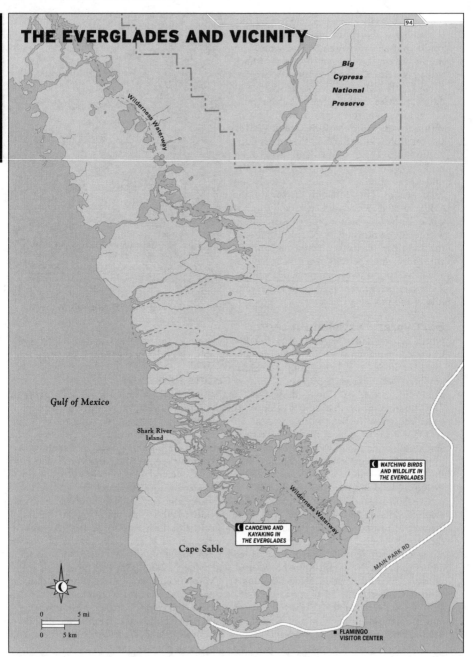

THE EVERGLADES AND VICINITY

94

Big Cypress National Preserve

Wilderness Waterway

Gulf of Mexico

Shark River Island

Wilderness Waterway

☾ WATCHING BIRDS AND WILDLIFE IN THE EVERGLADES

☾ CANOEING AND KAYAKING IN THE EVERGLADES

Cape Sable

MAIN PARK RD

0   5 mi
0   5 km

■ FLAMINGO VISITOR CENTER

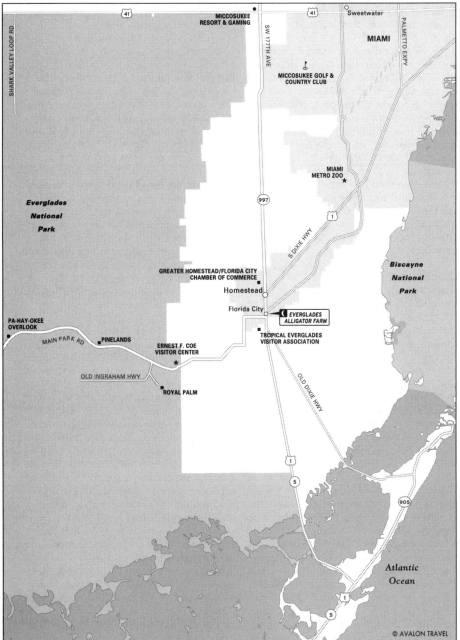

Farther west along the Tamiami Trail, the 7,270-acre **Collier-Seminole State Park** (20200 E. Tamiami Trail, Naples, 239/394-3397, www.floridastateparks.org/colliersemi-nole, 8 A.M.–sunset daily, $5 vehicles w/2–8 passengers, $4 motorcycles and single-occupant vehicles, $2 pedestrians, bikers, and extra passengers) offers even more outdoor diversions. Here, visitors can canoe through mangrove swamps, hike or bike amid pine flatwoods, camp beneath majestic royal palm trees, fish in the Blackwater River, or simply take a stroll through the on-site nature center. Obviously, wildlife-watching opportunities abound in this bountiful park, which also offers picnic areas, playgrounds, a boat ramp, and guided tours along the nature trail and boardwalk. As a bonus, leashed, well-behaved pets are welcome here.

Biscayne National Park

Water enthusiasts should venture east of the Everglades to Biscayne National Park (9700 SW 328th St., Homestead, 305/230-1144, www.nps.gov/bisc, 7 A.M.–5 P.M. daily, free), a stunning wonderland of aquamarine waters, peaceful islands, and living coral reefs, all within sight of downtown Miami. To explore this 172,000-acre park, **Biscayne National Underwater Park, Inc.** (305/230-1100, www.biscayneunderwater.com, 9 A.M.–5 P.M. daily, rates vary) offers canoe and kayak rentals as well as scuba-diving and snorkeling trips in Biscayne Bay, around the islands inside the park, and to the fascinating underwater coral reefs. Of course, if you'd prefer a less active experience, you're welcome to board a glass-bottom boat tour, which provides a wonderful glimpse of the coral reefs as well as frolicking dolphins and other marine creatures.

The islands, which are only accessible via canoe, kayak, or boat, are also worth exploring. Once a thriving community of wreckers, sponge makers, and pineapple farmers and now the park's largest island, **Elliott Key** offers ample picnicking, swimming, hiking, camping, fishing, and wildlife-viewing opportunities. Meanwhile, on **Boca Chita Key,**

the park's most popular island, you can enjoy a relaxing picnic, stroll along a half-mile hiking trail, or tour the 65-foot ornamental lighthouse, which is open intermittently and affords a fantastic view of nearby islands, Biscayne Bay, and the Miami skyline. One way to reach Boca Chita is via the Boca Chita Island Adventure ($35 adults, $25 seniors and military personnel, $20 children 2–12, children under 2 free), a three-hour boat ride and island tour through Biscayne National Underwater Park, Inc. Although the water portion of Biscayne National Park is open 24 hours daily, be advised that the keys have different operating hours. Adams Key, for instance, is a day-use area only. Keep in mind, too, that there are no bridges or ferries to the islands and, consequently, no RV camping facilities on the islands themselves. For more information about tours and activities, consult the **Dante Fascell Visitor Center** (305/230-7275, 9 A.M.–5 P.M. daily) near Convoy Point (9700 SW 328th St., Homestead) on the mainland.

Museums and Historic Sites

The Everglades, despite being a recreationist's paradise, aren't without their share of cultural diversions. The **Coral Castle Museum** (28655 S. Dixie Hwy., Homestead, 305/248-6345, www.coralcastle.com, 8 A.M.–6 P.M. Sun.–Thurs., 8 A.M.–8 P.M. Fri.–Sat., $9.75 adults, $6.50 seniors 62 and over, $5 children 7–12, children under 7 free), for instance, invites visitors to solve a long-standing mystery: How could a diminutive man like Edward Leedskalnin carve and sculpt 1,100 tons of coral all on his own? Erected secretly between 1923 and 1951, at a time when no modern construction conveniences existed, this strange sculpture garden has sparked countless debates over the years, and to this day, scientists and thinkers have yet to discern Edward's methods. While visiting this marvel, you can either take a guided tour or listen to a self-paced audio tour, available in English, Spanish, French, or German. Note, too, that the Coral Castle is part of the **Historic Redland Tropical Trail** (www.redlandtrail.com), created to promote

passing through Homestead's historic district

the agricultural heritage of the unique region between Miami and the Florida Keys.

To the west of Krome Avenue, on the south side of the Tamiami Trail in the Everglades, you'll encounter another cultural gem, the **Miccosukee Indian Village** (MM 70 U.S. 41, Miami, 305/552-8365, www.miccosukee. com, 9 A.M.–5 P.M. daily, $8 adults, $5 children 6–11, children under 6 free). Here, you can observe live alligator demonstrations, take an airboat ride into the Everglades, view historical artifacts and photographs at the Miccosukee Museum, and taste authentic cuisine at the on-site restaurant. In addition, you're welcome to observe Miccosukee Indians as they weave baskets, craft dolls, carve wood, and fashion colorful beadwork and patchwork, much of which you can purchase at the on-site gift shop. Two annual festivals here also highlight such handmade crafts: the Miccosukee Indian Arts Festival (late December to early January) and Miccosukee Everglades Music & Crafts Festival (mid-July).

For more Native American history,

specifically about the Calusa Indians, as well as tales of southwestern Florida's pioneers, head farther west to the **Museum of the Everglades** (105 W. Broadway, Everglades City, 239/695-0008, www.evergladesmuseum. org, 9 A.M.–5 P.M. Tues.–Fri., 9 A.M.–4 P.M. Sat., free), which features both permanent and traveling displays of artifacts, sketches, photographs, and the like. In addition, the on-site Pauline Reeves Gallery presents monthly exhibits from local and regional painters, photographers, and artisans. One of four Collier County Museums (www.colliermuseums.com) in the region, the Museum of the Everglades is housed within an old laundry building that was built in 1927 by Barron Gift Collier, who had purchased the village in 1922 from the Storter family in order to create a company town that would serve as the new county seat and the engineering headquarters for the construction of the Tamiami Trail. It's only appropriate then that this museum, the former laundry for Collier's company town, opened its doors on April 26, 1998, the 70th anniversary of the opening of the Tamiami Trail.

Faithfully restored to its 1920s-era appearance, the museum is listed on the National Register of Historic Places. During certain events, such as artists' receptions, you can take a guided walking tour (ranging from 20 minutes to an hour) of the historic buildings near the museum, such as the landmark Everglades Rod and Gun Club, once known as the Allen House. Private tours can also be arranged. While admission and parking are free at this wheelchair-accessible museum, donations are gratefully accepted, even for the walking tours. Note, too, that no food, drink, or gum is allowed in the museum, and flash photography is prohibited in the galleries.

You can better understand the Seminole Indians by visiting the **Ah-Tah-Thi-Ki Museum** (34725 W. Boundary Rd., Clewiston, 863/902-1113, www.ahtahthiki.com, 9 A.M.–5 P.M. daily, $9 adults, $6 military personnel, seniors 55 and over, students 5–18, and children 5–18, children under 5 free) on the Big Cypress Seminole Indian Reservation north of I-75.

© LAURA MARTONE

Featuring the country's largest display related to the Florida Seminole culture, this spacious museum presents exhibits and artifacts that illustrate how the Seminoles' ancestors once lived in the Florida Everglades, from cooking customs to traditional Green Corn Ceremony dances. Besides perusing the exhibits, visitors can watch an orientation video, stroll along a one-mile boardwalk through a 60-acre cypress dome, experience a living village, and purchase authentic jewelry, carvings, beadwork, and patchwork clothing crafted by Seminole and Miccosukee tribes.

⟪ Everglades Alligator Farm

Here in the Florida Everglades, you'll encounter a number of airboat tour operators, alligator exhibits, and live animal shows. Some places, like the Everglades Alligator Farm (40351 SW 192nd Ave., Florida City, 305/247-2628, www.everglades.com, 9 A.M.–6 P.M. daily, $23 adults, $15.50 children 4–11, children under 4 free)—part of the **Historic Redland Tropical Trail** (www.redlandtrail.com) and situated

about 40 miles southwest of Miami—offer all three. Beginning in 1982 as a mere airboat ride attraction, it's since become southern Florida's oldest alligator farm. Besides taking a narrated airboat ride (roughly 30 minutes long) along curious canals in the nearby Everglades, today's visitors can witness riveting alligator feedings (noon and 3 P.M. daily) and snake shows (10 A.M., 1 P.M., and 4 P.M. daily), observe and perhaps even hold a baby alligator or two, and stroll amid more than 2,000 alligators, caimans, native snakes, and specimens of three crocodile species: American, Nile, and Orinoco.

The on-site gift shop (9 A.M.–5:30 P.M. daily) is also worth a quick visit, especially if you forgot to bring insect spray with you, which you'll need to deter mosquitoes for most of the year. Just be advised that the last airboat departs at 5:25 P.M. each day. In addition, wearing earplugs is strongly recommended, as airboats can be very loud. Note, too, that the basic admission price includes an airboat ride, a visit to the alligator farm, and access to all animal

an American alligator lounging amid a sawgrass marsh

© DANIEL MARTONE

© DANIEL MARTONE

taking an airboat ride through the Everglades

shows; if you're only interested in the farm and the shows, you can opt for a lower ticket price ($15.50 adults, $10.50 children 4–11, children under 4 free).

Other Animal Attractions

Besides the Everglades Alligator Farm, you'll find another animal attraction on the **Historic Redland Tropical Trail** (www.redlandtrail. com), created to promote the agricultural heritage of the unique region between Miami and the Florida Keys. Situated between Miami and Homestead, not far from Zoo Miami, lies the family-owned **Monkey Jungle** (14805 SW 216th St., Miami, 305/235-1611, www.monkeyjungle.com, 9:30 A.M.–5 P.M. daily, $30 adults, $28 seniors 65 and over, $24 children 3–9, children under 3 free), where, as the facility's slogan indicates, "humans are caged and monkeys run wild!" Home to nearly 400 primates, this 30-acre reserve features the natural, unrehearsed antics of 30 different species, including gibbons, guenons, spider monkeys, howler monkeys, gorillas, orangutans, endangered golden lion tamarins, and descendants

of the original Java monkeys that animal behaviorist Joseph DuMond released into a dense southern Florida hammock in 1933. There are no parking fees here, but be advised that the ticket office closes promptly at 4 P.M.

Of course, monkeys aren't the only creatures you'll find in southern Florida. In addition to the Everglades Alligator Farm, several other airboat tour operators present engrossing alligator exhibits and shows. Along the Tamiami Trail, for instance, you'll spy **Gator Park** (24050 SW 8th St., Miami, 305/559-2255 or 800/559-2205, www.gatorpark.com, 9 A.M.–5 P.M. daily, $22 adults, $11 children, children under 6 free), where, in addition to experiencing an airboat ride (roughly 40 minutes long) amid the birds, snakes, alligators, sawgrass, and hammocks of the nearby Everglades, you'll be able to observe a fascinating wildlife show, during which staff members capture alligators using a barehanded technique favored by the Native Americans of southern Florida. Also on the premises is a souvenir shop, an RV park ($30 daily, $180 weekly), and a restaurant that serves hamburgers, hot dogs, and regional delicacies like alligator sausage, catfish, and frog legs. The last wildlife show usually occurs at 4:30 P.M. daily, while the last airboat ride starts at 5 P.M.

A little farther west, the **Everglades Safari Park** (26700 SW 8th St., Miami, 305/226-6923 or 305/223-3804, www.evergladessafari-park.com, 9 A.M.–4 P.M. daily, $23 adults, $10 children 5–11, children under 5 free) offers an eco-adventure tour that includes a 30-minute, narrated airboat ride; a show featuring alligators, crocodiles, turtles, and other wildlife; a stroll along the Jungle Trail boardwalk and elevated observation platform; a glimpse at a replica Cheekee Village; and the chance to view more than 100 alligators on their very own island. The airboat tours here depart every half hour, and the last one leaves around 4 P.M. At both Gator Park and Everglades Safari Park, you'll even be able to hold a baby alligator, if you dare.

North of I-75, you'll find yet another intriguing animal attraction, albeit a bit more expensive. Situated on the 2,200-acre Big Cypress Seminole Indian Reservation, **Billie Swamp Safari** (30000 Gator Tail Trail, Clewiston, 863/983-6101 or 800/467-2327, www.swampsafari.net, 9:30 A.M.–6 P.M. daily) invites visitors to experience the Everglades via airboat (10 A.M.–4:30 P.M. daily, $15 pp) or swamp buggy (11 A.M.–5 P.M. daily, $25 adults, $23 seniors 62 and over, $15 children 4–12, children under 4 free), either of which offers you the chance to see native flora and fauna in an untamed landscape. The airboat ride is roughly 20 minutes long, while the swamp buggy tour takes an hour. While here, you can also watch a show about native and nonnative swamp critters (1:15 P.M. daily, $8 adults, $4 children, children under 4 free), as well as an up-close presentation about venomous snakes, nonvenomous snakes, and, of course, alligators (2:15 P.M. daily, $8 adults, $4 children, children under 4 free).

Other activities include campfire storytelling ($3.50 pp, children under 4 free), nighttime swamp buggy ecotours ($30 adults, $28 seniors 62 and over, $20 children 4–12, children under 4 free), and an overnight stay in a traditional chickee lodge ($35 per chickee), all of which require advance reservations. Various packages are also available for those hoping to save a few bucks, and you'll find both a gift shop (8:30 A.M.–6 P.M. daily) and a restaurant, the Swamp Water Café (7 A.M.–6 P.M. daily, $4–21), on the premises. Children must be at least four years old to ride an airboat.

Fruit and Spice Park

If your interests lean more toward flora than fauna, you'll be pleased to know that the area near Homestead is home to a plethora of plant nurseries. One particularly curious stop is the Fruit and Spice Park (24801 SW 187th Ave., Homestead, 305/247-5727, www.fruitand-spicepark.org, 9 A.M.–5 P.M. daily, $8 adults, $1.50 children 6–12, children under 6 free), a 37-acre tropical botanical garden that hosts more than 500 varieties of plants, fruits, vegetables, spices, herbs, and nuts, including several varieties of mangoes, bananas, and bamboo trees. Visitors can have a picnic on the premises or eat lunch at the on-site café. In addition, guided tours are conducted every day at 11 A.M., 1:30 P.M., and 3 P.M., and various events regularly take place at the park, including the Redland International Orchid Show ($7 pp) in mid-May and the Redland Summer Fruit Festival ($8 pp) in mid-June.

Marco Island

Along the coast of southwestern Florida lies a chain of islands and mangrove islets known as the Ten Thousand Islands region—despite the fact that the islands actually number in the hundreds, not the thousands. Marco Island (www.marco-island-florida.com), the largest, northernmost island in this chain, is a popular locale for outdoor enthusiasts, especially anglers, boaters, kayakers, bird-watchers, and beachcombers. In fact, Marco Island features two public beaches, **Tigertail Beach** (Spinnaker Dr. and Hernando Dr., 8 A.M.–sunset daily, $8 parking) and **South Marco Beach** (Collier Blvd. and Swallow Ave., 8 A.M.–sunset daily, $8 parking). While South Marco offers no facilities, Tigertail features a concession stand, a playground, a butterfly garden, volleyball courts, public restrooms, and watersports rentals.

Besides outdoor diversions, Marco Island also boasts several specialty shops and waterfront restaurants, including those at **The Esplanade Shoppes, Residences and Marina** (760 N. Collier Blvd., Marco Island, 239/394-7772, www.esplanadeshoppes.com, hours vary daily), an Italian-style village on Smokehouse Bay.

To reach Marco Island, head into the Everglades via the Tamiami Trail (U.S. 41), turn south onto Collier Boulevard, and continue until you reach the island.

ENTERTAINMENT AND EVENTS

While Miami offers a greater variety of entertainment options and annual events, the Everglades aren't without a dose of culture.

Nightlife

Among the handful of bars you'll encounter in the Everglades, one lively option is the **Iron Rhino Saloon** (19800 E. Tamiami Trail, Naples, 239/393-3974, www.ironrhinosaloon.com, hours vary Tues.–Sun.), not far from Collier-Seminole State Park and the turnoff for Marco Island. Besides offering happy-hour beer and drink specials (5–7 P.M. Mon.–Fri.), this popular, air-conditioned watering hole features an ever-changing menu, two-for-one burgers and draft beers on Wednesday (5 P.M.–close), live rockabilly music and dancing on Sunday (2–6 P.M.), and occasional bikini and tattoo contests. Another fun joint is the **Wharf Lounge** (1 SE 1st Ave., Florida City, 305/245-3377, www.mutineer.biz, 11 A.M.–2 A.M. daily), located at the Mutineer Restaurant and offering live rock music on Friday and Saturday nights (9 P.M.–1 A.M.).

Unlike other parts of Florida, the area between Miami and the Everglades offers few options for gamblers. One such option is the **Miccosukee Resort & Gaming** (500 SW 177th Ave., Miami, 305/925-2555, www.miccosukee.com, 24 hours daily), a casino resort

the Miccosukee gaming resort, west of Miami

© DANIEL MARTONE

that lies west of Miami and is operated by the Miccosukee Tribe of Indians of Florida, who separated from the native Seminole Indians in the 1950s. Here, visitors can enjoy live entertainment, various dining options, cocktails in the Cypress Lounge and Martini Bar, and, of course, an assortment of gaming options, including a high-stakes bingo hall, a 58-table poker room, and more than 1,790 video slot machines.

Festivals and Events

For more than 35 years, Everglades City has hosted the annual **Everglades Seafood Festival** (239/695-4100, www.evergladesseafoodfestival.com, free admission though fees apply for some activities), a family-friendly event that usually occurs during the first weekend of February. Besides carnival rides, arts and crafts, and live music, attendees will be treated to plenty of delicious food, including standard American fare like hamburgers and corn-on-the-cob. Of course, fresh seafood is the main event; highlights include fresh shrimp, catfish, lobster, stone crabs, and fish chowder.

Another curious event usually happens from late December to early January. Over the course of nine days, the **Miccosukee Indian Arts Festival** (305/223-8380, http://miccosukeeresortgaming.webpanl.com, $10 adults, $7 children 7–12, children under 7 free) welcomes visitors to the Miccosukee Indian Village (MM 70 U.S. 41, Miami, 305/552-8365, www.miccosukee.com, 9 A.M.–5 P.M. daily), where you can experience Native American dances and musical performances, marvel at traditional costumes, enjoy authentic foods, browse genuine arts and crafts from various Native American tribes, observe alligator demonstrations, and perhaps even take an airboat ride into the Everglades. As a bonus, proceeds from the festival help to fund educational programs for Native American youth. A similarly long-standing event, the **Miccosukee Everglades Music & Crafts Festival** (305/223-8380, www.miccosukee.com/festival, $25 pp, children under 7 free), also occurs at the Miccosukee Indian Village. Usually occurring on a weekend in mid-July, this festival features similar crafts, fashions, demonstrations, tours, and food, plus live performances from various musical groups that, in the past, have included The Little River Band and The Neville Brothers.

SHOPPING

Though most folks don't venture into the Everglades on a shopping quest, there are nevertheless several spots worth visiting. Headed south of downtown Miami, toward Homestead, you'll encounter the nostalgic **Cauley Square Historic Railroad Village** (22400 Old Dixie Hwy., Miami, 305/258-3543, www.cauleysquare.com, 11 A.M.–6 P.M. Tues.–Sat., noon–5 P.M. Sun.), part of the **Historic Redland Tropical Trail** (www.redlandtrail.com), which was created to promote the agricultural heritage of the unique region between Miami and the Florida Keys. Here, you can stroll along garden paths, enjoy tea and sandwiches at the on-site, Victorian-style Tea Room Restaurant (305/258-0044, www.tearoombakery.com, 11 A.M.–4 P.M. Mon.–Thurs., 11 A.M.–5 P.M. Fri.–Sun.), and browse a variety of quaint cottages, housing a cornucopia of jewelry, candles, handmade crafts, antique furniture, and other specialty items. Also on the premises, you'll find the cozy Village Chalet Restaurant (305/258-8900, www.villagechalet.com, 11 A.M.–3 P.M. Mon., 11 A.M.–9 P.M. Tues.–Thurs. and Sun., 11 A.M.–10 P.M. Fri.–Sat.), which features salads, sandwiches, steaks, and seafood entrées, plus live jazz on occasion.

Farther south, you can shop for bargain, name-brand clothes, shoes, jewelry, and perfume at **Prime Outlets Florida City** (250 E. Palm Dr., Florida City, 305/248-4736 or 888/545-7198, www.primeoutlets.com, 10 A.M.–9 P.M. Mon.–Sat., 11 A.M.–6 P.M. Sun.). Not far away, the **Schnebly Redland's Winery** (30205 SW 217th Ave., Homestead, 305/242-1224 or 888/717-9463, www.schneblywinery.com, 10 A.M.–5 P.M. Mon.–Fri., 10 A.M.–6 P.M. Sat., noon–5 P.M. Sun.), also part of the Historic Redland Tropical Trail, invites visitors to sample handcrafted fruit wines amid coral waterfalls.

The area in and around Homestead, especially along Krome Avenue (S.R. 997/SW 177th Ave.), is also known for its bountiful nurseries, including the **Santa Barbara Nursery** (20425 SW 177th Ave., Miami, 305/256-7577, www.santa-barbaranursery.com, 7:30 A.M.–5:30 P.M. Mon.–Sat., 8 A.M.–5:30 P.M. Sun.), which offers a wide assortment of trees, plants, and flowers. In addition, the Historic Redland Tropical Trail features three other agricultural delights, including **Miami Tropical Bonsai** (14775 SW 232nd St., Miami, 305/258-0865, www.miamitropicalbonsai.com, 9 A.M.–4:30 P.M. Mon.–Sat.), which sells an assortment of bonsai trees and supplies, and **R.F. Orchids** (28100 SW 182nd Ave., Homestead, 305/245-4570, www.rforchids.com, 9 A.M.–5 P.M. Tues.–Sun.), which, as the name indicates, provides an array of vibrant orchids. Closer to Florida City is the third option, the **Robert Is Here Fruit Stand and Farm** (19200 SW 344th St., Homestead, 305/246-1592, www.robertishere.com, 8 A.M.–7 P.M. daily Nov.–Aug.). Established in 1960, this store offers a range of seasonal produce and products, from oranges and mangoes to preserves and salsas.

Along the Tamiami Trail (U.S. 41), farther into the wetlands and hammocks of the Everglades, you'll spy the **Big Cypress Gallery** (MM 54.5 U.S. 1, Ochopee, 239/695-2428, www.clydebutcher.com, 10 A.M.–5 P.M. daily) on the south side of the highway, roughly 37 miles west of Krome Avenue and only half a mile east of the Big Cypress National Preserve Oasis Visitor Center. Featuring the black-and-white landscape photography of Clyde and Niki Butcher, this art gallery and studio also offers guided swamp walks behind the on-site cottage every Saturday (10 A.M. and 2 P.M., $50 adults, $25 children), from mid-September through late March. Hats, long pants, old sneakers, and insect repellent are recommended for such tours.

RECREATION

It perhaps goes without saying that most visitors venture to the Everglades for recreational reasons, whether planning a long-distance hike, scheduling a canoe trip, or simply hopping to glimpse as many birds and alligators as possible.

Hiking and Biking

Given the wide array of habitats in the Everglades, hikers and bikers will encounter no shortage of fascinating opportunities. In **Everglades National Park** (40001 S.R. 9336, Homestead, 305/242-7700, www.nps.gov/ever, visitor center 9 A.M.–5 P.M. daily, park 24 hours daily, $10 vehicles, $5 motorcycles, pedestrians, and bikers), for instance, you'll find several hiking trails, two of which allow bicycles. These multipurpose trails include the 1.6-mile **Snake Bight Trail** and the 2.6-mile **Rowdy Bend Trail,** which, if combined with the main park road, form a 12.6-mile, round-trip biking excursion from the Flamingo Visitor Center. Bicycle rentals ($15 for two hours, $20 per half day) are available in the park, but be advised that pets are not allowed on any park trails.

An even bigger challenge awaits in **Big Cypress National Preserve** (33100 E. Tamiami Trail, Ochopee, 239/695-2000, www.nps.gov/bicy, headquarters 8:30 A.M.–4:30 P.M. Mon.–Fri., preserve 24 hours daily, free), where long-distance hikers can enjoy three different sections of the **Florida National Scenic Trail,** which incidentally connects with Gulf Islands National Seashore, a park that stretches alongside southern Mississippi and the Florida Panhandle. The longest section in Big Cypress, which extends for roughly 28 miles between the Big Cypress Visitor Center on U.S. 41 and the rest area at mile marker 63 on I-75, passes through a rugged, often overgrown habitat of pinelands, prairies, cypress swamps, and hardwood hammocks. Only experienced hikers should attempt this route. Make sure, too, to bring enough drinking water with you, especially during the dry season (Nov.–Apr.).

Although you're welcome to use your own bicycle along the available trails in the Everglades, rentals are available, too. In the Everglades, for instance, the full-service **Glades Haven Marina** (801 S. Copeland Ave., Everglades City, 239/695-2628 or

ALIENS IN THE EVERGLADES

A **native species** is one that occurs in a particular habitat, ecosystem, or region without direct or indirect human actions. Every organism on the planet — whether plant, animal, insect, fungi, or bacteria — is native to some locale, where it's probably existed for thousands of years due to natural forces like climate, storms, moisture, fire, soil, and species interactions. In North America, native species are considered those that occurred prior to European settlement. Approximately 18,000 plants are native to this continent, serving as the foundation for a variety of landscapes as well as providing sources of food, fiber, and other necessities.

Nonnative species, meanwhile, are organisms that occur artificially in locales beyond their natural ranges. Also known as exotic, foreign, introduced, nonindigenous, and alien species, such nonnatives can do irreparable damage to fragile ecosystems in the United States, whether they're accidentally or intentionally transported between continents or from one part of the country to the other. In America, nonnative invaders and habitat destruction have led to the extinction of roughly 200 native plant species since the 1800s.

In **Everglades National Park** (40001 S.R. 9336, Homestead, 305/242-7700, www.nps. gov/ever), several invasive plant species are currently threatening native plant populations. These alien invaders include:

- **Australian pine** (*Casuarina equisetifolia*): Native to Australia, Malaysia, and southern Asia, this tall, fast-growing pine tree was introduced to Florida in the late 1800s for the purposes of ditch and canal stabilization, shade, and lumber. Today, dense thickets have displaced native dune and beach vegetation; radically altered the light, temperature, and soil chemistry of beach habitats; inhibited the growth of native plants, upon which native insects and other wildlife depend; and increased beach and dune erosion, which has affected the nesting activities of sea turtles and American crocodiles.

- **Brazilian pepper** (*Schinus terebinthifolius*): As the name indicates, this bushy, spreading evergreen tree hails from Brazil, Argentina, and Paraguay. Given its aromatic leaves, white flowers, and red berries, it's no wonder that the Brazilian pepper was imported as an ornamental in the 1840s. Since then, however, the seeds of this fire-resistant, salt-tolerant plant have spread, resulting in the formation of dense monocultures in farmlands, pinelands, hardwood hammocks, and mangrove forests. As an unfortunate bonus, chemicals in the lovely leaves, flowers, and berries can irritate human skin and respiratory passages.

- **Latherleaf** (*Columbrina asiatica*): Found along coastal areas of eastern Africa, India, Southeast Asia, Australia, and the Pacific Islands, this sprawling bush was brought from Asia to Jamaica by immigrants in the 1850s. From there, the seeds, which can be dispersed by tides and storms, probably floated to southern Florida on ocean currents. Nowadays, latherleaf has invaded coastal beaches and dunes, pine and hardwood forests, and mangrove estuaries, smothering native vegetation and

239/695-2746, www.theevergladesflorida.com, 6 A.M.–6 P.M. Sun.–Thurs., 6 A.M.–9 P.M. Fri.–Sat.) offers top-quality trail bicycles for rent ($15 hourly, $20 per half day, $25 daily). As an alternative, **Everglades Area Tours** (238 Mamie St., Chokoloskee Island, 239/695-3633, www.evergladesareatours.com) features guided Everglades bicycle tours ($99 pp) for which reservations are required. Riders must be at least 12 years old, and the tours can accommodate a maximum of 20 people at a time.

◖ Bird-Watching and Wildlife-Viewing

The Everglades, which constitute one of the largest tracts of wilderness in the United

threatening to form a monoculture if left uncontrolled.

· **Melaleuca** *(Melaleuca quinquenervia):* Originally from Australia, New Guinea, and the Solomon Islands, this subtropical tree was introduced to southern Florida in the early 1900s for landscaping and "swamp drying" purposes. Today, the fast-spreading melaleuca is the greatest threat to the Everglades ecosystem, which faces extreme and perhaps irreversible alteration because of the tree's ability to convert native plant communities like sawgrass marshes and wet prairies into impenetrable thickets.

· **Old World climbing fern** *(Lygodium microphyllum):* Native to Australia, Africa, and tropical Asia, this intertwining vine was introduced to Florida in the 1960s as a landscape ornamental. Since then, the climbing fern, which has a dense root system, has blanketed pine forests, cypress swamps, and other Floridian habitats; altered the water flow through streams and wetlands; and provided fuel for fires that would not normally spread through a wetland area.

· **Seaside mahoe** *(Thespesia populnea):* Indigenous to the tropical seashores of Africa and India, this tall, flowering tree was brought to Florida as an ornamental for coastal landscapes in the 1920s. Since then, the seaside mahoe has invaded shoreline habitats, where its dense shade has smothered its competitors. Unfortunately, its seeds float in seawater, which means it can also ride the ocean currents to colonize other unsuspecting shores.

While management methods, such as herbicide and nonnative insects, vary from plant to plant, you can take certain actions to prevent the introduction or spread of all invasive alien plants into natural areas. Such actions include:

· Avoiding disturbance to natural areas, such as clearing native vegetation, planting nonnatives, and dumping yard wastes

· Refraining from the use of exotic species in your landscaping, land restoration, or erosion control projects

· Using ornamentals that are native to your local region

· Consulting a local university, arboretum, nature center, native plant society, or Department of Agriculture office if you have any concerns about a plant that you intend to grow

· Using techniques such as cutting, mowing, pruning, or herbicide to remove or manage any invasive exotics

· Asking local nurseries and garden shops not to sell invasive exotic plants

· Notifying land managers about invasive exotic plant occurrences

· Assisting in exotic plant removal projects

· Working with your local government to encourage the use of native plants in urban and suburban landscapes

States, boast a number of diverse habitats, from sawgrass marshes to tropical hardwood hammocks. Consequently, this massive region is home to hundreds of bird, fish, reptile, amphibian, and mammal species. In fact, whether you choose to explore the **East Everglades Expansion Area** via airboat, take a canoe trip through **Everglades National Park** (40001 S.R. 9336, Homestead, 305/242-7700, www.nps.gov/ever, visitor center 9 A.M.–5 P.M. daily, park 24 hours daily, $10 vehicles, $5 motorcycles, pedestrians, and bikers), or simply stroll along the 2,000-foot **Big Cypress Bend Boardwalk** in **Fakahatchee Strand Preserve State Park** (137 Copeland Dr., Copeland, 239/695-4593, www.floridastateparks.org/

fakahatcheestrand, 8 A.M.–sunset daily, free), you're bound to encounter an array of curious birds and other wild animals, including great blue herons, American alligators, various snakes and turtles, and, for the lucky few, the elusive Florida panther.

Although some conservationists worry about the presence of airboats in the Everglades, citing reasons like noise pollution and wildlife disturbance, most airboat operators are exceedingly passionate and knowledgeable about this fragile landscape. For those visitors who have little or no experience with activities like canoeing and kayaking, airboat tours provide a good opportunity to learn about this unique environment firsthand. Luckily, you'll find at least a dozen operators willing to guide you through this "river of grass" for an up-close look at birds, alligators, and other native inhabitants.

Along the Tamiami Trail, for instance, you'll encounter **Coopertown Airboats** (22700 SW 8th St., Miami, 305/226-6048, www.

© DANIEL MARTONE

Birding opportunities abound in the Everglades.

coopertownairboats.com, 8 A.M.–6 P.M. daily, $22 adults, $17 children 7–11, children under 7 free), which offers 40-minute narrated tours through a sawgrass marsh and an alligator hole; **Gator Park Airboat Tours** (24050 SW 8th St., Miami, 305/559-2255 or 800/559-2205, www.gatorpark.com, 9 A.M.–5 P.M. daily, $22 adults, $11 children, children under 6 free), which also features an exciting wildlife show; and **Wooten's Everglades Airboat Tour** (32330 E. Tamiami Trail, Ochopee, 239/695-2781 or 800/282-2781, www.wootensairboats. com, 8:30 A.M.–4:30 P.M. daily, $25 adults, $21 children 4–12), which also provides 45-minute swamp buggy rides.

Several more operators are in Everglades City, including **Speedy's Airboat Tours** (621 Begonia St., Everglades City, 239/695-4448 or 800/998-4448, www.speedysairboattours.com, 9 A.M.–5 P.M. daily, $40 adults, $25 children 3–10, children under 3 free); **Captain Doug's Everglades Tours** (200 S.R. 29, Everglades City, 800/282-9194, www.captaindougs.com, 9 A.M.–5 P.M. daily, $37.50 adults, $22.50 children under 13), situated one mile past the main bridge; and **Jungle Erv's Airboat Tours** (31222 Tamiami Trail, Everglades City, 877/695-2820, www.jungleervairboatworld. com, 9 A.M.–5 P.M. daily, $37.50 adults, $25 children 3–10, children under 3 free), located a half mile west of S.R. 29.

I-75 offers access to airboat tours, too. **Billie Swamp Safari** (30000 Gator Tail Trail, Clewiston, 863/983-6101 or 800/467-2327, www.swampsafari.net, 9:30 A.M.–6 P.M. daily), for instance, is located on the 2,200-acre Big Cypress Seminole Indian Reservation north of the interstate. Besides taking an airboat tour (10 A.M.–4:30 P.M. daily, $15 pp) here, you'll also be able to spot wildlife on a swamp buggy ecotour (11 A.M.–5 P.M. daily, $25 adults, $23 seniors 62 and over, $15 children 4–12, children under 4 free) through the wetlands or watch the on-site animal and reptile shows (1:15 P.M. and 2:15 P.M. daily, $8 adults, $4 children, children under 4 free). The airboat ride is roughly 20 minutes long, while the swamp buggy tour takes an hour.

An even more unusual wildlife-watching opportunity awaits through **Everglades Area Tours** (238 Mamie St., Chokoloskee Island, 239/695-3633, www.evergladesareatours.com, times vary Nov.–May), which offers flights via an Alaskan float plane from the **Everglades City Airpark** (650 E.C. Airpark Rd., Everglades City, 239/695-2778) and across various destinations, including Everglades National Park and Big Cypress National Preserve. Some of the flights include the 20-minute Everglades City Tour ($100 per adult or two children, $150 per two adults), the 45-minute Marco Island Tour ($192 per adult or two children, $288 per two adults), the hourlong Everglades National Park Tour ($250 per adult or two children, $375 per two adults), the 90-minute Area Grand Tour ($375 per adult or two children, $563 per two adults), and the 10-hour Key West and Fort Jefferson Tour ($919 per adult or two children, $1,489 per two adults). For each flight, there are extra fees for additional passengers; up to four guests can be accommodated on each flight.

Fishing and Boating

Since roughly one-third of **Everglades National Park** (40001 S.R. 9336, Homestead, 305/242-7700, www.nps.gov/ever, visitor center 9 A.M.–5 P.M. daily, park 24 hours daily, $10 vehicles, $5 motorcycles, pedestrians, and bikers) is covered by water, it's no wonder that fishing and boating have long been popular activities in this region. Anglers, in fact, will find both saltwater and freshwater fishing opportunities here, especially via boat, which allows access to a multitude of channels, shallow flats, and mangrove keys, not to mention Florida Bay. Depending on the time of year, you're likely to find snapper, redfish, bass, bluegill, and other varieties in these waters. Just be aware that saltwater and freshwater fishing require separate Florida fishing licenses, and remember that collecting plants and animals, such as orchids and conch, is forbidden in protected waters.

Even if you don't like to fish, traversing the Everglades via boat can be a rewarding experience—though it's only advisable for skilled boaters. There are, after all, innumerable obstacles in the Everglades, from seagrass banks to oyster reefs. It helps, then, to know the draft of your vessel, be able to "read" the water for signs of shallow areas, and adhere to slow speed zones at all times. The same rules apply for boaters in **Biscayne National Park** (9700 SW 328th St., Homestead, 305/230-7275, www.nps.gov/bisc, 7 A.M.–5 P.M. daily, free admission though tour and rental fees may apply), where it's also critical to understand the shifting tides.

Although having your own vessel might make boating in Everglades National Park and Biscayne National Park a bit more convenient, it's possible to rent one, too. In the Everglades, for instance, the full-service **Glades Haven Marina** (801 S. Copeland Ave., Everglades City, 239/695-2628 or 239/695-2746, www.theevergladesflorida.com, 6 A.M.–6 P.M. Sun.–Thurs., 6 A.M.–9 P.M. Fri.–Sat.) offers boat rentals ($50–75 hourly, $150–250 per half day, $225–300 daily, plus fuel charges), plus an easy-access boat ramp, plenty of docking space, a full-time mechanic, an on-site deli, and a bait and tackle shop that provides lures, bait, and fishing gear. As an alternative, **Chokoloskee Charters** (239/695-9107, www.chokoloskeecharters.com), helmed by Captain Charles Wright, provides guided, light-tackle fishing and fly-fishing trips into the Everglades backcountry. The rates depend on the trip length and the number of anglers. For two people, for example, a half-day trip costs $375, while a full-day trip costs $575. Six anglers, meanwhile, can expect a rate of $675 per half day and $900 daily. All charters include the necessary bait, tackle, gear, coolers, licenses, insurance, and safety equipment.

◀ Canoeing and Kayaking

The region between Miami and the Florida Keys offers a wealth of opportunities for canoeists and kayakers. With its sawgrass marshes, cypress swamps, and mangrove forests, the Everglades provide ideal spots for paddlers, especially those who enjoy observing or photographing wild animals in their element. In **Fakahatchee Strand Preserve State Park** (137 Copeland Dr., Copeland, 239/695-4593, www.floridastateparks.org/fakahatcheestrand, 8 A.M.–sunset daily, free), for instance, you can paddle amid a linear swamp forest, while **Collier-Seminole State Park** (20200 E. Tamiami Trail, Naples, 239/394-3397, www.floridastateparks.org/collierseminole, 8 A.M.–sunset daily, $5 vehicles w/2–8 passengers, $4 motorcycles and single-occupant vehicles, $2 pedestrians, bikers, and extra passengers) offers a 13.6-mile canoe trail along the Blackwater River, lined by interlocked mangrove trees.

If you don't have a canoe or kayak of your own, don't worry. From November to mid-April, **North American Canoe Tours** (107 Camellia St., Everglades City, 239/695-3299, www.evergladesadventures.com) provides canoe ($20–25 per half day, $28–35 daily) and kayak rentals ($28–45 per half day, $36–65 daily) as well as guided kayaking trips ($99–124) through mangrove tunnels, cypress swamps, and sawgrass prairies. The full-service **Glades Haven Marina** (801 S. Copeland Ave., Everglades City, 239/695-2628 or 239/695-2746, www.theeverglades-florida.com, 6 A.M.–6 P.M. Sun.–Thurs., 6 A.M.–9 P.M. Fri.–Sat.) also provides canoe rentals ($25 per half day, $35 daily) and kayak rentals ($30–45 per half day, $45–55 daily). In addition, **Everglades Area Tours** (238 Mamie St., Chokoloskee Island, 239/695-3633, www.evergladesareatours.com) provides canoes ($45 daily), recreational kayaks ($35–45 per half day, $45–65 daily), fishing kayaks ($35–55 per half day, $45–70 daily), and sea kayaks ($55–60 per half day, $75–80 daily).

You can even rent canoes ($16 for two hours, $22 per half day, $32 daily) and kayaks ($22.50–28.50 for two hours, $35–45 per half day, $45–55 daily) through **Everglades National Park** (40001 S.R. 9336, Homestead, 305/242-7700, www.nps.gov/ever, visitor center 9 A.M.–5 P.M. daily, park 24 hours daily, $10 vehicles, $5 motorcycles, pedestrians, and bikers), where well-equipped, well-prepared paddlers can explore a labyrinth of water and mangroves

in the Ten Thousand Islands area. Another option is a guided kayaking trip through **Crystal Seas Kayaking** (360/378-4223 or 877/732-7877, www.crystalseas.com, times vary daily Dec.–Apr., rates vary).

Of course, the Everglades don't have a monopoly on paddling adventures. **Biscayne National Underwater Park, Inc.** (305/230-1100, www.biscayneunderwater.com, rates vary) also offers canoe and kayak rentals for those hoping to explore the islands and coral-rich waters of **Biscayne National Park** (9700 SW 328th St., Homestead, 305/230-7275, www.nps.gov/bisc, 7 A.M.–5 P.M. daily, free).

Diving and Snorkeling

Despite all of the outdoor activities available in the Everglades, diving and snorkeling aren't common here. That's not the case, however, in **Biscayne National Park** (9700 SW 328th St., Homestead, 305/230-7275, www.nps.gov/bisc, 7 A.M.–5 P.M. daily, free), which is accessible via boat from the coast near Homestead. If you don't have a boat of your own, you can simply board a guided scuba-diving or snorkeling tour through **Biscayne National Underwater Park, Inc.** (305/230-1100, www.biscayneunderwater.com, $40–99 pp), which offers excursions around Biscayne Bay and trips to the offshore coral reefs that are part of the national park.

ACCOMMODATIONS

For the most part, the Everglades offer quiet inns, chain hotels, and campgrounds—ideal for those on a budget. Of course, even here, you'll find a few resort-style choices, too.

Under $100

Southeast of Miami, the communities of Homestead and Florida City offer several affordable lodging options—ideal for those hoping to explore Everglades National Park, Biscayne National Park, and the Florida Keys. Continuously operated since 1904, the historic, smoke-free **Redland Hotel** (5 S. Flagler Ave., Homestead, 305/246-1904 or 800/595-1904, www.redlandhotel.com, $70–130 d), for instance, offers nicely decorated rooms, free cable television, complimentary wireless Internet access, and the on-site, seasonal Downtown Bar and Grill (11:30 A.M.–7 P.M. Mon.–Thurs., 11:30 A.M.–8 P.M. Fri.), which specializes in old-fashioned comfort food. Just be advised that the closer your room is to the street, the noisier it may be.

If you're more comfortable with chain establishments, consider staying at the pet-friendly **Travelodge Florida City/Homestead** (409 SE 1st Ave., Florida City, 305/248-9777 or 800/758-0618, www.tlflcity.com or www. travelodge.com, $50–75 d), which offers ample parking, free high-speed Internet access, and a heated pool.

$100-200

If you're looking for a familiar chain option, reserve a room at the **Holiday Inn Express Hotel & Suites Florida City/Gateway to the Keys** (35200 S. Dixie Hwy., Florida City, 305/247-3414 or 800/315-2621, www. hiexpress.com, $110–140 d), which provides guests with complimentary breakfast, high-speed Internet access, an outdoor pool, and an on-site fitness center.

At the intersection of Krome Avenue and the Tamiami Trail, you'll be hard-pressed to miss the enormous (**Miccosukee Resort & Gaming** (500 SW 177th Ave., Miami, 305/925-2555 or 877/242-6464, www.miccosukee.com, $140–155 d). Part of a complex that includes a 24-hour casino, a well-equipped fitness center, an indoor heated pool, a full-service European spa, and five dining options, the hotel features 302 comfortable rooms and suites, all of which include wireless Internet access, premium cable television, 24-hour room service, and 24-hour laundry services, among other amenities.

Farther west along the Tamiami Trail, the family-owned, ecofriendly **Ivey House Bed & Breakfast** (107 Camellia St., Everglades City, 239/695-3299 or 877/567-0679, www. iveyhouse.com, $70–175 d) encompasses a variety of accommodations, including a lovely inn, historic lodge, and cozy cottage. In addition, guests can relax in a tropical pool, rent a canoe, join a guided kayaking trip, and enjoy

free wireless Internet access in limited areas. The facilities here are nonsmoking, and pets are not allowed.

The landmark (**Everglades Rod and Gun Club** (200 Riverside Dr., Everglades City, 239/695-2101, www.evergladesrodandgun. com, $95–140 d), situated on the Barron River, borders Everglades National Park. Formerly known as the Allen House and converted to a private club in the 1920s, this historic building has hosted a number of famous guests over the years, including Ernest Hemingway, President Eisenhower, John Wayne, Jack Nicklaus, Mick Jagger, and Sean Connery. Inside, the hunting lodge–style decor includes dark, wood-paneled walls, old-fashioned furniture, and mounted tarpon, deer, and alligator trophies, while outside, the airy, screened porch entices guests to relax in the white, wicker furniture and watch passing boats in the adjacent river. Overnight guests can choose from one of several private, air-conditioned cottages—essentially cozy, raised, modern-looking structures with small porches, hardwood floors, comfortable beds, and convenient bathrooms. While here, you can enjoy access to an on-site restaurant and lounge, a convenient marina, and an outdoor pool with a picturesque waterfall.

Camping

Between Miami and the Everglades, not far from the Monkey Jungle, lies the appropriately named **Miami Everglades Campground** (20675 SW 162nd Ave., Miami, 305/233-5300 or 800/917-4923, www.miamicamp.com, $34–65 daily). Here, you'll find 330 spacious RV and tent sites, some of which include patios and picnic tables, plus several different air-conditioned cabins and lodges ($49–179 daily) that can also be rented by the week or month. Campers will enjoy an array of recreational facilities, including a heated pool and hot tub, a large playground, a paved walking/jogging track, bicycle rentals, horseshoes, as well as volleyball, basketball, and shuffleboard courts. Other amenities include shady tiki huts, a recreation hall, a well-stocked camp store, a casual eatery, a propane filling station, modern restrooms, laundry facilities, wireless Internet access, and free U-pick avocados and mangoes.

For a more unusual experience, consider camping on the islands of **Biscayne National Park** (9700 SW 328th St., Homestead, 305/230-7275, www.nps.gov/bisc, 7 A.M.–5 P.M. daily, free admission though tour and rental rates apply), which lies between Key Biscayne and Key Largo. Tent camping ($15 daily) is available on both popular **Boca Chita Key,** which features a grassy waterside camping area with picnic tables, grills, and toilets, and spacious **Elliott Key,** which offers waterside and forested camping areas, picnic tables, grills, drinking water, and restrooms with cold showers. Group camping ($30 daily) is also available, and boaters are welcome to stay in either of the two harbors for a fee ($20 daily). Just be advised that RV camping isn't possible in the park, and any vessel still in the harbor after 5 P.M. is presumed to be staying overnight and will be charged as such. The islands are only accessible via boat; if you don't have your own, you can easily arrange transportation through **Biscayne National Underwater Park, Inc.** (305/230-1100, www.biscayneunderwater.com, rates vary).

Along the Tamiami Trail (U.S. 41), you'll find a slew of camping options, including the six campgrounds available within **Big Cypress National Preserve** (33100 E. Tamiami Trail, Ochopee, 239/695-2000, www.nps.gov/bicy, headquarters 8:30 A.M.–4:30 P.M. Mon.–Fri., preserve 24 hours daily, free), two of which are seasonal and four of which are open all year. While most of these are primitive campgrounds with no available drinking water, the year-round **Midway Campground** features a dump station, restrooms, drinking water, a day-use area, 10 tent sites ($16 daily), and 26 RV sites ($19 daily) with electric hookups. All campgrounds are available on a first-come, first-served basis. For more information about campground availability and potential closures, contact the **Oasis Visitor Center** (239/695-1201, 9 A.M.–4:30 P.M. daily).

Farther west, alongside the Barron River,

you'll find relative luxury at **Everglades Isle** (803 Collier Ave., Everglades City, 239/695-2600, www.evergladesisle.com, $125–150 daily), an exclusive motorhome retreat offering 61 landscaped and paved sites. Each site includes a social membership in the Lighthouse Club and the option of having your own wet slip at the on-site marina. Other amenities include a pool and hot tub, a movie theater, a fitness center, a restaurant and lounge, a boat launch, spa treatment salons, golf cart rentals, satellite television, and wireless Internet access.

Along U.S. 41 is **Collier-Seminole State Park** (20200 E. Tamiami Trail, Naples, 239/394-3397, www.floridastateparks.org/collierseminole, 8 A.M.–sunset daily, $5 vehicles w/2–8 passengers, $4 motorcycles and single-occupant vehicles, $2 pedestrians, bikers, and extra passengers), which offers a 120-site, pet-friendly campground ($22 daily) and primitive camping for hikers and canoeists. Nestled amid gumbo limbo trees and royal palms, the official campground can accommodate tents as well as motorhomes. Every site offers water and electric service, and other amenities include an activity building as well as restrooms with showers. For reservations, contact **ReserveAmerica** (800/326-3521, www.reserveamerica.com).

Naturally, **Everglades National Park** (40001 S.R. 9336, Homestead, 305/242-7700, www.nps.gov/ever, visitor center 9 A.M.–5 P.M. daily, park 24 hours daily, $10 vehicles, $5 motorcycles, pedestrians, and bikers) offers several camping options as well, including two front-country campgrounds ($16 daily): the **Long Pine Key Campground** (305/242-7873), which provides 108 tent and RV sites on a first-come, first-served basis, plus restrooms, a dump station, a picnic area, and a fishing pond, and the **Flamingo Campground,** where reservations are strongly recommended for the 274 available tent and RV sites. At the Flamingo Campground, which is situated alongside Florida Bay, campers can utilize cold showers, two dump stations, picnic tables, an amphitheater, and several nearby hiking and canoe trails. Everglades National Park also allows backcountry camping ($10 per permit, plus $2 pp daily), though a permit must be secured at least 24 hours in advance.

If you'd prefer to stay closer to I-75, you can always opt for the year-round **▐ Big Cypress RV Resort** (34950 Hall's Rd., Clewiston, 800/437-4102, www.bigcypressrvresort.com), which lies 19 miles north of the interstate on S.R. 833. Situated on the Big Cypress Seminole Indian Reservation, this campground offers easy access to Billie Swamp Safari and the Ah-Tah-Thi-Ki Museum. Facilities here include tent sites ($26 daily, $150 weekly), RV sites ($30 daily, $200 weekly, $545 monthly), and air-conditioned cabins ($65–75 daily)—all of which typically require reservations. All tent sites include water and electric service, while RV sites feature water and electric service, plus sewer access. Other amenities include a heated pool and hot tub, a general store, a clubhouse, an exercise room, a playground, a miniature golf course, basketball courts, a propane/dump station, and laundry facilities.

FOOD

Although you'll find a greater variety of restaurants in Miami and the Florida Keys, the Everglades do indeed offer their share of dining options, including the **Mutineer Restaurant** (1 SE 1st Ave., Florida City, 305/245-3377, www.mutineer.biz, 11 A.M.–9:30 P.M. daily, $14–28), a nautically themed eatery offering an assortment of dishes and treats, including hickory-smoked baby back ribs, lobster and shrimp pasta, well-prepared steaks, and key lime pie.

The popular chain restaurant **Sonny's Real Pit Bar-B-Q** (33505 S. Dixie Hwy., Florida City, 305/245-8585, www.sonnysbbq.com, 11 A.M.–10 P.M. daily, $12–22) will satisfy your craving for barbecue beef, pork, and chicken, not to mention Southern-style sweet tea. On the adjacent street, the family-owned **Capri Restaurant** (935 N. Krome Ave., Florida City, 305/247-1542, www.dinecapri.com, 11 A.M.–9:30 P.M. Mon.–Thurs., 11 A.M.–10:30 P.M. Fri.–Sat., 4–9 P.M. Sun., $9–27) serves fine Italian cuisine, from traditional dishes like

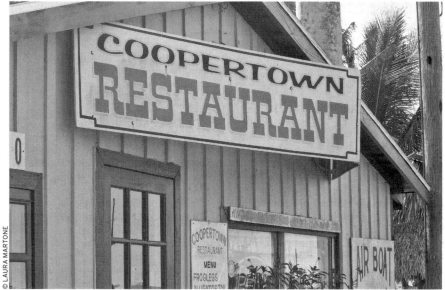

Visitors often stop at the Coopertown Restaurant before joining an airboat tour.

chicken marsala to unique concoctions such as Shrimp Casino, which features sautéed shrimp, onions, peppers, bacon, and garlic butter, served over angel hair pasta.

From Florida City, head north to the Tamiami Trail and drive west into the Everglades, where you'll find the **Coopertown Restaurant** (22700 SW 8th St., Miami, 305/226-6048, www.coopertownairboats.com, 8 A.M.–6 P.M. daily, $8–14), a convenient stop before taking a Coopertown airboat ride. Offering an authentic taste of the Everglades, this no-frills eatery serves standard fare as well as frog legs and alligator tail.

Everglades City features several options, including the **Island Cafe** (305 Collier Ave., Everglades City, 239/695-0003, 6 A.M.–3 P.M. daily, $5–14), which prepares decent breakfast dishes, plus inexpensive sandwiches, burgers, and seafood. Just down the street, the Spanish-style **Everglades Seafood Depot Restaurant** (102 Collier Ave., Everglades City, 239/695-0075, www.evergladesseafooddepot.com, 10:30 A.M.–9 P.M. daily, $5–20) offers similar cuisine in a waterfront setting beside Lake Placid.

INFORMATION AND SERVICES

Even in the vast, largely undeveloped Florida Everglades, you'll find useful services, from welcome centers to gas stations.

Tourism and Government Offices

For maps, brochures, and information about the Everglades, consult the **Naples, Marco Island, Everglades Convention & Visitors Bureau** (2800 Horseshoe Dr., Naples, 239/225-1013 or 800/688-3600, www.paradisecoast.com, 9 A.M.–5 P.M. Mon.–Fri.), the **Everglades Area Chamber of Commerce Welcome Center** (S.R. 29 and U.S. 41, Everglades City, 239/695-3941, www.evergladeschamber.net, 9 A.M.–4 P.M. daily), **Everglades National Park** (40001 S.R. 9336, Homestead, 305/242-7700, www.nps.gov/ever, 9 A.M.–5 P.M. daily), and the **Greater Homestead/Florida City Chamber of Commerce** (212 NW 1st Ave.,

Homestead, 305/247-2332, www.chamberinaction.com, 9 A.M.–5 P.M. Mon.–Fri.).

The nonprofit **Tropical Everglades Visitor Association (TEVA)** (160 U.S. 1, Florida City, 305/245-9180 or 800/388-9669, www.tropicaleverglades.com, 8 A.M.–5 P.M. Mon.–Sat., 10 A.M.–2 P.M. Sun.), which is part of the Historic Redland Tropical Trail (www.redlandtrail.com), is a helpful resource, too. In addition, *The Mullet Rapper* (www.evergladesmulletrapper.com), a local newspaper available at establishments throughout Everglades City and Chokoloskee, as well as websites like www.florida-everglades.com, may prove useful.

For government-related issues, you'll have to first figure out which county you need to contact. The Everglades, after all, constitute a large area—so large in fact that it extends across three different counties: **Miami-Dade County** (www.miamidade.gov), **Monroe County** (www.monroecounty.gov), and **Collier County** (www.colliergov.net). You can also call the local governments directly, such as the **City of Homestead** (www.cityofhomestead.com).

Mail

If you need to purchase stamps or send packages while you're in the Everglades, you'll find a handful of **post offices** (800/275-8777, www.usps.com) in the area, including one in Everglades City (601 Collier Ave., 239/695-2174, 10 A.M.–noon and 1–3 P.M. Mon.–Fri.).

Groceries and Supplies

Though the Everglades may seem to be filled with flyspeck towns and undeveloped hinterlands, there are several groceries and other helpful stores here. **Publix** (www.publix.com), for instance, offers several branches in Homestead, including one within the **Homestead Towne Square** (891 N. Homestead Blvd., 305/242-1500, 7 A.M.–11 P.M. Mon.–Sat., 7 A.M.–10 P.M. Sun.). Even isolated Marco Island has a **Winn-Dixie** (625 N. Collier Blvd., 239/642-9126, www.winndixie.com, 7 A.M.–11 P.M. daily), which features a deli, a bakery, fresh seafood, ATMs, and an on-site pharmacy (239/393-

0843, 8 A.M.–8 P.M. Mon.–Fri., 8 A.M.–6 P.M. Sat., 9 A.M.–2 P.M. Sun.).

Emergency Services

In case of an emergency that requires police, fire, or ambulance services, dial **911** from any cell or public phone. For nonemergency assistance, contact the **Miami-Dade Police Department** (9105 NW 25th St., Doral, 305/476-5423 or 305/471-1780, www.miami-dade.gov/mdpd, 8 A.M.–5 P.M. Mon.–Fri.) or the **Collier County Sheriff's Office** (3301 E. Tamiami Trail, Bldg. J, Naples, 239/774-4434, www.colliersheriff.org, 8 A.M.–5 P.M. Mon.–Fri.). If you're seeking medical assistance, simply consult one of several hospitals in southern Florida, including **Mercy Hospital** (3663 S. Miami Ave., Miami, 305/854-4400, www.mercymiami.org) or the **NCH Downtown Naples Hospital** (350 N. 7th St., Naples, 239/436-5000, www.nchmd.org).

GETTING THERE
By Air

To reach the Everglades by plane, you can either fly major carriers into the **Miami International Airport (MIA)** (4200 NW 21st St., Miami, 305/876-7000 or 800/825-5642, www.miami-airport.com) or commuter flights into the **Naples Municipal Airport (APF)** (160 N. Aviation Dr., Naples, 239/643-0733, www.flynaples.com). From either one, you can rent a vehicle through such agencies as **Avis** (800/331-1212, www.avis.com), **Enterprise** (800/325-8007, www.enterprise.com), **Hertz** (800/654-3131, www.hertz.com), or **Thrifty** (800/367-2277, www.thrifty.com).

By Bus or Train

If you don't have a vehicle of your own and would prefer not to fly, you can take a bus or train into the area and then rent a vehicle to reach the Everglades. **Greyhound** (800/231-2222, www.greyhound.com) offers service to several different stations, including the **Miami Greyhound Station** (4111 NW 27th St., Miami, 305/871-1810, 24 hours daily) and the **Central Park Bus Terminal** (2669 Davis

Blvd., Ste. 1, Naples, 239/774-5660, 7:30–10:30 A.M. and 1:30–5 P.M. Mon.–Sat.).

Amtrak (800/872-7245, www.amtrak.com) offers service via its Silver Service/Palmetto route. The three southernmost stations include **Fort Lauderdale (FTL)** (200 SW 21 Terrace, Fort Lauderdale, 8:30 A.M.–6:15 P.M. daily), **Hollywood (HOL)** (3001 Hollywood Blvd., Hollywood, 8:30 A.M.–6:20 P.M. daily), and **Miami (MIA)** (8303 NW 37th Ave., Miami, 7 A.M.–9 P.M. daily).

By Car

The Everglades region is accessible via several major roads, including I-75 from Tampa, U.S. 41 from Miami, and U.S. 1 from the Florida Keys. No matter how you get here, though, be sure to call **511** for an up-to-the-minute traffic report.

GETTING AROUND
By Car

In lieu of a kayak or airboat, the most efficient way to travel through the Florida Everglades is via car, truck, RV, or motorcycle—all of which offer easy access to major highways as well as detours to places like Marco Island. Essentially, you can traverse the Everglades via two main routes, both of which offer access to the Big Cypress National Preserve. Interstate 75 (I-75), also known as Alligator Alley or the Everglades Parkway, runs from Naples to Fort Lauderdale, while U.S. 41, more commonly called the Tamiami Trail, connects Tampa to Miami.

By Boat

Of course, you can also experience the Everglades via canoe, kayak, or airboat. Although having your own vessel makes navigating these waters even easier, you can easily rent one from several different outfitters, including **North American Canoe Tours** (107 Camellia St., Everglades City, 239/695-3299, www.evergladesadventures.com), which provides canoe ($20–25 per half day, $28–35 daily) and kayak rentals ($28–45 per half day, $36–65 daily) from November to mid-April.

KEY LARGO

Nestled between the Everglades and the continental United States' only living coral reef, Key Largo is the northernmost community in the Florida Keys. It's also the largest island in this one-of-a-kind archipelago. Although Key Largo, which also includes part of the community of Tavernier (the rest of which lies on Plantation Key), has gradually become a getaway town for southern Floridians and northern snowbirds alike—and, as a result, has suffered a bit from overcrowding and overdevelopment—it's still a quieter, more laid-back destination than Miami or even Key West, that infamously eccentric city at the southern end of the Overseas Highway.

Here, locals can dock their boats just steps from their favorite waterfront eateries or tiki bars, and visitors can stay at any number of intimate inns and posh resorts, some of which are linked to well-equipped marinas. But, of course, the area's biggest claim to fame is its wealth of outdoor diversions, including sportfishing, snorkeling, and scuba diving. In fact, thanks to the fascinating underwater coral reefs, shipwrecks, and landmarks, such as the *Christ of the Abyss* statue, that extend along the Atlantic shoreline—part of the Key Largo National Marine Sanctuary, established in 1975—Key Largo is also the self-proclaimed "diving capital of the world."

No first-time visitor should skip the John Pennekamp Coral Reef State Park, America's first undersea park and one of the jewels of Florida's state park system. Beyond informative marine exhibits in the visitor center, the park offers daily glass-bottom boat tours, snorkeling

© DANIEL MARTONE

HIGHLIGHTS

◖ Dagny Johnson Key Largo Hammock Botanical State Park: Given its location in the northern part of Key Largo, this 2,421-acre preserve receives fewer visitors than other state parks in the Florida Keys, but those who appreciate solitude and serenity will relish wandering these backcountry trails, which offer a chance to spy endangered species like the Key Largo woodrat and the American crocodile (page 86).

◖ John Pennekamp Coral Reef State Park: Perhaps the most popular state park in the Florida Keys, this lively place lures a wide array of outdoor enthusiasts with its pleasant beaches, reasonable canoe and kayak rentals, snorkeling and diving excursions, and glass-bottom boat tours atop the fascinating offshore coral reefs (page 87).

◖ Dolphin Attractions: Animal lovers will find two incredible dolphin facilities in Key Largo, Dolphin Cove and Dolphins Plus, both of which feature a variety of interactive programs, including structured swims with the resident dolphins as well as full-day, behind-the-scenes activities (page 88).

◖ Key Largo Pirates Fest: While Fantasy Fest is happening down in Key West, revelers in Key Largo celebrate the region's curious past with this four-day event, featuring zany activities like pirate costume contests, a pirate bazaar and thieves market, and an underwater treasure hunt (page 93).

◖ Canoeing and Kayaking Around Key Largo: The islands, patch reefs, tidal flats, and mangrove creeks of the Upper Keys are ideal places to explore by canoe or kayak, which allows nature lovers a leisurely, up-close way to observe wild dolphins, various birds, and, for the lucky ones, a gentle manatee or two (page 98).

◖ Diving and Snorkeling amid Wrecks and Reefs: Key Largo, the self-proclaimed "diving capital of the world," offers a variety of snorkeling and scuba-diving operators, all of which can assist visitors in exploring the underwater coral reefs east of town, part of the 220-mile-long Florida Keys National Marine Sanctuary (page 99).

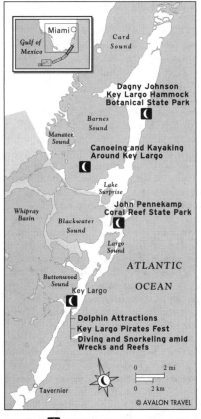

LOOK FOR ◖ TO FIND RECOMMENDED SIGHTS, ACTIVITIES, DINING, AND LODGING.

trips, and scuba-diving excursions. In addition, visitors can opt to rent a canoe, kayak, or paddle boat for a bird-watching adventure in the park's winding mangrove creeks.

Other enticing attractions in Key Largo include interactive dolphin programs, a wild bird center, a wooded state park at the northern end of the island, not to mention the weathered old boat used famously in the Bogart-Hepburn film *The African Queen*. Of course, if you desire a taste of the zaniness you'll encounter farther south, you might want to plan your vacation around the annual Key Largo Pirates Fest, a lively October event that presents pirate costume contests, a "thieves market," and an underwater treasure hunt.

HISTORY

As with the rest of the Florida Keys, local historians believe that the earliest residents of Key Largo were the Calusa Indians and other Native American tribes common to southern Florida. Most of these native inhabitants eventually moved or died out by the 1820s—about the time the U.S. Navy managed to scare away most of the marauding pirates that once roamed these waters. Permanent settlers soon followed, many of whom farmed the land, producing key lime groves, tamarind groves, and pineapple fields, among other produce. It was 16th-century Spanish explorers, however, who gave this lengthy island its name—Cayo Largo, which essentially means "long islet" in Spanish—even though there's no real evidence that they ever came ashore.

With little record of its early years, however, it's difficult to pinpoint the exact history of Key Largo prior to the mid-19th century, when various passengers aboard passing ships noted the presence of a small community on the island. But it seems that the prevalence of mosquitoes and the reality of hurricanes slowed the expansion of tiny settlements like Planter, Rock Harbor, Basin Hills, and High Mangroves. The 1870 census, for instance, revealed a population of merely 60 individuals, which only rose to 230 by 1885. During this time, there was no centralized community, as evidenced by

the repeated relocation of a communal post office, from Rock Harbor to Planter—the southern part of Key Largo, which is today known as Tavernier.

In 1908, scheduled daily train service via the Florida East Coast Railway helped to bring a few more settlers to the area—though, ultimately, the presence of the railroad merely shifted the primary mode of distribution and transportation from ships to trains. At that time, there were four stations: Jewfish Creek, Key Largo, Rock Harbor, and Tavernier. By the 1920s, the community of Key Largo was well established, and the population continued to grow, even after the destruction of the Overseas Railroad in the Labor Day hurricane of 1935.

Over the next few decades, tourism became an increasingly important factor in the growth of Key Largo, and even Hollywood took notice, highlighting this unique locale in the Bogart-Bacall film *Key Largo* (1948). Of course, it was the offshore coral reef that really set Key Largo apart from other vacation destinations in America. With the establishment of John Pennekamp Coral Reef State Park, America's first undersea park, in 1963 and the Key Largo National Marine Sanctuary in 1975, the island found its niche as a world-class underwater diving destination—a designation that has endured into the 21st century.

Today, Key Largo, a self-reliant community filled with as many family-owned businesses as corporate chains, has an estimated population of 18,530—due, in large part, to the town's status as a bedroom community for those escaping Miami's urban sprawl. Of course, the thriving tourism industry has certainly helped, too. For more information about Key Largo's past, consult the **Historical Preservation Society of the Upper Keys** (www.keyshistory.org).

PLANNING YOUR TIME

Despite being the largest island in the Florida Keys, Key Largo has fewer overall diversions than, for instance, Key West—and not much in the way of museums, historical districts, or

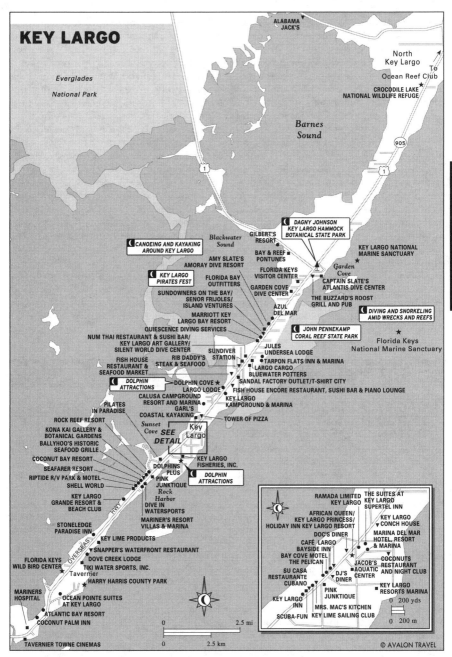

KEY LARGO

Everglades
National Park

North
Key Largo
To
Ocean Reef Club

ALABAMA
JACK'S

CROCODILE LAKE
NATIONAL WILDLIFE REFUGE

Barnes
Sound

905

1

1

DAGNY JOHNSON
KEY LARGO HAMMOCK
BOTANICAL STATE PARK

GILBERT'S
RESORT

Blackwater
Sound

CANOEING AND KAYAKING
AROUND KEY LARGO

KEY LARGO NATIONAL
MARINE SANCTUARY

BAY & REEF
PONTUNES

AMY SLATE'S
AMORAY DIVE RESORT

Garden
Cove

KEY LARGO
PIRATES FEST

FLORIDA BAY
OUTFITTERS

FLORIDA KEYS
VISITOR CENTER

CAPTAIN SLATE'S
ATLANTIS DIVE CENTER

SUNDOWNERS ON THE BAY/
SENOR FRIJOLES/
ISLAND VENTURES

GARDEN COVE
DIVE CENTER

THE BUZZARD'S ROOST
GRILL AND PUB

AZUL
DEL MAR

MARRIOTT KEY
LARGO BAY RESORT

DIVING AND SNORKELING
AMID WRECKS AND REEFS

QUIESCENCE DIVING SERVICES

JOHN PENNEKAMP
CORAL REEF STATE PARK

NUM THAI RESTAURANT & SUSHI BAR/
KEY LARGO ART GALLERY/
SILENT WORLD DIVE CENTER

Florida Keys
National Marine Sanctuary

SUNDIVER
STATION

JULES
UNDERSEA LODGE

FISH HOUSE
RESTAURANT &
SEAFOOD MARKET

RIB DADDY'S
STEAK & SEAFOOD

TARPON FLATS INN & MARINA

LARGO CARGO

DOLPHIN
ATTRACTIONS

DOLPHIN COVE

BLUEWATER POTTERS

SANDAL FACTORY OUTLET/T-SHIRT CITY

LARGO LODGE

FISH HOUSE ENCORE RESTAURANT, SUSHI BAR & PIANO LOUNGE

CALUSA CAMPGROUND
RESORT AND MARINA

KEY LARGO
KAMPGROUND & MARINA

PILATES
IN PARADISE

GARL'S
COASTAL KAYAKING

Sunset
Cove

TOWER OF PIZZA

ROCK REEF RESORT

Key
Largo

KONA KAI GALLERY &
BOTANICAL GARDENS

SEE
DETAIL

BALLYHOO'S HISTORIC
SEAFOOD GRILLE

KEY LARGO
FISHERIES, INC.

COCONUT BAY RESORT

DOLPHINS
PLUS

DOLPHIN
ATTRACTIONS

SEAFARER RESORT

PINK
JUNKTIQUE

RIPTIDE R/V PARK & MOTEL

SHELL WORLD

Rock
Harbor

KEY LARGO
GRANDE RESORT &
BEACH CLUB

DIVE IN
WATERSPORTS

STONELEDGE
PARADISE INN

MARINER'S RESORT
VILLAS & MARINA

KEY LIME PRODUCTS

SNAPPER'S WATERFRONT RESTAURANT

FLORIDA KEYS
WILD BIRD CENTER

DOVE CREEK LODGE

TIKI WATER SPORTS, INC.

Tavernier

HARRY HARRIS COUNTY PARK

MARINERS
HOSPITAL

OCEAN POINTE SUITES
AT KEY LARGO

ATLANTIC BAY RESORT

COCONUT PALM INN

TAVERNIER TOWNE CINEMAS

0   2.5 mi

0   2.5 km

[Detail inset]

RAMADA LIMITED
KEY LARGO

THE SUITES AT
KEY LARGO
SUPERTEL INN

AFRICAN QUEEN/
KEY LARGO PRINCESS/
HOLIDAY INN KEY LARGO RESORT

KEY LARGO
CONCH HOUSE

MARINA DEL MAR
HOTEL, RESORT
& MARINA

DOC'S DINER

CAFÉ LARGO

BAYSIDE INN

BAY COVE MOTEL

THE PELICAN

JACOB'S
AQUATIC
CENTER

COCONUTS
RESTAURANT
AND NIGHT CLUB

SU CASA
RESTAURANTE
CUBANO

DJ'S
DINER

KEY LARGO
RESORTS MARINA

PINK
JUNKTIQUE

KEY LARGO

MRS. MAC'S KITCHEN

0   200 yds

SCUBA-FUN

KEY LIME SAILING CLUB

0   200 m

© AVALON TRAVEL

KEY LARGO

cultural attractions. Still, the interactive dolphin programs, diverse state parks, and underwater coral reefs can keep you busy for at least a few days. If you choose to pursue outdoor activities like full-day fishing charters, kayaking excursions, and scuba-diving trips, you'll need to stay a few days more.

With access to a vehicle, this is an easy island to navigate—in spite of its large size and the spread-out nature of its attractions and lodgings. Stretching from mile markers 110 to 91, Key Largo is easily traversed via the Overseas Highway. Just be aware that much of the thoroughfare is divided by a wide median here, often making it necessary to use the center access roads to reach destinations on the opposite side of U.S. 1.

Given how popular Key Largo can be in the winter months, traffic congestion is often an issue from December to April, so be sure to give yourself plenty of time to get around, especially if you have tour reservations. During the winter, you're also sure to encounter higher lodging rates and more crowded attractions.

When planning a trip to Key Largo, you might also want to consider factors like annual events and fishing seasons. The weather is an equally important consideration. While usually comfortable, the climate can be a little too chilly for sunbathing in January and rather hot and humid from June to September—an ideal time for water-related activities like snorkeling.

As for safety, while Key Largo is relatively crime-free, certain outdoor activities—such as kayaking or scuba-diving—can be dangerous without proper instruction. It helps, too, to have a full understanding of any necessary guidelines or regulations before venturing out, especially if you're a first-timer.

For more information about Key Largo, consult the **Monroe County Tourist Development Council** (1201 White St., Ste. 102, Key West, FL 33040, 305/296-1552 or 800/352-5397, www.fla-keys.com) and the **Key Largo Chamber of Commerce** (106000 Overseas Hwy., Key Largo, FL 33037, 305/451-4747 or 800/822-1088, www.keylargo.org or www.key-largochamber.org).

Sights

◖ DAGNY JOHNSON KEY LARGO HAMMOCK BOTANICAL STATE PARK

If you're driving to Key Largo, as most people do, your first stop should be in the northern part of the island, north of the U.S. 1 turnoff and not far from the Crocodile Lake National Wildlife Refuge, which is closed to the public. Here, on the ocean side of the county road, lies the tranquil Dagny Johnson Key Largo Hammock Botanical State Park (C.R. 905, www.floridastateparks.org/keylargohammock, 8 A.M.–sunset daily, $2.50 pp). Spared from becoming a condominium development in the early 1980s and named after a local environmental activist, this 2,421-acre preserve now protects 84 plant and animal species, plus one of the country's largest tracts of West Indian tropical hardwood hammock.

Hikers, bikers, bird-watchers, photographers, and other wildlife lovers can, with a backcountry permit, explore the park's more than six miles of backcountry trails, where you might spot mahogany mistletoe, semaphore cactus, Key Largo woodrats, varied butterflies, migratory birds, or an American crocodile. If you have the time, consider bringing a picnic lunch and relaxing at one of the designated tables near the butterfly garden—and of course, don't forget to pack out any and all trash.

Unlike at other state parks in the Florida Keys, you'll find no on-duty park ranger near the front gate, so you're expected to use the honor box to pay the requisite park fee. Remember, too, that motorized vehicles are prohibited in the park, as is the collection of any plants or animals. Moreover, you should keep to the paved roadways and designated trail unless you have a backcountry permit, which is available through the John Pennekamp Coral Reef State Park office (305/451-1202). Leashed, well-behaved pets are welcome in the picnic areas and on the roadways and nature trail; service animals are, of course, welcome throughout the park.

◖ JOHN PENNEKAMP CORAL REEF STATE PARK

For nature lovers, one of the primary stops in Key Largo should be the incredible John Pennekamp Coral Reef State Park (102601 Overseas Hwy., 305/451-1202 or 305/451-6300, www.floridastateparks.org/pennekamp or www.pennekamppark.com, 8 A.M.–sunset daily, $8 vehicles w/2–8 passengers plus $0.50 pp, $4.50 motorcycles and single-occupant vehicles, $2.50 pedestrians, bikers, and extra passengers), America's first underwater park—and the perfect spot for a wide range of outdoor activities, from sunbathing to bird-watching to sportfishing. Established in 1963 and situated

© LAURA MARTONE

the rocky shoreline of John Pennekamp Coral Reef State Park

on the ocean side of U.S. 1, this well-favored park offers several picnic areas, pavilion rentals ($32–54 daily), a small campground (with modern restrooms), a souvenir and gift shop, a boat ramp ($10 per vessel), and convenient access to two sandy beaches, including Cannon Beach, which features the remnants of an old Spanish shipwreck.

Visitors enjoy swimming in the relatively warm waters here, plus paddling through the mangrove swamps. Luckily, you can even rent canoes, kayaks, and paddle boats on-site (8 A.M.–3:45 P.M. daily, $12–17 hourly). Also available are diving tours ($60 pp), glass-bottom boat tours ($24 adults, $17 children under 12) on the flagship *Spirit of Pennekamp*, and 2.5-hour snorkeling tours ($30 adults, $25 children under 18) amid the vibrant, shallow-water coral reefs of the Key Largo National Marine Sanctuary—part of the only living coral reef in the continental United States and a real treat for underwater explorers. Here, you'll likely spot parrotfish, yellow cherubfish, brain and staghorn coral, spotted spiny lobster, sea hermit crabs, and other amazing sealife, all of which are even more vibrant on a sunny, cloudless day.

While first-time snorkelers are common here, scuba divers must be certified to participate in the park's reef adventures. Fortunately, though, the park offers scuba instruction (305/451-6322 or 877/727-5348). Be advised, too, that all anglers must have a saltwater fishing license. Although this is definitely the spot for active visitors, disabled individuals are welcome aboard (free of charge) the glass-bottom boat tours and snorkeling trips, provided that they are able to get in and out of the water on their own—or with the assistance of accompanying helpers. For those who prefer a less up-close-and-personal underwater encounter, the park's visitor center (8 A.M.–5 P.M. daily) features several natural history exhibits as well as a 30,000-gallon saltwater aquarium, housing many of the tropical fish, sea creatures, and other organisms you might see in the ocean. Do yourself a favor, though: Don't leave this park without venturing into the sometimes

KEY LARGO

WHO IS JOHN PENNEKAMP?

Established in 1963, **John Pennekamp Coral Reef State Park** (102601 Overseas Hwy., 305/451-1202 or 305/451-6300, www.floridastateparks.org/pennekamp or www.pennekamppark.com, 8 A.M.-sunset daily, fees apply) lures a plethora of visitors every year. If you're one of them, you've probably come to snorkel amid the vibrant offshore coral reefs, peer at them from a glass-bottom boat, or kayak through seagrass beds and mangrove swamps. While doing so, you might, if ever so briefly, wonder about the name of the park.

Ultimately, this one-of-a-kind locale serves as a tribute to the late John D. Pennekamp, a longtime journalist, *Miami Herald* editor, and regional environmentalist who was instrumental in preserving the land that would eventually become Everglades National Park. Born in 1897, Pennekamp worked for 14 years at the *Cincinnati Post* before heading to southern Florida, where he joined the *Miami Herald* staff in 1925. First serving as a city editor and later

as the associate editor, Pennekamp stayed with the *Herald* until his retirement in 1976.

Beyond his editorial duties, however, Pennekamp had a passion for the environment – and a desire to help preserve it for future generations. So, following his efforts to establish Everglades National Park, he became a member of the Everglades National Park Commission from 1945 to 1947. In addition, he served as chairman of the Florida Board of Parks and Historic Memorials, the precursor to the Division of Recreation and Parks, from 1953 to 1976. During the 1960s, Governor LeRoy Collins honored the journalist's unwavering dedication to conservation by naming America's first undersea park after him. When Pennekamp died in 1978 at the age of 81, only two years after retiring from the *Herald*, he left behind a legacy of appreciation for the natural world, a legacy that endures today through the more than one million visitors who venture inside the park annually.

---

choppy waters of the Key Largo National Marine Sanctuary. The sight of all those kaleidoscopic fish—and perhaps a sand shark or two—is an experience you'll never forget.

◖ DOLPHIN ATTRACTIONS

Together, the sister facilities **Dolphin Cove** (MM 101.9 BS U.S. 1, 305/451-4060 or 877/365-2683, www.dolphinscove.com, 8 A.M.–5 P.M. daily, nonparticipating admission $10 adults, $5 children 6–12, children under 6 free) and **Dolphins Plus** (31 Corrine Pl., 305/451-1993 or 866/860-7946, www.dolphinsplus.com, 8 A.M.–5 P.M. daily, nonparticipating admission $10 adults, $5 children 7–17, children under 7 free) pursue marine mammal research, promote environmental awareness, and present year-round educational opportunities to the visiting public. At Dolphin Cove, visitors can touch bottlenose dolphins through shallow-water encounters (1 P.M. and 3:30 P.M. daily, $125 pp), experience dorsal tows and foot pushes in structured swims (9 A.M., 1 P.M., and

3:30 P.M. daily, $185 pp), or snorkel alongside dolphins in natural swims (9:45 A.M. daily, $135 pp).

Other activities include painting with dolphins (9 A.M., 1 P.M., and 3:30 P.M. daily, $175 pp), Captain Sterling's personalized Everglades and Florida Bay ecology tours, and the trainer-for-a-day program (8 A.M.–4 P.M. daily, $630 pp), which offers a behind-the-scenes look at this fascinating marine mammal facility, including the basics of animal training, dolphin behaviors, and food preparation, plus participation in various dolphin swims. Combo packages are also available, though be advised that, depending on the program, age, height, and physical restrictions may apply. Reservations are highly recommended.

A little farther south, Dolphins Plus is accessible via Ocean Bay Drive on the ocean side of U.S. 1, just south of mile marker 100. Here, visitors can also participate in structured (8:30 A.M., 12:45 P.M., and 3 P.M. daily, $185 pp) and natural swims (9:30 A.M. and 1:30 P.M.

© DANIEL MARTONE

experiencing a dorsal tow at Dolphins Plus

daily, $135 per half hour, $220 hourly) with bottlenose dolphins, plus an engrossing trainer-for-a-day program (8 A.M.–4 P.M. daily, $630 pp). In addition, animal lovers can opt for dolphin body language workshops (8 A.M.–noon daily, $395 pp), a combination structured and natural swim ($260 pp), or an educational, one-on-one swim (11 A.M. and 3 P.M. daily, $120 pp) with a frisky California sea lion named Wono—preceded by a 30-minute briefing about sea lion habitats, feeding habits, reproductive biology, and conservation, among other topics.

Truly passionate souls can also sign up for the full-day marine biologist program (8 A.M.–5 P.M. daily, $600 pp), during which they will learn about dolphin behavior and sampling techniques, participate in a study about mother-calf interactions, help to prepare fish and vitamin regimens for the on-site marine mammals, and engage in a private natural swim. Participants in this program must be at least 14 years of age, and anyone under the age of 18 must have a signed release form from a parent or legal guardian. Age and height restrictions may also apply with other activities,

and reservations are highly recommended, especially for the full-day programs.

FLORIDA KEYS WILD BIRD CENTER

While Key Largo is mainly known for its wide assortment of water-related activities, you should also consider taking a walk through the nonprofit Florida Keys Wild Bird Center (93600 Overseas Hwy., Tavernier, 305/852-4486, www.fkwbc.org, sunrise–sunset daily, $5 pp donation requested), which was founded in 1984 when veterinarian Bob Foley asked retired teacher Laura Quinn to assist with the rehabilitation of several wild birds that he had treated. Operated by volunteers and comprising natural habitats as well as open-air enclosures, the 5.5-acre center allows visitors to stroll along a narrow, shaded boardwalk, where you can observe a variety of caged species, from cormorants to laughing gulls to great horned owls—most of whom have been injured by manmade causes, such as mercury poisoning and fishing tackle entanglements, and are currently undergoing rehabilitation.

© DANIEL MARTONE

Birds literally flock to the open habitats of the Florida Keys Wild Bird Center.

In the adjacent black and red mangrove wetlands and along the Florida Bay shoreline, you'll spot a slew of native birds, including pelicans, common egrets, and great white herons, most of whom are usually waiting for the afternoon feeding. Almost more curious, though, is the innumerable mass of makeshift, wooden sponsor plaques affixed to the cages and boardwalk railing—a testament to all of the individuals and organizations who have helped to support the center—and the separate hospital space (93997 Overseas Hwy.)—over the years.

After visiting the bird center, consider heading south to mile marker 92.5, where you can cross the highway via Burton Drive. From here, continue on Burton to 1st Street, and take Beach Road to **Harry Harris County Park** (sunrise–sunset daily, $5 non–county residents 16 or older Sat.–Sun. and holidays, children under 16 and Monroe County residents free), a popular place on the weekends and the perfect spot to watch one of the Keys' notoriously sensational sunsets. Other amenities here include a sandy beach, a swimming area, a boat ramp, playground equipment, picnic tables, barbecue grills, and public restrooms.

Unfortunately, pets aren't allowed in the park or along the beach.

BOAT TOURS

Every day, the **Coral Reef Park Company** (305/451-6300) operates three separate 2.5-hour glass-bottom boat tours ($24 adults, $17 children under 12) out of **John Pennekamp Coral Reef State Park** (102601 Overseas Hwy., 305/451-1202, www.floridastateparks. org/pennekamp or www.pennekamppark. com, 8 A.M.–sunset daily, $8 vehicles w/2–8 passengers plus $0.50 pp, $4.50 motorcycles and single-occupant vehicles, $2.50 pedestrians, bikers, and extra passengers). Such excursions are offered via the flagship *Spirit of Pennekamp,* a 65-foot, high-speed catamaran that's capable of whisking up to 130 passengers toward the coral formations and vibrant sealife of the Florida Keys National Marine Sanctuary in the ocean waters east of Key Largo. All tours require a minimum number of passengers to leave the marina, and limited wheelchair accessibility is available on board.

Farther south, you'll find other glass-bottom boat tours, such as the *Key Largo*

© DANIEL MARTONE

The glass-bottom boat *Spirit of Pennekamp* returns from offshore coral reefs.

Princess (305/451-4655 or 877/648-8129, www.keylargoprincess.com, $30 adults, $17 children), a luxurious 70-foot, 125-passenger yacht that operates three daily two-hour excursions (10 A.M., 1 P.M., and 4 P.M.). Docked at the Holiday Inn Key Largo Resort & Marina (99701 Overseas Hwy., 305/451-2121, www.holidayinnkeylargo.com), the *Key Largo Princess* also offers sunset and cocktail cruises (complete with underwater lights). If you choose one of the daytime excursions, try to get a seat on the sun deck, which affords you a panoramic offshore view of the Florida Keys and the multicolored ocean waters around you. Once you reach the living coral reef, you'll be able to observe varied coral specimens and kaleidoscopic fish through a 280-square-foot viewing window below your feet.

Before heading out on the *Princess,* take note of the small, weathered boat docked beside her. Built in 1912 for service in Africa, the **African Queen** was used, until 1968, by the British East Africa Railway to ferry cargo passengers across Lake Albert. During that time, the *Queen* was featured in the eponymous 1951 John Huston film that also starred Humphrey Bogart and Katharine Hepburn. Feel free to take photographs of this famous vessel or step into Bogie's shoes and reserve an unforgettable ride (305/451-4655) aboard the *Queen* herself.

A little farther south, **Caribbean Watersports** (Key Largo Grande Resort & Beach Club, 97000 Overseas Hwy., 305/852-4707 or 800/223-6728, www.caribbeanwatersports.com, 9 A.M.–5 P.M. daily), which offers two-hour champagne sunset cruises ($60 pp) and two-hour private charters ($350 per group), also features **Enviro-Tours** (www.enviro-tours.com, $60 adults, $45 children under 17) across Florida Bay and into the Everglades. These personalized two-hour excursions, which can accommodate 2–6 passengers at a time, provide an intimate glimpse at the diverse ecosystems of southern Florida, from mangrove forests to shallow creeks and bays. Along the way, you may also encounter any number of wild creatures, including bottlenose dolphins, pygmy seahorses, laughing gulls, bald eagles, and endangered manatees. As a bonus, each tour includes free admission to Dolphins Plus in Key Largo.

KEY LARGO

Entertainment and Events

NIGHTLIFE

Key Largo isn't exactly a hotbed of nighttime activity—certainly not like Miami to the north or Key West to the south. Still, you will find several after-hours diversions here, mostly in the form of live entertainment—or, at the very least, curious people-watching opportunities—at area bars and restaurants. The **Caribbean Club** (MM 104 BS U.S. 1, 305/451-4466, 11 A.M.–2 A.M. daily) is one such joint. Although it may look like a typical Keys-style bar, you'll soon notice that it's filled with locals. Don't let the motorcycles parked outside dissuade you; this is a friendly place for cheap drinks and vittles. Besides, the bikers weren't the first tough guys to frequent the Caribbean Club. It was here, after all, that Humphrey Bogart and Lauren Bacall filmed their famous 1948 movie *Key Largo*. Just as in the days of Bogie, the club allows smoking inside, though the doors stay open to let in some fresh Florida air. So, order a burger and a cocktail, and enjoy the laid-back atmosphere.

A few miles south, the **Coconuts Restaurant and Night Club** (528 Caribbean Dr., 305/453-9794, www.coconutsrestaurant.com, 11 A.M.–2 A.M. daily) is another after-hours option. Situated on the ocean side of U.S. 1, near mile marker 100 and beside the Key Largo Resorts Marina, Coconuts offers, in addition to waterfront dining on the outdoor patio, a lively interior space, containing large television screens, a separate bar, and a roomy dance floor. Besides providing nightly entertainment, from rock bands to DJs to karaoke, as well as a late-night menu, Coconuts is the site of many spirited events, including the Lingerie Love Parade on Valentine's Day and the Naughty Santa Parade at Christmastime—not to mention the annual Coconuts Dolphin Tournament, a corporate-sponsored fishing competition in mid-May.

Situated at mile marker 94.5, **Snapper's Waterfront Restaurant** (139 Seaside Ave., 305/852-5956, www.snapperskeylargo.com,

the waterfront patio of Coconuts Restaurant and Night Club

© DANIEL MARTONE

11 A.M.–10 P.M. Mon.–Thurs., 11 A.M.–11 P.M. Fri.–Sat., 10 A.M.–10 P.M. Sun.) is another winning spot for nightly entertainment, from magic acts to blues, jazz, reggae, and classic rock musicians. In addition, on the last Sunday of every month, Snapper's hosts a "Turtle Club Party," a thematic daylong event featuring live music, games, giveaways, and specials, plus free food for all Turtle Club members. Past parties have revolved around everything from crawfish boils to Mardi Gras.

Also in Key Largo—and, really, throughout the Florida Keys—most bars and some restaurants offer regular happy hours, complete with appetizer and drink specials. For more information about such watering holes, consult **Happy Hour Keys** (www.happyhourkeys.com); just be advised that, when in doubt about the accuracy of information on third-party websites, you should always contact the bar or restaurant directly.

THE ARTS

Key West certainly boasts the lion's share of live music, dance performances, and theatrical venues in the Florida Keys, but that doesn't mean that Key Largo is without cultural diversions. Since 1978, the nonprofit **Key Players** (305/453-0997, www.thekeyplayers.org, show times and ticket prices vary) organization has presented live theater in the Upper Keys. The community troupe typically produces four shows each year, ranging from Broadway musicals to lesser-known comedies and dramas, in assorted venues, such as the Key Largo Lions Club.

On occasion, the **Keys Community Concert Band** (www.keyscommunityconcertband.org)—which was founded in 1992 by a small group of dedicated musicians and usually performs free family concerts at Islamorada's Founders Park (Nov.–Apr.)—offers an extra concert in the Key Largo Community Park. Check the band's online schedule for specific dates, and for information about other cultural events in the Upper Keys, consult the **Florida Keys Council of the Arts** (1100 Simonton St., Key West, 305/295-4369, www.keysarts.com).

If you enjoy arts of a more cinematic bent, you can always head to the **Tavernier Towne Cinemas** (91298 Overseas Hwy., Tavernier, 305/853-7003, show times and ticket prices vary), which is at the southern end of Key Largo. Although this isn't the fanciest movie theater you'll ever encounter, you'll certainly be able to catch the latest flicks here.

FESTIVALS AND EVENTS
◖ Key Largo Pirates Fest

For four fun-filled days in late October, the annual Key Largo Pirates Fest (305/394-3736, www.keylargopiratesfest.com, activity prices vary) invites visitors to celebrate the pirating lifestyle—and, in particular, the legend of the notorious pirate Black Caesar, who allegedly prowled Florida's coastal waters in the early 1800s. Before heading south to Key West for the annual Fantasy Fest extravaganza, which also takes place in late October, consider getting a taste of the island mayhem with this lively event. Festival activities include a pirate parade, pirate costume contests, a pirate bazaar and thieves market, an underwater poker tournament, an underwater treasure hunt, choreographed pirate shows, and various celebrations at area restaurants.

Other Area Festivals

Besides holiday gatherings like the St. Patrick's Day Parade and New Year's Eve fireworks display, Key Largo hosts several other annual events, including fishing tournaments and food festivals. During the last weekend in January, for instance, the **Key Largo Stone Crab & Seafood Festival** (www.fkrm.com/crabandseafood, $7 adults, $5 children under 12) features an array of fresh seafood, cooking demonstrations, fishing workshops, eating contests, arts-and-crafts vendors, live entertainment, and other distractions. Meanwhile, in late July and early August, the 10-day **Key Largo Food & Wine Festival** (www.fkrm.com/foodandwine, activity prices vary) lures gourmands with wine tastings, wine classes, cooking demonstrations, and progressive wine dinners.

In late April, the five-day **Key Largo Conch Republic Days** (305/394-3736, www.keylargoconchrepublicdays.com, activity prices vary) honors the 1982 ceremonial secession of the Florida Keys from the United States with a lineup of zany activities at area restaurants, such as a Jimmy Buffett impersonator contest, a key lime pie–eating contest, a conch and key lime cookoff, and an attempt at the world record for underwater ironing.

Another curious event is the **Key Largo Reef Fest** (800/822-1088, www.keylargowrecks.com, activity prices vary), which lures many eager scuba divers to the Upper Keys in early June. To celebrate the region's incredible coral reefs and shipwrecks, this six-day event offers dive-and-stay packages, environmental and underwater photography seminars, underwater treasure and photo scavenger hunts, and nightly gatherings at area restaurants and attractions.

Of course, if you're here in early or mid-December, consider watching the **Holiday Boat Parade** (www.keylargoboatparade.com, dates vary) on Blackwater Sound, near mile marker 104 on the bay side of U.S. 1. With a different theme each year, this magical, lighted boat parade, which typically occurs on a Saturday evening, is a festive, family-friendly way to kick off the holiday season—whether you decide to participate in the parade, view from your boat, or observe the proceedings from shore. Each year, cash prizes are awarded in various categories, including best use of the selected theme.

Shopping

In general, travelers flock to Key Largo for its bountiful outdoor diversions, not its shopping opportunities. That's probably because, beyond the Tradewinds Shopping Center and several diving emporiums, shoppers won't find as many options in this part of the Florida Keys as in, for instance, Key West. Nevertheless, there are several area stores worth mentioning.

ART GALLERIES

Although art aficionados will find more selections in Islamorada and Key West, they'll still appreciate places like the **Key Largo Art Gallery** (103200 Overseas Hwy., 305/451-0052, www.keylargoartgallery.com, 10 A.M.–5 P.M. Tues.–Sat., 10 A.M.–1 P.M. Sun.), which presents a wide array of kaleidoscopic paintings from artists like Jackie Campa and Teresa Kelley, and **Bluewater Potters** (102991 Overseas Hwy., Ste. A, 305/453-1920, www.bluewaterpotters.com, 11 A.M.–5 P.M. daily), which features on-site pottery production and kiln firing, the beach-inspired pottery of owners Kim and Corky Wagner, plus items from other local, regional, and national artists.

Stephen Frink Photography (102600 Overseas Hwy., 305/451-3737 or 800/451-3737, www.stephenfrink.com or www.stephenfrinkphoto.com, 10 A.M.–5 P.M. Mon., 8 A.M.–5 P.M. Tues.–Sat.) displays the stunning images of one of the world's most widely published underwater photographers.

You'll find the tastefully displayed paintings of several world-renowned artists at the **Gallery at Kona Kai** (97802 Overseas Hwy., 305/852-7200, www.g-k-k.com, 9 A.M.–7 P.M. daily or by appt.), an elegant gallery situated amid the lush foliage of the Kona Kai Resort.

For more information about these and other art galleries, consult the **Florida Keys Council of the Arts** (1100 Simonton St., Key West, 305/295-4369, www.keysarts.com).

GIFT AND SOUVENIR SHOPS

For gifts and souvenirs, you'll spot a handful of curious shops, including the **Florida Keys Gift Company** (MM 103 OS U.S. 1, 305/453-9229, www.keysmermaid.com, 9 A.M.–7 P.M. Mon.–Sat., 9 A.M.–6 P.M. Sun.), a repository of tropical jewelry, clothing, and decor, plus regional products like the aromatic roasts of Baby's Coffee, a store in the Lower Keys. Nearby, **Largo Cargo** (103101 Overseas Hwy., 800/795-8889, www.largocargo.com, 8:30 A.M.–8:30 P.M. daily) offers an assortment of tropical apparel, Panama Jack hats, Future Beach kayaks, island music, maps and books, and collectable coins, fragrances, and glassware.

You can peruse antique furniture and collectibles, plus vintage clothes, jewelry, and linens, at **Pink Junktique** (MM 98.2 OS U.S. 1, 305/853-2620, www.pinkjunktique.com, 10 A.M.–5 P.M. daily). Pick up any number of seashells, seasonal outfits, and other souvenirs at the 20,000-square-foot **Shell World** (97600 Overseas Hwy., 305/852-8245, www.shellworldflkeys.com, 9 A.M.–8 P.M. daily), which is situated on the median of U.S. 1 and has an alternative location on the northern end of Key Largo (106040 Overseas Hwy., 305/451-9797, 9 A.M.–5 P.M. daily).

If you're short on beach staples like towels,

AN EYE ON MAILBOXES

Given the varied landscapes, creatures, activities, and architectural styles that abound in the Florida Keys, it's no wonder that plenty of creative people have found their way here – including artists like John James Audubon, widely known for his bird paintings, and Robert Wyland, a marine conservationist celebrated around the world for his impressive Whaling Walls. While art galleries, filled with the work of local and regional visionaries, extend from Key Largo to Key West, one of the most wonderful aspects of this unique region is that art often exists where you least expect to find it – and life is certainly never dull in southern Florida. Everywhere you turn, for example, you're liable to spy a clever, colorful mailbox, inspired by this diverse place. From lighthouses and manatees on the Overseas Highway to fishing lures and mini-bungalows on the side streets, these photo-worthy mailboxes are a common sight. So, keep a sharp lookout for them as you venture through the Florida Keys – and if you decide you'd like a memorable mailbox of your own, simply contact companies like the **Ocean Gifts and Hammock Factory** (82237 Overseas Hwy., Islamorada, 305/664-2222, www.oceangifts.net, 9 A.M.–5 P.M. daily) – or better yet, ask the locals where they got theirs.

Clever mailboxes can be spotted throughout the Florida Keys.

sunglasses, hats, sandals, and other apparel—not to mention souvenirs—stop by the **Sandal Factory Outlet/T-Shirt City** (102411 Overseas Hwy., 305/453-9644, 9 A.M.–8 P.M. Mon.–Sat., 9 A.M.–6 P.M. Sun.), which also has locations in Islamorada and Marathon.

FOOD AND CIGAR EMPORIUMS

If you have a hankering for regional treats, head to **Key Lime Products** (95200 Overseas Hwy., 305/853-0378 or 800/870-1780, www.keylimeproducts.com, 9 A.M.–6 P.M. daily), which offers a wide assortment of tangy delights, from key lime iced tea to key lime thimble cookies to key lime shampoo.

If you're staying in a room, suite, or cottage

equipped with kitchen facilities, you might also want to partake of the fresh fish, crab, lobster, shrimp, and conch, as well as the key lime pie and other delectables, that **Key Largo Fisheries, Inc.** (1313 Ocean Bay Dr., 800/432-4358, www.keylargofisheries.com, 7 A.M.–5:30 P.M. Mon.–Sat.) has been serving since 1972.

Even cigar lovers will find shopping bliss in Key Largo. The **Island Smoke Shop** (103400 Overseas Hwy., 305/453-4014 or 800/680-9701, www.islandsmokeshop.com, 10 A.M.–6 P.M. daily) offers pipes, ashtrays, humidors, lighters, and over 1,200 brands and sizes of handmade, premium cigars, including El Original maduros. Besides its vast inventory, it also boasts the largest walk-in humidor in southern Florida.

KEY LARGO

© LAURA MARTONE

Sports and Recreation

GOLF

At the exclusive **Ocean Reef Club** (35 Ocean Reef Dr., 305/367-2611 or 800/741-7333, www.oceanreef.com) on the northern end of Key Largo, guests staying at the on-site inn have access to two championship 18-hole courses. Both the Hammock Course, which is partially situated within a mangrove and tropical hardwood hammock, and the Dolphin Course, with fairways that wind past mahogany trees and coconut palms, feature incredible vistas and challenging holes. Guests of the Ocean Reef Club may reserve tee times by contacting the Membership Office (305/367-5921, rates vary seasonally). Rental clubs are also available (starting from $20 guests, $15 members), as are instructional sessions (305/367-5912).

HIKING AND BIKING

Although Key Largo is primarily a water lover's playground, there are certainly some favored activities among landlubbers. Hikers, for instance, can experience the winding self-guided nature trail through **Dagny Johnson Key Largo Hammock Botanical State Park** (C.R. 905, www.floridastateparks.org/keylargohammock, 8 A.M.–sunset daily, $2.50 pp). Of course, to really experience the woods of this serene, 2,421-acre preserve, which protects more than 80 different plant and animal species, you should explore the six miles of backcountry trails, for which you'll need a backcountry permit, available through **John Pennekamp Coral Reef State Park** (102601 Overseas Hwy., 305/451-1202, www.floridastateparks.org/pennekamp or www.pennekamppark.com, 8 A.M.–sunset daily, $8 vehicles w/2–8 passengers plus $0.50 pp, $4.50 motorcycles and single-occupant vehicles, $2.50 pedestrians, bikers, and extra passengers). If you're a birding enthusiast, you'll especially appreciate Dagny Johnson State Park, where you're likely to spot a variety of species, from white-crowned pigeons to red-bellied woodpeckers to great blue herons. Rare sightings

might include mangrove cuckoos, masked boobies, black vultures, and great horned owls. With its two beaches and three nature trails, nearby John Pennekamp also offers a treasure trove of species for avid bird-watchers.

Bikers, too, will enjoy the backcountry trails of Dagny Johnson State Park (provided you secure a permit). In addition, there is a 15.5-mile bike path, part of the **Florida Keys Overseas Heritage Trail,** that runs past numerous businesses and parks in Key Largo, between mile markers 106.5 and 91. Bikes can be rented from the **Key Largo Resorts Boat & Bike Rental** (Key Largo Resorts Marina, MM 100 OS U.S. 1, 305/451-2241, 8 A.M.–5 P.M. daily, $5 hourly, $10 per half day, $15 daily) beside the Ramada Limited Key Largo. Baskets, locks, helmets, and touring maps are included with all rentals.

FISHING AND BOATING

While anglers and boaters will find even more options down south in Islamorada, the self-proclaimed "sportfishing capital of the world," Key Largo certainly features a wide array of fishing charters and boat rentals. The **Key Largo Resorts Marina** (MM 100 OS U.S. 1, 305/453-7171, www.keylargomarina.com)—hard to miss beside the Holiday Inn—is probably the best place to start your search for a fishing charter. Of the numerous options available, you'll find **Beaver Charters** (305/394-0679, www.sportfishinginthekeys.com), which offers half-day charters ($600), full-day charters ($900), evening tarpon trips ($350), and swordfishing excursions ($900). All charters include bait, tackle, ice, and fishing licenses. Other options range from the *Sailors Choice* Party Boat (305/451-1802, www.sailorschoicefishingboat.com, $40 pp), a 65-foot vessel offering three daily trips (9 A.M.–1 P.M., 1:30–5:30 P.M., and 7:30 P.M.–midnight) for snapper, grouper, barracuda, and other offshore fish, to **Key Largo Fishing Adventures** (305/923-9293, www.keyssportfishing.com),

© DANIEL MARTONE

Three fishing trips are offered daily on the *Sailors Choice* Party Boat.

which features the 38-foot *Fin Razer* ($700 per half day, $1,000 daily), ideal for reef and offshore fishing, plus swordfishing ($1,325 per trip) night or day.

Operating out of Dove Creek Lodge, near mile marker 94.5, **Blackfoot Charters** (305/481-0111, www.blackfootfishing.com, $375 per half day, $500 daily) offers backcountry, flats, and canoe fishing in the Upper Keys, the Everglades, and Biscayne National Park. Captain Mike Makowski, a native of southern Florida, invites novice and veteran anglers to seek out bonefish, tarpon, permit, snook, redfish, and other seasonal species—while listening to his colorful tales of local history. Other area charters include **Reel Chaos Charters** (Key Largo Resorts Marina, MM 100 OS U.S. 1, 305/587-1150, www.reelchaoscharters.com, $400 per half day, $550 daily), which specializes in backcountry and flats fishing for redfish, tarpon, shark, and other species; **Rodeo Charters** (Key Largo Fisheries, 1313 Ocean Bay Dr., 305/453-9614 or 305/522-2638, www.rodeocharters.com, $400–600 per half day, $600–800 daily), which has featured

offshore, reef, wreck, and backcountry fishing since 1973; and **Tails Up Fishing Charters** (305/394-1383, www.tailsupfishing.com, $375 per half day, $500 daily), which targets redfish, bonefish, snook, and tarpon in the backcountry and flats and, even better, will bring the boat directly to your doorstep.

If you'd prefer a private fishing trip, consider renting a boat from **Key Largo Resorts Boat & Bike Rental** (Key Largo Resorts Marina, MM 100 OS U.S. 1, 305/451-2241, 8 A.M.–5 P.M. daily), which offers three different boat styles: 19-foot ($140 per half day, $175 daily), 20-foot ($140 per half day, $175 daily), and 21-foot ($225 daily). Other boat rental companies include **Bay & Reef Pontunes** (MM 107.9 BS U.S. 1, 305/393-5593, www.pontunes.com, rates vary), which offers an assortment of vessels, from fishing boats to luxury pontoons ideal for snorkelers, and **Dive In Watersports** (Mandalay Marina, 80 E. 2nd St., 305/852-1919, www.divein-watersports.com, 8 A.M.–5 P.M. daily), which provides a variety of powerboats ($125–225 per two hours, $150–300 per half day, $185–385 daily, depending on vessel type) and Hobie Cat rentals ($70 per two hours, $125 per four hours, $175 daily). If you'd rather purchase a vessel while you're in the Keys, consult **Tiki Water Sports, Inc.** (94381 Overseas Hwy., 305/852-9298 or 800/726-2102, www.tiki-watersports.net, 8 A.M.–4:30 P.M. Mon.–Fri., 10 A.M.–2 P.M. Sat.), a one-stop shop that sells sailboats, kayaks, pedal boats, and canoes; offers a wide array of marine supplies, plus sailboat and kayak rentals; and provides boat maintenance, repairs, and dry boat storage.

C CANOEING AND KAYAKING

With access to mangrove swamps, the Atlantic Ocean, Florida Bay, and, of course, the wildlife-rich waterways of the Everglades, Key Largo provides an ideal landscape for canoeists and kayakers alike. Many first-timers head initially to **John Pennekamp Coral Reef State Park** (102601 Overseas Hwy., 305/451-1202, www.floridastateparks.org/pennekamp or www.pennekamppark.com, 8 A.M.–sunset daily, $8 vehicles w/2–8 passengers plus $0.50 pp, $4.50 motorcycles and single-occupant vehicles, $2.50 pedestrians, bikers, and extra passengers) in the northern part of Key Largo, where the **Coral Reef Park Company** (305/451-6300) offers enough canoe and kayak rentals ($12–17 hourly) to accommodate several individuals, couples, and families at any given time. No matter when you visit, it seems that you'll always spot a brightly colored kayak winding its way through the mangrove trees— the ideal mode of transport for those hoping to get an up-close, yet unobtrusive, look at area birds and other critters.

Of course, the Coral Reef Park Company isn't the only game in town. **Caribbean Watersports** (Key Largo Grande Resort & Beach Club, 97000 Overseas Hwy., 305/852-4707 or 800/223-6728, www.caribbeanwatersports.com, 9 A.M.–5 P.M. daily) offers both kayak ($12–30 hourly, $20–45 per two hours) and paddleboat rentals ($30–40 hourly, $45–55 per two hours). You can also rent a kayak from **Dive In Watersports** (Mandalay Marina, 80 E. 2nd St., 305/852-1919, www.

a guided kayaking trip amid the mangroves of the Upper Keys

© DANIEL MARTONE

divein-watersports.com, 8 A.M.–5 P.M. daily, $20 hourly), situated near mile marker 97.5 on the ocean side of U.S. 1.

Additionally, **Florida Bay Outfitters** (104050 Overseas Hwy., 305/451-3018, www.kayakfloridakeys.com, 8:30 A.M.–6 P.M. daily) and **Garl's Coastal Kayaking** (17 Poinciana Dr., 305/394-5046, www.coastal-kayaking.com, trip times vary) both provide guided kayak trips throughout the Upper Keys and the Everglades—and both typically offer pickup service to the launch point. In fact, Florida Bay Outfitters features a wide array of trips, from three-hour tours to Dusenberry Creek ($60 pp), where dolphin and manatee spottings are probable, to three-day kayak sailing excursions amid the islands of Florida Bay ($495 pp, incl. meals and camping gear). Free pickups and drop-offs at participating resorts are offered for most trips, and reservations are necessary for all of them. In addition to guided tours, Florida Bay Outfitters—Florida's largest paddle-sports retailer—also offers rental canoes, sea kayaks, pedal and sail kayaks, sit-on-tops, and rec boats ($30–100 per half day, $40–150 daily), plus three-hour instructional sessions ($75 pp w/rental gear) focused on specific topics like kayak basics, advanced skills, or rescue techniques.

Meanwhile, Garl's ocean trips ($100 per half day, $150 daily) allow you to explore Key Largo patch reefs, tidal flats and seagrass habitats, and perhaps even historic Indian Key Historic State Park near Islamorada. For the Everglades trips ($100 per half day, $150 daily), Garl can transport passengers (when there's room in his jeep) from Key Largo to Flamingo. Depending on the weather conditions and the type of trip, Garl guides paddlers on a combination of hikes to alligator holes, freshwater kayak excursions amid mangroves and crocodiles, and saltwater kayak tours at sunset. No matter which trip you choose, Garl encourages you to wear your swimsuit, as snorkeling is usually a possibility. Single and double kayaks are available, and reservations are required for all trips.

◖ DIVING AND SNORKELING

In the ocean waters east of Key Largo lies the Key Largo National Marine Sanctuary, part of the Florida Keys National Marine Sanctuary, a 220-mile-long coral reef ecosystem that stretches from the southern end of Key Biscayne to the Dry Tortugas— incidentally, the only living coral reef in the continental United States and the third largest coral reef system in the world. If you're new to snorkeling and scuba diving, head first to **John Pennekamp Coral Reef State Park** (102601 Overseas Hwy., 305/451-1202, www. floridastateparks.org/pennekamp or www. pennekamppark.com, 8 A.M.–sunset daily, $8 vehicles w/2–8 passengers plus $0.50 pp, $4.50 motorcycles and single-occupant vehicles, $2.50 pedestrians, bikers, and extra passengers). Through the **Coral Reef Park Company** (305/451-6300, 305/451-6322, or 877/727-5348), you can take diving instruction ($185–385 pp), earn PADI Open Water certification ($485 pp), and participate in 2.5-hour snorkeling trips ($30 adults, $25 children under 18, plus gear rentals) or scuba-diving

tours ($60 pp, plus $29 for gear rental) amid the vibrant coral reefs a few miles offshore.

Out here, you'll encounter amazing sealife like parrotfish, yellow cherubfish, brain and staghorn coral, spotted spiny lobster, and sea hermit crabs, plus formations such as **Grecian Rocks** and **Key Largo Dry Rocks,** which contains elkhorn coral and the ever-popular, often-photographed *Christ of the Abyss* statue. Before heading out on a snorkeling or diving trip, consider stopping by the park's visitor center (8 A.M.–5 P.M. daily), which features several saltwater aquariums, housing many of the kaleidoscopic tropical fish, coral formations, and other sea creatures you might see while exploring the ocean.

As with kayaking, the Coral Reef Park Company isn't the only diving outfitter in Key Largo. For instance, **Amy Slate's Amoray Dive Resort** (104250 Overseas Hwy., 305/451-3595 or 800/426-6729, www.amoray. com) offers an array of diving classes, from a half-day beginner's class ($75 pp) to a six-day divemaster class ($900 pp), plus twice-daily snorkeling excursions (8:30 A.M. and 1 P.M., $45–50 pp) and multiple-location diving trips (8:30 A.M. and 1 P.M. daily, $75 pp). The **Jules Undersea Lodge** (51 Shoreland Dr., 305/451-2353, www.jul.com), based in the **Key Largo Undersea Park,** also offers diving instruction, even for nonguests. Some of the classes include Discover Diving ($175 pp), Underwater Photography ($295 pp, plus boat fees), Open Water Certification ($595 pp, plus materials and boat fees), and Dive Master ($1,000 pp, plus materials and boat fees).

In addition to diving classes, operators such as the **Garden Cove Dive Center** (105664 Overseas Hwy., 305/451-5844, www.gardencovedivers. com, 9 A.M.–3 P.M. Mon.–Fri., 8 A.M.–5 P.M. Sat., 8 A.M.–3 P.M. Sun., trips 8:30 A.M. and 1:30 P.M. daily, $74–84 pp, $462 per charter), **Island Ventures** (103900 Overseas Hwy., 305/451-4957, www.islandventure.com, trips 8:30 A.M. and 1 P.M. daily, $80 pp), the well-favored **Silent World Dive Center** (103200 Overseas Hwy., 305/451-3252 or 800/966-3483, www.silent-worldkeylargo.com, 7:30 A.M.–5:30 P.M. daily,

PROTECTING FLORIDA'S CORAL REEFS

While visiting the **John Pennekamp Coral Reef State Park** (102601 Overseas Hwy., 305/451-1202 or 305/451-6300, www.floridastateparks.org/pennekamp or www.pennekamppark.com, 8 A.M.-sunset daily, fees apply), you should take a moment to stop by the on-site visitor center. Here, you'll learn more about the organisms you might see on a scuba-diving or snorkeling excursion amid the remarkable offshore coral reefs within and beyond the park. Besides featuring aquariums filled with eels, tropical fish, and spotted spiny lobsters, the center tries to educate people about proper coral reef etiquette in an effort to protect the fragile coral reef system that extends for 220 miles along the eastern side of the Florida Keys, constituting the 2,900-square-mile Florida Keys National Marine Sanctuary. In fact, some of the following boating and diving regulations are strictly enforced by state park officials, so remember them the next time you venture into the offshore waters of the Florida Keys:

- Whether or not you choose to operate your own boat, you should always consult weather conditions ahead of time, as it's best not to go out in rough seas; poor visibility, strong winds, and increased waves can hinder safe interaction with coral reefs.

- If you do use your own boat, be sure to maintain all equipment so as to avoid inadvertent discharges of oil and other toxic substances.

- Do not discharge any raw sewage into offshore waters; instead, use official pump-out facilities available throughout the Keys.

- Do not litter in the ocean or abandon structures on the seabed, especially near the reefs; if you see such debris, please retrieve it and properly dispose of it on land.

- Use nautical and tidal charts to practice safe navigation, know your boat's draft, and be aware of the variations in surface water color: Deep-water areas, for instance, are typically blue; shallower areas are often green; brown usually indicates shallow coral reefs and seagrass beds; and white signifies sandbars and rubble areas.

- Try to stay in marked channels, and do not approach lighthouses, reef light towers, shoal markers, and yellow buoys, which usually indicate shallow reef and seagrass areas.

- Slow down to an idle speed in dive areas, and stay at least 100 feet from a red-and-white, diver-down flag.

- Be careful while navigating a boat around coral reefs and seagrass beds, and do not

---

trips 8:30 A.M. and 12:30 P.M. daily, $80–105 pp), and the **Sea Dwellers Dive Center** (MM 100 BS U.S. 1, 305/451-3640 or 800/451-3640, www.seadwellers.com, 8 A.M.–5 P.M. daily, trips 8:30 A.M. and 1 P.M. daily, $65–80 pp) offer diving trips (and, in most cases, snorkeling excursions) to the reefs and wrecks that compose the Key Largo National Marine Sanctuary and all-encompassing Florida Keys National Marine Sanctuary. Such underwater sights include the *Duane* and the *Bibb,* two U.S. Coast Guard cutters used in World War II, and the USS *Spiegel Grove,* a 510-foot Navy transport ship originally launched in November 1955, prematurely sunk in June 2002 to create an artificial reef, and

thankfully shifted into an upright position by Hurricane Dennis in 2005. In this region, you might also see star coral, elkhorn coral, and other formations on the **Molasses Reef,** the *Benwood* shipwreck south of **Dixie Shoals,** the sea caves of **French Reef,** and the *City of Washington* shipwreck near **Elbow Reef.**

You'll also find a number of diving operators in the nearby **Key Largo Resorts Marina** (MM 100 OS U.S. 1, 305/453-7171, www.keylargomarina.com). Such options include **BlueWater Divers of Key Largo** (305/453-9600, www.bluewaterdiver.net, 8:30 A.M. and 1 P.M. daily, $80 pp), **Horizon Divers** (305/453-3535 or 800/984-3483, www.horizondivers.

drop anchors on, or near, living coral; instead, use the white-and-blue mooring buoys or anchor in the sandy patches adjacent to the reef.

- Do not damage or remove markers and mooring buoys.

- If you run aground, immediately turn the engine off and tilt the motor upward if possible; wait until high tide to remove the vessel by walking or poling, and if necessary, call the **Florida Fish and Wildlife Conservation Commission (FWC)** (888/404-3922) for assistance. Be prepared to incur towing fees as well as fines for damaging the seagrass habitat.

- To avoid standing on the coral, use inflatable vests (if snorkeling) and practice proper buoyancy control (if diving).

- Avoid touching, kicking, defacing, or sitting on living coral formations.

- Do not collect historic resources (such as parts of shipwrecks), plantlife, living coral, seashells, tropical fish, queen conch, sea stars, or other marine creatures near the reef.

- Do not engage in spearfishing or release exotic species near the reef.

- Resist the temptation to feed fish, seabirds, and marine mammals, and avoid any wildlife disturbance.

In other words, "Look, but don't touch." Additionally, you can assist in the welfare of such coral reefs even when you're not in the water. For instance, try to choose seafood from fisheries that have the least negative impact on the ocean, and minimize your use of chemically enhanced pesticides and fertilizers, which may end up in offshore waters. Also, avoid purchasing coral jewelry and souvenirs, unless you know for certain that such decorative objects were not illegally harvested. Be sure, too, to report all damage incurred by coral reefs to dive operators or conservation groups that monitor coral reef health. For more information about area coral reefs, consult the **Florida Keys National Marine Sanctuary** (305/852-7717 or 305/292-0311, www.floridakeys.noaa.gov). To learn how to protect these beautiful, complex, and surprisingly fragile formations, contact the **Project AWARE Foundation** (949/858-7657 or 866/802-9273, www.projectaware.org) or the **Reef Relief Environmental Center** (631 Greene St., Key West, 305/294-3100, www. reefrelief.org), two nonprofit organizations dedicated to preserving the living coral reef ecosystems around the world.

KEY LARGO

com, 8 A.M.–6 P.M. daily, $80–90 pp), the **Keys Diver & Snorkel Center** (305/451-1177 or 888/289-2402, www.keysdiver.com, 8 A.M.–5:30 P.M. daily, trips 8:30 A.M. and 1 P.M. daily, $75–80 pp), and **Ocean Divers** (522 Caribbean Dr., 305/451-1113 or 800/451-1113, www.oceandivers.com, 7:30 A.M.–5 P.M. daily, trips 8 A.M. and 1 P.M. daily, $85–90 pp). Other area operators that feature diving classes as well as diving excursions include **Captain Slate's Atlantis Dive Center** (51 Garden Cove Dr., 305/451-1325 or 800/331-3483, www.captain-slate.com, 7:30 A.M.–6 P.M. Mon.–Thurs. and Sun., 7:30 A.M.–9 P.M. Fri.–Sat., $80–110 pp), which hosts an annual Underwater Easter Egg

Hunt; **Quiescence Diving Services** (103680 Overseas Hwy., 305/451-2440, www.keylargo-diving.com, 8 A.M.–6 P.M. daily, $82 pp); and **Scuba-Fun** (99222 Overseas Hwy., 305/394-5046, www.scuba-fun.com, 8 A.M.–5 P.M. daily, $80–149 pp), which is hard to miss due to the stunning Wyland Whaling Wall on its exterior.

Of course, many of these operators also offer snorkeling as an option. In addition, you can board the *Sundiver III,* operated by the **Sundiver Station** (102840 Overseas Hwy., 305/451-2220 or 800/654-7369, www. snorkelingisfun.com, trips 9 A.M., noon, and 3 P.M. daily, $30–33 adults, $25–27 children under 13, plus gear rentals), as well as the **Reef Roamer** (MM 100 OS U.S. 1, 305/453-0110 or 877/453-0110, www.reefroamersnorkel.com, 8 A.M.–5 P.M. daily, trips 9 A.M. and 12:30 P.M. daily, $26–35 pp) and the **Morning Star** (Key Largo Fisheries, 1313 Ocean Bay Dr., 305/451-7057, www.morningstarcharters.com, trip 9 A.M.–1 P.M. daily, $75 pp)—all offer snorkeling excursions to the reefs within John Pennekamp Coral Reef State Park.

OTHER ACTIVITIES

As an alternative to activities like fishing or snorkeling, consider taking flight with **Key Largo Parasail** (305/747-0032, www.keylargoparasail.com, 10 A.M.–4 P.M. daily, $39–59 pp), which, weather permitting, welcomes people of all ages to fly 600 to 1,000 feet above the ocean. Boat trips leave from Sundowners on the Bay at mile marker 104, on the bay side of U.S. 1. Single and tandem rides are available on a first-come, first-served basis, though trips are usually unavailable during part of the off-season (Sept.–Oct.). Farther south, **Caribbean Watersports** (97000 Overseas Hwy., 305/852-4707 or 800/223-6728, www.caribbeanwatersports.com, 9 A.M.–5 P.M. daily), based out of the Key Largo Grande Resort & Beach Club, has offered parasailing flights ($70 per flyer, $140 per tandem) for more than 19 years. Caribbean Watersports also offers WaveRunner

rentals ($75 per half hour, $120 hourly), for which certain riders (ages 14–21) must have Florida-approved boater certification.

Located in Key Largo Community Park at mile marker 99.6, on the ocean side of U.S. 1, the **Jacobs Aquatic Center (JAC)** (320 Laguna Ave., 305/453-7946, www.jacobsaquaticcenter.org, 10 A.M.–7 P.M. daily, day passes $21–25 families, $8–10 adults, $6–8 children 11–17, and $5–6 children 3–10) offers three different swimming pools, each of which has separate temperature controls. One pool, ideal for children, features a "spray" gym and a pirate ship with water slides. Other amenities here include a multipurpose activity room, bathrooms with showers and lockers, and a wide array of activities and classes, including water aerobics, water polo, swimming lessons, pilates, and scuba certification. Multi-pass and long-term rates are also available.

You might find an even greater release at **Pilates in Paradise** (98840 Overseas Hwy., 305/453-0801, www.pilatesinparadise.net, times vary Mon.–Sat., $20–35 per class), where, depending on how long you'll be in the area, you can experience just one class or a series of them. Several options are available here, from a mat session that teaches breathing, stretching, and strengthening exercises to a Nia program that fosters a unified body-mind-spirit fitness and lifestyle practice.

Accommodations

UNDER $100

Initially built as a fishing camp in 1903, **Gilbert's Resort** (107900 Overseas Hwy., 305/451-1133, www.gilbertsresort.com, $69–140 d) presents a laid-back atmosphere that's especially apparent in the on-site tiki bar, which offers live music and a full menu. The standard rooms provide two double beds, air conditioners, small refrigerators, and cable television. Also available are bayside rooms, with waterfront patios, and spacious family suites. Unlike at many establishments in the Upper

Keys, pets are allowed here, though for an extra charge.

You can relish some quiet time near the poolside tiki bar at the **Ramada Limited Key Largo** (99751 Overseas Hwy., 305/451-3939, www.ramadakeylargo.com, $90–250 d), perhaps after returning from a dive or fishing adventure provided by one of the many guides in the adjacent marina. Every room features comfortable king-sized or queen-sized beds, cable television, and free wireless Internet access. The king Jacuzzi suites also include

THE BOGIE CONNECTION

the original *African Queen*

Several famous people, from novelists to singers to presidents, are inextricably linked to the Florida Keys. One such celebrity is Humphrey Bogart, whose 1948 film *Key Largo* was actually filmed on the northernmost island. Of course, this well-favored crime thriller, directed by John Huston, is not the only reminder of Bogart's connection to Key Largo. Over the years, Bogart has been such a legendary presence here that you'll even find pets named after him, such as Bogie, the beloved yellow-naped Amazon parrot at the Rock Reef Resort near mile marker 98. Even better, you can view the one-and-only *African Queen,* the actual vessel featured in the eponymous 1951 film starring Bogart and Katharine Hepburn. When not reserved for private rides, the small, weathered vessel is typically docked beside the aptly named **Bogie's Café,** a casual eatery at the Holiday Inn Key Largo Resort & Marina near mile marker 100.

conditioners. The hotel also provides free wireless Internet access to help you keep in touch with friends back home or plan your next Key Largo adventure. While staying here, take advantage of the bayfront beach, where gorgeous sunsets are common, or feel free to rest on one of the available hammocks. Anglers and boaters will also appreciate the on-site boat ramp and docks. Just a little farther south lies one of the few smoke-free hotels in Key Largo, the **Key Largo Inn** (99202 Overseas Hwy., 305/451-2478 or 866/488-3020, http://keylargoinn.com, $69–99 d), which features a clean, two-story, Caribbean-style building surrounded by a pool and a tropical courtyard. The rooms contain extra-long, queen-sized beds, and additional amenities include a complimentary breakfast and free wireless Internet access.

Perfect for divers, anglers, and snorkelers, the **Seafarer Resort** (97684 Overseas Hwy., 305/852-5349, www.seafarerresort.com, $65–175 d) features a private beach ideal for relaxing, watching a romantic sunset, or embarking upon a variety of water-related adventures. Here, you can choose to snorkel in the turquoise waters nearby, arrange a fishing trip with one of the many local guides, or enlist the help of the on-site dive center. With studio and standard rooms, as well as cottages ($105–200 daily), a family apartment ($105–180 daily), and a beach house ($110–190 daily), the resort can even accommodate large groups. Farther south, the low-key **Stoneledge Paradise Inn** (95320 Overseas Hwy., 305/852-8114, www.stoneledgeparadiseinn.com, $88–98 d) offers basic lodgings alongside Florida Bay. As with most places in the Keys, the rooms range in size, with some providing full kitchens, and for families, there's even a two-bedroom house ($185–250 daily) with an extra queen-sized sofabed.

$100-200

Among the moderately priced lodging options that Key Largo offers is the **Azul del Mar** (104300 Overseas Hwy., 305/451-0337, www.azulhotels.us, $120–320 d), a small, quiet, adults-only boutique hotel that features

wraparound balconies with spectacular views of the marina.

Not far away, **The Pelican** (99340 Overseas Hwy., 305/451-3576 or 877/451-3576, www.hungrypelican.com, rooms $60–160 d, suites $195–220, cottages $85–95) offers 23 rooms, suites, and cottages, all of which are equipped with cable television, refrigerators, and air

five suites with ocean or garden views, various water sports and eco-adventures, and a rejuvenating beach beside Florida Bay. Each room here provides a king-sized bed, a kitchenette, a large television, and wireless Internet access.

Situated beside Florida Bay, **《 Amy Slate's Amoray Dive Resort** (104250 Overseas Hwy., 305/451-3595 or 800/426-6729, www.amoray. com, $99–239 d) caters to the diving or snorkeling enthusiast. Peppered with palm trees, this breezy property offers a wide variety of airy accommodations, with ceiling fans, tropical decor, free wireless Internet access, and, in some cases, full kitchens. Even better, you can take a variety of scuba-diving classes on the premises, and while staying here, you'll be just steps away from the resort's two on-site boats: the 45-foot *Amoray Diver* and the 26-foot *Just-In-Time,* both of which deliver guests to the reefs and wrecks of John Pennekamp Coral Reef State Park and the Key Largo National Marine Sanctuary.

For a blend of Victorian charm and Caribbean flair, reserve a room at the year-round **《 Tarpon Flats Inn & Marina** (29 Shoreland Dr., 305/453-1313 or 866/546-0000, www.tarponflats.com, $160–220 d). This well-appointed bed-and-breakfast offers lovely rooms and suites, with British Colonial–style furnishings and intimate verandas that open onto stunning Largo Sound. Besides amenities like satellite television and kitchenettes, the inn's major claim to fame is its proximity to an assortment of natural pleasures and outdoor diversions. You'll find swimming, sailing, and kayaking opportunities right at your doorstep, and you'll be within walking distance of several tiki bars and waterfront restaurants. In addition, you're not far from the wonders of John Pennekamp Coral Reef State Park—not to mention that the Everglades are just a 30-minute boat ride away.

Near some of the best fishing and diving waters, the **Largo Lodge** (101740 Overseas Hwy., 305/451-0424, www.largolodge.com, $95–195 d) lies only a mile from the John Pennekamp Coral Reef State Park. Located on three acres alongside Florida Bay, the six cottages and

three units here offer free wireless Internet access, cable television, plus kitchenettes or full kitchens—making them especially economical for families.

The 130 rooms at the **Holiday Inn Key Largo Resort & Marina** (99701 Overseas Hwy., 305/451-2121, www.holidayinnkeylargo. com, $110–186 d) are all tropically themed, some with private balconies overlooking the oceanside marina and the fishing village that features Bogie's Café. The rooms offer queen-sized or king-sized beds, plus cable television and free wireless Internet access. Besides the immediately available water sports, the hotel features two freshwater pools.

If you're traveling with your cat or dog, the **Marina Del Mar Hotel, Resort & Marina** (527 Caribbean Dr., 305/451-4107, www. marinadelmarkeylargo.com, $109–290 d) offers 76 pet-friendly rooms, studios, or apartments. Queen-sized or king-sized beds are provided, as well as cable television and free wireless Internet access. Other amenities include a heated pool, tennis courts, and a free continental breakfast.

The 56-unit, pet-friendly **Bayside Inn** (99490 Overseas Hwy., 305/451-4450, www. baysidekeylargo.com, $140–300 d) contains one-bedroom waterfront suites, bay-view rooms, and island-view rooms. Each includes a small refrigerator and a large flat-screen television, and the suites also have full kitchens. In addition, the property features a relaxing pool.

In the heart of Key Largo, on Florida Bay, the **Bay Cove Motel** (99446 Overseas Hwy., 305/451-1686, www.baycovemotel.com, $100–325 d) provides accommodations to suit every kind of traveler. The single and double cottages, efficiencies with kitchens, and spacious house (which accommodates up to eight people) are all within walking distance of many restaurants and shops. Guests can utilize the boat ramp and large dock, and after a long day of boating or fishing, you can relax under a palm tree on the private beach.

If you're an experienced sailor who's come to the Keys without a boat of your own, the **Key**

Lime Sailing Club (99306 Overseas Hwy., 305/451-3438, www.keylimesailingclub.com, $140–300 d) has one at your disposal. For a smaller vessel, try one of the available kayaks, canoes, paddleboats, or rowboats. With a variety of cottages on-site, this hideaway has something for every occasion. Be aware, though, that each cottage charges a one-time cleaning fee, the amount of which depends upon the size of the cottage.

The **Rock Reef Resort** (97850 Overseas Hwy., 305/852-2401 or 800/477-2343, www.rockreefresort.com, $85–195 d) is a year-round oasis beside Florida Bay that was once part of an old key lime grove. Operated since 1989 by on-site owners Linda and David Adams, this low-key resort offers a wide range of comfortable accommodations. Beyond the main hotel, a white, two-story building that contains standard and deluxe rooms as well as efficiencies, lie the lush, spacious grounds, where amid shady palm trees and vibrant bougainvillea are more intimate lodgings, from well-furnished apartments ($143–295 daily) to beachside cottages ($165–260 daily). With several hammocks among the trees, numerous lounge chairs on the beach, a fishing pier with docking facilities ($15 daily), a hot tub in the garden, a waterfront tiki hut, and a communal picnic and barbecue area, it's no wonder that the 21-unit resort is a popular option for wedding parties and family reunions. Other amenities include cable television, laundry services, wireless Internet access, and on-site parking. Those seeking romance and relaxation will also appreciate the no-pet and no-fireworks policies.

Offering suites, cottages, villas, and efficiencies—all with full kitchens—the lush, 2.5-acre **Coconut Bay Resort** (97702 Overseas Hwy., 305/852-5695 or 800/385-0986, www.coconutbaykeylargo.com, rooms $75–185 d, cottages $145–235, suites $230–310, villas $195–445) can accommodate any type of Upper Keys vacation. Every room has cable television, barbecue grills, and shady huts. A phone-free and smoke-free environment, the resort also provides free wireless Internet access in selected areas.

KEY LARGO

© DANIEL MARTONE

the lush setting of Rock Reef Resort

For townhouse-style lodging, the 40 suites at **Suites at Key Largo Supertel Inn** (201 Ocean Dr., 305/451-5081, www.suitesofkeylargo.com, $108–120 d) each have a queen-sized bed, a sofa sleeper, two bathrooms, and a well-equipped kitchen. Extended stay rates and boat dockage are available. Beyond comfortable accommodations at the **Ocean Pointe Suites at Key Largo** (500 Burton Dr., Tavernier, 800/882-9464, www.opsuites.com, $138–158 d), the resort specializes in arranging snorkeling, fishing, and ecotours as package deals. Spend the day at the private beach or the freshwater pool, then grab a bite to eat at the on-site café and lounge.

Situated on Florida Bay, the **Atlantic Bay Resort** (160 Sterling Rd., Tavernier, 305/852-5248 or 866/937-5650, www.atlanticbayresort.com, rooms $79–159 d, suites $119–325, cottages $159–199) features 500 feet of relaxing waterfront, plus 19 efficiencies, cottages, and suites, all of which have full kitchens. In addition, guests can utilize the boat ramp and dock.

As one of the Keys' most unique hotels, the pet-friendly **Coconut Palm Inn** (198 Harborview Dr., Tavernier, 305/852-3017 or 800/765-5397, www.coconutpalminn.com, $129–399 d) offers 20 rooms and suites—varying between standard rooms with garden views, patio rooms with bay views and screened porches, and suites with separate living areas, bay views, and balconies or decks. Here, you'll also enjoy a sandy beach hidden among a grove of coconut trees, some of which have hammocks hanging between them.

OVER $200

The **Marriott Key Largo Bay Resort** (103800 Overseas Hwy., 305/453-0000 or 866/849-3753, www.marriottkeylargo.com, rooms $140–409 d, suites $499–649) offers a complete resort experience with full watersports facilities, a full-service day spa, and access to the Keysgate championship 18-hole golf course only 25 minutes away. In addition, the property houses three separate eateries: the open-air Breezer's Bar and Grill, ideal

for sunset-watching; Flipper's Poolside Tiki Bar (11 A.M.–sunset daily); and Gus' Grille (7 A.M.–11 P.M. daily), featuring award-winning Floribbean cuisine. The rooms here range from standard accommodations, with two double beds, to a two-bedroom suite, and all include cable television, small refrigerators, and wireless Internet access.

Formerly an underwater research habitat, the **(C** **Jules Undersea Lodge** (51 Shoreland Dr., 305/451-2353, www.jul.com, $375–475 pp) is now open to the public for a unique lodging experience. To enter the lodge, you must dive 21 feet beneath the sea, making this the perfect base camp for diving enthusiasts. The lodge consists of the same creature comforts you would expect above the sea: hot showers, a well-stocked kitchen, a common room for winding down after a long day of scuba diving, and two bedrooms with 42-inch windows, offering a fascinating glimpse of the ocean floor.

Barely visible from the highway, the **Kona Kai Resort, Gallery & Botanic Gardens** (97802 Overseas Hwy., 305/852-7200 or 800/365-7829, www.konakairesort.com, rooms $219–349 d, one-bedroom suites $269–559, two-bedroom suites $518–899) provides a lush, intimate setting with 11 guest rooms and suites. The grounds have been transformed into a beautiful botanic garden, offering a serene setting to relax and replenish. Guests can pamper themselves by tanning on one of the largest private beaches in Key Largo, swimming in the beachside pool, or napping in one of the shaded hammocks. The property also features an elegant art gallery.

To take advantage of the self-proclaimed "diving capital of the world," head to the **Mariner's Resort Villas & Marina** (97501 Overseas Hwy., 305/853-1111 or 305/853-5000, www.keycaribbean.com, $200–350 d), which, as the name indicates, features direct access to a beautiful marina. Luxury town homes and villas offer a quiet escape in this gated resort. The grounds also promise plenty of adventure, with two freshwater pools—one of which is supposedly the largest pool in the Keys.

Perhaps one of the Hilton chain's prettiest properties is the **Key Largo Grande Resort & Beach Club** (97000 Overseas Hwy., 305/852-5553 or 888/871-3437, www.keylargoresort.com, $160–300 d), hidden away on 13 acres of lush forestland. Boasting all of the expected amenities of any complete resort, the Key Largo Grande equally suits family vacations, with its impressive lineup of water sports, as well as romantic getaways, given the solitude offered by its sumptuous grounds. The rooms and suites all feature queen-sized or king-sized beds, cable television, free wireless Internet access, and private balconies with either bayside or forest views. Other on-site amenities include a beachside watering hole, a swimming pool and adjacent bar, and the Treetops Bar & Grill (7 A.M.–10 P.M. daily), which offers panoramic views of Florida Bay.

For an intimate island-style boutique hotel, try the **Dove Creek Lodge** (147 Seaside Ave., 305/852-6200 or 800/401-0057, www.dovecreeklodge.com, $175–325 d), where you'll find one-bedroom and two-bedroom suites, with small refrigerators, cable television, free wireless Internet access, and lockers to store your fishing, boating, or diving equipment. The two luxury suites each have a well-equipped kitchen, a separate dining area, and two full bathrooms, and the deluxe one also features a full-sized pool table.

CAMPING

Key Largo offers several budget-friendly campgrounds, ideal for families and outdoor enthusiasts. Near the northern end of Key Largo, **John Pennekamp Coral Reef State Park** (102601 Overseas Hwy., 305/451-1202, www.floridastateparks.org/pennekamp or www.pennekamppark.com, 8 A.M.–sunset daily, $8 vehicles w/2–8 passengers plus $0.50 pp, $4.50 motorcycles and single-occupant vehicles, $2.50

pedestrians, bikers, and extra passengers) offers a full-facility campground for RVs and tents ($36 daily), with access to modern restrooms and hot showers. While the campground isn't as stunning as other state park campgrounds in the Florida Keys, it's a terrific home base for park activities, from sunbathing to snorkeling. Extensive renovations, which are scheduled to be completed by April 2011, will likely improve its facilities, though be advised that the campground will, as a consequence, be closed between August 2010 through March 2011. For reservations, contact **ReserveAmerica** (800/326-3521, www.reserveamerica.com) up to 11 months in advance.

Located on 40 acres alongside the Atlantic Ocean, the **Key Largo Kampground & Marina** (101551 Overseas Hwy., 305/451-1431 or 800/526-7688, www.keylargokampground.com, $35–75 daily, $220–470 weekly) presents a variety of campsites, from tent sites with no hookups to waterfront, full-hookup sites ideal for RVs. Amenities include laundry facilities, a general store for limited grocery needs, and a dock that offers boat owners easy access to the Atlantic Ocean.

The **Calusa Campground Resort and Marina** (325 Calusa St., 305/451-0232, www.calusacampground.com, $55–95 daily, $343–592 weekly, $1,320–2,280 monthly) features a relaxing pool, direct access to the marina, and three types of RV sites: inland, canal, and bayfront. The **Riptide R/V Park & Motel** (97680 Overseas Hwy., 305/852-8481, www.riptidervparkfloridakeys.com, $39–69 daily, $250–379 weekly, $450–900 monthly) offers over 30 palm-shaded sites with oceanfront views. Additional amenities include a beach pavilion, a shuffleboard area, a boat dock and launching ramp ($10 daily, $75 monthly), and a small motel. Pets are welcome for a one-time fee of $25.

Food

SEAFOOD

Considering Key Largo's allure for anglers and other water lovers, it surely comes as no surprise that seafood restaurants abound on this island. One such place is **Alabama Jack's** (58000 Card Sound Rd., 305/248-8741, www.alabamajacks.com, 11 A.M.–7 P.M. daily, $8–24), a family-owned eatery since 1947—the motto of which, "anything goes," could apply to the food as well as the country-western dancing on the weekends. Given the waterfront access, you can dock your boat and be eating in no time at all, and while the place doesn't have a complex menu, what the cooks do, they do well. The conch fritters, for instance, have been voted among the best in the Keys.

Just past the junction of U.S. 1 and C.R. 905, **The Buzzard's Roost Grill and Pub** (21 Garden Cove Dr., 305/453-3746, www.buzzardsroostkeylargo.com, 11 A.M.–9 P.M. Mon.–Thurs., 11 A.M.–10 P.M. Fri.–Sat., 10:30 A.M.–9 P.M. Sun., $9–30) offers an extensive menu, including many hook-and-cook options. Provided you catch a fish at its legal size and in its proper season, then clean and fillet it yourself, the staff will prepare it for you, whether you prefer your fish fried, grilled, or jerked.

On U.S. 1 is **Sundowners on the Bay** (103900 Overseas Hwy., 305/451-4502, www.sundownerskeylargo.com, 10 A.M.–10 P.M. daily, $14–36), one of the finest places to watch a sunset in the Upper Keys. Specializing in sandwiches, steaks, and, of course, seafood, Sundowners features many local favorites, including the island-style fish, poached in coconut milk with basil, chilies, garlic, and fresh ginger.

The Fish House Restaurant & Seafood Market (102401 Overseas Hwy., 305/451-4665, www.fishhouse.com, 11:30 A.M.–10 P.M. daily, $9–28) presents a relaxed atmosphere

the pet-friendly Key Largo Conch House

© DANIEL MARTONE

and specializes in yellowtail snapper, mahimahi, and other fresh local seafood. After sampling the smoked fish or homemade chowders at the Fish House for lunch, consider planning your dinner at **The Fish House Encore Restaurant, Sushi Bar & Piano Lounge** (102341 Overseas Hwy., 305/451-0650, www.fishhouse.com, 5–10 P.M. daily, $11–33), a fine-dining eatery that features seafood, steaks, pasta dishes, a raw bar, plus expertly prepared sushi—and, as with most Florida Keys restaurants, tangy key lime pie. Here, reservations are accepted—and recommended.

Whether it's for breakfast, lunch, or dinner, the airy, pet-friendly **【 Key Largo Conch House** (100211 Overseas Hwy., 305/453-4844, www.keylargocoffeehouse.com, 7 A.M.–10 P.M. daily, $9–30) offers an amazing menu in a lovely wooded setting. Try the cracked conch Benedict for breakfast, the fish tacos for lunch, or the mahi key lime almandine for dinner. Additional specialties include the conch chowder, conch fritters, and the lobster and conch ceviche. If the weather is pleasant, dine on the porch or relax in the courtyard, which is surprisingly pleasurable despite the eatery's proximity to busy U.S. 1. Feel free, too, to take advantage of the free wireless Internet access while you eat.

You can dine beside a lovely marina at the **【 Coconuts Restaurant and Night Club** (528 Caribbean Dr., 305/453-9794, www.coconutsrestaurant.com, 11 A.M.–2 A.M. daily, $8–27). Although the building admittedly looks unimpressive from the parking lot, it's the covered waterfront patio that's truly worth experiencing—for lunch as well as for dinner, especially when the outdoor temperature is mild. Besides tasty Keys standards like coconut shrimp and conch fingers, you'll find more curious fare, such as the stuffed artichoke hearts, fresh ahi tuna sashimi, and yellowtail Largo. While here, treat yourself to one of Coconuts' excellent mojitos or a slice of delicious key lime pie. Then, once your food has settled, stroll into the nightclub, where you can watch sporting events, listen to live musical performances, or perhaps even dance the night away.

If you appreciate a lovely view as much as good food, head to the **【 Bayside Grille** (99530 Overseas Hwy., 305/451-3380, www.keylargo-baysidegrill.com, 11:30 A.M.–10 P.M. daily, $8–28), the epitome of waterfront dining on Key Largo. Situated at Sunset Cove on Florida Bay, this family-owned eatery is an ideal spot to watch drifting sailboats, swaying palm trees, and incredible sunsets, and the fresh cuisine is exceptionally delicious. Lunchtime offerings include blackened mahimahi, coconut shrimp baskets, fried oyster baskets, and non-seafood dishes like maple-glazed meatloaf. The dinner menu is a bit more extensive, with everything from conch fritters to seafood enchiladas to filet mignon. The place prides itself on more than just fresh seafood, though—everything here is made on the premises daily, from the tuna salad to the grilled pineapple salsa. To enhance your experience, order a refreshing cocktail like Martha's Bayside Blue Margarita or Jim's Orange Blossom Mojito and watch the sun sink into the bay.

【 Mrs. Mac's Kitchen (99336 Overseas Hwy., 305/451-3722, www.mrsmacskitchen.com, 7 A.M.–9:30 P.M. Mon.–Sat., $8–27) is an extremely popular and often crowded joint, filled with as many locals as tourists. If you're looking for a meal like Mom used to make—especially if Mom was a gourmet chef—then look no farther than this casual eatery. Featuring plenty of Keys favorites, the extensive menu includes everything from "Konk" chowder to relleno-style hogfish. The decor is a winner, too. Making use of the entire space, inside and out, Mrs. Mac's feels like a kid's clubhouse, with beer bottles along the rafters, license plates all over the walls and ceiling, overhead lamps cleverly fashioned from similar license plates, and small aluminum-can planes hanging everywhere.

Nestled on the median, **Ballyhoo's Historic Seafood Grille** (97800 Overseas Hwy., 305/852-0822, www.ballyhoosrestaurant.com, 11 A.M.–10 P.M. daily, $8–33) sits in a lovingly preserved Conch-style structure that started as a fishing camp and now serves an array of seafood, steaks, and sandwiches. Try

© DANIEL MARTONE

the whimsical interior of Mrs. Mac's Kitchen

the Bimini stuffed shrimp, the Caribbean pan-fried scallops, fresh fish prepared in any number of interesting ways, and, when in season, all-you-can-eat stone crabs.

Following its opening in 1989, **Snapper's Waterfront Restaurant** (139 Seaside Ave., 305/852-5956, www.snapperskeylargo.com, 11 A.M.–10 P.M. Mon.–Thurs., 11 A.M.–11 P.M. Fri.–Sat., 10 A.M.–10 P.M. Sun., $12–25) quickly became one of Key Largo's busiest eateries—not to mention a hot spot for live nighttime entertainment. For a truly unique dish, try the key lime lobster or the Thai seared tuna.

AMERICAN AND EUROPEAN

While **Rib Daddy's Steak & Seafood** (102570 Overseas Hwy., 305/451-0900, www.ribdaddysrestaurant.com, 11 A.M.–9 P.M. Sun.–Thurs., 11 A.M.–10 P.M. Fri.–Sat., $16–35) provides standard Keys dishes and plenty of fresh fish, it's the barbecue that sets it apart from other area restaurants. For a taste of Memphis, head for the big yellow chuck wagon (a hard-to-miss landmark out front) and order a plate of baby back ribs.

The **Tower of Pizza** (100600 Overseas Hwy., 305/451-1461 or 305/451-3754, 11 A.M.–11 P.M. daily, $10–19) has never closed down, not even for a hurricane. In addition to excellent pizza, this eat-in, take-out, and delivery joint offers other Italian fare, from minestrone to veal parmesan. Of course, if you don't feel like dining out, simply have a large pepperoni pizza and, to appease the diet, a Caesar salad delivered to your hotel.

Bogie's Café (99701 Overseas Hwy., 305/451-2121, www.holidayinnkeylargo.com/restaurants.html, 7 A.M.–9 P.M. daily, $8–16) is part of the Holiday Inn complex and just steps from the historic *African Queen*. You can enjoy the American and continental-style dishes inside or in the garden patio, and the entire menu is also available at the nearby tiki bar (11 A.M.–9 P.M. daily).

The family-run **Doc's Diner** (99696 Overseas Hwy., 305/451-2895, www.docsdinerkeylargo.com, 6 A.M.–2 P.M. daily, $4–9) is a local favorite for breakfast and lunch. If you're here with your family, try Doc's Feast, which offers a huge assortment of the joint's most popular breakfast foods, including a dozen scrambled eggs. For a casual meal, stop by the 1950s-style **DJ's Diner** (99411 Overseas Hwy., 305/451-2999, 7 A.M.–9 P.M. Mon.–Fri.,

7 A.M.–3 P.M. Sat.–Sun., $6–14). Sample a burger or the meatloaf dinner while gazing at celebrity photos on the walls.

For a taste of Europe, stop by **Café Largo** (99530 Overseas Hwy., 305/451-4885, www.keylargo-cafelargo.com, 11 A.M.–10 P.M. daily, $8–24), which serves a fantastic assortment of Italian dishes, from traditional fare like littleneck clams and linguini to Conch-style items such as the yellowtail snapper. This family-run restaurant, established in 1992, also offers basic pizzas and subs for those in a hurry.

ASIAN AND LATIN AMERICAN

Two cuisines are better than one at the **Num Thai Restaurant & Sushi Bar** (103200 Overseas Hwy., 305/451-5955, 11 A.M.–9 P.M. daily, $8–16), where you can sample a spicy tuna roll or some excellent pad thai all in the same night. Of course, if you're in the mood for some killer Mexican food, head to **Señor**

Frijoles (103900 Overseas Hwy., 305/451-1592, www.senorfrijolesrestaurant.com, 11 A.M.–10 P.M. daily, $6–18), which has been serving delicious Mexican food and fantastic margaritas since 1979. One local favorite is the steak fajita burrito, served wet with grilled skirt steak, pico de gallo, frijoles, and a tasty chipotle sour cream—all wrapped in a large tortilla, topped with ranchero sauce, and covered with Monterey jack and cheddar cheese. Wednesday night features all-you-can-eat tacos for only $9.

The **Su Casa Restaurante Cubano** (99246 Overseas Hwy., 305/453-0939, 7 A.M.–10 P.M. daily, $4–14) serves large portions of authentic Cuban food for a reasonable price. Open for breakfast, lunch, and dinner, Su Casa also features live music every night. Try the delicious pork chop dinner with plantains, black beans, and rice, and finish off your meal with a homemade flan.

Information and Services

INFORMATION

For brochures, maps, and other information about Key Largo, stop by the **Key Largo Chamber of Commerce and Florida Keys Visitor Center** (106000 Overseas Hwy., 305/451-4747 or 800/822-1088, www.keylargo.org or www.keylargochamber.org, 9 A.M.–6 P.M. daily), a two-story yellow building on the bay side of U.S. 1, near mile marker 106—inside of which you'll spy an 18th-century British cannon, one of several found in an offshore patch reef. You can also consult the **Monroe County Tourist Development Council** (1201 White St., Ste. 102, Key West, 305/296-1552 or 800/352-5397, www.fla-keys.com, 9 A.M.–5 P.M. Mon.–Fri.) for questions about Key Largo and the rest of the Florida Keys. For government-related issues, contact the **Monroe County offices** (1100 Simonton St., Key West, 305/294-4641, www.monroecounty-fl.gov, 8 A.M.–5 P.M. Mon.–Fri.).

For local news, consult *The Reporter* (www.keysnet.com), the *Upper Keys Free Press* (www.keysnews.com), and *The Weekly Newspapers* (www.keysweekly.com). The daily *Miami Herald* (www.miamiherald.com), the daily *Key West Citizen* (www.keysnews.com), and the biweekly *Florida Keys Keynoter* (www.keysnet.com) are additionally available throughout the Keys.

In Key Largo, you'll also have access to several radio stations, including **Thunder Country** (WCTH-FM 100.3, www.thundercountry.com) and the **SUN** (WFKZ-FM 103.1, www.sun103.com) for classic rock. For other stations, visit www.keysradio.com.

SERVICES

Given its large size, Key Largo offers plenty of necessary services for residents and travelers alike.

Money

For banking needs, stop by the **TIB Bank** (103330 Overseas Hwy., 305/451-2000

Stop by the Key Largo visitor center for maps and brochures.

or 800/233-6330, www.tibbank.com, 9 A.M.–4 P.M. Mon.–Thurs., 9 A.M.–6 P.M. Fri., extended drive-through hours) and the **First State Bank of the Florida Keys** (97670 Overseas Hwy., 305/852-2070, www.keysbank. com, 9 A.M.–4 P.M. Mon.–Thurs., 9 A.M.–6 P.M. Fri., extended drive-through hours), which offers foreign currency exchange.

Mail

For shipping, faxing, copying, and other business-related services, visit **The UPS Store** (99611 Overseas Hwy., 305/453-4877, www. theupsstore.com, 8 A.M.–6 P.M. Mon.–Fri., 9 A.M.–3 P.M. Sat.). You'll also find two **post offices** (800/275-8777, www.usps.com) in the area: one in Key Largo (100100 Overseas Hwy., 305/451-3155, 8 A.M.–4:30 P.M. Mon.–Fri., 10 A.M.–1 P.M. Sat.) and one in Tavernier (91220 Overseas Hwy., 305/853-1052, 9 A.M.–4:30 P.M. Mon.–Fri.).

Groceries and Supplies

If you require groceries and other supplies, head to **Winn-Dixie** (105300 Overseas Hwy., 305/451-0328, www.winndixie.com, 7 A.M.–10 P.M. daily), which houses an on-site

pharmacy (305/451-3591, 8 A.M.–8 P.M. Mon.–Fri., 9 A.M.–6 P.M. Sat., 10 A.M.–5 P.M. Sun.).

In the Tradewinds Shopping Center, you'll spot a **Publix** (101437 Overseas Hwy., 305/451-0808, www.publix.com, 7 A.M.–10 P.M. daily), which, in addition to groceries and other services, includes an on-site pharmacy (305/451-5338, 9 A.M.–9 P.M. Mon.–Fri., 9 A.M.–7 P.M. Sat., 10 A.M.–5 P.M. Sun.). **Walgreens** (99501 Overseas Hwy., 305/451-4385, www.walgreens. com, 7 A.M.–10 P.M. daily) offers a pharmacy drive-through (9 A.M.–5 P.M. daily) as well as a full liquor department.

Laundry

If you need to clean some clothes during your trip, you'll find several coin-operated laundromats in the area, including the **Waldorf Plaza Coin Laundry** (MM 100 OS U.S. 1, 305/451-4575, 7:30 A.M.–9 P.M. Sun.–Fri., 7:30 A.M.–8 P.M. Sat.).

Internet Access

For Internet access, head to the **Key Largo Conch House** (100211 Overseas Hwy., 305/453-4844, www.keylargocoffeehouse. com, 7 A.M.–10 P.M. daily), which offers free wireless Internet access with the purchase of a meal. **Snapper's Waterfront Restaurant** (MM 94.5 OS U.S. 1, 305/852-5956, www. snapperskeylargo.com, 11 A.M.–10 P.M. Mon.–Thurs., 11 A.M.–11 P.M. Fri.–Sat., 10 A.M.–10 P.M. Sun.) provides free wireless Internet access throughout the entire property.

You'll also find useful services at the **Key Largo Branch Library** (101485 Overseas Hwy., 305/451-2396, www.keyslibraries. org, 9:30 A.M.–6 P.M. Tues. and Thurs.–Fri., 9:30 A.M.–8 P.M. Wed., 10 A.M.–6 P.M. Sat.) in the Tradewinds Shopping Center.

Emergency Services
In case of an emergency that requires police, fire, or ambulance services, dial **911** from any cell or public phone. Even in less critical situations, you can consult the **Key Largo Volunteer Fire-Rescue Department** (305/451-2700, www. keylargofire.com), which operates two fire stations at mile markers 99 and 106. For nonemergency assistance, contact the **Monroe County Sheriff's Office** (Roth Bldg., 50 High Point Rd., Ste. 100, Tavernier, 305/853-3211, www. keysso.net, 8 A.M.–5 P.M. Mon.–Fri.).

For medical assistance, consult the **Mariners Hospital** (91500 Overseas Hwy., Tavernier, 305/434-3000, www.baptisthealth.net). Foreign visitors—seeking help with directions, medical concerns, business issues, law enforcement needs, or other problems—can receive **multilingual tourist assistance** (800/771-5397) 24 hours daily.

Getting There and Around

GETTING THERE
By Air
Despite the presence of a private airport at the **Ocean Reef Club** (35 Ocean Reef Dr., 305/367-2611, www.oceanreef.com), Key Largo has no major airport of its own. To travel here by plane, you'll need to fly into the **Fort Lauderdale-Hollywood International Airport (FLL)** (320 Terminal Dr., Fort Lauderdale, 866/435-9355, www.broward. org/airport), the **Miami International Airport (MIA)** (4200 NW 21st St., Miami, 305/876-7000 or 800/825-5642, www.miami-airport. com), the **Key West International Airport (EYW)** (3491 S. Roosevelt Blvd., Key West, 305/809-5200 or 305/296-5439, www.key-westinternationalairport.com), or the **Florida Keys Marathon Airport (MTH)** (9400 Overseas Hwy., Marathon, 305/289-6060). From there, you can rent a vehicle from agencies like **Avis** (800/331-1212, www.avis.com), **Budget** (800/527-0700, www.budget.com), **Enterprise** (800/325-8007, www.enterprise. com), **Hertz** (800/654-3131, www.hertz.com), or **Thrifty** (800/367-2277, www.thrifty.com) in order to reach Key Largo.

By Bus or Train
The **Miami-Dade County Metrobus** (305/891-3131, www.miamidade.gov/transit) operates the **301 Dade-Monroe Express** between Florida City and Marathon (5:15 A.M.–8:40 P.M. daily, $2.35 per one-way trip), with stops in Key Largo and Tavernier until 10:55 P.M. and 11:10 P.M., respectively. In addition, **Greyhound** (800/231-2222, www.greyhound.com) offers limited bus service to Key Largo. **Amtrak** (800/872-7245, www.amtrak.com), however, provides train service only as far south as Miami. Of course, you can always rent a car or hop a shuttle to reach the Florida Keys.

Transport from Airports and Stations
If you arrive in the Fort Lauderdale–Miami area via plane, bus, or train—or Key West via plane or bus—you can either rent a car or hire a shuttle service to reach Key Largo. Some of these companies include **Keys Shuttle** (305/289-9997 or 888/765-9997, www.keysshuttle.com, $60–70 per shared ride, $275–325 for exclusive service) and **Keys Tropical Transportation** (305/852-3595, www.keystropicaltransportation.com,

KEY LARGO

starting at $130 or $165 per ride, depending on the airport of origin), both of which provide service from the Miami and Fort Lauderdale airports; **SuperShuttle** (305/871-2000 or 954/764-1700, www.supershuttle.com, $102 pp, $165 per group of four or more), which only serves visitors flying into Miami; and **TO'n'FRO** (305/852-4514, www.tonfro.com, $55–65 per shared van ride, $160–180 per luxury sedan ride), a personalized van and car service that offers transportation between the airports in Fort Lauderdale, Miami, and Key West and any destination in the Keys.

By Car

To reach Key Largo from Miami, simply head south on U.S. 1 (Overseas Hwy.) and continue through Key Largo to your destination. If you're headed from the Everglades via I-75 (Everglades Pkwy.), drive south on U.S. 27, veer right onto S.R. 997 (Krome Ave.), and follow the signs to U.S. 1. From U.S. 41 (Tamiami Trail) in the Everglades, head south on S.R. 997 and continue toward U.S. 1. If you arrive during the peak season (Dec.–Apr.), be sure to call **511** for an up-to-the-minute traffic report.

GETTING AROUND
By Car

The best way to travel through Key Largo is via car, truck, RV, or motorcycle—all of which offer easy access to U.S. 1 and other roads, such as C.R. 905, which traverses the northern part of Key Largo, where you'll find the Dagny Johnson Key Largo Hammock Botanical State Park and the exclusive Ocean Reef Club.

By Van Service

If, while staying in Key Largo, you have a sudden desire to head to Key West for the evening—and would rather leave your vehicle at the hotel, resort, or campground where you're staying—consider boarding **Sea the Keys** (305/896-7013, www.keywestdaytrip.com, rates vary), a passenger van service that will pick you up from your hotel in the Upper Keys and drop you off in Key West around 11 A.M. While down there, you'll be free to explore

any number of restaurants, bars, museums, and other attractions, before making the return trip around 9 P.M.

By Taxi

Taxicab companies such as **Key Largo Cabs** (305/451-9700, $7 per pickup, $2.50 per mile) and **Mom's Taxi** (305/852-6000, $7 per pickup, $2.50 per mile) can help you get around Key Largo and Tavernier.

By Bike or Boat

While you can certainly traverse Key Largo via bicycle, the sprawling nature of this region makes it challenging for novice riders. Nevertheless, it's a lovely, ecofriendly way to experience the northernmost island, and there's even a 15.5-mile bike path that runs past numerous businesses and parks between mile markers 106.5 and 91. Bikes can be rented from places like **Key Largo Resorts Boat & Bike Rental** (Key Largo Resorts Marina, MM 100 OS U.S. 1, 305/451-2241, 8 A.M.–5 P.M. daily, $5 hourly, $10 per half day, $15 daily) beside the Ramada Limited Key Largo. Baskets, locks, helmets, and touring maps are included with all rentals.

Of course, you can also experience Key Largo via boat. Having your own vessel might make navigating these waters a bit easier, and you'll find no shortage of boat ramps and marina slips in Key Largo. If you'd rather rent a boat, contact **Key Largo Resorts Boat & Bike Rental** (Key Largo Resorts Marina, MM 100 OS U.S. 1, 305/451-2241, 8 A.M.–5 P.M. daily), which offers three different boat styles: 19-foot ($140 per half day, $175 daily), 20-foot ($140 per half day, $175 daily), and 21-foot ($225 daily). Other boat rental companies include **Dive In Watersports** (Mandalay Marina, 80 E. 2nd St., 305/852-1919, www.divein-watersports.com, 8 A.M.–5 P.M. daily, $125–225 per two hours, $150–300 per half day, $185–385 daily, depending on vessel type), which provides a variety of powerboats, WaveRunners, and kayaks, and **Bay & Reef Pontunes** (MM 107.9 BS U.S. 1, 305/393-5593, www.pontunes.com, rates vary), which offers an assortment of vessels, from fishing boats to luxury pontoons.

ISLAMORADA

South of Key Largo, most of the remaining Upper Keys have become part of Islamorada (pronounced *eye-lah-more-AH-dah*), an incorporated town long celebrated for its bountiful sportfishing opportunities. Its name—derived from the Spanish phrase *islas moradas,* which means "purple islands," as termed by European explorers centuries ago—might refer, depending on the resident you ask, to the region's incredible violet-tinted sunsets or the brilliant flowers that blossom here or even the purplish snail shells that once peppered the shores of these islands.

Regardless of its origins, however, this "Village of Islands," allegedly the oldest inhabited place in the Florida Keys, includes several keys that are accessible via the Overseas Highway—namely, Plantation Key (which includes part of the Tavernier community), Windley Key, Upper Matecumbe Key, and Lower Matecumbe Key—plus two state-park islands only reachable by boat. If you have the time, in fact, you should definitely venture to these two remote locales: the Indian Key Historic State Park, site of a former 19th-century settlement, and the Lignumvitae Key Botanical State Park, home to a virgin tropical hardwood hammock.

Islamorada, one of the wealthier areas in the Florida Keys, boasts several high-end art galleries, boutiques, and full-service spas as well as sophisticated restaurants and resorts, but it's the sportfishing that lures most people. The clear, warm waters around Islamorada—the self-proclaimed "sportfishing capital of the world"—teem with tarpon, trout, redfish,

© DANIEL MARTONE

ISLAMORADA

HIGHLIGHTS

◖ Theater of the Sea: Established in 1946, the world's second oldest marine mammal facility invites visitors to view birds, alligators, sea turtles, and other marine creatures, swim with dolphins and sea lions, watch them frolic and paint, and even take a snorkeling cruise to an offshore coral reef (page 120).

◖ History of Diving Museum: Sea lovers will appreciate this curious collection of diving paraphernalia, which includes fantastic diving machines, old-fashioned scuba tanks, hand-cranked air pumps, underwater cameras, and diving helmets from around the world, plus valuable treasures and historic artifacts recovered from the ocean (page 122).

◖ Indian Key Historic State Park: Once the site of a lucrative shipwreck-salvaging business and only accessible via canoe, kayak, or boat, this lovely offshore island lures hikers, swimmers, sunbathers, bird-watchers, snorkelers, scuba divers, and anglers alike (page 125).

◖ Lignumvitae Key Botanical State Park: Located on the bay side of Islamorada and only accessible via boat, canoe, or kayak, this wooded offshore island, once home to a

wealthy Miami chemist, features the kind of virgin tropical hardwood hammock that formerly thrived in the Upper Keys (page 127).

◖ Fishing and Boating near Islamorada: The self-proclaimed "sportfishing capital of the world" boasts several full-service marinas and an enormity of fishing charters, independent fishing guides, and boat rentals, ideal for those who hope to search the bountiful backcountry and offshore waters of the Upper Keys (page 132).

◖ Kayaking Around Islamorada: Besides being popular with anglers from around the world, Islamorada also offers a wealth of opportunities for kayakers, who can either rent kayaks or opt for a guided kayaking excursion amid backcountry waters and offshore islands (page 136).

◖ Spas and Yoga in Islamorada: Filled with upscale accommodations and restaurants, the Village of Islands also provides other pampering places, such as several rejuvenating spas, where you can enjoy refreshing facials, body treatments, massages, and, sometimes, beachside yoga lessons (page 137).

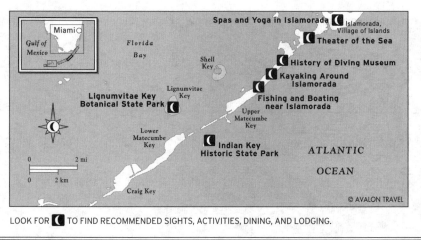

LOOK FOR ◖ TO FIND RECOMMENDED SIGHTS, ACTIVITIES, DINING, AND LODGING.

snapper, sailfish, and other worthy species. It's a snap to rent a boat, hire a fishing guide, or charter a full crew—if you so desire.

Of course, if fishing is not your preference, you'll find several other distractions in the area, including a geological state park on Windley Key that was once linked to Henry Flagler's ill-fated Overseas Railroad. In addition, you can watch entertaining dolphins and sea lions at a year-round marine-mammal center; peruse one of the world's largest collections of diving helmets and artifacts; feed wild tarpon at Robbie's of Islamorada; and explore an underwater archaeological state park, which preserves the wreck of a Spanish treasure-fleet ship that sank here nearly three centuries ago.

HISTORY

Despite the commonly heard claim that Islamorada is the oldest inhabited place in the Florida Keys, it's difficult to know the exact origins of the community that now thrives here. As with the rest of the Florida Keys, the four livable islands, two remote state parks, and one private key that compose this "Village of Islands"—Plantation Key, Windley Key, Upper Matecumbe Key, Lower Matecumbe Key, Indian Key, Lignumvitae Key, and Teatable Key—were likely frequented by the Calusa and Tequesta Indians, as well as other Native American tribes, long before Europeans, Floridians, and other Americans encountered them.

Nevertheless, local historians believe that the earliest community in the Upper Keys existed on Indian Key—which the Spanish originally termed Cayuelo de Matanza (Small Slaughter Key) during the salvage operations of the *San Pedro,* a Spanish ship that wrecked during a 1733 hurricane and now forms the basis of an archaeological state park. In 1836, Indian Key became the first county seat of Dade County. At that time, this diminutive island, which lies on the ocean side of the Overseas Highway, was also the site of John Jacob Housman's lucrative cargo-salvaging business—that is, until 1840, when, during the Second Seminole War, Seminole Indians invaded the island, plundered

the buildings, and allegedly killed several settlers, despite the presence of Fort Paulding on nearby Teatable Key. Today, Indian Key is a historic state park, while Teatable has become a private residence.

The other islands that compose Islamorada have equally curious histories. Once the site of a large Indian mound, Plantation Key has had many names over the years, from Bull Island to Long Island to Vermont Key, and in 1935, it was home to a large coral rock quarry operated by World War I veterans. Windley Key, to the south, was also once the site of a rock quarry enterprise. Formerly two islands, known as the Umbrella Keys, Windley Key became one island in the early 20th century, when workers for Henry Flagler's ill-fated Overseas Railroad filled in the space between the two keys. At that time, there were three separate quarries in operation on Windley Key, the fossilized coral from which was used to build the railroad. Today, the former quarry complex has become a geological state park, one that explores the island's critical role in the Overseas Railroad, which was effectively destroyed by the Labor Day hurricane of 1935.

According to historical documents, Upper Matecumbe Key and Lower Matecumbe Key were both settled in the late 1800s. It wasn't until 1907, however, that the name "Islamorada" reemerged. Although it's actually a Spanish term, meaning "purple islands" and attributed by early explorers, William Krome was the first to use it in an official capacity, when he planned a subdivision on Upper Matecumbe Key called the "Townsite of Islamorada." Soon, the moniker spread, inspiring the name of the railroad depot and, in 1908, the Islamorada Post Office. Islamorada was eventually incorporated on December 31, 1997, as "Islamorada, Village of Islands." Today, with a population of more than 7,030, it includes all of the aforementioned keys— even Lignumvitae Key, the wooded offshore island on the bay side of U.S. 1. Once known as Jenkinson Island, Lignumvitae (which means "tree of life") has been home to various individuals since at least the 1830s, including William

ISLAMORADA

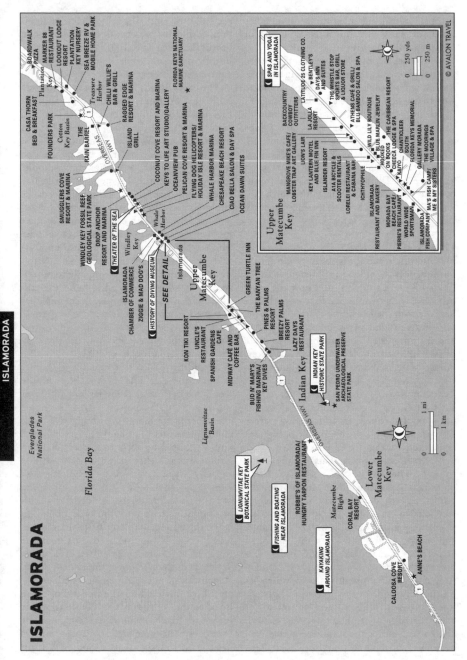

ISLAMORADA

Everglades
National Park

Florida Bay

Lignumvitae
Basin

BOARDWALK
PIZZA
MARKER 88
RESTAURANT
LOOKOUT LODGE
RESORT
PLANTATION
KEY NURSERY
SEA BREEZE RV &
MOBILE HOME PARK
Plantation
Key
CASA THORN
BED & BREAKFAST
FOUNDERS PARK
Treasure
Harbor
CHILI WILLIE'S
BAR & GRILL
RAGGED EDGE
RESORT & MARINA
Cotton
Key Basin
THE
RAIN BARREL
ISLAND
GRILL
COCONUT COVE RESORT AND MARINA
KEYS TO LIFE ART STUDIO/GALLERY
FLORIDA KEYS NATIONAL
MARINE SANCTUARY
OCEANVIEW PUB
PELICAN COVE RESORT & MARINA
FLYING DOG HELICOPTERS/
HOLIDAY ISLE RESORT & MARINA
WHALE HARBOR MARINA
CHESAPEAKE BEACH RESORT
CIAO BELLA SALON & DAY SPA
OCEAN DAWN SUITES

SMUGGLERS COVE
RESORT & MARINA
WINDLEY KEY FOSSIL REEF
GEOLOGICAL STATE PARK
DROP ANCHOR
RESORT AND MARINA
THEATER OF THE SEA
Windley
Key
Whale
Harbor

ISLAMORADA
CHAMBER OF COMMERCE
ZIGGIE & MAD DOG'S
HISTORY OF DIVING MUSEUM
Islamorada
SEE DETAIL
Upper
Matecumbe
Key

GREEN TURTLE INN
THE BANYAN TREE
PINES & PALMS
RESORT
BREEZY PALMS
RESORT
LAZY DAYS
RESTAURANT

KON TIKI RESORT
UNCLE'S
RESTAURANT
SPANISH GARDENS
CAFE
MIDWAY CAFÉ AND
COFFEE BAR
BUD N' MARY'S
FISHING MARINA/
KEY DIVES

INDIAN KEY
HISTORIC STATE PARK
Indian Key
SAN PEDRO UNDERWATER
ARCHAEOLOGICAL PRESERVE
STATE PARK

LIGNUMVITAE KEY
BOTANICAL STATE PARK

FISHING AND BOATING
NEAR ISLAMORADA

ROBBIE'S OF ISLAMORADA/
HUNGRY TARPON RESTAURANT

Lower
Matecumbe
Key

Matecumbe
Bight

KAYAKING
AROUND ISLAMORADA

CORAL BAY
RESORT

ANNE'S BEACH

CALOOSA COVE RESORT

0   1 mi
0   1 km

Upper Matecumbe Key (detail)

SPAS AND YOGA
IN ISLAMORADA

BACKCOUNTRY
COWBOY
OUTFITTERS
LATITUDE 25 CLOTHING CO.
BENTLEY'S
DAYS INN
AND SUITES
THE WHISTLE STOP
SPORTS BAR, GRILL
& LIQUOR STORE
LA JOLLA
RESORT
ATHENS CAFE & GRILL/
BLU BAMBOO SALON & SPA

MANGROVE MIKE'S CAFE/
LOBSTER TRAP ART GALLERY
LION'S LAIR
KEY LANTERN MOTEL
AND BLUE FIN INN
ISLANDER RESORT
A1A BICYCLE &
SCOOTER RENTALS
LORELEI RESTAURANT
& CABANA BAR
ICHTHYOPHILE
ISLAMORADA
RESTAURANT AND BAKERY
MORADA BAY
BEACH CAFE
PIERRE'S RESTAURANT
WORLD WIDE
SPORTSMAN
ISLAMORADA
FISH COMPANY

WILD LILY BOUTIQUE
BLUE MARLIN JEWELRY
HOOKED
ON BOOKS
KAIYO
GALLERY MORADA
FLORIDA KEYS MEMORIAL
THE CARIBBEAN RESORT
CHEECA LODGE & SPA
CHANTICLEER
SOUTH
THE MOORINGS
VILLAGE & SPA
MA'S FISH CAMP/
ME & MY SISTERS

Upper
Matecumbe
Key

0   250 yds
0   250 m

© AVALON TRAVEL

J. Matheson, a wealthy Miami chemist who bought the island in 1919 and whose former hideaway is now the visitor center within a botanical state park. For more information about Islamorada's past, consult the **Historical Preservation Society of the Upper Keys** (www.keyshistory.org).

PLANNING YOUR TIME

Though Islamorada comprises several islands between mile markers 91 and 72, with attractions and resorts stretching from Plantation Key to Lower Matecumbe Key, it's fairly simple—as with the rest of the Florida Keys—to navigate this area by car, via the Overseas Highway. In fact, the only main attractions that will require a boat ride are the underwater coral reefs and the two island state parks: Indian Key and Lignumvitae Key.

In Islamorada, you'll find a wide range of diversions, from marine mammal shows to day spas to a diving museum, so you could conceivably spend a few days here—even longer if you plan to hire a fishing charter or visit the offshore state parks. As with other parts of the Keys, you may encounter traffic congestion, crowded restaurants and attractions, and higher lodging rates during the peak tourist season—from December to April—so plan accordingly.

When scheduling a trip to Islamorada, you might also want to consider factors like annual events, fishing seasons, and climate. For instance, while the hot, humid summer months can be less popular among tourists, those who favor snorkeling and scuba diving might appreciate the warmer waters. No matter when you visit, however, it's important to understand the risks of outdoor activities like kayaking and scuba diving, which can be dangerous without proper instruction and preparation.

For more information about Islamorada, consult the **Monroe County Tourist Development Council** (1201 White St., Ste. 102, Key West, FL 33040, 305/296-1552 or 800/352-5397, www.fla-keys.com) and the **Islamorada Chamber of Commerce** (P.O. Box 915, Islamorada, FL 33036, 305/664-4503 or 800/322-5397, www.islamorada-chamber.com).

Sights

PLANTATION KEY

If you're driving to Islamorada from Key Largo, you'll first encounter Plantation Key, just west of mile marker 91, across Tavernier Creek. Primarily a residential area that includes part of Tavernier, Plantation Key contains a handful of curious diversions, including several art galleries, the Tavernier Creek Marina, and **Founders Park** (87000 Overseas Hwy., Plantation Key, 305/853-1685, www.islamorada.fl.us, 8 A.M.–6 P.M. daily, $8 adults, $5 children 3–17 and seniors 65 and over, children under 3 and residents free)—a 42-acre public park on the bay side of U.S. 1. Its many features include a large, heated, Olympic-style swimming pool and children's water park, a playground and skateboard park, an open-air amphitheater, a sandy beach, a dog park, and access to a marina, the Plantation Yacht Harbor Marina, which also offers a boat ramp (8 A.M.–6 P.M. daily). In addition to family-friendly diversions like water-sports rentals, fitness and walking trails, tennis and basketball courts, and multi-use fields, Founders Park hosts events throughout the year, from the "Pops in the Park" concert series (Nov.–Apr.) to an underwater Easter egg hunt. For a current schedule of events, contact the park directly, and be advised that there's a fee for use of the pool and skate park (hours vary daily, $3 adults, $2 children 3–17 and seniors 65 and over, children under 3 free).

WINDLEY KEY
Windley Key Fossil Reef Geological State Park

Once two separate islands, known as the

ISLAMORADA

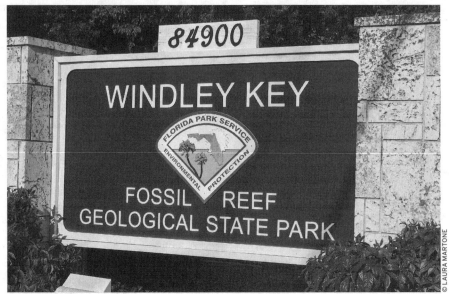

© LAURA MARTONE

Visitors can explore the old coral rock quarries at Windley Key.

Umbrella Keys, Windley Key is one of the highest islands in the Florida Keys archipelago—which was formed of Key Largo limestone (fossilized coral) over 125,000 years ago. In the mid-1800s, the Russell family homesteaded the easterly Umbrella Key, until it was sold to the Florida East Coast Railway in 1908. Soon afterward, railroad workers filled in the gap between the two Umbrella Keys, forming the Windley Key of today. From 1908 until the completion of Henry Flagler's Overseas Railroad in 1912, the three coral rock quarries on the eastern end of Windley Key were used to supply thousands of tons of limestone for the railbed and bridges that eventually stretched all the way to Key West.

Today, the Windley Key Fossil Reef Geological State Park (MM 84.9 BS U.S. 1, Windley Key, 305/664-2540, www.floridastateparks.org/windleykey, 8 A.M.–5 P.M. Thurs.–Mon., education center 8 A.M.–5 P.M. Fri.–Sun., $2.50 pp, children under 6 free) invites visitors to walk along self-guided trails through the former quarries: the Windley Quarry, the Flagler Quarry, and the Russell Quarry. Here, you can view old mining equipment and walk along eight-foot-high quarry walls to see cross-sections of the ancient coral. In addition, the Alison Fahrer Environmental Education Center features informative exhibits about the connection between the quarry complex and the ill-fated railroad, which came to an end with the Labor Day hurricane of 1935. One-hour guided tours ($1 pp, children under 6 free) are available Friday–Sunday at 10 A.M. and 2 P.M., though reservations are suggested. Given the small size and limited nature of this park, it's best to visit when you can take full advantage of the education center and guided tours.

(Theater of the Sea

Around mile marker 84.5 on Windley Key, you'll be hard-pressed to miss the enormous sign for Theater of the Sea (84721 Overseas Hwy., Windley Key, 305/664-2431, www.theaterofthesea.com, 9:30 A.M.–5 P.M. daily, $26.95 adults, $19.45 children 3–10, children under 3 free), the second oldest marine mammal facility in the world. Established in 1946, this lush 17-acre marine animal park features

© DANIEL MARTONE

Talented sea lions paint for the public at Theater of the Sea.

entertaining dolphin, sea lion, and parrot shows every day of the year. Such shows integrate lessons about anatomy, physiology, husbandry, natural history, and conservation in an informative, interactive, and often hilarious presentation. In addition to watching the varied shows, you can stroll amid habitats containing enormous sea turtles, alligators, tropical birds, reptiles, and other marine creatures—and perhaps catch a glimpse of a free-roaming iguana.

Some visitors choose to take a guided bottomless boat ride or board a four-hour adventure and snorkeling cruise (8:30 A.M. and 1 P.M. daily), which includes visits to an offshore coral reef, two island state parks, and Robbie's of Islamorada. Of course, many visitors come to Theater of the Sea to interact with the animals themselves. Here, you can watch dolphins and sea lions paint colorful, abstract pictures, learn the hand signals for natural behaviors like waving and kissing, and even swim with the resident dolphins, sea lions, and stingrays in the on-site lagoon.

The cost of admission includes access to the lagoon-side beach, the guided marinelife tour, the bottomless boat ride, snorkel gear, and the dolphin, sea lion, and parrot shows. Additional charges apply for special programs, such as swimming with the rays ($55 pp), meeting a sea lion or dolphin ($75 pp), swimming with a sea lion ($135 pp), wading with a dolphin ($165 pp), swimming with a dolphin ($175 pp), and the adventure cruise ($69 adults, $45 children 5–12). Reservations may be required for certain programs, and restrictions such as age and physical fitness may apply, so be sure to call ahead. Be aware, too, that the shows run continuously, so you can simply join the one in progress as soon as you arrive. Allow 2.5 hours to experience everything save for the adventure cruise.

Flying Dog Helicopters

Based on the lower end of Windley Key, at the Holiday Isle Resort & Marina, Flying Dog Helicopters (MM 84 OS U.S. 1, Windley Key, 866/435-4743, www.flyingdoghelicopters.com, flight times vary) enables visitors to get a bird's-eye view of the islands, beaches, coral reefs, and bountiful waters that the

ISLAMORADA

THE FACTS ABOUT DOLPHINS AND SEA LIONS

Situated on Windley Key, the **Theater of the Sea** (84721 Overseas Hwy., 305/664-2431, www.theaterofthesea.com, 9:30 A.M.–5 P.M. daily, fees apply) features daily Atlantic bottlenose dolphin and California sea lion shows that, along with entertaining antics, provide lessons about anatomy, physiology, husbandry, natural history, and conservation. You'll learn, for instance, that dolphins and sea lions are both marine mammals, which means they are warm-blooded creatures who breathe air, have hair or fur, give birth to live young, and care for their offspring until maturity. While dolphins and sea lions tend to be friendly attention-seekers, these two species are quite different from each other.

ATLANTIC BOTTLENOSE DOLPHIN

Belonging to the order Cetacea and the family Delphinidae, the Atlantic bottlenose dolphin *(Tursiops truncatus)* inhabits temperate, coastal waters throughout the world. Here are some other curious facts about these playful creatures:

• Active predators who feed on small, schooling fish, bottlenose dolphins can live into their 40s, grow to 10 feet in length, weigh up to 600 pounds, and reach sexual maturity between ages 5 and 12.

• Calves, which are born after a yearlong gestation period and can be three feet long and 30 pounds at birth, will typically nurse for two to four years and begin to eat fish at a few months of age.

• The bottlenose, or rostrum, is used for touching and pushing, while the small, cone-

shaped teeth, of which dolphins typically have 88, are used for grasping and tearing food, not chewing.

• The blowhole on the top of each dolphin's head serves as a nostril, through which the dolphin typically breathes twice per minute.

• Dolphins can conveniently breathe and eat at the same time, and they can hold their breath for eight minutes if necessary.

• The blowhole, not the throat, produces their vocalizations, which they can manipulate to mimic other sounds, such as human laughter.

• The pectoral fins, which contain all the bones of a land animal's forelimbs and are located on the dolphin's sides, are used for steering, while the dorsal fin, which is made entirely of cartilage and is located on the dolphin's back, is used for balance.

• The peduncle is the muscular area that powers the flukes, or two halves of the tail, allowing dolphins to swim up to 17 miles per hour.

• Dolphins can only swim forward, not backward, and they can shut down half of their brains while resting and still manage to swim, hunt, and communicate.

• Although Atlantic bottlenose dolphins have no sense of smell, they have excellent eyesight above and below the water, and they can also hear well, especially below the water, where they navigate, detect prey, and

Upper Keys comprise. Truly an incredible experience, such tours promise animal lovers a chance to spot dolphins, sharks, stingrays, turtles, and other sea creatures from far above the Atlantic Ocean. Specific tours include the Sand Bar Loop ($70 pp); Alligator Reef Lighthouse ($100 pp); Shark Hunt ($100 pp); Lighthouse and Shark Hunt ($130 pp); Sandbar, Lighthouse, and Shark Hunt ($155 pp); Molasses Reef ($155 pp); 50 Mile Trip (rate varies); and 100 Mile Trip (rate varies).

UPPER MATECUMBE KEY
History of Diving Museum

On the bay side of mile marker 83 on Upper Matecumbe Key, sea lovers will enjoy the

locate other objects by utilizing echolocation – a sonar-like system whereby high-pitched sounds are emitted, reflected off other surfaces, and interpreted by sensory receptors, typically the jowls.

• Dolphins appreciate eye contact, which is why they tend to be more motivated when you look at and speak to them directly.

CALIFORNIA SEA LION

The California sea lion (Zalophus californianus), which belongs to the order Carnivora and the family Otariidae, is considered a pinniped, along with seals, walruses, and four other types of sea lions. Typically, California sea lions inhabit the temperate coastline and islands of the western Americas, from British Columbia to Ecuador, spending much time at sea and coming ashore frequently to sleep or bask in the sun. Although related to seals, sea lions are markedly different in that they tend to have external ear flaps, possess much larger fore flippers, and move about on land by walking on all fours, as opposed to seals' customary wriggling, much like an inchworm. In addition, while sea lions move their fore flippers in an up-and-down, flying-like motion to propel themselves through the water, seals move their hind flippers in a side-to-side, fish-like motion. Here are some other curious facts about California sea lions:

• Agile, active predators who feed on squid, octopus, and fish, California sea lions maneuver well both on land and in water, and they can live for roughly 25 years.

• Male sea lions usually have a darker fur coat than females and weigh up to 900 pounds, three times the weight of female sea lions.

• Breeding season typically occurs between May and August, and pups are born after a yearlong gestation period; weighing roughly 13 pounds at birth, these pups can nurse for up to a year.

• Sea lions have 34 to 38 teeth that, as with dolphins, are designed for grasping and tearing food, not chewing.

• Although they usually stay submerged three minutes or less, they can hold their breath for up to 15 minutes.

• Sea lions, which are tactile, social creatures, communicate with one another through vocalizations and postural displays, and they have 25 whiskers that they use to explore objects on land and in water.

• The fore flippers contain all the bones of a land animal's forelimbs but are modified to allow for swimming at speeds of up to 23 miles per hour.

• The hind flippers, meanwhile, are used for steering and can be rotated underneath the body, enabling them to walk on all fours.

• Three nails on the hind flippers are used in grooming, and a small, flattened tail can be found between the flippers.

• California sea lions see well on land and in water, and their large eyes are very light-sensitive; although they have a poor sense of taste, their hearing and sense of smell are both keen.

interactive, educational History of Diving Museum (82990 Overseas Hwy., Upper Matecumbe Key, 305/664-9737, www.diving-museum.org, 10 A.M.–5 P.M. daily, $12 adults, $11 seniors, $6 children 5–12, children under 5 free). Even non-divers might appreciate this well-designed attraction, which packs a lot of information and artifacts into a deceivingly small space.

Following an orientation video, you'll be able to stroll amid a curious collection of diving paraphernalia, including improbable diving machines, rare diving helmets, armored diving suits, vintage U.S. Navy diving gear, underwater photographs, old-fashioned scuba tanks, recovered coins, and other treasures relating to sea exploration. Here, you'll even be able

© DANIEL MARTONE

Curiosities abound at the History of Diving Museum.

to test your breath-holding abilities, sit inside Halley's enormous diving bell, crank several hand-operated air pumps, view a reef aquarium from inside a diving helmet, and check out Captain Nemo's submarine and diving helmet from the Disney film *20,000 Leagues Under the Sea* (1954).

Founded by Dr. Joseph A. Bauer Jr. and his wife, Dr. Sally E. Bauer, whose extensive personal collection forms the basis of these engrossing exhibits, the museum is intended to demonstrate "man's quest to explore under the sea" over the course of 4,000 years, from the ancient times of Gilgamesh to the modern days of recreational diving. Ask the museum staff about free monthly programs, which can range in topics from the 1733 Spanish galleon treasure fleet to life as a female Navy diver.

Florida Keys Memorial

While traveling across Upper Matecumbe Key, most people whiz right past the Florida Keys Memorial at mile marker 81.6, on the ocean side of U.S. 1. It's easy to do, after all. The memorial itself is fairly simple and nondescript, but still, if you have a moment, you ought to stop and take a look; it's even free to do so. Dedicated in 1937 and now listed on the National Register of Historic Places, the memorial commemorates the fateful Labor Day hurricane that took many lives, caused much property damage, and effectively destroyed Henry Flagler's Overseas Railroad. As the bronze plaque says, the memorial is "dedicated to the memory of the civilians and war veterans whose lives were lost in the hurricane of September Second, 1935"—a sobering reminder of nature's power over humanity.

LOWER MATECUMBE KEY
Robbie's of Islamorada

At the northern end of Lower Matecumbe Key, on the bay side of U.S. 1 near mile marker 77.5, you'll find Robbie's of Islamorada (77522 Overseas Hwy., Lower Matecumbe Key, 305/664-8070, 877/664-8498, or 800/979-3370, www.robbies.com, 7 A.M.–sunset daily), a full-service, family-friendly marina that has been offering outdoor distractions since 1976. Here, you can rent boats, board an offshore

© DANIEL MARTONE

Robbie's of Islamorada offers souvenirs, kayak rentals, Jet Ski tours, and more.

sportfishing charter, opt for a snorkeling excursion, peruse crafts and souvenirs in an open-air market, and grab a bite in the Hungry Tarpon restaurant (305/664-0535). In addition, you can feed visiting schools of tarpon from the dock ($1 pp, $3 per bucket of fish) or take advantage of the marina's status as the official tour operator (800/979-3370) for two remote islands: **Indian Key Historic State Park** and **Lignumvitae Key Botanical State Park.** Typically, the marina is open from sunrise to sunset year-round, which means you can expect later hours during the spring, summer, and fall months, following the daylight saving time change in mid-March.

Anne's Beach

On the ocean side of Lower Matecumbe Key lies Anne's Beach (MM 73.5 OS U.S. 1, Lower Matecumbe Key, sunrise–sunset daily, free), a peaceful place to watch the sunrise or sunset, swim in the Atlantic Ocean, give kiteboarding a try, or spend some quiet time with your friends and loved ones. Dedicated to local environmentalist Anne Eaton, this pet-friendly beach features several covered picnic tables, plus a half-mile boardwalk that allows access to more secluded stretches of sand. Public restrooms and ample parking are also available.

OFFSHORE STATE PARKS
◖ Indian Key Historic State Park

Supposedly, the earliest Upper Keys community existed on this 11-acre island, which, in 1830, became site of John Jacob Housman's lucrative cargo-salvaging business. In 1836, it was designated the first county seat of Dade County, and in 1840, during the Second Seminole War, Seminole Indians invaded the island, plundered the buildings, and allegedly killed several settlers, despite the presence of Fort Paulding on nearby Teatable Key. From the early 1900s until it became a state park, Indian Key was uninhabited.

Today, the lovely Indian Key Historic State Park (MM 78.5 OS U.S. 1, Indian Key, www.floridastateparks.org/indiankey, 8 A.M.–sunset daily, free), which lies on the ocean side of the Overseas Highway and is only accessible via canoe, kayak, or boat, lures hikers, swimmers, sunbathers, bird-watchers, and anglers alike. In addition, the park offers an interpretive trail through a re-created street system and also features one of the few close-to-shore areas where snorkelers and scuba divers can explore living coral. Although visitors have access to an observation tower and a boat dock, there are no restrooms or picnic facilities on-site, and most facilities are not wheelchair-accessible. To reach the island, you can rent a kayak or powerboat from **Robbie's of Islamorada** (77522 Overseas Hwy., Lower Matecumbe Key, 305/664-8070 or 877/664-8498, www.robbies.com, 7 A.M.–sunset daily) or opt for a 2.5-hour historic island tour (800/979-3370, 9 A.M. daily, $35 adults, $20 children) aboard the *Happy Cat* snorkeling catamaran. Just remember, pets are not allowed on the island, though service animals are permitted. Also, if you head to the island via your own vessel and plan to dive or snorkel in the offshore waters, you must use a red-and-white diver-down flag. For more information, contact the **Windley Key Fossil Reef Geological State Park** (305/664-2540).

San Pedro Underwater Archaeological Preserve State Park

South of Indian Key lies the San Pedro Underwater Archaeological Preserve State Park (www.floridastateparks.org/sanpedro, 8 A.M.–sunset daily, free), site of the *San Pedro,* a 287-ton Spanish ship that wrecked here during a hurricane on July 13, 1733. Discovered in 1960, the wreck site underwent major salvaging efforts over the subsequent decade, so today, all that remains is a large pile of ballast stones. Since enhanced with seven replica cannons and an anchor, the site, which lies in 18 feet of water, now forms an artificial reef, home to many tropical fish and, therefore, popular among snorkelers and scuba divers. Swimmers, kayakers, and boaters also favor this site. Listed on the National Register of Historic Places, the San Pedro Underwater Archaeological Preserve State Park is also officially part of the Florida Keys National Marine Sanctuary Shipwreck Trail. For more information, contact the **Windley Key Fossil Reef Geological State Park** (305/664-2540).

LIGNUMVITAE KEY CHRISTMAS

While the wooded **Lignumvitae Key Botanical State Park** (MM 78.5 BS U.S. 1, www.floridastateparks.org/lignumvitaekey, 9 A.M.–5 P.M. Thurs.-Mon.) is fun to explore all year long, visiting this historic island at Christmastime can be even more magical. During the first weekend of December, the Lignumvitae Key Christmas, which is presented by the park staff and the Friends of Islamorada Area State Parks for the benefit of the park, invites visitors to step back in time and experience the holiday traditions of the early 20th century. As part of this annual event, dulcimer players welcome arriving visitors, who can then take ranger-guided walking tours of the historic Matheson House, which is typically decorated for the holidays with tropical greenery, handmade ornaments, and other Keys-inspired decora-

tions. Visitors can also take a guided tour of the nearby virgin hardwood hammock, enjoy free key limeade, coffee, and homemade cookies, and paint holiday themes on sea beans, oyster shells, and sea grape leaves to create souvenir ornaments.

On each day of the event, which usually runs from 9 A.M. to 3 P.M., catamaran rides ($20 adults, $15 children under 13) operate from **Robbie's of Islamorada** (77522 Overseas Hwy., Lower Matecumbe Key, 305/664-8070 or 800/979-3370, www.robbies.com) in the morning and afternoon. Although the park is normally free to visit, a nominal fee – usually $2-5 per person, though it can vary annually – is charged during this event. For more information, contact the **Windley Key Fossil Reef Geological State Park** (305/664-2540).

◀ Lignumvitae Key Botanical State Park

Situated on the bay side of the Overseas Highway and only accessible via boat, canoe, or kayak, the wooded Lignumvitae Key Botanical State Park (MM 78.5 BS U.S. 1, www.floridastateparks.org/lignumvitaekey, 9 A.M.–5 P.M. Thurs.–Mon., free) features the kind of virgin tropical hardwood hammock that once thrived in the Upper Keys. Formerly known as Jenkinson Island, Lignumvitae (pronounced *lig-num-VIE-tee* and meaning "tree of life") has been home to various individuals since at least the 1830s—including William J. Matheson, a wealthy Miami chemist who bought the island in 1919 and, soon afterward, built a caretaker's home, with a cistern for rainwater and a windmill for electricity. Today, Matheson's former hideaway is now the park's visitor center.

Here, you can take a one-hour, ranger-guided tour ($1 pp) amid the peaceful foliage or inside the Matheson house. The tours, which are offered twice daily (10 A.M. and 2 P.M.) from Friday to Sunday, enable you to access trails through the preserve that would normally be off-limits to visitors. To reach the island, you can rent a kayak or powerboat from **Robbie's of Islamorada** (77522 Overseas Hwy., Lower Matecumbe Key, 305/664-8070 or 877/664-8498, www.robbies.com, 7 A.M.–sunset daily) or opt for a 1.5-hour state park tour (800/979-3370, $20 adults, $15 children under 13), which, when available, includes the hourlong, ranger-led walking tour and transportation to and from the island. Just remember, pets are not allowed in this remote park, though service animals are permitted. While the boat is wheelchair-accessible, arrangements must be made in advance; unfortunately, accessibility is limited on the island itself. For more information, contact the **Windley Key Fossil Reef Geological State Park** (305/664-2540).

Entertainment and Events

ISLAMORADA

NIGHTLIFE

As with much of the Florida Keys region, most of the nightlife options in Islamorada consist of bars and restaurants that offer live entertainment or a chance to watch televised sports with like-minded folks. The **Island Grill** (85501 Overseas Hwy., Plantation Key, 305/664-8400, www.keysislandgrill.com, 7 A.M.–10 P.M. Sun.–Thurs., 7 A.M.–11 P.M. Fri.–Sat.), for instance, features nightly performers, from local funk and blues singers to rock-'n'-roll and magicians. Just down the road, the long-standing **Oceanview Pub** (MM 84.5 BS U.S. 1, Windley Key, 305/664-8052, www.theocean-view.com, 7 A.M.–2 A.M. daily) has the distinction of securing the first liquor license in the Florida Keys. For well over a decade, it's been co-owned by former NFL players Gary Dunn and Dennis Harrah, who, despite extensive renovations, have maintained the casual vibe that residents and local anglers have adored for years. Stop by for some cold beer and your favorite televised sporting event.

The **Holiday Isle Resort & Marina** (84001 Overseas Hwy., Windley Key, 305/664-2321, www.holidayisle.com) boasts six different bars, including the **Tiki Bar** (11 A.M.–midnight Sun.–Thurs., 11 A.M.–1 A.M. Fri.–Sat.), where live rock and pop bands perform on the weekends (8 P.M.–close Fri.–Sat.); the multilevel, thatched-roof **Rumrunners Island Bar** (10 A.M.–midnight daily), where locals and tourists can enjoy balmy breezes, frozen drinks, as well as live pop, rock, folk, and country music Thursday–Saturday (8 P.M.–close); and the **Kokomo Beach Bar** (noon–6 P.M. Sat.–Sun.), which features live reggae and island music. The other on-site bars are the **Floaters Pool Bar** (noon–5 P.M. Mon.–Fri., 11 A.M.–6 P.M. Sat.–Sun.), the **Wreck Bar** (11 A.M.–5 P.M. Fri., 11 A.M.–6 P.M. Sat.–Sun.), and the **Jaws Raw Bar** (8 A.M.–9 P.M. Sun.–Thurs., 8 A.M.–11 P.M. Fri.–Sat.), all of which feature tropical drinks and stunning views.

On the ocean side of U.S. 1, **The Whistle Stop Sports Bar, Grill & Liquor Store**

(82685 Overseas Hwy., Upper Matecumbe Key, 305/664-2623 or 305/664-4246, www. keyswhistlestop.com, 10 A.M.–3 A.M. daily) has been luring night owls for over 25 years, with its full-service bar and array of distractions, from pool to darts to televised sports. At **Lorelei Restaurant & Cabana Bar** (81924 Overseas Hwy., Upper Matecumbe Key, 305/664-2692, www.loreleifloridakeys.com, 7 A.M.–10 P.M. daily), you can enjoy happy hour specials every day (4–6 P.M.) and live pop, rock, country, folk, or rhythm-and-blues every night (6–10 P.M.).

The **Morada Bay Beach Café** (81600 Overseas Hwy., Upper Matecumbe Key, 305/664-0604, www.moradabay-restaurant. com, 11:30 A.M.–close daily) presents an array of activities, including happy hour (4–6 P.M. Mon.–Fri.), featuring $2 domestic beers, $3 imported beers, and $4 well drinks, and open jam sessions around a bonfire every Friday night (10:30 P.M.–close). Of course, the most popular event at Morada Bay is surely the well-publicized Full Moon Party (dates vary, $15 cover) each month. Essentially a large beach bash, this lively event consists of multiple bonfires, specialty drinks at the indoor and outdoor bars, and an array of live performers, from flamenco guitarists to electric reggae bands to stilt walkers.

THE ARTS

While cultural enthusiasts will definitely find more live music, dance performances, and theatrical venues in Key West, Islamorada still offers a few options for those seeking an alternative to outdoor activities. Since 1978, the nonprofit **Key Players** (305/453-0997, www.thekeyplayers.org, show times and ticket prices vary) troupe has presented live comedies, dramas, and Broadway musicals in venues throughout the Upper Keys, from the Key Largo Lions Club to the San Pedro Catholic Church in Tavernier. The community troupe typically produces four shows every year.

From November to April, the **Keys Community Concert Band** (www.key-scommunityconcertband.org)—which was founded in 1992 by a small group of dedicated

musicians—features "Pops in the Park," a free monthly concert series at the open-air TIB Amphitheater in Founders Park, near mile marker 87 on Plantation Key. The performances are held on a Saturday afternoon each month during the concert season, and attendees are welcome to bring chairs and blankets, as there are no seats on the lawn. Check the band's online schedule for specific dates.

In addition, **Islamorada Community Entertainment (ICE)** (305/395-6344, www. keysice.com, show times and ticket prices vary) helps to bring plays, operas, concerts, and film festivals to the TIB Amphitheater in Founders Park and the Coral Shores High School Performing Arts Center (89901 Old Hwy., Tavernier, 305/853-3222, http://csh. monroe.k12.fl.us/pac) on Plantation Key. For information about other cultural events in the Upper Keys, consult the **Florida Keys Council of the Arts** (1100 Simonton St., Key West, 305/295-4369, www.keysarts.com).

If you're craving a bit of cinematic entertainment, head just east of Plantation Key, where you'll find the **Tavernier Towne Cinemas** (91298 Overseas Hwy., Tavernier, 305/853-7003, show times and ticket prices vary). Although this isn't the fanciest movie theater in southern Florida, you'll at least be able to catch the latest flicks here.

FESTIVALS AND EVENTS

Besides numerous annual fishing competitions—such as the four-day **Islamorada Sailfish Tournament** (305/852-2102, www.is-lamoradasailfishtournament.com), which takes place in early December—Islamorada hosts several popular events throughout the year. In mid-January, for instance, art lovers are invited to spend the Saturday prior to Martin Luther King Day perusing the arts and crafts at **Art Under the Oaks** (www.artundertheoaks. com, free admission), a long-standing community event at the San Pedro Catholic Church (MM 89.5 BS U.S. 1, Tavernier, 305/852-5372, www.sanpedroparish.org) on Plantation Key. Beyond fine art and original crafts, you'll be treated to local musicians, specialty food booths, and a self-guided nature walk. Parking is available on-site ($5 donation requested) or at the nearby Coral Shores High School (89901 Old Hwy., Tavernier, free parking and shuttle service), also on Plantation Key.

In late February, locals flock to Founders Park (87000 Overseas Hwy., Plantation Key) for the two-day **Gigantic Nautical Flea Market** (305/712-1818, www.giganticnauticalfleamarket.org, free admission), where you'll find bargains on new and used boats, marine and dock equipment, diving and fishing gear, clothing, electronics, antiques, and nautical arts and crafts. Free parking and shuttle service are available at the Coral Shores High School on Plantation Key, and all the proceeds from the flea market benefit area youth.

Additionally, **Islamorada Community Entertainment (ICE)** (305/395-6344, www. keysice.com, show dates and ticket prices vary) hosts several events throughout the year, including the annual **Bay Jam,** a premier, one-day music fest that typically occurs in Founders Park in mid-March. If you're here in early December, consider attending the full-day **Florida Keys Holiday Festival,** which takes place every year in Founders Park (87000 Overseas Hwy., Plantation Key) and features a holiday parade, an arts-and-crafts bazaar, and carolers singing around an enormous holiday tree. For more information about the holiday festival and other area events, contact the **Islamorada Chamber of Commerce** (MM 83.2 BS U.S. 1, Upper Matecumbe Key, 305/664-4503 or 800/322-5397, www.islamoradachamber.com).

Shopping

Although many avid shoppers head straight to Key West, Islamorada lures quite a few eager spenders with its assortment of art galleries, clothing boutiques, gift shops, and other unique emporiums.

ART GALLERIES

You'll find it hard to miss Betsey, the giant lobster sculpture that welcomes art lovers to **The Rain Barrel** (86700 Overseas Hwy., Plantation Key, www.keysdirectory.com/rainbarrel, 9 A.M.–5 P.M. daily), a working village of artists situated in a lush, rustic setting on the bay side of U.S. 1. A popular stop for locals and tourists alike, this unusual complex features several eye-popping galleries, including **Rain Barrel Treasures** (305/852-3084), the barn-like structure marking the entrance, and the **Rain Barrel Sculpture Gallery** (305/852-8935, www.rainbarrelsculpture.com), situated at the rear of the property and offering bronze statues and stoneware items fashioned by gallery owners Dwayne and Cindy King. Among other options here is **Out on a Whim** (305/852-7676), a gallery operated by artist Janet Doto and displaying the work of her fellow creators, including the well-traveled painter and illustrator Cynthia Ré Robbins (479/244-6746, www. art4spirit.com).

The **Keys to Life Studio/Gallery** (84771 Overseas Hwy., Windley Key, 954/290-4262, www.artbypasta.com, 10 A.M.–5 P.M. daily) is home to the colorful paintings and wooden sculptures of marinelife artist Pasta Pantaleo.

Farther south, on Upper Matecumbe Key, the **Stacie Krupa Studio Gallery of Art** (82935 Overseas Hwy., Upper Matecumbe Key, 305/942-0614, www.staciekrupa.com, 10 A.M.–6 P.M. daily) presents Krupa's expressionistic visions of animals, while the unique **Lobster Trap Art Gallery** (82200 Overseas Hwy., Upper Matecumbe Key, 305/664-0001, www.lobstertrapart.com, 8 A.M.–4 P.M. daily) features the vivid, sea-inspired paintings of local artists Nadine and Glenn Lahti. Interestingly, all the wooden frames in this gallery have been crafted from old lobster traps that were once used throughout the Florida Keys.

As the name indicates, **Ichthyophile** (81904 Overseas Hwy., Upper Matecumbe

© DANIEL MARTONE

A giant lobster beckons art lovers to The Rain Barrel.

Key, 305/664-8960, www.ichthyophile.com, 10 A.M.–5 P.M. daily) is an ideal gallery for fish lovers, as every painting, antique print, wall fixture, lamp, hanging mobile, cookbook, novel, and piece of jewelry or pottery in the store focuses on fish or fishing enthusiasts. The **Gallery Morada** (81611 Overseas Hwy., Upper Matecumbe Key, 305/664-3650, www.gallerymorada.com, 10 A.M.–6 P.M. daily) represents the imaginative jewelry, dishware, lamps, clocks, glass sculptures, and other creations of more than 200 artisans.

For more information about these and other art galleries, consult the **Florida Keys Council of the Arts** (1100 Simonton St., Key West, 305/295-4369, www.keysarts.com).

CLOTHING BOUTIQUES

Whether you're a serious clotheshorse or just in need of a casual outfit, you'll find a handful of clothing boutiques in Islamorada, including the **Latitude 25 Clothing Co.** (82748 Overseas Hwy., Upper Matecumbe Key, 866/664-4421, www.floridakeysstore.net, 9:30 A.M.–5:30 P.M. daily), which offers a wide array of women's

and men's apparel, from Body Glove bikinis to Tommy Bahama shirts, plus shoes, accessories, sunscreen, pet toys, and tropical gifts.

The **Lion's Lair** (82185 Overseas Hwy., Upper Matecumbe Key, 305/664-9921 or 800/220-1691, www.lionslairdesigns.com, 9:30 A.M.–7 P.M. daily) features an assortment of ladies' swimwear and lingerie. The one-of-a-kind **Wild Lily Boutique** (81933 Overseas Hwy., Upper Matecumbe Key, 305/517-9222, www.wildlilyboutique.com, 10 A.M.–6 P.M. Mon.–Fri., 10 A.M.–5 P.M. Sat., 11 A.M.–5 P.M. Sun.) lures shoppers with its ever-changing collection of youthful apparel, creative jewelry, and island-style accessories.

GIFT AND BOOK SHOPS

For those who hope to bring a special souvenir home with them, Islamorada doesn't disappoint. You'll find a wide array of emporiums in the Village of Islands, all of which commemorate a particular aspect of this unique region. The **Plantation Key Nursery** (MM 88 OS U.S. 1, Plantation Key, 305/852-9190, 9 A.M.–5 P.M. daily), for instance, offers native

Hooked on Books offers plenty of local guidebooks.

plants and colorful accessories for garden lovers, while **Blue Marlin Jewelry** (81915 Overseas Hwy., Upper Matecumbe Key, 305/664-8004 or 888/826-4424, www.bluemarlin-jewelry.com, 9:30 A.M.–5:30 P.M. Mon.–Sat., 11 A.M.–5 P.M. Sun.) features nautical-inspired jewelry, from swordfish pendants to earrings made of salvaged treasure coins.

Hooked on Books (81909 Overseas Hwy., Upper Matecumbe Key, 305/517-2602, www.hookedonbooksfloridakeys.com, 10 A.M.–5:30 P.M. daily) provides a wealth of Florida-related selections, including regional travel guides, novels by Florida-based writers, and books about Florida Keys history, cuisine, activities, and wildlife. Near mile marker 81.6 on the ocean side of U.S. 1, **Me & My Sisters** (105 Palm Ave., Upper Matecumbe Key, 305/664-5575, www.meandmysistersonline.com, 10 A.M.–5 P.M. Tues.–Sat., 11 A.M.–5 P.M. Sun.) carries an impressive assortment of whimsical items, from tiki clocks to ceramic kitty banks to insulting parrot key chains. As a bonus, all proceeds from the store are split between two nonprofit organizations: Caring for Cats in the Upper Keys and the Florida Keys Wild Bird Center.

On the bay side of the highway, the two-story **World Wide Sportsman** (81576 Overseas Hwy., Upper Matecumbe Key, 305/664-4615, www.basspro.com, 9 A.M.–8:30 P.M. Sun.–Thurs., 9 A.M.–9 P.M. Fri.–Sat.) looms large in a sprawling complex that includes the Bayside Marina and the Islamorada Fish Company. Inside this vast, well-designed store, you'll find casual clothes and shoes, inshore and offshore fishing gear, as well as souvenirs. In addition, you can peruse the displayed memorabilia, mounted fish, and engrossing aquariums; visit an elegant art gallery; step aboard the *Pilar*, the sister ship to Ernest Hemingway's famous fishing boat; and relax on the balcony of the Zane Grey Long Key Lounge. For something a bit more intimate, head to **The Banyan Tree** (81197 Overseas Hwy., Upper Matecumbe Key, 305/664-3433, www.banyantreegarden.com, 10 A.M.–5:30 P.M. Mon.–Sat., 11 A.M.–4 P.M. Sun.), which features a plethora of antiques, linens, housewares, ceramics, home furnishings, garden fixtures, and exotic plants and flowers.

Sports and Recreation

HIKING AND BIKING

While Islamorada doesn't offer much for long-distance hikers, you can certainly enjoy a pleasant stroll through places like **Indian Key Historic State Park** (MM 78.5 OS U.S. 1, www.floridastateparks.org/indiankey, 8 A.M.–sunset daily, free), which has an interpretive trail, and **Lignumvitae Key Botanical State Park** (MM 78.5 BS U.S. 1, www.floridastateparks.org/lignumvitaekey, 9 A.M.–5 P.M. Thurs.–Mon., free), which features guided ranger walks. Both islands are only accessible by boat, and neither has a direct phone number. For more information about either island, contact the Windley Key Fossil Reef Geological State Park (305/664-2540).

Given Islamorada's sprawling nature and numerous bridges, bikers will undoubtedly appreciate the region even more—though care should always be taken on the Overseas Highway, and a proper helmet should be worn at all times. Between mile markers 91 and 71, you'll even find 10 miles of actual bike paths, part of the **Florida Keys Overseas Heritage Trail.** Bikes can be rented from **A1A Bicycle & Scooter Rentals** (81984 Overseas Hwy., Upper Matecumbe Key, 305/664-4535, www.keyswatersports.com, 9 A.M.–5 P.M. daily, rates vary), which offers daily, weekly, and monthly rates and even provides delivery service. In addition, **Backcountry Cowboy Outfitters** (82240 Overseas Hwy., Upper Matecumbe Key, 305/517-4177, www.backcountrycowboy.com, 10 A.M.–6 P.M. Mon.–Sat., 10 A.M.–5 P.M. Sun., $15–20 per half day, $20–25 daily, $35–100 for multiple days, $95–115 weekly) offers both one-speed and three-speed bicycle rentals—plus helmets, combination locks, and copies of the state's bicycle laws.

(FISHING AND BOATING

Anglers and boaters will find a treasure trove of options in the Islamorada area. Boasting one of the largest fishing fleets in Florida, it

The Tavernier Creek Marina is home to several fishing and diving operators.

© DANIEL MARTONE

ZANE GREY: AUTHOR AND ANGLER

While Ernest Hemingway is undoubtedly the most famous novelist ever to be linked to the Florida Keys, he is most certainly not the only one. As evidenced by places like the **Zane Grey Long Key Lounge** (81576 Overseas Hwy., Upper Matecumbe Key, 305/517-2190, www.basspro.com, 11 A.M.-10 P.M. daily) in Islamorada's World Wide Sportsman complex and the **Zane Grey Master Suite** at the Lime Tree Bay Resort (MM 68.5 BS U.S. 1, Layton, 305/664-4740, www.limetreebayresort.com) on Long Key, it's apparent that American novelist Zane Grey was also part of this archipelago's colorful history.

After discovering the Florida Keys in the early 1900s, Grey began fishing the local waters of Long Key, Duck Key, and Grassy Key. In 1910, he first stayed at the Long Key Fishing Club, a luxurious fishing resort built by Henry Flagler on the ocean side of Long Key. Featuring a large wooden lodge, a store, a post office, a railroad station, roughly 30 small cottages, and a tunnel beneath the roadbed connecting the camp with the bayside docks, the resort attracted famous, wealthy sportfishermen such as Andrew Mellon, William Hearst, Herbert Hoover, Franklin D. Roosevelt, and, of course, Zane Grey.

Born Pearl Zane Grey in 1872 in Zanesville, Ohio, Grey wrote his first novel in 1903. By the 1920s, he was earning half a million dollars per year from his writing career, and he owned several homes in California, fishing camps in Oregon and New Zealand, and a hunting lodge in Arizona. Although he traveled throughout the world, from Catalina Island to Mexico to Tahiti, he always returned to Long Key, where he favored not only the marvelous fishing but also the quietude, which allowed him to write such Western classics as *Wild Horse Mesa* (1928) and *Code of the West* (1934).

Though Grey was best known for his novels about the American West, some fans still prefer his real-life fishing adventures, including *Tales of Fishes* (1919), in which he wrote about

light-tackle fishing for sailfish and kingfish near Long Key and the surrounding islands, and *The Bonefish Brigade* (1922), in which he described his companions at the Long Key Fishing Camp and their obsessive quest for the elusive bonefish. In fact, it was such pioneering accounts that helped to lure more wealthy sportfishermen to the region, at a time when most local residents were using spears and harpoons to snag their supper from the passes between the keys.

To reach the Long Key Fishing Camp, Grey and his fellow anglers would travel on the Key West extension of the Florida East Coast Railway. While staying at the camp, he would dine on such delicacies as stone crab, grouper chowder, conch fritters, broiled king mackerel, coconut pudding, and key lime pie — cuisine that's still popular today. In fact, Grey loved the camp so much that, after the terrible Labor Day hurricane of 1935 destroyed the lodge, the buildings, and roughly 30 miles of Henry Flagler's railroad tracks, he honored the vacation spot in the foreword of a saltwater fishing book. "It is sad to think that Long Key, doomed by a hurricane, is gone forever," he wrote. "But the memory of that long white winding lonely shore of coral sand, and the green reef, and the blue Gulf Stream will live in memory, and in such fine books as this."

Four years after the storm that destroyed the Long Key Fishing Camp, Grey passed away in Altadena, California, having sold more than 27 million copies of his novels and nonfiction books. Since then, that number has risen dramatically, and in addition, more than 110 movies have been made from his stories, including a silent D. W. Griffith short called *Fighting Blood* (1911) as well as the most recent version of *Riders of the Purple Sage* (1996), which stars Ed Harris and Amy Madigan. While Grey's beloved Long Key Fishing Camp was eventually replaced by a state park, sportfishing is still popular in the Upper and Middle Keys — for the rich and the not-so-rich alike.

ISLAMORADA

SAFETY TIPS FOR UNDERWATER ENTHUSIASTS

Thousands upon thousands of snorkelers and scuba divers flock to the Florida Keys every year to explore the underwater coral reefs that lie within six nautical miles of the shore and comprise the 2,900-square-mile Florida Keys National Marine Sanctuary. Although taking care not to touch or damage these fragile, living coral reefs is an important aspect of proper underwater etiquette, human safety is also a top priority. Here are several precautions that all underwater enthusiasts should take:

- Check weather conditions before venturing out, as strong winds and rough seas can create unsafe conditions.

- If operating your own vessel, make sure you stay at least 300 feet from diver-down flags in open water and at least 100 feet from flags in rivers and inlets; if you cannot maintain such distance, slow down to an idle speed when passing other divers.

- Make sure you've had proper snorkeling and/or scuba-diving instruction.

- When in doubt about your abilities, don't

hesitate to join a professional guide or tour.

- Always tell someone on land where you're planning to go and when you intend to return.

- If you plan to be in the water for a while, apply ample waterproof sunscreen or wear a T-shirt to avoid sunburn.

- Make sure your mask and flippers fit properly, and check that you have all necessary equipment, such as inflatable vests for snorkelers and weights and tanks for scuba divers.

- If you find it difficult to walk on the boat while wearing flippers, carry them into the water before putting them on.

- Never snorkel or dive without displaying a proper red-and-white, diver-down flag on your vessel, and always remove said flag when all divers have returned to the boat.

- Always snorkel or dive with a buddy, and try to stay together.

might just be, as residents claim, the "sport-fishing capital of the world." Just consider all of the resorts that offer access to fishing charters and boat rentals, such as the **Ragged Edge Resort & Marina** (243 Treasure Harbor Rd., Plantation Key, 305/852-5389, www.ragged-edge.com) and **Smugglers Cove Resort & Marina** (MM 85.5 BS U.S. 1, Windley Key, 305/664-5564, www.smug-scove.com). In fact, Windley Key offers a slew of such fishing-friendly resorts, including the **Drop Anchor Resort and Marina** (MM 85 OS U.S. 1, 305/664-4863, Windley Key, www.dropanchorresort.com), **Coconut Cove Resort and Marina** (84801 Overseas Hwy., Windley Key, 305/664-0123, www.coconutcove.net), **Pelican Cove Resort & Marina** (84457 Overseas Hwy., Windley Key, 305/664-4435, www.pcove.com), and

Holiday Isle Resort & Marina (84001 Overseas Hwy., Windley Key, 305/664-2321, www.holidayisle.com).

Farther south, on Upper Matecumbe Key, lies **Bud N' Mary's Fishing Marina** (MM 79.8 OS U.S. 1, Upper Matecumbe Key, 305/664-2461, www.budnmarys.com), which has been serving the public since 1944 and now features more than 40 fishing captains and guides, making it the oldest and largest fishing fleet in the Florida Keys. Here, anglers can find backcountry fishing expeditions ($375–450 per half day, $550–650 daily), offshore fishing charters (rates vary), and a 65-foot party fishing boat, the *Miss Islamorada,* plus a tackle and bait shop, boat storage, diving excursions, and an outdoor eatery. Of the many boats docked here, you'll encounter the 44-foot *Redfish* (305/664-

- Plan your entry and exit points before jumping into the water.

- Swim into the current upon entering the water and then ride the current back to your exit point.

- Don't touch any tempting sea creatures, as they may sting you.

- Look above the water every now and again to ensure that you haven't drifted too far away from the boat; try to stay within 300 feet of the diver-down flag when in open water and within 100 feet when in a river or inlet.

- If you have a diving emergency, dial 911 from your cell phone, or use a VHF radio to signal a "MAYDAY."

A helpful saying to remember is "Snorkel aware, dive with care!" For scuba divers, another helpful saying is "Dive ALIVE," with the letters in "ALIVE" standing for:

- **Air:** Monitor your air supply, always surface with at least 500 PSI, and practice out-of-air procedures.

- **Lead Weights:** Wear only enough lead to achieve proper buoyancy, and know how to release your and your buddy's weight systems.

- **Inspection:** Inspect your gear before every dive trip, replace missing or worn gear, replace batteries in any electronics, and have regulators serviced annually.

- **Verification:** Verify your dive skills, and review your dive plan, signals, and lost buddy procedures with your diving buddy.

- **Escape:** Always dive with surface signaling devices; if you become entangled, remain calm and do what you can to free yourself; and if you're lost on the surface, inflate your buoyancy compensation device (BCD), remain calm, maintain your position if possible, and try to attract others' attention.

For more safety tips, consult area diving operators or the **Florida Keys National Marine Sanctuary** (305/852-7717 or 305/292-0311, www.floridakeys.noaa.gov).

8497, www.redfishsportfishing.com, hours and rates vary), operated by veteran Captain Merv Finch and featuring offshore trips in search of (depending on the season) mahi-mahi, sailfish, wahoo, snapper, grouper, marlin, tuna, permit, tilefish, amberjack, swordfish, and king mackerel.

Another option, of course, is to visit one of the non-resort marinas in the area, such as the **Tavernier Creek Marina** (90800 Overseas Hwy., Tavernier, 305/852-5854, www.tavernercreek-marina.com), which lies on the bay side of Plantation Key and boasts the largest dry storage facility in the Florida Keys. Here, you can hire such charters as **Blue Water Blues** (305/731-9612, www.bluewaterblues.com, hours and rates vary), operated by Captain George Coffey, who offers reef trips for grouper, snapper, and kingfish,

plus evening excursions for tarpon and shark. Farther south, on Upper Matecumbe Key, lie two more impressive fleets: one at the **Whale Harbor Marina** (83413 Overseas Hwy., Upper Matecumbe Key, 305/664-4959, www.whaleharborinn.com, trips and rates vary) and the other at the **World Wide Sportsman Bayside Marina** (81576 Overseas Hwy., Upper Matecumbe Key, 305/394-0106, www.islamoradafishingguidesandcharters.com, trips and rates vary). Of course, many anglers head even farther south to **Robbie's of Islamorada** (77522 Overseas Hwy., Lower Matecumbe Key, 305/664-8070 or 877/664-8498, www.robbies.com, 7 A.M.–sunset daily), which offers an array of backcountry, patch-reef, and offshore fishing opportunities (trips and rates vary). In addition, Robbie's provides boat rentals, including 18-foot Wagner skiffs ($150 per half day, $200 daily), 18-foot Wagner powerboats ($135 per half day, $185 daily), and 23-foot deck boats ($185 per half day, $235 daily).

◖ KAYAKING

While sportfishing is indeed the most popular activity in Islamorada, kayakers also appreciate the bountiful waters surrounding this Village of Islands. After all, some attractions—such as Indian Key Historic State Park, San Pedro Underwater Archaeological Preserve State Park, and Lignumvitae Key Botanical State Park—are only accessible via kayak, canoe, or boat.

Even if you haven't lugged your own kayak with you, you're in luck. There are several kayaking outfitters in the region, including **Founders Park Watersports** (87000 Overseas Hwy., Plantation Key, 305/434-8984, www.the-helm.com, 11 A.M.–5 P.M. Mon.–Fri., 11 A.M.–6 P.M. Sat.–Sun., $15–35 hourly), operating from the beach in Founders Park and offering kayak, pedal boat, and Hobie Wave rentals.

You can also rent a single or double kayak from **Backcountry Cowboy Outfitters** (82240 Overseas Hwy., Upper Matecumbe Key, 305/517-4177, www.backcountrycowboy.com, 10 A.M.–6 P.M. Mon.–Sat., 10 A.M.–5 P.M. Sun.) for a half day ($45–60), a full day ($60–80), multiple days ($85–165), or an entire week ($165–195). In addition, Backcountry Cowboy offers three different two-hour guided kayaking excursions: the backcountry nature tour ($45 adults, $22.50 children under 13), the sunset tour ($45 pp), and the historical Indian Key tour ($45 pp).

Based out of the local Days Inn, **A1A Watersports** (82749 Overseas Hwy., Upper Matecumbe Key, 305/664-8182, www.keyswatersports.com, 7 A.M.–9 P.M. daily, rates vary) offers single and double kayaks for half-day, daily, multi-day, weekly, and monthly rentals, all of which include instruction, seat backs, paddles, life jackets, and a navigational chart. Local delivery and pickup is possible for multi-day rentals. As a bonus, A1A provides several

other locations in the Florida Keys, including the Keys Motel (90611 Overseas Hwy., Tavernier, 305/664-8182) and the Fiesta Key RV Resort (70001 Overseas Hwy., Fiesta Key, 305/664-9192).

Located at Robbie's of Islamorada, **Florida Keys Kayak** (77522 Overseas Hwy., Lower Matecumbe Key, 305/664-4878, www.kayakthefloridakeys.com, 9 A.M.–sunset daily) provides single and double kayaks ($40–55 per half day, $50–65 daily), stand-up paddleboards ($50 per half day), single and double Hobie pedal kayaks ($50–65 per half day, $60–75 daily), and canoes ($60 per half day). Free delivery is available to local resorts and residences, and earlier hours (such as sunrise) are possible with 24-hour notice. Florida Keys Kayak features three two-hour guided excursions: the backcountry tour ($45 pp), the sunset tour ($45 pp), and the Indian Key snorkeling tour ($45 pp).

DIVING AND SNORKELING

Whether you're a novice or an experienced underwater explorer, you should definitely reserve part of your trip for the waters east of Islamorada, an area filled with shallow coral reefs, curious wall formations, and shipwrecks. Through the **Conch Republic Divers** (Tavernier Creek Marina, 90800 Overseas Hwy., Tavernier, 305/852-1655 or 800/274-3483, www.conchrepublicdivers.com) or the **Florida Keys Dive Center** (90451 Old Hwy., Tavernier, 305/852-4599 or 800/433-8946, www.floridakeysdivectr.com)—both of which are based on the northern end of Plantation Key—you can take various diving classes, rent scuba-diving gear, and join twice-daily diving excursions (8:30 A.M. and 1 P.M., $80 pp) to explore many of the nearby underwater attractions.

Some of the sights you might encounter include the **Conch Wall,** noted for barrel sponges, rare pillar coral, and, of course, conch; the **Davis Reef,** an ideal spot to observe green moray eels; the **Crocker Wall,** home to gorgonian coral and eagle rays; **Hens and Chickens,** an area that offers mounds of star and plate coral; and **Little Conch Reef,** adjacent to the wrecked *El Infante,* a Spanish galleon that sank in the 1733 hurricane. In these waters, you'll also find the **Alligator Reef,** site of the shipwrecked **USS** *Alligator,* and the *Eagle,* a 287-foot freighter donated by the Eagle Tire Company as an artificial reef in 1985, and now teeming with countless fish.

Besides Conch Republic Divers and the Florida Keys Dive Center, there are several other diving operators in the area. Such alternative options, all of which provide instructional scuba-diving programs, include the **Holiday Isle Dive Shop** (84001 Overseas Hwy., Windley Key, 305/664-3483, www.diveholidayisle.com, 8 A.M.–6 P.M. daily, $75 pp), based out of the tropical-style Holiday Isle Resort & Marina, and **Key Dives** (79851 Overseas Hwy., Upper Matecumbe Key, 305/664-2211 or 800/344-7352, www.key-dives.com, 8 A.M. and 12:30 P.M. daily, $85–110 pp), which offers professional underwater tour guides for small groups of up to six divers. All four of the aforementioned dive operators also offer affordable, daily snorkeling excursions ($30–40 adults, $25–40 children).

In addition, you can opt for a private, two-hour snorkeling trip through the **Bay and Reef Company** (81801 Overseas Hwy., Upper Matecumbe Key, 305/393-1779 or 305/393-0994, www.bayandreef.com, $250 per group, $75 hourly beyond the initial two hours), which is based out of the Cheeca Lodge & Spa, or board the *Happy Cat* at **Robbie's of Islamorada** (77522 Overseas Hwy., Lower Matecumbe Key, 800/979-3370, www.robbies.com, 9 A.M., noon, 3 P.M., and 6 P.M. daily, $35 adults, $20 children).

Snorkelers and scuba divers can also rent a kayak or boat from Robbie's (305/664-8070 or 305/664-9814, rates vary) and head toward the **San Pedro Underwater Archaeological Preserve State Park** (305/664-2540, www.floridastateparks.org/sanpedro, 8 A.M.–sunset daily, free), south of Indian Key. Here, underwater explorers will find the remains of the *San Pedro,* a 287-ton Spanish ship that wrecked in this location during a 1733 hurricane. Since its

discovery in 1960, it's undergone several salvaging attempts and now forms an artificial reef, home to plenty of tropical fish.

◖ SPAS AND YOGA

Save for Key West, Islamorada is surely the best locale in the Florida Keys to seek pampering rejuvenation for the body, mind, and soul. The **Cheeca Lodge & Spa** (81801 Overseas Hwy., Upper Matecumbe Key, 305/664-4651, www.cheeca.com, spa 9 A.M.–8 P.M. daily, fitness center 6 A.M.–midnight daily, rates vary), for instance, features a 5,700-square-foot "oasis of relaxation and rejuvenation." Here, resort guests (age 18 or older) can choose from an array of fitness classes, steam rooms, salt scrubs, skin and body treatments, refreshing facials, and massage therapies—in private treatment rooms, poolside cabanas, or an oceanside tiki hut.

Unlike the Cheeca Lodge, however, **The Moorings Village & Spa** (123 Beach Rd., Upper Matecumbe Key, 305/664-4708, www.mooringsvillageandspa.com) allows nonguests to partake of the facials, massages, and beachside yoga lessons provided at the on-site **Island Body & Sol Spa** (305/664-3264, www.islandbodyandsolspa.com, by appt. daily, $50–190 per treatment).

Beyond such resort-type facilities, however, you'll find several day spas in the area, including the appointment-only **Kiki's Spa** (89240 Overseas Hwy., Ste. 2, Tavernier, 305/852-0011, www.tavernierspa.com, 10 A.M.–6 P.M. Tues.–Sat.) on Plantation Key, where you can opt for manicures ($15–35 pp), pedicures ($25–45 pp), facials ($45–200 pp), massages ($15–125 pp), waxing treatments ($12–70 pp), tanning services ($45–70 pp), and other options. On Upper Matecumbe Key, the European-style **Ciao Bella Salon & Day Spa** (82913 Overseas Hwy., 305/664-4558, www.theislamoradaspa.com, 9 A.M.–6 P.M. Tues.–Sat.) specializes in hair care (rates vary), natural manicures and pedicures ($20–50 pp), clean waxing treatments (rates vary), clinical facials ($85–125 pp), and healing massages for both men and women ($45–250 pp).

© LAURA MARTONE

Rejuvenation awaits at The Moorings' on-site spa.

Appointments are recommended, and a 24-hour cancellation notice is required.

Just down the road, the **Blu Bamboo Salon & Spa** (82205 Overseas Hwy., Upper Matecumbe Key, 305/664-9342, 9 A.M.–6 P.M. Tues.–Sat.) encourages you to "indulge your senses and soothe your soul" with an array of facials ($15–135 pp), waxing services ($10–65 pp), hand treatments ($5–50 pp), foot treatments ($5–80 pp), and massages ($80–90 pp). Appointments are recommended, and a 24-hour cancellation notice is required.

Accommodations

UNDER $100

As Islamorada's only B&B, the pet-friendly **Casa Thorn Bed & Breakfast** (114 Palm Ln., Plantation Key, 305/852-3996, www.casa-thorn.com, $79–239 d) presents five comfortable rooms, ranging from the moderate Secret Garden Room, equipped with a small refrigerator, to the Moroccan Room, with its king-sized, four-poster bed and a tub made for two. Other on-site amenities include a lovely tropical garden and a refreshing swimming pool. Situated on a large grassy property alongside the Atlantic Ocean, the **Ragged Edge Resort & Marina** (243 Treasure Harbor Dr., Plantation Key, 305/852-5389, www.ragged-edge.com, $69–259 d) offers standard motel rooms with small refrigerators, efficiencies with kitchenettes, large studios with full kitchens and balconies or screened porches, plus a deluxe two-bedroom suite with two bathrooms, a full kitchen, a balcony, and a large family room. Anglers will especially like this resort, which offers access to a full-service marina and a fishing pier. Clang the cowbell when you arrive and the manager will be with you shortly.

The **Coconut Cove Resort and Marina** (84801 Overseas Hwy., Windley Key, 305/664-0123, www.coconutcove.net,

$75–195 d) presents three types of accommo-dations: the Captain's Cottages, each of which includes a single bed, a queen-sized bed, and a kitchen; the General Quarters, which also boast luxurious hot tubs; and the Admiral's Accommodations, each containing two queen-sized beds, a queen-sized sleeper sofa, and a kitchen. In addition, the resort's friendly staff can help you arrange any kind of fishing ex-cursion in the area.

The **La Jolla Resort** (82216 Overseas Hwy., Upper Matecumbe Key, 305/664-9213 or 888/664-9213, www.lajollaresort.com, $79–329 d) provides both garden-facing rooms and bayfront rooms. Some offer only basic ameni-ties, while others sport well-equipped kitch-ens and porches with hammocks and barbecue grills. Free wireless Internet access is available throughout the property.

If you're looking for basic lodgings at an affordable price, consider the **Sunset Inn** (82200 Overseas Hwy., Upper Matecumbe Key, 305/664-3454, www.sunsetinnkeys.com, $75–85 d), which offers rooms with either one king-sized bed or two double beds, plus effi-ciencies with full kitchens. Every room has cable television and small refrigerators. When not exploring Islamorada, take a dip in the on-site freshwater pool. For an even better deal, stay at the **Key Lantern Motel and Blue Fin Inn** (82150 Overseas Hwy., Upper Matecumbe Key, 305/664-4572, www.keylantern.com, $39–68 d), perhaps the cheapest place in the entire Florida Keys archipelago. Here, you'll find basic rooms with kitchenettes and free wireless Internet access.

More difficult to categorize—at least where cost is concerned—the **Pines & Palms Resort** (80401 Overseas Hwy., Upper Matecumbe Key, 305/664-4343, www.pinesandpalms.com, rooms and suites $89–239 d, cottages $139–299, houses and villas $359–579) en-compasses a variety of accommodations, from a budget-priced efficiency with a queen-sized bed to an enormous, three-bedroom villa, fea-turing two king-sized beds and a sofa bed. All rentals come with well-equipped kitchens and free wireless Internet access. The property also includes an oceanfront freshwater pool, a free boat ramp, and dockage at no extra charge.

$100-200

If you hope to visit upscale Islamorada with-out blowing your entire vacation budget, consider moderately priced lodgings like the pet-friendly **Lookout Lodge Resort** (87770 Overseas Hwy., Plantation Key, 305/852-9915 or 800/870-1772, www.lookoutlodge.com, $100–399 d), which presents one-bed-room and two-bedroom suites with bay views, mini-suites with bay or garden views, and two-bedroom garden suites, all equipped with kitchenettes. The resort also features a relaxing private beach area, with swimming access, as well as assistance in arranging diving, snorkel-ing, or fishing excursions.

On Windley Key, the peaceful **⟨ Smugglers Cove Resort & Marina** (MM 85.5 BS U.S. 1, Windley Key, 305/664-5564, www.smugscove.com, $119–139 d) offers con-venient access to both the Atlantic Ocean and the Gulf of Mexico. At Smugglers Cove, you'll find not only 11 clean, comfortable rooms and one spacious suite, but also a 30-slip, deep-wa-ter marina, a fully stocked bait and tackle shop, a gas station for boats, a waterfront bar and res-taurant, plus several dependable fishing char-ters. Other amenities include air conditioning, wireless Internet access, cable television, and stunning views.

✦ Also on Windley Key, the **Drop Anchor Resort and Marina** (84959 Overseas Hwy., 305/664-4863 or 888/664-4863, Windley Key, www.dropanchorresort.com, $125–219 d) has 18 individualized rooms, ranging from basic lodgings, with a mini-fridge and a cof-feemaker, to a two-bedroom suite, with a full kitchen, living room, and dining area. This oceanfront hideaway also offers a nice private beach, a heated freshwater pool, a boat launch, and bulkhead docking.

The **Pelican Cove Resort & Marina** (84457 Overseas Hwy., Windley Key, 305/664-4435 or 800/445-4690, www.pcove.com, $169–279 d) offers standard hotel rooms with mini-re-frigerators and private balconies, as well as efficiencies with full kitchens, plus a luxury suite ($369–389 daily). Despite mixed reviews about the management and a need to update the furnishings, a bonus for many travelers is that certain rooms are pet-friendly (though there is a fee per pet), which is not always the case in the Florida Keys. The entire resort features free wireless Internet access, and other amenities include a tennis court, an oceanfront hot tub, a freshwater pool, water-sports equipment, and an on-site restaurant called the Cabana Club.

The spacious **◖ Holiday Isle Resort & Marina** (84001 Overseas Hwy., Windley Key, 305/664-2321 or 800/327-7070, www.holidayisle.com, $149–229 d) features a range of accommodations, from standard rooms with queen-sized beds to oceanfront suites with kitchenettes. In this laid-back, palm-studded setting, guests can easily while away their vacation, relaxing by the pool or sunning themselves on the beach. Of course, if you have a little more energy, be sure to take advantage of the available personal watercraft rentals, sportfishing charters, scuba-diving trips, and snorkeling excursions. Pets, up to 45 pounds, are allowed, provided that you're willing to part with a small, nonrefundable deposit. In addition, while you'll find several fine restaurants in Islamorada, you'll surely appreciate the presence of the on-site Sportfish Grill, not to mention six tropical bars, including the multilevel Rumrunners, reminiscent of the Swiss Family Robinson's island home.

The pet-friendly **Days Inn and Suites Key Islamorada** (82749 Overseas Hwy., Upper Matecumbe Key, 305/664-3681, www.daysinnflakeys.com, rooms $109–209 d, suites $169–339) houses an array of accommodations, from courtyard efficiencies with two double beds and a kitchenette to a two-bedroom, 2,000-square-foot, oceanfront suite ($368–508 daily) with two bathrooms and a full kitchen. The property also features a boat ramp, boat dockage up to 21 feet, personal watercraft and boat rentals, and an oceanside tiki bar.

The first thing you'll notice as you arrive at the **Kon Tiki Resort** (81200 Overseas Hwy.,

Upper Matecumbe Key, 305/664-4702, www.kontiki-resort.com, rooms $129–285 d, villas and houses $298–427) is the lush tropical landscape, featuring tempting hammocks, a barbecue grill and picnic area, and a heated freshwater pool alongside a private lagoon. Here, guests can dock and launch their boats on-site, and the 27 uniquely decorated rooms and villas provide enough options and amenities, from cable television to screened porches, to suit any vacationer.

Avid anglers can certainly plan a memorable fishing trip at **Bud N' Mary's Fishing Marina** (79851 Overseas Hwy., Upper Matecumbe Key, 305/664-2461 or 800/742-7945, www.budnmarys.com, $120 d), where, in addition to lodgings, you'll find a spacious marina, housing a fleet of more than 40 fishing boats, plus a tackle shop and outdoor eatery. Beyond comfortable, standard rooms, the complex offers a penthouse with a full kitchen ($300 daily) and a two-bedroom beach house ($400 daily) with a full kitchen, a backyard, and access to a dock. In addition, Bud N' Mary's provides a houseboat rental that contains a queen-sized bed and a small kitchenette.

The family-friendly **Breezy Palms Resort** (80015 Overseas Hwy., Upper Matecumbe Key, 305/664-2361 or 877/412-7339, www.breezypalms.com, $100–269 d) is a terrific home base for your Florida Keys adventures. Offering boat rentals and dockage, the resort can easily assist you in arranging your next fishing excursion. The accommodations, meanwhile, range from a standard motel room, with one bedroom, one bath, and a small refrigerator, to a two-bedroom suite, with king-sized and queen-sized beds, a sofa sleeper, a full kitchen, and a dining room.

Lined by hibiscus and bougainvillea, the **Coral Bay Resort** (75690 Overseas Hwy., Lower Matecumbe Key, 305/664-5568, www.coralbayresort.com, rooms $119–179 d, one-bedroom apartments $139–199, two-bedroom apartments $189–305, cottages $210–305) features everything from a standard bedroom with a small refrigerator to a comfortable cottage with four double beds, two bathrooms, and a well-equipped kitchen. Each unit includes cable television, as well as a cozy patio or covered porch.

Situated on a 10-acre estate, the **Caloosa Cove Resort** (73801 Overseas Hwy., Lower Matecumbe Key, 888/297-3208, www.caloosacove.com, $195–275 d) houses 30 rooms, including luxury efficiencies and one-bedroom suites, all with kitchen areas and private balconies. In addition, the resort features a full-service marina, a bait and tackle shop, boat rentals, tennis courts, a heated freshwater pool, and a large sandy beach.

OVER $200

Islamorada presents some of the most upscale, exclusive resorts in the entire Florida Keys archipelago. One such option is the tranquil **Chesapeake Beach Resort** (83409 Overseas Hwy., Upper Matecumbe Key, 305/664-4662 or 800/338-3395, www.chesapeake-resort.com, rooms $210–340 d, villas $225–450) on Upper Matecumbe Key. Providing a quiet place to relax and replenish, this luxurious, well-landscaped property features a variety of accommodations, from tastefully furnished hotel rooms with garden views to premium ocean villa suites. In addition to the 6.5-acre tropical garden, the resort offers two heated oceanfront pools, a hot-water spa, tennis and shuffleboard courts, and a tiki-style observation deck, plus the ubiquitous kayaks, lounge chairs, and hammocks.

Ocean Dawn Suites (82885 Overseas Hwy., Upper Matecumbe Key, 305/664-4844 or 866/540-5520, www.oceandawnsuites.com, $200–275 d) presents eight Caribbean-style luxury suites alongside the Atlantic Ocean. Possible amenities include giant plasma televisions, full kitchens, or private balconies. While staying here, feel free to cook the day's catch on a communal barbecue grill, relax beneath an oceanside tiki hut, or watch the sunset from the resort's private beach.

Situated on 25 lush acres, the **Islander Resort** (82100 Overseas Hwy., Upper Matecumbe Key, 305/664-2031, www.islanderfloridakeys.com, $235–285 d) provides full

kitchens, screened lanais, free Internet access, and free continental breakfasts daily. Three lodging types are available here: courtyard rooms with a lanai and one double bed, ocean view rooms with two double beds, and poolside rooms with a lanai and two double beds. The resort also features a lanai courtyard room where pets are allowed with a nonrefundable fee. Other amenities here include two heated pools, a hot tub, the Bluewater Tiki Bar, and 1,300 feet of sandy beach, with a shallow snorkeling area.

If you're looking for all the comforts of a well-appointed, oceanfront home, look no farther than **The Caribbean Resort** (117 S. Carroll St., Upper Matecumbe Key, 305/664-2235 or 800/799-9175, www.thecaribbean-resort.com, one-bedroom homes $350–400 d, two-bedroom homes $400–500, three-bedroom homes $1,500), situated far enough from U.S. 1 that it's easy to forget about the traffic for a while, especially during the peak winter months. This sumptuous property contains an array of spacious homes, each with its own unique style. On-site amenities include lush gardens filled with tropical flowers and banana trees; a gorgeous pool and spa oasis, graced with waterfalls and arching coconut palms; as well as private sun decks, gazebos, tables, and lounge chairs scattered throughout the grounds.

Established in 1946, the lavish **C Cheeca Lodge & Spa** (81801 Overseas Hwy., Upper Matecumbe Key, 305/664-4651 or 800/327-2888, www.cheeca.com, rooms $209–490 d, suites $259–899, two-bedroom suites $559–998, bungalows $319–597) has lured an array of U.S. presidents and movie stars since its opening. Today, the recently renovated resort provides guests with a relaxing, pampering, tropical playground, where you can play tennis or golf, fish from the 525-foot pier, relax on the private beach, or seek rejuvenation in the incredible on-site spa. You may just feel like royalty in the spacious, Caribbean-style rooms, suites, and adults-only bungalows, which include 42-inch televisions, wet bars, luxurious furniture, and marvelous views of the ocean,

ISLAMORADA

The Moorings Village provides a wide array of well-appointed cottages and vacation homes.

beach, lagoon, and resort. In fact, it's the varied views, as well as the shifting seasons, that determine the wide range in lodging rates. Besides the lovely surroundings, the amenities here include two fine restaurants, Atlantic's Edge and Nikai Sushi, and an adults-only pool.

Perhaps the best example of Islamorada's luxury and seclusion is (**The Moorings Village & Spa** (123 Beach Rd., Upper Matecumbe Key, 305/664-4708, www.mooringsvillageandspa. com, one-bedroom inland homes $250–750 daily, two-bedroom oceanfront bungalow $3,150–4,550 weekly, two-bedroom inland homes $3,850–5,600 weekly, one-bedroom oceanfront home $4,200–5,775 weekly, two-bedroom oceanfront homes $6,650–9,100 weekly), a serene, splendidly lush property on the ocean side of U.S. 1, near mile marker 81.6. Once part of a coconut plantation in the 1930s, the verdant 18-acre resort offers 18 private homes and cottages (which greatly range in price depending on the season), from small, brightly painted Caribbean bungalows tucked amid the foliage to a three-bedroom, French Colonial plantation house ($7,700–10,500

weekly) directly beside the ocean. These self-sufficient residences, many of which lure the same travelers year after year, contain televisions, telephones, well-equipped kitchens, luxurious beds, and, sometimes, washers and dryers. All lodgings require a two-night or one-week minimum stay, and all are only a short stroll from a private Polynesian-style beach—complete with swaying palm tress, cushioned lounge chairs, relaxing hammocks, and complimentary kayaks. It's no wonder, then, that the beach is often used as a backdrop in movies and catalog photo shoots.

Other on-site amenities include tennis courts, a stunning pool area, and the **Island Body & Sol Spa** (305/664-3264, www.islandbodyand-solspa.com, $50–190 per treatment), which offers a selection of rejuvenating facials and massages. The family-owned resort also boasts two of the finest eateries in the Keys—the Morada Bay Beach Café, ideal for light lunches beside the beach, and Pierre's Restaurant, perfect for a romantic dinner. Both restaurants lie on the bay side of the Overseas Highway, only a short drive from the Moorings.

CAMPING

Despite its plethora of accommodations, Islamorada has few options for campers, especially those hoping to stay awhile. The **Sea Breeze RV & Mobile Home Park** (87425 Old Hwy., Plantation Key, 305/852-3358, www.seabreezervlots.com), situated on the ocean side of U.S. 1, is one such option. Essentially a residential mobile home park, Seabreeze offers several full-hookup RV lots, including some with oceanfront views, on a month-to-

month basis (starting from $650 May–Oct., $900 Nov.–Apr.). The park is conveniently located across the street from Islamorada's Founders Park and only a few miles northeast of attractions like Windley Key Fossil Reef Geological State Park and Theater of the Sea. Other amenities include on-site laundry facilities, a boat ramp, a fish-cleaning station, cable television, phone service, boat dockage ($135 monthly), and dry-dock storage ($80 monthly).

Food

SEAFOOD

Given Islamorada's focus on fishing and boating, the prevalence of seafood restaurants should be less than surprising. Seafood lovers should head first to the **Island Grill** (85501 Overseas Hwy., Plantation Key, 305/664-8400, www.keysislandgrill.com, 7 A.M.–10 P.M. Sun.–Thurs., 7 A.M.–11 P.M. Fri.–Sat.,

$11–33), which features a fried seafood platter for two, complete with shrimp, scallops, mahimahi, crab clusters, and crab cakes—more than enough to satisfy a pair of seafood gourmands. Come for dinner, and you'll be treated to live music from one of the local bands that perform here nightly.

In the **Whale Harbor Restaurants and**

© DANIEL MARTONE

casual waterfront dining at Wahoo's Bar & Grill

Marina complex (83413 Overseas Hwy., Upper Matecumbe Key, www.whaleharborinn.com) on Upper Matecumbe Key, you'll find three unique restaurants, anchored by the **Whale Harbor Restaurant** (305/664-4959, www.whaleharborrestaurant.com, 4–9 P.M. Mon.–Thurs., 4–10 P.M. Fri., 2–10 P.M. Sat., noon–9 P.M. Sun., $29 adults, $14.50 children), which offers one of the Florida Keys' most popular seafood buffets, with everything from snow crab to whole fried yellowtail snapper. Also on the premises are **Wahoo's Bar & Grill** (305/664-9888, www.wahoosbarandgrill.com, 11 A.M.–10 P.M. Sun.–Thurs., 11 A.M.–11 P.M. Fri.–Sat., $12–26), an ideal spot to enjoy fresh seafood and waterfront views, and the **Braza Leña Brazilian Steakhouse** (305/664-4940, www.brazalena.com, 5–9:30 P.M. Tues.–Sun., $42 adults, $20 children 6–12, children under 6 free), which features a fixed-price dinner menu that includes an extensive salad bar plus an assortment of meat selections, from pork ribs to lamb chops to filet mignon. Of course, seafood lovers will be happy to hear that Braza also offers à la carte specialties like tiger prawns, a 16-ounce lobster tail, or a fresh local catch.

Perhaps aiming to, as Chef Emeril Lagasse says, "kick it up a notch" with its New Orleans cuisine and Bahamian-style cooking, it's easy to see why **Bentley's** (82779 Overseas Hwy., Upper Matecumbe Key, 305/664-9094, 11 A.M.–9 P.M. daily, $9–29) is considered one of the top seafood restaurants in the Upper Keys. For a real treat, order the Louisiana spicy shrimp à la carte or over a bed of linguini.

Mangrove Mike's Cafe (82200 Overseas Hwy., Upper Matecumbe Key, 305/664-8022, www.mangrovemikes.com, 6 A.M.–2 P.M. daily, $6–22) offers more than just a meal. With breakfast and lunch, you might also receive a history lesson about the Conchs. Still, the food is paramount here. Many locals, in fact, believe Mike's has one of the best breakfast menus in the Keys. Among favored dishes is the Mangrove Oscar, a toasted English muffin with sautéed spinach, poached eggs, and your choice of blue crab, grilled shrimp, or grilled mahimahi, covered in a béarnaise sauce.

© LAURA MARTONE

Situated beside Florida Bay, Pierre's offers fine dining in a plantation-style mansion.

While they may share the same beach, (**Morada Bay Beach Café** (81600 Overseas Hwy., Upper Matecumbe Key, 305/664-0604, www.moradabay-restaurant.com, 11:30 A.M.– 10 P.M. Sun.–Thurs., 11:30 A.M.–11 P.M. Fri.– Sat., $11–33) and (**Pierre's Restaurant** (81600 Overseas Hwy., Upper Matecumbe Key, 305/664-3225, www.pierres-restaurant.com, 5–10 P.M. Sun.–Thurs., 5–11 P.M. Fri.–Sat., $34–40) offer far different dining experiences. With several colorful tables set upon the sand— in addition to its indoor and patio seating, of course—Morada Bay takes full advantage of its laid-back beachside setting. Although this breezy eatery does many dishes well, from the island-style conch chowder to fresh salads and sandwiches, a definite highlight is the seared jumbo scallops in a coconut pad thai sauce. If you're not hungry enough for an entrée, try the tapas menu, which includes dishes like Fritto Mediterraneano with calamari, shrimp, zucchini, and chipotle aioli in a tangy marinara sauce. The bar is open later than the dining areas, and if you're here at the right time, be sure to stick around for Morada Bay's Friday night jam sessions and monthly Full Moon Parties.

Housed within a picturesque French Colonial–style mansion—which is, incidentally, identical to the plantation house on offer at the affiliated Moorings Village across the highway—Pierre's provides one of the best fine dining experiences in the Keys. With an interior that blends sailing motifs with an exotic Moroccan-themed decor (which even pervades the restrooms), the first-floor lounge and second-floor dining area are, at once, comfortable and elegant. Of course, your meal will be especially memorable on the candlelit balcony that overlooks Florida Bay and the beach below, which is often lined with alluring tiki torches. Pierre's features a small but eclectic menu, the star of which is the tempura lobster tail over hearts of palm hash—truly, a heavenly dish that's been popular ever since it was initially offered. Reservations are recommended here, though the dress code is decidedly casual. Be advised, however, that the wine list is on the pricey side.

The historic Green Turtle Inn has long served fresh seafood and other delicacies.

For a no-frills seafood dining experience, head to **Ma's Fish Camp** (105 Palm Ave., Upper Matecumbe Key, 305/517-9611, 11 A.M.–9 P.M. daily, $6–16), which offers simple, yet tasty, meals for an affordable price. Favored for its excellent service, this popular eatery promises a laid-back atmosphere in which to dine on delectable dishes like coconut curry shrimp, grilled fish tacos, and key lime pie.

The World Wide Sportsman complex (now part of the Bass Pro Shops chain) features the waterfront **Islamorada Fish Company** (81532 Overseas Hwy., Upper Matecumbe Key, 305/664-9271, www.fishcompany.com, 11 A.M.–11 P.M. daily, $9–21). With 175 outdoor seats overlooking the beach, this exceptional eatery provides the perfect spot to watch the sunset or host a party. Serving classic Florida Keys cuisine, the Fish Company excels with its fried baskets and grilled platters. For lighter fare, consider venturing to the adjacent World Wide Sportsman, which features the **Zane Grey Long Key Lounge** (81576 Overseas Hwy., Upper Matecumbe Key, 305/517-2190, www.basspro.com, 11 A.M.–10 P.M. daily, $10–16) on the upper level. Here, after returning from a long day of fishing, you can relax on the open-air balcony that overlooks the marina, have a cocktail, and sample seafood treats like coconut shrimp and lobster salad.

Serving both classic and contemporary cuisine, the **Green Turtle Inn** (81219 Overseas Hwy., Upper Matecumbe Key, 305/664-2006, www.greenturtlekeys.com, 6 A.M.–10 P.M. Tues.–Sun., $10–35) serves breakfast, lunch, and dinner in a historic, recently renovated building. For breakfast, try the Keys Benedict, featuring two poached eggs, crab cakes, tomatoes, and Hollandaise sauce, then later, return for dinnertime delicacies like the herb-seared tuna served over hearts of palm hash. The **Lazy Days Restaurant** (79867 Overseas Hwy., Upper Matecumbe Key, 305/664-5256, www.lazydaysrestaurant.com, 11 A.M.–9:30 P.M. Sun.–Thurs., 11 A.M.–10 P.M. Fri.–Sat., $6–25) provides, as the name indicates, a relaxing oceanfront dining experience, where you can relish a fried oyster sandwich for lunch or jumbo stuffed shrimp for dinner.

Although open for both breakfast and lunch, the **Hungry Tarpon Restaurant** (77522 Overseas Hwy., Lower Matecumbe Key, 305/664-0535, www.hungrytarpon.com, 6:30 A.M.–close daily, $12–27) lures even more diners, especially locals, for the dinner menu. Based at Robbie's of Islamorada, the Tarpon serves favorites like the Purple Island Mahi-Mahi, topped with a brandy lobster sauce, or the Filet à la Annie, with a mushroom, shallot, and red wine demi-glace. Come down for Robbie's famous tarpon feedings and stay to feed yourself.

AMERICAN

Overlooking Florida Bay, the **Marker 88 Restaurant** (88000 Overseas Hwy., Plantation Key, 305/852-9315, www.marker88.info, 11 A.M.–11 P.M. daily, $11–36) is a wonderful place to relax for a while and relish dishes like cheeseburgers and poached Florida lobster. Dine indoors or sit outside to enjoy a beautiful view of the ocean. Just down the road, you can sample chicken wings, burgers, or barbecue ribs at **Chilli Willie's Bar & Grill** (86701 Overseas Hwy., Plantation Key, 305/852-8786, www.keysdining.com/chilliwillies, 11 A.M.–10 P.M. daily, $6–20). In addition, you can watch your favorite sporting event on at least one of the restaurant's 14 televisions.

Another fun-loving spot is the **Hog Heaven Sports Bar & Grill** (85361 Overseas Hwy., Windley Key, 305/664-9669, www.hogheavensportsbar.com, 11 A.M.–3:30 A.M. daily, $7–19). Situated just opposite Windley Key Fossil Reef Geological State Park, this late-night joint features happy-hour specials, beachfront dining, and a range of vittles, from tuna melts to barbecue rib platters.

Ziggie & Mad Dog's (83000 Overseas Hwy., Upper Matecumbe Key, 305/664-3391, www.ziggieandmaddogs.com, 11:30 A.M.–10 P.M. Sun.–Thurs., 11:30 A.M.–11 P.M. Fri.–Sat., $16–42) serves a variety of soups, salads, seafood dishes, steaks, and chops. One of several favorite dishes is the key lime chipotle chicken with sausage and cornbread stuffing. For something budget-friendly, visit **The Whistle Stop Sports Bar, Grill & Liquor Store** (82685 Overseas Hwy., Upper Matecumbe Key, 305/664-2623, www.keyswhistlestop.com, 11:30 A.M.–2 A.M. daily, $5–12), a popular locals' hangout and a good option for night owls. Check out daily specials like Mom's meatloaf and chicken pot pie, and be advised that the on-site bar has longer hours (10 A.M.–3 A.M. daily).

For tasty, inexpensive breakfast, lunch, or dinner, try the **Lorelei Restaurant & Cabana Bar** (81924 Overseas Hwy., Upper Matecumbe Key, 305/664-2692, www.loreleifloridakeys.com, 7 A.M.–10 P.M. daily, $4–23). Between three-egg omelets, spinach salads, cracked conch sandwiches, and baby back ribs, there's surely something for everyone.

If you're staying at the exclusive Cheeca Lodge & Spa or looking for a fine dining alternative, consider **Atlantic's Edge** (81801 Overseas Hwy., Upper Matecumbe Key, 305/664-4651, www.cheeca.com, 7 A.M.–10 P.M. daily, $23–52). With indoor and outdoor seating—most of which offers remarkable ocean views—it can be a pleasant place for the discerning gourmand, especially if you don't mind the slightly elevated prices—on both the menu and the wine list. Specialties include the dry aged bone-in ribeye steak and the Florida Keys barrel fish.

Open for breakfast and lunch, the **Islamorada Restaurant and Bakery** (81620 Overseas Hwy., Upper Matecumbe Key, 305/664-8363, www.bobsbunz.com, 6 A.M.–2 P.M. daily, $2–8) is one of those places that locals would prefer to keep a secret. Although the popular eatery offers a hundred different breakfast and lunch items, most people come for Bob's Bunz. Taste one, and you, too, will be hooked. Meanwhile, excellent coffee, breakfast selections, and vegetarian dishes make a trip to the **Midway Café and Coffee Bar** (80499 Overseas Hwy., Upper Matecumbe Key, 305/664-2622, 6 A.M.–9 P.M. daily, $5–14) equally worthwhile.

EUROPEAN AND ASIAN

For fine Italian dining, visit the **Old Tavernier Restaurant** (90311 Overseas Hwy., Tavernier, 305/852-6012, www.oldtavernier.com, 4–11 P.M. daily, $12–46) on Plantation Key, which provides both indoor and outdoor seating. Although the portions here aren't enormous, the quality is topnotch, especially if you enjoy sampling inspired dishes like scallops de Provence. If you have a hankering for more basic Italian cuisine, try **Boardwalk Pizza** (20 High Point Rd., Plantation Key, 305/853-3800, www.boardwalkpizzainthekeys.com, 11 A.M.–9 P.M. Mon.–Fri., 11 A.M.–10 P.M. Sat.–Sun., $4–17), which serves tasty pizzas, subs, salads, and pasta. If you'd prefer to stay in your hotel, remember that Boardwalk will deliver to any location in Islamorada.

If, while in the land of fresh seafood, you get a sudden craving for some excellent Greek cuisine, stop by the **Athens Café & Grill** (82205 Overseas Hwy., Upper Matecumbe Key, 305/664-0848, 11 A.M.–10 P.M. Mon.–Fri., 11 A.M.–6 P.M. Sat., $4–17), where you'll be treated to inexpensive Mediterranean salads, hummus wraps, pita sandwiches, and heftier dishes such as the Greek-style rack of lamb. For those in a hurry, the café also offers carry-out service and free delivery between mile markers 74 and 90.

Kaiyó (81701 Overseas Hwy., Upper Matecumbe Key, 305/664-5556, www.kaiyokeys.com, 11 A.M.–11 P.M. daily, $13–36) considers itself a Florida-inspired Asian cuisine restaurant. Besides sushi, Kaiyó offers a lunch buffet that features a variety of alternating dishes, plus dinner entrées like the macadamia yellowtail with Jean's famous mango sauce. You can continue with the macadamia theme by trying the white chocolate macadamia pie for dessert.

Several countries over—at least in spirit—the contemporary French menu at **Chanticleer South** (81671 Overseas Hwy., Upper Matecumbe Key, 305/664-0640, www.chanticleer-south.com, 6–10 P.M. daily mid-Nov.–May, $19–58) features the well-favored cuisine of Chef Jean-Charles Berruet. Classic

ISLAMORADA

dishes include regional Floridian touches, such as the filet of monkfish wrapped in bacon, roasted with vegetables, cognac, port, and cream, baked in a puff pastry, and served with lime beurre blanc. Unfortunately, Chanticleer is closed during the off-season, usually from late May to mid-November. Luckily, however, you can opt for the year-round **Uncle's Restaurant** (80939 Overseas Hwy., Upper Matecumbe Key, 305/664-4402, www.unclesrestaurant.com, 5–10:30 P.M. Tues.–Sun., $12–26), which specializes in ample portions of fresh seafood and classic Italian cuisine. With its soft lighting, laid-back patio, and fishing snapshots galore, this casual, friendly eatery might remind you of eating at your uncle's house—if, that is, your uncle were a longtime fishing guide turned award-winning restaurateur who boasts his own herb garden and has over 40 nieces and nephews. Although it's difficult to choose just one entrée, you can't go wrong with authentic dishes like bouillabaisse, pasta primavera, veal marsala, rack of lamb with port wine demi-glace, or chargrilled teriyaki tuna with wasabi aioli.

The **Spanish Gardens Cafe** (80925 Overseas Hwy., Upper Matecumbe Key, 305/664-3999, www.spanishgardenscafe.com, 11 A.M.–9 P.M. daily, $6–22) serves sandwiches and salads for lunch, plus a dinner menu that includes a variety of tapas, ranging from mussels marinara to bison empanadillas. The seafood paella comes in various sizes—depending, naturally, on how many of you will be sharing it.

Information and Services

INFORMATION
For brochures, maps, and other information about Islamorada, stop by the **Islamorada Chamber of Commerce and Visitors Center** (MM 83.2 BS U.S. 1, Upper Matecumbe Key, 305/664-4503 or 800/322-5397, www.islamoradachamber.com, 9 A.M.–5 P.M. Mon.–Fri., 9 A.M.–4 P.M. Sat., 9 A.M.–3 P.M. Sun.) or consult the **Monroe County Tourist Development Council** (1201 White St., Ste. 102, Key West, 305/296-1552 or 800/352-5397, www.fla-keys.com, 9 A.M.–5 P.M. Mon.–Fri.). For government-related issues, contact the **Islamorada Village Administration Center & Public Safety Headquarters** (86800 Overseas Hwy., Plantation Key, 305/664-6400, www.islamorada.fl.us, 8 A.M.–5 P.M. Mon.–Fri.) or the **Monroe County offices** (1100 Simonton St., Key West, 305/294-4641 or 305/852-1469, www.monroecounty-fl.gov, 8 A.M.–5 P.M. Mon.–Fri.).

For local news, consult *The Reporter* (www.keysnet.com), the *Upper Keys Free Press* (www.keysnews.com), and *The Weekly Newspapers* (www.keysweekly.com). The daily *Miami Herald* (www.miamiherald.com), the daily *Key West Citizen* (www.keysnews.com), and the biweekly *Florida Keys Keynoter* (www.keysnet.com) are additionally available throughout the Keys.

In Islamorada, you'll also have access to several radio stations, including the **SUN** (WAIL-FM 99.5, www.wail995.com), which offers a classic rock format. For other stations, visit www.keysradio.com.

SERVICES
Spread across multiple islands, Islamorada offers plenty of necessary services for both residents and travelers—as does Tavernier to the north.

Money
For banking needs, stop by the **TIB Bank** (80900 Overseas Hwy., Upper Matecumbe Key, 305/664-4483 or 800/233-6330, www.tibbank.com, 9 A.M.–4 P.M. Mon.–Thurs., 9 A.M.–6 P.M. Fri., extended drive-through hours) or the **First State Bank of the Florida Keys** (81621 Overseas Hwy., Upper Matecumbe Key, 305/664-9070, www.keysbank.com, 9 A.M.–4 P.M. Mon.–Thurs., 9 A.M.–6 P.M.

Fri., extended drive-through hours), which offer foreign currency exchange.

Mail

For shipping, faxing, copying, and other business-related services, visit **PostNet** (88005 Overseas Hwy., Plantation Key, 305/853-1101, www.postnet.com, 9 A.M.–5 P.M. Mon.–Fri., 10 A.M.–1 P.M. Sat.). Of course, you can also package and ship items at the local **post office** (82801 Overseas Hwy., Upper Matecumbe Key, 305/664-4738 or 800/275-8777, www. usps.com, 8 A.M.–4:30 P.M. Mon.–Fri., 9 A.M.– noon Sat.).

Groceries and Supplies

For groceries, baked goods, and other supplies, head to the nearest **Winn-Dixie** (92100 Overseas Hwy., Tavernier, 305/852-5904, www.winndixie.com, 7 A.M.–11 P.M. daily), which houses an on-site pharmacy (305/852-5069, 8 A.M.–8 P.M. Mon.–Fri., 9 A.M.–6 P.M. Sat., 10 A.M.–5 P.M. Sun.). A **CVS/pharmacy** (82894 Overseas Hwy., Upper Matecumbe Key, 305/664-2576, www.cvs.com, 8 A.M.– 10 P.M. daily) offers limited supplies as well as an on-site pharmacy (8 A.M.–8 P.M. Mon.–Fri., 8 A.M.–7 P.M. Sat., 9 A.M.–6 P.M. Sun.).

Laundry

If you need to clean some clothes during your trip, you'll find several coin-operated laundries in the area, including the **Coral Shores Coin Laundry** (90071 Old Hwy., Tavernier, 305/852-5497, 8 A.M.–7 P.M. Mon.–Fri., 8 A.M.–5 P.M. Sat., 9 A.M.–4 P.M. Sun.) on Plantation Key.

Internet Access

For wireless Internet access, consult your hotel or resort, as many offer free access nowadays. You'll also find useful services at the **Islamorada Branch Library** (81830 Overseas Hwy., Upper Matecumbe Key, 305/664-4645, www.keyslibraries.org, 9:30 A.M.–8 P.M. Tues., 9:30 A.M.–6 P.M. Wed.–Fri., 10 A.M.–6 P.M. Sat.).

Emergency Services

In case of an emergency that requires police, fire, or ambulance services, dial **911** from any cell or public phone. For nonemergency assistance, contact the **Monroe County Sheriff's Office** (87000 Overseas Hwy., Plantation Key, 305/853-7021, www.keysso.net, 8 A.M.–5 P.M. Mon.–Fri.). For medical assistance, consult the **Mariners Hospital** (91500 Overseas Hwy., Tavernier, 305/434-3000, www.baptisthealth. net). Foreign visitors—seeking help with directions, medical concerns, business issues, law enforcement needs, or other problems— can receive **multilingual tourist assistance** (800/771-5397) 24 hours daily.

Getting There and Around

GETTING THERE
By Air

Despite the presence of a private airstrip at the **TavernAero Airport Park** (MM 90 BS U.S. 1, www.tavernaero.com) on Plantation Key, Islamorada has no major airport of its own. To travel here by plane, you'll need to fly into the **Fort Lauderdale-Hollywood International Airport (FLL)** (320 Terminal Dr., Fort Lauderdale, 866/435-9355, www.broward. org/airport), the **Miami International Airport (MIA)** (4200 NW 21st St., Miami, 305/876-7000 or 800/825-5642, www.miami-airport. com), the **Key West International Airport (EYW)** (3491 S. Roosevelt Blvd., Key West, 305/809-5200 or 305/296-5439, www.keywestinternationalairport.com), or the **Florida Keys Marathon Airport (MTH)** (9400 Overseas Hwy., Marathon, 305/289-6060). From there, you can rent a vehicle from agencies like **Avis** (800/331-1212, www.avis.com), **Budget** (800/527-0700, www.budget.com), **Enterprise** (800/325-8007, www.enterprise. com), **Hertz** (800/654-3131, www.hertz.com),

ISLAMORADA

or **Thrifty** (800/367-2277, www.thrifty.com) in order to reach Islamorada.

By Bus or Train

The **Miami-Dade County Metrobus** (305/891-3131, www.miamidade.gov/transit) operates the **301 Dade-Monroe Express** between Florida City and Marathon (5:15 A.M.–8:40 P.M. daily, $2.35 per one-way trip), regularly stopping in Islamorada. In addition, **Greyhound** (800/231-2222, www.greyhound.com) offers bus service to the Burger King in Islamorada (82201 Overseas Hwy., Upper Matecumbe Key). **Amtrak** (800/872-7245, www.amtrak.com), however, only provides train service as far south as Miami. Of course, you can always rent a car or hop a shuttle to reach the Florida Keys.

Transport from Airports and Stations

If you arrive in the Fort Lauderdale–Miami area via plane, bus, or train—or Key West via plane or bus—you can either rent a car or hire a shuttle service to reach Islamorada. Some of these companies include **Keys Shuttle** (305/289-9997 or 888/765-9997, www.keysshuttle.com, $70–80 per shared ride, $300–350 for exclusive service) and **Keys Tropical Transportation** (305/852-3595, www.keystropicaltransportation.com, starting at $130 or $165 per ride, depending on the airport of origin), both of which provide service from the Miami and Fort Lauderdale airports; **SuperShuttle** (305/871-2000 or 954/764-1700, www.supershuttle.com, $205 for up to 10 passengers), which only serves visitors flying into Miami; and **TO'n'FRO** (305/852-4514, www.tonfro.com, $55–65 per shared van ride, $160–180 per luxury sedan ride), a personalized van and car service that offers transportation between the airports in Fort Lauderdale, Miami, and Key West and any destination in the Keys.

By Car

To reach Islamorada from Miami, simply head south on U.S. 1 (Overseas Hwy.) and continue through Key Largo, toward your destination

on the islands of Islamorada. If you're headed from the Everglades via I-75 (Everglades Pkwy.), drive south on U.S. 27, veer right onto S.R. 997 (Krome Ave.), and follow the signs to U.S. 1. From U.S. 41 (Tamiami Trail) in the Everglades, head south on S.R. 997 and continue toward U.S. 1. If you arrive during the peak season (Dec.–Apr.), be sure to call **511** for an up-to-the-minute traffic report.

GETTING AROUND
By Car

The best way to travel through Islamorada is via car, truck, RV, or motorcycle—all of which offer easy access to U.S. 1 as well as the side roads.

By Van Service or Tour Bus

If, while staying in Islamorada, you have a sudden desire to head to Key West for the evening—and would rather leave your vehicle at the hotel, B&B, resort, or campground where you're staying—consider boarding **Sea the Keys** (305/896-7013, www.keywestdaytrip.com, rates vary), a passenger van service that will pick you up from your hotel in the Upper Keys and drop you off in Key West around 11 A.M. While down there, you'll be free to explore any number of restaurants, bars, museums, and other attractions, before making the return trip around 9 P.M.

An alternative is the **KuKu KonKanut** (305/432-3202, www.kukukonkanut.com, Thurs.–Sat., $45 pp). Rain or shine, this bar-hopping tour bus picks up passengers at several stops in Islamorada (MM 86–72) from approximately 1:45 to 2:15 P.M. Amid island tunes and history lessons, the tour bus guides passengers to Mallory Square in Key West, where you can stroll around the attractions and watering holes of Old Town, before making the return trip at 11 P.M. Needless to say, you must be at least 21 years old to ride the party bus.

By Taxi

Taxicab companies such as **Mom's Taxi** (305/852-6000, $7 per pickup, $2.50 per mile), **Islamorada Taxi** (305/664-4100, $7 per pickup, $2.50 per mile), and **Spring's Island Taxi** (305/664-4331, www.springsislandtaxi.com, $7 per pickup, $3 per mile after initial two miles) can help you get around Islamorada.

By Bike or Boat

While you can certainly traverse Islamorada via bicycle, the region's sprawling nature and numerous bridges make it challenging for novice riders. Nevertheless, it's a lovely, ecofriendly way to experience the Upper Keys. Between mile markers 91 and 71, you'll even find 10 miles of actual bike paths.

Bikes can be rented from **A1A Bicycle & Scooter Rentals** (81984 Overseas Hwy., Upper Matecumbe Key, 305/664-4535, www.keyswatersports.com, 9 A.M.–5 P.M. daily, rates vary), which offers daily, weekly, and monthly rates and even provides delivery service. In addition, **Backcountry Cowboy Outfitters** (82240 Overseas Hwy., Upper Matecumbe Key, 305/517-4177, www.backcountrycowboy.com, 10 A.M.–6 P.M. Mon.–Sat., 10 A.M.–5 P.M. Sun., $15–20 per half day, $20–25 daily, $35–100 for multiple days, $95–115 weekly) offers both one-speed and three-speed bicycle rentals—plus helmets, combination locks, and copies of the state's bicycle laws.

Of course, you can also experience the islands of Islamorada via boat. In fact, certain locales, such as Indian Key Historic State Park, are only accessible via boat, canoe, or kayak. Having your own vessel might make navigating these waters a bit easier, and you'll find no shortage of boat ramps and marina slips in Islamorada. If you'd rather rent a boat, just head to **Robbie's of Islamorada** (77522 Overseas Hwy., Lower Matecumbe Key, 305/664-8070 or 877/664-8498, www.robbies.com, 7 A.M.–sunset daily), which offers an array of vessels ($135–185 per half day, $185–235 daily), ranging from 18 to 23 feet in length. As an alternative, you can rent a kayak from **Backcountry Cowboy Outfitters** (82240 Overseas Hwy., Upper Matecumbe Key, 305/517-4177, www.backcountrycowboy.com, 10 A.M.–6 P.M. Mon.–Sat., 10 A.M.–5 P.M. Sun., $45–60 per half day, $60–80 daily, or $165–195 weekly).

ISLAMORADA

MARATHON AND THE MIDDLE KEYS

For those seeking some peace and quiet, the Middle Keys definitely have their appeal. Beyond the bridges south of Islamorada and the minuscule community of Layton, the first stop—Long Key State Park, which is often claimed by the Upper Keys—is an idyllic place to escape the crowds of other islands. Hiking, canoeing, kayaking, snorkeling, and picnicking are favored pastimes here, and unlike other public beaches in the region, the narrow stretch of sand at Long Key is only available to overnight campers, making it decidedly more tranquil than the beaches of Key West.

After crossing the Long Key Viaduct, you'll be in the "Heart of the Keys"—a transitional, middle-of-the-road space between the outdoor pleasures of Key Largo and the unabashed revelry of Key West. Family-friendly activities seem to reign supreme in the Middle Keys, from up-close dolphin encounters on Duck Key to the playground and picnic areas of Sombrero Beach, popular among swimmers and windsurfers alike and site of an annual dragon boat festival. Past Duck Key, you'll encounter the town of Marathon, an unassuming 13-mile-long community that stretches from Grassy Key to Knight's Key.

Besides casual seafood eateries and motel hideaways, this sleepy region offers several wildlife-oriented activities, from dolphin swims to bird-watching haunts. On Grassy Key, you'll find a nonprofit dolphin and sea lion center that offers tours and interactive programs, and farther south lie the islands that make up a 260-acre state park especially favored among kayakers, who frequently spot

© LAURA MARTONE

HIGHLIGHTS

Long Key State Park: Situated between Layton and Marathon and occupying most of Long Key, this tranquil park, once the site of a posh fishing resort, contains a campground, a canoe/kayak launching area, several picnic pavilions, two nature trails, and a narrow beach that offers easy ocean access for swimmers, snorkelers, and anglers (page 156).

Dolphin Research Center: Once home to the frisky dolphins that starred in the 1963 film *Flipper,* this nonprofit marine mammal facility on Grassy Key offers a variety of educational experiences, including brief dolphin dips, deep-water dolphin encounters, and day-long research programs (page 158).

Curry Hammock State Park: Comprising several islands near Marathon, this family-friendly park features a campground, several picnic tables, a 1.5-mile nature trail through a preserved hardwood hammock, and a pleasant beach and playground area that entices swimmers, kayakers, anglers, and bird-watchers alike (page 160).

Sombrero Beach: Part of a public park in southern Marathon that provides picnic pavilions, volleyball courts, and a small playground, this curvy, palm-lined expanse of sand is a preferred spot among swimmers, beach-

combers, and, from April to October, nesting turtles (page 161).

Pigeon Key: South of Marathon and accessible via ferry or the defunct Old Seven Mile Bridge, this tiny coral island invites history buffs to stroll amid several picturesque buildings that collectively served as the base camp for Henry Flagler's railroad workers in the early 20th century (page 162).

Battle in the Bay: Every May, spectators flock to Sombrero Beach to watch this lively, colorful dragon boat race, the organizers of which typically donate part of the proceeds to various local nonprofit organizations (page 167).

Fishing and Boating Around the Middle Keys: Like the Upper and Lower Keys, the Marathon area offers full-service marinas, fishing charters, and boat rentals, all of which can help anglers in search of permit, bonefish, tarpon, and other fish in the offshore and back-country waters of the Middle Keys (page 170).

Diving near Sombrero Reef: With the help of area operators, first-timers can learn the ropes of scuba diving before venturing out to explore the elkhorn coral and tropical fish of this spur-and-groove reef formation, designated by a 142-foot tower (page 172).

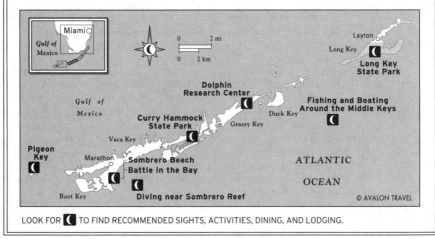

LOOK FOR **(** TO FIND RECOMMENDED SIGHTS, ACTIVITIES, DINING, AND LODGING.

manatees, raptors, herons, egrets, and other birds in the area.

In addition, Marathon has relaxing spas, a public golf course, several campgrounds, a commuter airport featuring sightseeing tours, and numerous adventure outfitters and operators that assist visiting bikers, anglers, boaters, and scuba divers. A popular attraction among children is the Crane Point Museum and Nature Center, which encompasses a natural history museum, a bird center, a nature trail, and one of the oldest houses in the Florida Keys.

En route to the Lower Keys, you'll cross the Seven Mile Bridge—a long stretch across open water that's unnerving for some. Along the way, you'll pass tiny Pigeon Key, a historic, early 20th-century work camp situated beside the Old Seven Mile Bridge, an engineering marvel that was once considered the Eighth Wonder of the World.

HISTORY

The original inhabitants of the islands that now constitute the Middle Keys were, as on the rest of the Florida Keys, Native American tribes who probably came to the region as early as 2000 B.C. Primarily hunters and gatherers, these Indians relied on food from the ocean, including manatees, which were, at that time, more plentiful in these waters. Given that manatees are also known as "sea cows" and that the Spanish word for "cow" is *vaca*, it's no wonder that the earliest known name for Marathon's biggest island was Key Vaca.

According to many historical accounts, New England fishermen ventured to Key Vaca in the early 1800s. Here, they spent the winter months fishing the surrounding waters in order to sell their catches in Cuba. It's believed that, eventually, these fishermen relocated to Key West, which offered a much better harbor.

The next settlers to arrive on Key Vaca were undoubtedly former Bahamian nationals who moved here to fish, farm, and salvage wrecks. By 1840, the settlement known as Conch Town encompassed 50 homes and a school, but the community's existence was short-lived. When, in August of that year, Seminole Indians raided

Indian Key to the north, the Conch Town inhabitants fled south to Key West.

Once the threat of Indian attacks had subsided, roughly 20 families returned to Key Vaca in the late 1840s, but by 1870, the island was once more deserted. Over three decades later, a group of black Bahamians settled at what is now Crane Point Hammock. The settlement, known as Adderley Town, was named after the group's leader, George Adderley, and now stands as the oldest house in the Keys outside of Key West.

In 1904, construction of Henry Flagler's Overseas Railroad commenced on Key Vaca. Here, the Florida East Coast Railway erected construction headquarters, central supply facilities, shops, a church and a school, a hospital and a hotel, as well as living quarters for hundreds of railroad workers. According to legend, Flagler was pushing his workers so hard to complete the railroad that one worker exclaimed, "Building this railroad has become a regular marathon!" Soon afterward, the town's name changed from Key Vaca to Marathon— though it's interesting to note that the largest island in the Middle Keys is still known as Vaca Key.

Following the 1912 completion of the railroad, the population of Marathon quickly declined. By World War II, Marathon experienced a resurgence due, in large part, to additions like electricity, a water pipeline, an airport, and the overseas highway. Attracted to the region by its pleasant climate and excellent fishing opportunities, new residents sparked the area's growth in the 1950s, and today, the population of Marathon—which consists of the islands between Grassy Key and Knight's Key—now exceeds 10,600.

PLANNING YOUR TIME

Like Islamorada and the Lower Keys, Marathon and the rest of the Middle Keys are made up of numerous islands, most of which are easily accessible by car, via the Overseas Highway. Given the sheer variety of attractions, extending from Long Key at mile marker 67 to Pigeon Key near mile marker

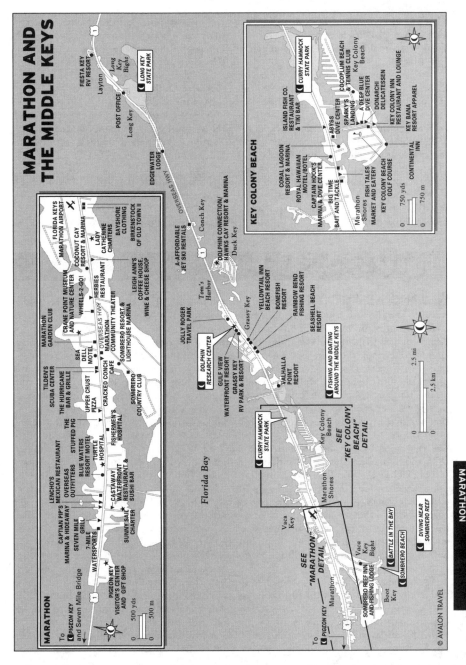

MARATHON AND THE MIDDLE KEYS

MARATHON

To ◄ PIGEON KEY
and Seven Mile Bridge

PIGEON KEY
VISITOR'S CENTER
AND GIFT SHOP

0   500 yds
0   500 m

LENCHO'S
MEXICAN RESTAURANT
CAPTAIN PIP'S
MARINA & HIDEAWAY
SEVEN MILE
GRILL
7-MILE
WATERSPORTS
BLUE WATERS
RESORT MOTEL
OVERSEAS
OUTFITTERS
THE
STUFFED PIG
TURTLE
HOSPITAL
SUNNY SAIL
CHARTER
CASTAWAY
WATERFRONT
RESTAURANT &
SUSHI BAR
FISHERMEN'S
HOSPITAL
SOMBRERO
COUNTRY CLUB
TILDEN'S
SCUBA CENTER
THE HURRICANE
BAR & GRILLE
UPPER CRUST
PIZZA
CRACKED CONCH
CAFE
SOMBRERO RESORT &
LIGHTHOUSE MARINA
SEA
DELL
MOTEL
MARATHON
COMMUNITY THEATER
MARATHON
GARDEN CLUB
CRANE POINT MUSEUM
AND NATURE CENTER
OVERSEAS HWY
LEIGH ANN'S
COFFEE HOUSE,
WINE & CHEESE SHOP
HERBIES
RESTAURANT
WHEELS-2-GO!
COCONUT CAY
RESORT & MARINA
LADY
CATHERINE
CHARTERS
BAYSHORE
CLOTHING
BIRKENSTOCK
OF OLD TOWN II
FLORIDA KEYS
MARATHON AIRPORT

KEY COLONY BEACH

CORAL LAGOON
RESORT & MARINA
ROYAL HAWAIIAN
MOTEL/MOTEL
CAPTAIN HOOK'S
MARINA & DIVE CENTER
BIG TIME
BAIT AND TACKLE
Marathon
Shores
FISH TALES
MARKET AND EATERY
KEY COLONY BEACH
GOLF COURSE
ISLAND FISH CO.
RESTAURANT
& TIKI BAR
ABYSS
DIVE CENTER
A DEEP BLUE
DIVE CENTER
SPARKY'S
LANDING
DONARCHI
DELICATESSEN
KEY COLONY INN
RESTAURANT AND LOUNGE
COCOPLUM BEACH
Key Colony
Beach
SPARKY'S
& TENNIS CLUB
KEY BANA
RESORT APPAREL
CONTINENTAL
INN
◄ CURRY HAMMOCK
STATE PARK

0   750 yds
0   750 m

FIESTA KEY
RV RESORT
Long
Key
Bight
Layton
◄ LONG KEY
STATE PARK
POST OFFICE
Long Key
EDGEWATER
LODGE
OVERSEAS HWY
Conch Key
A-AFFORDABLE
JET SKI RENTALS
DOLPHIN CONNECTION/
HAWKS CAY RESORT & MARINA
Duck Key
Tom's
Harbor
◄ DOLPHIN
RESEARCH CENTER
JOLLY ROGER
TRAVEL PARK
GULF VIEW
WATERFRONT RESORT
GRASSY KEY
RV PARK & RESORT
VALHALLA
POINT RESORT
Grassy Key
YELLOWTAIL INN
BEACH RESORT
BONEFISH
RESORT
RAINBOW BEND
FISHING RESORT
SEASHELL BEACH
RESORT
◄ FISHING AND BOATING
AROUND THE MIDDLE KEYS
◄ CURRY HAMMOCK
STATE PARK
Key Colony
Beach
SEE
"KEY COLONY
BEACH"
DETAIL
Marathon
Shores
Florida Bay
Vaca Key
SEE
"MARATHON"
DETAIL
Marathon
Vaca
Key
Bight
Boot
Key
To
◄ PIGEON KEY
SOMBRERO REEF INN
AND FISHING LODGE
◄ SOMBRERO BEACH
◄ BATTLE IN THE BAY
◄ DIVING NEAR
SOMBRERO REEF

0   2.5 mi
0   2.5 km

© AVALON TRAVEL

MARATHON

45, a proper visit may take a few days—even longer if you plan to add activities like fishing, kayaking, camping, windsurfing, and golf to your itinerary.

Just be prepared, as with other parts of the Florida Keys, to deal with traffic congestion, crowded restaurants and attractions, and higher lodging rates during late winter and early spring. When planning a trip to the Middle Keys, you should also consider factors like climate, fishing seasons, and annual events such as the Battle in the Bay, a dragon boat race that takes place at Sombrero Beach every May. If you're a novice to certain activities, such as scuba diving, you might also want to allow for proper instruction time.

Where you decide to stay, however, is entirely up to you. With a car, it's easy enough to navigate the entire region, so whether you choose a resort near mile marker 68 or a campground near mile marker 47, you should be able to reach everything you hope to see and experience in the Middle Keys.

For more information about Marathon and the Middle Keys, consult the **Monroe County Tourist Development Council** (1201 White St., Ste. 102, Key West, FL 33040, 305/296-1552 or 800/352-5397, www.fla-keys.com) and the **Greater Marathon Chamber of Commerce** (12222 Overseas Hwy., Marathon, FL 33050, 305/743-5417 or 800/262-7284, www.floridakeysmarathon.com).

Sights

◖ LONG KEY STATE PARK

Between the flyspeck community of Layton and the lengthy town of Marathon lies Long Key, a strangely shaped island that, from above, appears to resemble the open jaws of a vicious snake. Perhaps that's why Spanish explorers originally called this island Cayo Vivora, which means "Rattlesnake Key." In the early 20th century, it was the site of a luxurious fishing resort that was favored by the author Zane Grey and other saltwater anglers. Eventually, the resort was wiped away by the Labor Day hurricane of 1935, the same terrible tempest that destroyed Henry Flagler's Overseas Railroad. Nowadays, Long Key often appears on maps of the Upper Keys, but given that it's not technically part of Islamorada and that its upscale past has now been usurped by a quiet, nature-oriented vibe, it seems more suited for the Middle Keys. Just bear in mind that not everyone will agree with such a sentiment.

Today, Long Key is home to the aptly titled Long Key State Park (67400 Overseas Hwy., Long Key, 305/664-4815, www.floridastateparks.org/longkey, 8 A.M.–sunset daily, $5 vehicles w/2–8 passengers plus $0.50 pp, $4.50 motorcycles and single-occupant

vehicles, $2.50 pedestrians, bikers, and extra passengers), a popular place among anglers, swimmers, snorkelers, picnickers, and campers since it was established in 1969. Encompassing roughly 1,000 acres, this pleasant preserve features a variety of foliage, including mangrove forests, lush vegetation, scrubby grass, vibrant wildflowers, and dense, inland trees like poisonwood, gumbo limbo, and coconut palm. Given such greenery, hikers may appreciate the two on-site nature trails—the **Golden Orb Trail,** which was named after a native spider and offers a 1.2-mile stroll through various plant communities, and the **Layton Trail,** a 0.3-mile walk on the bay side of the park—while bird-watchers will relish spying a wide array of vibrant species, from wading egrets to red-bellied woodpeckers, which are particularly prevalent during the winter months.

Of course, canoeists especially favor this tranquil place, which features the leisurely **Long Key Lakes Canoe Trail** through a shallow lagoon. Canoe rentals ($5 hourly, $10 daily) and a self-guided brochure make this a relatively easy diversion for novices, too. For some visitors, another highlight is the narrow, rocky, grass-lined beach on the ocean side of

MARATHON

the park, not far from picnic pavilions, public showers, and a canoe/kayak launching area. Only open to those staying in the state park campground, it tends to be more peaceful than the beaches farther south, though it can also be rather muddy at times. Guided trail walks (10 A.M. Wed. Dec.–May, free) and interpretive programs (10 A.M. Thurs. year-round, free), from bird-watching talks to snorkeling excursions, are periodically available, and be aware that, while leashed, well-behaved pets are ostensibly permitted here, they are not allowed on the beaches, in the picnic shelters, or in the restrooms. Fireworks and hunting are also prohibited.

DOLPHIN ATTRACTIONS
Dolphin Connection

If you're driving west from Long Key, you'll cross the Long Key Channel and pass through the Conch Keys before encountering the secluded, 60-acre island known as Duck Key on the ocean side of the highway. Situated here is the luxurious **Hawks Cay Resort** (61 Hawks Cay Blvd., Duck Key, 305/743-7000, www. hawkscay.com), which offers a slew of diversions, from water sports and spa services to the Dolphin Connection (888/313-5749, www. dolphinconnection.com, 9 A.M.–5 P.M. daily), which was established in 1990 as a marine mammal education, breeding, and research facility. Like the other interactive dolphin facilities in the Florida Keys, the Dolphin Connection allows visitors to interact with these friendly marine mammals from the dock or within the on-site saltwater lagoon.

Three basic programs are available here. The 30-minute Dockside Dolphins program ($60 pp) allows you to feed, play with, and interact with the dolphins without ever getting in the water, though splashing may still be involved; all ages are welcome, though children under 6 must be accompanied by a paid adult. The 25-minute Dolphin Discovery program ($155 pp), meanwhile, offers you the chance to touch, kiss, hug, splash, and swim with the dolphins; although there are no age restrictions, participants must be at least 4.5 feet tall. Lastly, the

© DANIEL MARTONE

rewarding dolphins at the Dolphin Research Center

MARATHON

MANATEE RESCUE

While visiting the Florida Keys, you may be fortunate enough to spy an endangered **West Indian manatee,** also known as a "sea cow," in the warm coastal waters surrounding this archipelago – especially during the winter months, when ocean temperatures drop. A giant yet gentle creature and the state's official marine mammal, the manatee inhabits shallow estuaries and saltwater bays, feeds on aquatic vegetation, and has sadly been diminished by boat collisions, propeller injuries, rope and fishing line entanglements, vandal attacks, poachers, habitat destruction, oil spills, and cold stress.

Although protected from harassment, hunting, capture, or murder by the Marine Mammal Protection Act of 1972 and the Endangered Species Act of 1973, the manatee continues to suffer from human actions – despite the fact that anyone convicted of violating such federal laws may face a fine of up to $100,000 and/or a year in prison. In fact, it's believed by many experts that there are only 3,300 of these precious mammals left in the wild. Luckily, nonprofit organizations like the **Save the Manatee Club (SMC)** (500 N. Maitland Ave., Maitland, FL 32751, 407/539-0990 or 800/432-5646, www.savethemanatee.org), begun in 1981 by singer/songwriter Jimmy Buffett and former Florida governor and U.S. senator Bob Graham, are doing what they can to protect these endangered creatures and their habitat for future generations.

In addition to providing a wide array of interactive dolphin and sea lion programs, the **Dolphin Research Center (DRC)** (58901 Overseas Hwy., Grassy Key, 305/289-1121 or 305/289-0002, www.dolphins.org, 9 A.M.-4:30 P.M. daily, fees apply) is also actively involved in manatee conservation efforts. The DRC even has a Manatee Rescue Team, nicknamed the Gray Cross, but naturally, the efforts of the SMC and DRC are greatly enhanced by assistance from the public. Here are just a few ways that you can protect endangered manatees and aid in conservation efforts:

- Try to stay in marked, deep-water channels, where manatees are less likely to be.

- Obey all signage and speed laws when boating in coastal waters; as the SMC encourages, "Navigate with care. Manatees are there."

- Drive slowly and designate a lookout person, who will watch for wildlife, swimmers, boaters, and obstructions.

- Do not enter designated manatee sanctuaries for any reason.

- Wear polarized glasses to improve visibility and make it easier to spot the surface swirls that indicate a manatee is near.

- If you see wild manatees while swimming, snorkeling, diving, boating, or operating other watercraft, please observe them from the water's surface and at a distance of at least 50 feet.

- Avoid excessive noise and splashing if a manatee appears in your swimming area,

engrossing Trainer for a Day program ($295 pp) offers participants (who must be at least 10 years of age and 4.5 feet tall) a three-hour, behind-the-scenes look at the daily activities of the training team; Dockside Dolphins and Dolphin Discovery are both included with this program. Advance reservations (operators available 8 A.M.–9 P.M. Mon.–Fri., 9 A.M.–7 P.M. Sat.–Sun.) are required for all programs, all of which are preceded by a proper orientation, and short-style wetsuits are provided free of charge to those entering the water. Also note that, unlike other dolphin facilities in the Florida Keys, the Dolphin Connection does not charge for merely observing the programs.

◖ Dolphin Research Center

On the bay side of Grassy Key, you'll spot the hard-to-miss sign for the Dolphin Research Center (DRC, 58901 Overseas Hwy., Grassy

and use snorkel gear, in lieu of noisier scuba gear, when observing the manatees.

- Do not touch, poke, hook, ride, chase, surround, feed, or give water to wild manatees, as such actions can put them on the defensive, alter their natural behavior, and ultimately cause them to vacate warmer areas for fear of being harassed.

- Never isolate an individual or separate a mother and her calf.

- If you spot an injured, entangled, tagged, orphaned, or deceased manatee, call the **Florida Fish and Wildlife Conservation Commission (FWC)** (888/404-3922) or use VHF Channel 16 on your marine radio, which will launch a trained, authorized response to aid the animal.

- Do not approach or try to assist the manatee, which can put you at risk and potentially scare away the injured animal.

- Report any criminal activities involving these marine mammals.

According to the DRC, concerned Florida Keys citizens and visitors have made hundreds of calls over the years to report manatees in distress, resulting in the successful rescue, treatment, and release of many of these gentle giants. Still, you can do even more to help endangered manatees as well as other at-risk marine creatures, such as threatened and endangered sea turtles, by simply preserving their habitat. With an increased number of boaters and anglers every year, it's imperative that you do your part to keep the waters clean and safe for the organisms that live there. Here are some of the precautions you can take:

- Use onshore restrooms and pump-out facilities in lieu of discharging treated or untreated sewage into offshore waters.

- Do not discard trash, fishing gear (such as nets, hooks, or monofilament line), fish waste, or other pollutants (such as fuel and oil) into the water, which can harm manatees as well as sea turtles.

- Use oil-absorbent materials in your bilge and for cleanups, and recycle used oil, antifreeze, oil filters, and batteries.

- Rely on the smallest amount of the least toxic products, and wipe up, rather than hose off, any spills.

- Do not spill cleaners, detergents, paints, or solvents overboard or wash them down drains.

- Keep your vessel clean and well maintained, and if possible, do all painting, pressure-washing, and repairs while in dry dock.

- Report oil spills and debris violations to the proper authorities.

- Minimize your wake near shore to prevent erosion, avoid disturbing submerged aquatic vegetation, and adhere to all posted "no wake" zones.

Key, 305/289-1121 or 305/289-0002, www.dolphins.org, 9 A.M.–4:30 P.M. daily, $19.50 adults, $16.50 seniors 55 and over, $13.50 children 4–12, children under 4 free), a nonprofit education, research, and rescue facility that "promises peaceful coexistence, cooperation, and communication between marine mammals, humans, and the environment." Adhering to this mission statement, DRC features a wide array of programs—from brief dolphin dips to daylong research programs—that could easily be classified as "edutainment."

Founded in 1984, the facility that is now DRC has, in fact, a much longer history. Despite a shift in ownership over the years, this site has been a continuously operated marine mammal facility since 1956, when fisherman Milton Santini captured several bottlenose dolphins, including one he called "Mitzi," and formed Santini's Porpoise School. In 1963,

Mitzi starred in the original *Flipper* movie, along with five other resident dolphins. When Mitzi passed away in 1972, Santini sold the property to an entertainment conglomerate that operated the site as Flipper's Sea School. It wasn't until 1977, however, that the facility began to shift its purpose to the one upheld today—that of, among other things, cultivating environmental ambassadors among the visiting public.

Today, visitors can watch a variety of educational shows and demonstrations, during which dolphins get a chance to display their learned behaviors, while trainers can offer a bit of insight into caretaking aspects that are rarely seen by the public, such as administering medicine to a sick dolphin. In addition, guests can opt to meet a dolphin from the dock ($25 pp), hug a sea lion ($30 pp), toss toys to the dolphins ($50 pp), paint with a dolphin ($55 pp), experience a group dip with the dolphins ($104 pp), or have a shallow-water or deep-water dolphin encounter ($189 pp). Truly immersive activities include the trainer-for-a-day ($650 pp) and researcher-for-a-day ($500 pp) programs, both of which provide an intensive, all-day look into the folks that operate DRC. Age restrictions may apply for some of these programs, and almost all of the programs require advance reservations. DRC welcomes guests with disabilities, and staff members will do their best to accommodate them.

◖ CURRY HAMMOCK STATE PARK

West of Grassy Key is the largest uninhabited parcel of land between Key Largo and Big Pine Key. True, it's composed of several wooded islands, with names like Crawl Key, Little Crawl Key, Long Point Key, Deer Key, and Fat Deer Key, but nonetheless, Curry Hammock State Park (56200 Overseas Hwy., Marathon, 305/289-2690, www.floridastateparks.org/curryhammock, 8 A.M.–sunset daily, $5 vehicles w/2–8 passengers plus $0.50 pp, $4.50 motorcycles and single-occupant vehicles, $2.50 pedestrians, bikers, and extra passengers) constitutes an impressive, nearly development-free

the beach at Curry Hammock State Park
© DANIEL MARTONE

place in the heart of a fairly populated region. Encompassing more than 1,000 acres, Curry Hammock protects sizable seagrass beds, mangrove swamps, and rockland hammocks, including one of the country's largest populations of thatch palms.

Established in 1991 and named after Lamar Louise Curry—a respected Miami teacher whose father, Thomas, purchased large tracts of land in the Upper and Middle Keys—this popular park offers a full-facility campground, picnic tables and pavilions, and easy access to swimming, windsurfing, canoeing, and kayaking opportunities. Visitors can even rent single and double kayaks on-site ($17.20–21.50 per two hours). In addition, hikers can stroll along a 1.5-mile **nature trail** through a preserved hardwood hammock on Fat Deer Key. Little Crawl Key features a pleasant beach and playground area, which is accessible by overnight campers and day-use visitors alike.

Fishing and beachcombing are popular activities here, and bird-watchers will also appreciate this park, which lies on a critical bird migration route and hosts the annual Florida Keys Birding and Wildlife Festival. The beaches, hammock, and grass flats are home to a wide array of herons, egrets, plovers, sanderlings, white-crowned pigeons, pelicans, osprey, and bald eagles. Wildlife lovers might also spot Key Vaca raccoons, nurse sharks, spotted rays, dolphins, and manatees.

Bikers are welcome to ride along the park roads as well as a two-mile stretch of the **Florida Keys Overseas Heritage Trail,** which leads to and from Marathon. Just remember to wear a helmet at all times, and be advised that biking is not permitted on the boardwalks, foot paths, or nature trail inside the park. You should be aware, too, that while leashed, well-behaved pets are ostensibly permitted here, they are not allowed along the shoreline, in the water, or in the picnic area and restrooms. Fireworks and hunting are also prohibited.

CRANE POINT MUSEUM AND NATURE CENTER

Near mile marker 50, on the bay side of U.S. 1 in the heart of Marathon, lies the Crane Point Museum and Nature Center (5550 Overseas Hwy., Marathon, 305/743-9100, www.cranepoint.net, 9 A.M.–5 P.M. Mon.–Sat., noon–5 P.M. Sun., $12 adults, $10 seniors over 65, $8 children 6–12, children under 6 free), a sprawling, 63-acre preserve that families with young children especially favor. Your first stop is typically the **Museum of Natural History,** where you can learn about the human history of the Florida Keys, including facts about the Calusa Indians that once inhabited these islands, the Spanish and British explorers that later discovered them, and the Bahamian pioneers that eventually called them home. Here, you'll also discover stories about various shipwrecks and the ill-fated Overseas Railroad. Other dioramas and exhibits explore the flora, fauna, and geology that define this diverse region, including mangroves, butterflies, sea turtles, and coral reefs.

From the museum, most visitors venture outside, where you can view a 10-minute orientation video, watch daily fish feedings in the saltwater lagoon, and interact with marine creatures like conch and starfish in the on-site touch tanks. Afterward, you can explore ever-changing creature exhibits in a Cracker-style bungalow, venture across a butterfly meadow peppered with aromatic flowers, and stroll amid thatch palm trees and mangroves. Additionally, nature trails lead to three curious destinations, including the historic **Adderley House,** an open, weathered, Bahamian-style structure built in the early 1900s by Bahamian immigrant George Adderley. Formed from Tabby, a concrete-like material made of burned conch and other shells, the Adderley House is the oldest house in the Florida Keys north of Key West and now invites visitors to wander amid old-fashioned beds, chests, and other furnishings, reminiscent of those used by George and Olivia Adderley when they lived here between 1902 and 1949.

Other accessible stops along the way include the **Wild Bird Center,** which aims to rescue, rehabilitate, and release injured gulls, osprey, and other native birds, and the art deco–style **Crane House,** constructed in the 1950s and once home to Francis and Mary Crane, a Massachusetts couple who purchased the land here in 1949. Both passionate conservationists and horticulturists, the Cranes worked hard to preserve and enhance the preserve with flowering trees and shrubs. The family retained the property until the late 1970s, and by 1989, it was purchased by the Florida Keys Land and Sea Trust in order to spare it from impending development. Eventually, this preserve of palm and hardwood hammocks, mangrove forests, tidal lagoons, and wetland ponds was named for Francis and Mary Crane, whose former home isn't far from **Crane Point** itself, where you can observe pelicans, raptors, and other native bird species along the shore of Florida Bay. If possible, try to visit the nature preserve on a sunny day, when the foliage looks infinitely better than on an overcast one.

◖ SOMBRERO BEACH

Located at the end of Sombrero Beach Road, near mile marker 50 in Marathon, Sombrero

© DANIEL MARTONE

strolling along Sombrero Beach, home to the Battle in the Bay

Beach (305/292-4560, free) is definitely one of the more popular beaches in the Florida Keys. Part of a public park that offers picnic pavilions, volleyball courts, public restrooms, and a small playground, this curving, palm-lined expanse of sand is also a preferred spot for nesting turtles from April to October. Favored among swimmers, snorkelers, picnickers, wind-surfers, and volleyball enthusiasts, Sombrero Beach is home to the annual Battle in the Bay, a dragon boat race that typically takes place in May. Although there are no concessions, equipment rentals, or camping facilities on-site, families, couples, and active individuals simply adore this place, especially on a sunny, cloudless day—and unlike many beaches in the Keys, Sombrero allows pets, provided they're well-behaved.

TURTLE HOSPITAL

Situated on the western end of Vaca Key and dedicated to ensuring the survival of sea turtles, the Turtle Hospital (2396 Overseas Hwy., Marathon, 305/743-2552, www.turtlehospital.

org, 9 A.M.–6 P.M. daily, $15 adults, $7.50 children 4–12, children under 4 free) is the only state-certified veterinary hospital of its kind in the world. Featuring up-to-date medical equipment, the nonprofit facility strives to rescue and rehabilitate injured sea turtles, with the goal of releasing them back into the wild. The turtle species typically found in the Florida Keys include the threatened loggerhead turtles as well as the endangered green, hawksbill, leatherback, and Kemps Ridley turtles. In recent years, threats to such turtles have encompassed fishing line and net entanglements; boat strikes; oil spills; coastal development, which damages nesting sites; and intestinal impaction due to the ingestion of floating debris. The hospital can receive as many as 70 turtles yearly—even more during particularly cold winters when hundreds of stunned sea turtles have been found floating in the ocean. To date, this working hospital has successfully released more than 1,000 sea turtles.

As part of its educational outreach component, the Turtle Hospital features an education center (plus gift shop) and invites guests to take a guided 1.5-hour tour of the facility. Three such tours are offered daily (10 A.M., 1 P.M., and 4 P.M.) and consist of a slide show presentation, a behind-the-scenes look at the hospital facilities, a visit to the outdoor turtle rehabilitation area, and an opportunity to feed the permanent residents. Bear in mind that this tour will require a minimal amount of walking; limited wheelchair access is available. Reservations for these tours are highly recommended, given space limitations, but be advised that poor weather and turtle emergencies may supersede any scheduled tour. All minors under the age of 18 must be accompanied by an adult.

◖ PIGEON KEY

To reach the Lower Keys from Marathon, simply head west across the **Seven Mile Bridge.** Along the way, you'll spy an isolated, palm-dotted island tucked beside the **Old Seven Mile Bridge,** once considered an engineering marvel and, by some historians, the Eighth Wonder of the

MARATHON

FROM CAPTIVITY TO THE WILD

The primary mission of the **Turtle Hospital** (2396 Overseas Hwy., 305/743-2552, www.turtlehospital.org), a nonprofit facility on Vaca Key in southern Marathon, is to rescue, rehabilitate, and reintroduce injured sea turtles into the wild. While this particular organization has successfully released more than 1,000 sea turtles into the waters surrounding the Florida Keys, not all captive animals, such as the dolphins that reside at the **Dolphin Connection** (61 Hawks Cay Blvd., Duck Key, 888/313-5749, www.dolphinconnection.com) and the **Dolphin Research Center** (58901 Overseas Hwy., Grassy Key, 305/289-1121 or 305/289-0002, www.dolphins.org), can or should be released into the wild.

For one thing, reintroducing an animal must be done in a manner that protects wild populations as well as the individual being released. Though the marine mammal community returns hundreds of stranded animals to the wild each year, it can be dangerous to reintroduce one that's been in long-term human care. Such dangers include disease transmission, unwanted genetic exchange, the inability for the released animal to nourish and defend itself, and, perhaps most notably, the fact that said animal has lost its natural fear of humans.

Typically, wild animals keep their distance from people, but a marine mammal accustomed to interacting with and being fed by humans can become vulnerable to a variety of problems. Such animals may, for instance:

- Spend a lot of time near boats, where they can be struck by hulls and cut by propellers

- Learn to steal fish from fishing lines, thereby ingesting monofilament line and hooks

- Eat inappropriate food, such as spoiled fish, beer, ice cream, or nonedible items

- Get pushy and aggressive when they don't get the handouts they've come to expect

- Encounter people who view them as nuisances, which can get them shot or otherwise injured

In the gulf and ocean waters surrounding the Florida Keys, you'll find plenty of opportunities to see wild dolphins, whether from shore or by boat. Although watching them in their natural habitat can be an amazing experience, it's important that you practice responsible viewing. Approaching such creatures too closely, moving too quickly, or making too much noise can increase the risk of harassment and possibly disrupt natural behaviors like migration, sheltering, breeding, nursing, feeding, and breathing – which is actually against federal law. For more information about the responsible viewing of wild dolphins in the Florida Keys National Marine Sanctuary, consult **Dolphin SMART** (www.dolphinsmart.org), a program that promotes:

- **S**taying at least 50 yards from dolphins

- **M**oving away cautiously if dolphins show signs of disturbance

- **A**lways putting one's engine in neutral when dolphins are near

- **R**efraining from feeding, touching, or swimming with wild dolphins

- **T**eaching others to be Dolphin SMART

World. This tiny coral island, known as Pigeon Key, has been lovingly preserved by the Pigeon Key Foundation (305/289-0025)—in order to capture the atmosphere of the early 1900s, when it served as a base camp for railroad workers. Here, you can take a self-guided walking tour of the grounds, which includes educational facilities, a small museum, and, of course, the historic buildings that once housed more than 400 workers, who labored 14 hours a day, six days a week, to construct Henry Flagler's ill-fated Overseas Railroad. Besides the history lesson, you might also enjoy picnicking on this lovely little island. Snorkeling is also a possibility; you can either bring your own snorkel and mask or borrow the gear that's available on Pigeon Key.

MARATHON

a former workers' camp on Pigeon Key

You can purchase tickets to Pigeon Key at the **Pigeon Key Visitor's Center and Gift Shop** (1 Knight's Key Blvd., Knight's Key, 305/743-5999, www.pigeonkey.net, 9:30 A.M.–2:30 P.M. daily, $11 adults, $8.50 Monroe County residents and children 5–13, children under 5 free), which is housed in a silver train car near mile marker 47. The admission price grants you access to Pigeon Key all day and includes a guided ferry ride from Knight's Key to the island (10 A.M., 11:30 A.M., 1 P.M., and 2:30 P.M. daily) and back again (10:30 A.M., noon, 1:30 P.M., 3 P.M., and 4 P.M. daily). Reservations for the ferry are definitely advised, especially on holidays and weekends. Of course, you can also access this historic site by walking or biking down a 2.2-mile segment of the Old Seven Mile Bridge from Knight's Key; in addition, you can reach the island via private boat. If you opt against the ferry service and choose to come by foot, bicycle, or private vessel, admission fees and docking charges will still apply, so be sure to stop by

the gift shop to make advance arrangements for your visit.

BOAT AND AIR TOURS

For a relaxing tour of the surrounding waters, consider heading to the Seascape Motel and Marina (1275 E. 76th St. Ocean, Marathon), where you can hire **Lady Catherine Charters** (305/743-5544, www.diveandfishmarathon. com, hours vary daily, $200 per cruise) for a private, two-hour sunset cruise. Such cruises can be customized, whether you'd like to toast the occasion with champagne or even, as other guests have done, renew your marital vows in the midst of a glorious Florida Keys sunset. The boat can accommodate up to 22 passengers, so bring your friends and loved ones along for the ride. As an alternative, you can board a 43-foot sailing ketch through **Sunny Sail Charters** (Marathon Marina and Boat Yard, 1021 11th St., Marathon, 305/394-4319, www.sunny-sailcharters.com), a seasonal touring company that offers couples or small groups the chance to journey across ocean waters for two-hour sunset sails (times vary daily depending on the sunset, $150 couples), four-hour luncheon sails (10 A.M. daily, $300 couples, $75 additional couples), four-hour sunset dinner cruises (times vary daily depending on the sunset, $350 couples, $100 additional couples), or customized trips. Reservations are a must for both companies.

Between Key Colony Beach and the Crane Point Museum, you'll surely spot the Florida Keys Marathon Airport, from which **Conch Air** (Marathon Airport, Marathon, 305/395-1117, www.conch-air.com) offers exhilarating, open-air biplane rides high above the Florida Keys and the shimmering waters of the Atlantic Ocean and the Gulf of Mexico. Besides the basic scenic ride ($74 pp, based on two passengers), Conch Air offers mile-high flights, scenic aerobatic flights, and romantic sunset flights at varying rates and times. From the Marathon airport, you can also opt for the **Keys Heli Tour** (9850 Overseas Hwy., Marathon, 305/393-5645, www.keyshelitour.

com), which offers a helicopter adventure high above the beaches, coral reefs, and aquamarine waters of the Middle Keys. Besides customized tours, you can opt for a 10-minute, 15-mile trip ($75 pp) or a 20-minute, 30-mile trip ($125 pp). Just be advised that there must be a minimum of two passengers, and all tours are limited to three passengers, with a maximum combined weight of 550 pounds.

For a completely different experience, board one of the three vintage World War II airplanes operated by **History Flight** (MM 52 BS U.S. 1, Marathon, 888/743-3311, www.historyflight. com, times and rates vary). Under the guidance of a certified flight instructor, you can fly the flagship *Mitchell,* a North American B-25 bomber; the *Texan,* a North American AT-6 trainer; or the *Stearman,* a Boeing N2S biplane. While you're learning to fly, know that you're helping a worthy cause, since all flight proceeds fund the nonprofit organization's ongoing research efforts and recovery expeditions dedicated to bringing missing-in-action servicemen home.

Entertainment and Shopping

NIGHTLIFE

If you're looking for a plethora of dance clubs and late-night bars, heading south to Key West might be your best bet. That doesn't mean, however, that you won't find nighttime diversions in the Middle Keys. As on the Upper and Lower Keys, several area bars and restaurants feature live music throughout the week.

At **The Hurricane Bar & Grille** (4650 Overseas Hwy., Marathon, 305/743-2220, www.thehurricanegrille.com, 11 A.M.–midnight daily), for instance, patrons can watch televised sports and enjoy nightly entertainment, from blues bands to country rock performers. Farther down the road, Barbara and Johnny Maddox invite nighttime revelers to their ever-popular **Porky's Bayside BBQ Restaurant** (1410 Overseas Hwy., Marathon, 305/289-2065, www.porkysbaysidebbq.com, 11 A.M.–10 P.M. daily), which offers a daily

happy hour (4–7 P.M.) and live bluegrass, country, or rock-'n'-roll nightly (6:30–9:30 P.M.) in a classic, laid-back Keys atmosphere.

In Key Colony Beach, near mile marker 53.5, you'll find two winning spots to while away the evening. Owned and operated by Matt and Carolyn Anthony, the rustic **Sparky's Landing** (400 Sadowski Cswy., Key Colony Beach, 305/289-7445, www.sparkyslanding. com, 11 A.M.–10 P.M. daily) provides locals and tourists a quintessential Florida Keys experience, featuring a daily happy hour (4–6 P.M.) as well as live folk, rock, country, and reggae music Wednesday–Saturday. Not far away, the family-owned **Key Colony Inn Restaurant and Lounge** (700 W. Ocean Dr., Key Colony Beach, 305/743-0100, www.kcinn.com, 11 A.M.–9:30 P.M. daily) has been a favorite among residents and visitors for well over 15 years—not just for the delicious cuisine, but

MARATHON

also for the live piano music in the on-site lounge every night.

THE ARTS

Though cultural enthusiasts will definitely find more concerts, dance performances, and theatrical venues in Key West, the Middle Keys still offer a few options for those seeking an alternative to outdoor activities. The **Marathon Garden Club** (5270 Overseas Hwy., Marathon, 305/743-4971, www.marathongardenclub.org), for example, has been known to host live performances, such as productions by the Island Opera Theatre (show times and ticket prices vary). In addition, the club features exhibits, workshops, educational programs, flower shows, and home and garden tours, not to mention an on-site garden and gift shop (10 A.M.–2 P.M. Mon.–Fri.).

The **Marathon Community Theater** (5101 Overseas Hwy., Marathon, 305/743-0994, www.marathontheater.org) has presented live theater and other entertainment to the Middle Keys since 1944. In addition to offering dance classes, readings, and screenings, such as classic movies every Wednesday at 2 P.M. (305/743-0288 for schedule), the theater features live performances (show times vary, $18 for plays, $24 for musicals), including modern farces, comedies, thrillers, and dramas, plus Broadway musicals. Recent productions have included the musical *Guys and Dolls* and the comedy-thriller *Deathtrap*. Performances are usually held Thursday–Saturday in the winter months, though events occur throughout the year. Student tickets ($9) are available for nonmusical performances, and patrons can purchase season passes ($54–70 pp) every year.

Near mile marker 49, the **Marathon Community Park** (200 36th St. OS, Marathon, 305/743-6598, www.ci.marathon.fl.us, 7 A.M.–10 P.M. daily) contains, among other facilities, an amphitheater for live performances. Call the park for current events. In addition, the **Middle Keys Concert Association** (www.marathonconcerts.com) has been hosting live musical performances, from piano concerts to string quartets, for more than four

decades. Seasons usually run from January to March, and most performances take place at the San Pablo Catholic Church (550 122nd St. OS, Marathon, 305/289-0636, www.sanpablo1.hypermart.net) near mile marker 53.5.

For information about other cultural events in the Middle Keys, consult the **Florida Keys Council of the Arts** (1100 Simonton St., Key West, 305/295-4369, www.keysarts.com).

FESTIVALS AND EVENTS

While Key West offers the lion's share of annual festivals and events—some of which even lure visitors during the hottest parts of the year—you'll certainly encounter a few curious celebrations in the Middle Keys.

Pigeon Key Art Festival

For over 15 years, art lovers have ventured to Marathon for the Pigeon Key Art Festival ($7 adults, $3 students, children under 13 free), hosted annually by the Pigeon Key Foundation (1 Knight's Key Blvd., Knight's Key, 305/743-5999, www.pigeonkey.net). Established by a gathering of local artists in 1995, this well-favored art show spent the first decade of its existence on Pigeon Key, the small, isolated island that sits beside the Old Seven Mile Bridge west of Marathon. For logistical reasons, the well-attended art festival, which typically takes place during the first weekend of February, shifted venues in 2005 to the Marathon Community Park on the ocean side of U.S. 1, near mile marker 49, where the attendance has continued to rise, even without the ambience of Pigeon Key.

Presented by volunteers, this annual event features live music, art raffles, and the artwork of roughly 85 artists from around the country—artwork that usually includes photography, jewelry, sculpture, glassware, fine crafts, and graphic arts, as well as watercolor, acrylic, and oil paintings. Food and beverages are often available, and the admission price includes a ferry ride to historic Pigeon Key—an excellent deal, considering that ferry tickets usually cost $11 for adults and $8.50 for children. Pets, save for service animals, are not allowed during the festival.

◀ Battle in the Bay

Each May, visitors flock to Marathon's Sombrero Beach, an oceanside stretch of sand accessible via Sombrero Beach Road near mile marker 50, to watch the Battle in the Bay Dragon Boat Festival (www.battle-inthebay.org), an annual race of festively decorated dragon boats. Launched directly from the beach, the colorful boats constitute more than just a heated competition on the water. Every year, the dragon boat teams are encouraged to gather pledges for the charities of their choice.

In addition, race organizers typically donate part of the proceeds from this event to local nonprofit organizations, such as Reef Relief. Although it costs a considerable amount to register a team for the race, it's absolutely free to watch the festivities—good news for locals and visitors alike. Parking ($3) is available at Marathon High School, located on Sombrero

Beach Road about a mile from the race site, and the flaming pink **KuKu KonKanut** bus (305/432-3202, www.kukukonkanut.com) provides free shuttle service from the parking lot to the beach. Typically, the one-day event occurs on a Saturday in early or mid-May, and area bars usually host fun-filled parties before and after the race.

Florida Keys Birding and Wildlife Festival

In late September, animal lovers head to the Middle Keys for the Florida Keys Birding and Wildlife Festival (305/852-4486, www. keysbirdingfest.org). Typically based out of Curry Hammock State Park (56200 Overseas Hwy., Marathon, 305/289-2690, www.flori-dastateparks.org/curryhammock), the five-day festival, which began in 1999, usually features an environmental fair and a series of field trips. Such educational excursions—some of which

DUANWU FESTIVAL

Though Marathon's **Battle in the Bay Dragon Boat Festival** (www.battleinthebay.org) epitomizes the spirited vibe of the Florida Keys, dragon boat festivals are certainly not unique to this part of the world. In fact, dragon boat racing is an ancient Chinese tradition. For more than 5,000 years, dragon boats have been used for ceremonial purposes in China, though it wasn't until the death of the beloved scholar, statesman, and poet Qu Yuan roughly 2,300 years ago that the Duanwu Festival was born.

As the story goes, Qu Yuan, a loyal minister to the King of Chu, was favored by the Chinese people, but his erudite ways greatly unnerved the other court officials, so much so that he was framed for conspiracy and exiled from his home. During the exile, he wrote numerous poems to express his ire and despair over his king, his country, and his people. Then, in the year 278 B.C., at the age of 37, he attempted to drown himself in a nearby river. Because he was still considered a righteous man by the people, several individuals leaped into

their boats and searched the waters for him, but their efforts were futile. Since then, the Dragon Boat Festival has commemorated this ill-fated attempt to rescue Qu Yuan.

Celebrated annually in various Asian countries, including Taiwan, Singapore, and Malaysia, the festival typically occurs on the fifth day of the fifth month of the lunar calendar and, among other activities, always features dragon boat racing. In the 1970s, Hong Kong was instrumental in the development of dragon boat racing as a modern sport. Today, the Duanwu Festival is an official national holiday in China, and the sport, which is governed by the **International Dragon Boat Federation** (www.idbf.org), enthralls more than 50 million people worldwide. For more information about dragon boat racing in southern Florida, contact the **Florida Keys Dragon Boat Club** (305/304-5100, www.floridakeysdragonboat. com) – and be sure to visit during Marathon's one-day version of the Dragon Boat Festival in early or mid-May.

MARATHON

are free and several of which range in price—may include a biking tour of the Florida Keys Overseas Heritage Trail, a self-guided stroll through the Florida Keys Wild Bird Center, a snorkeling trip to the Looe Key National Marine Sanctuary, or an all-day bird-watching journey to Dry Tortugas National Park.

Other Annual Events

Besides community events like the annual **Key Colony Beach Boat Parade** (305/743-7214)—a nighttime procession that usually takes place in mid-December and features lighted, decorated vessels amid the canals and cuts of Key Colony Beach—the Middle Keys host numerous fishing tournaments throughout the year. In early March, for instance, anglers can participate in the three-day **Leon Shell Memorial Sailfish Tournament** (www.leonshelltournament.com), which honors the late Captain Leon Shell—who died of brain cancer in 1997, while in the care of hospice workers—by benefiting the Hospice of the Florida Keys and Visiting Nurse Association (www.hospicevna.com).

Champions of the Leon Shell tournament are usually awarded a variety of trophies, prizes, and cash purses at Sparky's Landing in the Key Colony Beach Marina.

Other popular fishing events include the three-day **Marathon International Tarpon Tournament** (305/289-2248) in early May, the three-day **Burdines Waterfront Dolphin & Blackfin Tuna Fun Fishing Tournament** (305/743-5317, www.burdineswaterfront. com) in late June, and the four-day **Marathon International Bonefish Tournament** (305/743-7368) in mid-September.

SHOPPING

Truly dedicated shoppers will surely make a beeline for Key West, a town that abounds in art galleries, clothing shops, and other unique emporiums. Here in the Middle Keys, outdoor diversions, family-friendly attractions, and practical chain stores are definitely more prevalent than unique shopping opportunities. In fact, for the most part, you'll find little more than souvenir stores in the Marathon area.

the marina beside Sparky's Landing, site of the Leon Shell tournament

© DANIEL MARTONE

© LAURA MARTONE

shopping options in Marathon

On Vaca Key, for instance, you'll find a slew of gifts and souvenirs at the **Tropical Island Outlet** (305/289-0250, 10 A.M.–6 P.M. daily) and **Marooned in Marathon** (305/743-3809, 10 A.M.–6 P.M. daily), which share the same building (11528 Overseas Hwy., Marathon) and, together, offer T-shirts, beach towels, puzzles and games, tropical art and ornaments, and fine cigars.

Also on Vaca Key, you can shop for Birkenstocks, Teva sandals, Crocs, and other footwear at **Birkenstock of Old Town II** (8915 Overseas Hwy., Marathon, 305/289-9999, 9:30 A.M.–5 P.M. Mon.–Sat.), peruse the women's, men's, and children's apparel at **Bayshore Clothing** (8911 Overseas Hwy., Marathon, 305/743-8430, www.bayshoreclothing.com, 9:30 A.M.–5:30 P.M. Mon.–Sat. in summer, 9:30 A.M.–5:30 P.M. daily in winter), and stock up on hats, sunglasses, sandals, beach towels, souvenirs, and other island necessities at the **Sandal Factory Outlet/T-Shirt City** (5195 Overseas Hwy., Marathon, 305/743-5778, 9 A.M.–8 P.M. Mon.–Sat., 9 A.M.–6 P.M. Sun.),

which also has locations in Key Largo and Islamorada.

Of course, for a real taste of the Florida Keys, you should stop by the **Blond Giraffe Key Lime Pie Factory** (5187 Overseas Hwy., Marathon, 305/743-4423, www.blondgiraffe. com, noon–6 P.M. Mon.–Fri., 10 A.M.–6 P.M. Sat.–Sun.), which offers award-winning key lime pies, key lime pie cookies, key lime juice, key lime taffy, and other tangy products.

Even Key Colony Beach, which is accessible via the Sadowski Causeway at mile marker 53.5, features a worthwhile boutique near the intersection of Key Colony Beach Causeway and West Ocean Drive. For more than 25 years, locals and tourists have frequented **Key Bana Resort Apparel** (MM 53.5 OS, Key Colony Beach Causeway, Key Colony Beach, 305/289-1161, www.keybana.com, 9:30 A.M.–5:30 P.M. Mon.–Sat.) for women's and men's tropical-style clothes and other accessories, which nowadays might include Beer Can Island shorts, Tommy Bahama swimwear, designer suits, shoes, sunglasses, and more.

MARATHON

Sports and Recreation

GOLF

Established in the 1950s, the **Sombrero Country Club (SCC)** (4000 Sombrero Blvd., Marathon, 305/743-2551, www.sombrerocc.com) allows its members, many of whom don't even live in the Keys year-round, access to lighted tennis courts, an 18-hole golf course, and an active clubhouse. In lieu of purchasing a membership to SCC, which can require a $10,000 initiation fee, you can simply stop by the **Key Colony Beach Golf Course** (8th St., Key Colony Beach, www.keycolonybeach.net/recreation.html, 7:30 A.M.–sunset daily, $11), which offers a nine-hole, par-three golf course, plus tennis courts that are free for the public to use. Golf memberships ($265–385 yearly) are available, as are club rentals ($3) and pull carts ($2).

HIKING AND BIKING

Like much of the Florida Keys, the greater Marathon area doesn't typically appeal to long-distance hikers. Nevertheless, you can certainly enjoy a pleasant stroll through places like **Long Key State Park** (67400 Overseas Hwy., Long Key, 305/664-4815, www.floridastateparks.org/longkey, 8 A.M.–sunset daily, $5 vehicles w/2–8 passengers plus $0.50 pp, $4.50 motorcycles and single-occupant vehicles, $2.50 pedestrians, bikers, and extra passengers), which features two nature trails: the 1.2-mile Golden Orb Trail, named after a native spider, and the shorter 0.3-mile Layton Trail, located on the bay side of the park.

Curry Hammock State Park (56200 Overseas Hwy., Marathon, 305/289-2690, www.floridastateparks.org/curryhammock, 8 A.M.–sunset daily, $5 vehicles w/2–8 passengers plus $0.50 pp, $4.50 motorcycles and single-occupant vehicles, $2.50 pedestrians, bikers, and extra passengers) contains a 1.5-mile nature trail that winds through the hardwood hammock preserved by the park. In the heart of Vaca Key, the **Crane Point Museum and Nature Center** (5550 Overseas Hwy.,

Marathon, 305/743-9100, www.cranepoint.net, 9 A.M.–5 P.M. Mon.–Sat., noon–5 P.M. Sun., $12 adults, $10 seniors over 65, $8 children 6–12, children under 6 free) even features a 1.5-mile nature trail through palm trees and mangroves, alongside historic structures, and not far from Florida Bay.

Given the Middle Keys' numerous bridges and sprawling nature, bikers will undoubtedly relish the region even more—though care should always be taken on the Overseas Highway, and a proper helmet should be worn at all times. Between mile markers 58 and 40, you'll find an 11-mile bike path, part of the **Florida Keys Overseas Heritage Trail,** plus a wide shoulder along the **Seven Mile Bridge.** Bikes can be rented from **Bike Marathon Bike Rental** (305/743-3204, www.bikemarathonbikerentals.com, 8 A.M.–6 P.M. daily, $35 weekly, $99 monthly), Marathon's first and oldest bicycle rental company, which also offers free delivery and free pickup service in Marathon and Key Colony Beach. Each rental includes a free basket and lock.

You can also rent bicycles from **Wheels-2-Go!** (5994 Overseas Hwy., Marathon, 305/289-4279, www.wheels-2-go.com, 10 A.M.–6 P.M. daily, $10–15 daily, $65 weekly), which also supplies free helmets, locks, baskets, and car racks if needed. The family-owned **Overseas Outfitters** (1700 Overseas Hwy., Marathon, 305/289-1670, www.overseasoutfitters.com, 9 A.M.–6 P.M. Mon.–Fri., 9 A.M.–3 P.M. Sat., $10 daily, $60 weekly) features a wide array of bicycle rentals and sales, plus repair service. In addition, the vast inventory includes sandals, sunglasses, athletic clothing and shoes, and plenty of other sporting goods, from volleyballs and tennis rackets to pool cues and snorkel masks. Free bicycle delivery is available.

◖ FISHING AND BOATING

While perhaps not as abundant as in Islamorada, fishing charters and boat rentals are available throughout the Middle Keys. If you're new to the area, your best bet would be to stop by one of the many marinas down here. Several area resorts, for instance, feature on-site marinas, where guests and nonguests can book offshore and backcountry fishing charters. Some of these include **Hawks Cay Resort & Marina** (61 Hawks Cay Blvd., Duck Key, 305/743-7000, www.hawkscay.com), **Coral Lagoon Resort & Marina** (12399 Overseas Hwy., Marathon, 866/904-1234, www.coral-lagoonresort.com), and **Captain Pip's Marina & Hideaway** (1410 Overseas Hwy., Marathon, 305/743-4403 or 800/707-1692, www.captain-pips.com).

Another option is **Burdine's Waterfront Marina** (1200 Oceanview St., Marathon, 305/743-5317, www.burdineswaterfront.com, 6:30 A.M.–6 P.M. daily), which not only assists with fishing charters, but also offers a bait and tackle shop, fishing and boating equipment, picnic supplies, and boat dockage that includes bathrooms, showers, water and electric service, cable television, and laundry facilities. As a bonus, you can relax at the ChikiTiki Bar & Grille (11:30 A.M.–9 P.M. daily), which serves cheeseburgers, fresh sandwiches, key lime pie, and cold beer. Return after your fishing trip, and the restaurant will cook your fresh, cleaned catch any way you like it.

The Middle Keys house entirely too many fishing charters to name them all, but there are at least two stand-outs. **Sweet E'Nuf Fishing Charters** (1406 Ocean View Ave., Marathon, 305/610-4778, www.sweetenufcharters.com, $450 per half day, $550 per six hours, $650–850 daily, $100 per additional hour, fuel charges apply) offers both sportfishing and reef-fishing trips, while **Flat Out Sportfishing** (941 E. 75th St. Ocean, Marathon, 305/743-7317 or 305/395-1228, www.floridakeysflats.com, trips and rates vary daily) enables anglers to fish for permit, bonefish, tarpon, and shark in the backcountry.

Lady Catherine Charters (305/743-5544, www.diveandfishmarathon.com, daily, $550 per half day, $850 daily), situated at the Seascape Motel and Marina (1275 E. 76th St.

OS, Marathon), offers diving excursions and sunset cruises in addition to offshore, reef, and bay fishing, while the **Marathon Lady** (MM 53 OS U.S. 1, Marathon, 305/743-5580, www.marathonlady.net, 8:30 A.M., 12:30 P.M., 1:30 P.M., and 5:30 P.M. daily, $45 pp, $5 per rod and reel) provides a party boat fishing experience that's ideal for families on a budget. Reservations are highly recommended—and, oftentimes, absolutely necessary—for all fishing charters. Also, take note that, while the cost for most charters includes a fishing license fee, you should always ensure such details when booking your trip.

If, however, you'd rather venture out on your own, you can simply rent a boat from **Fish 'n Fun Boat & Watersports Rentals** (4590 Overseas Hwy., Marathon, 305/743-2275 or 800/471-3440, http://fishnfunrentals.com, 8 A.M.–6 P.M. daily), which offers vessels from 19 feet ($140 per half day, $190 daily, $965 weekly) to 26 feet in length ($235 per half day, $285 daily, $1,565 weekly). Other options include **Tropical Boat Rentals** (91 Ave. A, Marathon, 305/481-7006, www.tropicalboatrentals.com, 8 A.M.–8 P.M. daily, rates vary daily and weekly) and **Boat Rentals in Paradise** (Captain Hook's Marina & Dive Center, 11833 Overseas Hwy., Marathon, 305/393-7399 or 305/743-2444, www.boatrentalsmarathon.com, 6 A.M.–7 P.M. daily, $125–200 per half day, $165–375 daily, $794–1,804 weekly), both of which offer a wide array of vessels, plus delivery service. For live, fresh, or frozen bait, plus fuel, apparel, rod and reel rentals, and other supplies, stop by **Big Time Bait and Tackle** (11499 Overseas Hwy., Marathon, 305/289-0199, www.bigtimetackle.com, 6:30 A.M.–6 P.M. daily) on Vaca Key before heading out on your fishing trip.

CANOEING AND KAYAKING

As with the rest of the Florida Keys, paddling enthusiasts won't be disappointed in the greater Marathon area. There are not only plenty of nooks and crannies for you to explore via kayak, but also several operators and guides to help you navigate these bountiful waters.

MARATHON

© DANIEL MARTONE

kayaking amid the mangroves of the Middle Keys

At **Long Key State Park** (67400 Overseas Hwy., Long Key, 305/664-4815, www.floridastateparks.org/longkey, 8 A.M.–sunset daily, $5 vehicles w/2–8 passengers plus $0.50 pp, $4.50 motorcycles and single-occupant vehicles, $2.50 pedestrians, bikers, and extra passengers), for instance, canoeists can enjoy a leisurely trip along the **Long Key Lakes Canoe Trail** through a shallow lagoon. Canoe rentals ($5 hourly, $10 daily) and a self-guided brochure make this a relatively easy diversion even for novices. Meanwhile, at Hawks Cay Resort, **Sundance Watersports** (61 Hawks Cay Blvd., Duck Key, 305/743-0145, www.sundancewatersports.net, 8 A.M.–5 P.M. daily) provides single and double kayak rentals by the hour ($20–25), half day ($40–45), and full day ($65–69). You can also rent single and double kayaks ($17.20–21.50 per two hours) from the ranger station at **Curry Hammock State Park** (56200 Overseas Hwy., Marathon, 305/289-2690, www.floridastateparks.org/curryhammock, 8 A.M.–sunset daily, $5 vehicles w/2–8 passengers plus $0.50 pp, $4.50 motorcycles and single-occupant vehicles, $2.50

pedestrians, bikers, and extra passengers), a wonderful place to paddle in the shallow waters that surround several wooded islands.

On Vaca Key, **Wheels-2-Go!** (5994 Overseas Hwy., Marathon, 305/289-4279, www.wheels-2-go.com, 10 A.M.–6 P.M. daily) offers free delivery for all single and double kayaks, which you can rent by the hour ($10–15), day ($29–55), or week ($129–195). Besides paddleboard rentals ($15 hourly), Wheels-2-Go! also provides three-hour guided kayak tours ($49 pp) through the mangrove islands and backcountry waters. Near mile marker 49.5, **Fish 'n Fun Boat & Watersports Rentals** (4590 Overseas Hwy., Marathon, 305/743-2275 or 800/471-3440, http://fishnfunrentals.com, 8 A.M.–6 P.M. daily) offers a range of vessels, including single kayaks ($30 per half day, $45 daily) and tandem kayaks ($45 per half day, $60 daily), plus pedal boats and Hobie Cat sailboats. Anchors and diver-down flags are provided with all rentals.

◖ DIVING AND SNORKELING

Whether you're a first-time snorkeler or an experienced scuba diver, you should take some

MARATHON

© DANIEL MARTONE

Dive shops abound in the Florida Keys.

time to explore the waters east of the Middle Keys. Situated in the heart of Vaca Key, **Tilden's Scuba Center** (4650 Overseas Hwy., Marathon, 305/743-7255 or 888/728-2235, www.tildensscubacenter.com, 8 A.M.–6 P.M. daily), a full-service diving facility and retail store, provides equipment rentals and Snuba diving ($100–190 pp), a patented, deep-water form of snorkeling. In addition, you can take a scuba-diving classes through Tilden's, including an introduction course ($126 pp), a first-aid course ($151 pp), an advanced certification course ($350 pp), a rescue diver course ($451 pp), an open water certification course ($400–600 pp), and several other specialty options; just be advised that some classes have age restrictions. Through Tilden's, you can also participate in snorkeling ($36–46 pp) and scuba-diving adventures ($61–116 pp), even wreck ($86 pp) and night dives ($81–91 pp).

Other area operators include **Dive Duck Key** (Hawks Cay Resort, 61 Hawks Cay Blvd., Duck Key, 305/289-4931 or 877/386-3483, http://experience.hawkscay.com/diving, 8 A.M.–6 P.M. daily), **A Deep Blue Dive Center** (400 Sadowski Cswy., Key Colony Beach, 800/978-3483, www.adeepbluedive.com, 8 A.M.–5 P.M. daily), the **Abyss Dive Center** (12565 Overseas Hwy., Marathon, 305/743-2126 or 800/457-0134, www.abyss-dive.com, 8 A.M.–5 P.M. daily), and **Captain Hook's Marina & Dive Center** (11833 Overseas Hwy., Marathon, 305/743-2444 or 800/278-4665, www.captainhooks.com, 6 A.M.–7 P.M. daily)—all of which offer lessons, equipment rentals, and daily snorkeling and diving trips to area reefs. For snorkel-only excursions, consider boarding catamarans like the **Spirit** (MM 47.5 BS U.S. 1, Marathon, 305/289-0614, www.spiritsnorkeling.net) or **Starfish** (MM 47.5 BS U.S. 1, Marathon, 305/481-0407, www.starfishsnorkeling.com); each offers two trips daily (9 A.M. and 1 P.M., $30 pp) in addition to seasonal sunset cruises (times vary depending on sunset, $35 pp) and specialty trips.

Of the more than 25 underwater sites that you might see on such diving and snorkeling tours, two of the most popular ones include the **Delta Shoals,** a network of coral canyons that nurture star, elkhorn, and brain coral heads,

MARATHON

HOW ARTIFICIAL REEFS WORK

The 2,900-square-mile Florida Keys National Marine Sanctuary encompasses more than just living coral reefs. This incredible preserve also contains several artificial reefs – essentially, manmade underwater structures that have been utilized around the world for a variety of purposes. Centuries ago, ancient Persians and Romans used such reefs to defend waterways or trap enemy ships. In more recent times, they've been employed to improve fishing, control beach erosion, enhance hydrodynamics for surfing, or, as is typically the case in the Florida Keys, promote marinelife in areas of featureless bottom.

While artificial reefs can be erected using various materials, including rubble, tires, concrete, and construction debris, those that you'll find in the Florida Keys are usually one of two varieties: actual shipwrecks or intentional vessel sinkings. Once preserved on the sea floor, these structures lure algae, barnacles, oysters, sponges, coral formations, and other invertebrates. The gradual, natural accumulation of such diverse marinelife then provides an intricate structure as well as sustenance for a variety of tropical fish, game fish, and other marine creatures.

Naturally, such lively artificial reefs lure both anglers and scuba divers to the Florida Keys – albeit for different reasons – and plenty of local fishing and diving charters can guide you to these fascinating locales, which stretch from one end of this island chain to the other. Near Key Largo, for instance, you'll encounter the **USS *Spiegel Grove***, a 510-foot Navy transport ship originally launched in November 1955, prematurely sunk in June 2002 to create an artificial reef, and thankfully shifted into an upright position by Hurricane Dennis in 2005. Closer to Key West lies the 522-foot **USNS *General Hoyt S. Vandenberg***, a former troop transport ship used during World War II, intentionally sunk in May 2009 as an artificial reef, and now a marinelife habitat that offers a fascinating look at the developing stages of coral growth. Even the Marathon area has its share of enticing artificial reefs, including the ***Thunderbolt***, a 188-foot steel ship built in 1942, purposely sunk in 1986 four miles south of Key Colony Beach, and now

encrusted with coral and sponges, which attract deep-water fish like jacks and angelfish.

Although recreationists adore such artificial reefs, it's important to remember that they provide a necessary service for the ocean environment, offering a home to countless fish and marine creatures. While the public is welcome to explore and enjoy them, conservation is still a top priority. To that end, scuba divers should avoid defacing or damaging these reefs and refrain from collecting any natural or historical resources found there. Likewise, anglers should avoid anchoring too close to such reefs and, whenever possible, practice catch-and-release fishing in these areas, which helps to protect fisheries from excessive harvest. If you're not familiar with catch-and-release fishing, follow these simple guidelines:

- Use artificial lures, barbless hooks, and fishing line that's strong enough to bring in the fish quickly.

- Wet your hands before handling the fish, and minimize the time that it's out of the water.

- Be gentle and keep your fingers away from the gills and eyes.

- Measure and photograph the fish while it's in the water.

- Use long-nosed pliers to back the hook out of its entrance hole, and if possible, remove the hook quickly and gently while keeping the fish in the water.

- Cut the line near the hook if the fish is hooked deeply.

- Move the fish back and forth until it is revived and swims from your hands.

For more information about catch-and-release fishing, consult the **Florida Fish and Wildlife Conservation Commission (FWC)** (850/488-6058, www.myfwc.com), and for more information about artificial reefs in this region, consult the **Florida Keys National Marine Sanctuary** (305/852-7717 or 305/292-0311, www.floridakeys.noaa.gov).

and **Sombrero Reef,** a spur-and-groove reef formation featuring elkhorn coral and designated by a 142-foot tower. Also in these waters lie two curious shipwrecks: the **Adelaide Baker,** the remains of a three-masted, iron-rigged ship now lying in 25 feet of water, and the **Thunderbolt,** a 188-foot ship sunk in 1986 and now encrusted with coral and sponges, which lure deep-water fish like jacks and angelfish.

A helpful resource for divers is **Teall's Guides,** a detailed nautical map prepared by Keys Charts, Inc. (305/872-3123) that indicates water depths throughout the Middle Keys as well as official dive sites—from East Turtle Shoal to Sombrero Reef.

OTHER ACTIVITIES

If you're hoping to travel the waters of the Middle Keys on something faster than a kayak, you're in luck. Several area companies provide personal watercraft rentals, which can be ideal for both swimmers and snorkelers. **A-Affordable Jet Ski Rentals** (3 N. Conch Ave., Conch Key, 305/304-8733, www.a-affordablejetskirentals.com, 10 A.M.–5 P.M. daily, hours can vary depending on demand), based near mile marker 63, offers WaveRunners for the half day ($39) or full day ($69), plus guided tours ($119 pp) through the surrounding mangroves. Life jackets are included with every rental, and delivery service is available throughout the Florida Keys for daylong or multi-day rentals.

At nearby Hawks Cay Resort, **Sundance Watersports** (61 Hawks Cay Blvd., Duck Key, 305/743-0145, www.sundancewatersports.net) provides Jet Ski rentals (9 A.M.–5 P.M. daily, $149 pp) for all ages, though solo riders must be at least 22 years old or, alternatively, 18–21

years old with a safe boaters card. Sundance Watersports also offers wakeboard experiences (8:30 A.M.–5 P.M. daily, $89 per half hour, $129 per 45 minutes, $149 hourly, $199 per 90 minutes, $259 per two hours, $359 per three hours) for riders that are at least 8 years old, plus parasailing adventures (9 A.M.–5 P.M. daily) for single fliers ($79) or tandem trips ($139).

Other area operators include **Fish 'n Fun Boat & Watersports Rentals** (4590 Overseas Hwy., Marathon, 305/743-2275 or 800/471-3440, http://fishnfunrentals.com, 8 A.M.–6 P.M. daily), which provides anchors and diver-down flags with every Yamaha WaveRunner rental ($85 hourly, $275 per half day, or $500 daily), and the family-operated **7-Mile Watersports** (1090 Overseas Hwy., Marathon, 305/743-2015, www.7milewatersports.com, 9 A.M.–6:30 P.M. daily, $85 hourly), which offers Sea-Doo personal watercraft for riders that are at least 14 years old.

Those hoping to experience a little less activity, or simply relax after a long day in the sun, should consider making an appointment at the **Calm Waters Spa** (61 Hawks Cay Blvd., Duck Key, 305/289-4810, www.hawkscay.com/spa.php, 9 A.M.–7 P.M. daily) at Hawks Cay Resort. Featuring an array of island-inspired manicures and pedicures ($30–140 pp), facials ($70–200 pp), massages ($110–280 pp), body exfoliation treatments ($70–180 pp), and other services, the Calm Waters Spa also offers daily exclusives, such as Sea Stone Saturday, during which patrons can receive complimentary aromatherapy with every sea stone massage or a complimentary eye treatment with every Sun N' Sea facial. Appointments are highly recommended, and cancellations must be made at least four hours prior to your scheduled treatment time.

MARATHON

Accommodations

UNDER $100

The **Edgewater Lodge** (65656 Overseas Hwy., Long Key, 305/664-2662, www.edge-waterlodge.com, $89–110 d) offers standard motel rooms, plus efficiencies and two-bedroom cottages with full kitchens. On-site amenities include large sun decks, a freshwater pool, a fishing pier, and a boat ramp. While the Edgewater offers dockage for a daily fee, the quiet, inexpensive **Valhalla Point Resort** (56223 Ocean Dr., Marathon, 305/360-2726, www.keysresort.com, $80–155 d) provides a free boat launch and dockage to all guests. Here, you can choose from eight comfortable motel rooms, suites, and efficiencies, all of which feature waterfront views. Don't be shy about using the complimentary kayaks and canoes on the private beach.

In Key Colony Beach, the **Continental Inn** (1121 West Ocean Dr., Key Colony Beach, 305/289-0101 or 800/443-7352, www.mara-thonresort.com, $95–152 d) invites you to a secluded retreat on the Atlantic Ocean. The one-bedroom and two-bedroom apartments all have full kitchens and cable television. In addition, the inn offers free boat dockage, access to a par-three golf course, and assistance in satisfying all of your water-sports needs.

On Vaca Key, the **Coconut Cay Resort & Marina** (7196 Overseas Hwy., Marathon, 877/354-7356, www.coconutcay.com, $69–179 d) possesses all the charms of a Bahamian resort. The accommodations vary from standard rooms, with one or two double beds and a small refrigerator, to the Coral Cove rental, with three bedrooms and a full kitchen. Pleasantly lined with palm trees, the lovely property features a swimming pool with a 4,000-square-foot sunning deck. Kayak and boat rentals are also available.

Offering nightly, weekly, and monthly rates, the **Sombrero Reef Inn and Fishing Lodge** (17–18 Man O War Dr., Marathon, 305/743-4118, www.sombreroreefinn.com, $90–145 d) is also an ideal location from which to base your next fishing adventure. Situated south of U.S. 1 and accessible via Sombrero Beach Road, this small, low-key hideaway offers a range of accommodations, from standard motel rooms to two-bedroom suites, all of which are equipped with a mini-refrigerator and a coffee maker. Each guest is allowed to launch and dock one boat in the small marina. In addition, fishing guide and outfitting services are available.

On U.S. 1, the clean, affordable units at the **Sea Dell Motel** (5000 Overseas Hwy., Marathon, 305/743-5161 or 800/648-3854, www.seadellmotel.com, $89–159 d) include refrigerators and a variety of bed sizes. The pet-friendly, "waterview" efficiency, which is also available for weekly rentals, features two double beds and a full kitchen. Other amenities include a heated freshwater pool, picnic tables, and a barbecue area.

Just east of the Seven Mile Bridge, the **Blue Waters Resort Motel** (2222 Overseas Hwy., Marathon, 800/222-4832, www.bluewatersre-sortmotel.com, $89–159 d) provides deep-water access to Florida Bay, the Atlantic Ocean, and the only living coral reef in U.S. waters. In addition, the property features efficiencies with full kitchens, a freshwater pool, protected boat dockage, and access to area fishing and water sports.

$100-200

Nestled amid palm trees and flowering plants on the bay side of Long Key, the intimate **Lime Tree Bay Resort** (MM 68.5 BS U.S. 1, Layton, 305/664-4740, www.limetreebayre-sort.com, rooms $89–129 d, studios $129–184, mini-suites $129–194, suites $189–304, townhouses $200–365) features 44 different units, ranging from standard rooms to townhouses. Certain lodgings are pet-friendly, for a daily fee of $15 per pet. In addition, guests have free use of the sunning beach, swimming pool and heated spa, boat dockage, wireless Internet access, kayaks, hammocks, and barbecue grills.

The secluded **C** **Conch Key Cottages**

Morning breaks at the peaceful Conch Key Cottages.

(62250 Overseas Hwy., Walker's Island, 305/289-1377 or 800/330-1577, www.conchkeycottages.com, $159–399 d) is a small, tranquil boutique resort far enough from the highway to make you feel as though you're on your own private island. Each unit has its own unique ambience, from the stilted two-bedroom cottages to the beachfront bungalows, and each features a well-equipped kitchen and amenities like plush robes, cable television, and free continental breakfasts. Guests are welcome to relax in the gated swimming pool or launch complimentary, two-seater kayaks from the private beach for a bird-watching excursion among the mangroves. For a fee, you can also launch and dock your own boat during your stay. In addition, the beach and lounging tiki area are ideal places from which to watch a gorgeous sunrise or sunset.

On Grassy Key, the **Gulf View Waterfront Resort** (58743 Overseas Hwy., Marathon, 305/289-1414 or 877/289-0111, www.gulfviewwaterfrontresort.com, $110–214 d) features 11 units, ranging from guest rooms with refrigerators to two-bedroom apartments with full kitchens. This pet-friendly resort also has one of the largest freshwater pools in the Florida Keys, plus complimentary canoes, kayaks, and pedal boats. If you just want to relax, feel free to take advantage of one of the on-site hammocks or tiki huts. For a no-frills place at a reasonable price, check out the **Yellowtail Inn Beach Resort** (58162 Overseas Hwy., Marathon, 305/743-8400 or 800/605-7475, www.yellowtailinn.com, $100–220 d), also on Grassy Key. The traditional guest rooms have one queen-sized bed or two double beds, a small refrigerator, and a microwave oven. The efficiencies and cottages, meanwhile, feature full kitchens, and some even boast private balconies or porches. Other on-site amenities include a small swimming pool, a private beach, and a fishing pier.

Farther west on Grassy Key, the quiet ◖ **Rainbow Bend Fishing Resort** (57784 Overseas Hwy., Marathon, 305/289-1505 or 800/929-1505, www.rainbowbend.com, $150–270 d) houses one-bedroom and two-bedroom oceanfront suites and one-bedroom patio efficiencies with full kitchens. As a bonus, a full

MARATHON

complimentary American breakfast is served at the Hideaway Café each morning. Given that it's a fishing resort, it's probably no surprise that Rainbow Bend also offers free use of the on-site motorboats. In addition, the staff can easily arrange a fishing charter for you.

As the only "botel" in this part of the Florida Keys, the **Royal Hawaiian Motel/Botel** (12020 Overseas Hwy., Marathon, 305/743-7500, www.royalhawaiianmotelbotel.com, $109–200 d) promises easy access to the Gulf of Mexico and Atlantic Ocean through the Vaca Cut. Each standard room contains two double beds and a small refrigerator, while each kitchenette comes with two double beds and a full kitchen. In addition, guests are entitled to free boat dockage during their stay.

If you're looking for a one-stop vacation shop, consider the **Sombrero Resort & Lighthouse Marina** (19 Sombrero Blvd., Marathon, 800/433-8660, www.sombreroresort.com, $159–299 d), which offers standard rooms and efficiencies. While here, you can satisfy all of your water-sports needs at slip #53, where you can rent a canoe, kayak, or fishing boat. After playing a few sets on the lighted tennis courts, take a dip in the heated pool, then sip a piña colada while relaxing at the poolside tiki-hut bar. If you get hungry, you're in luck: The on-site Marathon Pizza & Pasta serves an array of salads, pizzas, and pasta dishes. In addition, the cooking staff will prepare your day's catch any way you like it.

OVER $200

Located on 60-acre Duck Key, **(Hawks Cay Resort & Marina** (61 Hawks Cay Blvd., 305/743-7000 or 888/313-5749, www.hawkscay.com, $225–450 d) almost lulls you into believing you're on a luxurious Caribbean island. With gorgeous rooms and villas, five unique eateries (including Tom's Harbor House), five different swimming pools, a world-class spa, a slew of water-related activities, and its own interactive dolphin facility, Hawks Cay promises a unique, all-encompassing experience in the Florida Keys. Beyond well-appointed, West Indies–style hotel rooms and suites,

the resort offers luxury villas in four separate areas: Sunset Village, Marina Village, Harbor Village, and Sanctuary Village.

Situated on Grassy Key, the **Bonefish Resort** (58070 Overseas Hwy., Marathon, 305/743-7107 or 800/274-9949, www.bonefishresort.com, $299–399 d) offers an assortment of accommodations to suit a variety of vacation needs. Beyond standard guest rooms, efficiencies, and deluxe efficiencies, you'll find deluxe oceanfront efficiencies that offer full kitchens, queen-sized beds, and spacious living areas. Anglers will especially appreciate the chance to fish right from the property. For a taste of "old Florida," head to the **Seashell Beach Resort** (57612 Overseas Hwy., Marathon, 305/289-0265, www.seashellbeachresort.com, $299–399 d), a Grassy Key property that attempts to transport you to the simple, hospitable days of the 1950s. The on-site efficiencies and suites all have full kitchens, and guests will surely enjoy the private beach, the 100-foot and 300-foot fishing docks, and the complimentary kayaks.

A bit off the beaten path lies the stunning **CocoPlum Beach & Tennis Club** (109 Coco Plum Dr., Marathon, 305/743-0240 or 800/228-1587, www.cocoplum.com, $107–425 d), which features 20 separate two-bedroom villas. Each elevated unit consists of three stories: The ground floor has a washer and dryer, plus storage units; the first floor contains the kitchen and dining room, as well as a large screened porch; and the second floor features two bedrooms, two bathrooms, and a living room. Other on-site amenities include a beachfront swimming pool featuring a zero-edge concept, plus a nine-slip docking area designed for boats up to 40 feet in length.

The **Coral Lagoon Resort & Marina** (12399 Overseas Hwy., Marathon, 866/904-1234, www.corallagoonresort.com, $299–399 d) presents Conch-style villas and detached marina homes. All of the two-bedroom villas, three-bedroom villas, and single family homes feature 2.5 bathrooms, full kitchens, lower and upper porches, and excellent views, in addition to cable television and free wireless Internet access. The on-site water-sports program offers everything you'll need to fish, snorkel, dive, or simply enjoy the water.

Given that most of its guest rooms are named after fish, it's no wonder that ◖ **Captain Pip's Marina & Hideaway** (1410 Overseas Hwy., Marathon, 305/743-4403 or 800/707-1692, www.captainpips.com, $225–450 d) specializes in arranging the ultimate fishing vacation. This low-key resort near the western end of Vaca Key even offers a few boats that are free for guests to enjoy, and the adjacent marina features a variety of boat rentals, plus fishing guides that can show you the best spots in the bay, ocean, or reefs. Lodgings range from waterfront guest rooms to comfortable efficiencies to spacious apartments. Other on-site amenities include the popular Porky's Bayside BBQ Restaurant.

CAMPING

Campers will find plenty of options in the Middle Keys. Just south of Islamorada is the **Fiesta Key RV Resort** (70001 Overseas Hwy., Fiesta Key, 305/664-4922, www.fiestakeyrvresort.com, $40–100 daily), which offers tent sites, RV sites with water and electricity, and full-hookup RV sites on a day-to-day basis. The 28-acre property also features an Olympic-sized freshwater pool and a complete marina with available slip rentals.

Long Key State Park (67400 Overseas Hwy., Long Key, 305/664-4815, www.floridastateparks.org/longkey, 8 A.M.–sunset daily, $5 vehicles w/2–8 passengers plus $0.50 pp, $4.50 motorcycles and single-occupant vehicles, $2.50 pedestrians, bikers, and extra passengers) presents 60 campsites ($36 daily), each with water and electricity, overlooking the Atlantic Ocean. In addition, the park offers a canoe trail and two land-based nature trails. As a bonus to campers, the beach is only open to those staying in the campground, so you'll surely find this to be one of the more private beaches in the Keys. Reservations can be made up to 11 months in advance through **ReserveAmerica** (800/326-3521, www.reserveamerica.com).

© DANIEL MARTONE

the Curry Hammock State Park campground

On Grassy Key, the **Jolly Roger Travel Park** (59275 Overseas Hwy., Marathon, 800/995-1525, www.jrtp.com, $50–75 daily) has full-hookup RV sites, van sites with optional water and electric service, and tent spaces. The park offers daily, weekly, and monthly rates. On-site amenities include high-speed wireless Internet access, cable television hookups, snorkeling and swimming areas, a boat dock with slip rentals, and a free boat ramp for guests.

The **Grassy Key RV Park & Resort** (58671 Overseas Hwy., Marathon, 305/289-1606, www.grassykeyrvpark.com, $50–110 daily, $300–715 weekly, $720–2,310 monthly) accepts RVs of all sizes, including the "big rig" motor coaches. The waterfront, premium, and standard sites are all equipped with water, sewer access, 30/50-amp electricity, and cable television. Other on-site amenities include a freshwater pool, a lounging beach, a clubhouse, laundry facilities, and new boat dockage ($1.25 per foot daily, $6 per foot weekly, $10 per foot monthly) that allows access to both the Gulf of Mexico and the Atlantic Ocean. Pets are welcome here with some restrictions. Please be aware that camping rates can vary greatly depending on the specific site and season; also note that multi-month rates are available.

Another state park option is **Curry Hammock State Park** (56200 Overseas Hwy., Marathon, 305/289-2690, www.floridastateparks.org/curryhammock, 8 A.M.–sunset daily, $5 vehicles w/2–8 passengers plus $0.50 pp, $4.50 motorcycles and single-occupant vehicles, $2.50 pedestrians, bikers, and extra passengers), which has a 28-site campground ($36–39 daily) equipped with picnic tables, charcoal grills, water service, and 20/30/50-amp electricity. A dump station is available at the park. No motorized vessels can be launched here—only kayaks and canoes. Leashed pets are allowed in the campground, but not on the beach. Although bikers, anglers, swimmers, paddlers, and picnickers favor this park, Curry Hammock is especially popular with birding enthusiasts, who will often spot herons, egrets, ibises, plovers, and sanderlings along the shore. Reservations can be made up to 11 months in advance through **ReserveAmerica** (800/326-3521, www.reserveamerica.com).

On the western end of Marathon, beside the Seven Mile Bridge, you'll spot the **Knights Key RV Resort & Marina** (1 Knight's Key Blvd., Knight's Key, 305/743-4343 or 800/348-2267, www.keysdirectory.com/knightskeycampground, $46–93 daily), which has provided affordable accommodations here since 1962. Offering spacious RV sites with lovely ocean views, this breezy campground also provides tent sites ($35–45 daily), boat dockage, a private beach, and easy access to the Pigeon Key ferry.

Food

SEAFOOD

As with the Upper and Lower Keys, it's probably no surprise that the Middle Keys—also popular among anglers and boaters—offer a wealth of seafood options. At Hawks Cay Resort & Marina, **Tom's Harbor House** (61 Hawks Cay Blvd., Duck Key, 305/743-7000, www.hawkscay.com, 4–11 P.M. Mon.–Fri., 11 A.M.–2 P.M. and 4–11 P.M. Sat.–Sun., $9–32) exudes the elegance of a seaside grill and the laid-back vibe of a fishing village. The menu is loaded with fresh fish dishes, and the "you hook it, we'll cook it" policy delights vacationing anglers who hope to taste their bounty sooner rather than later. But even if you're not bringing your own catch, you'll certainly be able to taste the fruits of the sea, including Keys favorites like grouper, hogfish, and, when in season, Florida lobster and stone crab.

Other delightful seafood restaurants include the laid-back ◖ **Island Fish Co. Restaurant & Tiki Bar** (12648 Overseas Hwy., Marathon, 305/743-4191, www.islandfishco.com, 11:30 A.M.–close daily, $8–32), which features one of the largest menus in the Keys, including burgers, sandwiches, fried island platters, and fried key lime pie, among other items. The house specialties feature some winning choices, among them a particularly tasty Caribbean dish consisting of seasoned pan-seared grouper, served with island rice, black beans, and pineapple salsa. If you favor alcoholic drinks, be sure to try the key lime pie martini, in a glass that's cleverly ringed with graham cracker crumbs. The spacious, island-style restaurant offers rustic indoor seating as well as outdoor seating alongside the water.

If you return from a long day of fishing empty-handed, never fear. Less than a mile west of the Island Fish Co., the family-owned **Fish Tales Market and Eatery** (11711 Overseas Hwy., Marathon, 305/743-9196 or 888/662-4822, www.floridalobster.com, 10 A.M.–6 P.M. Mon.–Sat., $4–10) offers plenty of fresh, locally caught seafood, from fish and lobster to shrimp and stone crabs. In addition, the market offers hand-cut steaks, plus a whole slew of spices, spreads, rubs, and hot sauces, not to mention suggested recipes. Before or after making your purchases, be sure to stay for a meal in the cozy, inexpensive eatery; if you're a seafood lover, you surely won't regret sampling everything from the red conch chowder to steamed shrimp to a grilled yellowfin tuna sandwich.

If you have a hankering for conch—indeed a popular item in southern Florida—there's probably no place in the Keys that boasts as many conch-related dishes than the aptly named **(Cracked Conch Cafe** (4999 Overseas Hwy., Marathon, 305/743-2233, www.conchcafe.com, 9:30 A.M.–10:30 P.M. Mon.–Thurs., 7 A.M.–10:30 P.M. Fri.–Sun., $16–28), which lies just west of the Crane Point nature preserve. Popular with locals for more than three decades, this casual eatery offers delicious conch fritters, both cream-based and tomato-based conch chowders, and several conch specialties, including "conch in the weeds," a conch dish that features spinach and mushrooms. With a relaxing outdoor patio and a simple interior that sports an "old Florida"

© DANIEL MARTONE

MARATHON

filling an order at the Fish Tales Market

vibe, the Cracked Conch even relies on ceiling fans—in lieu of an air conditioner—to keep the joint cool during the warm months.

Another popular seafood eatery is the **Keys Fisheries Market & Marina** (3502 Gulfview Ave., Marathon, 305/743-4353 or 866/743-4353, www.keysfisheries.com, 11 A.M.–9 P.M. daily, $9–29), which lies roughly half a mile west of the Cracked Conch and features picnic tables overlooking the marina. Try the famous lobster Reuben, the key lime scallops over linguini, or the whiskey peppercorn snapper. For a more eclectic menu, head to the spacious ◖ **Castaway Waterfront Restaurant & Sushi Bar** (1406 Oceanview Ave., Marathon, 305/743-6247, www.jonesn4sushi.com, 11 A.M.–10 P.M. daily, $14–40), which, prior to a massive renovation that dramatically expanded and modernized the space, was the oldest intact building on the island. Owned for the past decade by ever-present husband-and-wife duo John and Arlene, Castaway can get fairly crowded with tourists and locals (including other area restaurant owners) during the high season, despite its hidden location on a side street in western Marathon. The menu boasts such tasty dishes as the hogfish stuffed with shrimp and scallops, premium queen conch lightly egg-battered and fried, and sautéed alligator tail smothered in mushrooms and scallions—not to mention a full lineup of topnotch sushi. Beyond the incredible food and outdoor seating alongside the adjacent marina, Castaway even offers a casual outer bar where you can listen to live music before or after your meal.

AMERICAN

South of mile marker 53.5, you'll spot ◖ **Sparky's Landing** (400 Sadowski Cswy., Key Colony Beach, 305/289-7445, www.sparkyslanding.com, 11 A.M.–10 P.M. daily, $7–29), a popular local hangout situated beside the Key Colony Beach Marina. This rustic, unassuming eatery offers an extremely eclectic menu, with everything from standard burgers to bacon-wrapped scallops. Even the appetizers are varied, ranging from shrimp potstickers to

blue cheese chips, essentially homemade potato chips covered in blue cheese and drizzled with an herb vinaigrette. The shrimp and bacon pizza, fish tacos, and key lime pie are also worth a try. Like several other restaurants in the Florida Keys, Sparky's promises to cook whatever you catch. As a bonus, the low-key eatery features live music Wednesday–Saturday and hosts the annual Leon Shell Memorial Sailfish Tournament.

The **Donarchi Delicatessen** (301 Sadowski Cswy., Key Colony Beach, 305/743-6676, 7 A.M.–8 P.M. Mon.–Sat., 8 A.M.–8 P.M. Sun., $4–12) offers both breakfast and lunch to locals and tourists alike. Although you'll find a decent variety of made-to-order sandwiches here, this is no fast-food joint, so be prepared for a long wait.

On the main drag, you'll be hard-pressed to miss the giant teacup-shaped sign at **Leigh Ann's Coffee House, Wine & Cheese Shop** (7537 Overseas Hwy., Marathon, 305/743-2001, www.leighannscoffeehouse.com, 7 A.M.–5 P.M. Mon.–Fri., 7 A.M.–3 P.M. Sat., 8 A.M.–noon Sun., $4–12), a quaint, eco-friendly eatery that serves freshly baked pastries for breakfast and scrumptious salads, like the chicken and tuna with mango slaw, for lunch. If you have a chance, be sure to sample the Italian-style spinach pie during your visit.

While the decor at **Herbies Restaurant** (6350 Overseas Hwy., Marathon, 305/743-6373, 11 A.M.–11 P.M. Tues.–Sat., $9–22) may not win the Vaca Key eatery any awards anytime soon, it's the delicious food that ensures return customers. Among the offerings is one of the best conch chowders in the Florida Keys, plus popular dishes like sautéed fish and a burger with onion rings. Be prepared, though: Herbies only accepts cash. Beside Boot Key Harbor, the **Dockside Bar & Grill** (35 Sombrero Dr., Marathon, 305/743-0000, www.docksidebarandgrill.com, 11 A.M.–11 P.M. daily, $6–28) allows you to relax with a cold beer or, if you're hungry, enjoy an assortment of delicious appetizers, sandwiches, seafood baskets, and daily lunch and dinner specials. Try Monday's seafood combo platter or, as an alternative, the chicken Sappora, a lightly grilled chicken breast brushed with teriyaki and finished with sautéed peppers, onions, and mushrooms.

On U.S. 1, **The Hurricane Bar & Grille** (4650 Overseas Hwy., Marathon, 305/743-2220, www.thehurricanegrille.com, 11 A.M.– midnight daily, $7–19) serves salads, sandwiches, and entrées like the Hurricane Chicken, topped with shrimp and crabmeat stuffing. In addition, you can enjoy live music here Tuesday–Saturday. You can relish a dynamite breakfast at **◖ The Stuffed Pig** (3520 Overseas Hwy., Marathon, 305/743-4059, www.thestuffedpig.com, 5 A.M.–2 P.M. Mon.–Sat., 6 A.M.–noon Sun., $6–18), which offers lunch, too. Locals especially favor this casual joint, where you dine indoors, on the side patio, or beneath the enormous tiki hut. Winning items include the blueberry pancakes, the popular Pig's Breakfast, and the seafood Benedict, which is served with two poached eggs, crab, shrimp, and scallops.

While traditional Florida Keys–style dishes are available at **Porky's Bayside BBQ Restaurant** (1410 Overseas Hwy., Marathon, 305/289-2065, www.porkysbaysidebbq.com, 11 A.M.–10 P.M. daily, $9–18), it's the exceptional barbecue, as the name indicates, that separates this popular eatery from other area restaurants. While here, try the Citrus Mojo Marinade Cuban Pork or, if you've come with a friend, the BBQ Dinner for Two, which includes chicken, spareribs, and pork or beef, plus your choice of four sides.

If you're planning an afternoon trip to Pigeon Key or the Lower Keys, you might want to head to the well-favored **Seven Mile Grill** (1240 Overseas Hwy., Marathon, 305/743-4481, www.keysdining.com/7milegrill, 7 A.M.–9 P.M. daily, $4–11), located just east of the bridge that inspired its name. The friendly staff here will make you feel like a regular, and the food is prepared and served with little delay. For more than 45 years, the Seven Mile Grill has offered large portions at reasonable prices. The extensive menu features everything from three-egg omelets to deluxe cheeseburgers to seafood

© DANIEL MARTONE

the popular Stuffed Pig restaurant

MARATHON

baskets—ideal for breakfast, lunch, or dinner. Consider trying the excellent conch chowder before heading out on your next adventure.

EUROPEAN AND MEXICAN

A wonderful place for a romantic meal, the **Hideaway Café** (57784 Overseas Hwy., Marathon, 305/289-1554, www.hideawaycafe. com, 7 A.M.–5 P.M. Mon.–Fri., 7 A.M.–3 P.M. Sat., 8 A.M.–noon Sun., $7–19), located at the Rainbow Bend Fishing Resort on Grassy Key, offers both a unique menu and a relaxing atmosphere. Try the escargot appetizer and the Hideaway seafood special: the day's catch sautéed with shrimp and scallops in a scampi sauce. As an alternative, try the filet medallions à la "beurre noir," essentially slices of filet mignon flambéed with cognac, garlic, and shrimp. Enjoy your meal while gazing out at the palm-lined ocean from this true island "hideaway."

Head to Key Colony Beach for a tasty espresso martini at the **Key Colony Inn** (700 W. Ocean Dr., 305/743-0100, www.kcinn. com, 11 A.M.–9:30 P.M. daily, $12–29), where you'll find plenty of seafood, often merged with French and Italian cuisine. The New Brunswick baked sea scallops, for instance, feature bacon in a light cream sauce with a hint of rosemary, while the baked lasagna seafood contains layers of noodles, local snapper, scallops, shrimp, cheese, and sauce.

Even in the seafood capital of the world, you might sometimes have a craving for pizza. Luckily, **Upper Crust Pizza** (3740 Overseas Hwy., Marathon, 305/743-7100, 11 A.M.–11 P.M. daily, $8–20) can satisfy any such craving. Situated on Vaca Key, this roomy, super-casual joint serves traditional Italian dishes in addition to pizza, and if you'd rather not eat out, you're in luck. Upper Crust happily offers both take-out and delivery service.

Lencho's Mexican Restaurant (1622 Overseas Hwy., Marathon, 305/743-4500, www.lenchosrestaurant.com, 11 A.M.–10 P.M. daily, $9–19) is considered by many locals to be the best Mexican eatery in the Keys. With dine-in and take-out options, this popular joint features such winners as chimichangas, enchiladas, and unique entrées like the El Oaxaqueno, a flame-grilled New York steak served with two flautas covered in mole sauce.

Information and Services

INFORMATION

For brochures, maps, and other information about Marathon and the Middle Keys, stop by the **Greater Marathon Chamber of Commerce and Visitors Center** (12222 Overseas Hwy., Marathon, 305/743-5417 or 800/262-7284, www.floridakeysmarathon. com, 9 A.M.–5 P.M. daily), near mile marker 53 on the bay side, or consult the **Monroe County Tourist Development Council** (1201 White St., Ste. 102, Key West, 305/296-1552 or 800/352-5397, www.fla-keys.com, 9 A.M.–5 P.M. Mon.–Fri.). For government-related issues, contact the **City of Marathon** (9805 Overseas Hwy., Marathon, 305/743-0033, www.ci.marathon.fl.us, 8 A.M.–5 P.M. Mon.–Fri.) or the **Monroe County offices**

(1100 Simonton St., Key West, 305/294-4641 or 305/743-0079, www.monroecounty-fl.gov, 8 A.M.–5 P.M. Mon.–Fri.).

For local news, consult the *Marathon & Big Pine Free Press* (www.keysnews. com) and *The Weekly Newspapers* (www. keysweekly.com). The daily *Miami Herald* (www.miamiherald.com), the daily *Key West Citizen* (www.keysnews.com), and the biweekly *Florida Keys Keynoter* (www.keysnet.com) are also available throughout the Keys.

In Marathon, you'll also have access to several radio stations, including **WGMX** (94.3 FM) and **WAVK** (97.7 FM), which offer an adult contemporary format, as well as **WFFG** (1300 AM), which provides news and talk radio.

SERVICES

Spread across multiple islands, Marathon and the Middle Keys offer plenty of necessary services for residents and travelers alike.

Money

For banking needs, stop by one of the two local branches of **TIB Bank** (800/233-6330, www.tibbank.com). There's one in Marathon Shores (11401 Overseas Hwy., 305/743-7845, 9 A.M.–4 P.M. Mon.–Thurs., 9 A.M.–6 P.M. Fri., extended drive-through hours) and one in Marathon (2348 Overseas Hwy., 305/743-0072, 9 A.M.–4 P.M. Mon.–Thurs., 9 A.M.–6 P.M. Fri., extended drive-through hours). For foreign currency exchange, visit the **First State Bank of the Florida Keys** (6900 Overseas Hwy., Marathon, 305/289-4393, www.keysbank.com, 9 A.M.–4 P.M. Mon.–Thurs., 9 A.M.–6 P.M. Fri., extended drive-through hours).

Mail

For shipping, faxing, copying, and other business-related services, visit **The UPS Store** (5409 Overseas Hwy., Marathon, 305/743-2005, www.theupsstore.com, 8 A.M.–6 P.M. Mon.–Fri., 9 A.M.–5 P.M. Sat.). Of course, you can also package and ship items at the four area **post offices** (800/275-8777, www.usps.com). There's one on Long Key (68340 Overseas Hwy., 305/664-4112, 8 A.M.–4:30 P.M. Mon.–Fri.), another in Marathon Shores (11400 Overseas Hwy., Ste. 120, 305/743-6050, 9:30 A.M.–12:30 P.M. Mon.–Fri.), one in Key Colony Beach (600 W. Ocean Dr., 305/743-2249, 11 A.M.–1 P.M. and 2–4 P.M. Mon.–Fri.), and another in Marathon (5171 Overseas Hwy., 305/743-5238, 8:30 A.M.–5 P.M. Mon.–Fri., 9 A.M.–noon Sat.).

Groceries and Supplies

For groceries, baked goods, and other supplies, head to the nearest **Winn-Dixie** (5585 Overseas Hwy., Marathon, 305/743-3636, www.winndixie.com, 7 A.M.–10 P.M. daily), not far from the local **Publix** (5407 Overseas Hwy., Marathon, 305/289-2920, www.publix. com, 7 A.M.–10 P.M. Mon.–Sat., 7 A.M.–9 P.M. Sun.), which includes an on-site pharmacy (305/289-3192, 9 A.M.–9 P.M. Mon.–Fri., 9 A.M.–7 P.M. Sat., 10 A.M.–5 P.M. Sun.). The area also features a **CVS/pharmacy** (5575 Overseas Hwy., Marathon, 305/743-9484, www.cvs.com, 8 A.M.–10 P.M. daily), which offers limited supplies as well as an on-site pharmacy (8 A.M.–8 P.M. Mon.–Fri., 8 A.M.–7 P.M. Sat., 9 A.M.–6 P.M. Sun.).

Laundry

If you need to clean some clothes during your trip, you'll find coin-operated machines and dropoff service at **Maytag Coin Laundry** (5998 Overseas Hwy., Marathon, 305/743-3448, 9 A.M.–7 P.M. Mon.–Sat., 9 A.M.–4 P.M. Sun.).

Internet Access

For wireless Internet access, consult your hotel or resort, as many offer free access nowadays, and you can typically use the Internet at the **Marathon Branch Library** (3251 Overseas Hwy., Marathon, 305/743-5156, www. keyslibraries.org, 9:30 A.M.–6 P.M. Tues. and Thurs.–Fri., 9:30 A.M.–8 P.M. Wed., 10 A.M.–6 P.M. Sat.).

Emergency Services

In case of an emergency that requires police, fire, or ambulance services, dial **911** from any cell or public phone. For nonemergency assistance, contact the **Monroe County Sheriff's Office** (Marathon Substation, 3103 Overseas Hwy., Marathon, 305/289-2430, www.keysso. net, 8 A.M.–5 P.M. Mon.–Fri.). For medical assistance, consult the **Fishermen's Hospital** (3301 Overseas Hwy., Marathon, 305/743-5533, www.fishermenshospital.com). Foreign visitors—seeking help with directions, medical concerns, business issues, law enforcement needs, or other problems—can receive **multilingual tourist assistance** (800/771-5397) 24 hours daily.

Getting There and Around

GETTING THERE
By Air

Although you can fly small planes directly into the **Florida Keys Marathon Airport (MTH)** (9400 Overseas Hwy., Marathon, 305/289-6060), most travelers reach the Middle Keys by first flying into one of the other area airports, including the **Fort Lauderdale-Hollywood International Airport (FLL)** (320 Terminal Dr., Fort Lauderdale, 866/435-9355, www.broward.org/airport), the **Miami International Airport (MIA)** (4200 NW 21st St., Miami, 305/876-7000 or 800/825-5642, www.miami-airport.com), or the **Key West International Airport (EYW)** (3491 S. Roosevelt Blvd., Key West, 305/809-5200 or 305/296-5439, www.keywestinternational-airport.com). From there, you can rent a vehicle from agencies like **Avis** (800/331-1212, www.avis.com), **Budget** (800/527-0700, www.budget.com), **Enterprise** (800/325-8007, www.enterprise.com), **Hertz** (800/654-3131, www.hertz.com), or **Thrifty** (800/367-2277, www.thrifty.com) in order to reach the Marathon area.

By Bus or Train

The **Miami-Dade County Metrobus** (305/891-3131, www.miamidade.gov/transit) operates the **301 Dade-Monroe Express** between Florida City and Marathon (5:15 A.M.–8:40 P.M. daily, $2.35 per one-way trip), with several stops in between. In addition, the **Key West Department of Transportation (KWDoT)** (305/600-1455, www.kwtransit.com, $3 per ride, $16 weekly, $50 monthly) provides bus service from Key West to Marathon between 5 A.M. and 11 P.M. daily. Reduced fares may apply for students under 22 years old, senior citizens over 59 years old, military personnel, and disabled individuals.

In addition, **Greyhound** (800/231-2222, www.greyhound.com) offers bus service to Marathon (12222 Overseas Hwy., 305/296-9073). **Amtrak** (800/872-7245, www.amtrak.

com), however, only provides train service as far south as Miami. Of course, you can always rent a car or hop a shuttle to reach the Florida Keys.

Transport from Airports and Stations

If you arrive in the Fort Lauderdale–Miami area via plane, bus, or train—or Key West via plane or bus—you can either rent a car or hire a shuttle service to reach the Marathon area. Some of these companies include **Keys Shuttle** (305/289-9997 or 888/765-9997, www.keysshuttle.com, $70–80 per shared ride, $300–350 for exclusive service) and **Keys Tropical Transportation** (305/852-3595, www.keystropicaltransportation.com, starting at $130 or $165 per ride, depending on the airport of origin), both of which provide service from the Miami and Fort Lauderdale airports; **SuperShuttle** (305/871-2000 or 954/764-1700, www.supershuttle. com, $255 per ride for up to 10 passengers), which only serves visitors flying into Miami; and **TO'n'FRO** (305/852-4514, www.tonfro. com, starting at $55–65 per shared van ride, $190–200 per luxury sedan ride), a personalized van and car service that offers transportation between the airports in Fort Lauderdale, Miami, and Key West and any destination in the Keys.

By Car

To reach the Middle Keys from Miami, simply head south on U.S. 1 (Overseas Hwy.), drive through Key Largo and Islamorada, and continue toward your destination. If you're headed from the Everglades via I-75 (Everglades Pkwy.), drive south on U.S. 27, veer right onto S.R. 997 (Krome Ave.), and follow the signs to U.S. 1. From U.S. 41 (Tamiami Trail) in the Everglades, head south on S.R. 997 and continue toward U.S. 1. If you arrive during the peak season (Dec.–Apr.), be sure to call **511** for an up-to-the-minute traffic report.

MARATHON

GETTING AROUND
By Car
The best way to travel through the Middle Keys is via car, truck, RV, or motorcycle—all of which offer easy access to U.S. 1 as well as the side roads, such as Sombrero Beach Road.

By Tour Bus
If, while staying in the Middle Keys, you have a sudden desire to head to Key West for the evening—and would rather leave your vehicle at the hotel, resort, or campground where you're staying—consider boarding the **KuKu KonKanut** (305/432-3202, www.kukukonkanut.com, Thurs.–Sat., $45 pp). Rain or shine, this bar-hopping tour bus picks up passengers at several stops in the Middle Keys (MM 67–46) from approximately 2:30 to 3:15 P.M. Amid island tunes and history lessons, the tour bus guides passengers to Mallory Square in Key West, where you're free to visit the attractions, restaurants, and watering holes of Old Town, before making the return trip at 11 P.M. Needless to say, you must be at least 21 years old to ride the party bus.

By Taxi
Taxicab companies such as **On Time Taxi** (305/289-5656, $4 per pickup, $1 per mile after initial two miles) can help you get around the Middle Keys.

By Bike or Boat
While you can certainly traverse the Middle Keys via bicycle, the region's sprawling nature and numerous bridges make it challenging for novice riders. Nevertheless, it's a lovely, eco-friendly way to experience the Middle Keys. Between mile markers 58 and 40, you'll even find an 11-mile bike path, plus a wide shoulder along the Seven Mile Bridge. Bikes can be rented from **Bike Marathon Bike Rental** (305/743-3204, www.bikemarathonbikerentals.com, 8 A.M.–6 P.M. daily, $35 weekly, $99 monthly), Marathon's first and oldest bicycle rental company, which also offers free delivery and free pickup service in Marathon and Key Colony Beach.

Of course, you can also experience the Middle Keys via boat. Having your own vessel makes navigating these waters even easier, and you'll find no shortage of boat ramps and marina slips in the Marathon area, a region popular among boating enthusiasts. If you'd rather rent a boat or kayak for the day, stop by **Fish 'n Fun Boat & Watersports Rentals** (4590 Overseas Hwy., Marathon, 305/743-2275 or 800/471-3440, http://fishnfunrentals.com, 8 A.M.–6 P.M. daily), near mile marker 49.5, which offers a range of vessels, including single and tandem kayaks ($30–45 per half day, $45–60 daily), personal watercraft ($85 hourly, $275 per half day, $500 daily), 19-foot fishing boats ($140 per half day, $190 daily, $965 weekly), and 26-foot fishing boats ($235 per half day, $285 daily, $1,565 weekly). While Fish 'n Fun provides kayak and personal watercraft rentals for up to a full day, you can rent six varieties of fishing boats on a day-to-day or weekly basis.

MARATHON

BIG PINE AND THE LOWER KEYS

Stretching from Little Duck Key to Boca Chica Key, the Lower Keys are the largest and least developed part of the Florida Keys archipelago. Composed of numerous keys and island clusters, the Lower Keys possess a far more sedate vibe than that of Key West to the south. In this region, beaches, campgrounds, and a host of animals—including birds, snakes, alligators, rabbits, and raccoons—take precedence over tourists and museums, making the Lower Keys the ideal place to escape from the world for a while, even in the winter months, when snowbirds help to increase the population.

West of the Seven Mile Bridge, the first major stop, Bahia Honda State Park, is one of the most popular parks in the Keys. Its three sandy beaches, which allow access to the Atlantic Ocean and the Gulf of Mexico, are routinely voted the best in the state and are well favored among photographers. Soft, white sand and calm, shallow waters make this the perfect place for swimmers, snorkelers, and kayakers. Fishing, boating, biking, and hiking are also favored pastimes here.

Among the remaining islands, Big Pine Key boasts the lion's share of diversions. From here, visitors can take biking and diving trips, glass-bottom boat tours, deep-sea fishing charters, full-day kayaking adventures, and island excursions. Also on Big Pine lies part of the 84,351-acre National Key Deer Refuge, established in the late 1950s to preserve the dwindling population of the petite Key deer. Nowadays, this amazing refuge protects several other threatened plants and animals as well, many of which you might spot at the

HIGHLIGHTS

◖ **Bahia Honda State Park:** A jewel of Florida's state park system, this recreational treasure, which encompasses all of Bahia Honda Key, offers ideal waters for snorkelers, kayakers, and swimmers and boasts some of the most photographed beaches in the Florida Keys (page 192).

◖ **National Key Deer Refuge:** Established in 1957, this 84,351-acre sanctuary comprises mangrove and pine forests, freshwater and salt-marsh wetlands, and tropical hardwood hammocks, providing critical habitat for hundreds of native and migratory species, including the diminutive Key deer (page 193).

◖ **Blue Hole:** Once an active limestone quarry, this tranquil, well-visited body of water nurtures an array of creatures, from green herons to turtles to alligators, luring bird-watchers, wildlife lovers, and photographers alike (page 194).

◖ **Fantasy Dan's Airplane Rides:** Operating from Sugarloaf Key Airport, one of the Keys' longest-running sightseeing tours provides an aerial view of the magnificent is-

lands, coral reefs, lighthouses, and marinelife that define this region (page 195).

◖ **Underwater Music Festival:** For over two decades, this whimsical event has lured numerous divers and snorkelers to Looe Key Reef, to enjoy underwater musical performances and promote the preservation of the Florida Keys' unique coral reef ecosystem (page 197).

◖ **Boating and Kayaking Around Big Pine Key:** Various outfitters and tour operators enable visitors to experience the backcountry islands, assorted habitats, bountiful waters, and amazing creatures of the Lower Keys — via kayak, skiff, powerboat, or glass-bottom catamaran (page 200).

◖ **Diving and Snorkeling near Looe Key Reef:** Created in 1981 and located about five nautical miles offshore of Big Pine Key, the Looe Key National Marine Sanctuary invites scuba divers and snorkelers to explore the parrotfish, barracuda, moray eels, and varied sharks that dwell within this classic spur-and-groove formation (page 200).

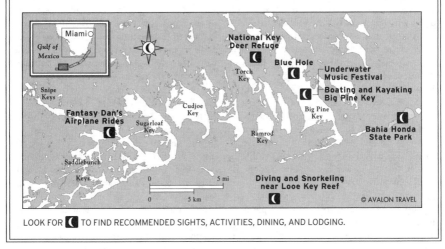

LOOK FOR ◖ TO FIND RECOMMENDED SIGHTS, ACTIVITIES, DINING, AND LODGING.

Blue Hole, the largest freshwater source in the Keys.

While adjacent Little Torch Key offers access to the exclusive Little Palm Island Resort & Spa, it's still a laid-back locale and a terrific jumping-off point for scuba divers and snorkelers. Part of the Florida Keys National Marine Sanctuary, the incredible Looe Key Reef—named after a long-ago shipwreck—sits amid several historic wreck sites and is home to the fascinating Underwater Music Festival every July. Other keys—such as Ramrod, Summerland, Cudjoe, and Sugarloaf—offer their own share of diversions, from fishing charters to airplane rides. Of course, even though outdoor diversions are paramount here, you're not so far away from Key West that you can't make a day trip to the bars, museums, and people-watching hot spots that await.

HISTORY

As with other parts of the Florida Keys, it's believed that American Indians, specifically tribes like the Calusa and Tequesta, were the original inhabitants of the Lower Keys. The memoirs of a shipwrecked Spaniard, dated in the mid-1500s, have revealed the presence of such tribes, who supposedly subsisted on fish, lobster, turtles, snails, raccoons, and manatees.

Unfortunately, little is known about the Lower Keys until the 1800s, long after many of the Indian tribes had either moved or died out. Only the remnants of shipwrecks, such as the HMS *Looe,* which crashed against the eponymously named Looe Key Reef in February 1744, sheds some light on the 18th century. After all, the lack of bridges, the presence of mosquitoes, and the inability to make a living in the untamed Lower Keys made it difficult to settle here.

During the second half of the 19th century, however, settlements began to expand on places like No Name Key—filled both with wealthy part-time residents of Key West, who would travel by boat to their country homes in the Lower Keys, and with hardy full-time inhabitants, who managed to eke out a living

by farming, fishing, collecting sponges, and producing charcoal. For instance, Sugarloaf Key—which was once called Glenn Key and, later, Perkey—became a grower and supplier of sugarloaf pineapples.

With the fulfillment, however, of Henry Flagler's lifelong dream to construct an Overseas Railroad, linking the Florida Keys to the mainland, the Lower Keys finally began to flourish. Between 1905 and 1912, during construction of the railroad, buildings were being erected in the Lower Keys to serve as train stations, residences for station agents, and homes for settlers. The railroad, which took seven years, much of Flagler's fortune, and hundreds of workers to build, operated from 1912 until it was destroyed by the terrible Labor Day hurricane of 1935. Soon afterward, what remained of the railroad was sold to the state of Florida. During its operation, however, islands like Bahia Honda Key became legitimate settlements.

In the years that followed the destruction of the Overseas Railroad, developments such as the state-funded Overseas Highway (which was initially an arduous combination of roads and ferries), the 1957 establishment of the National Key Deer Refuge, and the 1981 designation of the Looe Key National Marine Sanctuary helped to bring attention to the Lower Keys. Still, in many areas, this part of the Florida Keys is even less developed and less populated than it was in the early 20th century.

PLANNING YOUR TIME

Although many travelers simply pass through this region on their way to Key West, the Lower Keys are definitely worth a look. You might not find museums or historic districts here, but you'll certainly encounter a wealth of outdoor sights and activities, from underwater coral reefs to fishing charters to kayaking excursions. While the attractions and lodgings are spread across numerous islands, it's not terribly difficult to traverse this region via car, especially since the Overseas Highway links several of the main islands, such as Bahia Honda Key, Big Pine Key, and Sugarloaf Key.

BIG PINE AND THE LOWER KEYS

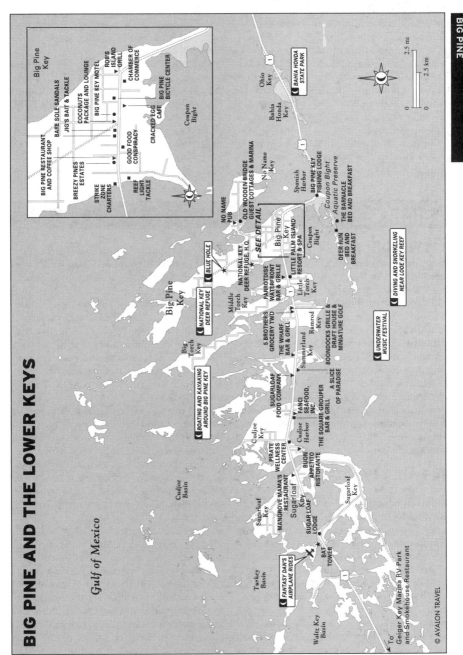

© AVALON TRAVEL

Still, some places, like the No Name Pub, can be a bit challenging to find.

Most people only need a day or two to hit the highlights of this region, such as Bahia Honda State Park and the Blue Hole. The length of your stay, however, depends upon your chosen activities. Fishing, kayaking, snorkeling, and diving—all popular activities here—could easily fill a few days.

Luckily, you won't often face crowds and congestion in the Lower Keys, unless you head to a Bahia Honda beach on a particularly warm, sunny day. Of course, while crime isn't really an issue, you should still stay alert in the more isolated areas.

For more information about Big Pine Key and the Lower Keys, consult the **Monroe County Tourist Development Council** (1201 White St., Ste. 102, Key West, FL 33040, 305/296-1552 or 800/352-5397, www.fla-keys.com) and the **Lower Keys Chamber of Commerce** (31020 Overseas Hwy., Big Pine Key, FL 33043, 305/872-2411 or 800/872-3722, www.lowerkeyschamber.com).

Sights

LITTLE DUCK KEY BEACH

Just past the western end of Seven Mile Bridge lies Little Duck Key, a small island that features **Veterans Memorial Park** (MM 39 BS/OS U.S. 1, Little Duck Key, 305/295-4385, 24 hours daily, free), formerly known as Little Duck Key County Park. Although most people bypass this key for the well-visited Bahia Honda State Park farther down the Overseas Highway, it's a pleasant stop for those who appreciate a quiet beach, with access to the Gulf of Mexico and the Atlantic Ocean. Amenities here include picnic pavilions, grills, restrooms, a small parking lot, and a paved boat ramp. Just remember that dogs must be leashed at all times, and no overnight parking is allowed.

◖ BAHIA HONDA STATE PARK

From the Seven Mile Bridge, you'll cross three tiny islands—Little Duck Key, Missouri Key, and Ohio Key—before encountering one of southern Florida's recreational jewels. Encompassing all of Bahia Honda Key, the 524-acre Bahia Honda State Park (36850 Overseas Hwy., Bahia Honda Key, 305/872-2353 or 305/872-3210, www.floridastateparks.org/bahiahonda or www.bahiahondapark.com, 8 A.M.–sunset daily, $8 vehicles w/2–8 passengers plus $0.50 pp, $4.50 motorcycles and single-occupant vehicles, $2.50 pedestrians, bikers, and extra passengers) features three breezy, coconut palm–studded beaches that, together, offer access to the Atlantic Ocean as well as the Gulf of Mexico. The smallest beach, Calusa, provides several small picnic pavilions and shares a bathhouse and outdoor, freshwater showers with Loggerhead Beach, considered the shallowest of the three. Sandspur, the largest and most popular beach, has three picnic pavilions, plus restrooms with outdoor showers. It's a perfect place to relax, enjoy the warm waters, and watch one of the Keys' notoriously magnificent sunsets.

Ideal for swimmers, the park also provides kayak and snorkel gear rentals, a concession building, three campgrounds, vacation cabins, and two-hour snorkeling excursions (305/872-3954, 9:30 A.M. and 1:30 P.M. daily, $30 adults, $25 children under 18, plus gear rentals) to the offshore Looe Key National Marine Sanctuary. In addition, bikers can utilize the paved 3.5-mile road that runs the length of the island, while anglers can fish from shore or launch their own boats at the on-site boat ramps ($10 per launch). Nature lovers might also appreciate the small on-site Sand and Sea Nature Center (305/872-9807, 9 A.M.–5 P.M. Thurs.–Mon., free), which offers exhibits about offshore coral formations and the island's native plants and animals, from mangroves to iguanas.

Of course, the park's three nature trails offer bird-watchers and wildlife lovers the

sandpipers, laughing gulls, mourning doves, mangrove cuckoos, red-bellied woodpeckers, brown pelicans, turkey vultures, and bald eagles.

Other activities here include ranger-led beach walks (9 A.M. Tues. June–July), nature programs (1 P.M. Fri. June–July), and, in late January, a reenactment of the first train ride on Flagler's former railroad. Reservations are recommended for campgrounds, cabin rentals, boat slips, and snorkeling excursions. Unlike at many places in the Florida Keys, pets are welcome at Bahia Honda, though their access is limited, and they must be well behaved and kept on six-foot, hand-held leashes at all times.

BIG PINE KEY

As the largest island in the Lower Keys, Big Pine Key anchors a region defined by its numerous island clusters and bountiful natural resources—a region that remains the last undeveloped holdout of the Florida Keys. While Big Pine Key, the second largest island in the entire archipelago, contains the lion's share of attractions, shops, services, and the like, it still represents the laid-back vibe prevalent throughout the Lower Keys, a place where people come to escape the more commercialized—and often more crowded—communities of Key West and Islamorada.

◖ National Key Deer Refuge

Founded in 1957, this 84,351-acre sanctuary encompasses mangrove and pine forests, freshwater and salt-marsh wetlands, and tropical hardwood hammocks on 25 islands in the Lower Keys. The primary purpose of the refuge is to provide critical habitat for hundreds of native and migratory species, including the docile Key deer, a miniature version of the white-tailed deer, who only grow to 26–32 inches tall and whose diminishing population was the original inspiration for the creation of the National Key Deer Refuge (28950 Watson Blvd., Big Pine Key, 305/872-2239, www.fws.gov/nationalkeydeer, free).

Nevertheless, visitors are welcome 24 hours

© LAURA MARTONE

remnants of the railroad at Bahia Honda State Park

opportunity to see real specimens in action. One trail, called the Silver Palm Trail, is situated near the Sandspur area and offers a look at mangrove trees, sand dunes, and a tropical hardwood hammock, while another winds through the Wings and Waves Butterfly Garden, planted in 1998 beside the Loggerhead parking lot and now frequented by vibrant butterflies, including the zebra longwing butterfly and the endangered Miami blue butterfly. The third trail, situated beside the Calusa beach, leads to the top of the Old Bahia Honda Bridge, a seemingly unfinished concrete-and-steel structure that once spanned the Bahia Honda Channel as part of Henry Flagler's Overseas Railroad. Built in the early 1900s, the bridge was partially destroyed in the infamous Labor Day hurricane of 1935, and today, it affords a panoramic view of the entire island as well as the surrounding waters. From here, you may spot fish, eagle rays, sea turtles, bottlenose dolphins, West Indian manatees, and an array of wading birds, shorebirds, and raptors, including great white herons, spotted

NO SNORKELING FOR FIDO

In general, it's rather difficult to travel with your pets in the Florida Keys, including the islands that the Lower Keys comprise. Only a handful of Big Pine-area hotels – such as the **Sugar Loaf Lodge** (17001 Overseas Hwy., Sugarloaf Key, 800/553-6097, www.sugarloaflodge. net) and the **Old Wooden Bridge Guest Cottages and Marina** (1791 Bogie Dr., Big Pine Key, 305/872-2241, www.oldwood-enbridge.com) – are pet-friendly, so it's always best to call ahead if you're considering bringing your cat or dog with you.

Although it's often easier for pet owners to stay in a campground, such as those available at **Bahia Honda State Park** (36850 Overseas Hwy., Big Pine Key, 305/872-2353 or 305/872-3210, www.floridastateparks.org/bahiahonda or www.bahiahondapark.com), certain restrictions still do apply. While service and guide dogs, with proper identification, are welcome in all areas of the park, pets are typically not allowed in cabins, bathhouses, pavilions, or the concession building. They're also not allowed on the beaches or in the water, which unfortunately means you won't be able to swim or snorkel with your pet.

In the limited areas where pets are permitted – such as the campgrounds – they must be well behaved and kept on a six-foot, hand-held leash at all times. Perhaps it goes without saying, but owners must always pick up and properly dispose of their pets' waste – no matter where they leave it.

daily in at least part of the refuge, most notably within designated areas of Big Pine Key and No Name Key. Here, you'll find the wheelchair-accessible, 0.1-mile Mannillo Nature Trail and the 0.7-mile Jack C. Watson Nature Trail, both of which offer photographers and nature lovers the opportunity to observe many different species of birds, reptiles, and

mammals, including great white herons, brown pelicans, various raptors and songbirds, lizards, turtles, alligators, and Key deer, which, though said to swim easily between the islands, mainly dwell on Big Pine. Early morning and late afternoon are typically the best times to spot a Key deer, especially at the northern end of Key Deer Boulevard.

The wheelchair-accessible **visitor center** (179 Key Deer Blvd., Big Pine Key, 305/872-0774, 9 A.M.–4:30 P.M. Mon.–Fri.) is in the Big Pine Shopping Center near the intersection of U.S. 1 and Key Deer Boulevard. Here, you'll also find information about the **Great White Heron National Wildlife Refuge** (www.fws. gov/nationalkeydeer/greatwhiteheron) and the **Key West National Wildlife Refuge** (www. fws.gov/nationalkeydeer/keywest), two protected areas that encompass numerous backcountry islands in Florida Bay and the Gulf of Mexico, set aside by the federal government to maintain a preserve and breeding ground for native birds. Unlike the National Key Deer Refuge, these two are only accessible via boat.

BLUE HOLE

Once an active limestone quarry—utilized during the construction of Henry Flagler's ill-fated Overseas Railroad in the early 20th century—this tranquil, well-visited body of water nurtures an array of creatures, from green herons to turtles to alligators. Situated within the National Key Deer Refuge on Big Pine Key and free to visit, it lures bird-watchers, wildlife lovers, and photographers alike. The observation platform offers an unobstructed view of the water, where, if you're lucky, you might spot a Key deer stopping for a refreshing drink. To reach the Blue Hole, take U.S. 1 to mile marker 30, turn northwest onto Key Deer Boulevard, continue past Watson Boulevard, and look for the sign on the left, near Big Pine Street.

SUGARLOAF KEY

En route to Key West, you'll encounter several quiet residential areas on islands like Little Torch Key and Big Coppitt Key, all the way to the Key West Naval Air Station on Boca

RULES OF THE REFUGE

Created in 1957 to protect endangered Key deer and other precious wildlife resources, the **National Key Deer Refuge** (28950 Watson Blvd., Big Pine Key, 305/872-2239 or 305/872-0774, www.fws.gov/nationalkeydeer) now preserves roughly 84,351 acres in the Lower Keys. Unlike in some national wildlife refuges, however, visitors (and leashed pets) are allowed within its boundaries. Though public access is prohibited in much of the refuge – in order to protect wildlife and critical habitat, as well as visitors – you'll find walking and hiking trails, a visitor center, and opportunities for fishing, biking, wildlife-watching, and noncommercial photography on Big Pine Key and No Name Key. Surprisingly, you can even drive in parts of the refuge.

Of course, despite such accessibility, certain activities are prohibited, including:

- Bringing weapons onto refuge lands, unless they are unloaded, cased, and secured in vehicles or boats

- Using metal detectors to search for antiquities or treasure

- Bringing horses onto refuge lands, as their manure might carry the seeds of invasive plants

- Camping on refuge lands, since there are no sanitary facilities for campers

- Using poles or pipes, such as beach umbrellas, which might penetrate turtle nests

- Campfires, which can start destructive wildfires

- Storing equipment or property on refuge lands

- Feeding wildlife, which can cause animals to become less wary and subsequently increase the risk of poaching, spreading diseases, and being struck by vehicles

- Injuring or harassing wildlife

- Removing wildlife, plants, or natural items from refuge lands

- Introducing exotic plants or wildlife, which can cause competition with existing native species

In addition, you're expected to drive carefully throughout the refuge – even on the Overseas Highway, which crosses several of the 25 islands contained within the preserve. You must stay alert for Key deer at all times, though especially at sunrise and sunset, when they're more likely to emerge. The speed limit, which is 35 miles per hour at night, is strictly enforced, and tickets can be costly. Vehicle collisions are one of the leading threats to these endangered animals, and of course, killing one on purpose can result in steep fines and possible imprisonment.

Chica Key. Along this route lies Sugarloaf Key, a charming residential island that contains its share of friendly eateries, laid-back campgrounds, and curious attractions—plus a small airport of its own.

◖ Fantasy Dan's Airplane Rides

Operating out of the Sugarloaf Key Airport, Fantasy Dan's Airplane Rides (MM 17 BS U.S. 1, Sugarloaf Key, 305/745-2217 or 305/304-1214, www.floridaairplanetours.com, times vary) is one of the Keys' longest-running sightseeing tours, guided by a pilot with over three

decades' worth of experience. The plane can accommodate up to three passengers, who can choose from a variety of experiences. The 35-minute Key West Aerial Nature Tour ($150 per ride) offers a bird's-eye view of backcountry islands, pristine coral reefs, offshore lighthouses, and Key West's coastal attractions. The hourlong Boca Grande Flight ($200 per ride) includes all of the sights observed on the Key West tour, plus shipwrecks and marinelife, from dolphins to sharks to sea turtles. Dan also offers a 45-minute Sunset Flight ($180 per ride), plus customized tours of area lighthouses and, for anglers, special trips to spot the best fishing holes. Reservations are recommended—and absolutely required for the Sunset Flight, especially if you choose the champagne package.

Bat Tower

At mile marker 17, those headed to the Sugarloaf Key Airport must turn northwest onto Bat Tower Road. En route to the airport, you should stop for an up-close look at the weather-beaten Bat Tower, erected in 1929 by entrepreneur Richter Clyde Perky as part of a pesticide-free plan to eliminate mosquitoes from his tourist attractions in the Lower Keys. Based on the theory that bats have a notoriously ravenous appetite for mosquitoes and other insects, the 30-foot-tall pine tower was intended to house a colony of imported bats who would, in turn, solve Perky's pest problem. Despite his creative thinking, however, the bats didn't stay, and the plan subsequently failed. Today, the defunct tower, which is listed on the National Register of Historic Places and costs nothing to view, serves as a monument to one man's inability to control nature.

Entertainment and Shopping

NIGHTLIFE

If you're looking for a vivacious nightlife, with an assortment of dancing and drinking options, then head south to Key West, where the "Duval crawl" can keep you busy all night. But if you just need a place to unwind, the Lower Keys can certainly satisfy you. For over 20 years, **Coconuts Package and Lounge** (30535 Overseas Hwy., Big Pine Key, 305/872-3795, 7 A.M.–close daily) has lured night owls with beer, liquor, and pool tables, and the fact that it's air-conditioned is a big plus in the summertime. In addition, this casual lounge stays open until at least 2 A.M. every night, though a 4 A.M. closing time is not unusual. The **Parrotdise Waterfront Bar & Grille** (183 Barry Ave., Little Torch Key, 305/872-9989, www.parrotdisewaterfront.com, 11 A.M.–10 P.M. Sun.–Thurs., 11 A.M.–close Fri.–Sat.) offers a daily happy hour (3–7 P.M.), plus two-for-one Martini Mondays and Saturday beach parties.

The **Looe Key Tiki Bar/Restaurant** (27340 Overseas Hwy., Ramrod Key, 305/872-2215 or 800/942-5397, www.diveflakeys.com, 11 A.M.–11 P.M. daily) features a daily happy hour (4–7 P.M.) and live entertainment nightly (usually 7–11 P.M.), from acoustic guitarists to funk bands to karaoke. Across the highway, **Boondocks Grille & Draft House**

& Miniature Golf (27205 Overseas Hwy., Ramrod Key, 305/872-4094, www.boondocks.us.com, 11 A.M.–close daily) provides an open-air tiki bar, where you can enjoy happy hour (4–6 P.M.) on weekdays as well as contests and

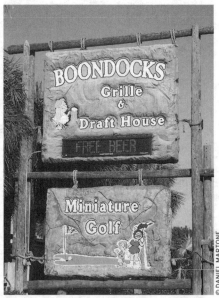

Boondocks Grille & Draft House features live music.

© DANIEL MARTONE

live folk, country, and rock music throughout the week.

Mangrove Mama's Restaurant (MM 20 BS U.S. 1, Sugarloaf Key, 305/745-3030, www.mangrovemamasrestaurant.com, 11:30 A.M.–10 P.M. daily) offers a daily happy hour (4–6 P.M.), plus live blues on Friday and Saturday. Closer to Key West, the **Geiger Key Marina RV Park** (5 Geiger Rd., Geiger Key, 305/296-3553, www.geigerkeymarina.com) also features live music—typically laid-back tunes from the 1970s, '80s, and '90s—on Friday, Saturday, and Sunday nights at the on-site Smokehouse Restaurant (305/294-1230, 8 A.M.–10 P.M. daily).

FESTIVALS AND EVENTS
◖ Underwater Music Festival

For more than 25 years, the Lower Keys have promoted the preservation of the spectacular Looe Key Reef with a unique summertime event, the whimsical, daylong Underwater Music Festival, which usually takes place in mid-July. This annual underwater concert features an array of seaworthy tunes, from humpback whale songs to ditties by Jimmy Buffett, the Beatles, and other legendary musicians. Every year, hundreds of snorkelers and scuba divers flock to the area for this one-of-a-kind celebration—an ideal time for you to explore this vibrant coral reef, home to a wide variety of tropical fish, while listening to an uninterrupted underwater broadcast of the concert, presented by various guitarists, percussionists, and other musicians who are literally playing their instruments beneath the waves. For more information, contact the **Lower Keys Chamber of Commerce** (31020 Overseas Hwy., Big Pine Key, 305/872-2411 or 800/872-3722, www.lowerkeyschamber.com).

Big Pine and the Lower Keys Island Art Festival

Typically held on the first Saturday in December, the Big Pine and the Lower Keys Island Art Festival features a full day of arts, crafts, exhibits, and live music on the grounds of the **Lower Keys Chamber of Commerce**

(31020 Overseas Hwy., Big Pine Key, 305/872-2411 or 800/872-3722, www.lowerkeyschamber.com) near mile marker 31, on the ocean side of the Overseas Highway. Food and beverages are available on-site, and admission and parking are free. For more information, contact the chamber of commerce or the **Florida Keys Council of the Arts** (1100 Simonton St., Key West, 305/295-4369, www.keysarts.com).

Other Annual Events

The Lower Keys host a wide array of other annual events, including the one-day **Outdoor Art Show** in mid- to late January—a collaboration between the Artists in Paradise Gallery (221 Key Deer Blvd., Big Pine Key, 305/872-1828, www.artistsinparadise.com) and the Boondocks Grille & Draft House & Miniature Golf (27205 Overseas Hwy., Ramrod Key, 305/872-4094, www.boondocks.us.com), where the show usually takes place. Also in mid- to late January is the **Big Pine & Lower Keys Nautical Flea Market,** typically held on a Saturday at the Lower Keys Chamber of Commerce (31020 Overseas Hwy., Big Pine Key, 305/872-2411 or 800/872-3722, www.lowerkeyschamber.com, free admission and parking) and featuring an emporium of boats, motors, and other nautical items, plus live music, food, and beverages.

In early April, the **Lower Keys Music Festival** (305/872-2411 or 800/872-3722, www.lowerkeyschamber.com, $20–25 adults and children over 10, free parking) features a full day of reggae music, crafts, food, and beverages at Camp Sawyer near mile marker 34.5 on West Summerland Key. Anglers might also enjoy area fishing tournaments like the three-day **Lower Keys & Key West Reef Shootout** (305/395-3474) in mid-May, which targets bottomfish, kingfish, and wahoo and benefits the Lower Keys Chamber of Commerce, and the three-day **Big Pine & Lower Keys Dolphin Tournament** (305/872-2411 or 800/872-3722, www.lowerkeyschamber.com) in mid-June, which typically offers over $25,000 in prizes.

BIG PINE

SHOPPING

Although avid shoppers will find a slew of options farther south in Key West, the pickings are much slimmer in this part of the Lower Keys. Still, there are at least a few shops worth mentioning.

Near mile marker 30.4 on Big Pine Key, the **Big Pine Shopping Center** (www.bigpine-shopping.com) houses several choices, including clothing boutiques and specialty shops like the **Key West Key Lime Pie Co.** (225 Key Deer Blvd., Big Pine Key, 305/872-7400 or 877/882-7437, www.keywestkeylimepieco.com, 10 A.M.–6 P.M. Mon.–Sat., noon–5 P.M. Sun.), which sells award-winning key lime pies in addition to gourmet jellies, marinades, cookies, candies, spices, cookbooks, and other treats. Here, you'll also spot the **Artists in Paradise Gallery** (221 Key Deer Blvd., Big Pine Key, 305/872-1828, www.artistsinparadise.com, 10 A.M.–6 P.M. daily), a co-op gallery that spotlights the jewelry, photography, sculptures, stained glass, mixed media, watercolor paintings, and other artwork of over 30 local artists. Created in 1994, the gallery also provides framing services and hosts periodic demonstrations, workshops, auctions, and other events—such as Walk on Winn-Dixie, which features art exhibitions, live music, and receptions throughout the shopping center on the first Friday of every month, from October to June.

For last-minute shoe needs, head to nearby **Bare Sole Sandals** (30313 Overseas Hwy., Big Pine Key, 305/872-1882, www.baresole-sandals.com, 10 A.M.–5:30 P.M. Mon.–Fri., 9 A.M.–5 P.M. Sat.), where you can peruse a large selection of sandals, clogs, flip-flops, and water shoes for men, women, and children, plus jewelry, handbags, hats, and other accessories. Not far away lies the **Good Food Conspiracy** (MM 30.2 OS U.S. 1, Big Pine Key, 305/872-3945 or 305/872-9119, www.goodfoodconspiracy.com, 9:30 A.M.–7 P.M. Mon.–Sat., 11 A.M.–5 P.M. Sun.), which sells natural foods, vitamins, herbs, and oils in addition to offering a juice bar and a holistic health center.

Depending on the season, **Fanci Seafood, Inc.** (MM 22.5 OS U.S. 1, Cudjoe Key, 305/745-3887, www.fanciseafood.com, 10 A.M.–6 P.M. Mon.–Sat.) provides seafood lovers with fresh fish, shrimp, lobster, and stone crab. Art lovers might also appreciate **Island Iron & Ink** (MM 21.5 BS U.S. 1, Cudjoe Key, 305/744-9196, by appt.), an out-of-the-way studio and gallery, housed within a barn and offering original metalwork and custom-designed mixed media by longtime local artist Reen Stanhouse, who specializes in large, one-of-a-kind creations like sculptures and fountains. Near mile marker 15 on the ocean side of U.S. 1, you can choose from a range of roasts at the highly touted **Baby's Coffee** (3178 Overseas Hwy., Saddlebunch Keys, 305/744-9866 or 800/523-2326, www.babyscoffee.com, 6:30 A.M.–6 P.M. Mon.–Fri., 7 A.M.–5 P.M. Sat., 8 A.M.–5 P.M. Sun.), which serves many area establishments, including Key West's Eden House. Choices include the nutty Baby's Key West Old Town Roast, the full-bodied Hemingway's Hair of the Dog, and other cleverly named concoctions. In addition to gourmet coffee, Baby's offers a wide selection of beer, wine, sodas, fruit juices, chocolate, pastries, and gourmet sandwiches—all you might need for a picnic by the sea.

Sports and Recreation

BIKING

In the Lower Keys, biking enthusiasts can explore a variety of different bike paths on Big Pine Key, No Name Key, the Saddlebunch Keys, and Big Coppitt Key. Many of these short paths connect to county roads, allowing for longer bike rides and terrific opportunities to view wildlife, from herons to Key deer. Eventually, the **Florida Keys Overseas Heritage Trail** will make it much easier for bikers to traverse the Lower Keys, from the Seven Mile Bridge to Stock Island. For now, you must venture along the shoulder of the Overseas Highway, which can be dangerous at times. No matter where you travel, though, always wear a helmet.

If you didn't bring a bike of your own, don't fret. The **Big Pine Bicycle Center** (31 County Rd., Big Pine Key, 305/872-0130, 9 A.M.–5 P.M. Mon.–Fri., 9 A.M.–3 P.M. Sat., closed Mon. in summer, $8 per half day, $10 daily) offers rentals, in addition to repairs, parts, and accessories. All bicycle rentals include helmets, baskets, and locks.

FISHING

While anglers tend to favor the bountiful waters of Islamorada, the Lower Keys certainly offer their share of fishing opportunities. **Strike Zone Charters** (MM 29.5 BS U.S. 1, Big Pine Key, 305/872-9863 or 800/654-9560, www.strikezonecharter.com, 8 A.M.–5 P.M. daily, $650–850) provides, among other excursions, deep-sea fishing trips for up to six people. Half-day and full-day trips are available, as are backcountry fishing excursions. Reservations are highly recommended.

Some area fishing guides have no specific port, but can still be reached to arrange a variety of charters. Two such companies include **Key Flat Charters** (305/304-3152, www.lowerkeysflatsfishing.com, $375–500), operated by Captain Luke Kelly and covering the flats and backcountry inshore waters, and **Last Cast Charters** (305/744-9796, www.

lastcastcharters.net, $400–1,250), operated by Captain Andrew Tipler and featuring offshore fishing, flats fishing, and swordfish excursions. Also in the area, you'll find **Sea Boots Charters** (MM 24.5 OS U.S. 1, Summerland

---

WILD ANIMAL ENCOUNTER

Lizards, iguanas, roosters, and feral cats roam freely in the Florida Keys. You'll see them everywhere – in parking lots, on porches, even amid the foliage. Because such creatures are so accustomed to people, it's sometimes easy to forget how to handle an encounter with truly wild animals.

Whether you spot a lounging alligator, a tiny Key deer, or something else entirely, you should adhere to the following rules:

- Observe wildlife from a distance; do not follow or approach the animals.

- Never feed wildlife; feeding wild animals can damage their health, alter their natural behaviors, and expose them to predators.

- Never taunt or disturb wildlife.

- Protect wildlife by storing your food and trash securely.

- Control pets at all times, or leave them at home.

- Avoid wildlife during sensitive phases, such as mating or nesting.

For more information about respecting wildlife, consult the recreation and parks division of the **Florida Department of Environmental Protection** (850/245-3029 or 850/245-2157, www.dep.state.fl.us or www.floridastateparks.org) or contact the Colorado-based **Leave No Trace Center for Outdoor Ethics** (303/442-8222 or 800/332-4100, www.lnt.org).

Key, 305/745-1530 or 800/238-1746, www.sea-boots.com, $700–1,100), operated by Captain Jim Sharpe and featuring big game fishing, from wahoo to sharks.

There are also several bait shops in the Lower Keys, including **Jig's Bait & Tackle** (30321 Overseas Hwy., Big Pine Key, 305/872-1040, http://jigsbaitandtackle.com, 7 A.M.–7 P.M. Mon.–Sat., 7 A.M.–5 P.M. Sun.), a one-stop shop for fishing equipment, bait, tackle, firearms, and charts, and **Reef Light Tackle** (29770 Overseas Hwy., Big Pine Key, 305/872-7679, www.reeflighttackle.com, 6 A.M.–6 P.M. daily), which offers fishing reels and rods in addition to bait. Another option is **Fanci Seafood, Inc.** (MM 22.5 OS U.S. 1, Cudjoe Key, 305/745-3887, www.fanciseafood.com, 8 A.M.–6 P.M. daily), which provides anglers with bait, chum, and ice throughout the day, not to mention fresh seafood for retail customers beginning at 10 A.M. each morning.

◖ BOATING AND KAYAKING

Given the topography of the Lower Keys, which contains plenty of open water, curious islands, and backcountry channels, this is truly a water lover's playground and an ideal place for boating and kayaking. **Strike Zone Charters** (MM 29.5 BS U.S. 1, Big Pine Key, 305/872-9863 or 800/654-9560, www.strikezonecharter.com, 8 A.M.–5 P.M. daily, $55 pp) offers all-inclusive island excursions on glass-bottom catamarans. Such trips combine a breezy boat ride with history and ecology lessons, bird-watching, light-tackle fishing, a fish cookout, and a snorkeling experience amid the offshore coral reefs, part of the Looe Key National Marine Sanctuary. Reservations are recommended.

Boat owners who would prefer to explore this region on their own will find several marinas and public boat ramps at their disposal. Of course, if you didn't bring a boat with you, you can easily rent one from **Big Pine Key Boat Rentals** (MM 33 OS U.S. 1, Big Pine Key, and 24326 Overseas Hwy., Summerland Key, 305/745-1505, www.bigpineboatrentals.com, 8 A.M.–5 P.M. daily, $200–395) and go cruising, fishing, and snorkeling at your own

pace. Just be advised that reservations are a must; typically, the hours of operation are flexible, and help is only available if the staff knows you're coming. Meanwhile, **Blu Waters Rentals** (MM 24.5 OS U.S. 1, Summerland Key, 305/923-3323, www.bluwatersrental.com, 9 A.M.–6 P.M. daily), based at the Summerland Cove Marina, offers both personal watercraft rentals ($75 hourly, $110 per two hours, $145 per half day, $225 daily) as well as boat rentals ($150–175 per half day, $250–275 daily, $900–1,000 weekly).

For kayak rentals, guided kayaking nature tours, skiff ecotours, and backcountry catamaran cruises, consult **Big Pine Kayak Adventures** (Old Wooden Bridge Marina, 1791 Bogie Dr., Big Pine Key, 305/872-7474, www.keyskayaktours.com, 8 A.M.–5 P.M. daily, rentals $20 per two hours, $5 for each additional hour, guided tours start at $50 pp), operated by Captain Bill Keogh, a well-respected naturalist, educator, photographer, and author who has lived in the Lower Keys for more than two decades. In addition, the **Coral Reef Park Company** (305/872-3210) offers kayak rentals at **Bahia Honda State Park** (36850 Overseas Hwy., Bahia Honda Key, 305/872-2353, www.floridastateparks.org/bahiahonda or www.bahiahondapark.com, 8 A.M.–sunset daily, $8 vehicles w/2–8 passengers plus $0.50 pp, $4.50 motorcycles and single-occupant vehicles, $2.50 pedestrians, bikers, and extra passengers), including single kayaks ($10 hourly, $30 per half day) and those meant for two passengers ($18 hourly, $54 per half day).

◖ DIVING AND SNORKELING

Roughly five nautical miles south of Big Pine Key lies one of the finest and most diverse coral reefs in the Florida Keys. Established in 1981, following the success of the Key Largo National Marine Sanctuary, which was created in 1975, the **Looe Key National Marine Sanctuary,** part of the Florida Keys National Marine Sanctuary, features a 33-acre, spur-and-groove network of coral fingers, sand channels, and turtle grass that abound with over 150 species of fish, including parrotfish,

© DANIEL MARTONE

snorkeling in the Lower Keys

angelfish, yellowtail, barracuda, grouper, turtles, eagle rays, whale sharks, and moray eels. The U-shaped reef—long ago named after the HMS *Looe,* which supposedly ran aground here in February 1744—comprises patch reefs as well as outside reefs, and has depths that vary from 8 to 40 feet, making it ideal for first-time snorkelers as well advanced scuba divers. Either way, visitors will get an up-close look at a variety of coral, including elkhorn, staghorn, star, fire, and brain. For most of the year, the water clarity is excellent, and the sea conditions are moderate; January is often the only month during which visibility can be less than ideal. No matter when you visit, however, certain activities are absolutely prohibited, including spearfishing and the collecting of shells and tropical fish.

Several area operators provide tours to this one-of-a-kind reef, including the **Looe Key Reef Resort & Dive Center** (27340 Overseas Hwy., Ramrod Key, 305/872-2215, www.diveflakeys.com, 7:30 A.M.–8 P.M. Sun.–Thurs., 7:30 A.M.–9 P.M. Fri.–Sat.), which has offered scuba-diving instruction and three-hour

diving and snorkeling trips (10 A.M. and 3 P.M. Thurs.–Tues., $84 divers, $44 snorkelers, $34 children under 7, $29 passengers) to Looe Key Reef since 1978. Through the dive center, you're also able to experience the **Adolphus Busch,** a 210-foot freighter that was intentionally sunk in 1998 to create an artificial reef. Upright in 120 feet of water, the intact shipwreck has become a haven for a wide variety of marine invertebrates and fish, from moray eels to the 250-pound grouper often seen in the wheelhouse or cargo holds. Typically, the dive center offers a wreck trip on Wednesday, which includes a dive on the *Adolphus Busch,* plus two dives on Looe Key Reef ($84 divers for all three dives, $69 divers for two reef dives, $39 snorkelers for two reef dives, $29 passengers and snorkeling children under 7). All trip prices include tanks, weights, masks, snorkels, and fins; gas fills, equipment rentals, and repair services are also available on-site.

Other area operators include the **Coral Reef Park Company** (MM 37 OS U.S. 1, Bahia Honda Key, 305/872-3210 or 305/872-3954, www.bahiahondapark.com, 8 A.M.–5 P.M. daily,

the dive shop at Strike Zone Charters

© DANIEL MARTONE

$30 adults, $25 children under 18, $4 snorkel, $2 mask, $2 fins), which provides twice-daily, two-hour snorkeling trips (9:30 A.M. and 1:30 P.M.) from Bahia Honda State Park to the Looe Key Reef, and **Strike Zone Charters** (29675 Overseas Hwy., Big Pine Key, 305/872-9863 or 800/654-9560, www.strikezonecharter.com, 8 A.M.–5 P.M. daily, reservation required), which offers PADI instruction ($175–395 pp) and daily two-hour snorkeling and diving trips ($25–45 pp, plus gear rental) to the Looe Key Reef on roomy glass-bottom catamarans. Even in the waters near Bahia Honda, though, you're bound to see curious marine creatures, including queen conch, red rock urchin, spiny lobster, sea cucumbers, seahorses, horseshoe crabs, cushion sea stars, tubed sponges, moon jellies, and nurse sharks. Luckily, snorkel gear rentals ($6 wetsuit, $6 diver-down flag, $5 snorkel, $5 safety vest, $4–5 mask, $4 fins) are available daily in the park.

OTHER OUTDOOR ACTIVITIES

If you're looking for a land-based diversion in this watery playground, stop by **Boondocks** Grille & Draft House & Miniature Golf (27205 Overseas Hwy., Ramrod Key, 305/872-0265, www.boondocks.us.com, 10 A.M.–10 P.M. daily), where you can play an 18-hole round of golf ($9 adults, $7 children under 13) amid the caves and waterfalls of this tropical setting, then enjoy some snacks and libations at the 19th Hole Party Zone. It's an ideal activity for travelers with children.

For a more exhilarating experience, head to the Sugarloaf Key Airport at mile marker 17 on Sugarloaf Key, where **Sky Dive Key West** (305/745-4386, www.skydivekeywest.com, by appt. daily, $245–265 pp) offers tandem jumps for an aerial view of the Lower Keys from two miles above the earth. Skydivers must be at least 18 years old, and certain weight restrictions could apply. Reservations are necessary for all jumps; note that cash transactions will save you $20 per person.

SPAS AND YOGA

Although outdoor activities are paramount in the Lower Keys, you'll also find more relaxing pursuits like yoga and massage. The

KEYS NAMED AFTER WRECKS

With more than 800 islands in the Florida Keys, you're bound to find some curious names. People, animals, topographic features, even objects – such as money or teakettles – have inspired many of the monikers that you might spot on a typical map of the region.

Two islands in the Lower Keys – **Ramrod Key** and the submerged **Looe Key Reef** – were named after a pair of sunken ships. Originally known as Roberts Island, Ramrod Key – which serves scuba divers and snorkelers headed for the Looe Key Reef – apparently derives its modern moniker from a Spanish vessel that wrecked on an offshore coral reef in the early 19th century. Little is generally known about the ship itself, or the circumstances of its demise.

Such is not the case, however, for the HMS *Looe,* the 44-gun British frigate that eventually inspired the name of the Looe Key Reef. According to Bob "Frogfoot" Weller – the author of such books as *Famous Shipwrecks of the Florida Keys* (1990) and *Galleon Alley: The 1733 Spanish Treasure Fleet* (2001) – the HMS *Looe* was outfitted in Longreach, England, with 190 crewmen and spent the first years of her service patrolling the English Channel and searching for Barbary pirates. After her crew captured four Spanish vessels in Vigo Bay, Spain began attacking Fort Frederick in Georgia and harassing British settlers along America's East Coast. When the governor of South Carolina petitioned to have a warship protect the coastline, Captain Ashby Utting took the *Looe* on its final voyage.

After the ship reached Charleston, a four-day storm damaged the *Looe*'s rigging and main mast. With orders to seek out and destroy enemy ships near Florida, the *Looe* headed to Jamaica for repairs. By December 3, 1743, the ship was again ready to sail, and by February 4, 1744, she was in the Bahama Channel when an enemy ship was sighted. The *Looe* wasted little time in capturing the *Snow,* which, upon closer examination, turned out to be a British ship, the *Billander Betty,* that had been taken by the Spanish. When important French and Spanish documents were tossed overboard by the enemy and subsequently recovered by Utting's crew, the captain decided to escort the ship back to Charleston. Before retiring for the night, he ordered that the lead line be thrown every 30 minutes to sound for depth.

Around 1 A.M., the on-duty crewmen tossed the lead line and found no bottom at 300 feet. Not 15 minutes later, however, the officer of the watch was alarmed to spot breakers directly ahead. Despite a valiant attempt to veer the ship away from harm, a crosswind caught the sails and the stern subsequently collided with the reef. Soon afterward, the *Looe* began to fill with water. Recognizing that the ship was lost, Utting ordered that his men save as much of the bread and gunpowder as possible. Meanwhile, the *Snow* allegedly met a similar fate against a nearby reef.

By morning, Utting and his men found themselves on a small, sandy key, which they rightly assumed would soon be underwater. When they sighted a sloop offshore, Utting armed his small boats and sent them in pursuit. The next morning, the boats returned with the sloop in tow, and by February 8, the entire crews of the two fallen ships – 274 men in all – were rescued. Before leaving, Utting set fire to the *Looe,* which subsequently exploded into several pieces.

Although Utting and his crew arrived in Jamaica on February 13, 1744, the wreck wasn't discovered until 1951, when Art McKee, Mendel Peterson, Dr. Barney Crile, and his wife dove down to the wreck site and managed to recover one of the *Looe*'s cannons, plus a number of artifacts. The next year, the group returned and recovered additional artifacts from the *Looe,* including cannonballs, coins, buttons, and a pewter teapot. While down there, they supposedly located one of the *Snow*'s anchors (although there's still some debate as to whether the *Looe* was even towing the *Snow* at the time of its demise). In the early 1970s, Art Hartman and Bobby Jordan explored the site and recovered even more artifacts, from utensils to pewter mugs to silver candlestick holders.

Nowadays, the wreck site – including any remaining artifacts – and living coral reef are protected by the Looe Key National Marine Sanctuary, part of the Florida Keys National Marine Sanctuary. As Bob "Frogfoot" Weller has written, "Salvaging artifacts is illegal, but sightseeing is encouraged."

Good Food Conspiracy (MM 30.2 OS U.S. 1, Big Pine Key, 305/872-9119, www.goodfoodconspiracy.com, 9:30 A.M.–7 P.M. Mon.–Sat., 11 A.M.–5 P.M. Sun.), for instance, offers massage, reflexology, facials, as well as light and raindrop therapies. The **Pirate Wellness Center** (21460 Overseas Hwy., Cudjoe Key, 305/744-3348, www.piratewellnesscenter.com, 5 A.M.–9 P.M. Mon.–Fri., 8 A.M.–4 P.M. Sat.–Sun.), which offers short-term memberships, provides a range of holistic treatments, including Swedish massage, deep tissue massage, shiatsu massage, acupressure, and reflexology, plus various yoga, tai chi, and pilates classes.

Accommodations

While places like Islamorada and Key West boast a wider range of lodging choices, including chain hotels, the Lower Keys still have their share of options—from intimate bed-and-breakfasts to affordable campgrounds—almost all of which are privately owned. Just remember that, as with most of the Florida Keys, accommodations are far less expensive in the off-season, which is typically May–November, though it depends on the establishment.

UNDER $200

In general, vacations can be expensive in the Florida Keys, but luckily, you'll find a handful of bargain-friendly lodgings in the Lower Keys, including the **(Big Pine Key Fishing Lodge** (33000 Overseas Hwy., Big Pine Key, 305/872-2351, $109–149 d), a laid-back, waterfront establishment on Spanish Harbor that's been family-owned and operated since 1972. Besides efficiencies, lodge and loft rooms, and mobile homes, amenities here include a heated pool, a recreation room, a convenience store and gift shop, laundry facilities, wireless Internet access, diving equipment, camping and fishing supplies, a marina with boat dockage and rentals, plus fishing charters and diving excursions.

South of the Big Pine Key Fishing Lodge,

the Big Pine Key Fishing Lodge

© LAURA MARTONE

a long, scenic route winds past mangrove trees and beachfront hideaways, such as **The Barnacle Bed and Breakfast** (1557 Long Beach Dr., Big Pine Key, 305/872-3298 or 800/465-9100, www.thebarnacle.net, $145–205 d), a lush inn that offers four comfortable, air-conditioned rooms, with color television, beach towels, Bahama fans, private bathrooms, and a full breakfast. Other amenities include a hot tub, a relaxing hammock, a tiki hut, and a private, sandy beach that inspires guests to swim, snorkel, or simply relax. Just remember: Pets and smoking are not allowed here.

The no-frills **Big Pine Key Motel** (30725 Overseas Hwy., Big Pine Key, 305/872-9090 or 888/872-9191, www.bigpinekeymotel.com, $69–139 d) offers 32 units, including efficiencies and apartments, with cable television, air conditioning, and access to a swimming pool. Visitors might also appreciate the spacious boat parking area and the motel's proximity to the Cracked Egg Cafe. North of the highway lies the **Old Wooden Bridge Guest Cottages and Marina** (1791 Bogie Dr., Big Pine Key, 305/872-2241, www.oldwoodenbridge.com, $95–215 d), a resort and marina facility on five waterfront acres. Situated at the intersection of Watson Boulevard and Bogie Drive, just west of the No Name Key Bridge, this peaceful resort provides 14 efficiency cottages, a boat ramp, a swimming pool, laundry facilities, cable television, and on-site kayak rentals and tours.

On adjacent Little Torch Key, near mile marker 28.5, you'll find two more laid-back, waterfront choices: the pet-friendly **Dolphin Marina and Cottages** (28530 Overseas Hwy., Little Torch Key, 305/872-2685 or 800/553-0308, www.dolphinmarina.net, $99–219 d) on the ocean side and **Parmer's Resort** (565 Barry Ave., Little Torch Key, 305/872-2157, www.parmersresort.com, $99–264 d) on the gulf side, both of which are ideally situated for people hoping to explore the National Key Deer Refuge and the Looe Key National Marine Sanctuary. While Dolphin Marina offers a boat ramp, a marina store, boat rentals, and well-landscaped, air-conditioned cottages,

with cable television, screened porches, and, in some cases, full kitchens, Parmer's provides a complimentary breakfast, tiki-style picnic pavilions, hammocks and barbecue grills, a private boat dock, a swimming pool, and a variety of comfortable accommodations.

Just as fishing enthusiasts have several suitable choices in the Lower Keys, so can snorkelers and scuba divers pursue their passion at the spacious **Looe Key Reef Resort & Dive Center** (27340 Overseas Hwy., Ramrod Key, 305/872-2215 or 800/942-5397, www.diveflakeys.com, $80–199 d). In addition to comfortable, air-conditioned rooms—equipped with cable television, telephone service, and free wireless Internet access—the resort offers a dive shop, a swimming pool, an on-site restaurant and tiki bar, varied scuba-diving courses, plus snorkeling and diving excursions to nearby coral reefs and shipwrecks.

The pet-friendly **Sugar Loaf Lodge** (17001 Overseas Hwy., Sugarloaf Key, 800/553-6097, www.sugarloaflodge.net, $115–165 d) houses 31 waterfront rooms, which, though somewhat outdated, are each equipped with air conditioning and cable television. Other amenities include tennis and shuffleboard courts, a miniature golf course, a heated swimming pool, an on-site tiki bar, a recently renovated restaurant, a fully equipped marina, and a nearby airstrip.

OVER $200

Although Key West features many more high-priced hotels, inns, and resorts than the rest of the Lower Keys, you'll encounter at least two expensive options in this region. South of the Big Pine Key Fishing Lodge, the remote, ecofriendly **Deer Run Bed and Breakfast** (1997 Long Beach Dr., Big Pine Key, 305/872-2015, www.deerrunfloridabb.com, $200–355 d) provides a serene oasis beside the Atlantic Ocean. The four rooms—with names like Atlantis, Utopia, Heaven, and Eden—are each decorated in a unique way, though all include organic linens, private baths, screened porches, original artwork, and a hot vegetarian breakfast. Other amenities include a sandy beach, a pool and hot tub, and on-site massage therapy. Guests may also enjoy biking and kayaking during their visit. Take note, however, that pets, children, and smoking aren't permitted here.

Of course, the pinnacle of luxury can be found at the secluded **((Little Palm Island Resort & Spa** (28500 Overseas Hwy., 305/872-2524 or 800/343-8567, www.littlepalmisland. com, bungalows $595–990, suites $1,290–1,860), once the site of a family-owned fishing village and now an award-winning, private, five-acre island getaway south of Little Torch Key, only accessible via private yacht, ferry, or seaplane. Filled with swaying Jamaican palm trees, surrounded by aquamarine waters, and favored by presidents, movie stars, famous athletes, and countless other celebrities, Little Palm Island is probably the most gorgeous and certainly one of the most unique locales in the entire Florida Keys archipelago.

Here, you'll encounter white sandy beaches, a stunning outdoor pool, cushioned lounge chairs, two grand suites, and 28 thatched-roof, oceanfront bungalows—many of which have Polynesian-style furnishings, lawn furniture, hammocks, as well as private showers, hot tubs, and verandas. Besides the remote location, incredible views, and opportunity to spot Key deer frolicking on the lawn, other amenities include free wireless Internet access, complimentary valet parking on Little Torch Key, a boutique and gift shop, a romantic on-site spa (SpaTerre) that provides exotic, spirit-revitalizing massages and treatments, and an on-site restaurant that features gourmet "Floribbean" cuisine in a candlelit dining room, on the breezy terrace, or, if you're truly daring, directly on a sandbar. Activities range from yoga classes to kayaking to sailing, fishing, and scuba-diving excursions. What you won't find here are phones, televisions, vehicles, and folks under 21. No wonder it's a popular place for weddings.

CAMPING

The Lower Keys contain several laid-back campgrounds, including the **((Sunshine Key RV Resort and Marina** (38801 Overseas Hwy., Ohio Key, 305/872-2217 or 877/570-2267, www.rvonthego.com/ Sunshine-Key-RV-Resort.html, $65–97 daily, $390–592 weekly, $875–2,160 monthly), situated on the gulf side of Ohio Key, southwest of the Seven Mile Bridge. A private 75-acre island resort, Sunshine Key offers a wide array of full-hookup campsites, with 30/50-amp electric service and cable television. Picnic tables, waterfront views, and pull-through sites are available. Other amenities include a 172-slip marina, a fishing pier and boat ramp, a heated 24-hour outdoor pool, sandy volleyball courts, a shuffleboard area, tennis and basketball courts, ping-pong tables, an on-site restaurant and a poolside café, a convenience store and gas station, a fitness center, a coin-op laundry, barbecue and kennel facilities, high-speed Internet access, watercraft rentals, a video game center, a dump station, restrooms, rental cottages, sightseeing tours, and on-site activities, such as weekly potlucks and dances. Leashed pets are welcome, though some restrictions may apply.

A couple miles west, the year-round **((Bahia Honda State Park** (36850 Overseas Hwy., Bahia Honda Key, 305/872-2353 or 305/872-3210, www.floridastateparks.org/bahiahonda or www.bahiahondapark.com, 8 A.M.–sunset daily, $8 vehicles w/2–8 passengers plus $0.50 pp, $4.50 motorcycles and single-occupant vehicles, $2.50 pedestrians, bikers, and extra passengers) offers three budget-friendly campgrounds—Buttonwood, Sandspur, and Bayside—which collectively contain 80 campsites for tent and RV campers ($36 daily). Buttonwood has gravel sites, each with electric and water service, a picnic table, and access to a dump station, restrooms, and hot showers. Some of the sites are situated beside the water, and all can accommodate a variety of setups, from small tents to 40-foot RVs. Sandspur, located in a hardwood hammock, has much smaller sites, with lower clearance—ideal for tents and RVs less than 14 feet in length. Some of the sites have electricity and waterfront views, and all have a picnic table, a grill, and water service. Bayside is the smallest campground, with eight sites and a tiny restroom, though all campers are allowed to use the dump station and restrooms in Buttonwood.

To reach Bayside, your vehicle must be able to travel under the new Bahia Honda Bridge, which has a height restriction of six feet, eight inches. Also available for rent near the Bayside campground are three stilted duplex cabins ($120–160 daily) that overlook the bay. Each of the six cabins has a full bath, a kitchen/dining room, a living room with a sofa bed, one or two bedrooms, and central heating and cooling; five of the cabins accommodate up to six people, and one is wheelchair-accessible. Although pets are prohibited in the cabins, they're permitted in the campgrounds, provided they're confined, leashed, or otherwise kept under control. In addition to campgrounds and cabins, Bahia Honda provides 19 boat slips for overnight rental ($2 per foot, $30 minimum), which includes water, electricity, and the use of park facilities such as restrooms, showers, and trash disposal. For reservations, contact **ReserveAmerica** (800/326-3521, www.reserveamerica.com).

Near mile marker 33 on the ocean side of U.S. 1, the family-owned, year-round **Big Pine Key Fishing Lodge** (33000 Overseas Hwy., Big Pine Key, 305/872-2351, $39–57 daily, $246–360 weekly, $936–1,370 monthly) offers a 114-site campground in addition to its motel-style rooms. Rustic, full-hookup, pull-through, and shaded sites are available. Amenities include 30-amp electric service, cable television, phone access, propane gas, a heated swimming pool, a recreation room, a convenience store and gift shop, laundry facilities, a marina, boat dockage, boat rentals, and restrooms with showers. Anglers and scuba divers will especially appreciate the easy access to the ocean, as well as the availability of fishing charters and diving excursions to the nearby Looe Key National Marine Sanctuary. With its helpful staff and neighborly atmosphere, the campground is popular among families and long-term RVers, many of whom are repeat visitors. Tents are welcome here, but dogs are not allowed.

Recently renovated **Breezy Pines Estates** (29859 Overseas Hwy., Big Pine Key, 305/872-9041, www.breezypinesrv.com, $33–50 daily, $250–350 weekly, $1,250 monthly) is on the

© DANIEL MARTONE

the campground and marina at the Big Pine Key Fishing Lodge

gulf side of U.S. 1, not far from the National Key Deer Refuge. In fact, Key deer are often spotted at Breezy Pines. An ideal base for fishing, kayaking, diving, and snorkeling, this park—which, despite the name, is filled with palm trees, not pines—offers full-hookup, gravel sites, equipped with 30/50-amp electric service, wireless Internet access, cable television, and phone service. Other amenities here include a laundry and an outdoor pool. As with other RV parks in this region, leashed pets are allowed here, and many of the lots are for sale.

Near mile marker 20, the beachfront **Sugarloaf Key/Key West KOA** (251 S.R. 939, Sugarloaf Key, 305/745-3549 or 800/562-7731, www.keywestkoa.com, $55–90 daily)— home to the annual **12 Step Music Fest** (www.12stepmusicfest.com), a four-day, drug-free campout in early November that's only open to 12-step fellowships—contains both RV and tent spaces, some of which offer 30/50-amp electric service, cable television, waterfront views, or pull-through access. This tropical resort provides easy access to a private sandy beach, where visitors can savor gorgeous sunsets and warm ocean breezes, as well as snorkeling, fishing, and ecotour excursions. Other amenities include a heated swimming pool and hot tub, air-conditioned trailer rentals ($170–195 daily), clean restrooms and hot showers, wireless Internet access, propane gas, a pet playground, beach volleyball, a snack bar, an open-air pavilion with a pub and a restaurant, a full-service marina with boat rentals, ramps, and slips, a floating water trampoline and banana bike rentals, seasonal activities, and shuttle service to Key West.

On the ocean side of Sugarloaf Key, near mile marker 19.8, is the picturesque 28-acre **Lazy Lakes RV Resort** (311 Johnson Rd., Sugarloaf Key, 305/745-1079 or 866/965-2537, www.lazylakeskeyscamping.com, $40–115 daily, $240–690 weekly, $800–1,580 monthly), which offers 99 RV/tent spaces, some of which have full hookups with water, sewer access, 30/50-amp electric service, cable television, and wireless Internet access. Lakefront sites are also available. Other amenities include

seasonal trailer rentals ($125 daily, $750 weekly, $2,200 monthly Apr.–Nov.), a clubhouse, a camp store, a heated pool, laundry facilities and clean restrooms, paddle boats, and complimentary kayaks. In addition, visitors can swim, fish, and snorkel in the seven-acre saltwater lake and participate in on-site activities like bingo, darts, horseshoes, game and movie nights, potluck dinners, and ice cream socials. A limited number of sites are available for ownership. Both of the Sugarloaf campgrounds allow leashed pets, although Lazy Lakes does not permit pets in the trailer rentals.

Closer to Key West, near mile marker 14.3, you'll encounter the **Bluewater Key RV Resort** (U.S. 1 and Bluewater Dr., Saddlebunch Keys, 305/745-2494 or 800/237-2266, www.bluewaterkey.com, $55–140 daily, $372–709 weekly), which offers spacious, individually owned lots for rent. Divided into waterfront, poolside, and canal sites, all are landscaped with shady, tropical foliage and equipped with tiki huts, picnic tables, cable television, wireless Internet access, water, sewage access, and 30/50-amp electric service. Fishing, snorkeling, and sunbathing are popular pastimes here, and amenities include a swimming pool, clubhouse, bathhouse, laundry, and boat dock.

For those who want to be as close to Key West as possible, without surrendering the unhurried vibe of the Lower Keys, the pet-friendly **C Geiger Key Marina RV Park** (5 Geiger Rd., Geiger Key, 305/296-3553, www.geigerkeymarina.com, $70–105 daily, $420–630 weekly, $1,260–1,890 monthly) offers the best of both worlds. Founded over five decades ago by two fishermen, Geiger Key still has the vibe of old Florida. An off-the-beaten-path oasis and a terrific base for snorkeling, scuba diving, and deep-sea fishing, Geiger Key is the sort of place where locals arrive by boat, just to enjoy a relaxing breakfast, lunch, or dinner at the on-site Smokehouse Restaurant and Tiki Bar. Amenities here include full-hookup sites, waterfront spaces with boat slips ($28 daily, $85 weekly, $170 monthly), laundry and shower facilities, and live music on the weekends.

Food

SEAFOOD

Like the rest of the Florida Keys, the Lower Keys boast several seafood options. Near mile marker 28.5 on the gulf side of U.S. 1, for instance, the island-style 【 **Parrotdise Waterfront Bar & Grille** (183 Barry Ave., Little Torch Key, 305/872-9989, www.parrotdisewaterfront.com, 11 A.M.–10 P.M. Sun.–Thurs., 11 A.M.–close Fri.–Sat., $15–30) serves beer, martinis, tropical cocktails, "Big Pecker Wines," soups and salads, steaks, fresh seafood, and signature sandwiches like the Mahi Mahi Reuben in Parrotdise. Diners arrive by car or by boat, and anglers can even bring in the day's catch (already cleaned, of course), to be prepared however they wish. As the menu says, "You hook it, we cook it." In addition to a daily happy hour (3–7 P.M.), other highlights include Martini Mondays, Saturday beach parties, live entertainment, and waterfront views.

On the Overseas Highway, the **Looe Key Tiki Bar/Restaurant** (27340 Overseas Hwy., Ramrod Key, 305/872-2215, www.diveflakeys.com, 11 A.M.–11 P.M. daily, $5–17) is part of a resort and dive center on the ocean side of U.S. 1. In addition to a daily happy hour (4–7 P.M.) and live entertainment, the restaurant features soups, salads, sandwiches, burgers, and seafood baskets. It's hard to miss the thatched tiki-style structures of the **Boondocks Grille & Draft House & Miniature Golf** (27205 Overseas Hwy., Ramrod Key, 305/872-4094, www.boondocks.us.com, 11 A.M.–11 P.M., $8–22), which offers an open-air, fully-stocked bar, plus burgers, sandwiches, soups, salads, seafood baskets, and entrées like broiled lobster tail. You can also enjoy a weekday happy hour (4–6 P.M.) as well as random contests and live musical performances.

On the gulf side of U.S. 1, near mile marker 25.5, **The Wharf Bar & Grill** (25163 Overseas Hwy., Summerland Key, 305/745-3322, www.wharfbarandgrill.com, 11 A.M.–10 P.M. daily, $10–18) houses a marina, a fish market, and a seafood restaurant, serving fresh fish, seafood sandwiches and baskets, and Sunday brunch 10 A.M.–2 P.M. Anglers can also purchase bait, ice, beer, and additional supplies on the premises. For innovative cuisine in a contemporary setting, look no farther than 【 **The Square Grouper Bar & Grill** (MM 22.5 OS U.S. 1, Cudjoe Key, 305/745-8880, 11 A.M.–2:30 P.M. and 5–10 P.M. Tues.–Sat., $9–32), a favorite among residents and tourists alike. Housed in an inconspicuous, two-story building beside the highway and jokingly named for the compressed bales of marijuana that used to wash ashore in the Lower Keys, this curious eatery spotlights Floribbean dishes like toasted, almond-crusted grouper with warm Caribbean-style pineapple relish; be sure, too, to save room for the chocolate fondue.

Besides a daily happy hour (4–6 P.M.) and live music on the weekends, **Mangrove Mama's Restaurant** (MM 20 BS U.S. 1, Sugarloaf Key, 305/745-3030, www.mangrovemamasrestaurant.com, 11:30 A.M.–10 P.M. daily, $8–29) offers a wide array of dishes, including salads, sandwiches, steaks, seafood dishes, all-you-can-eat fish fry on Fridays, Saturday hog roasts, classic key lime pie, and Sunday brunch.

AMERICAN

Besides several seafood restaurants, the Lower Keys present an array of casual all-American eateries, such as **Rob's Island Grill** (31251 Ave. A, Big Pine Key, 305/872-3022, 11 A.M.–close Mon. and Wed.–Fri., noon–close Sat.–Sun., $9–16). Essentially a spacious sports bar, featuring pool tables, dartboards, and 15 televisions tuned to a variety of spectator sports, Rob's offers a full menu of steaks, pizzas, sandwiches, burgers, and local seafood, plus a daily happy hour (3–6 P.M.). Adjacent to the Big Pine Key Motel, the **Cracked Egg Cafe** (MM 30.5 BS U.S. 1, Big Pine Key, 305/872-7030, 6 A.M.–7 P.M. Fri.–Mon., 6 A.M.–3 P.M. Tues.–Thurs., $4–10) is popular with the breakfast crowd, who especially favor the pancakes, omelets, and hot coffee; in addition, you'll find soups, sandwiches, beer, wine, and daily specials, including an all-you-can-eat fish fry every Friday. Though the food is usually tasty, the service here is rather unpredictable; on some days, you might encounter lukewarm dishes and rude servers.

The **Big Pine Shopping Center** (MM 30.4 BS U.S. 1, Big Pine Key, www.bigpineshopping.com) houses several restaurants, including the **Bagel Island Coffee & Deli** (205 Key Deer Blvd., Big Pine Key, 305/872-9912, www.bagelislandcoffee.com, 7 A.M.–2 P.M. Mon.–Fri., 7 A.M.–1 P.M. Sat., $4–8), which serves salads, sandwiches, desserts, smoothies, coffee, and more. Vegetarians, meanwhile, will appreciate the low-key ◖ **Good Food Conspiracy** (MM 30.2 OS U.S. 1, Big Pine Key, 305/872-3945 or 305/872-9119, www.goodfoodconspiracy.com, 9:30 A.M.–7 P.M. Mon.–Sat., 11 A.M.–5 P.M. Sun., $6–9), a health food store and juice bar that serves smoothies, fresh juices, homemade soups, raw desserts, vegetarian sandwiches, organic salads, and other healthy treats. Of course, if you have a hankering for something a little less diet-conscious, the nearby **Big Pine Restaurant and Coffee Shop** (MM 30 BS U.S. 1, Big Pine Key, 305/872-2790, 6 A.M.–9 P.M. Tues.–Sat., 6 A.M.–2 P.M. Sun., $4–24) offers a wide array of homey dishes, from omelets to fried chicken to barbecue pork ribs.

Another favored neighborhood place is the ◖ **No Name Pub** (30813 N. Watson Blvd., Big Pine Key, 305/872-9115, www.nonamepub.com, 11 A.M.–11 P.M. daily, $8–15), a friendly, out-of-the-way joint that's been luring locals and tourists alike since 1936. Considered the oldest bar on Big Pine Key, this former bait-and-tackle shop certainly has a rough-hewn appeal, with its gravel parking lot, shady patio area, private garden, and no-frills interior, the walls and ceiling of which are plastered with autographed dollar bills (what the owner calls "early and late American clutter")—a common feature in similarly casual hangouts throughout the Keys. Besides beer and other libations, you'll find basic vittles like pizza, meatballs, smoked fish dip, and seafood baskets—not

No Name Pub, the oldest bar on Big Pine Key

© DANIEL MARTONE

to mention some interesting local characters. To reach this long-standing haunt, take U.S. 1 to mile marker 30 on the gulf side, turn northwest on Key Deer Boulevard, turn right onto Watson Boulevard, and veer to the north, toward (but not past) the No Name Key Bridge.

You'll find even cheaper vittles at the **5 Brothers Grocery Two** (27023 Overseas Hwy., Ramrod Key, 305/872-0702, 6 A.M.–6:30 P.M. Mon.–Sat., 7 A.M.–2 P.M. Sun., $2–7), which sells breakfast dishes, daily soups, and various sandwiches, including a traditional *cubano*. The **Sugarloaf Food Company** (24171 Overseas Hwy., Summerland Key, 305/744-0631, www.sugarloaffood.com, 6:30 A.M.–3 P.M. Mon.–Sat., $5–10) prepares salads, sandwiches, and baked goods for breakfast or lunch.

A local favorite is the ◖ **Geiger Key Marina Smokehouse Restaurant and Tiki Bar** (5 Geiger Rd., Geiger Key, 305/294-1230, www.geigerkeymarina.com, 8 A.M.–10 P.M. daily, $6–19), a family-friendly eatery well off the beaten path. Serving breakfast, lunch, and dinner, this popular joint features Southern favorites like fried green tomatoes, fish tacos, shrimp po'boys, and crab cakes. On the weekends, you'll be treated to live music and a Sunday barbecue—a 20-year tradition that includes barbecue chicken, smoked ribs, jalapeño cornbread, cole slaw, island rice, and barbecue beans ($16.95 pp).

EUROPEAN

If you have a desire for fine Italian dining, make a reservation at **Buon Appetito Ristorante** (457 Drost Dr., Cudjoe Key, 305/745-1711, www.buonappetitoinc.com, 5–10 P.M. Mon. and Wed.–Fri., 5–11 P.M. Sat.–Sun., $16–29), which offers daily specials plus traditional dishes like baked ziti and veal parmesan. Those who enjoy more casual Italian cuisine will encounter at least two options in the Lower Keys. Situated in the Big Pine Shopping Center, **Pizzaworks** (229 Key Deer Blvd., Big Pine Key, 305/872-1119, 11 A.M.–9 P.M. Mon.–Thurs., 11 A.M.–10 P.M. Fri.–Sat., noon–9 P.M. Sun., $8–19) can deliver salads, pizzas, subs,

pasta dishes, and key lime pie right to your hotel, while **A Slice of Paradise** (24458 Overseas Hwy., Summerland Key, 305/744-9718, 11 A.M.–9 P.M. Sun.–Thurs., 11 A.M.–11 P.M. Fri.–Sat., $6–23) offers salads, hot and cold subs, and specialty pizzas.

For an exceptionally elegant meal, take a boat ride from Little Torch Key to the exclusive **(Little Palm Island Resort & Spa** (28500 Overseas Hwy., Little Torch Key, 305/872-2551, www.littlepalmisland.com, 8–10:30 A.M. and noon–9 P.M. daily, prices vary depending on the menu), which welcomes the public to its on-site, waterfront restaurant for breakfast, lunch, and dinner daily as well as Sunday brunch. Although the French-Latin fusion cuisine is ever-evolving, sample dishes might range from shrimp and yellowtail snapper ceviche to coriander-crusted elk with dried fruit compote, toasted asparagus, and port wine sauce. The only snag for many Keys vacationers is that proper attire is required, and children under 16 are not allowed, making it a poor choice for families

© DANIEL MARTONE

outdoor dining at the Little Palm Island Resort & Spa

with kids but an ideal spot for a romantic meal for two. You can make it even more memorable by requesting the Chef's Table in the kitchen, where Chef Luis Pous will attend to you personally, preparing and presenting a multi-course tasting menu paired with the perfect wine selection. You can also dine outside on the sandbar, an especially exotic choice for dinner, when the romantic atmosphere is enhanced by cool night breezes and flaming tiki torches. Of course, no matter how you choose to enjoy this one-of-a-kind dining experience, advance reservations are required, and while the prices vary daily, a couple can expect to pay at least $250 for a multi-course dinner, excluding alcohol.

Information and Services

INFORMATION

For brochures, maps, and other information about Big Pine Key and the Lower Keys, consult the **Lower Keys Chamber of Commerce** (31020 Overseas Hwy., Big Pine Key, 305/872-2411 or 800/872-3722, www.lowerkeyschamber.com, 9 A.M.–5 P.M. Mon.–Fri., 9 A.M.–3 P.M. Sat.), near mile marker 31, or the **Monroe County Tourist Development Council** (1201 White St., Ste. 102, Key West, 305/296-1552 or 800/352-5397, www.fla-keys.com, 9 A.M.–5 P.M. Mon.–Fri.). For government-related issues, contact the **Monroe County offices** (1100 Simonton St., Key West, 305/294-4641, www.monroecounty-fl.gov, 8 A.M.–5 P.M. Mon.–Fri.).

For local news, consult the **Marathon & Big Pine Free Press** (www.keysnews.com), **The Weekly Newspapers** (www.keysweekly.com), the **News-Barometer** (www.news-barometer.com), and www.bigpinekey.com. The daily **Miami Herald** (www.miamiherald.com), the daily **Key West Citizen** (www.keysnews.com), and the biweekly **Florida Keys Keynoter** (www.keysnet.com) are also available throughout the Keys.

SERVICES
Money

Although the Lower Keys have fewer businesses than the rest of the Keys, you'll still find helpful resources in—or near—the region. For banking needs, stop by **TIB Bank** (30480 Overseas Hwy., Big Pine Key, 305/872-0295 or 800/233-6330, www.tibbank.com,

8 A.M.–4 P.M. Mon.–Thurs., 8 A.M.–6 P.M. Fri.). If you require foreign currency exchange, visit the **First State Bank of the Florida Keys** (30515 Overseas Hwy., Big Pine Key, 305/872-4778, www.keysbank.com, 9 A.M.–5 P.M. Mon.–Thurs., 9 A.M.–6 P.M. Fri.).

Mail

For shipping, faxing, and copying needs, visit **Big Pine Shipping** (30440 Overseas Hwy., Big Pine Key, 305/872-5733, 8 A.M.–6 P.M. Mon.–Fri., 10 A.M.–2 P.M. Sat.). You'll also find two **post offices** in the area: one on Big Pine Key (29959 Overseas Hwy., 305/872-2531, www.usps.com, 8:30 A.M.–5 P.M. Mon.–Fri., 8:30 A.M.–noon Sat.) and one on Summerland Key (24700 Overseas Hwy., 305/745-3391, www.usps.com, 8:30 A.M.–5 P.M. Mon.–Fri., 8:30 A.M.–noon Sat.).

Groceries and Supplies

For groceries, head to the **Winn-Dixie** (251 Key Deer Blvd., Big Pine Key, 305/872-4124, www.winndixie.com, 7 A.M.–11 P.M. daily) in the **Big Pine Shopping Center** (MM 30.4 BS U.S. 1, Big Pine Key, www.bigpineshopping.com), a complex that offers a number of useful services, including hair salons, a laundromat, and a public library (213 Key Deer Blvd., Big Pine Key, 305/292-3595, www.keyslibraries.org, noon–8 P.M. Tues., 10 A.M.–6 P.M. Wed.–Sat.). In addition, the Winn-Dixie features an on-site pharmacy (305/872-4850, 8 A.M.–8 P.M. Mon.–Fri., 9 A.M.–6 P.M. Sat., 10 A.M.–5 P.M. Sun.).

Emergency Services

In case of an emergency that requires police, fire, or ambulance services, dial **911** from any cell or public phone. For nonemergency assistance, contact the **Monroe County Sheriff's Office** (Freeman Substation, 20950 Overseas Hwy., Cudjoe Key, 305/745-3184, www.keysso.net, 8 A.M.–5 P.M. Mon.–Fri.). For medical assistance, consult the **Fishermen's Hospital** (3301 Overseas Hwy., Marathon, 305/743-5533, www.fishermenshospital.com) or the **Lower Keys Medical Center** (5900 College Rd., Key West, 305/294-5531, www.lkmc. com). Foreign visitors—seeking help with directions, medical concerns, business issues, law enforcement needs, or other problems—can receive **multilingual tourist assistance** (800/771-5397) 24 hours daily.

Getting There and Around

GETTING THERE
By Air

Despite the presence of small airports like the **Sugarloaf Key Airport** (MM 17 BS U.S. 1, Sugarloaf Key), out of which touring planes operate, the Lower Keys have no major airport of their own. To travel here by plane, you'll need to fly into the **Fort Lauderdale-Hollywood International Airport (FLL)** (320 Terminal Dr., Fort Lauderdale, 866/435-9355, www. broward.org/airport), the **Miami International Airport (MIA)** (4200 NW 21st St., Miami, 305/876-7000 or 800/825-5642, www.miami-airport.com), the **Key West International Airport (EYW)** (3491 S. Roosevelt Blvd., Key West, 305/809-5200 or 305/296-5439, www.keywestinternationalairport.com), or the **Florida Keys Marathon Airport (MTH)** (9400 Overseas Hwy., Marathon, 305/289-6060) and then rent a vehicle from agencies like **Avis** (800/331-1212, www.avis.com), **Budget** (800/527-0700, www.budget.com), **Enterprise** (800/325-8007, www.enterprise. com), **Hertz** (800/654-3131, www.hertz.com), or **Thrifty** (800/367-2277, www.thrifty.com) in order to reach the Lower Keys.

By Bus or Train

To reach the Lower Keys via the regional bus system, you can take the **Miami-Dade County Metrobus** (305/891-3131, www.miamidade. gov/transit), which operates the **301 Dade-Monroe Express** between Florida City and Marathon (5:15 A.M.–8:40 P.M. daily, $2.35 per one-way trip). From Marathon, you can then use the **Lower Keys Shuttle,** which is operated by the **Key West Department of Transportation (KWDoT)** (305/600-1455, www.kwtransit.com, $3 per ride, $16 weekly, $50 monthly) to complete the rest of your journey. The shuttle runs from Marathon to Key West between 5:30 A.M. and 11:15 P.M. daily, and from Key West to Marathon between 5 A.M. and 11 P.M. daily. Other stops include Sunshine Key, Bahia Honda State Park, Big Pine Key, Little Torch Key, Ramrod Key, Sugarloaf Key, and several other Lower Keys. Reduced fares may apply for students under 22 years old, senior citizens over 59 years old, military personnel, and disabled individuals.

In addition, **Greyhound** (305/296-9072 or 800/231-2222, www.greyhound.com) offers bus service to the Lower Keys by making regular bus stops at the Big Pine Key Motel (30725 Overseas Hwy., Big Pine Key). **Amtrak** (800/872-7245, www.amtrak.com), however, only provides train service as far south as Miami. Of course, you can always rent a car or hop a shuttle to reach the Florida Keys.

Transport from Airports and Stations

If you arrive in the Fort Lauderdale/Miami area via plane, bus, or train—or Key West via plane or bus—you can either rent a car or hire a shuttle service to reach the Lower Keys. Some of these companies include **Keys Shuttle** (305/289-9997 or 888/765-9997, www.keysshuttle.com, $80–100 per shared ride, $325–450 for exclusive service) and **Keys Tropical Transportation** (305/852-3595, www.keystropicaltransportation.com, starting at $130 or $165 per ride, depending on the airport of origin), both of which provide service from the Miami and Fort Lauderdale airports; **SuperShuttle** (305/871-2000 or 954/764-1700, www.supershuttle.com, $280 per ride for up to 10 passengers), which only serves visitors flying into Miami; and **TO'n'FRO** (305/852-4514, www.tonfro.com, starting at $55–65 per shared van ride, $300–350 per luxury sedan ride), a personalized van and car service that offers transportation between the airports in Fort Lauderdale, Miami, and Key West and any destination in the Keys.

By Car

To reach the Lower Keys from Miami, simply head south on U.S. 1 (Overseas Hwy.), continue through Key Largo, Islamorada, and Marathon, and cross the Seven Mile Bridge. If you're headed from the Everglades via I-75

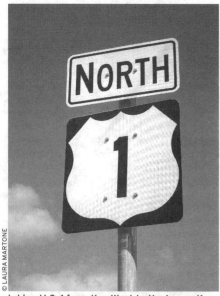

© LAURA MARTONE

taking U.S. 1 from Key West to the Lower Keys

(Everglades Pkwy.), head south on U.S. 27, veer right onto S.R. 997 (Krome Ave.), and follow the signs to U.S. 1. From U.S. 41 (Tamiami Trail) in the Everglades, head south on S.R. 997 and continue toward U.S. 1. If you arrive during the peak season (Dec.–Apr.), be sure to call **511** for an up-to-the-minute traffic report.

GETTING AROUND
By Car

The best way to travel through the Lower Keys is via car, truck, RV, or motorcycle—all of which offer easy access to U.S. 1 and the smaller roads, such as Key Deer Boulevard on Big Pine Key, Watson Boulevard on No Name Key, and Sugarloaf Boulevard on Sugarloaf Key.

By Tour Bus

If, while staying in the Lower Keys, you have a sudden desire to head to Key West for the evening—and would rather leave your vehicle at the hotel, B&B, resort, or campground where you're staying—consider boarding the **KuKu KonKanut** (305/432-3202, www.kukukonkanut.com, Thurs.–Sat., $45 pp). Rain or shine, this bar-hopping tour bus picks up passengers at several stops between Islamorada and the Boondocks Grille & Draft House on Ramrod Key, from which it leaves at 5 P.M. Amid island tunes and history lessons, the tour bus guides passengers to Mallory Square in Key West, where you're free to explore the watering holes of Old Town before making the return trip at 11 P.M. You must be at least 21 years old to ride the party bus.

By Taxi

Taxicab companies such as **Big Pine Taxi** (305/872-2662, $2 per mile, flat rates available) can help you get around the Lower Keys.

By Bike or Boat

While you can certainly traverse the Lower Keys via bicycle, the sprawling nature of this region makes it challenging for novice riders. Nevertheless, it's a lovely, ecofriendly way to experience the major islands. The **Big Pine Bicycle Center** (31 County Rd., Big Pine Key, 305/872-0130, 9 A.M.–5 P.M. Mon.–Fri., 9 A.M.–3 P.M. Sat., closed Mon. in summer, $8 per half day, $10 daily), near mile marker 30.9 on the gulf side, offers rentals as well as repairs.

Of course, biking will only get you so far. Most of the islands down here stand alone, and without the benefit of roads or bridges, you can only reach them via boat. Having your own boat makes navigating these islands, especially those in the backcountry, even easier, and you'll find no shortage of boat ramps and marina slips in the Lower Keys. If you'd rather rent a boat, contact **Blu Waters Rentals** (MM 24.5 OS U.S. 1, Summerland Key, 305/923-3323, www.bluwatersrental.com, 9 A.M.–6 P.M. daily, $150–175 per half day, $250–275 daily, $900–1,000 weekly). To explore the Lower Keys via kayak, contact **Big Pine Kayak Adventures** (Old Wooden Bridge Marina, 1791 Bogie Dr., Big Pine Key, 305/872-7474 or 877/595-2925, www.keyskayaktours.com, 8 A.M.–5 P.M. daily, $20 per two hours, $5 for each additional hour), which even offers kayak rentals for multiple days.

KEY WEST

At the end of the Overseas Highway lies the southernmost point in the continental United States—on a quirky little island known as Key West, where biking and walking are the preferred modes of transportation. Residents here are proud to call themselves "conchs"—a remnant of the past, when Bahamian immigrants called this unique place home. To many, the Conch Republic is more than just an excuse for souvenirs; it's a symbol of the island's distinctive vibe. No wonder famous visionaries like Ernest Hemingway, Tennessee Williams, Robert Frost, and John James Audubon had such an affinity for this town.

These days, Key West is home to a blend of varied folks, including vacationing families, retired couples, eccentric artists, newlyweds, adventurers, corporate escapees, and hardy natives who can withstand the humidity, isolation, and hurricane season. There's also a sizable gay population here—as evidenced by male-only resorts, gay-themed tours, and raucous events like Fantasy Fest.

Those who have heard of Key West but never seen it for themselves often liken it to a 24-hour Mardi Gras celebration in the New Orleans French Quarter, but the Southernmost City is not so easy to characterize. In fact, it's as diverse as the rest of the Keys. While there's indeed a party vibe in some of the Old Town bars and restaurants—such as Sloppy Joe's, home to the famous Hemingway Look-Alike Contest during the city's annual Hemingway Days—that's not all that Key West has to offer.

Old Town contains a number of Victorian inns, tropical gardens, and luxurious spas—not

© DANIEL MARTONE

HIGHLIGHTS

◖ **Mallory Square:** Situated in Key West's Old Town, this waterfront plaza presents several eateries, shops, monuments, and attractions, including the daily Sunset Celebration (page 225).

◖ **Mel Fisher Maritime Museum:** Besides educating visitors about marine archaeology, this impressive repository highlights many of the treasures that Mel Fisher's crew discovered in the famous *Atocha* shipwreck (page 226).

◖ **Ernest Hemingway Home and Museum:** Surrounded by lush gardens, this 19th-century mansion was once home to novelist Ernest "Papa" Hemingway, who wrote *To Have and Have Not* in the backyard studio (page 231).

◖ **Key West Butterfly and Nature Conservatory:** Housing an art gallery, gift shop, and learning center, this fascinating place invites visitors to stroll amid hundreds of vibrant flowers, birds, and butterflies in a glass-enclosed habitat (page 233).

◖ **Fort Zachary Taylor Historic State Park:** Centered around an intriguing Civil War fort, Florida's southernmost state park features bike paths, nature trails, picnic areas, a popular beach, and access to incredible snorkeling opportunities (page 234).

◖ **Train and Trolley Tours:** First-time visitors will enjoy a 90-minute narrated tour aboard either the Conch Tour Train or the Old Town Trolley, both of which provide an overview of the city's major sights and diversions (page 239).

◖ **Hemingway Days:** In honor of Key West's most famous former resident, this annual summertime event offers an array of activities, from a marlin tournament to a Hemingway Look-Alike Contest (page 247).

◖ **Fantasy Fest:** Leading up to Halloween, this zany event provides a quintessential look at Key West culture, complete with outrageous costumes, colorful parades, brazen drag queens, and toga parties (page 248).

◖ **Biking Around Key West:** Residents and visitors alike enjoy touring this one-of-a-kind town via bicycle, an ideal way to experience its historic homes, lovely gardens, scenic beaches, and main attractions (page 259).

◖ **Spas and Yoga in Key West:** Befitting this tropical paradise, several resorts and day spas provide rest and rejuvenation with a variety of massages, body treatments, and, sometimes, yoga lessons (page 267).

KEY WEST

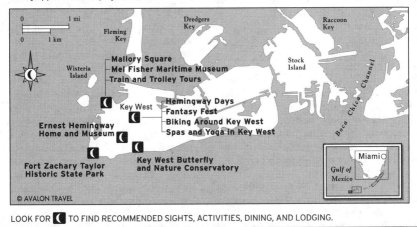

LOOK FOR ◖ TO FIND RECOMMENDED SIGHTS, ACTIVITIES, DINING, AND LODGING.

to mention a plethora of reliable restaurants, offering everything from fresh seafood to Caribbean cuisine to tangy key lime pie. Of course, historic attractions abound here, too—from the Ernest Hemingway Home and Museum to the Audubon House and Tropical Gardens. Other curious diversions, like trolley tours, maritime museums, sunset celebrations at Mallory Square, and the Key West Butterfly and Nature Conservatory, can keep history buffs, relentless revelers, and nature lovers busy for days on end.

In addition, shoppers will find an array of enticing boutiques and emporiums. Cultural enthusiasts will be delighted by the variety of concerts and plays available. Recreationists can play golf, rent a kayak, embark on a fishing excursion, snorkel in the surrounding waters, or venture to the Dry Tortugas, and if that's not enough, Key West also hosts an assortment of festivals and events throughout the year, from the Conch Republic Independence Celebration to the Lighted Boat Parade during the winter holiday season.

Still, while Key West isn't as easy to characterize as some may believe, it is indeed a laidback locale, where the island time seems to move at a pace all its own. As if to accentuate this easygoing persona, the tunes of Jimmy Buffett—the quintessential mascot for Key West and the Florida Keys—seem to feature prominently in every bar, restaurant, and local performer's repertoire, no matter the time of day or night.

HISTORY

During pre-Columbian times, the Calusa Indians inhabited the island now known as Key West. Although Spanish explorer Juan Ponce de León was probably the first European to visit the island during his second expedition to Florida in 1521, it wasn't until Florida became a Spanish colony that a fishing and salvaging village was established here.

When initially settled by the Spanish, the island was apparently littered with bones, a fact that sparked its name: Cayo Hueso (Bone Island). In 1763, the British took control of Florida and relocated the community of Spaniards and Native Americans to Havana. Even after Florida returned to Spanish control in the 1780s, the island was only informally used by Cuban and Bahamian fishermen.

Key West then passed through several different hands before U.S. businessman John W. Simonton—who had been informed of the deep harbor and strategic location by his friend John Whitehead—was able to gain title to the "Gibraltar of the West." In 1822, Matthew C. Perry, who reported on piracy problems in the Caribbean, planted the U.S. flag on the island, symbolically claiming the Florida Keys for America. Although Perry tried renaming it Thompson's Island for Secretary of the Navy Smith Thompson, the name never stuck.

Soon after his purchase, Simonton subdivided the island into plots and sold some of the land to John Whitehead, John Fleming, and two men who quickly resold their share to Pardon C. Greene. Today, all four of these early developers have been immortalized on the city grid in the form of street names. Other early residents of Key West include black Bahamian immigrants, known as "Conchs," who came in even larger numbers after 1830 and claimed an area west of Old Town now known as Bahama Village.

In the early 1800s, major industries in Key West included fishing, salt production, and cargo salvaging. By 1860, Key West had become the largest and richest city in Florida, mainly due to the fact that most of the inhabitants were salvaging high-priced cargo from shipwrecks on nearby reefs.

The latter half of the 19th century was an active period for Key West. During the American Civil War, the island remained in Union hands because of the presence of a naval base, even though the rest of Florida joined the Confederate States of America. Fort Zachary Taylor, which was erected and fortified near Key West between 1845 and 1866, became a significant outpost during the Civil War. Meanwhile, Fort Jefferson, which was constructed in the Dry Tortugas about 68 miles west of the Southernmost City, became a military prison during and after the war. In addition, the 1860s and 1870s witnessed a rise in Cuban refugees, who were responsible for pioneering Key West's cigar-making industry, which eventually upstaged the flagging cargo-salvaging and salt-producing industries in the late 1800s.

In spite of such prosperity, the city of Key West suffered a setback in the mid-1880s. During the early morning hours of April 1, 1886, a fire began in the San Carlos Hall on Duval Street. Due to high winds and inadequate fire-fighting equipment, the fire quickly spread through the downtown area, ultimately killing four people and destroying more than six wharves and 50 buildings, including St. Paul's Episcopal Church. Following the Great Fire of 1886, the area now known as Old Town underwent several years of restoration, resulting in such architectural gems as the red-brick Custom House on Front Street.

Despite being the largest and wealthiest city in Florida in the 1890s, Key West remained fairly isolated until it was linked to the Florida mainland via the Overseas Railroad in 1912. Although the Labor Day hurricane of 1935 essentially destroyed the railroad and killed hundreds of residents, Key West did not remain isolated for long. By 1938, the U.S. government had completed the Overseas Highway, an extension of U.S. 1. It was also in the 1930s, and later in the 1940s, that Key West began to see an influx of celebrities, from President Harry S. Truman to writer Tennessee Williams.

Key West's most famous resident, Ernest Hemingway, actually lived on the island during the 1930s, in a lovely, two-story home on Whitehead Street, which is now a tourist attraction. It was during this time, in fact, that Hemingway published several of his most famous novels, including *A Farewell to Arms* (1929), *To Have and Have Not* (1937), and *For Whom the Bell Tolls* (1940).

Despite its widespread appeal, Key West suffered a financial slump in the 1930s, which was remedied by the expansion of the naval base. By World War II, the U.S. Navy had increased its presence from 50 to 3,000 acres, which included the Naval Air Station on Boca Chica Key and the Fort Taylor Annex—later renamed the Truman Annex, after President Harry S. Truman, who used the commandant's house as his wintertime White House. It was also in the 1940s that the island literally doubled in size, due to a landfill now known as New Town.

By the late 1960s, tourism was beginning to take hold in Key West. The 1970s saw an increase in cruise ships, hotels, and other tourism-related establishments. Of course, the area also saw a rise in drug trafficking during this decade, and as a result, the growing tourism industry was hit hard in the early 1980s, when a U.S. Border Patrol blockade near Florida City caused an enormous traffic jam for those leaving the Florida Keys via U.S. 1. In response to this disruptive search for illegal aliens and possible drug runners, Key West and the rest of the Florida Keys briefly declared their secession from the Union in 1982, subsequently forming the Conch Republic. Today, this incident, which successfully ended the Border Patrol blockade, is celebrated with an annual Conch Republic Independence Celebration in Key West and a similar event in Key Largo.

Nowadays, tourism is still the lifeblood of Key West, whose population of about 22,360 is the largest in the Florida Keys. Nearby Stock Island and faraway Dry Tortugas National Park also benefit from tourists' dollars. Once favored among marauding pirates, the small island of Key West is today divided into two distinct halves. On the western side lies Old Town, a historic district that includes most of the city's major tourist destinations, such as Mallory Square, Fort Zachary Taylor, Duval and Whitehead Streets, and the oceanside beaches. Meanwhile, the eastern side of the island, known as New Town, comprises shopping centers, residential areas, schools, and the Key West International Airport.

PLANNING YOUR TIME

With its plethora of beaches, museums, nature centers, cultural events, trolley tours, sunset cruises, and other outdoor activities, Key West

KEY WEST

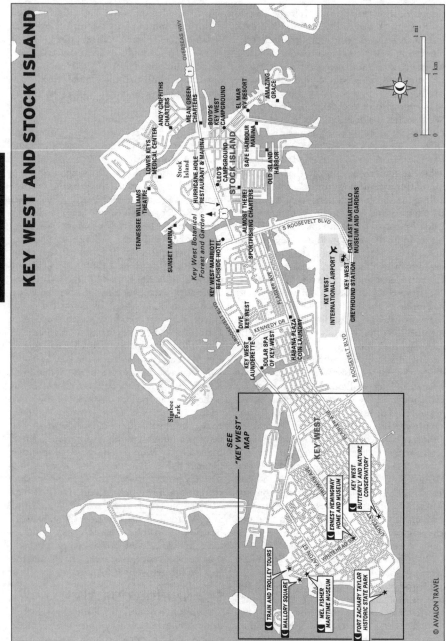

KEY WEST AND STOCK ISLAND

OVERSEAS HWY

ANDY GRIFFITHS CHARTERS

MEAN GREEN CHARTERS

BOYD'S KEY WEST CAMPGROUND

EL MAR RV RESORT

LOWER KEYS MEDICAL CENTER

TENNESSEE WILLIAMS THEATRE

Stock Island

AMAZING GRACE

HURRICANE HOLE RESTAURANT & MARINA

LEO'S CAMPGROUND

SAFE HARBOUR MARINA

STOCK ISLAND

OLD ISLAND HARBOR

SUNSET MARINA

ALMOST THERE! SPORTFISHING CHARTERS

Key West Botanical Forest and Garden

KEY WEST MARRIOTT BEACHSIDE HOTEL

S ROOSEVELT BLVD

FORT EAST MARTELLO MUSEUM AND GARDENS

ROOSEVELT BLVD

DIVE KEY WEST

KENNEDY DR

FLAGLER AVE

KEY WEST INTERNATIONAL AIRPORT

KEY WEST LAUNDERETTE

SOLAR SPA OF KEY WEST

HABANA PLAZA COIN LAUNDRY

KEY WEST GREYHOUND STATION

S ROOSEVELT BLVD

Sigsbee Park

SEE "KEY WEST" MAP

KEY WEST

FLAGLER AVE

EATON ST

WHITEHEAD ST

UNITED ST

ERNEST HEMINGWAY HOME AND MUSEUM

KEY WEST BUTTERFLY AND NATURE CONSERVATORY

TRAIN AND TROLLEY TOURS

MALLORY SQUARE

MEL FISHER MARITIME MUSEUM

FORT ZACHARY TAYLOR HISTORIC STATE PARK

DUVAL ST

1 mi

1 km

© AVALON TRAVEL

is definitely the most active of the Florida Keys. It's no surprise, in fact, that many travelers bypass the other islands to make Key West their primary destination.

Ironically, despite its diversions, it's also the most compact region in the Florida Keys. Including adjacent Stock Island, the area stretches from mile markers 5 to 0 on the Overseas Highway, which makes this an incredibly easy town to navigate. You can walk, bike, or drive around at your own pace. In addition, taxicabs and pedicabs are available day and night—which means you can stay wherever you want, from an Old Town bed-and-breakfast to a coastal resort.

Given all that there is to see and do, you could conceivably stay a long weekend in America's southernmost city—a week if you plan an extra trip to Dry Tortugas National Park. Of course, deciding when to visit Key West will depend on several factors, not the least of which is whether or not you hope to catch annual events like Hemingway Days, which usually takes place in late July, or Fantasy Fest, which typically occurs in late October. Since Key West is popular at such times, as well as during the winter months, you should be prepared for higher lodging rates, crowded restaurants and bars, and the need for reservations.

While crime is not a huge problem in the Florida Keys, bear in mind that Key West is a city, where anything is possible. As with many other tourist havens, muggings do occur from time to time, so it's advisable to stay alert and avoid walking on desolate, poorly lit streets at night.

For more information about Key West, consult the **Monroe County Tourist Development Council** (1201 White St., Ste. 102, Key West, FL 33040, 305/296-1552 or 800/352-5397, www.fla-keys.com) and the **Key West Chamber of Commerce** (510 Greene St., 1st Fl., Key West, FL 33040, 305/294-2587, www.keywestchamber.org).

KEY WEST

Sights

Of all the inhabited Florida Keys, Key West has, by far, the most museums, cultural attractions, and sightseeing tours, many of which are suitable for the entire family. Although New Town and Stock Island have a few curious locales between them, most of the tourist-friendly spots can be found in Old Town, Key West's original settlement.

OLD TOWN

Just a self-guided stroll through Old Town, part of which is a National Historic District, is a worthy attraction in itself, especially for architecture lovers. Along the way, you'll spot historic buildings like the majestic **Old City Hall** (510 Greene St.), constructed in 1891; the red-brick **Custom House** (281 Front St.), also erected in 1891 and once the workplace of Thomas Edison; and innumerable Conch-style homes, ornate Victorian mansions, and unusual eyebrow houses.

While wandering the streets of Key West, you're sure to find myriad worthy attractions to entice you off the sidewalk—at least for a little while.

Flagler Station Over-Sea Railway Historeum

Although technically not part of Old Town, the **Historic Seaport at the Key West Bight,** which lies along the edge of this historic district, lures many a visitor onto the picturesque harbor walk—especially on sunny days, when it's pleasant just to amble along the waterfront, taking in the sights of majestic schooners, private yachts, and other boats in the harbor. Before completing this stroll, which stretches from Grinnell Street to Simonton, take a short detour inland to the corner of Caroline and Margaret Streets, where you'll spot the Flagler Station Over-Sea Railway Historeum (901 Caroline

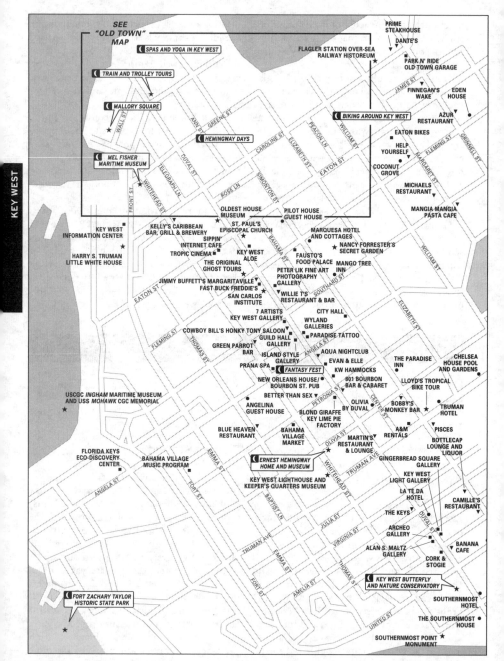

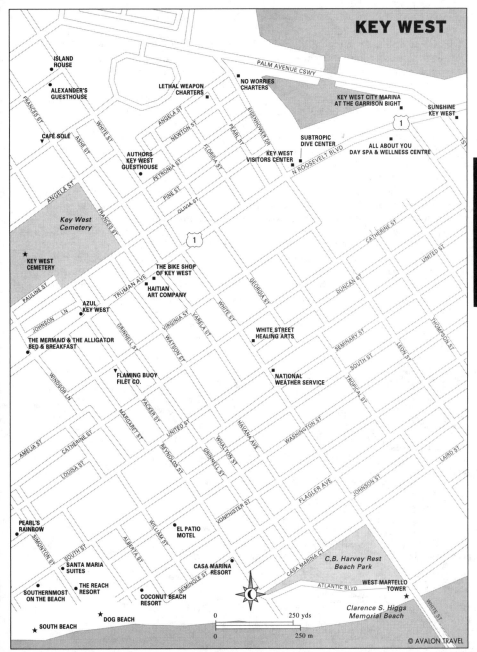

KEY WEST

St., 305/293-8716, www.flaglerstation.net, 9 A.M.–5 P.M. daily, $5 adults, $2.50 children). Completed in January of 1912, the station now serves as a tribute to Henry Flagler's determination to construct a 130-mile extension of the Florida East Coast Railway all the way to Key West.

In spite of his many critics, Flagler achieved his dream, with the help of hundreds of tireless workers. Although the Labor Day hurricane of 1935 effectively destroyed the Overseas Railroad, this historic feat is still worthy of exploration, and at the Flagler Station, that's exactly what visitors can do. Here, you'll encounter an assortment of intriguing artifacts, photographs, memorabilia, and eyewitness accounts. After passing through a reconstruction of the original station and a themed mercantile store, you'll step inside an actual railroad car, listen to informative storytellers, and watch various film presentations—including one about the construction of "Flagler's Folly" and another about the celebrations that took place on the day that Flagler and his wife arrived in Key West after riding the train all the way from New York.

Pirate Soul Museum

At the corner of Front and Ann Streets is the Pirate Soul Museum (524 Front St., 305/292-1113, www.piratesoul.com, 9 A.M.–5 P.M. Mon.–Fri., 10 A.M.–5 P.M. Sat.–Sun., $14 adults, $8 children), a Disney-esque repository of pirate-related paraphernalia, from authentic cutlasses to classic Jolly Roger flags. Despite the amusement park vibe of this museum, complete with canned soundtracks and fake twinkling lanterns, it's a fascinating look at the rough-and-tumble lifestyle of those who survived—and, in many cases, thrived—on the high seas, and the artifacts here are the sort that you might see at a venerable institution like the Smithsonian.

Upon entering this compact museum on your self-guided tour, you'll find yourself on a cobblestoned street in Port Royal, once known as the "world's most wicked city." With the random sounds of a busy village in the background, you'll stroll by old-fashioned storefront windows displaying artifacts from the late 1600s and early 1700s, such as pistols, swords, pewter dishes, physician's tools, and navigational instruments. From Port Royal,

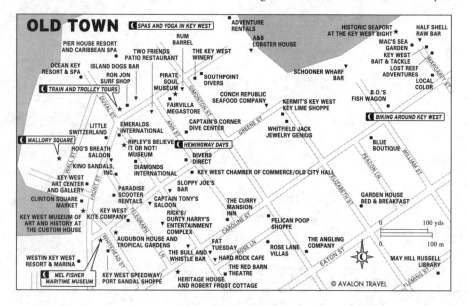

you'll pass into several interesting chambers, including a tavern, a darkened wharf, a captain's cabin, and a cave featuring shipwreck treasures. One especially curious exhibit invites you to sit inside a darkened cargo hold and experience, through voices and sound effects, Blackbeard's final battle.

Ripley's Believe It or Not! Museum

Half a block southeast of Front and Duval Streets, you'll encounter the two-story, 8,000-square-foot Ripley's Believe It or Not! Museum (108 Duval St., 305/293-9939, www.ripleyskeywest.com, 9:30 A.M.–11 P.M. daily, $15 adults, $12 children 5–12, children under 5 free) on Duval. While not the most unique place in town, Ripley's is still very popular among visitors, especially children. Boasting over 500 unusual exhibits in 13 themed galleries, this bizarre attraction features everything from a stuffed rare white buffalo to a portrait fashioned from butterfly wings. Also on display are some of Ernest Hemingway's former belongings, including a typewriter and a shrunken torso.

◖ Mallory Square

Nestled alongside the Gulf of Mexico, between Duval and Front Streets, lies Mallory Square (1 Whitehead St., www.mallorysquare.com), a popular destination for residents and tourists alike. Stretching from the Ocean Key Resort to the cruise ship pier, this open-air district features several eateries and shops, such as those enclosed within the air-conditioned **Clinton Square Market.** You'll also find several attractions, including the **Key West Historical Memorial Sculpture Garden,** which features 36 bronze busts of the town's pioneers, and the **Key West Military Memorial,** which honors the city's involvement in America's major wars.

Also located here is the **Key West Shipwreck Museum** (1 Whitehead St., 305/292-8990, www.shipwreckhistoreum.com, 9:40 A.M.–5 P.M. daily, $12 adults, $5 children 4–12, children under 4 free), where, through the use of live performers, films, and actual artifacts, visitors can experience a 19th-century wrecker's warehouse and learn about the 1856 *Isaac Allerton* shipwreck and subsequent salvage. In addition, you can discover how Key West once became the richest city in America and even pretend to spot wrecks from the 65-foot lookout tower atop the museum, the last of 20 such towers in Key West. Just steps from the Shipwreck Museum, the **Key West Aquarium** (1 Whitehead St., 305/296-2051 or 800/868-7482, www.keywestaquarium.com, 10 A.M.–6 P.M. daily, $12 adults, $5 children 4–12, children under 4 free) presents daily shark and turtle feedings as well as hands-on touch tanks featuring starfish, queen conch, and other regional marinelife. Opened in 1934, the aquarium also offers visitors the chance to observe moray eels, barracuda, grouper, tarpon, parrotfish, sea turtles, alligators, and other sea creatures in a 50,000-gallon tank that represents a typical mangrove ecosystem in the Florida Keys.

At least once during your visit to Key West,

the Key West Shipwreck Museum

© DANIEL MARTONE

KEY WEST

© LAURA MARTONE

the daily Sunset Celebration at Mallory Square

stroll to Mallory Square in the late afternoon, when artists, musicians, acrobats, and tourists converge to pay homage to Key West's gorgeous sunsets during the daily **Sunset Celebration.** To avoid the crowds along the shore, head to The Westin Key West Resort & Marina at 245 Front Street, where you can watch the sunset while sipping cocktails on the aptly named **Sunset Deck.**

Key West Museum of Art and History at the Custom House

Beside the Clinton Square Market in Mallory Square stands the Custom House, a gorgeous, red-brick structure erected in 1891 and once home to a post office, a courthouse, and a government center during a time when salvaging cargo from nearby shipwrecks had made Key West the wealthiest city per capita in the United States. By the 1930s, the city had gone bankrupt, and the Custom House was eventually abandoned. Following a nine-year, $9-million restoration project, the Key West Art & Historical Society opened the historic building

to the public in 1999 as the Key West Museum of Art and History at the Custom House (281 Front St., 305/295-6616, www.kwahs.com/customhouse.htm, 9:30 A.M.–4:30 P.M. daily, $10 adults, $9 seniors 62 and over and Key West residents, $5 children and students, children under 6 free), which is listed in the National Register of Historic Places. Among the fascinating exhibits here, you'll see Paul Collins's portraits of famous Key West residents, from Henry Flagler to Ernest Hemingway; Mario Sanchez's brightly colored wood paintings of life in Key West during the early 1900s; and various artifacts from Ernest Hemingway's adventurous life before and during his time on the island. You'll also learn about the pirates that once prowled the waters of the Florida Keys and how the U.S. Navy eventually expunged these looters and marauders from the region.

◀ Mel Fisher Maritime Museum

Not far from the hard-to-miss Custom House on Front Street stands the massive Mel Fisher Maritime Museum (200 Greene St., 305/294-2633, www.melfisher.org, 8:30 A.M.–5 P.M. Mon.–Fri., 9:30 A.M.–5 P.M. Sat.–Sun., $12 adults, $10.50 students, $6 children), one of the most impressive treasure collections and marine archaeology museums in the world. After passing through the gift shop just beyond the front entrance, you'll encounter an array of fascinating exhibits, the first of which explains Mel Fisher's 16-year search for the *Nuestra Señora de Atocha* and the *Santa Margarita,* two Spanish galleons that shipwrecked off the coast of the Florida Keys in 1622. Both vessels were part of a treasure fleet bound for Spain. Loaded with gold, silver, copper, tobacco, indigo, gems, and other valuables, the ships encountered a severe hurricane in early September of 1622, driving them onto the coral reefs near the Dry Tortugas and drowning many of those on board. Although Spain managed to recover some of the cargo from the *Santa Margarita,* salvagers were never able to locate the *Atocha,* which had apparently sunk in more than 50 feet of water. The shipwreck attained legendary status when Fisher's determination finally prevailed.

Subsequent museum displays feature a mere fraction of the multimillion-dollar treasures that Fisher and his crew uncovered and preserved after the 1985 discovery. Here, you'll see practical items such as daggers, corroded skillets, olive jars, shackles, thimbles, even an enormous anchor. In the adjacent chamber, you'll find it hard not to be awed by the varied treasures, from gold chains and silver coins to copper chunks and tobacco leaves. Especially intriguing is the 78-carat emerald that seems to glow like plutonium.

Following an exhibit about Mel Fisher's life, you'll head upstairs for the La Plata del Mar exhibit, highlighting the diverse collection of silver artifacts that were carried aboard the 1622 Spanish fleet. With holy music playing in the background, you'll stroll past enormous silver bars and varied display cases filled with silver reales, goblets, mirror frames, and other intriguing items. In the adjacent rooms, you'll

learn about other sunken vessels, including the 1715 Plate Fleet and the *Henrietta Marie* slave ship. If, after your comprehensive tour, your yen for treasure hunting has yet to be sated, consider stopping by Mel Fisher's Treasures, a separate jewelry store in the rear of the museum. And if that's not enough, you can opt to be an investor in the ongoing salvaging efforts of the *Atocha,* which is still yielding interesting, and often incredibly valuable, finds.

Audubon House and Tropical Gardens

Directly opposite the Mel Fisher museum on Greene Street—and, oddly enough, a gigantic water tank—you'll spot the Audubon House and Tropical Gardens (205 Whitehead St., 305/294-2116 or 877/294-2470, www.audubonhouse.com, 9:30 A.M.–5 P.M. daily, $12 adults, $7.50 students, $5 children 6–12, children under 6 free), one of several tranquil, historic properties in Key West. Built in 1847 by Captain John H. Geiger, a shipwreck salvager and the city's first harbormaster, this gorgeous

© DANIEL MARTONE

the Audubon House and Tropical Gardens

three-story home is a quintessential example of 19th-century architecture, with a symmetrical, tropical-style design that features first-floor porches, second-level balconies, white walls and columns, and dark wooden shutters. Interestingly, John James Audubon never lived here, although the celebrated naturalist presumably visited the property in 1832, during a research trip to the Florida Keys and Dry Tortugas.

Inside the lovely mansion, you'll see plenty of antiques and period furniture, though the most interesting items are the numerous original renditions and reprints of Audubon's ornithological paintings throughout the second and third floors. Among the regional species on display are roseate spoonbills, Florida cormorants, booby gannets, brown pelicans, mangrove cuckoos, blue-headed pigeons, noddy terns, reddish egrets, and mango hummingbirds.

Following your tour of the house, feel free to meander along the brick pathways through the ecofriendly tropical gardens, shaded by palm trees and bursting with vibrant orchids and bromeliads. On your way out, take a moment to peruse the **Audubon House Gallery of Natural History,** a small art gallery near the entrance.

Harry S. Truman Little White House

Just south of Caroline and Front Streets, the Truman Annex features the Harry S. Truman Little White House (111 Front St., 305/294-9911, www.trumanlittlewhitehouse.com, 9 A.M.–5 P.M. daily, $15 adults, $13 seniors, $5 children 5–12, children under 5 and Key West residents free), another remarkable example of Key West architecture and a fascinating piece of the town's history. This breezy, white structure, which was constructed in 1890 and once served as the command headquarters for the Key West Naval Station, became Truman's wintertime White House from 1946 to 1952 and, later, a retreat for five other U.S. presidents.

Now serving as Florida's only presidential museum and listed on the National Register

of Historic Places, this restored home invites visitors to amble amid original furnishings and learn about President Truman's personal and professional life, the politics of the Cold War, the naval history of Key West, and the origin of the Department of Defense. Guided tours are offered every 15 minutes, between 9 A.M. and 4:30 P.M. daily, and usually last between 45 and 55 minutes; scripts are available for the hearing-impaired. Guests can also take free, self-guided tours of the adjacent botanical gardens, usually between 7 A.M. and 6 P.M. daily. In addition, the museum offers wheelchair-accessible restrooms and allows service animals to accompany their owners onto the premises. Incidentally, parking is only available at Mallory Square or the Westin parking garage.

Oldest House Museum

Currently operated by the **Old Island Restoration Foundation (OIRF),** the Oldest House Museum (322 Duval St., 305/294-9501, www.oirf.org/museum.htm, 10 A.M.–4 P.M. Mon.–Tues. and Thurs.–Sat., free) is literally the oldest house in southern Florida. Supposedly erected in 1829 by Richard Cussans, a Bahamian builder and merchant, and moved to its current location in the mid-1830s, this white, one-story, country-style structure was the longtime home of Captain Frances Watlington, a sea captain, shipwreck salvager, and one-time state senator. The historic home remained in the Watlington family until 1972, when it was purchased by an individual and, soon afterward, deeded to the Historic Key West Preservation Board.

Over the decades, the stalwart house has survived fires, hurricanes, financial hardships, even the occupation of Union troops. Though docents and staff members are available to provide historical information about the property, visitors are free to roam through the tranquil rear garden as well as the house itself, which features many family portraits, original furnishings, plus other period pieces, ship models, and documents that relate to wrecking activities.

St. Paul's Episcopal Church

No matter how you choose to explore Duval, Old Town's main drag, you'll find it hard to miss the imposing white structure on the southeastern corner of Duval and Eaton Streets. Founded in 1831, St. Paul's Episcopal Church (401 Duval St., 305/296-5142, www. stpaulskeywest.org, 9 A.M.–5:30 P.M. daily, free) is the oldest church community south of St. Augustine, though the building itself is far younger. Originally constructed in 1839, the first church, made of coral rock, was leveled in an 1846 hurricane. Rebuilt in 1848, the second church, a wooden structure, was destroyed by the city's Great Fire of 1886. The third church, also made of wood, was completed in 1887 and taken by a hurricane in 1909.

The fourth incarnation of the church, the concrete structure that exists today, was designed in 1911, completed in 1919, and heavily renovated in 1993. With a striking frame, gorgeous stained-glass windows, and a traditional tin roof, St. Paul's is truly a magnificent building and the widely accepted centerpiece of downtown Key West. No wonder it's often photographed by both residents and out-of-towners. Music lovers will especially appreciate this historic sanctuary, where the organist offers free lunchtime concerts, and musical events are featured throughout the year.

San Carlos Institute

Just over a block southeast of the prominent St. Paul's Episcopal Church, you'll spot another fine example of Floridian architecture. Founded in 1871 by Cuban exiles and featuring an ornate, Spanish-style facade, the San Carlos Institute (516 Duval St., www.institutosancarlos.org, noon–6 P.M. Fri.–Sun., free) is one of the state's most historic landmarks. Dubbed "La Casa Cuba" by Cuban poet José Martí, the San Carlos was the site of Martí's 1892 attempt to unite the politically divided Cuban exile community in a bid for Cuba's independence. Today, this venerable institution serves as a nonprofit, multipurpose facility, featuring a museum, a library, a school, an art gallery, and a 360-seat theater that often hosts seminars and live concerts. Of particular interest to most visitors are the permanent exhibits relating to the history of Cuba and Florida's Cuban-American community, such as the photographs of poet José Martí and the portraits of Cuba's constitutional presidents.

Nancy Forrester's Secret Garden

Two blocks east of Duval Street lies a private tropical oasis that, for years, has been open to the public. Also known as Key West's Exotic Tropical Botanical Garden, Nancy Forrester's Secret Garden (1 Free School Ln., 305/294-0015, www.nfsgarden.com, 10 A.M.–5 P.M. daily, $10 pp) is widely celebrated for its gorgeous landscape of ferns, aroids, shade palms, edible fruits, medicinal plants, and other rare foliage—an ideal home for the macaws who live here. In the center of this enticing sanctuary stands a small cottage that has often served as an inspiring artist's studio—and can even be rented by those hoping to escape amid nature for a while.

Created by local artist and environmental educator Nancy Forrester, this lush garden is more than just a tourist attraction. It's also meant to represent the artist's wish for humanity to restore balance to the natural world. Unfortunately, this lovely spot—the last undeveloped, wooded acre in the heart of Old Town—needs the public's help to remain open, so if you relish this peaceful place, consider contributing to the capital campaign on your next visit.

Key West Cemetery

On the eastern side of Old Town, you'll find the intriguing, palm-lined Key West Cemetery (701 Passover Ln., 305/292-8177, www.keywestcity.com, 7 A.M.–7 P.M. daily in summer, 7 A.M.–6 P.M. daily in winter, free). Established in 1847, following a disastrous 1846 hurricane that unearthed the original cemetery, this fenced, 19-acre property now contains beautiful statuary, historic gravestones, amusing epitaphs, and the remains of more than 80,000 Bahamian mariners, Cuban cigar makers, Spanish–American War veterans, soldiers

© DANIEL MARTONE

Visitors can take a guided or self-guided walking tour of the Key West Cemetery.

and civilians, millionaires and paupers, whites and blacks, Catholics, Protestants, and Jews, and other unique individuals, illustrating Key West's incredibly diverse heritage.

Bordered by Windsor Lane and Angela, Frances, and Olivia Streets, the front entrance actually lies near the intersection of Angela and Margaret, where you can pick up a free, comprehensive, self-guided tour map from the office (8:30 A.M.–3:30 P.M. Mon.–Fri.). Guided one-hour tours (9:30 A.M. Tues. and Thurs., $15 pp donation suggested) are also available through the **Historic Florida Keys Foundation** (Old City Hall, 510 Greene St., 305/292-6718, www.historicfloridakeys.org), though reservations are required. Whether you come alone or as part of a tour group, remember that the cemetery is still active, so be respectful of mourners when visiting.

Key West Lighthouse and Keeper's Quarters Museum

Near the intersection of Truman Avenue and Whitehead Street, it's difficult to ignore the stately, white lighthouse towering above the trees. Here, at the Key West Lighthouse and Keeper's Quarters Museum (938 Whitehead St., 305/294-0012, www.kwahs.com/light-house.htm, 9:30 A.M.–4:30 P.M. daily, $10 adults, $9 seniors 62 and over and Key West residents, $5 students and children, children under 6 free), you'll learn about yet another facet of the coastal town's riveting history.

Erected in 1847 on a spot 14 feet above sea level, the 66-foot-tall brick lighthouse effectively replaced the original, 46-foot wooden tower on Whitehead Point, which had been built in 1825 to aid ships navigating the dangerous offshore reefs and was unfortunately destroyed in 1846 by a hurricane. In 1894, the city added a 20-foot extension to the second lighthouse, which was decommissioned by the U.S. Coast Guard in 1969. After an expensive restoration by the Key West Art & Historical Society two decades later—the same year that it was featured in a pivotal scene in *Licence to Kill* (1989)—it became the tourist attraction it is today.

Now, visitors can climb the dizzying, 88-step spiral staircase to a wraparound observation deck—just beneath the active 175-watt metal halide light—for an incredible, 360-degree view of the verdant city. Helpful cards indicate important locales throughout Key West, including the Casa Marina Resort in the distance and the grounds of the Ernest Hemingway Home down below. Also on the well-manicured grounds lies a small gift shop, plus the former keeper's quarters, constructed in 1887 to replace the original keeper's dwelling. Today, the faithfully restored quarters serve as a museum, offering a look at turn-of-the-20th-century life with historic furniture, period furnishings, and old photographs. In addition, you'll find a collection of lighthouse artifacts, instruments, maps, and photographs within various exhibits that shed some light on the maritime history of the Florida Keys.

◖ Ernest Hemingway Home and Museum

Directly across the street from the Key West Lighthouse lies the Ernest Hemingway Home and Museum (907 Whitehead St.,

305/294-1136, www.hemingwayhome.com, 9 A.M.–5 P.M. daily, $12 adults, $6 children, children under 5 free), one of the most popular attractions in all of Key West. Built in 1851 by Asa Tift, a marine architect and salvage wrecker, the airy, two-story structure features white walls and olive-green shutters, wraparound porches on both the lower and upper levels, and arched windows and doors on all sides, which invite a lot of natural light. Curiously, this island-style domicile once housed the city's most famous resident, Papa Hemingway himself, and has since become a registered National Historic Landmark. Situated amid picturesque palm trees and blooming foliage, the home invites visitors to retrace the footsteps of Ernest Hemingway, an American novelist and short-story writer known all around the world as a big-game hunter, sportfisherman, war veteran, and unabashed adventurer.

Inside the mansion, you'll see a cornucopia of memorabilia, including period furnishings, family photographs, original artwork, and war medals. The lovingly preserved home

© DANIEL MARTONE

the Ernest Hemingway Home and Museum

KEY WEST

HEMINGWAY'S KEY WEST

Historic homes and structures in Old Town constitute a huge facet of Key West's tourism industry. The **Old Island Restoration Foundation (OIRF)** (322 Duval St., 305/294-9501, www.oirf.org), a nonprofit organization responsible for the preservation of many of these architectural gems, even provides a pamphlet that outlines a self-guided walking tour of 50 unique sights along the "Pelican Path." This brochure, which is available through OIRF or the **Key West Chamber of Commerce** (510 Greene St., 1st Fl., 305/294-2587, www.keywestchamber.org, 8 A.M.–6:30 P.M. daily), includes several key buildings, such as the Oldest House (1829), the Heritage House and Robert Frost Cottage (1834), the Audubon House (1847), the Harry S. Truman Little White House (1890), and St. Paul's Episcopal Church (1919). One house, however, is conspicuously missing.

Perhaps Key West's most popular attraction, the **Ernest Hemingway Home and Museum** (907 Whitehead St., 305/294-1136, www.hemingwayhome.com, 9 A.M.–5 P.M. daily, fees apply) lures curious sightseers every day. Built in 1851 by marine architect Asa Tift, this two-story mansion became home to Ernest Hemingway and his second wife, Pauline Pfeiffer, in 1931. Today, visitors can see descendants of his six-toed felines, plenty of original artwork and family photographs, as well as the separate writing studio where the Nobel Prize-winning novelist penned several famous short stories and books, including *To Have and Have Not* (1937), the story of a fishing boat captain who runs contraband between Cuba and Florida.

Naturally, this isn't the sole remnant of Hemingway's time in Key West. Not only does every train, trolley, and walking tour mention his name, but you'll also find some of his former belongings in places like the **Ripley's Believe It or Not! Museum** (108 Duval St.) and the **Key West Museum of Art and History at the Custom House** (281 Front St.). In addition, several hotels and watering holes claim ties to Papa Hemingway. The private Mediterranean Revival-style home known as **Casa Antigua** (314 Simonton St.), for instance, was once a residential hotel above a Ford dealership, and it was here that Hemingway and Pauline stayed during their first visit to Key West. He even finished the initial draft of *A Farewell to Arms* (1929) while awaiting the delivery of his new Model A. Supposedly, Hemingway also stayed at the **Southernmost House** (1400 Duval St.), and he frequented **Captain Tony's Saloon** (428 Greene St.) when it was the original location of Sloppy Joe's. Today, you'll even catch a glimpse of Hemingway's former bar stool. Meanwhile, the most recent incarnation of **Sloppy Joe's Bar** (201 Duval St.) features the famous Hemingway Look-Alike Contest, part of the annual **Hemingway Days** celebration in July.

Hemingway, who was born in Oak Park, Il-

looks much as it did during the 1930s, when Hemingway and his wife Pauline lived here. Some of the docents, while happy to share stories about Hemingway, joke that they wish Hemingway's wife hadn't replaced all of the original ceiling fans with chandeliers—a decision that seems regrettable on the hottest days, when box fans can be found throughout the house.

If you're a first-time visitor to the Hemingway Home, you should definitely opt for a guided, 30-minute tour, available throughout the day, before exploring the grounds on your own.

Beyond the house, you'll encounter a lovely pool, quiet garden nooks, a bookstore, and the Nobel Prize winner's well-preserved studio, where he spent his most productive years. It was here, after all, that he wrote and published some of his most enduring novels, nonfiction books, and short-story collections, including *A Farewell to Arms* (1929), *Death in the Afternoon* (1932), *Green Hills of Africa* (1935), and *To Have and Have Not* (1937). While here, you'll also see a plethora of six-toed felines, the descendants of Hemingway's legendary, polydactyl cats—many of whom bear the names

linois, in 1899, first came to Key West in 1928 at the urging of a fellow writer. For the next few years, he and Pauline spent winters in the Florida Keys and summers in Europe and Wyoming. Then, in 1931, they acquired the house at 907 Whitehead Street, where they raised their sons, Patrick and Gregory. During this prolific period, his schedule consisted of writing every morning and relaxing every afternoon and evening with his friends, with whom he drank, swam, fished, and boxed. One particularly close pal was Joe Russell, an irascible fisherman and owner of Sloppy Joe's, initially a speakeasy that moved to 428 Greene Street in 1933. Russell introduced Hemingway to one of his lifelong passions – deep-sea fishing – and he repaid the favor by immortalizing his friend as Harry Morgan, captain of the *Queen Conch* charter boat in *To Have and Have Not*. Interestingly, the backyard drinking fountain that Hemingway built for his cats is actually a refurbished urinal from Sloppy Joe's, which was also where, in 1936, Hemingway met reporter Martha Gellhorn, who would later become his third wife.

Originally, Hemingway's home was surrounded by a chain-link fence, but in 1935, he erected the perimeter wall that exists today, in the hopes of providing his family a modicum of privacy from gawking tourist hordes. Between 1937 and 1938, while Hemingway was serving as a war correspondent for the Spanish Civil War, Pauline supervised the construction of the first residential swimming pool in Key West. When he returned, he was shocked by the final price tag of $20,000, at which point he removed a penny from his pocket and told her that she might as well take his last cent. Today, you can see this supposed penny embedded beside the pool.

Hemingway stayed in Key West for well over a decade before divorcing Pauline in 1940, marrying Martha, and heading to Cuba. Pauline, meanwhile, stayed in the Key West house until her death in 1951. Although Hemingway still lived in Cuba, he and his fourth wife, Mary, visited Key West often during the 1950s. In 1959, the Cuban Revolution sent them to Idaho, where he died in 1961. Upon his death, the Key West home was sold to local businesswoman Bernice Dickson, who lived in the main house until turning it into a museum in 1964. The home, which was designated a National Historic Landmark in 1968, remains the property of Dickson's family, though Hemingway's spirit is alive and well.

For more information about Hemingway's time in Key West, consult *Michael Palin's Hemingway Adventure* (New York: St. Martin's Press, 1999), an engrossing look at the novelist's world travels, including his ties to Key West. You'll also discover some intriguing tales in Stuart B. McIver's book *Hemingway's Key West* (Sarasota, FL: Pineapple Press, Inc., 2002), which even offers a two-hour Walk with Papa tour of the city.

of famous movie stars, from the calico called Audrey Hepburn to a much-photographed black-and-white cat named after classic film star Charlie Chaplin.

◖ Key West Butterfly and Nature Conservatory

Situated near the southern end of Duval Street, the Key West Butterfly and Nature Conservatory (1316 Duval St., 305/296-2988 or 800/839-4647, www.keywestbutterfly.com, 9 A.M.–4:30 P.M. daily, $12.50 adults, $9 military personnel and seniors, $8.50 children 4–12, children under 4 free) invites visitors to take a stroll through a vibrant, glass-enclosed, climate-controlled habitat, filled with waterfalls, trees, flowering plants, and hundreds of colorful birds and butterflies. While here, you can also learn about butterfly anatomy, physiology, life cycles, feeding, and migration in the **Learning Center,** which offers a 15-minute orientation film and an up-close view of caterpillars feeding and developing on their host plants. In addition, you can peruse Sam Trophia's kaleidoscopic creations—essentially, a variety of encased butterfly displays—inside

the glass-enclosed habitat at the Key West Butterfly and Nature Conservatory

the art gallery, **Wings of Imagination** (9 A.M.–5:30 P.M. daily). Before leaving the nature center, be sure to browse through the wide assortment of butterfly-related items and other souvenirs in the on-site gift shop (9 A.M.–5:30 P.M. daily). As a bonus feature, visitor parking is available in the lot behind the conservatory, but be advised that the gate closes at 6 P.M. every day.

SOUTHERN SHORE

Along the Atlantic Ocean side of Key West lie several interesting attractions, from military monuments to marine exhibits to fantastic beaches.

Fort Zachary Taylor Historic State Park

Accessible via the western end of Southard Street, Fort Zachary Taylor Historic State Park (305/292-6713 or 305/295-0037, www.floridastateparks.org/forttaylor or www.fortzacharytaylor.com, 8 A.M.–sunset daily, $6 vehicles w/2–8 passengers plus $0.50 pp, $4.50 motorcycles and single-occupant vehicles, $2.50 pedestrians, bikers, and extra passengers) is, in fact, the southernmost state park in Florida—and, for that matter, the continental United States. It's also a well-favored destination among history buffs and recreationists alike.

Situated at the convergence of the Gulf of Mexico and the Atlantic Ocean—where the clear, deep waters nurture living coral, yellowtail snapper, tropical fish, lobster, and other marine creatures—the 54-acre park is especially favored by swimmers, snorkelers, scuba divers, sunbathers, and picnickers—not to mention wedding parties. Enhanced by imported sand, the beach here is generally considered the finest in Key West—and an ideal place to watch an incredible Florida Keys sunset. Bikers, hikers, anglers, and bird-watchers also enjoy spending time in this beautiful place. Beyond bike paths and wooded nature trails, other amenities include picnic tables, barbecue grills, public restrooms, outdoor showers, ample parking, as well as beach equipment and water-sports rentals, such as chairs, rafts, and snorkeling gear. In addition, the Cayo Hueso Café offers refreshments from 10 A.M. to 5 P.M. daily.

But, of course, it's the 19th-century fort—completed in 1866, critical during the American Civil War and Spanish-American War, and designated a National Historic Landmark in 1973—that lures many of the visitors to this historic state park. Although you're free to wander through the fort on your own, you can also opt for one of the narrated, 30-minute tours, which are available daily at noon and 2 P.M. You'll especially enjoy visiting Fort Zachary Taylor during annual events, such as Civil War Days in February, the Conch Republic Independence Celebration in April, and Pirates in Paradise in November, so be sure to plan your visit accordingly.

Florida Keys Eco-Discovery Center

From Southard Street, you can head west toward the Truman Waterfront, where you'll spy the Florida Keys Eco-Discovery Center (35 E. Quay Rd., 305/809-4750, www.floridakeys. noaa.gov/eco_discovery.html, 9 A.M.–4 P.M.

Tues.–Sat., free). The 6,000-square-foot nature center features an array of interactive exhibits, dioramas, and displays about the Keys' varied ecosystems, including upland pinelands, hardwood hammocks, beach dunes, mangrove shores, seagrass flats, and coral reefs. Visitors can take a virtual 1,600-foot dive to the deep shelf; learn why a fort was built in the isolated Dry Tortugas; view a 2,500-gallon reef tank, filled with living coral and tropical fish; and walk through a mock-up of Aquarius, the world's only underwater ocean laboratory. Free parking is available on-site, and all net proceeds from the gift shop directly fund educational programs at the Eco-Discovery Center.

USCGC Ingham Maritime Museum

Military history enthusiasts might enjoy a quick detour to Memorial Park, which holds the USCGC Ingham Maritime Museum (Truman Waterfront, Old U.S. Navy Pier, 305/292-5072, http://uscgcingham.org, 10 A.M.–4 P.M. daily, $12 adults, $3 children

KEY WEST

Not far from Fort Zachary Taylor, the Florida Keys Eco-Discovery Center explores the varied ecosystems of southern Florida.

© DANIEL MARTONE

10–18, children under 10 and military personnel free), a historic, 327-foot U.S. Coast Guard cutter that was built in 1935 and served the nation from 1936 to 1988. Visitors can take a self-guided tour of the ship, which includes authentic artifacts, historic photographs, and interpretive signs outlining the ship's history. While on board, you'll be able to see where the men ate, slept, and played, and for an added fee ($20 pp), you can take a guided tour that includes additional chambers like the boiler room and engine room.

Nearby is the floating **USS Mohawk CGC Memorial Museum** (305/292-5072, www.ussmohawk.org, 10 A.M.–4 P.M. daily, $6 adults, $3 children 10–18, children under 10 and military personnel free), a former World War II combat ship that was involved in 14 attacks against Nazi submarines. Built in 1934, this historic U.S. Coast Guard cutter now serves as a memorial to the battles fought in the Atlantic Ocean. Though retired from active duty, the 165-foot-long *Mohawk* is still fully operational,

a rarity among decommissioned World War II vessels. Visitors here can watch a brief orientation film, then take a self-guided tour of various chambers, featuring artifacts, photographs, and interpretive signs. The main deck, which is accessible to wheelchairs, also welcomes strollers, making this an ideal stop for families on vacation. Combination adult tickets ($15 pp) are available for those wanting to visit both ships. In addition, parking is available on-site, though you can also walk to the floating maritime museums from Southard Street.

Southernmost Point Monument

Located at the corner of South and Whitehead Streets, right beside the Atlantic Ocean, stands an enormous replica of a marine buoy that marks the southernmost point in the continental United States. Once designated by a mere sign, the spot gained the now-famous monument in 1983, when city officials grew tired of replacing the oft-stolen sign. Colorfully painted in red, yellow, black, and white, the marker

Tourists flock to the southernmost point, which features one of the most well-photographed monuments in town.

simply reads "Southernmost Point Continental U.S.A." Also emblazoned on the monument are the phrases "The Conch Republic," "90 Miles to Cuba," and "Key West, FL, Home of the Sunset." Today, it's one of the most photographed attractions in all of Key West, as evidenced by the frequently long line of visitors, waiting for their chance to pose in front of the colorful buoy—smaller versions of which are often seen throughout the city, on everything from shot glasses to key chains to playing cards.

Beaches

Several public beaches (www.keywestcity.com), ranging in size and appeal, stretch along the southern shore of Key West. The good news is that all of them are free and open daily, but the bad news is that they're often crowded, especially on a gorgeous weekend during the peak winter season. Just remember that, given the absence of lifeguards, swimming is at your own risk. In addition, just because Key West has several clothing-optional resorts doesn't mean that such a flexible policy extends to the beaches down here; topless and nude sunbathing is actually illegal. Alcohol, drugs, campfires, glass containers, and overnight camping are also not allowed on the public beaches of Key West.

At the terminus of Duval Street, you'll first encounter **South Beach** (7 A.M.–11 P.M. daily, free), a cute patch of sand that's a far cry from the similarly named one in Miami. While it offers shallow waters, a pleasant pier, and an incredible view of the ocean, it's much smaller—and calmer—than its northern counterpart. Nevertheless, it's a favorite among locals, despite the lack of restrooms and facilities. East of Simonton, the somewhat rocky **Dog Beach** (7 A.M.–11 P.M. daily, free) is obviously popular among pet owners, though it has no restrooms or other facilities. Farther east, alongside Atlantic Boulevard between Reynolds and White Streets, lies another popular Key West beach, the wide, sandy **Clarence S. Higgs Memorial Beach** (6 A.M.–11 P.M. daily, free), where, in addition to swimming

and sunbathing, sun-worshipers can rent water-sports equipment or stroll amid pelicans and seagulls on the adjacent swimming pier. Other on-site amenities include covered picnic tables, public restrooms, a playground, and chair rentals.

Even farther east, near Atlantic Boulevard and White Street, the wheelchair-accessible **C. B. Harvey Rest Beach** (7 A.M.–11 P.M. daily, free) offers sandy dunes, picnic tables, public restrooms, a fishing pier, a yoga deck, and a bike path. Of course, on warm, sunny days, crowds flock to lengthy, manmade **Smathers Beach** (7 A.M.–11 P.M. daily, free) alongside Roosevelt Boulevard, a popular spot for spring breakers and an ideal place to watch the sunrise, have a picnic, or play a volleyball game. Water-sports and chair rentals, bike paths, concession stands, public restrooms, a boat ramp, and ample parking are also available here. **Sunset Watersports** (305/296-2554, www.sunsetwatersportskeywest.com, 9 A.M.–6 P.M. daily, $39 pp) even offers parasailing excursions from here.

enjoying Higgs Beach on a sunny day in winter

© DANIEL MARTONE

KEY WEST

West Martello Tower

On Higgs Beach, where White Street meets the Atlantic Ocean, stands the West Martello Tower, a Civil War–era fort that, as with the Fort East Martello Museum, was inspired by the round, stalwart fortress at Mortella Point in Corsica, an island in the Mediterranean Sea. Constructed during the 1860s by the U.S. Army Corps of Engineers, the West Martello Tower was never fully completed, and in the late 1940s, it was nearly leveled for aesthetic reasons. Luckily, demolition plans were thwarted, and it has since been listed on the National Register of Historic Places.

Home to the **Key West Garden Club** (southern end of White St., 305/294-3210, www.keywestgardenclub.com, 9:30 A.M.–5 P.M. daily mid-Jan.–mid-Apr., 9:30 A.M.–3:15 P.M. Tues.–Sat. mid-Apr.–Dec., free) since 1955, this historic locale entices visitors to stroll along brick pathways, amid graceful arches and lush, colorful foliage, which features a rare collection of blooming orchids, bromeliads, and other native and exotic flora. Here, you can simply sit beside a water lily pond or butterfly garden, enjoy balmy breezes from an oceanfront gazebo, and temporarily trade the hustle and bustle of places like Mallory Square and Duval Street for the tranquil seclusion of a fort by the sea. Just be advised that the facility is closed during the first two weeks of January.

NEW TOWN AND STOCK ISLAND

Although the bulk of Key West's attractions are spread throughout Old Town, you'll find a few worthy stops in New Town, the eastern half of the island, as well as on adjacent Stock Island.

Fort East Martello Museum and Gardens

South of the **Key West International Airport** stands the Fort East Martello Museum and Gardens (3501 S. Roosevelt Blvd., 305/296-3913, www.kwahs.com/martello.htm, 9:30 A.M.–4:30 P.M. daily, $6 adults, $5 seniors 62 and over and Key West residents, $3 children and students, children under 6 free). Modeled after the nearly impenetrable Martello watchtowers of Corsica and other places around the world, Fort East Martello, which was constructed during the Civil War, never actually witnessed hostile action. A testament to military engineering, the fort now serves as the country's best-preserved example of the Martello style of military architecture. Today, its citadel, courtyard, and casemates house a vast array of regional artifacts, historical records, and military memorabilia, in addition to the state's largest collection of drawings and painted wood carvings by artist Mario Sanchez, mainly known for his vivid depictions of life in Key West during the early 1900s. While here, visitors can also tour an 80-year-old playhouse and enjoy panoramic views from atop the central tower.

Key West Tropical Forest and Botanical Garden

Besides the plethora of flowers, trees, and creatures throughout Key West, nature lovers will find several intriguing attractions—not the least of which is the Key West Tropical Forest and Botanical Garden (5210 College Rd., Stock Island, 305/296-1504, www.keywestbotanicalgarden.org, 10 A.M.–4 P.M. Mon.–Sat., noon–4 P.M. Sun., suggested donation $5 adults, $4 children 12–18), the only frost-free botanical garden in the continental United States. Host to various events throughout the year, including Gardenfest Key West, Hot Havana Nights, and the Doo Wop Party, this tropical oasis nurtures rare flora and fauna and serves as a migratory stop for a variety of neotropical birds. After viewing a short orientation film, visitors are welcome to take a self-guided tour of the grounds, featuring a one-acre butterfly habitat, a lush canopy of tropical palms, and two of the last remaining freshwater ponds in the Florida Keys. Parking is free here, and the garden boardwalk is wheelchair-accessible.

ISLAND TOURS

If you're a first-time visitor to Key West, you might benefit from one of the many available sightseeing tours, which will help orient you to the island and its surrounding waters. So, before you explore the area on your own, consider choosing from an array of trolley excursions, guided strolls, sunset cruises, or other informative tours.

❰ Train and Trolley Tours

Before exploring the town on foot, consider taking a 90-minute narrated excursion on the **Conch Tour Train** (305/294-5161 or 888/916-8687, www.conchtourtrain.com, 9 A.M.–4:30 P.M. daily, $29 adults, $14 children 4–12, children under 4 and Key West residents free), which offers a look at most of Key West's major attractions, including Mallory Square, the Custom House, and the Ernest Hemingway Home. Since 1958, friendly train "engineers" have been guiding visitors around the Southernmost City and, along the way, sharing snippets of the town's history—real and legendary.

Train tours depart every 30 minutes from the Front Street depot (501 Front St.), where you can purchase tickets beforehand. You can also pick up tickets at three other locations: Mallory Square (303 Front St.), Flagler Station (901 Caroline St.), and 3840 North Roosevelt Boulevard. To save some money, purchase your tickets online or consider buying packages that also include admission to attractions like the Key West Aquarium and the Harry S. Truman Little White House.

As an alternative, you can take the 90-minute **Old Town Trolley Tour** (305/296-6688 or 888/910-8687, www.trolleytours.com, 9 A.M.–4:30 P.M. daily, $29 adults, $14 children 4–12, children under 4 free), which offers a comprehensive tour of Old Town, fully narrated by expert conductors. Along the route, you'll get an earful of curious anecdotes and well-researched historical tidbits. At no extra charge, you're welcome to get on and off the trolley at a dozen convenient stops, including the Bahama Village Market. The ubiquitous, orange-and-green trolleys pick up and drop off passengers every 30 minutes at each location. Tickets can be purchased at four different stops: Mallory

© DANIEL MARTONE

Conch Tour Train station

Square (No. 1) near Wall and Whitehead Streets, Simonton Row (No. 3) at Greene and Simonton Streets, Truval Village (No. 11) at Truman Avenue and Duval Street, and Angela Street (No. 12) between Duval and Whitehead Streets. As with the Conch Tour Train, you can save a little money by purchasing tickets online. Ticket packages and wheelchair-accessible vehicles are also available.

Bike and Walking Tours

For a more active exploration of the city, consider taking **Lloyd's Tropical Bike Tour** (601 Truman Ave., 305/294-1882 or 305/304-4700, www.lloydstropicalbiketour.com, $39 pp w/ bike rental), a leisurely, ecofriendly ride along Key West's quiet streets and secret lanes, amid tropical gardens, historic architecture, and the exotic scents of jasmine and gardenias. Led by a longtime resident of Key West, these one-of-a-kind, two-hour tours even enable you to taste a variety of local fruit, such as mangoes, coconuts, and key limes. The bicycles included on this tour are single-speed beach cruisers, equipped with foot brakes, fat tires, wide seats, and convenient baskets—ideal features for novice riders. Children, accompanied by at least one adult, are welcome, and reservations are a must. Be sure to wear comfortable clothes and shoes, and bring your own hat, sunglasses, and sunscreen.

If you'd prefer a two-hour walking tour instead, you're in luck. There are several such tours available in Key West, including the **Historic Key West Walking Tour** (305/292-8990, www.trustedtours.com, 10 A.M., 2 P.M., and 4 P.M. daily Nov.–Apr., 9:30 A.M. daily May–Oct., $18 adults, $9 children 4–12, children under 4 free), an entertaining tour of Old Town's lush foliage, unique architecture, varied districts, and diverse culture. Along the tour, guides will share stories about the town's early inhabitants, famous and notorious Key West personalities, historic incidents like the Great Fire of 1886, and the island's varied phases, from its wrecking and cigar-making days to its involvement in both World Wars. Tours depart from the Key West Shipwreck Museum

in Mallory Square. Given the limited group size, reservations are recommended. In addition, visitors should wear comfortable shoes, bring bottled water, and check in 15 minutes before departure time.

As an alternative, you can opt for **Trails and Tales of Key West** (305/292-2040, www.trailsandtalesofkeywest.net, 4 P.M. daily, $20 pp, children under 12 free), a zany two-hour walking tour that begins at Captain Tony's Saloon, winds through Old Town and alongside the Historic Seaport, and ends at Jimmy Buffett's Margaritaville. En route, you'll learn about the history of the Conch Republic, including stories about the city's celebrated former residents, from novelist Ernest Hemingway to treasure hunter Mel Fisher to the ever-popular singer/songwriter Jimmy Buffett. Given the limited group size, reservations are required, and comfortable shoes are highly recommended.

If your interests run toward the paranormal, you may appreciate a nighttime stroll via **The Original Ghost Tours of Key West** (423 Fleming St., 305/294-9255, www.hauntedtours.com, 8 P.M. and 9 P.M. nightly, $15 adults, $10 children). Founded in 1996 by David L. Sloan, author of *Ghosts of Key West*, and featured in numerous television programs, this lantern-led walking tour departs nightly from the Crowne Plaza Key West at 430 Duval Street. With a colorful history that includes pirates, smugglers, and wreckers, the town formerly known as Bone Island has its share of curious hauntings, in places as varied as the Banyan Resort, St. Paul's Episcopal Church, the Fort East Martello Museum, and Captain Tony's Saloon—all of which this 90-minute, wheelchair-accessible tour encompasses. Reservations are recommended. Many of the same sites are visited through **The Ghosts & Legends of Key West** (305/294-1713, www.keywestghosts.com, 7 P.M. and 9 P.M. nightly, $18 adults, $10 children), a narrated, 90-minute tour along the shadowy streets and lanes of Old Town. Along this route, you'll learn about Key West's most intriguing legends and bizarre ghost stories, including tales of island pirate lore, haunted Victorian mansions, and voodoo rituals. The tour departs from the Porter House Mansion at Duval and Caroline Streets, and as with the other walking tours, reservations are recommended.

Boat Tours

Since many of Key West's most memorable attractions actually lie in the waters surrounding the island, you should make some time for one of the many sightseeing cruises available, such as a two-hour, glass-bottom boat tour with **Fury Water Adventures** (305/296-6293 or 877/994-8898, www.furycat.com, noon–2 P.M. and 2–4 P.M. daily, $40 adults, $20 children 6–12, children under 6 free). From aboard *The Pride of Key West,* a modern, smooth-sailing catamaran, you'll be able to gaze at dolphins, sharks, and other marine creatures from the comfort of an upper sun deck or, for an even better experience, observe the colorful coral and tropical fish *below* the boat via the enclosed, air-conditioned viewing area. Other on-board amenities include restrooms and a snack bar. The catamaran leaves twice daily from the marina at 2 Duval Street, between the Ocean Key Resort and the Pier House Resort.

For a more romantic adventure, spend the evening on a sunset cruise. Among those available, Fury offers the two-hour Commotion on the Ocean (305/294-8899 or 877/994-8898, 5:30–7:30 P.M. daily late Jan.–mid-Mar., 6:30–8:30 P.M. daily mid-Mar.–mid-Sept., 6–8 P.M. daily mid-Sept.–Oct., 5–7 P.M. daily Nov.–late Jan., $49 adults, $24.50 children 6–12, children under 6 free), which, in conjunction with the Hog's Breath Saloon, features appetizers, beer, margaritas, and live music amid a famous Key West sunset. As a bonus, Fury donates a percentage of all sales to coral reef conservation.

As an alternative, **Sunset Watersports** (201 William St., 305/296-2554, www.sunsetwatersports.info, times vary seasonally, $49 pp) offers a daily, two-hour sunset yacht excursion that features a tropical buffet and a variety of libations, from soft drinks to champagne. Couples will especially enjoy watching

the sunset together and dancing on the lighted dance floor. Reservations are required for the sunset dinner cruise as well as for the basic, two-hour sunset cruise ($30 pp w/o dinner).

Other area possibilities include **Sebago Watersports** (201 William St., 305/292-4768 or 800/507-9955, www.keywestsebago.com, 5–7 P.M. daily late Oct.–late Feb., 5:30–7:30 P.M. daily late Feb.–early Mar., 6:30–8:30 P.M. daily early Mar.–mid-Sept., 5:30–7:30 P.M. daily mid-Sept.–late Oct., $39 pp), which includes free champagne, margaritas, and other libations on its catamaran champagne sunset sail. If you need to accommodate a large party, **Key West Tiki Charters** (Hurricane Hole Marina, 5130 Overseas Hwy., Stock Island, 305/896-3458, www.keywesttikicharters.com, trip lengths and rates vary) provides private sunset and dinner cruises for 6–20 passengers.

A truly memorable experience awaits you aboard a classic schooner, such as the 80-foot, square-rigged, Caribbean-style **Schooner *Jolly II Rover*** (800/979-3370, www.schoonerjollyrover.com), which offers two-hour sunset sails (times vary seasonally, $39 pp) and 1.5-hour stargazer sails (8:30 P.M., $39 pp) every day, all of which depart from the Historic Seaport at the Key West Bight. You can also opt for sunset and stargazer sails aboard the **Schooner *Western Union*** (305/292-1766, www.schoonerwesternunion.com, times vary daily, $55 adults, $25 children 5–12, children under 5 free), a historic tall ship and floating maritime museum that also docks at the Historic Seaport. Unlike the *Jolly II Rover,* which invites you to bring your own food and beverages, the *Western Union,* which is listed on the National Register of Historic Places, provides complimentary libations, conch chowder, and live, island-style music with each sail.

Among other excursions, **Sebago Watersports** (201 William St., 305/292-4768 or 800/507-9955, www.keywestsebago.com) features two-hour day sails (2–4 P.M. daily, $45 pp) and champagne sunset sails (5–7 P.M. daily in winter, 6:30–8:30 P.M. daily in summer, $49 pp) aboard the **Schooner *Appledore.*** Other

KEY WEST

The *Adirondack II* heads out for a sunset cruise.

© DANIEL MARTONE

possible adventures include a daily, two-hour Wind and Wine Sunset Sail through **Danger Charters** (305/304-7999, www.dangercharters.com, times vary seasonally, $70 adults, $45 children 4–12, children under 4 free), based out of the Westin Hotel Marina at Whitehead and Greene Streets, as well as 1.5-hour mimosa morning sails (11 A.M. daily, $34 pp), classic 1.5-hour day sails (1:30 P.M. daily, $34 pp), and two-hour champagne sunset sails (times vary seasonally, $49 pp) aboard the **Schooner Adirondack II** (305/293-7245, www.sail-key-west.com), which is based out of the Historic Seaport at the Key West Bight and limited to a November–April sailing season. Most of the sails offered in Key West feature online discounts and recommend advance purchases.

Air Tours

If you'd like to experience an aerial tour of Key West and its surrounding waters, consider taking a biplane ride through **Conch Republic Air Force Biplane Rides** (3469 S. Roosevelt Blvd., 305/851-8359 or 305/294-8687, www. keywestbiplanes.com, 10 A.M.–sunset daily). Flying out of the Key West International Airport, each narrated tour invites two passengers (besides the pilot) to view coral reefs, shipwrecks, lighthouses, uninhabited islands, and various marine creatures from aboard an original, open-air 1942 World War II Waco biplane, at a smooth, 500-foot cruising altitude. You can choose from three different flights: an 18-minute Island Biplane Ride ($135 per ride) that offers a look at nearby shipwrecks; a 35-minute Island and Reef Tour ($260 per ride) that surveys coral reefs as well as Key West attractions; and a romantic, 35-minute Sunset Flight ($310 per ride), which is essentially the Island and Reef Tour at sunset. Tour times are flexible, and each quoted price includes two passengers. In addition, cloth helmets, headsets, and goggles are provided with all flights—all of which are wheelchair-accessible—and as a bonus, an on-board camera system can record your flight for posterity. Although walk-ins are welcome, reservations will ensure availability.

Entertainment and Events

NIGHTLIFE

If you like to prowl the streets at night, seeking out spirited bars, live music, and the like, then you've come to the right town. With a slew of late-night watering holes and entertainment options at your fingertips, Key West promises the most fun you'll have outside of the New Orleans French Quarter. Of course, Duval Street offers the largest concentration of nightlife selections—hence the term "Duval crawl," a popular activity whereby locals and visitors alike endeavor to stop by every bar along the street, from the Atlantic Ocean to the Gulf of Mexico.

Beyond the late-night chain establishments on Duval, such as the **Hard Rock Cafe Key West** (313 Duval St., 305/293-0230, www.hardrock.com, 11 A.M.–close daily) and **Jimmy Buffett's Margaritaville Key West** (500 Duval St., 305/292-1435, www.margaritavillekeywest.com, 11 A.M.–midnight daily), you'll spot unique, laid-back establishments like **Willie T's Restaurant & Bar** (525 Duval St., 305/294-7674, www.williets.com, 11 A.M.–2 A.M. daily), a popular watering hole that features an enormous selection of mojitos, a daily happy hour (4–7 P.M.), and live acoustic music on the patio at 1 P.M. and 7 P.M. every day.

Farther down Duval stands the inimitable **Sloppy Joe's Bar** (201 Duval St., 305/294-5717, www.sloppyjoes.com, 9 A.M.–close daily), which has been luring patrons to the corner of Greene and Duval (supposedly even Ernest Hemingway) since 1937 and is now listed on the National Register of Historic Places. Home to the annual Hemingway Look-Alike Contest, Sloppy Joe's offers terrific food, televised sports, plenty of libations, and live rock, country, or funk music all day long, which often entails three different bands or solo artists from noon to 2 A.M.

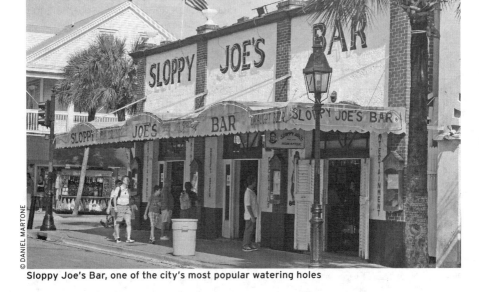

Sloppy Joe's Bar, one of the city's most popular watering holes

Across the street from Sloppy Joe's, the **Rick's/Durty Harry's Entertainment Complex** (202–208 Duval St., 305/296-5513, www.ricksanddurtyharrys.com, 11 A.M.–close daily) encompasses eight separate late-night options, including a Mardi Gras–style daiquiri bar, a strip club called the Red Garter, and Durty Harry's, which features several televisions and live rock music 8 P.M.–4 A.M. daily. At Duval and Caroline Streets, you'll encounter the clothing-optional **Garden of Eden** atop **The Bull and Whistle Bar** (305/296-4545, www.bullkeywest.com, 10 A.M.–4 A.M. Mon.–Sat., noon–4 A.M. Sun.), where body painting is a frequent activity. **Fat Tuesday Key West** (305 Duval St., 305/296-9373, www.fattues-daykeywest.com, 10 A.M.–close daily) claims to have the world's best selection of frozen drinks, including rumrunners, piña coladas, and New Orleans–style hurricanes.

Also on Duval, **Cowboy Bill's Honky Tony Saloon** (610½ Duval St., 305/295-8219, www.cowboybillskw.com, 11 A.M.–4 A.M. daily) invites you to watch televised sporting events, enjoy a specialty tequila, ride the mechanical bull, or boogie on Key West's largest dance floor.

You can also groove the night away at the predominantly gay **Aqua Nightclub** (711 Duval St., 305/294-0555, www.aquakeywest. com, 2:30 P.M.–3 A.M. daily), which features a daily happy hour (2:30–8 P.M.) in addition to karaoke, live piano and Caribbean-style music, and drag shows ($15 pp). Not far away lie two more gay hot spots: the **Bourbon St. Pub** (724 Duval St., 305/293-9800, www.bourbonst-pub.com, 10 A.M.–4 A.M. daily), which offers three inner bars, a clothing-optional garden bar, and sexy male dancers, and **801 Bourbon Bar & Cabaret** (801 Duval St., 305/294-9354, www.801bourbon.com, 10 A.M.–close daily), which features multiple bars, happy-hour specials (10 A.M.–6 P.M. daily), karaoke (6 P.M. Thurs. and Sun.), drag queen bingo (5 P.M. Sun.), and a twice-nightly drag show (9 P.M. and 11 P.M.). Both of these lively complexes factor heavily into annual events like Fantasy Fest and New Year's Eve.

For a less rowdy atmosphere, head to **The Keys** (1114 Duval St., 305/294-8859, www. akeywestpianobar.com, 5 P.M.–close daily, no cover), a piano bar that showcases a variety of sounds, from Broadway tunes to jazz standards, and invites novice singers to the stage for a nightly open mic. As an alternative, the **Pier House Resort** (1 Duval St., 305/296-4600, www.pierhouse.com) presents the **Wine Galley Piano Bar** (6 P.M.–close Fri.–Mon.), which offers martini specials and live nightly entertainment on the waterfront. Other enticing hotel options include the weekend cabaret show (9 P.M. Fri.–Sat., $26 pp) at the **La Te Da Hotel** (1125 Duval St., 305/296-6706, www.lateda. com); a full bar inside the **Rambler Lounge** (6:30–10 P.M. daily) at the **Casa Marina Resort** (1500 Reynolds St., 305/296-3535, www.casamarinaresort.com); and **Pearl's Patio** (305/293-9805, www.pearlspatio.com, noon–10 P.M. Sun.–Thurs., noon–midnight Fri.–Sat.), the women-only tropical bar at **Pearl's Rainbow** (525 United St., 305/292-1450, www.pearlsrainbow.com) that offers wireless Internet access, a happy hour (5–7 P.M. Mon.–Sat.), and special events.

Also off Duval, the **Bottlecap Lounge and Liquor** (1128 Simonton St., 305/296-2807, www.bottlecaplounge.com, noon–4 A.M. daily) lures revelers with pool tables, comfortable lounge chairs, oodles of beer, late-night vittles, and live blues and rock music. **Bobby's Monkey Bar** (900 Simonton St., 305/294-2655, www.bobbysmonkeybar.com, noon–4 A.M. daily) invites patrons to shoot some pool, play some free Wii games, and try their hand at karaoke (9:30 P.M. Sun.–Mon. and Thurs.–Fri.).

Over on Whitehead, the **Green Parrot Bar** (601 Whitehead St., 305/294-6133, www. greenparrot.com, 10 A.M.–4 A.M. Mon.–Sat., noon–4 A.M. Sun.) has been luring night owls since 1890. Today, you'll encounter a daily happy hour (4–7 P.M.), an awesome jukebox, and, of course, live blues, jazz, rock, and acoustic music almost every night.

Closer to the gulf, you can enjoy live rock and country music, plus a raw bar, at the **Hog's**

Breath Saloon (400 Front St., 305/296-4222, www.hogsbreath.com, 10 A.M.–2 A.M. daily), plus annual events like a bikini contest in October and a Parrot Head tribute party to Jimmy Buffett in November. The **Rum Barrel** (528 Front St., 305/292-7862, www.pirate-soul.com/rumbarrel, 11 A.M.–1 A.M. Mon.–Sat., 11:30 A.M.–1 A.M. Sun.) provides, as the name implies, a comprehensive rum selection, in addition to live folk, reggae, or classic rock music on an open-air rooftop deck, typically on Thursday, Friday, and Saturday nights.

Captain Tony's Saloon (428 Greene St., 305/294-1838, www.capttonyssaloon.com, 10 A.M.–2 A.M. Mon.–Sat., noon–2 A.M. Sun.), a Key West tradition since 1851 and the original location of Sloppy Joe's from 1933 to 1937, promises, among other things, live contemporary, classic rock, and country music every day, not to mention a glimpse at Ernest Hemingway's former stool. Typically, you can expect solo acoustic performers on weekdays and a house band on the weekend.

Beside the Historic Seaport at the Key West Bight, locals flock to the funky **Schooner Wharf Bar** (202 William St., 305/292-3302, www.schoonerwharf.com, 7:30 A.M.–4 A.M. daily), a weathered, open-air joint that offers excellent seafood, tropical drinks, and live acoustic music three times daily (noon, 7 P.M., and 9 P.M.). If you haven't had your fill of live entertainment yet, stroll over to the open-air **B.O.'s Fish Wagon** (801 Caroline St., 305/294-9272, www.bosfishwagon.com, 11 A.M.–9 P.M. daily) for the Friday night jam session. Closer to Grinnell, **Dante's** (955 Caroline St., 305/953-5123, www.dantes-key-west.com, 11 A.M.–10 P.M. daily) features a weekday happy hour (4–8 P.M.), daily raw bar specials (4–8 P.M.), live entertainment (Thurs.–Sun.), and access to a pool (11 A.M.–sunset daily).

You can enjoy some authentic Irish cuisine and live entertainment at **Finnegan's Wake** (320 Grinnell St., 305/293-0222, www.key-westirish.com, 11 A.M.–close daily), a lively, old-fashioned pub offering an enormous beer, wine, and hot toddies menu. During the peak tourist season, from November to May, you can usually expect Irish music on Friday and Saturday nights, while during the slower summer months, you might encounter local contemporary musicians on a Friday evening. For a more sensual, late-night experience, stop by **Better Than Sex** (411 Petronia St., 305/296-8102, www.betterthansexkw.com, 6 P.M.–1 A.M. Tues.–Sun. Christmas–Easter, 6 P.M.–1 A.M. Wed.–Sun. Apr.–Dec.), an intimate, dimly lit, bordello-style lounge and restaurant that features live jazz and acoustic music and focuses exclusively on wine and decadent desserts. Even Stock Island has a nightlife option: the casual **Hogfish Bar and Grill** (6810 Front St., 305/293-4041, www.hogfish-bar.com, 11 A.M.–11 P.M. Mon.–Sat., 9 A.M.–11 P.M. Sun.), which provides waterfront views and live blues, rock, and country music on the weekend (Thurs.–Sat.).

THE ARTS

While the rest of the Florida Keys host their fair share of plays, concerts, and screenings, most cultural enthusiasts head first to Key West—and with good reason. Despite its small size, America's Southernmost City nurtures a number of winning theatrical venues and musical organizations.

Theater and Cinema

Situated on the Florida Keys Community College (FKCC) campus, the **Tennessee Williams Theatre** (5901 College Rd., Stock Island, 305/296-1520, www.tennesseewilliamstheatre.com, show times and ticket prices vary) was saved from permanent closure in 2002 by the newly formed, nonprofit Performing Arts Centers for Key West (PACKW). Since then, this fantastic venue has featured a variety of nationally recognized performers and productions, from Lily Tomlin's one-woman show to Patti Lupone's musical reviews. To purchase tickets for events at the Tennessee Williams Theatre and other area venues, contact **KeysTix.com** (305/295-7676, http://keystix.ticketforce.com, 10 A.M.–2 P.M. Mon.–Fri.).

Mallory Square features the nonprofit **Waterfront Playhouse** (310 Wall St.,

305/294-5015, www.waterfrontplayhouse.org, show times and ticket prices vary), home to the Key West Players. From November to May, theater lovers are treated to a variety of cutting-edge productions, from rowdy musical comedies like *Reefer Madness* to classic dramas such as *Twelve Angry Men.*

The Red Barn Theatre (319 Duval St., 305/296-9911 or 866/870-9911, www.redbarntheatre.com, show times and ticket prices vary) has celebrated live theater for more than three decades. From November to May, theater showcases a wide array of modern comedies, dramas, and musicals, plus the springtime Short Attention Span Theatre, a well-favored event featuring an assortment of 10-minute plays.

Occasionally, live dance, musical, and theatrical performances take place at the nonprofit **San Carlos Institute** (516 Duval St., www.institutosancarlos.org, show times and ticket prices vary), a stunning, multipurpose facility that was founded by Cuban exiles and now features a museum, a library, an art gallery, a school, and a lovely, 360-seat theater. Contact the Institute or **KeysTix.com** (305/295-7676, http://keystix.ticketforce.com) for upcoming events.

Even movie lovers won't be disappointed in Key West. The relatively new **Tropic Cinema** (416 Eaton St., 877/761-3456, www.tropiccinema.com, show times and ticket prices vary) offers four different screening rooms—the Natella Carper Theater, the Frank Taylor Cinematheque Theater, the George Digital Theater, and the Peggy Dow Theater—and a spacious lobby (dubbed the Sussman Lounge) that have not only played host to the latest independent, alternative, and foreign films, but also community events, from jazz concerts to literary lectures to songwriting festivals. For information about other cultural events in Key West, consult the **Florida Keys Council of the Arts** (1100 Simonton St., 305/295-4369, www.keysarts.com).

Music

If you appreciate live classical music, then you're in luck. For well over a decade, the **Key West Symphony Orchestra (KWSO)** (305/292-1774, www.keywestsymphony.com, show times and ticket prices vary) has offered remarkable performances to the small community of Key West. Now composed of about 90 orchestral musicians and soloists from around the world, the KWSO splits its time between the **Tennessee Williams Theatre** (5901 College Rd., Stock Island, 305/296-1520, www.tennesseewilliamstheatre.com) and the **Broward Center for Performing Arts** (201 SW 5th Ave., Fort Lauderdale, 954/462-0222, www.browardcenter.org).

Typically from October to March, the nonprofit **Key West Pops Orchestra** (305/296-6059, www.keywestpops.org, show times and ticket prices vary) presents operas, Broadway musicals, and other musical performances at the Tennessee Williams Theatre and other area venues. Past shows have included *My Fair Lady, A Little Night Music,* and *The Pajama Game.* Also featured at the Tennessee Williams Theatre is the **FKCC Keys Chorale** (Florida Keys Community College, www.keyschorale.com, show times and ticket prices vary), Monroe County's only major vocal ensemble, which has been performing everything from pop songs to show tunes for more than 20 years. To purchase tickets for all three of these musical organizations, consult **KeysTix.com** (305/295-7676, http://keystix.ticketforce.com, 10 A.M.–2 P.M. Mon.–Fri.).

The **Key West Council on the Arts** has offered **Impromptu Concerts** (www.keywestimpromptu.org, show times and ticket prices vary) for more than 35 years. These concerts, which can range from solo piano performances to brass quintets to world-renowned operas, usually take place at the Tennessee Williams Theatre or at **St. Paul's Episcopal Church** (401 Duval St., 305/296-5142, www.stpaulskeywest.org). For tickets, contact the Tennessee Williams Theatre (305/296-1520).

Another curious option is the **Bahama Village Music Program** (727 Fort St., 305/292-9628, www.bvmpkw.org), a nonprofit group that offers free musical education to the children of Bahama Village, a historic community of multigenerational Bahamian Conchs. The students, who range in age from 6 to 13 and learn various styles of music, from piano to percussion, offer free concerts and recitals throughout the year. For more information about musical events in the Key West area, consult the **Florida Keys Council of the Arts** (1100 Simonton St., 305/295-4369, www.key-sarts.com).

FESTIVALS AND EVENTS

Key West may have many facets, but above all, it's still a town that knows how to party. Just consider the numerous festivals and events that lure revelers down here, sometimes even during the hottest months. Beyond fishing tournaments and New Year's Eve bashes, you'll find a number of art and heritage festivals, food events, and other exciting celebrations and competitions throughout the year. Perhaps you can even plan your next trip around such unabashed festivities.

Conch Republic Independence Celebration

On April 23, 1982, the U.S. Border Patrol set up a blockade near Florida City to search for illegal aliens and possible drug runners. Following the subsequent traffic jam on U.S. 1, the people of the Florida Keys briefly declared their secession from the United States, forming the "Conch Republic," a mock micronation, and successfully ending the disruptive blockade. Since then, for roughly three decades, the people of Key West have honored the 1982 ceremonial secession with the 10-day Conch Republic Independence Celebration (www.conchrepublic.com).

Every spring, in late April, residents and visitors can enjoy a lineup of varied activities around the city, such as the raising of the Conch Republic flag at Fort Zachary Taylor Historic State Park and the Great Conch Republic Drag Race, featuring competing drag queens, on Duval Street. Throughout the celebration, you can enjoy an array of events at area bars and restaurants, from the conch shell–blowing contest at the Schooner Wharf Bar to a fiddler's contest at the Green Parrot Bar. Other events include bed and dinghy races, car and crafts shows, mini-golf challenges, a pirate's ball, and, of course, the Conch Republic Naval Parade and Great Battle for the Conch Republic—a mock, on-the-water confrontation between the Conch Republic's "armed forces" and the "U.S. Border Patrol," an homage to the April 1982 protest. Needless to say, the Conch Republic is always victorious in the Great Battle that takes place in the Key West Bight.

◖ Hemingway Days

The spirit of Ernest Hemingway, one of Key West's most beloved former residents, endures in the Southernmost City—and not just through the popular Ernest Hemingway Home and Museum or because of the numerous establishments, such as Sloppy Joe's Bar and Captain Tony's Saloon, that claim to have been the famous novelist's favorite watering hole. Every summer, in late July, residents and visitors alike celebrate this fascinating man with the annual Hemingway Days (800/352-5397, www.fla-keys.com/hemingwaymedia), a six-day event that commemorates Hemingway's lust for life; his passion for activities like writing and fishing; his adoration of Key West, where he spent the better part of the 1930s; and, of course, his literary works, several of which he wrote while living on this very island.

Scheduled events typically include a literary competition; a Caribbean-style street fair; dramatic performances about Hemingway's life; a museum exhibit of rare Hemingway memorabilia; a three-day marlin tournament; and, perhaps most famous, the Hemingway Look-Alike Contest, for which upwards of 150 stocky, white-bearded old men flock to town to demonstrate their uncanny resemblance to this one-of-a-kind American writer. Another not-to-be-missed event is the wacky "Running of the Bulls," a slow-moving parade that features the "Papa" Hemingway look-alikes, dressed in Pamplona-style apparel, including khaki shorts and red berets, and riding or strolling beside

phony bulls-on-wheels—a silly photo opportunity for residents and tourists alike.

Fantasy Fest

Every October, tons of revelers pour into Key
West for Fantasy Fest (1111 12th St., Ste. 211,
305/296-1817, www.fantasyfest.net), a spirited
10-day event that nearly rivals the Big Easy's
annual Mardi Gras celebration. With colorful
parades, outrageous costumes, and oodles of
drag queens, this is surely Key West's grand-
est—and gayest—party of the year. Initiated in
the late 1970s to help the local economy during a traditionally slow period, Fantasy Fest has
now become such a successful event that it often
sustains the hotels, restaurants, and other local
establishments until the winter holiday season. Usually held in late October, culminating
with Halloween, this hallowed event features
everything from a children's costume contest
to a two-day goombay street fair in Bahama
Village—essentially, a Bahamian celebration
that highlights the calypso-style music and
dancing associated with goombay drums. In
addition, Fantasy Fest revelers will experience

fetish and toga parties, headdress balls, pet
masquerades, various costume and wet T-shirt
contests, body-painting displays, and plenty
of other hedonistic activities. Though not for
the faint of heart, Fantasy Fest is indeed a bash
worth observing—if not participating in.

Heritage Festivals

With a past that includes pirate legends,
Bahamian immigrants, Civil War skirmishes,
Cuban refugees, and other alluring facets, it's
little surprise that Key West plays host to a
number of cultural events throughout the year.
On multiple weekends from late December to
mid-March, for instance, those interested in
Key West's unique architecture and gardens
can take a **Key West House and Garden Tour**
($25 pp) through the historic Old Town dis-
trict. Sponsored by the **Old Island Restoration
Foundation** (322 Duval St., 305/294-9501,
www.oirf.org) for the past five decades, these
beloved tours allow both residents and visitors
a chance to peer beyond the front porches of
some of Key West's most one-of-a-kind homes.
Each tour features five private domiciles, all of

mock ballerinas frolicking during the annual Fantasy Fest masquerade

which reflect the varied tastes of their owners and many of which feature authentic restorations, creative renovations, and impressive art and antique collections.

Meanwhile, in late February, the **Key West Tropical Forest and Botanical Garden** (5210 College Rd., Stock Island, 305/296-1504, www.keywestbotanicalgarden.org) celebrates the island's bountiful flora with **Gardenfest Key West** (prices vary), a three-day event that typically includes raffles, demonstrations, lectures, nature-oriented artwork, and a plant sale, featuring fruit trees, exotic palms, orchids, bromeliads, and native plants. Also in late February, the city celebrates a three-day event known as **Civil War Days** (www.forttaylor.org/hfest.html, fees apply for some activities) with candlelit tours of Fort Zachary Taylor (western end of Southard St., 305/292-6713, www.floridastateparks.org/forttaylor), artillery demonstrations, a military parade down Duval Street, and reenacted engagements between Union soldiers and Confederate blockade runners in authentic, 19th-century schooners.

In early March, the Old Island Restoration Foundation (322 Duval St., 305/294-9501, www.oirf.org) hosts a popular, one-day **Conch Shell Blowing Contest** (free), also known as the "Conch Honk," during which children, teenagers, adults, and senior citizens alike demonstrate their shell-blowing skills in order to highlight the significance of the conch in Key West's past. Meanwhile, the Key West Tropical Forest and Botanical Garden (5210 College Rd., Stock Island, 305/296-1504, www.keywestbotanicalgarden.org) honors the town's Cuban heritage with **Hot Havana Nights** ($25–30 pp), a single-evening, mid-March display of Cuban music, dancing, and cuisine; later in March, the Botanical Garden also features an annual **Doo Wop Party** ($20–25 pp), a one-day celebration of the 1950s and 1960s with classic tunes, classic cars, and costume contests.

Typically in late April, music lovers will encounter the curious **Key West Songwriters' Festival** (www.kwswf.com, show times and ticket prices vary), a five-day event that presents more than 30 live concerts at popular locales throughout the city, from the Ocean Key

Fort Zachary Taylor, home to events like Civil War Days

Resort to the San Carlos Institute to Jimmy Buffett's Margaritaville. In late May, residents and visitors celebrate the influence of Cuban culture on the development of Key West with the three-day **Cuban American Heritage Festival** (5570 3rd Ave., 305/295-9665, www.cubanfest.com, prices vary), which typically includes activities like a coast-to-coast conga line, a Latin dance party, a Cuban cigar dinner, a domino tournament, and a progressive dinner at various Cuban restaurants.

Besides Hemingway Days, other popular summertime events include the five-day **Key West Pridefest** (305/294-4603, www.pridefestkeywest.com, fees apply for some activities) in mid-June and the four-day **Mel Fisher Days** (Mel Fisher's Treasures, 200 Greene St., 800/434-1399, www.melfisher.com, fees apply for some activities) in mid-July. In a town that possesses a healthy share of gay-friendly bars and hotels—and whose motto is "one human family"—it's no wonder that Pridefest is a much-anticipated event, filled with contests, shows, tours, dance and cocktail parties, a street fair, and a "pride" parade along Duval Street. A month later, Mel Fisher Days honors a different aspect of the city's heritage—its lust for treasure hunting. To honor the anniversary of Mel Fisher's discovery of the *Atocha* mother lode, this event features, among other activities, a parade, a poker tournament, and a bikini contest that offers authentic treasure coins as prizes.

Later in the year, two more events highlight the laid-back yet zany vibe of this island paradise. In early November, **Parrot Heads in Paradise, Inc.** (www.phip.com), the nonprofit, international organization of Parrot Head Clubs—the official fan clubs of singer/songwriter Jimmy Buffett and the carefree, tropical lifestyle he exemplifies—hosts a four-day **Meeting of the Minds** for all members in good standing, whether they be members of the virtual club or one of the more than 200 actual clubs that exist around the world. Typically in late November and early December, the 10-day **Pirates in Paradise** (305/296-9694, www.piratesinparadise.com, fees apply for some activities) lures a host of pirate lovers to the streets of Key West, where highlights include pub strolls, tall-ship sea battles, a walk-the-plank championship, a "most buxom wench and best bad ass pirate" contest, and a Fort Zachary Taylor pirate invasion, which features a village thieves' market, strolling minstrels, and storytelling pirates.

Food Events

In a city that celebrates so many hedonistic pleasures, it's no wonder that food plays a major role in so many annual events. Some even focus exclusively on the local cuisine. In mid-January, for instance, the one-day, family-friendly **Florida Keys Seafood Festival** (www.fkcfa.org/events.aspx, prices vary) highlights the region's commercial fishing industry by offering the freshest local seafood available, from crab to lobster. Later in January, the four-day **Key West Food & Wine Festival** (305/395-8611 or 800/474-4319, www.keywestfoodandwinefestival.com, prices vary) celebrates an assortment of local delicacies, including seafood, Cuban cuisine, tapas dishes, fine wine, and tropical ice cream at various local bars and restaurants. Other activities may include a coconut bowling tournament and a tea dance at La Te Da.

In mid-April, another annual food extravaganza, the one-day **Taste of Key West** ($1 per food/wine ticket), celebrates the cuisine of more than 100 vineyards and 50 local restaurants while benefiting the efforts of **AIDS Help** (1434 Kennedy Dr., 305/296-6196, www.aidshelp.cc). A few months later, in early August, residents and visitors celebrate one of their favorite crustaceans with the **Key West Lobsterfest** (Key West Promotions, Inc., 422 Fleming St., 305/744-9804, www.keywestlobsterfest.com, prices vary), a three-day event that features live music, cold drinks, and, naturally, fresh lobster.

Art Festivals

Given how influential Key West's landscape has been on local and visiting musicians, writers, and artists, it seems only natural that the Southernmost City would host its share of art-related events during the peak tourist season. In late January, the long-standing **Key West Craft Show** (305/294-1243, www.keywestartcenter.com/craft.html, prices vary), a two-day juried outdoor craft festival, attracts over 100 potters, fabric experts, jewelry makers, glass sculptors, wood craftsmen, and other skilled artists to Key West's Old Town. For a more unusual experience, consider visiting during **Sculpture Key West** (305/295-3800, www.sculpturekeywest.com, admission fees may apply), an annual wintertime exhibition of contemporary outdoor sculpture throughout the city, namely at attractions like Fort Zachary Taylor Historic State Park, the West Martello Tower, and the Key West Tropical Forest and Botanical Garden. Typically, you can enjoy this event from mid-January to mid-April.

Usually held in late February, the nationally recognized **Old Island Days Art Festival** (305/294-1243, www.keywestartcenter.com/festival.html, prices vary) has, for well over four decades, celebrated various art forms amid the historic structures of Key West's Old Town. Originally held as a fundraising event for the building that now houses the **Key West Art Center and Gallery (KWAC)** (301 Front St., 305/294-1241, www.keywestartcenter.com, 10 A.M.–5 P.M. daily), this two-day juried, outdoor fine art festival features the work of over 100 painters, photographers, sculptors, and other artists, many of whom definitely favor tropical themes.

Fishing and Racing Events

As in other parts of the Florida Keys, outdoor events are popular in Key West, perhaps none more so than the fishing tournaments and racing championships that take place throughout the year. In late January, thousands of sailors from around the world flock to Key West for the **Key West Race Week** (781/639-9545, www.premiere-racing.com, entry fees apply), a five-day international sailing competition in the waters surrounding the Southernmost City. Beginning in mid-March, men, women, juniors, and young children compete to catch and release more than 40 different fish species

in the nine-month-long **Key West Fishing Tournament (KWFT)** (www.keywestfishingtournament.com, entry fees apply).

In mid-April, elite anglers also compete in the prestigious, five-day **World Sailfish Championship** (866/550-5580, www.worldsailfish.com, entry fees apply), which typically awards cash prizes that total roughly $125,000. From mid-September to early November, celebrities and ordinary fishing enthusiasts come together for the **Redbone Celebrity Tournament Series** (305/664-2002, www.redbone.org, entry fees apply), a trio of three-day "Catch the Cure" competitions throughout the Keys that seek out permit, tarpon, bonefish, and redfish—ultimately benefiting cystic fibrosis research. Also in early November, a slew of high-speed powerboats race across the waters of Key West to vie for the world championship title in the eight-day **Key West World Championship** (www.keywestpowerboatraces.com or http://superboat.com/key-west, entry fees apply)—a competition that's equally appealing to spectators.

Holiday Celebrations

A year in Key West wouldn't be complete without experiencing the city's annual holiday celebrations. In early December, residents and visitors, often dressed in shorts and sandals, line up along Duval Street for the **Key West Holiday Parade** (free), a family-friendly event that usually occurs on a Saturday evening and features decorated floats, marching bands, and perhaps a few Santas holding fishing poles. On a Saturday evening in mid-December, locals "deck the hulls" for the **Key West Lighted Boat Parade** (free), a maritime tradition that features a procession of vessels in the Key West Bight. All the boats, most of which are owned by Florida Keys–based residents, are enhanced by bright lights, holiday decorations, and live music, from choirs to steel drums. Families especially favor this festive event.

For four enchanted evenings (typically, two weekends) in mid-December, the self-guided **Holiday Historic Inn Tour** (www.keywestinntour.com, $20 pp) highlights some of the city's loveliest properties, all of which are decorated for the holiday season with twinkling lights, poinsettia plants, and festooned palm trees. Often, you'll be able to step inside such historic inns as the Cypress House, the Curry Mansion, and The Mermaid & The Alligator B&B. In addition, fine food and beverages are usually available throughout the tour.

Not surprisingly, **New Year's Eve** is a popular holiday in the Southernmost City. Among the various midnight celebrations on December 31st, you'll spy a conch shell dropping from the roof of Sloppy Joe's Bar, a pirate wench descending the mast of a schooner at the Historic Seaport, and a local drag queen being lowered from a Duval Street balcony in an enormous, high-heeled shoe. Many of the bars are open into the wee hours, so the celebrating doesn't typically stop at midnight.

Shopping

With its cornucopia of art galleries, gift and souvenir shops, clothing boutiques, jewelry stores, and food emporiums, Key West promises you the most engrossing treasure hunt in the Florida Keys—at least on land. Here, shoppers will find all manner of items for sale, from hammocks to erotic literature to pendants fashioned from sunken Spanish coins. While such diverse shopping opportunities exist throughout the city, certain areas—such as Mallory Square and the rest of Old Town—offer the lion's share of options, especially for tourists.

Naturally, the suggestions listed here merely scratch the surface of Key West's shopping scene. For even more ideas, consult www.shopkeywest.com—or just take a stroll around the neighborhoods.

BAHAMA VILLAGE

Southwest of Whitehead Street, and roughly bordered by Southard, Fort, and Louisa Streets, lies a historic neighborhood known as Bahama Village. Named for its original inhabitants, many of whom were of Bahamian

© DANIEL MARTONE

crafts and souvenirs at the Bahama Village Market

ancestry, this residential area is a lively place in the daytime and rather quiet at night. Some visitors even find it a little too quiet once the sun goes down. In fact, due to the occurrence of criminal activities, such as muggings and drug transactions, local police officers often advise outsiders against venturing into this area after dark.

Nevertheless, the presence of several interesting shops and restaurants, such as the dessert-only eatery Better Than Sex, makes Bahama Village an enticing place for tourists. Shoppers might especially appreciate the **Bahama Village Market,** an open-air flea market near the village entrance on Petronia Street. Here, you'll find a collection of colorful stalls, featuring typical souvenirs like straw hats, T-shirts, beads, sponges, and Caribbean crafts.

MALLORY SQUARE

Although technically part of Key West's Old Town, Mallory Square (1 Whitehead St., www.mallorysquare.com) operates as its own unique entity. Situated at the northernmost part of Duval and Whitehead Streets, this popular collection of shops, eateries, and attractions is perhaps best known for its daily Sunset Celebration, when hundreds of locals and tourists gather beside the shore to enjoy the antics of musicians, artists, acrobats, jugglers, and other street performers, while paying homage to the sun as it seemingly sinks into the Gulf of Mexico.

If you're in search of souvenirs, you're in luck here. Vendor carts present a variety of goods, from coconut pirates to colorful flip-flops. In Mallory Square, you'll also spot the long-standing **Shell Warehouse** (305/294-5168, 8:30 A.M.–9 P.M. daily), which offers an intriguing assortment of shells, jewelry, artwork, and decorations. Another favored tourist stop is the **Sponge Market** (305/294-2555, 8 A.M.–9 P.M. daily), which features a variety of local art, model ships, sea sponges, shipwreck treasure jewelry, and other maritime collectibles—not to mention an enormous "sponge man," the subject of many a tourist's photograph, just outside the doorway.

© LAURA MARTONE

KEY WEST

vendor carts in Mallory Square

Adjacent to Mallory Square stands the **Clinton Square Market** (291 Front St., 305/296-6825, 8:30 A.M.–6 P.M. daily), an air-conditioned, two-story mall that contains a variety of shops, featuring everything from jewelry and tropical clothing to toys and pet items. If it's hot outside, be sure to grab an ice cream cone from **Sweets of Paradise** (305/296-1611, www.sweetsofparadise.com, 10 A.M.–6 P.M. daily), a small first-level shop that also prepares key lime pie, rum cake, macadamia nut brittle, and Michigan-style fudge.

HISTORIC SEAPORT

From Mallory Square, head northeast to the renovated Historic Seaport district at the Key West Bight, home to dozens of yachts and tour operators. Generally, people come here to hire charters, board sailboats, stroll along the boardwalk, or dine at lively places like the Schooner Wharf Bar, but shoppers will also find a couple of curious stores in the vicinity. Difficult to miss is **Mac's Sea Garden** (208 Margaret St., 305/293-7240, 9 A.M.–9 P.M. daily), a rustic gift shop, with chimes hanging beneath the porch roof, an old, weathered pickup sitting in the front yard, and the distinct appearance of a Cajun fishing camp. Not far away, at the corner of Elizabeth and Greene Streets, **Kermit's Key West Key Lime Shoppe** (305/296-0806, www.keylimeshop.com, 9 A.M.–9 P.M. daily) offers a whole slew of key lime products, from key lime bath soap to key lime barbecue sauce to, of course, classic key lime pie.

OLD TOWN

Although Key West's Old Town is generally considered the western half of the island, most of the available shopping opportunities are concentrated on or near **Duval Street,** the main drag of this historic district. Here and on surrounding roads, like Greene and Whitehead Streets, you'll find a ton of places to satisfy your cravings for art, souvenirs, fashion, jewelry, food, and so much more.

Art Galleries

If you're an art lover, then you've come to the right place, for Key West boasts well over 30 art galleries—certainly more than any other place in the Florida Keys. Over half of these can be found on Duval Street, in two separate clusters.

On the upscale end of Duval, closer to the Atlantic Ocean, lie nearly a dozen elegant galleries, bunched together amid tropical foliage and historic buildings. At the **Archeo Gallery** (1208 Duval St., 305/294-3771, www.archeogallery.com, 11 A.M.–5 P.M. Tues.–Sat.), you'll find hand-chosen, primitive art from around the world, such as vibrant Gabbeh rugs from Iran, teak furniture from Indonesia, and masks, sculpture, pottery, and metalwork from Africa. Across the street stands the **Gingerbread Square Gallery** (1207 Duval St., 305/296-8900, www.gingerbreadsquaregallery. com, 10 A.M.–6 P.M. daily), which was established in 1974 by Key West's former mayor Richard Heyman, making it one of the oldest art galleries in town. Represented here are the paintings, sculptures, and glassware of several different artists, from Sal Salinero's lush

rainforest landscapes to Peter Greenwood's whimsical bubble bottles.

The **Key West Light Gallery** (1203 Duval St., 305/294-0566, www.kwlightgallery.com, 10 A.M.–5 P.M. daily) features contemporary photography and paintings that highlight Key West's architecture, explore Cuban culture, and exemplify the concept of light in its many forms. A block down the street, the **Alan S. Maltz Gallery** (1210 Duval St., 305/294-0005, www.alanmaltz.com, 10 A.M.–6 P.M. daily) displays the stunning images of Florida's official wildlife photographer.

Several blocks down Duval, closer to the rowdier Gulf of Mexico end, lie nearly 10 more winning galleries, including the **Island Style Gallery** (620 Duval St., 305/292-7800, www.islandstylegalleries.com, 10 A.M.–8 P.M. Mon.–Sat., 11 A.M.–6 P.M. Sun.), which presents artistic jewelry, handcrafted glass, and colorful, tropical-themed home furnishings. On the same side of the street, you'll find the **Guild Hall Gallery** (614 Duval St., 305/296-6076, www.guildhallgallerykw.com, 10 A.M.–8 P.M. daily), which has supported local artists since 1976 and today displays the watercolor and acrylic paintings, contemporary sculpture, and youthful jewelry of more than 20 artists. Just a few steps away, the cooperative **7 Artists Key West Gallery** (604 Duval St., 305/293-0411, www.7artistskeywest.com, 10 A.M.–10 P.M. daily) offers the fanciful creations of seven local artists, including Michael Sanders' island-themed shot glasses and shadow boxes. Farther down Duval, you'll enjoy the dramatically illumined **Peter Lik Fine Art Photography Gallery** (519 Duval St., 305/292-2550, www. peterlik.com, 10 A.M.–9 P.M. daily), one of 13 such galleries in the United States.

Perhaps the most famous gallery in town is the flagship store of **Wyland Galleries** (623 Duval St., 305/292-4998 or 888/292-4998, www.wylandkw.com or www.wylandgalleries. com, 9 A.M.–10 P.M. daily), the largest Wyland gallery in the world. Inside this spacious store, you'll see an array of impressive glass creations, bronze sculptures, and vibrant paintings by the prolific muralist and environmentalist, whose

WYLAND'S WHALING WALLS

© DANIEL MARTONE

A Wyland whaling wall graces the former Waterfront Market.

Robert Wyland, better known simply as Wyland, is indeed the most famous marinelife artist in the world. For more than 25 years, Wyland – an avid scuba diver, marine conservationist, painter, sculptor, photographer, and world traveler as well as the official U.S. artist of the Olympics – has used his artwork to spread awareness about the ocean, its inhabitants, and the need to preserve and protect this fragile environment. His oil and watercolor paintings, bronze and Lucite sculptures, and other creations – which typically feature magnificent whales, peaceful manatees, frisky dolphins, giant sea turtles, and kaleidoscopic tropical fish – are on display in galleries throughout the country, most notably in Florida, California, and Hawaii. He even has two **Wyland Galleries** (www.wylandkw.com) in Key West, including the flagship store (623 Duval St., 305/292-4998) and the one near Mallory Square (102 Duval St., 305/294-5240).

Nicknamed the "Marine Michelangelo" by *USA Today,* Wyland has been recognized for his conservation efforts by the United Na-

tions, the Sierra Club, and other public and private institutions throughout the world. In fact, he cares so deeply about the environment that, in 1993, he established the **Wyland Foundation** (www.wylandfoundation.org), a nonprofit organization that has supported numerous conservation programs, including his most famous endeavor: the monumental Whaling Wall mural project. Begun in 1981 in Laguna Beach, California, this impressive series of 100 life-sized marinelife murals now spans 12 countries on four continents, from America to Japan to New Zealand, and captures nearly 1 billion viewers per year. Interestingly, you'll even find several of these amazing murals in southern Florida, including *Minke Whales* (1990) at Crane Point's Museum of Natural History in Marathon and *Florida's Living Reef* (1993) on the exterior wall of the now-defunct Waterfront Market in Key West – both of which are indeed worth a look. For more information about Wyland's art and conservation efforts, visit www.wylandgalleries.com and www.wyland.com.

work typically focuses on photogenic marine-life like dolphins, manatees, orcas, and sea turtles. In addition, this incredible gallery features the work of Wyland's fellow artists, including David Wight's amazing glass wave sculptures. Near Mallory Square, you'll spot another Wyland gallery at 102 Duval Street (305/294-5240 or 888/294-5240, 9 A.M.–10 P.M. daily), so be sure to stop there, too.

Of course, there are also plenty of worthwhile art galleries off Duval. Near downtown Key West, the **Audubon House and Tropical Gardens** (205 Whitehead St., 305/294-2116 or 877/294-2470, www.audubonhouse.com, 9:30 A.M.–5 P.M. daily) includes the **Audubon House Gallery of Natural History,** which offers a number of limited editions of John James Audubon's famous ornithological paintings from the 19th century. Farther inland, the **Haitian Art Company** (1100 Truman Ave., 305/296-8932, www.haitian-art-co.com, 10 A.M.–6 P.M. daily) sells an array of colorful paintings from Haitian artists like Simeon Michel, who focuses on the verdant Haitian countryside, and Soliman Delva, who strives for social realism.

For more information about these and other art galleries, consult the **Florida Keys Council of the Arts** (1100 Simonton St., 305/295-4369, www.keysarts.com).

Gift and Souvenir Shops

Given Key West's supreme popularity among tourists, it surely comes as no surprise that gift and souvenir shops abound in Old Town. For one thing, there's a plethora of strategically placed museum shops in this part of town. In fact, whether they're situated just beyond the front entrance, as with the **Mel Fisher Maritime Museum** (200 Greene St., 305/294-2633, www.melfisher.org, 8:30 A.M.–5 P.M. Mon.–Fri., 9:30 A.M.–5 P.M. Sat.–Sun.), or located at the end of the tour, as with the **Pirate Soul Museum** (524 Front St., 305/292-1113, www.piratesoul.com, 9 A.M.–5 P.M. Mon.–Fri., 10 A.M.–5 P.M. Sat.–Sun.), you're usually forced to pass through an eclectic collection of books, DVDs, jewelry,

apparel, and the like. If you're interested in less nautically themed items, consider browsing the gift shop at the **Key West Butterfly and Nature Conservatory** (1316 Duval St., 305/296-2988, www.keywestbutterfly.com, 9 A.M.–5:30 P.M. daily), which features a wide selection of butterfly-themed jewelry, ceramics, books, and other souvenirs.

You'll find several other curious gift shops along Duval. **KW Hammocks** (717 Duval St., Ste. 2, 305/293-0008, www.kwhammocks.com, hours vary daily), for one, has been distributing hammocks and hammock-style porch swings, chairs, and rockers for over a decade, and while it's true that **Jimmy Buffett's Margaritaville** (500 Duval St., 305/296-3070, www.margaritavillekeywest.com, 9 A.M.–11 P.M. daily) is part of a famous bar and restaurant chain, that doesn't mean that the attached store isn't worth browsing. Here, you'll find all manner of souvenir hats, T-shirts, flip-flops, lawn chairs, dog collars, and, of course, Buffett's novels and CDs. Be sure to check out the wacky window display at **Fast Buck Freddie's** (500 Duval St., 305/294-2007, www.fastbuckfreddies.com, 10 A.M.–6 P.M. Mon.–Fri., 10 A.M.–10 P.M. Sat., 11 A.M.–6 P.M. Sun.), an enormous, long-standing tropical department store.

Not far away, you can pick up unique aloe-based fragrances, hair products, and skin creams for women and men at **Key West Aloe** (419 Duval St., 800/445-2563, www.keywestaloe.com, 8:30 A.M.–5 P.M. daily). Off Duval, another curious locale is the **Pelican Poop Shoppe** (314 Simonton St., 305/296-3887, www.pelicanpoopshoppe.com, 10 A.M.–7 P.M. daily), which presents an array of lamps, weathervanes, metal wall art, and other Caribbean-style crafts. Established in 1976, the same year as Fast Buck Freddie's, the **Key West Kite Company** (408 Greene St., 305/296-5483, www.keywestkitecompany.com, 9 A.M.–8:30 P.M. daily) provides colorful kites, flags, toys, and yard ornaments to residents and visitors alike.

Now, if you've come to Key West with more amorous amusements in mind, consider

© DANIEL MARTONE

A Conch Republic flag is proudly displayed at the Key West Kite Company.

stopping by the **Fairvilla Megastore** (520 Front St., 305/292-0448, www.fairvilla.com, 9 A.M.–midnight daily), where you'll find a wide selection of erotic gifts and games, fantasy fashions, and sensual accessories. Just a few blocks away lies a completely different megastore. With a view of Key West Harbor, the 4,000-square-foot **Saltwater Angler** (243 Front St., 305/294-3248 or 800/223-1629, www.saltwaterangler.com, 9 A.M.–8:30 P.M. daily) serves as a one-stop shop for anyone interested in saltwater fishing in the Florida Keys. Operated by Captain Tony Murphy and situated within The Westin Key West Resort & Marina, the Angler houses an extensive inventory of travel and fishing apparel for men and women, plus luggage, wind chimes, stained-glass fish art, rare books, and locally made jewelry. While you're here, you can even ask about fishing guide services.

Clothing and Shoe Boutiques

Most of the clothing and footwear stores in Key West focus on carefree island styles. The **Ron Jon Surf Shop** (503 Front St., 305/293-

8880 or 888/757-8737, www.ronjons.com, 9 A.M.–9 P.M. daily) is no exception. This two-story behemoth offers a wide array of apparel and accessories for the vacationer, from swimsuits to backpacks to sunglasses. In keeping with that laid-back vibe, **Kino Sandals, Inc.** (107 Fitzpatrick St., 305/294-5044, www.kinosandalfactory.com, 8:30 A.M.–5:30 P.M. Mon.–Fri., 9 A.M.–5:30 P.M. Sat., 10 A.M.–3 P.M. Sun.), established in 1966 by Cuban immigrants, invites visitors to watch the sandals being made by hand, before choosing from an array of men's and women's selections. You can also pick up a pair of sandals at the **Port Sandal Shoppe** (218 Whitehead St., Ste. 2, 305/296-0001, www.sandalshoppe.com, 9:30 A.M.–7:30 P.M. daily), which houses thousands of different styles from popular brands like Teva, Timberland, and Crocs. For a real island look, consider stopping by **Hair Wraps of Key West** (310 Duval St., 305/293-1133, www.hairwrapsofkeywest.com, 10 A.M.–10 P.M. daily) and let the staff adorn your hair with braids, corn rows, and beads. Henna tattoos, charms, and hair accessories are also available.

For fancier duds, visit **Evan & Elle** (725 Duval St., 305/295-3530, www.shopbiton. com, 10 A.M.–3 P.M. Mon.–Fri., longer hours Nov.–Apr.), which offers upscale clothing for men and women, ideal for those headed out on a cruise. Off Duval, the stylish **Blue Boutique** (718 Caroline St., 305/292-5172, www.blueislandstore.com, 10 A.M.–6 P.M. daily) features high-end, contemporary fashions from today's hottest designers, such as Nicole Miller and James Perse. If you want to match your new outfit with the perfect hat, purse, or necklace, stroll to The Westin Key West Resort & Marina, where the locally owned **Key West Madhatter** (253 Front St., 305/294-1364 or 888/442-4287, www.kw-madhatter.com, 9 A.M.–11 P.M. daily) offers, among other accessories, more than 2,000 hats for women, men, and children, from elegant straw hats to goofy holiday fedoras.

Jewelry Stores

You'll certainly find an impressive assortment of shiny, pretty things in Key West, including oodles of gemstones at **Diamonds International** (122 Duval St., 305/293-1111, www.shopdi.com, 11 A.M.–9 P.M. daily), the largest duty-free jeweler in the world, as well as emerald, conch pearl, and Australian black opal rings at **Emeralds International** (104 Duval St., 305/294-2060 or 877/689-6647, www. emeraldsinternational.com, 10 A.M.–6 P.M. daily). For more precious gemstones—plus Key West's largest supply of Swiss watches—head to **Little Switzerland** (423 Front St., 305/292-2345, www.littleswitzerland.com, 9 A.M.–5 P.M. daily).

If your interests run a little less expensive, visit **Local Color** (276 Margaret St., 305/292-3635, www.localcolorkeywest.com, 9 A.M.–10 P.M. daily), which features the silver and gold "KW" hook bracelets and rings originated by the **KW Bracelet Co.** (www.keywestbracelet.com). You could also try **Paradise Tattoo** (627 Duval St., 305/292-9002, www.paradisetattoo.com, 10 A.M.–10 P.M. daily), which offers basic jewelry in addition to tattoo and body-piercing services.

For valuables that will evoke memories of your trip to the Florida Keys, head to **Whitfield Jack Jewelry Genius** (200 Elizabeth St., 305/294-7092 or 800/845-2243, www.jewelrygenius. com, 10 A.M.–4 P.M. Mon.–Sat.), which features a vast array of sea-inspired creations from local artist Whitfield Jack. Here, you'll find nearly every aspect of island life represented, from dolphins and seahorses to sand dollars and crossbones. Most treasure seekers head to **Mel Fisher's Treasures** (200 Greene St., 305/296-9936 or 800/434-1399, www.melfisher.com, 9:30 A.M.–5 P.M. daily), situated at the rear of the Mel Fisher Maritime Museum. Here, you can purchase a piece of the famous *Nuestra Señora de Atocha* shipwreck, including pearls, iron spikes, musket balls, pieces of eight, and pendants and earrings crafted from old Spanish coins. In addition, you can speak with the staff about investing in the site—from which underwater explorers are still recovering hidden coins, artifacts, and other treasures. Just be prepared to spend a bundle. Being an investor isn't cheap, but neither are the goods in the store, where you might spot an encrusted mystery object with a tiny embedded emerald on sale for $19,999.

Food and Beverage Emporiums

Key West residents celebrate all aspects of life, not the least of which is fine food. If you're hoping to take a taste of the Conch Republic home with you, look no farther than the **Blond Giraffe Key Lime Pie Factory** (www. blondgiraffe.com), which offers five different locations in Key West: 802 Duval Street (305/293-7874, 10 A.M.–11 P.M. Mon.–Thurs., 10 A.M.–midnight Fri.–Sun.), 412 Greene Street (305/294-0080, 9 A.M.–10 P.M. Thurs.–Tues., 9 A.M.–9 P.M. Wed.), 511 Greene Street (305/294-0160, 10 A.M.–9 P.M. Mon.–Wed., 10 A.M.–10 P.M. Thurs.–Sun.), 614 Front Street (305/296-2020, 10 A.M.–10 P.M. daily), and 1209 Truman Avenue (305/295-6776, noon–8 P.M. Mon.–Fri., 10 A.M.–8 P.M. Sat.–Sun.). No matter which store you encounter, you're sure to find a tasty selection of key lime products, from key lime juice to key lime meringue pie to pie-on-a-stick—a scrumptious treat that features a frozen slice of key lime pie covered in dark chocolate.

Of course, key lime pie isn't all that Key West has to offer. Founded by Cuban immigrant and cigar maker Fausto Castillo, **Fausto's Food Palace** (www.faustos.com) has served the people of Key West with fine wines, gourmet cheeses, and other delicious vittles since 1926. Today, Fausto's, which has moved and expanded over the years, offers two locations: 522 Fleming Street (305/296-5663, 8 A.M.–8 P.M. Mon.–Sat., 8 A.M.–7 P.M. Sun.) and 1105 White Street (305/294-5221, 8 A.M.–8 P.M. Mon.–Sat., 8 A.M.–7 P.M. Sun.).

Wine lovers might also appreciate **The Key West Winery** (103 Simonton St., 305/292-1717 or 866/880-1717, www.thekeywestwinery.com, 10 A.M.–6 P.M. Mon.–Sat., noon–6 P.M. Sun.), which features unusual key lime, mango, and other tropical wines, plus a variety of key lime condiments. Another option is the **Cork & Stogie** (1218 Duval St., 305/517-6419, www.corkandstogie.com, 10 A.M.–11 P.M. daily), which offers a fine selection of wine and cigars, including those produced by **The Original Key West Cigar Factory** (305/517-7273, www.kwcigarfactory.com), whose history stretches back to the 1880s.

KEY WEST

Sports and Recreation

GOLF

While the Florida Keys archipelago isn't the golf mecca that other parts of the Sunshine State purport to be, that doesn't mean that golfers are without options. Besides private golf courses like those at the Ocean Reef Club in Key Largo and the Sombrero Country Club in Marathon, golfers will find a lovely, palm-studded golf course in the Lower Keys. Encompassing at least a third of Stock Island, the 200-acre **Key West Golf Club** (6450 E. College Rd., 305/294-5232, www.keywestgolf.com, $70–95 w/cart) features an 18-hole, 6,500-yard public golf course, set on the gulf side of U.S. 1, amid dense mangroves, tranquil lakes, varied wildlife, and the ever-present tradewinds. This year-round, full-service facility—incidentally, the southernmost golf course in the continental United States—also offers a driving range ($8 per bucket), rental clubs ($40), bag storage ($125 yearly), locker rentals ($80 yearly), a pro golf shop and clubhouse, golf instruction ($45–55 pp), and private parking.

◖ BIKING

Whether you're an experienced or novice rider, Key West is a lovely, welcoming place to traverse via bicycle. Just remember that you'll have to share the streets with cars and

other vehicles, so take care while you tour the neighborhoods—and wear a proper helmet at all times. Bikes can be rented from several different outfitters, including **Eaton Bikes** (830 Eaton St., 305/294-8188, www.eatonbikes.com, 9 A.M.–6 P.M. Mon.–Sat., 9 A.M.–4 P.M. Sun., $12–45 daily, $40–135 weekly), which offers a range of bicycles, from trikes to mountain bikes to tandems, plus free delivery and pickup service throughout Key West. **The Bike Shop of Key West** (1110 Truman Ave., 305/294-1073, www.thebikeshopkeywest.com, 9 A.M.–6 P.M. Mon.–Sat., 10 A.M.–4 P.M. Sun., $12 daily, $60 weekly, $180 monthly), the oldest in town, also provides a wide array of bicycles, plus accessories, bicycle sales, and a service/repair department. All rentals include locks, lights, baskets, and wide soft seats.

Another helpful source for bicycle rentals is **Paradise Scooter Rentals** (www.paradisescooterrentals.com, 9 A.M.–5 P.M. daily, $8–16 for two hours, $15–30 daily, $75–100 weekly), which offers two locations—112 Fitzpatrick Street (305/292-6441) and 430 Duval Street (305/293-1112)—and provides scooter rentals ($35–48 for three hours, $60–75 daily, $200–300 weekly, plus gas) as well. **Adventure Rentals** (305/293-8883, www.keywest-scooter.com, 9 A.M.–5 P.M. daily, $8

biking past the Harry S. Truman Little White House

per half day, $15 daily, $60 weekly) also provides bicycle rentals at multiple locations—0 Duval Street, 617 Front Street, 135 Simonton Street, and Cruise Ship Pier B—plus scooters ($40–55 for four hours, $50–70 daily), Harley motorcycles (starting from $203 for four hours, $268 daily, $935 weekly), and multi-passenger electric cars ($94–137 per two hours, $159–202 daily).

In addition, **A&M Rentals** (305/896-1921, www.amscooterskeywest.com, 8 A.M.–8 P.M. daily, $15–30 daily, $40–85 weekly) features three spots from which to rent kid-sized bicycles, cruisers, and tandems: 523 Truman Avenue, 513 South Street, and 500 Truman Avenue. You can also rent one-seater scooters ($35 daily, $99 weekly), two-seater scooters ($55–60 daily, $169–199 weekly), and multi-seater electric cars ($150–250 daily, $600–1,050 weekly)—all popular ways to get around town. Free customer pickup and drop-off services are available. Similarly, **Sunshine Key West** (1910 N. Roosevelt Blvd., 305/294-9990, www.sunshinekeywest.com, 8 A.M.–6 P.M. daily) offers bicycles ($10–15 for four hours, $15–20 daily),

single-seat scooters ($45–65 daily), double-seat scooters ($65–100 daily), Harley motorcycles ($200–225 daily), and electric cars ($100–120 for four hours, $150–175 daily) for rent.

Even Stock Island has a bicycle outfitter. Just north of the Hurricane Hole Marina, **Re-Cycle** (5160 Overseas Hwy., Stock Island, 305/292-3336 or 305/294-7433, www.recyclekw.com, 9 A.M.–9 P.M. daily, $12–45 daily, $40–135 weekly) offers a full-service shop and free delivery for its wide array of bicycles, so you'll find no shortage of ways to enjoy a bike ride around this lovely city.

FISHING AND BOATING

Anglers come from all over the world to explore the waters surrounding Key West, a place that boasts year-round fishing opportunities. Every month, several different fish species are in season, and anglers can choose from a variety of fishing locales, including deep harbors, backcountry flats, coral reefs, and offshore waters. No wonder Ernest Hemingway found fishing down here so appealing.

For a small city, Key West sure does have

BOATING SAFETY ADVICE

Throughout the year, boating enthusiasts relish exploring the relatively warm, aquamarine waters of southern Florida. On especially gorgeous days, you're likely to see a ton of powerboats, sailboats, yachts, kayaks, and other vessels in the offshore waters extending from Miami to the Dry Tortugas. With so much action in Florida Bay, the Gulf of Mexico, and the Atlantic Ocean, there's bound to be chaos — unless, of course, boaters obey the following safety guidelines, for the sake of themselves as well as their passengers.

- **Verify Vessel Safety:** Before heading out on the water, make sure that your vessel has been properly maintained, that it meets all local and state regulations, and that your registration numbers are displayed prominently.

- **Equip Yourself:** When planning a boating trip, double-check that you have the following items on board: proper vessel documentation and insurance information, nautical charts, a marine radio, an anchor, a first-aid kit, mounted fire extinguishers, navigation lights, visual distress signals, sound-producing devices, a marine sanitation device, drinking water, extra fuel, and enough personal flotation devices (PFDs) for you and all your passengers.

- **Wear Your Life Jacket:** While it might seem more liberating to ride, fish, or kayak without a personal flotation device (PFD), it's imperative that you actually wear one at all times. Not all boating accidents occur in bad weather and rough seas; many happen in shallow water on deceptively calm, clear days, so be sure to wear a life jacket — even a lightweight, inflatable one — whenever you're on the water.

- **Stay Safe and Sober:** Although many boaters will partake of beer and other alcoholic beverages while out on the water, it's simply not advisable to do so. Wind, noise, motion, and sunlight can intensify the effects of alcohol and prescription medications, making it exceedingly dangerous to operate a vessel while under the influence.

- **Monitor Your Propeller:** Unfortunately, boat propellers are responsible for numerous injuries and fatalities every year. To avoid being yet another statistic, purchase propeller safety devices such as sensors and propeller guards, and don't forget to wear an engine cut-off lanyard at all times — which will ensure that if you and, by extension, your lanyard are thrown from the boat, the engine will immediately power down.

- **Monitor Your Passengers:** To ensure your passengers' safety, never allow them to board or disembark while the engine is running, and insist that they remain seated (in proper seats and not on the bow or transom) while the boat is in motion. In an effort to avoid accidents, assign someone to keep watch around the propeller area whenever other passengers, especially children, are swimming in the surrounding waters. To protect the passengers of other boats, stay alert when operating in congested areas, avoid swimmers altogether, and be aware of boats that are towing skiers or tubers. If someone on your vessel falls overboard, stop immediately, turn the boat around, keep the person in sight as you approach, and shut the engine off before rescuing him or her.

For additional advice or information about boating safety courses, consult **BoatU.S.** (800/336-2628, www.boatus.com) or the **U.S. Coast Guard's Boating Safety Division** (www.uscgboating.org), which aims to prevent fatalities, injuries, and property damage on U.S. waterways by improving the knowledge and skills of recreational boaters.

KEY WEST

an impressive number of marinas, from the **Historic Seaport at the Key West Bight** (305/295-9225, www.seaportrealtorskeywest. com) near Old Town to the **Hurricane Hole Marina** (5130 Overseas Hwy., 305/294-8025, www.hurricaneholekeywest.com) on adjacent Stock Island. In fact, Stock Island features several marinas, including the deep-water **Old Island Harbor** (7009 Shrimp Rd., 305/294-2288, www.oldislandharbor.com) and the nostalgic **Safe Harbour Marina** (6810 Front St., 305/294-9797, www.safeharbourmarina.com). So, if you're planning to bring your own boat in order to fish the abundant backcountry and offshore waters of the Florida Keys, you'll find no shortage of boat slips and marine services in the area.

Most anglers come to Key West with sportfishing charters in mind, and here, too, you'll find no scarcity of options. At the **Key West City Marina at the Garrison Bight** (1801 N. Roosevelt Blvd., 305/809-3981, www. keywestcity.com), for instance, you can hire any number of boats from Charter Boat Row, including offshore fishing services like **Fishcheck Key West Fishing Charters** (Slip #1, 305/295-0484 or 877/434-7459, www. fishcheckcharters.com, $165–750 per half day, $200–900 for six hours, $250–1,100 daily) and **Wild Bill Sportfishing** (305/296-2533 or 305/744-7957, www.wildbillkeywest. com, $150–650 per half day, $185–750 for six hours, $225–900 daily), both of which offer individual seats as well as private charters for up to six passengers. Among the other deepsea fishing vessels docked at the City Marina, you'll spot the *Ramerezi* (305/294-0803 or 305/745-2789, www.ramerezi.com, $600 per half day, $900 daily) and the **Charter Boats Linda D.** (Slips #19 and #20, 305/296-9798 or 800/299-9798, www.charterboatlindad.com, $600–675 per half day, $900–975 daily), all of which are helmed by longtime local fishing captains and can accommodate up to six anglers at a time.

If you're interested in shallow-water flats fishing and saltwater fly-fishing, consider **Almost There! Sportfishing Charters** (5001 5th Ave., Stock Island, 305/295-9444 or 800/795-9448, www.almostthere.net, $450 per half day, $750 daily), Key West's largest charter company, or, as an alternative, **Sting Rea Charters** (305/744-0903, www.flyfishingthekeys.com, $400 per half day, $600 daily), which transports its vessel from Sugarloaf Key to various locations and leads anglers to the waters around the Lower Keys and the Marquesas in search of tarpon, barracuda, permit, and bonefish. For reef and wreck fishing—among other fishing styles—consult **Mean Green Charters** (Murray Marina, 5710 Overseas Hwy., Stock Island, 305/304-1922, www.meangreen-fishing.com, $600 per half day, $850 daily), **Cheerio Charters** (Hurricane Hole Marina, 5130 Overseas Hwy., Stock Island, 305/797-6446, www.cheeriocharters.com, $600 per half day, $900 daily), **Boo-Ya Charters** (Charter Boat Row, 1801 N. Roosevelt Blvd., 305/292-6692, www.booyakeywest.com, $600 per half day, $800 daily), or **Hit 'Em Hard Charters** (305/509-1760, www.hitemhardcharters.com, starting from $275 per half day), through which you'll possibly snag grouper, snapper, amberjack, kingfish, tuna, barracuda, permit, yellowtail, cobia, and sharks. Families may especially appreciate **No Worries Charters** (711 Eisenhower Dr., 305/393-2402, www.noworriescharters.com, $500–600 per half day, $800–900 daily), a company based in the Key West City Marina that allows pets on board; supports catch-and-release fishing, especially for children; and customizes trips to include boating, snorkeling, dolphin-watching, and light-tackle fishing. Rates are often negotiable.

In general, fishing trips are offered daily, and rates, which typically include bait, tackle, ice, and proper fishing licenses, are for the entire trip, not per angler. For most fishing charters, reservations are recommended and deposits are often required. Also, cancellation policies vary between operators, so be sure to check such details well in advance, or else you may lose your deposit.

As an alternative to bringing your own boat or hiring a fishing charter, you can always rent a seaworthy vessel from **Sunset Watersports**

(Hurricane Hole Marina, 5130 Overseas Hwy., Stock Island, 305/294-5500, www.sunsetwatersports.info, 9 A.M.–6 P.M. daily), which offers a range of vessels, from 17-foot fishing boats ($250 per half day, $325 daily) to 24-foot pontoons ($400 per half day, $500 daily). Boats come equipped with GPS, fish and depth finders, live bait wells, and bimini tops.

If you need to rent a fishing rod or stock up on essentials like live bait and cold beer, head first to the Historic Seaport district, where **Key West Bait & Tackle** (241 Margaret St., 305/292-1961, www.keywestbaitandtackle.com, 7 A.M.–7 P.M. daily) features a wide selection of fishing tackle, rods and reels, frozen bait, lures, hooks, sunglasses, towels, and other necessities. Other helpful fishing stores include **The Angling Company** (333 Simonton St., 305/292-6306, www.theanglingcompany.com, 9:30 A.M.–7 P.M. daily) and the **Saltwater Angler** (243 Front St., 305/294-3248 or 800/223-1629, www.saltwaterangler.com, 9 A.M.–8:30 P.M. daily), a one-stop shop for travel gear, fishing apparel, reels, rods, sunglasses, and other fishing accessories.

As a bonus, all three stores can help you arrange fishing charters. Through Key West Bait & Tackle, you can opt for a backcountry flats fishing charter ($375 per half day, $475 for six hours, $550 daily) in search of redfish, snook, permit, and bonefish; a deep-sea fishing excursion ($750 per half day, $950 for six hours, $1,150 daily) to snag tuna, wahoo, mahimahi, and other game fish, and a light-tackle saltwater fishing charter ($500 per half day, $700 for six hours, $800 daily), which allows you to fish for tarpon in the harbor, marlin and swordfish in the offshore waters, and yellowtail near the reefs. Through the Angling Company and Saltwater Angler, you'll also find a slew of professional guides for flats fishing ($400–600 for up to two anglers), offshore fishing ($800–1,200 for up to six anglers), and light-tackle fishing ($700–950 for up to four anglers).

KAYAKING

Paddling enthusiasts will find a number of helpful operators in Key West. Based at the

Hurricane Hole Marina, **Lazy Dog Adventure** (5130 Overseas Hwy., Stock Island, 305/295-9898, www.lazydog.com, 9 A.M.–5 P.M. daily) offers two-hour guided kayaking tours ($35 pp) through backcountry waters and winding mangrove creeks. Lazy Dog also features a four-hour kayaking and snorkeling trip ($60 pp) along the Mosquito Coast, plus single and double kayak rentals ($20 per half day, $30 daily), stand-up paddleboard rentals ($25 each), paddleboard tours ($40 pp), and paddleboard yoga ($20 pp). Reservations are required, and complimentary pickups are available. Area maps are provided with all rentals.

Similarly, **Blue Planet Kayak** (305/294-8087 or 800/979-3370, www.blue-planet-kayak.com) offers guided kayaking trips into the fascinating backcountry, such as the 2.5-hour Boca Chica Tour (10 A.M. and 12:40 P.M. in winter, 10 A.M. and 3 P.M. in summer, $50 pp) and the 2.5-hour Romantic Sunset & Moonlight Tour ($50 pp). Beginners and families are welcome, though advance reservations are required. Since tour guides will only lead a maximum of 10 passengers on each personalized trip, slots can fill up quickly. Complimentary transportation is available for all tour customers. In addition, Blue Planet provides rentals for sit-in single kayaks ($30 per half day, $40 daily), tandem kayaks ($40 per half day, $50 daily), and fishing kayaks ($30 per half day, $40 daily). For the fishing kayaks, only charts, anchors, and advice are included; anglers must bring their own tackle.

For an alternative experience, consider **Java Cat Charters** (305/294-7245, www.keywestkayak.com), situated in the Historic Seaport at the Key West Bight, behind the Turtle Kraals Restaurant and Bar at the end of Margaret Street. As part of a 4.5-hour ecotour ($95 adults, $75 children under 13) that includes sailing and coral reef snorkeling, Java Cat offers kayaking trips amid seagrass beds and winding mangrove creeks, where you'll get an up-close look at tropical fish, aquatic birds, sea turtles, spotted eagle rays, dolphins, crabs, sponges, and other marine wonders. Tours occur twice daily

(9 A.M.–1:30 P.M. year-round, 2 P.M.–sunset in winter, 3:30 P.M.–sunset in summer) and allow a maximum of six passengers. Double-seat, sit-on-top kayaks are provided.

Based out of The Westin Key West Resort & Marina at 245 Front Street, **Danger Charters** (305/304-7999 or 305/296-3272, www.dangercharters.com) operates daily sailing excursions amid pristine coral reefs, deserted mangrove islands, and sponge gardens in the backcountry. These half-day (9 A.M. and 2 P.M. in winter, 9:30 A.M. and 3:30 P.M. in summer, $75 pp) and full-day trips (9:30 A.M. in winter, 10 A.M. in summer, $90 pp) also feature kayaking and snorkeling and include snacks, beverages, and gear.

DIVING AND SNORKELING

Like the rest of the Florida Keys, Key West is surrounded by thriving coral reefs and fascinating shipwrecks. On your own, you can easily dive and snorkel amid the tropical fish and varied coral formations in the bountiful waters near **Fort Zachary Taylor Historic State Park** (western end of Southard St., 305/292-6713 or 305/295-0037, www.floridastateparks.org/forttaylor or www.fortzacharytaylor.com,

8 A.M.–sunset daily, $6 vehicles w/2–8 passengers plus $0.50 pp, $4.50 motorcycles and single-occupant vehicles, $2.50 pedestrians, bikers, and extra passengers) and the **Dry Tortugas National Park** (305/242-7700, www.nps.gov/drto/index.htm or www.dry.tortugas.national-park.com, sunrise–sunset daily, $5 weekly), roughly 68 miles to the west. Still, many of the underwater attractions this far south are only accessible via professional diving charters.

Besides offering scuba-diving instruction and equipment rentals, several local companies, such as **Southpoint Divers** (610 Front St., 800/891-3483, www.southpointdivers.com, 8:30 A.M.–noon and 1:30–5 P.M. daily), provide trips to two curious wrecks: the 187-foot **Cayman Salvage Master** ($85–120 pp) and the 522-foot **USNS General Hoyt S. Vandenberg** ($115–150 pp), a former troop transport ship during World War II, later the backdrop for the film *Virus,* and now the foundation for an artificial reef. Sunk in May 2009, the ship has since become a habitat for varied fish and offers a unique look at the developing stages of coral growth. Guides are required for all open water dives on the *Vandenberg.*

© HAIG JACOBS/FLORIDA KEYS NEWS BUREAU/HO

Divers explore the *Vandenberg,* an artificial reef near Key West.

Varied gear—including tanks, weights, regulators, wetsuits, and nitrox bottles—is available through Southpoint Divers, and classes range from a refresher course ($75 pp) to a PADI dive master course ($895 pp).

In addition to leading excursions to the Cayman and *Vandenberg* wrecks, the **Subtropic Dive Center** (1605 N. Roosevelt Blvd., 305/296-9914 or 800/853-3483, www.subtropic.com, 8:30 A.M.–12:30 P.M. and 1:30–6 P.M. daily, $80–150 pp) and **Dive Key West** (3128 N. Roosevelt Blvd., 305/296-3823 or 800/426-0707, www.divekeywest.com, 9 A.M.–1 P.M. and 2–6 P.M. daily, $69–164 pp)—one of the oldest and largest full-service diving facilities in the Florida Keys—each offer trips to other wrecks, such as **Joe's Tug**, a storm-battered vessel that sits in 65 feet of water and is now home to assorted coral formations and nosy eels.

Additional diving resources include **Lost Reef Adventures** (261 Margaret St., 305/296-9737 or 800/952-2749, www.lostreefadventures.com, 9 A.M.–1 P.M. and 1:30–5:30 P.M. daily, $65–170 pp) and the **Captain's Corner Dive Center** (125 Ann St., 305/296-8865 or 305/304-0437, 9:30 A.M.–1:15 P.M. and 2–5:30 P.M. daily, $65–130 pp), whose 60-foot, aluminum diving vessel was used in the film *Licence to Kill.* Some of these operators even offer night dives as well as trips to reef formations like the deep, spur-and-groove networks of **Sand Key, Rock Key,** the **Eastern Dry Rocks,** and the **Western Sambo Ecological Reserve.** Other curious habitats include the **Kedge Ledge,** a patch reef that contains coral-encrusted anchors from 18th-century schooners, and the **Ten-Fathom Ledge,** a series of coral ledges, caves, and outcroppings that nurture grouper, lobster, sharks, and eagle rays.

Like the rest of the Keys, Key West appeals to snorkelers, too. In fact, all of the aforementioned diving operators also cater to snorkelers, offering at least two trips daily ($40–50 adults, $35–45 children), with rental equipment usually included in the price. In addition, **Sebago Watersports** (201 William St., 305/292-4768 or 800/507-9955, www.keywestsebago.com,

9 A.M.–12:30 P.M. and 1–4:30 P.M. daily, $49 adults, $25 children), **Sunset Watersports** (201 William St., 305/296-2554, www.sunsetwatersportskeywest.com, 9 A.M. and 1 P.M. daily mid-Mar.–mid-Sept., 11 A.M. and 3:30 P.M. daily mid-Sept.–mid-Mar., $30–35 pp), and **Fury Water Adventures** (1 Duval St. and 245 Front St., 305/294-8899 or 877/994-8898, www.furycat.com, 9:30 A.M.–12:30 P.M. and 1–4 P.M. daily, $40–45 adults, $20–25.50 children 6–12) offer snorkeling trips, among other water-related activities. Instruction and necessary equipment are provided with all trips.

Based out of the Historic Seaport at the Key West Bight, **Sunny Days** (201 William St., 305/296-5556 or 800/236-7937, www.sunnydayskeywest.com) features an array of high-speed catamarans for varied snorkeling trips, including the *Fast Cat* (305/296-5556 or 800/236-7937, 8 A.M.–5 P.M. daily, $145 adults, $135 students, military personnel, and seniors 62 and over, $100 children 3–16, children under 3 free, plus $5 park entrance fee for guests 17 and over), which can whisk you to the waters surrounding Dry Tortugas National Park, and the *Island Express* (305/292-6100, 10 A.M. daily, $85 adults, $50 children 3–14, children under 3 free), which boasts the only Looe Key Reef trip from Key West. Other snorkeling catamarans include the *Reef Express* (305/294-7755, 9 A.M. and 1 P.M. daily, $38 adults, $22 children), the *Cruzan Cat* (305/295-7601, 11 A.M. and 3 P.M. daily, $38 adults, $22 children), and the *Dolphin Cat* (305/293-5144, 9 A.M. and 1 P.M. daily, $55 adults, $45 children), which, as the name implies, features a glimpse of native dolphins in the backcountry. All boats are docked near the intersection of Greene and Elizabeth Streets.

Two other noteworthy vessels, the *Echo* catamaran (Historic Seaport at the Key West Bight, 305/292-5044, www.dolphinecho.com, 9 A.M.–1 P.M. and 1:30–5:30 P.M. daily, $74–79 pp) and the smaller *Amazing Grace* (6000 Peninsula Ave., Stock Island, 305/294-5026 or 800/593-6574, www.wildaboutdolphins.com, 8 A.M.–noon and 1–5 P.M. daily, $85 pp), combine snorkeling trips with wild dolphin encounters. Both offer private charters as well.

You might also want to visit **Snuba of Key West** (Key West City Marina at the Garrison Bight, 1801 N. Roosevelt Blvd., 305/292-4616, www.snubakeywest.com, 9 A.M., 1 P.M., and 4 P.M. daily, $99 adults, $79 children 8–12, $44 riders or non-Snuba snorkelers), where you can try an unusual form of deep-water snorkeling that requires no dive certification. On these personal guided tours amid the offshore coral reefs, you'll be able to breathe easily underwater without wearing heavy, restrictive diving gear. Just note that children must be at least 8 years old to try Snuba snorkeling.

Though nearly all of the aforementioned diving and snorkeling outfitters should have the equipment and accessories that you need, you can also make a quick stop at **Divers Direct** (535 Greene St., 305/293-5122, www.diversdirect.com, 9 A.M.–7 P.M. Mon.–Thurs., 9 A.M.–8 P.M. Fri.–Sat., 10 A.M.–7 P.M. Sun.), a well-stocked scuba-diving retailer, for any last-minute items.

OTHER OUTDOOR ACTIVITIES

For thrills of a different kind, consider heading to the Sunset Marina, where you can board the year-round **White Knuckle Thrill Boat Ride** (5555 College Rd., Stock Island, 305/797-0459, www.whiteknucklethrillboatride.com, $59 pp), an exhilarating, wet-and-wild jet boat experience that features twists, slides, and 360-degree spins in the waters near Key West. If you'd prefer to be in control of your own white-knuckle experience, feel free to rent a Jet Ski, Sea-Doo, or WaveRunner from the following outfitters: **Barefoot Billy's** (The Reach Resort, 1435 Simonton St., 305/849-0815, www.barefootbillys.com, 9 A.M.–6 P.M. daily, $70 per half hour, $100 hourly), **Island Water Sports** (The Westin Key West Resort & Marina, 245 Front St., 305/296-1754, www.islandwatersports.us, 9 A.M.–sunset daily, $75 per half hour, $100 hourly, $10 per extra passenger), or **Key West Water Tours** (Hurricane Hole Marina, 5106 Overseas Hwy., Stock Island, 305/294-6790, www.keywestwatertours.com, $110–130

hourly). In addition, all three operators offer guided, two-hour tours around the island of Key West every day. Billy's tour times include 10 A.M., noon, 2 P.M., and 4 P.M. ($130–150 pp), while Island Water Sports leaves at 9:30 A.M., 11:30 A.M., 1:30 P.M., 3:30 P.M., and 5:30 P.M. ($125 pp, $10 per extra passenger). Key West Water Tours, meanwhile, leads tours at 10 A.M., 12:30 P.M., 3:30 P.M., and sunset ($135–155 pp).

Now, if you'd rather be *above* the water, you can always opt for a parasailing adventure. Three such companies operate out of the Historic Seaport at the Key West Bight: **ParaWest Parasailing** (700 Front St., 305/292-5199, www.parawestparasailing.com, 9 A.M.–6 P.M. daily, $30 pp for morning rides, $40 single riders, $75 double riders, $105 triple riders), **Sebago Watersports** (201 William St., 305/292-4768 or 800/507-9955, www.keywestsebago.com, 9 A.M.–4 P.M. daily in winter, 10 A.M.–5 P.M. daily in summer, $55 single riders, $85 tandem riders), and **Sunset Watersports** (201 William St., 305/296-2554, www.sunsetwatersportskeywest.com, 9 A.M.–6 P.M. daily, $39 pp), which also operates out of Smathers Beach. Another operator, **Fury Water Adventures** (305/294-8899 or 877/994-8898, www.furycat.com, 9 A.M.–6 P.M. daily, $40 pp), offers parasailing adventures from two locations: the Pier House Resort (1 Duval St.) and The Westin Key West Resort & Marina (245 Front St.). All four offer solo and tandem rides, and all promise smooth take-offs, gentle landings, breathtaking aerial views, and safe experiences. No matter which you choose, try to book your trip in advance, especially during the peak winter months.

For a combination of such activities, consider opting for Fury's **Ultimate Adventure** (10 A.M.–4 P.M. daily, $139 adults, $70 children 6–12, children under 6 free), an all-inclusive experience that features kayaking, reef snorkeling, Jet Skiing, parasailing, rock climbing, and access to a water trampoline, plus a complimentary meal and unlimited beverages. Sunset Watersports offers a similar package, the **"Do It All!" Party Boat Adventure**

(10 A.M.–4 P.M. daily, $129 adults, $59 seniors and children under 10), which includes snorkeling, kayaking, rafting, sunfish sailing, kneeboarding, waterskiing, windsurfing, and access to various water sports, plus a grilled lunch. Not to be outdone, Sebago Watersports features its own version of this all-day fun with the **Power Adventure** (10 A.M.–4 P.M. daily, $149 adults, $75 children), which encompasses reef snorkeling, a guided kayaking tour, parasailing, and access to personal watercraft, water trampolines, and other water sports—plus free meals, snacks, and beverages. For all three adventures, booking online will typically save you a bit of money.

◖ SPAS AND YOGA

What better way to relax after a hard day of golfing, biking, fishing, kayaking, diving, or parasailing than to experience a soothing massage treatment or beachside yoga lesson. Fortunately, Key West provides an array of such rejuvenating experiences.

Several area resorts, in fact, feature on-site spas. At the **Pier House Resort** (1 Duval St., 305/296-4600, www.pierhouse.com), the full-service **Caribbean Spa** (8:30 A.M.–7 P.M. daily) offers manicures ($35 pp), pedicures ($40–70 pp), restorative facials ($65–165 pp), tanning services ($60–140 pp), and moisturizing body treatments ($115 pp), such as the full-body detoxifying mud wrap. Several massages ($70–170 pp) are also available, including the 80-minute hot stone therapy massage and the 80-minute, head-to-toe Caribbean Spa Coma, which proves to be as mind-numbing as it sounds. Guests should reserve appointments in advance and provide at least four hours' notice for any cancellations.

Meanwhile, the adjacent **Ocean Key Resort & Spa** (0 Duval St., 305/296-7701 or 800/328-9815, www.oceankey.com) features the waterfront **SpaTerre** (305/295-7017, 9 A.M.–6 P.M. daily), which provides day spa services as well as spa vacation packages. At SpaTerre, men and women alike can experience various massages ($65–175 pp), refreshing body treatments ($70–110 pp), such as the Caribbean Seaweed Body Mask, and incredible Balinese and Thai spa rituals ($165–230 pp), such as the Javanese Royal Spa Treatment, which includes a Balinese spa massage, an herbal exfoliation, a cool yogurt splash, an aromatic shower, and a tub soaking amid rose petals and tropical fragrances. Face and body depilation (rates vary), facials ($60–150 pp), manicures ($20–50 pp), and pedicures ($20–100 pp), including the ultra-special Key Lime Margarita Pedicure, are also available. An adjacent fitness center even offers yoga classes and a stretching patio.

At **Southernmost on the Beach** (508 South St., 305/296-6577, www.southernmostresorts.com), the full-service **Paradise Day Spa** (305/879-7352, www.keywestparadisedayspa.com, 9 A.M.–9 P.M. daily) offers an array of salon and spa services. Here, hotel guests as well as nonguests can enjoy various manicures ($40–60 pp), pedicures ($50–100 pp), facials ($80–150 pp), massages ($50–130 pp), and body wraps and treatments ($100–150 pp). Other salon services, such as waxing ($20–100 pp) and electrolysis ($30–300 pp), are also available. As with most spas, appointment cancellations must be made 24 hours in advance.

Another topnotch spa can be found at the **Casa Marina Resort** (1500 Reynolds St., 888/303-5717, www.casamarinaresort.com). Only open to hotel guests at the Casa Marina and its sister facility, **The Reach Resort** (1435 Simonton St., 888/318-4316, www.reachresort.com), the **Spa al Mare** presents facials ($100–160 pp), massages ($60–180 pp), aromatherapy treatments ($100–210 pp), and yoga classes ($20–80 pp). Spa packages are also available. Note that all massages are offered either in the studio or on the beach, and bear in mind that guests must notify the spa 24 hours in advance to cancel an appointment.

Beyond luxurious resorts, Key West also contains several stand-alone day spas. The locally owned **Prana Spa** (625 Whitehead St., 305/295-0100, www.pranaspakeywest.com, 11 A.M.–7 P.M. Tues.–Sat., 11 A.M.–5 P.M. Sun.), for instance, lures both residents and tourists with its clinical skin care ($55–140 pp), exotic spa treatments ($25–300 pp), and massage therapy ($50–160 pp). Specialties include the Thai yoga massage and the Prana Decadence, a complete three-hour experience that includes a body polishing scrub, a 75-minute body massage, an ultimate foot treatment, a 60-minute ultimate rejuvenation facial, and a shirodhara warm oil hair and scalp treatment.

White Street Healing Arts (1217 White St., 305/393-4102, 305/296-5997, or 305/304-5891, www.whitestreethealingarts.com, by appt.) is a holistic professional group that provides massage therapy in addition to acupuncture, chiropractic and Chinese medicine, and intuitive healing. Offerings include Swedish, deep tissue, aromatherapy, and reflexology massage ($90 hourly, $110 per 75 minutes, $130 per 90 minutes), plus hot stone massage ($165 per 90 minutes) and couples massage ($180 hourly, $220 per 75 minutes, $260 per 90 minutes). The licensed massage therapists here are often willing to bring their skills directly to you, but a 24-hour cancellation policy is in effect for all appointments, whether inside or outside the office.

In New Town, on the eastern part of the island, the **All About You Day Spa & Wellness Centre** (1712–1714 N. Roosevelt Blvd., 305/292-0818 or 888/710-4300, www.allaboutyoukw.com, by appt. Mon., 7 A.M.–6 P.M. Tues.–Sat.) features an assortment of salon and spa services, including perms, glycolic peels, waxing, and permanent make-up. As at other Key West day spas, you can opt for manicures ($20–35 pp), pedicures ($30–65 pp), facials ($45–100 pp), body wraps ($75–150 pp), and massage treatments ($50–140 pp). Two favorites are the 90-minute hot rock massage and the 60-minute monkey-bar massage, during which a licensed massage therapist uses suspended parallel bars to perform a tabletop Shiatsu massage. Farther east, the **Solar Spa of Key West** (2824 N. Roosevelt Blvd., 305/292-6080, www.solarspaofkeywest.com, 10 A.M.–7 P.M. Mon.–Sat.), a day spa and tanning salon, offers standard services, such as hair care (rates vary), manicures ($25 pp), pedicures ($35 pp), facials ($75 pp), body treatments ($120 pp), and massages ($80–100 pp).

For relaxation of a more active variety, consider **Yoga on the Beach** (305/296-7352, www.yogaonbeach.com), which offers daily, year-round classes on the beach, either at the Fort Zachary Taylor Historic State Park or Southernmost on the Beach property. Classes at the state park, which can range between the hourlong Yoga Express and the 90-minute Yoga for Every Body, typically cost $15 per person and include the park entrance fee. Meanwhile, classes at Southernmost on the Beach, such as the hourlong Yin Yoga, typically cost $10 for hotel guests and $15 for drop-in clients. Mats, blankets, and props are provided for all classes, and instructors will make every effort to accommodate those with disabilities.

Accommodations

Key West has, by far, the greatest assortment of lodging options in the Florida Keys, from intimate bed-and-breakfasts to sprawling resorts—only some of which are listed here. Organizations like the **Key West Innkeepers Association (KWIA)** (316A Simonton St., 305/295-1334 or 800/492-1911, www.keywestinns.com) or **The Lodging Association of the Florida Keys and Key West** (3152 Northside Dr., Ste. 101, 305/296-4959, www.keyslodging.org) can help you choose the place that's right for you. No matter where you decide to stay, reservations are highly recommended, especially on weekends during the peak season (Dec.–Apr.).

UNDER $200

Conceived to honor the many literary masters who lived and worked in Key West, the **Authors Key West Guesthouse** (725 White

St., 305/294-7381 or 800/898-6909, www. authorskeywest.com, $100–135 d) provides a compound of Conch-style houses, suites, and rooms. Typically named after famous writers or artists, the accommodations range from the John James Audubon room, which contains a queen-sized bed and a private bath, to the Ernest Hemingway cottage, which offers, in addition to a queen-sized bed, a trundle bed, a living room, and a full kitchen. Whether you choose to swim in the heated pool or sip an evening cocktail in the garden, the Authors Guesthouse may be the perfect place to start that novel you've always wanted to write.

Nestled amid the varied lodgings on Fleming, the ecofriendly (**Eden House** (1015 Fleming St., 305/296-6868 or 800/533-5397, www.edenhouse.com, $100–330 d) offers the ideal setting for a wide variety of visitors, from couples on a romantic getaway to large family reunions. Composed of an art deco–style main building and several renovated Conch-style houses, the Eden House seems a world away from Duval Street, though it lies within

walking distance of the busy thoroughfare. While not technically a spa resort, this picturesque place—which once served as the backdrop for *CrissCross,* a film starring Goldie Hawn—certainly has the ambience of one. Surrounded by the lovely buildings, the main focus of the complex is the freshwater pool area, where you'll find shady palm trees, gurgling fountains, numerous tables and chairs, a peaceful gazebo, a sun deck, and a six-person hot tub. Although the rooms and suites vary in size and amenities—from a cozy spot beside the pool to a two-level house with a hot tub of its own—all guests can enjoy the hotel's varied features, including a comfortable library area, relaxing hammocks, wireless Internet access, beach towels that can be used off-site, a daily happy hour beside the pool, a 24-hour staff, and complimentary coffee and tea in the lobby. As a bonus, the Eden House will let you store your luggage even after you check out, so that you can savor a few more hours in Key West.

The motto at the **Garden House Bed & Breakfast** (329 Elizabeth St., 305/296-5368 or

a relaxing porch swing at the Eden House

800/695-6453, www.key-west-florida-bed-break-fast.com, $149–199 d) encourages guests to "leave the grumpy attitude at home." That's pretty easy to do when you spot the sumptuous grounds, which include an upper-level sun deck as well as a heated pool with spa jets and a cascading waterfall, all surrounded by lush tropical gardens. There are 10 uniquely decorated rooms on-site—ranging from the Gecko Grotto, with its queen-sized bed and private bath, to the Writer's King, with its Tiffany-style reading lamps and king-sized bed. Not far away, in a quiet area of Old Town, the **Rose Lane Villas** (522–524 Rose Ln., 305/292-2170, www.roselanevillas.com, one-bedroom villas $159–269 d, two-bedroom and three-bedroom villas $402–666) provide a tempting haven for those who want to stay within walking distance of the action. Though the one-bedroom, two-bedroom, and three-bedroom villas vary in size, each has a full kitchen, cable television, free wireless Internet access, and an allotted parking space. Before hitting the town, take an early morning swim in the beautiful pool, accented by a stunning mural of lush gardens. After a long day exploring Key West, finish your evening with a cocktail on one of the peaceful porches or balconies and listen to the murmur of Old Town fading into the night.

Between the grand two-story Victorian mansion and the poolside cabana, the **Pilot House Guest House** (414 Simonton St., 305/293-6600 or 800/648-3780, www.pilot-housekeywest.com, $115–190 d) encompasses a variety of accommodations to suit every traveler's needs, ranging from a standard room with a private bathroom, a kitchenette, a queen-sized bed, and a balcony to the King Cabana II, which contains a king-sized bed, a kitchenette, a Jacuzzi tub, and a private bathroom with a European shower. The grounds also feature a beautiful pool and a semi-private spa, both of which are clothing-optional. The **Mango Tree Inn** (603 Southard St., 305/293-1177, www.mangotree-inn.com, $129–189 d), constructed in 1858, is a gorgeous example of Old Town's historic architecture. Inside, the inn offers comfortable rooms, some with two bedrooms and full kitchens. Relax with a swim in the

pool, surrounded by lush gardens and tall palm trees, or chat with the resident celebrities: Jade the parrot and Leilani the cockatoo.

Just two blocks off Duval, **The Paradise Inn** (819 Simonton St., 305/293-8007 or 800/888-9648, www.theparadiseinn.com, $169–199 d) provides elegant suites, ranging from a mini-suite with two queen-sized beds to the Royal Poinciana Suite, featuring two bedrooms, two bathrooms with Jacuzzi tubs, and a wraparound porch. The grounds, teeming with tropical flora, include a Jacuzzi and a fountain-fed pool. What was once, in the 1920s, a bordello and gambling spot has become a simple and affordable place to stay in Key West. At the **Angelina Guest House** (302 Angela St., 305/294-4480 or 888/303-4480, www.angelinaguesthouse.com, $99–139 d), "simple" means having no phones or televisions, allowing you to truly escape your daily existence. Only two blocks from the hustle and bustle of Duval, you'll find infinite tranquility in the verdant garden and heated lagoon-style pool. Here, the accommodations vary from having a shared bathroom and full-sized beds to having a king-sized bed, a private bathroom, and a refrigerator.

The **Truman Hotel** (611 Truman Ave., 305/296-6700 or 866/487-8626, www.trumanhotel.com, $169–199 d), one of the newer boutique hotels in town, prides itself on being "South Beach hip with a Key West flair." With accommodations that range from a standard room to a suite featuring two king-sized beds and a living room, each selection contains swanky touches like zebra-striped rugs, leather chairs, and modern lighting. As a bonus, after a long day wandering around Key West, you'll relish a dip in the combination pool and spa.

Among the more reasonable offerings in the Old Town section of Key West is the historic ◖ **Chelsea House Pool and Gardens** (709 Truman Ave., 305/296-2211 or 800/845-8859, www.historickeywestinns.com, $170–220 d), which consists of two grand Victorian mansions on an acre of lush tropical gardens. Dating from 1888 and 1906, these two former homes now contain a variety of comfortable guest rooms and suites, with amenities like private bathrooms, cable television, and air conditioning. Other features include a continental breakfast, a heated pool, on-site parking, free wireless Internet access in the courtyard, and proximity to Key West's most popular restaurants and attractions. With advance arrangements, you might also be able to bring your pet during your stay. After all, the Chelsea House was named for a cat (a British shorthair named Chelsea) that lived here in the 1970s.

The adults-only **Azul Key West** (907 Truman Ave., 305/296-5152, www.azulhotels. us, $159–219 d) features 11 rooms and suites surrounding a beautiful freshwater pool. Each room includes a king-sized bed, a flat-screen television, and wireless Internet access. The suites, meanwhile, range from those possessing shared balconies, with views of the pool or Truman Avenue, to the Aria Suite, situated at treetop level and offering stunning views of the entire area. As an alternative, head toward the quieter end of Duval, where the **La Te Da Hotel** (1125 Duval St., 305/296-6706 or 877/528-3320, www.lateda.com, $100–200 d) features plenty of activities to distract you from the "Duval crawl." Two bars, a restaurant, and a cabaret only add to the charm of this beautiful hotel. The accommodations here range from standard rooms with two queen-sized beds, a refrigerator, and cable television to luxury rooms featuring extra touches like British Colonial–style furnishings and 800-thread-count linens.

The **El Patio Motel** (800 Washington St., 305/296-6531 or 866/533-5189, www.elpatiomotel.com, $96–169 d), a 30-room motel designed in the art deco style, features a lush, tropical garden, a serene fountain, and a freshwater swimming pool. Accommodations here range from a basic room with a refrigerator to an apartment with a full kitchen. In addition, limited wireless Internet access is available, depending on your location on the property.

$200-300

Given that it's also a respected museum, **The Curry Mansion Inn** (511 Caroline St.,

305/294-5349 or 800/253-3466, www.currymansion.com, $195–240 d) is surprisingly accommodating to its guests. The historic, 22-room property contains various types of lodgings, from standard deluxe bedrooms with king-sized beds and private bathrooms to magnificent master suites featuring large balconies, comfortable sitting rooms, and cable television. Situated within the bustling heart of Old Town, the Curry still allows you a modicum of peace and quiet, whether you're dining a full breakfast, enjoying an afternoon cocktail party, swimming in the on-site pool, or simply relaxing on the grounds.

Northeast of the Curry, the **Cypress House** (601 Caroline St., 305/294-6969, www.cypresshousekw.com, $155–325 d) offers comfortable, bed-and-breakfast accommodations in a historic, Conch-style building that was erected in 1888. Guests can expect spacious, high-ceilinged rooms with air conditioning, ceiling fans, cable television, refrigerators, bathrobes, and complimentary, high-speed wireless Internet access. Other amenities on this locked, gated property include lush tropical gardens, a heated swimming pool, bike rentals, parking ($10 daily), a continental breakfast buffet (8–11 A.M. daily), and complimentary cocktails (6–7 P.M. daily). Note that minimum stay requirements vary seasonally, and guests must be at least 16 years of age.

Two blocks south of the Cypress House, the white, casually elegant, Conch-style ◖ **Marquesa Hotel and Marquesa Cottages** (600 Fleming St., 305/292-1919, www.marquesa.com or www.keywestmarquesacottages. com, $190–345 d), originally built in 1884, provide luxuriously furnished hotel rooms and private, well-equipped cottages. All chambers are clean, comfortable, and airy, with tropical-style touches like wooden floors, ceiling fans, and vibrant paintings. Despite its proximity to Duval Street, the Marquesa still offers enough of a buffer to make it feel as though you've found a quiet little nook of your own. That's especially true in the well-landscaped pool and garden area, which features a waterfall, two freshwater pools, and numerous chaise lounges

KEY WEST

and shaded tables. Other property amenities include wireless Internet access and an up-scale restaurant, open to hotel guests as well as the public. Farther south, **The Mermaid & The Alligator Bed & Breakfast** (729 Truman Ave., 305/294-1894 or 800/773-1894, www.kwmermaid.com, $148–318 d) truly aspires to be "your home in Key West." This beautiful 1904 Victorian-style home offers eight unique rooms in the main house in addition to a Conch-style cottage on the grounds. Amenities include a full complimentary breakfast, a lush garden, and a heated pool, featuring built-in benches and whirlpool jets.

The stylish **Santa Maria Suites** (1401 Simonton St., 305/296-5678 or 866/726-8259, www.santamariasuites.com, $249–279 d) fea-ture accommodations with private balconies and terraces. Only a block from the Atlantic Ocean and not far from Duval, this lovely hotel provides an escape from the craziness of Key West. The accommodations vary from stan-dard one-bedroom suites to luxury two-bed-room, bilevel suites. Other amenities include flat-screen televisions and two heated, garden-enclosed swimming pools.

Closer to the ocean, the magnificent, Spanish-style ◖ **Casa Marina Resort** (1500 Reynolds St., 305/296-3535 or 888/303-5717, www.casamarinaresort.com, $239–279 d) beckons an upscale clientele with its cream-colored walls, red roof tiles, and arched en-tryways. Built in 1920 and now part of the Waldorf Astoria Collection, the largest resort in Key West comprises a wide array of elegantly furnished rooms and suites, from the Island Vista, with two double beds, to the Ocean Vista two-bedroom suite, featuring 900 square feet of space. All accommodations include a mini-refrigerator and wireless Internet ac-cess. This grand resort also encompasses two enormous pools, a beautiful, 1,100-foot beach with hammocks strung between palm trees, the Sun-Sun Beach Bar & Grill, and the Spa al Mare, where you can opt for massages, facials, aromatherapy, or a yoga session. In addition, guests can enjoy live entertainment in the on-site Rambler Lounge and savor a delicious steak

at the Strip House, located at the hotel's sister property, The Reach Resort.

Situated on seven waterfront acres on the eastern side of the island, the **Key West Marriott Beachside Hotel** (3841 N. Roosevelt Blvd., 305/296-8100 or 800/546-0885, www.beachsidekeywest.com, $179–349 d) features luxurious accommodations, a lush tropical garden, a waterfront swimming pool, a sandy tanning beach, complete spa services, and im-mediate access to the on-site Tavern N Town Restaurant. In addition, all guests can enjoy complimentary high-speed Internet service and flat-panel LCD televisions with cable.

OVER $300

Located on the gulf side of the island, ◖ **The Westin Key West Resort & Marina** (245 Front St., 305/294-4000 or 800/937-8461, www.westinkeywestresort.com, $450–575 d) provides splendid accommodations just steps from Mallory Square and the Custom House. This spacious resort features 178 luxurious guest rooms and suites, all of which include specially designed beds and showers, compli-mentary wireless Internet access, cable tele-vision, air conditioning, and 24-hour room service, among other amenities. Some rooms and suites include flat-screen televisions, vaulted ceilings, Jacuzzi tubs, balconies, patios, and terrific views of the ocean, pool, courtyard, or gardens. Five hundred yards off the coast, the Westin also boasts the **Sunset Key Guest Cottages** (305/292-5300 or 888/477-7786, www.westinsunsetkeycottages.com, $740–1,500), a sophisticated, seven-acre resort on Sunset Key, a 27-acre residential island, where cars are not permitted. Offering seclusion from the hustle and bustle of Key West, the Sunset Key Guest Cottages contain one, two, three, or four bedrooms and can only be reached via ferry. Whether you choose to stay in Key West or on Sunset Key, you'll have access to all the amenities that the Westin resort offers, includ-ing the on-site marina, various water sports, a 24-hour fitness room and massage studio, a heated, palm-shaded outdoor pool, and sev-eral dining options, such as Bistro 245 and

Latitudes. In addition, the Westin's Sunset Deck is an ideal spot from which to watch a famous Key West sunset.

Also within walking distance of Mallory Square, the ◖ **Ocean Key Resort & Spa** (0 Duval St., 800/328-9815, www.oceankey.com, $279–411 d) provides fantastic sunset views and easy access to the heart of Key West. The luxurious, tropical-style accommodations range from a 600-square-foot junior suite, with a king-sized bed, a spacious living room, plasma television, and a private balcony, to a two-bedroom, 1,200-square-foot suite that's purportedly the largest suite on the island. On-site amenities include a heated outdoor pool, water-sports rentals, sailing and fishing trips arranged through the marina, unbelievable body treatments at SpaTerre, and the waterfront Hot Tin Roof restaurant. Situated across the street, the **Pier House Resort and Caribbean Spa** (1 Duval St., 305/296-4600 or 800/723-2791, www.pierhouse.com, $299–480 d) has been serving guests since 1979. Known as the first true resort on the island, Pier House encompasses a private beach, a heated outdoor pool, and a private dock for charter pickups. While here, relax with a massage at the resort's world-class spa, savor a meal at the HarbourView Cafe or the Beach Bar and Grille, or consider deals like the Spa Honeymoon Package, which includes breakfast and a trip to the spa.

You'll be hard-pressed to miss the **Southernmost Hotel Collection** (305/296-6577 or 800/354-4455, www.southern-mostresorts.com, $300–435 d), sandwiched between Duval, United, and Simonton Streets. Each of the four hotels here—the airy, 127-room **Southernmost Hotel** (1319 Duval St.), the tropical, 123-room **Southernmost on the Beach** (508 South St.), and the elegant, side-by-side, Victorian-style boutique hotels, the 11-room **La Mer Hotel** and the eight-room **Dewey House** (508 South St.)—offers sophisticated accommodations, sometimes with stunning ocean views. No matter which property you choose, you'll be able to relax on the private

© DANIEL MARTONE

Four properties comprise the Southernmost Hotel Collection, including Southernmost on the Beach.

KEY WEST

beach, enjoy a dip in one of three pools, work out in the on-site fitness center, relish a delicious meal at the Southernmost Beach Café, sip cocktails at the Southernmost Tiki Bar, or, of course, venture onto nearby Duval. Other amenities include free parking, lush gardens, and complimentary wireless Internet access.

Situated near the quieter end of Duval and built as a private residence in 1896, the colorful, Victorian-style **(Southernmost House** (1400 Duval St., 305/296-3141, www.southernmosthouse.com, $280–385 d) has seen its share of dignitaries, from Presidents Truman, Nixon, Kennedy, Eisenhower, and Carter to Key West fixtures like Ernest Hemingway. The accommodations here vary from the Southernmost Point Room, with its private balcony overlooking the Atlantic Ocean, to the Royal Suite, one of Key West's most favored suites, featuring a separate sitting parlor, stunning ocean and island views, and a four-post, king-sized bed. While staying at the Southernmost House, refresh with a dip in the oceanside, heated pool, then relax with a drink at the poolside bar.

The Reach Resort (1435 Simonton St., 305/296-5000 or 888/318-4316, www.reachresort.com, $319–419 d), part of the Waldorf Astoria Collection, is essentially a tropical playground. This boutique hotel provides the same experience you might receive from a Caribbean resort, with access to a spacious, private beach; a variety of sailboats and water-sports gear; and a terrific spa (at its sister property, the Casa Marina Resort) to help renew your focus. Finish your evening with an exquisite meal at the on-site Strip House Steakhouse, before retiring to your luxury room or suite.

On the Atlantic Ocean, the **Coconut Beach Resort** (1500 Alberta St., 305/294-0057 or 800/835-0055, www.coconutbeachresort.com, studios $200–315 d, suites $310–550) contains a variety of accommodations, from studios to two-bedroom suites. In addition, the property features an open-deck pool and Jacuzzi, plus a small sandy beach. Farther inland, the adults-only **Olivia by Duval** (511 Olivia St., 305/296-5169 or 800/413-1978, www.oldtownsuites.com, $59–500 d) offers uniquely decorated rooms and suites, some of which include kitchenettes. Operated by Old Town Suites, this charming inn provides the perfect location for those hoping to experience the action of Duval while still enjoying the serenity of a private guesthouse. Amenities include cable television, air conditioning, and a clothing-optional pool. For even more solitude, Old Town Suites also operates two lovely cottages on Center and Petronia Streets.

GAY AND LESBIAN LODGING

Key West is definitely a gay-friendly destination, as evidenced by Old Town's numerous gay bars and the city's annual events, from Pridefest to the ultimate bacchanal, Fantasy Fest. There are even several inns and resorts that cater to a gay and/or lesbian clientele.

The 38-room **Island House** (1129 Fleming St., 305/294-6284 or 800/890-6284, www.islandhousekeywest.com, $249–319 d), for instance, is Key West's largest gay male resort—and, as some visitors have claimed, the classiest, most outrageous such place in the world. Within this secure, clothing-optional compound, gay men can relax and be themselves in an accepting environment, where a friendly all-male staff is available day and night. Here, you'll find a swimming pool, a health club, a poolside bar and café, and a spa that includes a sauna, a five-man shower, and a Jacuzzi. The accommodations, meanwhile, are enclosed within four separate buildings, which were formerly a private residence, a boarding house, a Laundromat, and a cigar factory. The uniquely furnished lodgings range in size, though all have comfortable beds, extra-large bath towels, air conditioning, and cable television.

In the same block, **Alexander's Guesthouse** (1118 Fleming St., 800/654-9919, www.alexanderskeywest.com, $120–175 d) welcomes a gay and lesbian clientele to a tranquil, comfortable setting, surrounded by lush tropical gardens. While here, you're free to enjoy the relaxing spa and sumptuous pool, which serves as the property's social center. Three levels of sun decks also allow guests a semi-private setting to catch some rays and forget daily cares. Evenings at

GAY AND LESBIAN HISTORIC TROLLEY TOUR

Featuring a plethora of gay bars, drag shows, gay and lesbian accommodations, and outrageous events like the annual Fantasy Fest, Key West is indeed a gay-friendly destination. That said, it seems appropriate that the Southernmost City would also be home to the nation's only Gay and Lesbian Historic Trolley Tour (www.gaykeywestfl.com/trolley.cfm, $25 pp), a fun, interesting, and often hilarious private charter tour that runs every Saturday at 10:50 A.M. This 70-minute narrated excursion, which typically leaves from the corner of Elizabeth and Angela Streets, invites visitors to hop aboard a rainbow-hued trolley and learn about the curious history of this spirited town, from its unique architecture to its wreck-salvaging heritage to its famous residents like Ernest Hemingway. Of course, given the tour's particular theme, you'll also see gay and lesbian hot spots, hear about previous homosexual visitors such as playwright Tennessee Williams and poet Elizabeth Bishop, and hopefully come to understand the impact that gays and lesbians have had on the culture, politics, and economy of the Florida Keys. For tour tickets as well as information about other gay-friendly establishments, events, and activities, consult the **Key West Business Guild** (513 Truman Ave., 305/294-4603, www.gaykeywestfl.com, 9 A.M.–5 P.M. Mon.–Fri.).

KEY WEST

Alexander's begin with poolside cocktails, while in the morning, guests are greeted by a continental breakfast. No matter how you spend the time in between, however, you'll be sure to find a room that's right for you, as the inn houses a wide selection of airy accommodations, all individually decorated. In all, you'll find 15 comfortable guest rooms, one well-lit suite ($205–305 d) with a private patio, and a gorgeous apartment ($275–410) with wooden floors, a full kitchen, a private sun deck, and a front porch with a hammock.

Sixteen elegantly decorated guest rooms and suites make up the men-only **Coconut Grove** (815 Fleming St., 305/296-5107 or 800/262-6055, www.coconutgrovekeywest.com, $139–299 d), set within, as the name indicates, a lovely coconut grove. Featuring a secluded, heated pool and outdoor Jacuzzi, the inn serves wine and hors d'oeuvres nightly and a complimentary continental breakfast every morning. The accommodations range from a standard deluxe room to a presidential suite with two bedrooms, and all guests are welcome to use the free wireless Internet access.

Given that the Big Easy and the Southernmost City share so many common elements, it seems only fitting that you'd find the **New Orleans House** (724 Duval St., 305/293-9800 or 888/293-9893, www.neworleanshousekw.com, rooms and suites $110–220 d, cottages $185–340) in Key West's Old Town. As the only gay, all-male guesthouse on the Duval, the New Orleans House puts you just steps away from all the action, including the on-site Bourbon St. Pub. Still, if you're looking to relax, you can do just that on the private sun deck overlooking the pool and hot tub. The accommodations here range from standard rooms with a shared bathroom to an intimate cottage, equipped with a full kitchen and a king-sized bed. In all, you'll find eight rooms, one suite, and three cottages here.

Closer to the ocean lies one of the world's largest inns for women, including lesbians and gay-friendly heterosexuals. Just two blocks away from the southernmost point in the continental United States, **(Pearl's Rainbow** (525 United St., 305/292-1450 or 800/749-6696, www.pearlsrainbow.com, rooms $89–269 d, suites $199–379 d) offers a wide variety of 38 rooms and suites, ranging from the Skyview Room, with an angled ceiling and a queen-sized bed, to the Deluxe Poolside Suite, equipped with a king-sized bed, a poolside porch, and a living room with hand-painted furniture, a sofa bed, and two televisions. The property includes five separate structures—the Marrero Building, the Surf Building, the Louisa Cottage, the East Cottage, and the West Cottage—plus a parking lot, two freshwater pools, and two rejuvenating spas. Pearl's also features free wireless Internet access, a restaurant, and Key West's only tropical bar just for women. For more gay-friendly establishments, consult the **Key West Business Guild** (513 Truman Ave., 305/294-4603, www.gaykeywestfl.com).

CAMPING

Although most people visiting Key West choose to stay in one of the city's varied inns, hotels, or resorts, campers will also find a few options on nearby Stock Island. South of the Key West Golf Club, **Boyd's Key West Campground** (6401 Maloney Ave., Stock Island, 305/294-1465, www.boydscampground.com, $55–120 daily) offers tent sites as well as RV spaces, many of which are equipped with water service, 30/50-amp electricity, sewer access, and cable television. Both inland and waterfront spots are available. In addition, the property features a heated swimming pool, a lounging beach, free wireless Internet access, and numerous planned activities, including craft and yoga classes, pot luck dinners, movie nights, line dancing, and casino cruises.

The intimate **El Mar RV Resort** (6700 Maloney Ave., Stock Island, 305/294-0857, www.elmarrvresort.com, $80–110 daily) caters to RV enthusiasts only. No tents, pop-ups, or truck campers are allowed. Situated on the ocean, the property offers 10 spaces in all, half of which have waterfront views. All of the lengthy, gravel sites in this park feature patios and full hookups, including 30/50-amp electricity. Closer to the Overseas Highway and not far from the Hurricane Hole Marina, the family-operated **Leo's Campground** (5236 Suncrest Rd., Stock Island, 305/296-5260, www.leoscampground.com, $39–62 daily) welcomes tent and RV campers alike. Pets, however, are only allowed in the RV portion of the park, at a daily fee of $1 per pet. There are also charges for extra people ($8 daily) and trailers ($7 daily). The tent sites, most of which have barbecue grills and picnic tables, are situated along a small, quiet lake, surrounded by mangroves, while the RV spaces feature picnic tables, 70-channel cable television, and full hookups with 30/50-amp electricity. Other on-site amenities include a barbecue area for RV campers, a laundry facility, and a bathhouse with hot showers. Monthly rates ($990–1,395) are also available.

Food

As with lodging options, Key West has the largest selection of restaurants in the Florida Keys, and the cuisine down here runs the gamut from fresh seafood to all-American hamburgers to upscale French and Italian dishes. So, whatever your mood, you're sure to find something tasty in the Southernmost City. Of course, only a small percentage of the available eateries are listed here. For more suggestions, consult the **Florida Keys Dining Guide** (www.keysdining.com).

SEAFOOD

Key West, like the rest of the Florida Keys, boasts a plethora of fresh seafood options, especially near the Historic Seaport at the Key West Bight. While meandering around this lively area, be sure to stop by the **Half Shell Raw Bar** (231 Margaret St., 305/294-7496, www.halfshellrawbar.com, 11 A.M.–10 P.M. daily, $7–21), a former shrimp-packing facility that has maintained its charm as an authentic fish house. Though offering fried dishes, this laid-back eatery really specializes in raw, steamed, broiled, and grilled seafood. After starting with a bucket of steamed clams, try the stuffed shrimp, prepared with crabmeat and spices and broiled with garlic butter, white wine, and lemon juice.

Along the boardwalk, you can enjoy fresh seafood on the breezy upper deck of the weathered ℂ **Schooner Wharf Bar** (202 William

KEY WEST

© DANIEL MARTONE

waterfront dining at the Half Shell Raw Bar

St., 305/292-3302, www.schoonerwharf.com, 7:30 A.M.–4 A.M. daily, $8–18). Here, you'll find standard Keys fare like the filling seafood sampler, featuring conch fritters, mahimahi, four kinds of shrimp, and fries. In addition, the Schooner Wharf now serves complete breakfasts, such as the shrimp Benedict Florentine. This casual, open-air watering hole also offers live music, starting at noon and continuing late into the night.

Also beside the harbor, the **Conch Republic Seafood Company** (631 Greene St., 305/294-4403, www.conchrepublicseafood.com, 11 A.M.–midnight daily, $8–28) provides a casual atmosphere for seafood lovers. Here, you'll enjoy raw oysters and clams, traditional dishes like grilled dolphin (mahimahi), 80 different varieties of rum, and daily entertainment, with musicians often playing late into the evening.

Within the **A&B Lobster House** (700 Front St., 305/294-5880, www.aandblobsterhouse. com, 6–11 P.M. daily, $18–68), a fancy, white-cloth restaurant that offers signature dishes like grouper Oscar and tuna au poivre, you'll find **Alonzo's Oyster Bar** (www.alonzosoysterbar.

com, 11 A.M.–10 P.M. Mon.–Sat., noon–10 P.M. Sun., $9–28), a casual eatery that serves key lime garlic oysters, steamed shrimp, roasted mussels, and other tasty treats.

Though not as old or as legendary as some Key West eateries, the family-owned **❨ Two Friends Patio Restaurant** (512 Front St., 305/296-3124, www.twofriendskeywest.com, 8 A.M.–close daily, $9–35), located just steps from the fascinating Pirate Soul Museum, is still a lively choice for breakfast, lunch, and dinner. Established in 1967, this open-air eatery prepares filling breakfast dishes like shrimp and crabmeat quiche and crab cake Benedict, as well as terrific "chargrilled" steaks, fresh seafood dishes, and tropical drinks later in the day. As a bonus, you'll find early-bird specials from 4 to 7 P.M. daily, plus live karaoke nightly. Even if you never work up the nerve to take the stage, you'll certainly enjoy the show, and if you're a seafood fan, you can't go wrong at a place that offers everything from conch fritters and raw oysters to a lobster combo platter that includes grilled gulf shrimp, broiled scallops, and a whole Florida lobster tail.

outdoor seating at the Schooner Wharf Bar

Closer to the ocean, you'll spot **Pisces** (1007 Simonton St., 305/294-7100, www.pisceskeywest.com, 6–11 P.M. daily, $18–44), another fine-dining seafood establishment. Here, you can enjoy a taste of New Orleans with the grilled shrimp Nola, or try the black grouper bouillabaisse with mussels, clams, and calamari. Other favorites include Lobster Tango Mango and Yellowtail Snapper Atocha. Pisces is the ideal place for a candlelit dinner, which might explain why reservations are recommended year-round. For an alternative experience, head to the **Hurricane Hole Restaurant & Marina** (5130 Overseas Hwy., Stock Island, 305/294-8025, www.hurricaneholekeywest.com, 11 A.M.–10 P.M. daily, $11–23), where you can enjoy fresh seafood, steak, and chicken, while overlooking the marina. Bring in some freshly caught fish, and the cooks will grill, blacken, or fry it for you.

AMERICAN AND VEGETARIAN

Seafood isn't the only option for gourmands in Key West. Burgers, steaks, barbecue, even vegetarian dishes are available, too. If you're looking for a well-prepared steak, head first to the **Prime Steakhouse** (951 Caroline St., 305/296-4000, www.primekeywest.com, 6–10:30 P.M. daily, $22–39), a fine-dining steakhouse that also offers an excellent selection of complementary wines. Begin with a signature martini before sampling one of the steak specials. Reservations are recommended, especially during the high season. The newly remodeled **Turtle Kraals Restaurant & Bar** (231 Margaret St., 305/294-2640, www.turtlekraals.com, 7 A.M.–10 P.M. daily, $8–22) serves typical Keys-style dishes for breakfast, lunch, and dinner, though it definitely specializes in barbecue. Both the quaint indoor dining area and the covered outdoor patio provide the ideal atmosphere for enjoying a barbecue beef brisket platter or one of several other choice selections.

Just a few steps from Duval Street, and not far from the Pirate Soul Museum, lies the **Island Dogs Bar** (505 Front St., 305/509-7136, www.islanddogsbar.com, 11 A.M.–4 A.M. daily, $8–15), one of the few late-night joints in town. So, when most restaurants are closed, head directly to this casual bar and eatery, which serves food until 3:30 A.M. every night. Here, you'll find all-American favorites like chicken wings, hot dogs, burgers, and sandwiches, not to mention an array of alcoholic libations. Both indoor and outdoor seating are available.

◖ Sloppy Joe's Bar (201 Duval St., 305/294-5717, www.sloppyjoes.com, 9 A.M.–close daily, $4–13)—a spacious, boxy, white building that's hard to miss with its red-brick columns and the bar's name in giant, black letters—has been a Key West tradition since 1933. Supposedly one of Ernest Hemingway's favorite Key West watering holes, Sloppy Joe's has run an annual Hemingway Look-Alike Contest since 1980. The menu is fairly extensive, with traditional Key West–style cuisine as well as the famous Original Sloppy Joe Sandwich, which features delicious ground beef in a rich tomato sauce with onions, peppers, and spices. The food isn't the only attraction here; various bands keep you entertained day and night.

If you enjoy listening to good music while noshing on good food, then you're in luck. Sloppy Joe's isn't the only game in town. **Willie T's Restaurant & Bar** (525 Duval St., 305/294-7674, www.williets.com, 11 A.M.–2 A.M. daily, $11–17) also offers live music, excellent food, and terrific libations. In fact, the menu includes 28 different mojitos, from key lime to ginger to espresso. As for the food, Willie T's provides an assortment of tasty dishes, from the goat cheese and avocado salad to the blackened dolphin with avocado butter and red pepper jam.

For an organic, vegetarian meal, stroll over to **Help Yourself** (829 Fleming St., 305/296-7766, www.helpyourselffoods.com, 8 A.M.–7 P.M. Mon.–Sat., 8 A.M.–3 P.M. Sun., $8–14), which features a fairly extensive menu, including lasagna made with layers of zucchini, brazil nut meat, spinach, pesto, fresh tomatoes, and marinara. If you're just looking for a quick snack, consider ordering a refreshing smoothie, such as the Chocolate Buzz, made with cacao powder, cacao nibs, and banana.

KEY WEST

© DANIEL MARTONE

Help Yourself offers smoothies, organic cuisine, and proximity to a late-night laundry.

CONTINENTAL

For a variety of options, stroll toward the Key West Bight, where **The Commodore Waterfront Restaurant** (700 Front St., 305/294-9191, www.commodorekeywest.com, 5:30–10:30 P.M. daily, $20–38) features traditional Florida Keys–style dishes, including seafood and steaks, in a fine-dining setting along the waterfront. Farther inland, you'll encounter another winning option, **Kelly's Caribbean Bar, Grill & Brewery** (301 Whitehead St., 305/293-8484, www.kellyskeywest.com, 11 A.M.–11 P.M. daily, $16–30). Known as the birthplace of Pan American Airlines and now home to the Southernmost Brewery, Kelly's presents a menu of island flavors with such tasty dishes as coconut shrimp and jerked chicken. The food is delicious, but the real draw is the beer, crafted by the on-site brewmaster. Be sure to try Kelly's flagship beer, the Havana Red Ale.

Only a block off Duval, the classy, often noisy, ◖ **Café Marquesa** (600 Fleming St., 305/292-1919, www.marquesa.com, 6–10 P.M. daily, $20–49) feels as though it could be in Manhattan. The 50-seat restaurant offers contemporary American cuisine like macadamia-crusted yellowtail or pan-roasted duck breast. Whether you're a guest of the adjacent Marquesa Hotel or you're just looking for a fantastic place to start the evening, this small hot spot provides an elegant alternative to Key West's casual waterfront eateries. Situated in a garden oasis, ◖ **Michaels Restaurant** (532 Margaret St., 305/295-1300, www.michaelskeywest.com, 5:30–10 P.M. daily, $7–19) provides one of the most romantic dining opportunities in Key West. The menu features a variety of dishes, from fondue to veal saltimbocca, featuring sautéed veal, topped with prosciutto di parma, yellow tomatoes, fresh sage, manchego cheese, and a velvety cream sauce. As a bonus, from 5:30 to 7:30 P.M., Michaels serves a new light-side menu, featuring smaller versions of all available dishes.

The **Blue Heaven Restaurant** (729 Thomas St., 305/296-8666, www.blueheavenkw.com, 8 A.M.–close, $7–20) has been serving breakfast, lunch, and dinner since 1992. The full menu features everything from pancakes to Caribbean barbecue shrimp. For dessert, try the Banana Heaven, a banana bread with bananas flamed in rum, served with vanilla ice cream. On Duval, you'll spot ◖ **Martin's Restaurant & Lounge** (917 Duval St., 305/295-0111, www.martinskeywest.com, 5:30–11 P.M. daily, $16–48), a stylish German fusion restaurant that offers scrumptious dinner options as well as a terrific weekend brunch, featuring specialties like grilled bratwurst, seafood crepes, and eggs Benedict with lobster medallions. Both the menu and the decor illustrate a superb blend of classical and tropical attributes, with a touch of European sophistication. The space is divided into three unique sections: the elegant dining room, the chic lounge, and the sumptuous garden. Unlike many fine restaurants, Martin's welcomes children, which means that, while busy parents can enjoy delicious food, couples without kids may find a quiet, romantic meal less than probable.

Headed toward the ocean side of Old Town, you'll spot **Camille's Restaurant** (1202 Simonton St., 305/296-4811, www.camilleskeywest.com, 8 A.M.–3 P.M. daily, 6–10 P.M. Tues.–Sat., $9–28), a fun, exotic eatery that features breakfast, lunch, and dinner. Unique dishes include a three-egg omelet made with fresh lobster, or the tender veal with an Asian panko crust. Despite the delicious food, though, the prevalent sexual innuendos in Camille's might not make it the most family-friendly establishment in town. As an alternative, stroll over to the **Flaming Buoy Filet Co.** (1100 Packer St., 305/295-7970, www.theflamingbuoy.com, 6–9:30 P.M. daily, $20–25), where you can savor a New York strip steak with blue cheese butter, or the mojito chicken with fried plantains and brown rice. If you'd prefer to stay in your hotel, take advantage of the Flaming Buoy's delivery option.

FRENCH

While you won't find too many options for French cuisine in the Southernmost City, there are definitely two standouts. The **Banana Cafe** (1215 Duval St., 305/294-7227, www.banana-cafe-key-west.com, 8 A.M.–3 P.M. daily,

6–10 P.M. Tues.–Sat., $7–19), for instance, is a popular French-style eatery that specializes in delectable crepes for breakfast, including the tasty La Ratatouille, which features cooked eggplant, zucchini, onions, tomatoes, and varied peppers, wrapped in a crepe and topped with a fried egg. The dinner menu is also divine, offering such winners as mussels Brittany or a Parisian-style ribeye. Popular with couples in a romantic mood, **Café Solé** (1029 Southard St., 305/294-0230, www.cafesole.com, 5:30–10 P.M. daily, $18–23) combines French sauces with locally caught seafood. Fish dominates the menu, which includes such favorites as grouper Romesco, served with garlic, tomatoes, and a spicy roasted red pepper and hazelnut sauce, and tuna seared in pistachios with wasabi cream and a hoisin garlic sauce.

MEDITERRANEAN

For authentic Italian cuisine, look no farther than **Mangia Mangia Pasta Cafe** (900 Southard St., 305/294-2469, www.mangia-mangia.com, 5:30–10 P.M. daily, $10–28). Situated in the heart of Old Town, this corner restaurant channels the ambience of a small Italian village. Here, you'll find an array of fresh pastas with delicious homemade sauces, such as the New Zealand mussels with spaghettini, prepared in a garlic-based marinara sauce and topped with shaved parmesan cheese.

If you have a craving for various Mediterranean flavors, visit the well-regarded **Azur Restaurant** (425 Grinnell St., 305/292-2987, www.azurkeywest.com, 8 A.M.–2 P.M. and 6–10 P.M. Mon.–Fri., 9 A.M.–2 P.M. and 6–10 P.M. Sat., 10 A.M.–2 P.M. Sun., $6–36) beside the Eden House. Serving breakfast, lunch, and dinner on the shaded terrace or in the dining room, Azur features such delicious creations as Brie and mushroom omelets; charred octopus marinated with garlic, lemon zest, and Italian parsley; and apple and almond tarts with cardamon ice cream.

DESSERT

If you're a dessert connoisseur, you'll definitely find a lot of key lime pie in the eateries of Key West, but that's not the only treat that the Southernmost City has to offer. For something cool on a warm afternoon, head to the **Key West Ice Cream Factory** (201 William

© LAURA MARTONE

scrumptious Peanut Butter Perversion at Better Than Sex

St., 305/295-3011, www.keywesticecream-factory.com, 11 A.M.–10 P.M. daily, $7–19). Offering 33 flavors of ice cream, including "Conchy" Cookies 'N Cream or Bermuda Triangle Chocolate, the shop also features 15 flavors of sorbet, including cantaloupe and watermelon. Later in the evening, you should skip dinner altogether and head directly to **Better Than Sex** (411 Petronia St., 305/296-8102, www.betterthansexkw. com, 6 P.M.–1 A.M. Tues.–Sun. Christmas–Easter, 6 P.M.–1 A.M. Wed.–Sun. Apr.–Dec., $9–13), a bordello-style lounge that prepares unforgettable desserts, such as Peanut Butter Perversion, the Missionary Crisp, and Kinky Key Lime, a creamy mousse concoction that just might be the best key lime pie in town. Enhance your visit to this exotic, infinitely romantic spot with a glass of dark chocolate–rimmed Merlot.

Information and Services

INFORMATION
Tourism and Government Offices
For brochures, maps, and other information about Key West, plus assistance with hotel and tour reservations, stop by the **Key West Visitors Center** (1601 N. Roosevelt Blvd., 305/296-8881 or 877/296-8881, www.keywest123.com, 8 A.M.–10 P.M. daily), the **Key West Chamber of Commerce** (510 Greene St., 1st Fl., 305/294-2587, www.keywestchamber.org, 8 A.M.–6:30 P.M. daily), or the **Key West Information Center** (201 Front St., Ste. 108, 888/222-5590, www.keywestinfo.com, 9 A.M.–5 P.M. Mon.–Sat.). In addition, you can consult the **Key West Attractions Association (KWAA)** (www.keywestattractions.org), **Key West's Finest** (1107 Key Plaza, Ste. 310, 305/296-0555 or 866/990-8700, www.keywestfinest.com), or the **Monroe County Tourist Development Council** (1201 White St., Ste. 102, 305/296-1552 or 800/352-5397, www.fla-keys.com, 9 A.M.–5 P.M. Mon.–Fri.). You can even save money on sightseeing adventures through online companies like **Trusted Tours and Attractions** (800/844-7601, www.trusted-tours.com).

For government-related issues, contact the **City of Key West** (525 Angela St., 305/809-3700, www.keywestcity.com, 8 A.M.–5 P.M. Mon.–Fri.) or the **Monroe County offices** (1100 Simonton St., 305/294-4641, www.monroecounty-fl.gov, 8 A.M.–5 P.M. Mon.–Fri.).

Media
For local news, consult the daily **Key West Citizen** (www.keysnews.com), the **Key West Keynoter** (www.keysnet.com), or **The Weekly Newspapers** (www.keysweekly.com). The daily **Miami Herald** (www.miamiherald.com) and the biweekly **Florida Keys Keynoter** (www.keysnet.com) are also available throughout the Keys.

In Key West, you'll also have access to several radio stations, including the popular **US-1 Radio** (104.1 FM, http://us1radio.com), which offers local news, including up-to-the-minute weather information during hurricane season. In addition, most hotels offer access to the major television stations in the Miami–Fort Lauderdale market.

SERVICES
As the largest community in the Florida Keys, it's no surprise that Key West offers a wide array of services for both residents and travelers.

Money
For banking needs, stop by one of the two local branches of **TIB Bank** (800/233-6330, www.tibbank.com). There's one on the eastern end of Key West (3618 N. Roosevelt Blvd., 305/292-0230, 9 A.M.–4 P.M. Mon.–Thurs., 9 A.M.–6 P.M. Fri., extended drive-through hours) and one in Old Town (330 Whitehead St., 305/294-6330, 9 A.M.–4 P.M. Mon.–Thurs., 9 A.M.–6 P.M. Fri., extended drive-through hours). For foreign currency exchange, visit

the **First State Bank of the Florida Keys** (www.keysbank.com). There are five locations in the Key West area, from Stock Island (5450 MacDonald Ave., 305/296-8535, 9 A.M.–4 P.M. Mon.–Thurs., 9 A.M.–6 P.M. Fri., extended drive-through hours) to Old Town (444 Whitehead St., 305/296-8535, 9 A.M.–4 P.M. Mon.–Thurs., 9 A.M.–6 P.M. Fri.).

Mail

For shipping, faxing, copying, and other business-related services, visit **The UPS Store** (2900 N. Roosevelt Blvd., Ste. 1107, 305/292-4177, www.theupsstore.com, 9 A.M.–6 P.M. Mon.–Fri., 10 A.M.–3 P.M. Sat.). You can also package and ship items at the two local **post offices** (800/275-8777, www.usps.com). You'll find one on the eastern end of the island (2764 N. Roosevelt Blvd., 305/296-7327, 8:30 A.M.–5 P.M. Mon.–Fri., 9 A.M.–noon Sat.) and one in Old Town (400 Whitehead St., 305/294-9539, 8:30 A.M.–5 P.M. Mon.–Fri., 9:30 A.M.–noon Sat.).

Groceries and Supplies

For groceries, baked goods, and other supplies, head to the nearest **Winn-Dixie** (2778 N. Roosevelt Blvd., 305/294-0491, www.winndixie.com, 7 A.M.–midnight daily), which has an on-site pharmacy (305/294-0658, 8 A.M.–8 P.M. Mon.–Fri., 9 A.M.–7 P.M. Sat.–Sun.). In Key West, you'll also find a **Publix** (3316 N. Roosevelt Blvd., 305/296-2225, www.publix.com, 7 A.M.–10 P.M. Mon.–Sat., 7 A.M.–9 P.M. Sun.), which includes an on-site pharmacy (305/296-3225, 9 A.M.–9 P.M. Mon.–Fri., 9 A.M.–7 P.M. Sat., 10 A.M.–5 P.M. Sun.). The area also features a **CVS/pharmacy** (530 Truman Ave., 305/294-2576, www.cvs.com, 24 hours daily), which offers limited supplies as well as an on-site pharmacy (9 A.M.–9 P.M. Mon.–Sat., 10 A.M.–6 P.M. Sun.).

Laundry

If you need to clean some clothes during your trip, you'll find several coin-operated laundries in the area, including two locations of **Key West Laundries** (www.keywestlaundry.com): the **Key West Launderette** (912 Kennedy Dr., 7 A.M.–10 P.M. daily) and the **Habana Plaza Coin Laundry** (3124 Flagler Ave., 7 A.M.–10 P.M. daily).

Internet Access

Using your own laptop, you can access high-speed wireless Internet service at any number of hotels and resorts in the Key West area. In addition, there are several charming Internet cafés, including the **Coffee Plantation** (713 Caroline St., 305/295-9808, www.coffeeplantationkeywest.com, 7 A.M.–6 P.M. daily) and the **Sippin' Internet Cafe** (424 Eaton St., 305/293-0555, www.sippinkeywest.com, 7 A.M.–11 P.M. daily). You'll also find useful services, including Internet access, at the **Monroe County May Hill Russell Library** (700 Fleming St., 305/292-3595, www.keyslibraries.org, 9:30 A.M.–6 P.M. Tues. and Thurs.–Fri., 9:30 A.M.–8 P.M. Wed., 10 A.M.–6 P.M. Sat.).

Emergency Services

In case of an emergency that requires police, fire, or ambulance services, dial **911** from any cell or public phone. For nonemergency assistance, contact the **Monroe County Sheriff's Office** (5525 College Rd., 305/292-7000, www.keysso.net, 8 A.M.–5 P.M. Mon.–Fri.). Likewise, if you witness a crime of any kind, contact **Crime Stoppers of the Keys** (800/346-8477, www.tipsubmit.com) to offer an anonymous tip. For medical assistance, consult the **Lower Keys Medical Center** (5900 College Rd., Stock Island, 305/294-5531, www.lkmc.com). Foreign visitors—seeking help with directions, medical concerns, business issues, law enforcement needs, or other problems—can receive **multilingual tourist assistance** (800/771-5397) 24 hours daily.

KEY WEST

Getting There and Around

GETTING THERE
By Air

Travelers can reach Key West directly by flying into the **Key West International Airport (EYW)** (3491 S. Roosevelt Blvd., 305/809-5200 or 305/296-5439, www.keywestinternational-airport.com). Besides major airlines, such as **US Airways** (800/428-4322, www.usairways.com) and **Delta Air Lines** (800/221-1212, www.delta.com), the Key West airport hosts smaller air carriers, like **Cape Air** (508/771-6944 or 800/352-0714, www.flycapeair.com, rates vary), which offers daily service between Fort Myers and Key West.

Other area airports include the **Florida Keys Marathon Airport (MTH)** (9400 Overseas Hwy., Marathon, 305/289-6060), the **Fort Lauderdale-Hollywood International Airport (FLL)** (320 Terminal Dr., Fort Lauderdale, 866/435-9355, www.broward.org/airport), and the **Miami International Airport (MIA)** (4200 NW 21st St., Miami, 305/876-7000 or 800/825-5642, www.miami-airport.com). From each airport, you can rent a vehicle from such agencies as **Avis** (800/331-1212, www.avis.com), **Budget** (800/527-0700, www.budget.com), **Enterprise** (800/325-8007, www.enterprise.com), **Hertz** (800/654-3131, www.hertz.com), or **Thrifty** (800/367-2277, www.thrifty.com) in order to reach your hotel or primary destination in Key West.

By Bus or Train

To reach Key West via the regional bus system, you can take the **Miami-Dade County Metrobus** (305/891-3131, www.miamidade.gov/transit), which operates the **301 Dade-Monroe Express** between Florida City and Marathon (5:15 A.M.–8:40 P.M. daily). From Marathon, you can then use the **Lower Keys Shuttle**, which is operated by the **Key West Department of Transportation (KWDoT)** (305/600-1455, www.kwtransit.com, $3 per ride, $16 weekly, $50 monthly) to complete the rest of your journey. The shuttle runs from Marathon to Key West between 5:30 A.M. and 11:15 P.M. daily. Other stops include Bahia Honda State Park, Big Pine Key, and several other Lower Keys. Reduced fares may apply for students under 22 years old, senior citizens over 59 years old, military personnel, and disabled individuals.

As for national transportation companies, while **Greyhound** (800/231-2222, www.greyhound.com) offers bus service to the **Key West Greyhound Station** (3535 S. Roosevelt Blvd., 305/296-9072, 7:30–11 A.M. and 3–6 P.M. daily) near the Key West International Airport, **Amtrak** (800/872-7245, www.amtrak.com) only provides train service as far south as Miami. Of course, you can always rent a car or hop a shuttle to reach the Florida Keys.

Transport from Airports and Stations

If you arrive in the Fort Lauderdale–Miami area via plane, bus, or train—or Key West via plane or bus—you can either rent a car or hire a shuttle service to reach your destination in the Key West area. Some of these companies include **Keys Shuttle** (305/289-9997 or 888/765-9997, www.keysshuttle.com, $90–100 per shared ride, $400–450 for exclusive service) and **Keys Tropical Transportation** (305/852-3595, www.keystropicaltransportation.com, starting at $130 or $165 per ride, depending on the airport of origin), both of which provide service from the Miami and Fort Lauderdale airports; **SuperShuttle** (305/871-2000 or 954/764-1700, www.supershuttle.com, $355 per ride for up to 10 passengers), which only serves visitors flying into Miami; and **TO'n'FRO** (305/852-4514, www.tonfro.com, starting at $55–65 per shared van ride, $300–350 per luxury sedan ride), a personalized van and car service that offers transportation between the airports in Fort Lauderdale, Miami, and Key West and any destination in the Keys.

By Car

To reach Key West from Miami, simply head south on U.S. 1 (Overseas Hwy.), drive through the Upper, Middle, and Lower Keys—roughly 110 miles from the mainland—and continue toward your destination, likely west of mile marker 5. If you're headed from the Everglades via I-75 (Everglades Pkwy.), drive south on U.S. 27, veer right onto S.R. 997 (Krome Ave.), and follow the signs to U.S. 1. From U.S. 41 (Tamiami Trail) in the Everglades, head south on S.R. 997 and continue toward U.S. 1. If you arrive during the peak season (Dec.–Apr.), be sure to call **511** for an up-to-the-minute traffic report.

By Boat

As an alternative to planes, buses, and the like, you can also reach Key West via boat. The **Key West Express** (888/539-2628, www.seakeywestexpress.com, $86–145 adults, $57–75 children under 13, $86–135 seniors 62 and over) offers a fleet of comfortable, jet-powered passenger ferries that provide year-round daily service from Fort Myers Beach to Key West—a ride that typically takes 3.5 hours. Passengers can opt for one-way travel, same-day return, or different-day return and, with certain restrictions, may be allowed to bring pets and bicycles on board. All passengers 18 years of age and older must present valid identification in order to ride.

GETTING AROUND
By Car

If not on foot or bicycle, the third best way to travel through Key West is via car or motorcycle—both of which offer easy access to U.S. 1 as well as the residential roads throughout this compact city. The smaller the vehicle, the easier it will be to find street parking when necessary; just remember to watch for parking signs and feed any required meters. Note, too, that Key West offers a few public parking areas in Old Town, including the **Park N' Ride Old Town Garage** (305/809-3910, www.keywestcity.com, $2 hourly, $13 daily) at the corner of Grinnell and Caroline Streets, not far

from the Historic Seaport. The garage provides covered, overnight parking and convenient access to tourist attractions, and as a bonus, parking here allows you free, same-day access to the city's public transportation.

By Tour or Public Transit

Since Key West is the most populated—and most popular—destination in the Florida Keys, it's not surprising that there are public transit options in addition to taxicabs, pedicabs, and vehicle rentals. Upon arriving in town, you might want to opt for the **Conch Tour Train** (888/916-8687, www.conchtourtrain.com, 9 A.M.–4:30 P.M. daily, $29 adults, $14 children 4–12, children under 4 and Key West residents free) or the **Old Town Trolley Tour** (305/296-6688 or 888/910-8687, www.trolleytours.com, 9 A.M.–4:30 P.M. daily, $29 adults, $14 children 4–12, children under 4 free), both of which offer guided excursions through the city—an ideal way to get an overview of all available attractions before exploring them in more depth. In addition, the **Key West Department of Transportation (KWDoT)** (305/600-1455, www.kwtransit.com, $2–3 per ride, $8–16 weekly, $25–50 monthly) provides bus service around Key West and the Lower Keys between 5 A.M. and 11 P.M. daily.

By Taxi

Taxicab companies—such as **Perfect Pedicab** (305/292-0077, $1.50 per minute), offering three-wheeled, open-air, human-operated vehicles, and **Five 6's** (305/296-6666, www.keywesttaxi.com, $2.75 for first 0.2-mile, $0.60 per each additional 0.2-mile), which provides 24-hour service via the pink, ecofriendly hybrids that you'll spot seemingly everywhere—can also help you get around Key West.

By Bike or Boat

Key West is a lovely, welcoming place to traverse via bicycle, whether you're an experienced rider or a novice. Just remember that you'll have to share the streets with cars and other vehicles, so take care while you tour the neighborhoods.

Pedicab service is available throughout Key West.

Bikes can be rented from several different outfitters, including **Eaton Bikes** (830 Eaton St., 305/294-8188, www.eatonbikes.com, 9 A.M.–6 P.M. Mon.–Sat., 9 A.M.–4 P.M. Sun., $12–45 daily, $40–135 weekly), which offers a range of bicycles, from trikes to mountain bikes to tandems, plus free delivery service throughout Key West. **The Bike Shop of Key West** (1110 Truman Ave., 305/294-1073, www.thebikeshopkeywest.com, 9 A.M.–6 P.M. Mon.–Sat., 10 A.M.–4 P.M. Sun., $12 daily, $60 weekly, $180 monthly), the oldest in town, also provides a wide array of bicycles, plus accessories, bicycle sales, and a service/repair department. All rentals include locks, lights, baskets, and wide soft seats.

Another helpful source is **Paradise Scooter Rentals** (www.paradisescooterrentals.com, 9 A.M.–5 P.M. daily, $15–30 daily, $75–100 weekly), which offers two locations—112 Fitzpatrick Street (305/292-6441) and 430 Duval Street (305/293-1112)—and provides scooter rentals ($60–75 daily, $200–300 weekly, plus gas) as well. **Adventure Rentals** (305/293-8883, www.keywest-scooter.com,

9 A.M.–5 P.M. daily, $15 daily, $60 weekly) also provides bicycle rentals at multiple locations—0 Duval Street, 617 Front Street, 135 Simonton Street, and Cruise Ship Pier B—plus scooters ($50–70 daily), Harley motorcycles (starting from $268 daily, $935 weekly), and multi-passenger electric cars ($159–202 daily).

In addition, **A&M Rentals** (305/896-1921, www.amscooterskeywest.com, 8 A.M.–8 P.M. daily, $15–30 daily, $40–85 weekly) features three spots from which to rent kid-sized bicycles, cruisers, and tandems: 523 Truman Avenue, 513 South Street, and 500 Truman Avenue. Here, you can also rent one-seater scooters ($35 daily, $99 weekly), two-seater scooters ($55–60 daily, $169–199 weekly), and multi-seater electric cars ($150–250 daily, $600–1,050 weekly)—all popular ways to get around town. Free customer pickup and drop-off services are available. Similarly, **Sunshine Key West** (1910 N. Roosevelt Blvd., 305/294-9990, www.sunshinekeywest.com, 8 A.M.–6 P.M. daily) offers bicycles ($10–15 for four hours, $15–20 daily), single-seat scooters ($45–65 daily), double-seat scooters ($65–100 daily), Harley motorcycles ($200–225 daily), and electric cars ($100–120 for four hours, $150–175 daily) for rent. Take note that such outfitters typically require that all electric car operators possess a valid driver's license and be at least 21 or 22 years old.

You can also experience Key West via boat. Having your own vessel makes navigating these waters even easier, and you'll find no shortage of marinas in the area. If you'd rather rent a boat, stop by **Sunset Watersports** (Hurricane Hole Marina, 5130 Overseas Hwy., Stock Island, 305/294-5500, www.sunsetwatersports.info), which offers a range of vessels, from 17-foot fishing boats ($250 per half day, $325 daily) to 24-foot pontoons ($400 per half day, $500 daily). Also at the Hurricane Hole Marina, you'll find **Lazy Dog Adventure** (305/295-9898, www.lazydog.com), which offers two-hour guided kayak tours ($35 pp) in addition to kayak rentals ($20 per half day, $30 daily).

Dry Tortugas National Park

Roughly 68 miles west of Key West lies a cluster of seven islands, composed of coral and sand, that are collectively known as the Dry Tortugas. Originally named Las Tortugas (The Turtles) by Spanish explorers, the islands eventually became "Dry Tortugas" on mariners' navigational charts to indicate the lack of fresh water here. Part of the 220-mile-long Florida Keys archipelago, these islands, in addition to the surrounding shoals and waters, comprise the 64,657-acre Dry Tortugas National Park, established in 1992 to preserve this unique area and now one of the most remote parks in the National Park System. In addition, Dry Tortugas has been listed on the National Register of Historic Places.

Celebrated for its diverse wildlife, its remarkable coral reefs, its enthralling shipwrecks, and its pirate legends and military past, Dry Tortugas is indeed a must-see destination, the kind of place that really makes you feel as though you're a world away from the Florida mainland. If you have the time, you should definitely board a ferry or come by private boat to this unique destination—popular among sunbathers, swimmers, snorkelers, kayakers, anglers, bird-watchers, photographers, and overnight campers.

SIGHTS

While visiting the Dry Tortugas, you should take a guided or self-guided tour of **Fort Jefferson,** the well-preserved Civil War fort on Garden Key, the centerpiece of these remote islands. Nicknamed the "American Gibraltar," the country's largest 19th-century, coastal fort was initially established in 1846 in order to control navigation in the Gulf of Mexico, though its construction was never quite completed. During and after the war, it served as a remote, Union-affiliated military prison for captured deserters. From 1865 to 1869, it was even home to Dr. Samuel Mudd, who was incarcerated here for setting the broken leg of assassin John Wilkes Booth and thereby participating in the assassination of President Abraham Lincoln. By the 1880s, the U.S. Army had abandoned the facility, which became a wildlife refuge in 1908 and a national monument in 1935. An interesting tidbit is that, in 1847, seven enslaved African Americans fled Garden Key in a dramatic self-emancipation attempt. Although they were ultimately caught, their daring effort has been officially acknowledged by the National Underground Railroad Network to Freedom Program.

Within the fortified walls of this historic citadel, you'll encounter such sites as the officers' quarters, soldiers' barracks, cistern, magazines, and cannons. The visitor center and park headquarters are also located here. Just be advised that, from November to May, parts of Fort Jefferson are closed to the public while mason crews work on much-needed preservation projects. Such temporary closures are not in effect during the hurricane season (June–Nov.), which might only add to the logistical difficulties of this remote marine environment. Note that pets, food, and drinks are not allowed inside the fort. In addition, service and residential areas are closed to the public.

While visiting Fort Jefferson, be sure to take a look at the **Fort Jefferson Harbor Light,** northeast of the boat dock. Established in 1825 and still operational today, the lighthouse, whose present tower was erected in 1876, is a favorite among photographers. In addition, Loggerhead Key, which once housed the Carnegie Institute's Laboratory of Marine Ecology and is only accessible via private boat or charter, features the **Loggerhead Light,** also established in 1825, with an existing tower that was erected in 1858. Just remember that all buildings and structures on Loggerhead Key are closed to visitors, unless accompanied by a park ranger.

RECREATION

Although visiting Dry Tortugas National Park is only possible by ferry or private boat, the isolated **Fort Jefferson Beach** is well worth the trip. Besides its proximity to historic Fort Jefferson, it's a terrific locale for swimming, snorkeling, kayaking, fishing, and bird-watching. Be advised, however, that while there's plenty to do here, certain activities are prohibited, such as spearfishing, lobstering, using personal watercraft, collecting artifacts and marinelife, bartering with commercial fishermen for seafood, or possessing loaded firearms in federal facilities.

Bird-Watching and Wildlife-Viewing

Many people come to Garden Key for the bird-watching opportunities, which are truly excellent out here. More than 200 varieties are spotted annually, especially from March through September, when nearby Bush Key serves as the nesting grounds for migratory birds. During April and May, over 85,000 brown noddies and sooty terns nest on Bush

Key. In the spring, you might spot herons, raptors, and shorebirds, while in summertime, you might observe frigatebirds and mourning doves. The fall and winter months bring such species as hawks, merlins, peregrine falcons, gulls, terns, American kestrels, and belted kingfishers. Other possible sightings include orioles, warbles, cormorants, masked boobies, black noddies, mangrove cuckoos, and white-crowned pigeons. Be sure to pick up an official bird checklist from the visitor center in Fort Jefferson, or consult the **Audubon Society of Florida** (Keys Environmental Restoration Trust, 11399 Overseas Hwy., Ste. 4E, Marathon, 305/289-9988, http://fl.audubon. org) for more information.

While you can spot many of these species during a short visit to Garden or Loggerhead Keys, you might have a better experience on board a bird-watching charter—though admittedly a pricier one as well. **Sea-Clusive Charters** (1107 Key Plaza, Ste. 315, Key West, 305/744-9928, www.seaclusive.com, $2,600–3,275 per trip) features such tailored excursions, led by professional bird guide Larry Manfredi (www.southfloridabirding.com). While on board, you might also spot other wildlife, such as sharks, dolphins, and, if you're lucky, gigantic sea turtles. These cruises can accommodate a minimum of eight passengers and a maximum of 11.

Boating and Kayaking

Since Garden Key and Loggerhead Key are both accessible via private boat, many boaters enjoy this park as well. Unfortunately, the dock on Loggerhead Key is only open to government vessels, but luckily, you're allowed to land south of the boathouse. Docking on Garden Key can also be problematic, as the public dock is often occupied by ferries and supply boats. Given that you can only tie up to the dock for two-hour increments between sunrise and 10 A.M. and then again between 3 P.M. and sunset, your best bet is to anchor in the harbor and use a dinghy to reach the island, which offers a dinghy beach for that exact purpose. Overnight anchoring, between sunset and sunrise, is only allowed in the designated anchorage area: the sand and rubble bottom within one nautical mile of the Fort Jefferson Harbor Light.

All boaters should have self-sufficient, fully-equipped vessels. Necessary items include life jackets, nautical charts, a tool kit with spare parts, plenty of fuel and drinking water, and a VHF radio to monitor weather forecasts. In addition, all vessels must conform to U.S. Coast Guard regulations.

Kayaking can also be a wonderful way to experience the islands, though you'll need to take care. The currents here can be very strong, making the area suitable for experienced sea kayakers only. If you do choose to tote kayaks along for the ride, make sure to bring a life vest, an anchor, a bailer, extra paddles, drinking water, and waterproof bags for gear. Other necessary safety equipment includes flares, bow and stern lines, a sound-producing device, a 360-degree light for operating at night, and the NOAA nautical chart #11438.

Fishing

Anglers are welcome to fish from the public dock on Garden Key, as well as the beach west of the dock. With the recent establishment of the 46-square-mile Research Natural Area (RNA), however, fishing from a boat is only permitted within a one-mile radius of Garden Key. Nevertheless, several local fishing charters operate multi-day trips to this area. With proper permits and licenses, these guides are allowed to fish in and around Dry Tortugas National Park. **Andy Griffiths Charters** (40 Key Haven Rd., Key West, 305/296-2639, www.fishandy.com), for instance, offers three-day, two-night excursions ($2,100–2,400 Jan.–Feb., $2,400–2,700 Mar.–Apr., $3,000–3,300 May.–July, and $2,400–2,700 Aug.–Dec.) to the Dry Tortugas for up to six anglers. These trips typically last from 10 A.M. on Friday to 2 P.M. on Sunday, or from noon on Monday to 2 P.M. on Wednesday.

Dream Catcher Charters (5555 College Rd., Stock Island, 305/292-7702 or 888/362-3474, www.chartersofkeywest.com),

meanwhile, offers 10-hour trips ($900–950) for up to six passengers as well as overnight excursions (trip times and rates vary). Other operators include **FishMonster Charters** (6000 Peninsula Ave., Stock Island, 305/432-0047, http://fishmonster.com, $2,200–3,200 per trip) and **Lethal Weapon Charters** (1418 Angela St., Key West, 305/296-6999 or 305/744-8225, www.lethalweaponcharters.com, trip times and rates vary).

If you choose to fish on your own, remember that Florida state laws, regulations, and licensing requirements apply in these waters. Commercial fishing, spearfishing, taking fish by sling or speargun, dragging a net, casting near sea turtles, collecting shells and artifacts, and possessing lobster, conch, or ornamental tropical fish are not allowed within the boundaries of Dry Tortugas National Park.

Diving and Snorkeling

With numerous patch reefs and shipwrecks, including the 19th-century Bird Key Wreck and early 20th-century Windjammer Wreck, within the boundaries of Dry Tortugas National Park, it's no wonder that snorkelers, scuba divers, and underwater photographers favor this area. Whether you arrive on Garden Key via ferry or private boat, you'll be able to snorkel directly off the beach, near the moat walls and coaling dock ruins, in warm, shallow waters that boast a cornucopia of kaleidoscopic tropical fish, conch shells, lobster and sponges, sea fans and sea anemones, staghorn coral clusters, and occasional sea turtles.

For access to even more snorkeling and scuba-diving sites around the Dry Tortugas—part of the Florida Keys National Marine Sanctuary—you can opt for half-day, full-day, and overnight charters with **Calypso Sailing** (305/896-8004, www.calypsosailing.com, trip times and rates vary). Another option is **Sea-Clusive Charters** (1107 Key Plaza, Ste. 315, Key West, 305/744-9928, www.seaclusive.com, $2,600–3,275 per trip), which offers multi-day diving excursions for 6–11 passengers. With Sea-Clusive, divers will be able to explore the Windjammer wreck site as well as the overhangs, caves, and swim troughs of these incredible coral reefs, which offer water depths of 45 to 80 feet. Here, you'll spot tropical fish, resident jewfish, black grouper, coral formations, and sponges.

If you choose to snorkel or dive on your own, you should be aware of certain offshore protection zones that are closed to the public. In addition, you need to prepare for potentially strong gulf currents. Remember, too, that dive flags are required beyond designated swimming channels at all times.

CAMPING

Since Dry Tortugas National Park has no public lodging, camping is the only option for those who hope to stay overnight on Garden Key. Just a short southwesterly walk from the public dock lies a primitive 10-site campground. Although the group site, which must be reserved in advance, can accommodate 10–40 people, most of the sites are available on a first-come, first-served basis and will suit up to six people and three tents. The campground is a self-service fee area, charging a nightly fee of $3 per person, and the sites offer little more than picnic tables and barbecue grills.

Be advised that grocery stores, fresh water, ice, and fuel are unavailable here, so plan accordingly. No trash receptacles are present either, which means that all visitors, boaters, and campers must pack out any and all trash. Unless you plan to anchor a private boat in the harbor near Garden Key, you'll probably be reaching the park via a commercial ferry. If so, be aware that most transportation companies have cargo weight restrictions. On the *Yankee Freedom II,* for instance, campers are limited to 60 pounds of gear plus water, while campers arriving aboard the Sunny Days *Fast Cat* are limited to 40 pounds of gear plus water. Neither ferry allows the transport of fuels like propane or lighter fluid, so campers are encouraged to use self-starting charcoal.

In order to make your camping trip as smooth as possible, there are several items you should be sure to pack, including picture identification, a fishing license, camping regulations,

and the current weather forecast. To make your stay more comfortable, bring along a tent, a sleeping bag and pad, rain gear, clothing for warm and cold weather, a wide-brimmed hat, and plenty of food, water, and ice. Cooking equipment should include a portable stove or grill, fuel of some kind, waterproof matches and a lighter, cooking utensils, biodegradable soap, and trash bags. Personal gear, such as medications, a first-aid kit, a knife, a flashlight and spare batteries, sunglasses, sunscreen, and insect repellent, will also prove to be helpful. Although you can bring pets with you, be advised that they are only allowed on Garden Key, outside Fort Jefferson, and must be leashed and well-behaved at all times. It probably goes without saying that owners must remove all pet waste from the park. Be advised, too, that campers are only allowed to stay for four days and three nights at a time.

INFORMATION

Technically, Dry Tortugas National Park is open all year, though restrictions are in effect on certain islands. Garden Key, which contains Fort Jefferson, is surely the most visited island in the park. Although the island itself is open year-round, Fort Jefferson is only open during daylight hours. Loggerhead is also open year-round during daylight hours. Middle and East Keys, however, are closed from April to mid-October during turtle nesting season, while Bush, Hospital, and Long Keys are closed all year, meaning that visitors should remain 100 feet offshore of these particular islands.

To visit the park, anyone 17 years of age or older must pay an entrance fee of $5. The pass, which is valid for seven days, is typically collected by commercial transportation operators; otherwise, you'll have to remit payment at the Garden Key visitor center. Annual passes, which can be purchased or procured at the **Florida Keys Eco-Discovery Center (FKEDC)** (35 E. Quay Rd., Key West, 305/809-4750, www.floridakeys.noaa.gov/eco_discovery.html, 9 A.M.–4 P.M. Tues.–Sat., free) with qualifying documentation, are all honored in Dry Tortugas. These include the

National Parks and Federal Recreational Lands Pass ($80) and the lifetime versions for senior citizens 62 years of age and older ($10), disabled visitors (free), and volunteers (free)—plus the now-discontinued Golden Eagle, Golden Age, and Golden Access Passports. All such passes are only eligible to legal U.S. citizens and permanent residents.

Be advised, however, that the recently designated, 46-square-mile Research Natural Area (RNA)—an ecological preserve that will encompass a little less than half of the park and serves to protect species affected by overfishing and loss of habitat—may eventually limit your fishing access to certain areas and require permits in other areas. For more information about Dry Tortugas National Park, including details about the RNA, contact the **park headquarters** (305/242-7700, www.nps.gov/drto/index.htm, 8 A.M.–4:30 P.M. Mon.–Fri.) or the Florida Keys Eco-Discovery Center. You can also consult websites like www.dry.tortugas.national-park.com. In addition, you can download park maps and regulations, plus information about camping, bird-watching, island history, and the RNA, from the official National Park Service website. Books such as Thomas Reid's *America's Fortress: A History of Fort Jefferson, Dry Tortugas, Florida* (Gainesville, FL: University Press of Florida, 2006) are also helpful resources.

GETTING THERE AND AROUND

Dry Tortugas National Park, which is approximately 68 miles west of Key West, is only accessible via ferry or private boat—all of which can be boarded in Key West. (Incidentally, seaplanes used to be a viable way to reach Garden Key, but the company has indefinitely suspended such trips, pending legal action.) To reach Garden Key by ferry, you can schedule a day trip via the 100-foot catamaran *Yankee Freedom II* (240 Margaret St., 305/294-7009 or 800/322-0013, www.yankeefreedom.com, 8 A.M.–5:30 P.M. daily, $160 adults, $150 students, military personnel, and seniors 62 and over, $120 children 4–16, children under 4

KEY WEST

© DANIEL MARTONE

headed for the Dry Tortugas aboard the *Yankee Freedom II*

free) or the **Fast Cat** through Sunny Days (305/296-5556 or 800/236-7937, www.sunnydayskeywest.com/fastcat.htm, 8 A.M.–5 P.M. daily, $145 adults, $135 students, military personnel, and seniors 62 and over, $100 children 3–16, children under 3 free), both of which are docked in the Historic Seaport at the Key West Bight.

Reservations are recommended for both ferries, and both will charge an additional $5 park entrance fee per person aged 17 or over. Cancellations must be made the day before your scheduled trip, and all passengers should arrive no later than 7:30 A.M. on the day of departure. In addition to day trips, both ferries offer overnight excursions, for which reservations are absolutely required. The *Yankee Freedom II* charges $180 for adult campers and $140 for children, while the *Fast Cat* charges $175 for adults, $165 for students and seniors aged 62 or older, and $130 for children 2–16; such rates do not include the requisite park entrance and camping fees.

For both ferries, each of which have comfortable, air-conditioned cabins, the day trip from Key West begins at 8 A.M. While you journey past the Marquesas, the famous *Atocha*

shipwreck, and various marinelife, you'll be treated to a complimentary continental breakfast. Once you arrive on Garden Key, you can opt for a 45-minute narrated tour of Fort Jefferson with one of the ferries' knowledgeable guides, after which you can relax on the pristine beach, go for a swim, have a picnic, or take a bird-watching nature stroll. In addition, you'll have free use of the on-board snorkeling equipment. It's recommended that you bring a swimsuit and towel, sun protection, a camera and batteries, binoculars, sunglasses, water shoes, a jacket, and a hat. A reliable watch is also necessary, as each ferry will leave around 3 P.M. in order to reach Key West by late afternoon.

If you choose to travel to Garden Key via private vessel, bear in mind the docking restrictions, which limit your use of the public dock between the hours of sunrise and 10 A.M., and between 3 P.M. and sunset. On Loggerhead Key, which is only accessible via private boat or charter, you can only land your vessel south of the dock and boathouse. Once on the island, you can explore the developed trails and shoreline, but remember that the dock and all structures are closed to the public.

BACKGROUND

The Land

GEOGRAPHY

Between 25 million and 70 million years ago, dramatic fluctuations in the sea level gradually formed the limestone upon which southern Florida now exists. Beyond the beaches and urban sprawl of Miami lies a fascinating region for nature lovers, most notably in the Everglades and the Florida Keys.

Shaped by water and fire, the Everglades are essentially **subtropical wetlands,** part of a massive watershed in southern Florida. Termed the "river of grass" by writer Marjory Stoneman Douglas in the late 1940s, the Everglades comprise a complex system of interdependent ecosystems, including sawgrass marshes, cypress swamps, mangrove forests, tropical hardwood hammocks, pine rocklands, coastal prairies, tidal mud flats, sloughs and estuaries, and the marine environment of Florida Bay.

The Florida Keys, meanwhile, are essentially a series of low, offshore islands composed of sand and coral. While the Upper and Middle Keys are principally made of **Key Largo limestone,** once the peaks of living coral forests, the Lower Keys are basically an enormous shoal, made of sand, compacted oolite, and Key Largo limestone and traversed by many channels—hence, the reason why the northernmost islands tend to be larger and longer, while the Lower Keys are smaller and

© DANIEL MARTONE

Mangrove forests are prevalent in southern Florida.

82°F. On occasion, temperatures can reach over 90°F, and cold fronts, though rare, are indeed possible. Although such cold snaps don't normally last too long, they can create near-freezing conditions, sometimes resulting in the loss of tropical fish, sea turtles, and manatees. Nevertheless, while frost is possible in the Everglades, there is no known record of such an occurrence in Key West.

Summers, meanwhile, are hot and humid, with temperatures usually ranging from 72°F to 90°F and humidity well over 90 percent. Unless you're an avid angler, snorkeler, or scuba diver, in fact, you might want to avoid the unbearable summer months, when mosquitoes are abundant and afternoon thunderstorms are common. Although prevailing easterly trade winds and sea breezes can suppress the summertime heat, Key West has been known, at various times, to reach 100°F.

Hurricane Season

In southern Florida, the **dry season** usually runs from November through April. During this time, you'll experience abundant sunshine and less than 25 percent of the annual rainfall. The **wet season,** meanwhile, runs from May through October and usually constitutes more than 75 percent of the annual rainfall. Part of this rainfall may include infrequent hurricanes that can occur during the **Atlantic hurricane season,** which typically runs from June through November. Although hurricanes can certainly happen at other times of the year as well, most residents and visitors don't worry about such potentially destructive storms until June 1.

Based on wind speeds, hurricanes are classified on a scale that ranges from a mild Category 1 to a powerful Category 5. While Miami, the Everglades, and the Florida Keys haven't been hit by hurricanes very often, southern Floridians have certainly experienced their share of terrible storms, including the Labor Day hurricane of 1935, which killed more than 400 people and destroyed the Florida Keys' Overseas Railroad; Hurricane Andrew, which hit the Miami area in 1992 and was considered,

more numerous. In the Keys, you'll also find hardwood hammocks, mangrove swamps, and beaches, though many visitors come to experience the ecosystems that can't be seen above the water. Along the Atlantic side of the 220-mile-long Florida Keys archipelago, which technically stretches from Key Biscayne to the Dry Tortugas, lies a series of living **coral reefs,** filled with tropical fish and varied coral formations, constituting the third largest coral reef system in the world—and the only one of its kind in the continental United States. While snorkelers and scuba divers enjoy exploring these offshore coral reefs, anglers appreciate the **patch reefs** closer to the coast, which are usually teeming with worthy game fish.

CLIMATE

Positioned between the Gulf of Mexico, Florida Bay, and the Atlantic Ocean, southern Florida tends toward a **subtropical climate.** Typically, the fall, winter, and spring months, from November to April, are mild and pleasant, with temperatures ranging from 59°F to

AVERAGE TEMPERATURES

The table below gives average high/low temperatures in degrees Fahrenheit.

Month	Miami	Key West
January	75/59	75/65
February	77/60	76/66
March	79/64	79/69
April	82/68	82/72
May	85/72	85/76
June	88/75	88/79
July	89/76	89/80
August	89/77	90/79
September	88/76	88/79
October	85/72	85/76
November	80/67	81/72
December	77/62	77/67

until Hurricane Katrina, the costliest hurricane in U.S. history; and Hurricane Wilma, which caused massive damage in the Everglades and some flooding in the Lower Keys during the 2005 season.

ENVIRONMENTAL ISSUES

In general, southern Florida is heavily dependent upon a healthy environment. The effects of water pollution, overdevelopment, overfishing, and overhunting can easily affect at least two of its major industries—agriculture and tourism—not to mention the fragile ecosystems that compose this fascinating region. Of course, it's these very industries that have, at times, overwhelmed the ecosystems down here, especially in the Everglades, where habitat loss and long-term drainage efforts—to satisfy agricultural needs and a growing population— have had long-term negative effects on native flora and fauna. Oftentimes, the welfare of keystone species, such as the American alligator, has helped to reveal the condition of the entire region.

Researchers and conservationists are equally concerned about the health of the Florida Keys. While visiting the area, you'll find several ecofriendly adventure operators, plus animal facilities, such as the Florida Keys Wild Bird Center in Key Largo and the Turtle Hospital in Marathon, that are doing what they can to save marine birds and animals from manmade detriments, such as mercury poisoning, fishing line and net entanglements, boat strikes, intestinal impaction due to the ingestion of floating debris, and oil spills, including the Deepwater Horizon catastrophe of April 2010. Be sure to visit such facilities to learn more about how you can help minimize your impact on the easily susceptible ecosystems of southern Florida.

Flora and Fauna

The varied habitats that extend from the Everglades to the Florida Keys are home to literally thousands of animal, insect, and plant species, more than can possibly be listed here. Nevertheless, consider this section a sampling of what you can expect to encounter while visiting the marshes, forests, beaches, and coral reefs of southern Florida.

TREES

The Everglades, part of a massive watershed and subtropical wilderness north of the Florida Keys, nurture well over 120 different tree species. In Everglades National Park, for instance, you'll spy numerous **wetland tree islands** and **upland hardwood hammocks,** both of which support various mammals and serve as critical rookeries for wading and migratory birds.

The tree islands typically consist of bay, willow, bald cypress, dwarf cypress, or pond apple trees. The **cypress,** perhaps the most recognizable tree in the Everglades, is curious in that it can live either on dry land or in water and, unlike many subtropical trees, tends to shed its leaves every autumn.

The hardwood hammocks, meanwhile, often consist of landlubbing trees such as slash pine, live oak, royal palm, cabbage palm, saw palmetto, and West Indian mahogany. Another intriguing tree often present in these drier hardwood hammocks, as well as throughout the Florida Keys, is the **gumbo limbo,** a fast-growing, salt-tolerant tropical tree that has featherlike leaves and a shiny red exfoliating bark. Interestingly, it's also called the "tourist tree" due to the bark's resemblance to a peeling sunburn.

Prevalent throughout the marshes and tidal shores of both the Everglades and the Florida Keys is the **mangrove,** a coastal tree noted for its vast, interlaced, aboveground root system. Mangroves, which constitute many of the smaller keys in this region, are a keystone plant community in southern Florida, where they serve as a buffer along the coast. Together, these interlocked trees protect the land from wind and waves, reduce soil erosion, build the soil through growth and decomposition, and provide a border between saline coastal waters and freshwater marshes. Intolerant of cold weather and typically classified as black, white, or red, mangroves are protected by law, so be sure not to damage or deface any while exploring the backcountry waters.

In the Florida Keys, you might also spy small, ornamental trees like the buttonwood, the palmlike coontie, and the coral bean, which has spiny, magenta-hued leaves and toxic seeds. Flowering trees also abound here, such as the geiger tree, the locust berry, the poisonwood, and the coco-plum, the fruit of which is often used in preserves. Other curious native species include the strangler fig, the wild coffee, and the silver palm. In addition, the Keys are well

© DANIEL MARTONE

a hibiscus in bloom

known for several nonnative tree species, such as mango, coconut palm, and key lime.

PLANTS AND FLOWERS

Oases for nature lovers, the Everglades and the Florida Keys boast a wide array of native plants. In the Everglades, for instance, you'll encounter more than 100 marsh plant species that live in water for most or all of the year. Perhaps the most prevalent of these is **sawgrass,** a hardy sedge named for its serrated leaf blade, which now constitutes thousands of acres of marshland in the Everglades. Here, you'll also spy cattails, algae, and a variety of floating aquatic plants like bladderwort, spatterdock, maidencane, and white water lily.

In addition, this warm, often humid region nurtures an assortment of **epiphytes,** plants that grow on the branches, trunks, and leaves of other trees. Deriving their water and nutrients from the air, epiphytes here include beautiful orchids, bromeliads, tropical ferns, and Spanish moss.

Along the beaches of southern Florida, even in the Florida Keys, you're likely to see sandspur plants, the seeds of which resemble little spiked balls, as well as sea grapes and sea oats, both salt-tolerant plants that help to stabilize sand dunes and prevent erosion. While exploring the Florida Keys, you're also bound to see vibrant tropical flowers, whether you're driving along the Overseas Highway or walking amid the lush gardens of a posh resort. Two of the most common flowering plants down here are the **hibiscus** and the **bougainvillea,** both of which are usually ablaze with white, pink, red, orange, purple, or yellow flowers.

MAMMALS

More than 40 mammal species call the Everglades home, including cotton mice, rice rats, skunks, raccoons, opossums, marsh rabbits, river otters, gray foxes, bobcats, and white-tailed deer. Of course, the most well-known and most elusive mammal in the Everglades is the endangered **Florida panther,** the official state animal and the symbol of this vast, fragile ecosystem. Typically, panthers live in

© DANIEL MARTONE

A bottlenose dolphin lurks in the Middle Keys.

the upland areas, where they feed on deer and other mammals.

Raccoons and opossums dwell in the Florida Keys as well, along with oodles of feral cats. The Lower Keys are also home to the diminutive **Key deer,** a subspecies of the Virginia white-tailed deer. Key deer, which typically weigh 65–80 pounds, tend to stand between 24 and 32 inches high. Researchers believe that the Key deer migrated from the Florida mainland to the Florida Keys thousands of years ago. Found nowhere else in the world, the Key deer were in danger of extinction in the 1940s, until the establishment of the National Key Deer Refuge in 1957.

Naturally, marine mammals are prevalent in the Florida Keys, too. On sightseeing cruises, you're bound to spot an **Atlantic bottlenose dolphin** or an **Atlantic spotted dolphin.** Rare sightings of the endangered **West Indian manatee,** or "sea cow," are also possible in the Florida Keys as well as the Everglades, especially in warmer waters. A giant yet gentle creature, favoring a vegetarian diet, the manatee is actually Florida's state marine mammal.

BIRDS

Boasting over 350 wading or migratory bird species, the Everglades and the Florida Keys constitute a bird-watcher's paradise. It's no wonder that the famous ornithologist John James Audubon traveled to southern Florida to paint the region's native birds. Although over-hunting and habitat destruction have caused a steep decline in the native bird population since Audubon's time, you'll still encounter plenty of wonderful species during your visit to southern Florida.

In the Everglades, for instance, you'll encounter a variety of wading birds, including the white ibis, glossy ibis, wood stork, green-backed heron, great white heron, great blue heron, great egret, snowy egret, reddish egret, and roseate spoonbill. Other commonly seen birds range from cardinals and meadowlarks to blue jays and red-bellied woodpeckers. If you're looking for raptors, you're likely to spot red-shouldered hawks, barred owls, ospreys, and, if you're lucky, a bald eagle or two.

To the south, the Florida Keys nurture many

Pelicans drift in an Islamorada marina.

© LAURA MARTONE

of the same bird species that you'll find in the Everglades. In addition, you might spot common sandpipers, double-crested cormorants, laughing gulls, mangrove cuckoos, mourning doves, turkey vultures, and white-crowned pigeons. Also, no matter where you travel in the Keys, you're bound to encounter the brown pelican, which you might see floating in a marina, standing on a beach, or coasting above the water.

REPTILES

While exploring the Everglades, keep an eye out for the more than 50 species of reptiles found here. Whether you're traveling by kayak, canoe, airboat, or foot, you're likely to see at least some of the 26 snake species, 16 turtle species, and various lizards that call the Everglades home. **Snakes** can be found in nearly every habitat, from brown water snakes in freshwater ponds to mangrove salt marsh snakes in the saltwater marshes. Of course, you'll also find several venomous varieties here, including the Florida cottonmouth, the multicolored eastern coral snake, and the pygmy rattler, so be aware at all times. Meanwhile, notable **turtle** species in the Everglades include the striped mud turtle, the peninsula cooter, the Florida

ALLIGATORS VS. CROCODILES

Southern Florida is home to a wide variety of reptiles, including snakes, iguanas, and sea turtles. Of course, the most well-known species are the **American alligator** *(Alligator mississippiensis)* and the **American crocodile** *(Crocodylus acutus)*. While these two carnivorous crocodilians – which are both members of the Reptilia class and the Crocodylia order – resemble each other greatly, there are a number of differences between them.

Typically, alligators dwell in freshwater habitats throughout the Everglades and the Lower Florida Keys. Their telltale characteristics include brown scales, a wide, U-shaped snout, and a hidden fourth tooth on the lower jaw. Crocodiles, meanwhile, tend to be more elusive – a threatened species within saltwater habitats in the Everglades and places like Dagny Johnson Key Largo Hammock Botanical State Park. Their telltale characteristics include grayish-green scales, a narrow, V-shaped snout, and a lower fourth tooth that juts out noticeably. As a rule, crocodiles are faster, more active, and more aggressive than alligators, and they tend to spend more time in the water.

Alligators can reach up to 15 feet in length, weigh up to 1,000 pounds, and live for up to 60 years. Normally, they reach maturity after 4-7 years and can lay 10-50 eggs, with hatching occurring after a 65-day incubation period. Crocodiles, conversely, can reach up to 20 feet in length, weigh up to 2,200 pounds, and live for up to 75 years. Unlike alligators, they reach maturity after 10-15 years and can lay 20-60 eggs, with hatching occurring after about 90 days.

Of course, alligators and crocodiles have plenty of common traits. For one thing, the location of their eyes, ears, and nostrils on the top of their heads allows them to conceal much of their bodies underwater, making it easier to sneak up on their prey, which consists of fish, reptiles, rodents, birds, insects, and other mammals – some of which can be half their size. In addition, all crocodilians lay their eggs on land, well above the water line, where the females guard them from predators that might try to unearth them. Despite such efforts, many crocodilian eggs fall prey to other animals.

Other similar traits include webbed feet, powerful jaws, keen eyesight, an excellent sense of smell and hearing, an armored exterior made up of overlapping scales, a broad tail that enables them to swim smoothly and quickly, and short legs that can move surprisingly fast on dry land. In fact, although both species tend to float listlessly in the water like drifting logs, they can actually swim up to 20 miles per hour and run up to 11 miles per hour – a fact that you should well remember the next time you venture into the wilderness.

red-belly turtle, and the yellow-bellied slider, all of which favor freshwater ponds and marshes. In the pinelands and hardwood hammocks, you may also spy tiny camouflaged **lizards,** such as native green anoles, exotic brown anoles, and Florida reef geckos, the smallest lizards in North America.

Naturally, most visitors come to the Everglades hoping to catch a glimpse of an **American alligator**—incidentally, the state reptile—several of which you might spot drifting in a slough, resting in an alligator hole, or sunbathing alongside Tamiami Trail. You're also likely to see these prehistoric-looking creatures in the Florida Keys, especially near places like the Blue Hole on Big Pine Key. In Dagny Johnson Key Largo Hammock Botanical State Park, you might even spy an **American crocodile.** Just be advised that crocodiles can be far more aggressive than alligators. Other commonly seen reptiles here include brown and green anoles, corn snakes, Mediterranean geckos, and the ever-present green iguana, which you'll surely encounter everywhere, from Islamorada's Theater of the Sea to the restful trees of Key West's Old Town.

While exploring the Florida Keys, you might also be lucky enough to spot a **sea turtle,** in either the offshore waters or an onshore facility, such as Theater of the Sea or the Turtle Hospital in Marathon. Some of these species include the Kemp's Ridley turtle, the hawksbill turtle, the leatherback turtle, the loggerhead turtle, and the green turtle—all of which are either threatened or endangered.

AMPHIBIANS

In addition to numerous birds and reptiles, the Florida Everglades are also home to nearly 20 species of **frogs, toads,** and **salamanders,** including the grass frog, supposedly the tiniest frog in North America, and the Everglades dwarf siren, a salamander that is only found in the Everglades. Of course, most amphibians are nocturnal, well-camouflaged creatures, so you're more likely to hear them than see them. That's certainly the case with pig frogs, whose grunts can be heard in freshwater marshes,

and noisy oak toads, which favor pinelands, hardwood hammocks, and wet sawgrass communities.

FISH AND SEALIFE

Given the prevalence of salt water, fresh water, and brackish water in and around the Everglades and the Florida Keys, it surely comes as no surprise that there are more than 600 species of tropical and game fish in southern Florida, some of which you might spy while snorkeling along an offshore coral reef and some of which you might snag from a fishing boat in the backcountry. Depending on the fishing season, you could encounter redfish (also known as "red drum"), red grouper, bonefish, permit, common snook, amberjack, Spanish mackerel, wahoo, yellowfin tuna, king mackerel (also known as "kingfish"), tarpon, sailfish, blue marlin, and mahimahi, which are also known as "dorado" or "dolphinfish." While snorkeling or diving, you might see some of these very same species, plus colorful Spanish hogfish and yellowtail snapper, torpedo-shaped barracuda, abundant nurse sharks, southern stingrays, spotted moray eels, and kaleidoscopic queen angelfish. In the Everglades, you might also spy freshwater fish like the Florida gar, the mosquitofish, and the official state freshwater fish, the largemouth bass.

Of course, fish aren't the only entities you'll observe while exploring the coral reefs of the Florida Keys National Marine Sanctuary. Here, you may also notice banded coral shrimp, stone crabs, fire sponges, sea cucumbers, sea anemones, long-spined urchins, jellyfish, sand dollars, sea fans, sea stars, the Portuguese man-of-war, the spiny lobster, the Florida fighting conch, and a variety of coral, including brain coral, fire coral, elkhorn coral, and staghorn coral. Remember: As tempting as it might seem, it is illegal to collect any and all coral formations.

INSECTS AND ARACHNIDS

Between the Everglades and the Florida Keys, there are literally hundreds of insect and arachnid species, ranging in size from the minuscule chigger to the giant diving beetle. In the

© LAURA MARTONE

There are more than 600 species of tropical and game fish in southern Florida.

Everglades, four of the most commonly spotted insects include the large **lubber grasshopper,** which has wings but cannot fly; the **golden orb weaver,** a beautiful spider that weaves intricate webs in the hardwood hammocks; the bloodsucking **mosquito,** which, though annoying to humans, is a critical part of the food chain in mangrove estuaries; and the gorgeous **dragonfly,** affectionately known as a "mosquito hawk." Other curious creatures in the Everglades include the apple snail and the Liguus tree snail.

Many of these insects, including the pesky mosquito, can be seen—and, in some cases, felt—in the Florida Keys. Besides the mosquito, other bloodthirsty critters include the **no-see-um,** or "punkie," a tiny biting gnat that thrives in coastal areas, especially during the summer months. Down here, you may also spy **woodland cicadas,** curious crablike **spiny orb weavers,** and **fire ants,** large, aggressive red ants that are prevalent in tropical areas, capable of building large mounds, and inclined to inflict painful stings.

In both the Everglades and the Florida Keys archipelago, some of the most beautiful insects are, of course, **butterflies,** more than 50 species of which can be spotted in southern Florida. Some commonly spotted species include the Florida purplewing, the hammock skipper, the mangrove skipper, the sleepy orange, the white peacock, and the zebra longwing, which is actually the official state butterfly.

ENDANGERED SPECIES

At least 70 animal species found in the Everglades and the Florida Keys are federally listed as threatened or endangered, largely due to habitat loss, urban development, water flow alteration, overhunting, and, in some cases, highway collisions. Some endangered creatures, such as the Schaus swallowtail butterfly, the Key Largo cotton mouse, the Key Largo woodrat, and the snail kite (a bird that survives exclusively on the apple snail) are perhaps less well known to outsiders. Others, however, such as the Florida panther, the West Indian manatee, the American crocodile, and the Key deer, receive a lot more attention from conservationists, media representatives, and government officials.

The **Florida panther,** a large, long-tailed cat of which there are only about 100 left in the wild, is perhaps the most at risk for extinction. Presently, conservation efforts include radio-tracking collared individuals and introducing other panther strains to increase the gene pool.

Meanwhile, the **West Indian manatee,** a gentle creature that feeds on aquatic vegetation and typically inhabits sloughs, shallow estuaries, and saltwater bays, has been systematically diminished by boat collisions, vandal attacks, poachers, habitat destruction, and cold stress. Although it's protected by the Marine Mammal Protection Act of 1972 and the Endangered Species Act of 1973, human actions continue to threaten, harm, or kill the manatee. Luckily, groups like the Save the Manatee Club, which is based in Maitland, Florida, are doing what they can to save these endangered creatures, though individuals can help by obeying speed laws, recording manatee sightings, and reporting criminal activities involving these gentle marine mammals.

Sea turtles, such as the Kemp's Ridley turtle, the hawksbill turtle, the leatherback turtle, the loggerhead turtle, and the green turtle, have long been endangered everywhere, though conservation efforts are underway throughout Florida and other parts of the world. Other endangered bird species in the Everglades include the Arctic peregrine falcon, the Cape Sable seaside sparrow, the southern bald eagle, and the wood stork.

REINTRODUCTION PROGRAMS

Following successful efforts to reintroduce the **eastern bluebird** to the Florida Everglades, the National Park Service is currently attempting to reintroduce the **Florida wild turkey** to Everglades National Park. Such reintroduction programs are critical for habitat restoration efforts. In the case of the Florida wild turkey, for example, this reintroduction program has a twofold benefit: to help restore the pine rocklands of the Everglades and to monitor the progress of said restoration.

Perhaps more well known, though, are the reintroduction programs that involve endangered **sea turtles.** In the Florida Keys, for instance, the Turtle Hospital, which opened in 1986, has endeavored to rehabilitate injured sea turtles and return them to the wild. In addition, the hospital educates the public about the plight of sea turtles, conducts helpful research, and strives for environmental legislation that will make beaches and offshore waters safer and cleaner for these endangered creatures.

History

EARLY CIVILIZATION

Even without written records, it's generally accepted among historians that Native American tribes have inhabited the region now known as southern Florida for thousands of years, perhaps as early as 10,000 B.C. As evidenced by archaeological finds and the accounts of Spanish explorers in the early 1500s, the predominant tribes in this region were the Tequesta Indians in the Biscayne Bay area near present-day Miami, the Seminole Indians in the Everglades, and the Calusa Indians in the Florida Keys. The first European explorer to encounter these native tribes was allegedly Juan Ponce de León, who traveled to these waters on behalf of Spain in 1513. Although there's no evidence that he actually interacted with the Indians, written accounts of his expedition indicate their presence in southern Florida, even amid the twisted islands that de León named Los Martires (The Martyrs), later known as the Florida Keys.

Once Spain claimed the Florida territory as

its own, European interactions with the native peoples increased—interactions that varied from tribe to tribe. While the Tequesta, for instance, welcomed the Spanish explorers that took refuge in Biscayne Bay in 1565, the fierce Calusa Indians subjected others to repeated attacks.

COLONIALISM

After Florida was claimed by Spain, life changed drastically for the native peoples here. Over the ensuing decades, many Indians died as a result of European diseases and various battles between the Spanish, French, and British. By the mid-1700s, in fact, most of the Tequesta and Calusa Indians had either moved elsewhere or been sold into slavery by the British. Those that remained were relocated to Cuba in 1763, when Spain transferred the Florida territory to Britain. Although the Seminole Indians were also adversely affected by the Europeans' presence, they nonetheless managed to survive in the Everglades.

By the 1780s, the United States had been formed, though Florida was once again under Spanish control. Given incidents like the First and Second Seminole Wars during the first half of the 19th century, it took some time for permanent settlements to take root. In fact, by the late 1830s, Miami was little more than a fort beside the sea.

While Europeans were trying to settle this diverse region, pirates were trolling the waters of the Florida Keys, plundering unsuspecting ships and salvaging cargo. By the 1820s, the U.S. Navy had managed to scare away most of the marauding pirates, and permanent settlers, from places like Cuba, the Bahamas, and the northeastern United States, were beginning to populate the Upper, Middle, and Lower Keys. One of the earliest settlements was that of Indian Key, which became, in 1836, the first county seat of Dade County and, by 1840, was destroyed by invading Indians during the Second Seminole War, a harrowing invasion that also caused the disbandment of Conch Town, a Bahamian settlement in the Middle Keys. In 1845, while Florida was becoming the 27th U.S. state, four main industries were

underway in the Florida Keys: farming, fishing, salt production, and cargo salvaging. By the mid-1800s, it was cargo salvaging that had become the most lucrative enterprise, helping to make Key West one of the richest cities in the country by the late 1800s.

CIVIL WAR

By 1860, the island of Key West had become the largest and richest city in the state, and although Florida joined the Confederate States of America during the American Civil War, the isolated Southernmost City remained in Union hands because of the presence of a naval base. Fort Zachary Taylor, constructed between 1845 and 1866, became an important outpost during the Civil War, while Fort Jefferson in the Dry Tortugas was used as a military prison during and after the conflict. Also in the 1860s and 1870s, many Cuban refugees escaped to Key West, where they initiated a thriving cigar-making industry, which ultimately helped to replace the dwindling salt and salvaging industries in the late 1800s.

THE 20TH CENTURY

By the 1890s, Miami, which was officially incorporated as a city in 1896, was experiencing a real estate boom and subsequent population growth. Meanwhile, the Florida Keys were thriving due to the sponging and cigar-making industries. By the turn of the 20th century, however, the expansion of this area was due, in large part, to Henry Flagler, who envisioned a 130-mile extension of the Florida East Coast Railway between the mainland and Key West. In 1904, railroad construction began on Key Vaca, now known as Marathon, and by 1908, scheduled daily train service was helping to bring more settlers to Key Largo, the largest and northernmost island in the Florida Keys. By 1912, after the tireless efforts of hundreds of workers, Flagler's costly **Overseas Railroad** had become a reality. Even Key West, which became a strategic training base for U.S. Army and Navy forces during World War I, benefited greatly from the Overseas Railroad. Even Prohibition didn't hinder the Southernmost

City, which soon witnessed a rise in rumrunning and bootlegging.

During the 1920s, Miami also thrived culturally and financially, earning its nickname "The Magic City." In addition, tourism began to expand in the Everglades, largely due to the Seminole Indians, who made their living from homemade crafts and alligator-wrestling spectacles, and the 1928 opening of the Tamiami Trail between Tampa and Miami, the first official road across the Everglades. At the same time, the state completed a highway and ferry service alongside the Overseas Railroad, which continued to bring settlers, tourists, and

THE FORT TAYLOR TIMELINE

Originally positioned 1,200 feet offshore of Key West, the fortress that would later become **Fort Zachary Taylor** (www.forttaylor.org) was constructed as part of America's Third System of fortifications – a plan hatched after the War of 1812 to build new fortresses or remodel old ones along the Eastern Seaboard. Eventually, Fort Taylor became one of the most important fortresses of the mid-19th century. The following timeline offers a glimpse at the history of this impressive fort.

- **1821:** After the United States acquires the Florida territory, the federal government considers extending the Third System to protect the Gulf Coast.

- **1836:** Following a survey of Key West to determine the possibility of building a fort between the Straits of Florida and the Gulf of Mexico, the U.S. Congress decides to allocate funds to begin construction.

- **1845:** After much delayed funding, construction of the fort finally begins. As planned by the U.S. Army Corps of Engineers, the granite foundation of the three-tiered fort is established in offshore waters on the southwestern side of the island. Construction of the fort, which will eventually be linked to Key West by a wooden causeway, proves to be a challenge. Materials and workers have to be shipped from the mainland, funding problems often suspend construction, and yellow fever is common among the workers.

- **1846:** A terrible hurricane hits Key West, toppling the lighthouse, taking at least 50 lives, and damaging almost every building in town. Construction of the fort continues soon afterward.

- **1850:** In November, the structure is named for President Zachary Taylor.

- **1859:** Much of the trapezoid-shaped fortress is complete, including some cannons, tidal flush latrines, and a drawbridge.

- **1860:** Though not finished, Fort Taylor is ready for occupancy. Following President Abraham Lincoln's election, southern politicians discuss seceding from the Union, and secessionists seize several federal forts. While Florida considers secession, Captain E. B. Hunt, the current commander of the fort project, meets with other officers to discuss securing Fort Taylor and nearby Fort Jefferson for the Union. On November 20, U.S. Artillery Captain John Brannan orders 20 men to move into the fort under the guise of a training mission. Hunt arrives on December 2 with another 60 laborers.

- **1861-1865:** In early January of 1861, Florida secedes from the Union, and when the news reaches Key West, Hunt orders Brannan to assume military command of Fort Taylor. Though the fort contains 60 mounted cannons, numerous troops and civilian laborers, and enough stores for four months, Brannan requests additional soldiers and supplies. All communications are now routed through Havana, and in the following months, the fort receives more cannons, black powder, ammunition, and supplies. Despite formidable seaward defenses, the fort is still vulnerable to a land attack from Key West, so the engineers strengthen the cover face and mount additional cannons. During the American Civil War, Fort Taylor serves as the headquarters for the Union Navy East Gulf Coast

cargo to the Florida Keys—until, that is, the Labor Day hurricane of 1935 brought an end to Flagler's dream. Without modern detection techniques, the people of the Upper and Middle Florida Keys were caught off guard by this powerful storm, eventually considered the first recorded Category 5 hurricane to hit the United States. Forming on August 29, 1935, during a relatively quiet season, this legendary hurricane began as a small tropical storm and grew explosively during the Labor Day weekend, eventually making landfall with winds as high as 200 miles per hour. The hurricane was so monstrous that it single-handedly destroyed

Blockading Squadron, which captures about 300 Confederate vessels. After the war ends in April of 1865, troops are transferred from Fort Taylor to other posts, though Army engineers remain to continue construction on the cover face. On October 23, 1865, a hurricane passes west of the fort, destroying part of the seawall and the bridge to Key West.

- **1866:** Technically, the fort is complete, though construction continues.

- **1871:** The Secretary of War approves a plan to modify Fort Taylor, calling for the addition of two barbettes and the fortification of the main magazines.

- **1875:** After years of inadequate funding, another destructive hurricane halts work on the fort.

- **1885:** Secretary of War William Endicott chairs a panel that revisits the nation's harbor defense system and decides to modernize Fort Taylor. Congress approves the plan, but funds are slow to come.

- **1896:** Given the likelihood of a war with Spain, funding becomes available for Fort Taylor.

- **1897:** Army engineers and civilian contractors begin the process of upgrading the Civil War fort and military reservation.

- **1898:** When the Spanish-American War erupts, soldiers again occupy the fort, and construction continues. After removing the top two tiers, the engineers create a new entrance, fortify the casemates, and construct two new batteries.

- **1902:** Laborers complete the batteries and mount seacoast mortars.

- **1903-1945:** The coastal weaponry, operated by the U.S. Army's Coastal Artillery Corps and the Florida National Guard, remains at Fort Taylor until mid-World War II, after which the Army builds new mounts for anti-aircraft guns. At the war's end, the Coastal Artillery Corps is abolished.

- **1947:** After assuming control of the property, the U.S. Navy removes the anti-aircraft guns.

- **1950:** No longer used for coastal defense, Fort Taylor is listed as government excess property and eventually relegated to a scrap metal yard.

- **1968:** Once the fort is landlocked in the mid-1960s by the Navy, volunteers excavate Civil War guns, cannons, and ammunition from long-abandoned sections.

- **1970:** The Navy transfers the property to the Department of the Interior.

- **1971:** Fort Taylor is listed on the National Register of Historic Places.

- **1973:** The fort becomes a National Historic Landmark.

- **1976:** The Florida Park Service acquires Fort Taylor.

- **1985:** The fort opens as a state park, and soon afterward, a moat is dug around the fortress – to prevent easy entry into the structure and to create the illusion of its early days.

the Overseas Railroad and claimed at least 400 people in Florida and other Eastern states.

Following the death and destruction caused by the hurricane, the Florida Keys experienced a financial downturn during the 1930s—also as a result of the collapse of trade with Cuba, the decline of the cigar industry, and the closing of the Key West Naval Station. Similarly, Miami experienced an economic decline because of the statewide real estate collapse, an equally devastating hurricane in the 1920s, and, of course, the Great Depression. Three factors, however, saved the Florida Keys: the state-funded creation of the Overseas Highway in 1938, the attention of famous residents like Ernest Hemingway and President Harry S. Truman, and the expansion of the U.S. Navy in the Lower Keys. Miami, too, benefited from World War II, and by the 1950s, tourism became the dominant industry throughout southern Florida.

A growing concern for conservation seemed to go hand in hand with this economic upswing. Everglades National Park, for instance, was established in 1947 to conserve this fragile ecosystem and prevent further degradation of its habitats, flora, and fauna. A decade later, in 1957, the same year that the Seminole Tribe of Florida officially formed, the federal government designated the National Key Deer Refuge in the Lower Keys.

During the 1960s, while many Cubans were emigrating to Miami and increasing the city's population, the focus in the Florida Keys began to shift to the offshore coral reefs along the eastern side of southern Florida, which together constitute the third largest coral reef system in the world. By 1963, John Pennekamp Coral Reef State Park had become America's first undersea park, and in 1968, Biscayne National Monument was established north of Key Largo, eventually to become Biscayne National Park in 1980. In 1974, Big Cypress National Preserve, which has long been home to the Seminole and Miccosukee Tribes, became one of the country's first federally protected preserves, and after the Key Largo National Marine Sanctuary was established in 1975 and the Looe Key National Marine

Sanctuary followed in 1981, the Florida Keys archipelago truly began to secure its niche as a world-class underwater diving destination.

Conservation efforts continued into the 1990s, with the establishment of the Florida Keys National Marine Sanctuary in 1990 and Dry Tortugas National Park in 1992. Even remnants of "Flagler's Folly" have become part of the tourism landscape, most notably places like the coral rock quarries of Windley Key Fossil Reef Geological State Park, the early 20th-century worker buildings on Pigeon Key, and the old railroad bridge that's now part of Bahia Honda State Park.

Unfortunately, this growing tourism industry experienced a temporary setback in April of 1982, when a U.S. Border Patrol blockade near Florida City caused an enormous traffic jam for those leaving the Florida Keys via U.S. 1. In response to this disruptive search for illegal aliens and potential drug runners, Key West and the rest of the Florida Keys briefly declared their secession from the United States, subsequently forming a micronation called the Conch Republic. Today, this incident, which successfully ended the Border Patrol blockade, is celebrated with an annual Conch Republic Independence Celebration in Key West and a similar event in Key Largo. Despite this upset, the Florida Keys continued to thrive, and by 1997, several Upper Keys were incorporated into the town of Islamorada.

Meanwhile, the 1980s and 1990s were not as kind to Miami, which experienced drug wars, hurricanes, and increased crime, among other crises. In fact, Miami is still one of the most dangerous cities in America.

CONTEMPORARY TIMES

In the 21st century, tourism has continued to be the lifeblood of southern Florida. Despite the impact of other industries, such as international trade in Miami, agriculture in the Everglades, and commercial fishing in the Florida Keys, southern Florida has endured as a popular vacation and recreation destination, making it, in fact, one of the more financially stable regions in a state that was hit hard by a nationwide economic downturn.

Government and Economy

LOCAL GOVERNMENT

In general, the political climate of southern Florida is heavily Democratic. Given the cultural diversity of this region, it might also come as no surprise that, over the years, several of Miami's mayors and commissioners have been Latinos. The local government of Key West, which also serves as the Monroe County seat, has been equally diverse. The mayors down here have included such colorful characters as Carlos Manuel de Céspedes (1875–1876), father of the Cuban Republic, and Richard A. Heyman (1983–1985 and 1987–1989), one of the country's first openly gay public officials.

ECONOMY

Throughout much of Miami's past, seasonal tourism has been the overriding industry. Nowadays, however, the local economy has diversified to include year-round tourism as well as international trade and international banking.

The economy of the Florida Everglades, meanwhile, has long revolved around agriculture, commercial fishing, recreation, and tourism. While some of these industries have become the subject of controversy over the years, due to the detrimental impact on the fragile Everglades ecosystem, perhaps no industry has been as controversial or as devastating as the production of drinking water. Over the years, water suppliers in southern Florida have systematically drained the Everglades, to such a degree that the state is now in the midst of a costly restoration effort. As of 2007, the state of Florida refused to issue new water supply permits for the region and instructed water utilities to develop alternative means of water production, such as desalination techniques, for the growing population of southern Florida, which has, in recent years, depended on an estimated daily supply of 500 million gallons of water from the Everglades.

© DANIEL MARTONE

Nurseries line Krome Avenue in the Everglades.

The economic history of the Florida Keys has been just as complicated. During the 19th century, the regional economy evolved from a dependence on cargo salvaging—which, incidentally, helped to make Key West one of the richest cities in America—to a reliance on sponging, cigar-making, and commercial fishing. By the 1930s, the Florida Keys were suffering a financial decline, soon to be remedied by the U.S. Navy, which expanded its presence in the Lower Keys during that time. Following World War II, fishing and tourism became the dominant industries in the Keys, which is still the case today.

Agriculture

Southern Florida is a bountiful place, so it's no surprise that agriculture plays a critical role in the local economy. The Everglades, for instance, have an abundance of plant nurseries, which literally line miles of Krome Avenue north of Homestead. The plethora of farmers markets in Miami-Dade County is also an indication of the region's agricultural abundance. The subtropical climate allows for a year-round growing season, resulting in a diverse agricultural industry that, according to county statistics, employs more than 20,000 people and amasses more than $2.7 billion annually.

Shipping and Fishing

Given that the Port of Miami is nicknamed the "cruise capital of the world," it makes sense that commercial shipping is a viable industry in southern Florida. In the Florida Keys, meanwhile, commercial fishing is a major part of the economy. Though plenty of fishing guides and charter services make their living from visiting tourists, several fishing companies actually rely on the wholesale seafood market for their livelihood. Depending on the season, such fisheries sell a variety of fish, shrimp, Florida lobster, and stone crabs.

Tourism

While agriculture and fishing are important facets of the southern Florida economy, it

Sightseeing tours abound in Key West.

© DANIEL MARTONE

surely comes as no surprise that Miami, the Everglades, and the Florida Keys rely heavily on the tourism industry for survival. The entire area boasts numerous hotels, resorts, fine restaurants, golf courses, sightseeing tours, fishing charters, diving operators, national and state parks, shopping districts, and annual events—all of which help to fund local communities. In the Florida Keys, the peak tourist season—which essentially runs from late December to early January and from mid-February through April—is often so lucrative that it helps to sustain residents through much leaner times, such as the month of September.

People and Culture

NATIVE PEOPLES

Long before Spanish explorers encountered the land now known as southern Florida, various American Indian tribes called this bountiful region home. Although it's difficult to pinpoint all the native peoples that once lived here, archaeological finds have indicated that three specific tribes once dominated the area.

Along the southeastern Atlantic coast of Florida, in the territories now known as Broward and Miami-Dade Counties, lived the **Tequesta Indians.** Also called the Tekesta, Chequesta, and Vizcaynos, the Tequesta inhabited this region from at least the 13th century to the mid-18th century—when they had all but disappeared. During that time, the Tequesta established towns and camps at the mouths of rivers, streams, and inlets, where they fished, hunted, and gathered fruit and roots. In general, their diet consisted of manatees, sharks, sailfish, porpoises, stingrays, sea turtles, snails, lobster, venison, saw palmettos, sea grapes, prickly pear fruit, and other plants. Given the generally mild climate, clothing was minimal, ranging from loincloths made of deer hide to skirts crafted from Spanish moss, and tools consisted of canoes, nets, spears, bows, arrows, and simple pottery. At the height of the mosquito season, the Tequesta would typically relocate to the Florida Keys or to barrier islands in Biscayne Bay.

The Everglades, meanwhile, constituted the home of the **Seminole Indians.** While researchers claim that the Seminole's ancestors lived in the area 12,000 years ago, it was in the early 1500s that Europeans first encountered the tribe that would become known as the Seminole, which, at that time, numbered nearly 200,000 people. Unfortunately, thousands of these Indians were killed by European diseases, such as measles and smallpox, as well as the resulting wars between the Spanish, English, and French. Unlike the Tequesta, however, the Seminole survived such intrusions and subsequently thrived in the virgin forests and grass flats of the Everglades.

In the early 1800s, the Seminole lived in chickee-style domiciles, essentially palmetto thatch over cypress log frames, and clothing tended to be more complicated and more colorful than that of the Tequesta. Like the Tequesta, however, the Seminole relied on the bountiful flora and fauna of southern Florida for sustenance, including native stone crabs. Although their customs have evolved over the years, some of their traditions still remain, such as an affinity for beadwork, the fashioning of palmetto fiber husk dolls, and the sacred springtime gatherings known as the Green Corn Dance.

Although the Tequesta sometimes inhabited the Florida Keys, it was the **Calusa Indians** that dominated the region between the southwestern coast of mainland Florida and the Florida Keys. As with the Tequesta, most of the Calusa tribe died out in the mid-1700s, and any remaining Indians were sold as slaves or sent to Cuba. Before that time, however, the Calusa Indians thrived in this part of Florida. Known as the "Shell Indians," the Calusa allegedly numbered 50,000 people at one time.

In the early 1500s, when Spanish explorers

first discovered them, they were known to be a fierce, warmongering people. Like other Indians in southern Florida, the Calusa lived along the coast and inner waterways, relying on fish, eels, turtles, conch, crabs, clams, lobster, oysters, and deer for sustenance. Their homes were typically built on stilts, with palmetto thatch roofs and no walls, and their tools consisted of nets, spears, dugout canoes, and arrowheads made of fish bones. In addition, archaeological finds indicate that the Calusa collected shells, which they used as tools, utensils, jewelry, and shrine ornaments—hence, the nickname "Shell Indians." They were also known to salvage the wealth from shipwrecks along the coast, much as Key West residents did in later centuries.

THE IMMIGRANTS

Of course, native peoples were not the only inhabitants of southern Florida. Immigrants from Europe, Cuba, Haiti, and the Bahamas helped to establish the communities that exist today. Miami, for instance, is a mosaic of various cultures and cuisines, as evidenced by neighborhoods like Little Havana and Little Haiti. The Florida Keys were also settled, in part, by immigrants. In the early 1800s, for example, Bahamian nationals came to these islands seeking autonomy. Evidence of their presence

WHAT'S IN A CONCH?

While visiting the Florida Keys, you're likely to hear or see the term "conch" (pronounced "conk") virtually everywhere. From menus that feature conch fritters and conch chowder to stores that offer Conch Republic souvenirs, this multipurpose term typically has one of three meanings in the Keys.

First of all, a conch can signify a marine gastropod, such as the large queen conch, the feisty Florida fighting conch, or the imported conch that's often found in Keys cuisine. Since the 20th century, however, the term "conch" has also been used to refer to a resident of Key West. Some residents even go so far as to differentiate between "saltwater conchs," or those residents actually born in Key West, and "freshwater conchs," or those who, though born elsewhere, have lived in Key West for at least seven years. While "conch" is now a widely used term for a Key West resident, regardless of his or her origin, the original meaning of "conch" solely applied to the Bahamian immigrants that arrived in Key West during the 18th and early 19th centuries and made their living by fishing, logging, and salvaging shipwrecks. Many of these so-called Conchs were descendants of European Loyalists who had fled to the Bahamas, the nearest British colony, during the American Revolution. After arriving in Key West, many of these im-

migrants established a neighborhood in the western part of Old Town that is still known today as Bahama Village.

There are many theories, of course, for why these Bahamian immigrants were called Conchs in the first place. One such theory is that the affluent British Loyalists who settled in the Bahamas looked down upon the native residents, calling them "conchs" because shellfish was an important aspect of their diet. Another theory suggests that Bahamians told British authorities that they'd rather "eat conch" than pay taxes levied by the British Crown. No matter the true inspiration, the fact is that the term "conch," while considered a derogatory expression for Bahamian immigrants in other parts of Florida, has become a source of pride for those who live in the Florida Keys. Just consider the events of April 23, 1982, when, in protest of a U.S. Border Patrol blockade near Florida City, the Florida Keys collectively declared their tongue-in-cheek secession from the United States, forming a micronation called the Conch Republic – an incident that's still celebrated today with such annual events as Key West's Conch Republic Independence Celebration, a zany 10-day festival that typically occurs in April and features everything from Conch Republic flag raisings to drag queen races to conch shell-blowing contests.

remains today in the form of specific buildings, such as the Adderley House in Marathon and the Oldest House Museum in Key West, as well as neighborhoods like Bahama Village, adjacent to Key West's Old Town.

MODERN DEMOGRAPHICS

Today, the influence of native peoples and varied immigrants is evident in the demographics of southern Florida. In the three-county metropolitan area (Miami-Dade, Broward, and Palm Beach Counties), for instance, Latinos comprise roughly 38 percent of the total population, which numbers around 5.4 million people. The Jewish community makes up around 10 percent of this heavily Democratic population, and other factions include Muslims, Canadians, Europeans, and Caribbean immigrants, plus former snowbirds from the Northeast who tend to be of Jewish, Muslim, Italian, Irish, African, Dominican, or Puerto Rican descent.

Although the population of the Florida Everglades is harder to assess, the people are predominantly Caucasian, Latino, and Native American, most notably Seminole or Miccosukee. The Florida Keys, meanwhile, encompass all of Monroe County; the county seat even lies in Key West. Overall, this archipelago has a population of about 74,700, 75 percent of which is Caucasian and 18 percent of which is Latino, with even smaller percentages of Asian and African American. Curiously, many of the residents here aren't native to the area. You'll find, for instance, that a lot of the locals are actually transplants from other parts of the United States, such as Midwestern snowbirds who decided to stay permanently in this subtropical paradise.

RELIGION

Given the ethnic diversity of southern Florida, it's no surprise that residents tend to practice a variety of religions, or none at all. While you'll find large Jewish and Catholic factions in Miami, for example, you'll also encounter, as with any multicultural American city, Methodists, Lutherans, Presbyterians,

© LAURA MARTONE

St. Paul's Episcopal Church on Duval Street in Key West

Buddhists, and Muslims. The same can be said for the Florida Keys, where you'll spot everything from the Key Largo Baptist Church to the Unitarian Universalist Fellowship of Key West to the iconic St. Paul's Episcopal Church on Duval Street in Old Town.

LANGUAGE

While English is the predominant language in most of Miami, the Everglades, and the Florida Keys, Spanish often seems to be a close second, perhaps reflecting the influence of Cuban, Mexican, and other Latino immigrants on the region. In places like Miami's Little Havana, for example, you're likely to hear more Spanish than English—given the prevalence of Cuban exiles and Cuban Americans. Miami's Little Haiti, meanwhile, contains a mixture of English, French, and Spanish speakers, plus a Creole dialect that combines French, African, Arabic, Spanish, and Portuguese. In Miami, you might also hear German, Italian, Russian, and Yiddish. Although many Miami residents are fluent in both English and Spanish—or at least a form of "Spanglish"—the Florida Keys are a different story. Here, you'll do more than survive with just a solid command of the English language, even though Spanish, French, Italian, and German can be heard on occasion.

The Arts

LITERATURE

Writers have long favored the inspiring landscapes and diverse communities of southern Florida. Miami, called the "Magic City" by some and a dangerous metropolis by others, has nurtured several contemporary crime and mystery novelists, including John Katzenbach, a *Miami Herald* crime reporter whose debut novel, *In the Heat of the Summer* (1982), focuses on a dangerous cat-and-mouse game between a clever serial killer and an ambitious Miami journalist. Other popular novelists include Carl Hiaasen, a Florida native and *Miami Herald* columnist whose various madcap novels take place throughout southern Florida, and Charles Willeford, whose well-known crime series about an unorthodox Miami homicide detective began with *Miami Blues* in 1984.

The Florida Everglades—which constitute that vast, mysterious, ever-evolving subtropical wilderness filled with freshwater prairies, cypress swamps, hardwood hammocks, mangrove forests, and coastal lowlands—have also inspired their share of modern literature, from Hiaasen's novel *Nature Girl* (2005) to Susan Orlean's *The Orchid Thief: A True Story of Beauty and Obsession* (1998), a quirky tale of orchid fanatics in the Fakahatchee Swamp.

But, of course, it's the isolated Florida Keys archipelago that has sparked the creativity of countless writers, including Pulitzer Prize winners like the playwright Tennessee Williams and the poets Robert Frost, Wallace Stevens, and Elizabeth Bishop—all of whom once called Key West home. Naturally, the most famous writer to have been touched by the Southernmost City was Ernest Hemingway, who lived in Key West with his second wife, Pauline, during most of the 1930s. It was here, in fact, that the Nobel Prize–winning novelist wrote and published *To Have and Have Not* (1937), the story of a fishing boat captain who runs contraband between Cuba and Florida—no doubt inspired by Hemingway's own fishing experiences in the Florida Keys, not to mention his interactions with the eccentric locals of Key West.

VISUAL ARTS

The varied landscapes and diverse cultures of southern Florida have influenced not only writers but visual artists as well, as evidenced by the variety of art galleries and museums throughout Miami and the Florida Keys. In Miami, home to a thriving community of artists, designers, and collectors, you'll find such engaging sights as the Wynwood Arts District, an entire area devoted to visual arts, boasting well over 30 galleries, studios, and collections all within walking distance. Art lovers might also appreciate the Bass Museum of Art in Miami Beach, which contains a vast accumulation of European paintings, sculptures, and textiles from the 15th to the 20th centuries.

Farther south, the Florida Keys also present a plethora of enticements for art aficionados, from Key Largo's Bluewater Potters to The Rain Barrel, a working village of artists in Islamorada. Of course, it's Key West that houses the greatest number of art galleries and museum exhibits, including the flagship store of Wyland Galleries, which displays several of the famous muralist's marine sculptures and paintings, and the Key West Museum of Art and History at the Custom House, which features Mario Sanchez's colorful wood paintings of life in Key West during the early 1900s. Another curious collection can be seen in the Audubon House, which presents numerous originals and reprints of John James Audubon's famous ornithological paintings, many of which he prepared after observing native birds in the Florida Keys during the 1830s. For information about other art galleries in the Florida Keys, consult the **Florida Keys Council of the Arts** (www.keysarts.com).

Besides offering year-round repositories of fine and contemporary art, southern Florida also features several annual art events, especially during the winter months. In Miami, for instance, you'll find celebrations like the Coconut Grove Arts Festival and Art Basel Miami Beach. Key West, meanwhile, stages events like the Key West Craft Show and the Old Island Days Art Festival, both of which attract numerous artists and artisans to historic Old Town.

PERFORMING ARTS

In addition to visual arts, the communities of southern Florida boast a variety of performing arts. The Adrienne Arsht Center for the Performing Arts of Miami-Dade County, for instance, presents everything from opera productions to jazz concerts to contemporary dance performances. You'll find a similar array of entertainment options throughout the Florida Keys, such as theater troupes like the Key Players and music organizations like the Middle Keys Concert Association. As with art galleries, Key West naturally offers the widest array of performance venues, including the Tennessee Williams Theatre on Stock Island, where you can see regular performances of the Key West Symphony Orchestra, the Key West Pops Orchestra, and the FKCC Keys Chorale. For information about other performance venues in the Florida Keys, consult the **Florida Keys Council of the Arts** (www.keysarts.com).

CINEMA

For the past seven decades, Miami, the Everglades, and the Florida Keys have featured prominently in various film productions, from *Key Largo* in 1948 to *Miami Vice* in 2006. Given the diversity of landscapes, architectural styles, and ethnic communities in southern Florida, it's easy to understand Hollywood's fascination with this unique region. What better place to set a zany, gay-friendly film like *The Birdcage* (1996) than in the colorful, gay-filled streets of South Beach's Art Deco Historic District? Likewise, *Adaptation* (2002), a bizarre interpretation of Susan Orlean's book *The Orchid Thief,* wouldn't be the same without the tangled foliage of the Fakahatchee Strand Preserve in the Everglades. Even in Key West, you may recognize former cinematic backdrops, from the Eden House, where Goldie Hawn's character and her son live in the movie *CrissCross* (1992), to the Ernest Hemingway Home, which appears at a pivotal moment in the James Bond flick *Licence to Kill* (1989).

Of course, those who'd prefer to *watch* movies while visiting the Florida Keys won't be disappointed either. In Key West, for instance, the Tropic Cinema offers four different screening rooms that have not only hosted the latest independent, alternative, and foreign films, but also presented community events such as jazz concerts and literary lectures.

Key West's Tropic Cinema

© DANIEL MARTONE

ARCHITECTURE

Those who appreciate alluring architecture will also enjoy a trip to southern Florida. Indeed, one of the most famous architectural districts in the country lies in Miami's South Beach. Listed on the National Register of Historic Places, the vibrant Art Deco Historic District is celebrated every January with the Art Deco Weekend Festival. Of course, it would also be difficult to leave Miami without visiting the historic Biltmore Hotel in Coral Gables, a favorite spot for politicians and celebrities since its opening in the 1920s.

With a rich history that stretches back to the early 1800s, the Florida Keys also feature their share of unique architecture. South of Marathon, for instance, history buffs will enjoy strolling among the early 20th-century buildings on Pigeon Key, a tiny coral island beside the Old Seven Mile Bridge, an engineering marvel in its day. Down in Key West's Old Town, you'll find a cornucopia of architectural gems, from Caribbean-style bungalows to eyebrow houses to Victorian-era gingerbread mansions, such as the colorful Southernmost House, built in 1896 and now a favored inn.

Other worthy sights include the Key West Lighthouse, erected in 1847 to replace the original lighthouse that was destroyed by a hurricane; the Ernest Hemingway Home and Museum, built in 1851 by a marine architect and once the domicile of Key West's most famous resident; the stately Old City Hall and Custom House, both of which were constructed in 1891; and the Harry S. Truman Little White House, a breezy structure that once served as the command headquarters for the Key West Naval Station. If you'd prefer to experience the architecture of Old Town on a guided excursion, you'll find several options in Key West, including two that feature the city's most haunted structures.

MUSEUMS

Although the various outdoor pleasures, from beaches and state parks to coral reefs and abundant fishing waters, make southern Florida extremely popular among recreationists, those

© DANIEL MARTONE

the impressive Mel Fisher Maritime Museum in Key West

who prefer cultural attractions will be equally impressed by the wealth of museums in Miami and the Florida Keys. At HistoryMiami, for instance, history buffs can learn about the various cultures that have made the subtropical city what it is today. Meanwhile, those curious about the ocean, both above and below, will find several unique museums in the Florida Keys, from the History of Diving Museum in Islamorada to the Pirate Soul Museum in Key West. In addition, treasure seekers will appreciate places like the Key West Shipwreck Museum, which sheds some light on the city's former cargo-salvaging trade, and the nearby Mel Fisher Maritime Museum, which displays many of the valuable finds uncovered from the famous *Atocha* shipwreck. Of course, Key West also boasts several attractions that capture the spirit of the town's incredible past, such as the Flagler Station Over-Sea Railway Historeum, where you can learn about Henry Flagler's ill-fated Overseas Railroad, and the Oldest House Museum, so named because it's allegedly the oldest home in southern Florida.

ESSENTIALS

Getting There

While international tourists will most likely arrive in Miami or the Florida Keys via plane or cruise ship, domestic travelers can reach southern Florida by air, water, rail, or road. Consider your budget, destination, and intended activities before choosing the method that's right for your trip.

BY AIR

With at least five different airports in the region, southern Florida is an easy place to access via airplane. Of course, the two biggest airports are the **Fort Lauderdale-Hollywood International Airport (FLL)** (320 Terminal Dr., Fort Lauderdale, 866/435-9355, www.broward.org/airport) and the **Miami International Airport (MIA)** (4200 NW 21st St., Miami, 305/876-7000 or 800/825-5642, www.miami-airport.com), both of which accommodate major air carriers, including **American Airlines** (800/433-7300, www.aa.com), **Continental Airlines** (800/523-3273, www.continental.com), **Air Canada** (888/247-2262, www.aircanada.com), **Caribbean Airlines** (800/920-4225, www.caribbean-airlines.com), **Avianca** (800/284-2622, www.avianca.com), and many more. To reach Key West, travelers can fly directly into the **Key West International Airport (EYW)** (3491 S. Roosevelt Blvd., Key West, 305/809-5200 or

305/296-5439, www.keywestinternationalairport.com), where you'll find major airlines like **US Airways** (800/428-4322, www.usairways.com) and **Delta Air Lines** (800/221-1212, www.delta.com), as well as smaller air carriers, such as **Cape Air** (508/771-6944 or 800/352-0714, www.flycapeair.com, rates vary), which offers daily service between Fort Myers and Key West, and **Air Key West** (305/923-4033, www.airkeywest.com), which features quick flights to and from places like Orlando ($1,700 pp), Miami ($900 pp), Naples ($800 pp), and Nassau in the Bahamas ($1,700 pp).

Other area airports include the **Naples Municipal Airport (APF)** (160 N. Aviation Dr., Naples, 239/643-0733, www.flynaples.com) and the **Florida Keys Marathon Airport (MTH)** (9400 Overseas Hwy., Marathon, 305/289-6060), both of which can accommodate commuter flights.

BY TRAIN

If you choose to travel to southern Florida by train, you'll find that **Amtrak** (800/872-7245, www.amtrak.com) offers train service to this region via the Silver Service/Palmetto route. The three southernmost stations include **Fort Lauderdale (FTL)** (200 SW 21 Terrace, Fort Lauderdale), **Hollywood (HOL)** (3001 Hollywood Blvd., Hollywood), and **Miami (MIA)** (8303 NW 37th Ave., Miami). Unfortunately, Miami is as far as Amtrak goes, so to reach the Everglades and the Florida Keys, you'll have to rent a car or find alternative transportation.

BY BUS

For those traveling from elsewhere in the country, **Greyhound** (800/231-2222, www.greyhound.com) offers bus service to locations throughout southern Florida. Some of these include the **Miami Greyhound Station** (4111 NW 27th St., Miami, 305/871-1810), the **Central Park Bus Terminal** (2669 Davis Blvd., Ste. 1, Naples, 239/774-5660), and the **Key West Greyhound Station** (3535 S. Roosevelt Blvd., Key West, 305/296-9072) near the Key West International Airport.

TRANSPORT FROM AIRPORTS AND STATIONS

If you arrive in Naples, Key West, or the Fort Lauderdale–Miami area via plane, bus, or train, you can either rent a car or hire a shuttle service to reach your destination in southern Florida. Some of these shuttle companies include **Keys Shuttle** (305/289-9997 or 888/765-9997, www.keysshuttle.com), **Keys Tropical Transportation** (305/852-3595, www.keystropicaltransportation.com), **SuperShuttle** (305/871-2000 or 954/764-1700, www.supershuttle.com), and **TO'n'FRO** (305/852-4514, www.tonfro.com), a personalized van and car service that offers transportation between the airports in Fort Lauderdale, Miami, and Key West and any destination in the Keys.

BY CAR

If you're driving to southern Florida, Miami is accessible via several major roads, including I-75 from Tampa, Florida's Turnpike from Orlando, and I-95 from Jacksonville. To reach the Everglades from the west, take I-75 through Fort Myers or U.S. 41 through

heading south on U.S. 1

© LAURA MARTONE

Naples. Alternatively, to reach the Everglades from the east, take I-75 from Fort Lauderdale or U.S. 41 from Miami.

If you're headed to the Florida Keys from Miami, simply drive south on U.S. 1 (Overseas Hwy.), pass through Homestead and Florida City, cross Barnes Sound to Key Largo, and keep a lookout for the telltale mile markers (MM)—the little green signs that indicate your position along the 110-mile-long Overseas Highway. Key Largo lies roughly between MM 110 and MM 91, while the islands of Islamorada lie between MM 91 and MM 72. From MM 70 to MM 45, you'll find the Middle Keys, and after crossing the Seven Mile Bridge, you'll encounter the Lower Keys between MM 40 and MM 5. Key West and adjacent Stock Island, which are the most compact areas in the Keys, lie between MM 5 and MM 0. If you're looking for a particular destination, be advised that most people in the Keys use mile markers to denote addresses, and that places are often indicated as lying on the bay side (BS) or ocean side (OS) of the highway. From the western end of Marathon to Key West, where Florida Bay gives way to the Gulf of Mexico, some residents use the term "gulf side" instead of "bay side."

To reach the Florida Keys from the Everglades, you can take I-75 (Everglades Pkwy.), drive south on U.S. 27, veer right onto S.R. 997 (Krome Ave.), and follow the signs to U.S. 1. From U.S. 41 (Tamiami Trail) in the Everglades, head south on S.R. 997 and continue toward U.S. 1.

If you arrive in the Keys during the peak season (Dec.–Apr.), be sure to call **511** for an up-to-the-minute traffic report.

BY BOAT

Given that southern Florida is surrounded by miles and miles of shoreline, plus a variety of marinas, it's no surprise that many visitors arrive by boat—whether via cruise ship, ferry, or private vessel. The **Port of Miami** (1015 N. America Way, Miami, 305/347-4800, www. miamidade.gov/portofmiami) is, after all, the "cruise capital of the world." In addition, the Florida Keys offer their share of deep-water marinas, including the **Key West Bight Marina** (305/809-3983, www.keywestcity.com) at the northwest end of Margaret Street in Key West, where the **Key West Express** (888/539-2628, www.seakeywestexpress.com) arrives from Fort Myers Beach daily.

The Key West Bight Marina offers a deep-water marina to boats such as the *Jolly II Rover.*

© DANIEL MARTONE

Getting Around

While a private vehicle is probably the most convenient mode of transportation in southern Florida, it's by no means the only way to get around this diverse region.

BY AIR

Several operators invite visitors to tour southern Florida via airplane. **Everglades Area Tours** (239/695-3633, www.evergladesareatours.com, Nov.–May), for instance, offers flights via an Alaskan float plane from the Everglades City Airpark and across various destinations, including Everglades National Park, Big Cypress National Preserve, Key West, and the Dry Tortugas. You can also hop aboard sightseeing flights in the Florida Keys—an ideal way to survey the islands, coral reefs, and lighthouses that compose this unique region. One such operator is **Conch Air** (305/395-1117, www.conch-air.com), which flies from the Florida Keys Marathon Airport in the Middle Keys.

BY CAR

Southern Florida is probably best navigated by vehicle—it's possible to rent cars, RVs, and motorcycles throughout the region. Once you've secured a vehicle, it's a snap to traverse the area's major roads and highways, such as I-75 and U.S. 41, which link the Everglades to Miami, and U.S. 1, which connects Homestead to the Florida Keys.

Rental Cars and Taxis

If you've arrived in southern Florida without a vehicle of your own, you'll easily be able to rent one from such agencies as **Avis** (800/331-1212, www.avis.com), **Enterprise** (800/325-8007, www.enterprise.com), **Hertz** (800/654-3131, www.hertz.com), or **Thrifty** (800/367-2277, www.thrifty.com), all of which are available at the airports in Naples, Fort Lauderdale, Miami, Marathon, and Key West. In addition, you can rely on various taxi services, such as Key West's **Five 6's** (305/296-6666, www.keywesttaxi.com), to help you navigate the region.

MILEAGE BETWEEN KEYS

If you have access to a vehicle, southern Florida is a relatively easy region to navigate, especially given that major highways link the Florida Keys to both Miami and the Everglades. Basic mileage is listed below, though bear in mind that distances between towns in the Florida Keys can vary greatly depending upon your specific origin and destination. For example, the distance between Key Largo and Marathon can range between 30 and 60 miles.

DISTANCE FROM KEY LARGO TO:

- Homestead: 30 miles
- Miami: 59 miles
- Fort Lauderdale: 92 miles
- Everglades City: 114 miles
- Naples: 142 miles
- Islamorada: 17 miles
- Marathon: 45 miles
- Big Pine Key: 69 miles
- Key West: 98 miles

DISTANCE FROM KEY WEST TO:

- Homestead: 128 miles
- Miami: 157 miles
- Fort Lauderdale: 190 miles
- Everglades City: 212 miles
- Naples: 240 miles
- Big Pine Key: 29 miles
- Marathon: 53 miles
- Islamorada: 81 miles
- Dry Tortugas: 68 miles

Electric cars are available for rent in Key West.

RV Rentals

Given the plethora of RV campgrounds in southern Florida, it's no wonder that it's a popular region to navigate via motorhome, travel trailer, or pop-up camper. If you don't have an RV of your own, you can rent one from companies like **Cruise America** (480/464-7300 or 800/671-8042, www.cruiseamerica.com), which offers a dozen locations in Florida, including Fort Myers, Fort Lauderdale, and Miami. Just remember that, as with rental cars, age restrictions may apply.

Motorcycles and Scooters

Traveling through southern Florida by motorcycle or scooter is also a viable option. In some places, you can even rent them. Key West's Adventure Rentals, for instance, provides Harley motorcycle rentals as well as scooters at multiple locations throughout Old Town. Similarly, Sunshine Key West offers single-seat scooters, double-seat scooters, and Harley motorcycles for rent.

BY TRAIN OR TROLLEY

If you visit Key West without a car, you'll have no problem getting around town. This fairly compact city is easy to navigate on foot. In addition, you can always opt for a train or trolley ride. The **Conch Tour Train** (305/294-5161 or 888/916-8687, www.conchtourtrain.com) offers a look at most of Key West's major attractions, while the **Old Town Trolley Tour** (305/296-6688 or 888/910-8687, www.trolleytours.com), which provides a comprehensive tour of Old Town, allows you to get on and off the trolley at a dozen convenient stops.

BY BUS OR RAIL

For those who would prefer to travel by bus, southern Florida features a convenient public transit system. In addition to offering routes throughout Miami, the **Miami-Dade County Metrobus** (305/891-3131, www.miamidade.gov/transit) provides service to the Florida Keys via the **301 Dade-Monroe Express** between Florida City, Key Largo, Tavernier, Islamorada, and Marathon. From Marathon, you can then use

purchasing tickets for the Conch Tour Train

the **Lower Keys Shuttle,** which is operated by the **Key West Department of Transportation (KWDoT)** (305/600-1455, www.kwtransit.com) to access Bahia Honda State Park, Big Pine Key, Key West, and other Lower Keys.

As an alternative, you can travel through Miami via the light-rail system. The **Miami-Dade County Metrorail** (305/891-3131, www. miamidade.gov/transit) features 22 stations, offering convenient access to stops such as the Civic Center and Coconut Grove.

BY BIKE

Miami, the Everglades, and the Florida Keys are all terrific areas for biking enthusiasts to explore. While having your own bicycle might make it more convenient to travel this way, you can easily rent one from several outfitters in the region.

Although the **Florida Keys Overseas Heritage Trail,** a planned 106-mile scenic corridor for bikers, pedestrians, and other recreationists, isn't yet complete, you can certainly travel from Key Largo to Key West using a combination of bike trails, highway stretches, and bridges. Just remember that you'll have to share the road with other vehicles, so take care while navigating the highway—and always wear a proper bike helmet. For more information about the Heritage Trail, contact the **Florida Department of Environmental Protection's Office of Greenways & Trails** (3 La Croix Ct., Key Largo, FL 33037, 305/853-3571, www.dep.state.fl.us/gwt).

BY BOAT

Given that water is so prevalent in southern Florida, it's no surprise that you can easily travel the region via boat. Those with private vessels will find plenty of available marinas, such as the Key Largo Resorts Marina, a full-service facility in the Upper Florida Keys. If you don't have a vessel of your own, you can rent one at places like Robbie's of Islamorada or from independent companies such as Sunset Watersports on Stock Island, which offers a range of vessels, from 17-foot fishing boats to 24-foot pontoons, for half-day or full-day rentals.

Passengers prepare for a Coopertown airboat ride.

Of course, tour boat operators are plentiful in these waters, too. In the Everglades, for instance, you'll find about a dozen airboat operators, including Coopertown Airboats, which offers numerous trips through the "river of grass." Down in the Florida Keys, you can even take a glass-bottom boat ride amid the offshore coral reefs via operators like the Coral Reef Park Company, based out of John Pennekamp Coral Reef State Park, or Key West's Fury Water Adventures. Sunset cruises, such as those offered by Sebago Watersports in Key West, are prevalent here, too.

Sports and Recreation

Although Miami and the Florida Keys boast a number of museums, art galleries, and other cultural attractions, it's the outdoor diversions and athletic endeavors that tantalize most visitors. One thing to keep in mind when making plans is that many activities, such as fishing and snorkeling excursions, are cheaper if you book them online or utilize brochure coupons, often available in area visitor centers and chambers of commerce. In addition, you should take safety precautions before embarking on any water-related adventure. If you're a first-timer to activities like kayaking and snorkeling, be sure to ask for instruction before venturing into the water, and no matter what your level of experience, you should always have a personal flotation device (PFD) handy.

NATIONAL AND STATE PARKS

Given the diversity of southern Florida's landscapes, which range from marshes to beaches to coral reefs, it's no surprise that you'll find three national parks, one national preserve, and five national wildlife refuges in the region between Naples, Miami, and the Dry

Tortugas. If you enjoy escaping into untamed places, consider taking a kayaking trip through **Everglades National Park,** diving amid the coral reefs of **Biscayne National Park,** or exploring the remote islands that compose the 84,351-acre **National Key Deer Refuge**—all of which are accessible to visitors every day. For more information about southern Florida's national parks, contact the **National Park Service** (100 Alabama St. SW, 1924 Bldg., Atlanta, GA 30303, 404/507-5600, www.nps. gov), and for more information about the region's wildlife refuges, contact the **U.S. Fish & Wildlife Service** (10426 NW 31st Terrace, Miami, FL 33172-1200, 305/526-2610, www. fws.gov/refuges).

Southern Florida also boasts 14 unique state parks, from recreationists' oases like **Collier-Seminole State Park** in the Everglades to cultural landmarks like Key West's **Fort Zachary Taylor Historic State Park.** For more information about the incredible state parks in this region, consult the **Florida State Parks Information Center** (3900 Commonwealth Blvd., Tallahassee, FL 32399, 850/245-2157, www.floridastateparks.org), part of the Florida Department of Environmental Protection's Division of Recreation and Parks.

BEACHES AND SWIMMING

Between Miami and the Florida Keys, you'll find plenty of sandy beaches, ideal for sunbathing, picnicking, and general relaxation. Given the typically warm, shallow waters of southern Florida, swimming is also a favored pastime down here.

Where you decide to go, though, will depend on your interests. If people-watching is your prime objective, you should head to the beaches of **Miami Beach** or even **Smathers Beach** down in Key West. But, if you're looking for a bit more peace and quiet, consider stopping by **Sandspur Beach** at Bahia Honda State Park, near mile marker 37 on the Overseas Highway.

No matter where you choose to go, however, make sure that you understand the rules of that particular beach. For instance, most beaches in

© LAURA MARTONE

the bayside beach at Bahia Honda

SOUTHERNMOST STATE PARKS

While southern Florida's national parks, especially the Everglades, receive the lion's share of media attention, the vibrant region between Miami and Key West also nurtures 14 state parks that are worth a look.

- **The Barnacle Historic State Park:** Located beside Biscayne Bay, this lovely locale preserves the former home and grounds of Ralph Middleton Munroe, a yacht designer and one of Coconut Grove's most influential pioneers.

- **Bill Baggs Cape Florida State Park:** Home to a historic lighthouse – the oldest standing structure in Miami-Dade County – this park is popular among picnickers, bikers, swimmers, kayakers, anglers, and overnight boat campers.

- **Fakahatchee Strand Preserve State Park:** Often called "the Amazon of North America," this linear swamp forest beckons wildlife lovers, who can take guided canoe trips amid bald cypress trees, royal palm groves, and colorful orchids – home to alligators, varied birds and snakes, Florida panthers, white-tailed deer, and other engaging creatures.

- **Collier-Seminole State Park:** Situated along the Tamiami Trail in the Everglades, this 7,270-acre park invites visitors to canoe through mangrove swamps, hike or bike amid pine flatwoods, camp beneath majestic royal palm trees, and fish in the Blackwater River.

- **Dagny Johnson Key Largo Hammock Botanical State Park:** Hikers, bikers, bird-watchers, and photographers enjoy the six miles of nature trails within this wooded park, situated in northern Key Largo and featuring 84 protected species of plants and animals, from semaphore cactus to American crocodiles.

- **John Pennekamp Coral Reef State Park:** People flock daily to America's first underwater park, where visitors can snorkel amid offshore coral reefs, kayak through mangrove swamps, fish or swim in the warm waters, and view tropical fish and other sea creatures in the on-site aquarium.

- **Windley Key Fossil Reef Geological State Park:** Located near Islamorada, this historical park offers self-guided trails through

---

this part of Florida have no on-duty lifeguards, which means that you'll be swimming at your own risk, so be aware of undertows, riptides, and other potential dangers. Remember, too, that nude sunbathing, overnight camping, alcohol, drugs, and campfires are illegal on all public beaches.

HIKING AND BIKING

While long-distance hikers might find fewer options in southern Florida than in other parts of the country, this bountiful region certainly offers a lot of opportunities for hiking enthusiasts to enjoy a range of unique landscapes. In **Big Cypress National Preserve,** for instance, hikers can either use designated trails—part of the **Florida National Scenic Trail**—or venture into unmarked territory. Just be advised that, during the dry season (Nov.–Apr.), you'll have to carry all necessary drinking water with you. Conversely, during the wet season (May.–Oct.), you may find yourself tromping through waist-deep water, so be prepared for such problematic conditions. For more information about the Florida National Scenic Trail, contact the **Florida Trail Association** (5415 SW 13th St., Gainesville, FL 32608, 352/378-8823 or 877/445-3352, www.floridatrail.org).

Bikers, too, will enjoy exploring southern Florida. Besides biking through Miami and the Everglades, recreationists can also explore the Florida Keys via bicycle. Even though the planned, 106-mile **Florida Keys Overseas**

the former coral quarry, plus educational exhibits about the connection between the quarry and Henry Flagler's Overseas Railroad in the early 1900s.

- **Lignumvitae Key Botanical State Park:** Not far from Islamorada and only accessible via boat, canoe, or kayak, this wooded offshore island features the kind of virgin tropical hardwood hammock that once thrived in the Upper Keys.

- **Indian Key Historic State Park:** Once the site of a lucrative shipwreck-salvaging business and only accessible via boat, canoe, or kayak, this lovely island near Islamorada lures hikers, swimmers, and anglers alike.

- **San Pedro Underwater Archaeological Preserve State Park:** South of Indian Key Historic State Park, snorkelers and scuba divers will find this underwater preserve, which features the remains of a Spanish ship that sank in a 1733 hurricane.

- **Long Key State Park:** Between Layton and Marathon lies this peaceful park, once the site of a luxurious fishing resort, which was destroyed in a 1935 hurricane, and now a popular place for canoeists, hikers, anglers, swimmers, snorkelers, and overnight campers.

- **Curry Hammock State Park:** Composed of several islands near Marathon, this park offers a campground, picnic tables and pavilions, playground equipment, and easy access to swimming and kayaking, not to mention a 1.5-mile nature trail through a preserved hardwood hammock.

- **Bahia Honda State Park:** Considered one of southern Florida's finest state parks, this gorgeous, breezy locale features three stunning beaches, a boat ramp, kayak rentals, snorkeling excursions, a small nature center, cabins and campgrounds, and hiking trails, among other diversions.

- **Fort Zachary Taylor Historic State Park:** History buffs and recreationists alike appreciate Florida's southernmost park, which offers access to the finest beach in town, plus guided tours of the 19th-century fort that was designated a National Historic Landmark in 1973.

Heritage Trail isn't yet complete, you can certainly travel from Key Largo to Key West using a combination of bike trails, highway stretches, and bridges. Just remember that you'll have to share the road with other vehicles, so take care while navigating the highway—and always wear a proper bike helmet. For more information about the Heritage Trail, contact the **Florida Department of Environmental Protection's Office of Greenways & Trails** (3 La Croix Ct., Key Largo, FL 33037, 305/853-3571, www.dep.state.fl.us/gwt).

BIRD-WATCHING AND WILDLIFE-VIEWING

The varied landscapes and surrounding waters of southern Florida nurture a wide array of bird species, fish, reptiles, mammals, and other wildlife. Between terns in the Dry Tortugas, alligators in the Everglades, sea turtles in the ocean, and Key deer on Big Pine Key, birdwatchers and wildlife lovers will find no shortage of sightings in this part of the state. While you can easily spot such creatures on self-guided excursions through the marshes, in the hammocks, and along the beaches of the Sunshine State, you might see even more on guided adventures, such as airboat rides through the Everglades via companies like Billie Swamp Safari, located on the Big Cypress Seminole Indian Reservation. Birding enthusiasts might also enjoy tailored excursions like those offered by professional bird guide Larry Manfredi (www.southfloridabirding.com)

FISHING SEASONS AND TOURNAMENTS

In general, outdoor activities prevail in the Florida Keys, a region that offers diverse landscapes and warm temperatures year-round. Given the abundant backcountry and offshore waters surrounding the Keys, it's no wonder that fishing happens to be one of the most popular diversions for residents and out-of-towners alike. In fact, fishing has been well favored here since the early 20th century, when authors like Zane Grey and Ernest Hemingway explored these very same waters. Today, thanks to widely practiced catch-and-release efforts, fishing is still plentiful in the Keys. From Key Largo to Key West, you'll find a wide array of full-service marinas, party boats, fishing charters, independent guides, boat rentals, and designated fishing bridges. While fishing opportunities abound throughout the year, many anglers plan their trips around the region's varied fishing seasons and tournaments.

FISHING SEASONS

In the Florida Keys, you can choose from an assortment of fishing styles, including flats, backcountry, light-tackle, deep-sea, wreck, reef, harbor, and bridge. What you catch, of course, will depend on the time of year. Although most species are available year-round, some are only prevalent or legal to catch in certain months. Here are some suggestions:

- African pompano: year-round
- amberjack: year-round
- barracuda: November–April
- blackfin tuna: October–April
- black grouper: May–December
- blue marlin: April–October
- bonefish: April–December
- cobia: year-round
- common snook: September–December
- goliath grouper: May–December
- hogfish: year-round
- king mackerel: mid-November–March
- mahimahi: year-round
- permit: year-round
- redfish: year-round
- red grouper: May–December
- red snapper: June–July
- sailfish: October–April
- shark: year-round
- Spanish mackerel: year-round
- swordfish: year-round
- tarpon: April–December
- wahoo: year-round

with Key West's Sea-Clusive Charters. Just remember to be respectful of all wildlife that you see. For their safety as well as yours, you should not feed, approach, or disturb them at any time.

HUNTING

Even hunters will find opportunities in southern Florida. In **Big Cypress National Preserve,** which hunters were instrumental in protecting, you'll find various seasons for archery, muzzle loading, and general firearms. Although alligator hunting is not allowed within the preserve, hunters can, depending on the time of year, pursue white-tailed deer, turkeys, and hogs. For more information about hunting regulations, including proper licenses, contact the **Florida Fish and Wildlife Conservation Commission (FWC)** (Farris Bryant Bldg., 620 S. Meridian St., Tallahassee, FL 32399-1600, 850/488-4676, www.myfwc.com).

- yellowfin tuna: October–April

- yellowtail snapper: year-round

ANNUAL FISHING TOURNAMENTS

Every month, at least one highly prized fishing tournament is happening somewhere in the Florida Keys. Here are some suggestions:

- **January:** the **Islamorada Fishing Club Sailfish Tournament** (305/664-4735, www.theislamoradafishingclub.com)

- **February:** the **Cheeca Lodge Presidential Sailfish Tournament** (800/327-2888, www.cheeca.com/fishing-and-recreation) in Islamorada

- **March:** the **Leon Shell Memorial Sailfish Tournament** (www.leonshelltournament.com) near the Key Colony Beach Marina and the nine-month-long **Key West Fishing Tournament (KWFT)** (www.keywestfishingtournament.com), during which anglers compete to catch and release more than 40 different fish species

- **April:** the prestigious **World Sailfish Championship** (866/550-5580, www.worldsailfish.com), which typically awards cash prizes totaling roughly $125,000

- **May:** the **Marathon International Tarpon Tournament** (305/289-2248) and the **Lower Keys & Key West Reef Shootout** (305/395-3474), which targets bottom fish, kingfish, and wahoo

- **June:** the **Burdines Waterfront Dolphin & Blackfin Tuna Fun Fishing Tournament** (305/743-9204, www.burdineswaterfront.com) and the **Lower Keys Dolphin Tournament** (305/872-2411, www.lowerkeyschamber.com), which typically offers over $25,000 in prizes

- **July:** the **Conch Republic Ladies' Dolphin Tournament** (305/304-7674)

- **August:** the **Islamorada Swordfish Tournament** (305/282-1006, www.islamoradaswordfish.com)

- **September–November:** the **Marathon International Bonefish Tournament** (305/743-7368) in September and the **Redbone Celebrity Tournament Series** (305/664-2002, www.redbone.org), a trio of competitions from September to November that seek out permit, tarpon, bonefish, and redfish

- **December:** the **Islamorada Sailfish Tournament** (305/852-2102, www.islamorada-sailfishtournament.com)

For more information about annual fishing tournaments and area fishing guides, consult the following websites: www.fla-keys.com/fishing, www.fishingfloridakeys.com, and www.fishfloridakeys.com.

FISHING AND BOATING

Throughout the year, anglers and boaters flock to southern Florida, most notably the Florida Keys, to explore the offshore and backcountry waters of this abundant region. Considering the variety of game fish in these waters, not to mention the incredible views and gorgeous sunsets, it's easy to see why it's such a well-favored place. From Key Largo to Key West, you'll find more party boats, private fishing charters, boat rentals, sunset cruises, and full-service marinas than you can probably count, especially in Islamorada, the self-proclaimed "sportfishing capital of the world." In addition, most of the hotels and resorts along the Overseas Highway (U.S. 1), many of which are situated beside marinas, are more than willing to help arrange fishing and boating excursions for you.

For safety tips and necessary regulations that apply to both anglers and boaters in the Florida Keys as well as up-to-date fishing information, consult the **Florida Fish and Wildlife Conservation Commission** (850/488-4676, www.myfwc.com), and call 888/347-4356 for round-the-clock licensing information. In addition, you'll find helpful resources through the **Florida Keys Fishing Directory** (www.fishfloridakeys.com), **Florida Keys Boating** (www.floridakeysboating.com), and the **U.S. Coast Guard's Boating Safety Resource Center** (www.uscgboating.org).

Useful periodicals include *Florida Sportsman* (www.floridasportsman.com) and *The Weekly Fisherman* (http://weeklyfisherman.com).

Also, whether you plan to bring your own properly registered boat to the Florida Keys, rent a vessel, or even charter a fishing trip, you might want to consider joining **Sea Tow** (305/451-3330 or 800/473-2869, www.seatow.com), a nationwide provider of marine assistance for recreational boaters. Membership

TIPS FOR THE PADDLER

Given the plethora of mangrove creeks and uninhabited islands in the Florida Keys, it's no surprise that canoeing and kayaking are popular activities down here. Options range from short, hourlong trips to a 110-mile kayaking journey from Key Largo to Key West via the **Florida Keys Overseas Paddling Trail.** Though some enthusiasts bring their vessels with them, you can easily rent a variety of canoes and kayaks at several different outfitters, from Miami to Everglades City to Key West. In addition, many hotels and resorts offer complimentary kayaks to their guests.

Paddling through the Keys can be a rewarding experience, but it can also be dangerous if you're ill-prepared. High winds and waves can make paddling conditions challenging; in fact, while beginners are welcome to give paddling a try, it's helpful if you've had at least some experience before attempting it here. No matter what your experience level, however, the following guidelines are necessary for all canoeists and kayakers to remember:

- Ensure that you've had proper instruction for the vessel that you plan to use.

- Check the daily weather forecast, especially predicted wind speeds, beforehand.

- Be aware of tidal conditions, currents, and water levels; under normal circumstances, you should allow for a minimum paddling time of two miles per hour.

- Inform someone on shore of your plans, especially your intended destination and ex-

pected return time; leave a float plan with a responsible individual, place said plan in a visible spot in your vehicle, and contact the onshore person when you do, in fact, return.

- Arrange to have a vehicle (if not yours) and dry clothes waiting at your take-out point.

- Secure a spare paddle to your vessel.

- Place your keys, identification, money, and other valuables in a waterproof bag and secure the bag to the vessel.

- Apply sunscreen and insect repellent, even on cloudy days.

- Wear appropriate clothing for weather and water conditions.

- Have a readily accessible, personal flotation device (PFD) with attached whistle for each occupant; children under six must wear PFDs at all times.

- Bring plenty of food and drinking water (one gallon per person per day) in nonbreakable, watertight containers.

- Bring a cell phone in case of an emergency, but do not rely solely on said phone, as reception can be sporadic in the backcountry and offshore waters.

- Pack up all trash and store it on board until you can dispose of it properly at your trip's end.

assures you such services as towing, prop disentanglements, fuel drops, and jump-starts—useful assistance to have when you're stranded in the backcountry.

CANOEING AND KAYAKING

Given its cornucopia of freshwater swamps, mangrove creeks, backcountry waters, and offshore islands, southern Florida is indeed a paddler's dream. Luckily, you don't even have to bring your own canoe or kayak to explore this fascinating region, as you'll find helpful outfitters between Miami and Key West. Some of these companies include Miami's Liquid Surf & Sail, which offers sit-on-top kayak rentals, and North American Canoe Tours in Everglades City, which provides canoe and kayak rentals from November to mid-April.

You'll find even more outfitters in the Florida Keys, some of which also offer guided

---

- Leave all historical resources, plants, birds, and marine creatures as you find them.

- Respect all wildlife; do not approach, harass, or feed any animals that you see.

- Be considerate of anglers and other paddlers, avoid crossing fishing lines, and stay to the right of motorboats.

- If you're taking an overnight paddling trip and plan to camp somewhere, be sure to camp on durable surfaces away from the water, and minimize the impact from campfires (if they're even allowed where you're staying).

Besides the items already mentioned, you should bring the following essentials with you:

- area maps and NOAA nautical charts

- compass or GPS

- bilge pump and sponge

- anchor (if you plan to snorkel or camp) and some rope

- extra waterproof bags

- VHF or weather radio to monitor weather forecasts

- signaling devices such as a flashlight, flare, mirror, or air horn

- 360-degree light for operating your vessel at night

- sunglasses

- wide-brimmed hat

- long-sleeved shirt for extra protection

- sunscreen

- lip balm with SPF

- insect repellent

- first-aid kit

- towels, extra clothing, and extra shoes in a waterproof bag

- binoculars

- camera and extra batteries

- pocketknife or multipurpose tool

- duct tape

- repair kit

For more information about canoeing and kayaking in the Florida Keys, consult the state's **Office of Greenways & Trails (OGT)** (3 La Croix Ct., Key Largo, FL 33037, 305/853-3571, www.dep.state.fl.us/gwt), the **Florida State Parks Information Center** (3900 Commonwealth Blvd., Tallahassee, FL 32399, 850/245-2157, www.floridastateparks.org/thingstodo/activities.cfm), and the **Florida Professional Paddlesports Association (FPPA)** (P.O. Box 1764, Arcadia, FL 34265, 800/268-0083, www.paddleflusa.com).

kayak rentals at John Pennekamp Coral Reef State Park

tours. Florida Bay Outfitters in Key Largo, for instance, provides an array of canoe and kayak rentals, in addition to three-hour instructional sessions and several guided kayaking trips, from three-hour tours to three-day sailing excursions. Free pickups and drop-offs at participating resorts are offered for most trips, and reservations are necessary for all of them. No matter where you rent your vessel, however, you should make sure that personal flotation devices (PFDs) are included with each rental or at least available on-site.

DIVING AND SNORKELING

Within the ocean waters east of southern Florida stretches the third largest coral reef system in the world. With **Biscayne National Park** southeast of Miami and the 220-mile-long series of coral reefs that constitute the **Florida Keys National Marine Sanctuary,** scuba divers and snorkelers will find no shortage of underwater delights, from brain coral formations to historic shipwrecks to oodles of tropical fish. While you can certainly bring or

rent a vessel to dive or snorkel on your own, you'll also have access to a wide array of operators offering snorkeling and diving excursions in addition to equipment rentals and instruction.

In the Miami area, for instance, the South Beach Dive and Surf Center, a PADI 5 Star facility, provides a variety of courses, including an introduction class, a divemaster class, and a digital underwater photography class—plus snorkeling and diving trips in the waters near Key Largo. Of course, you'll also find an assortment of similar operators throughout the Florida Keys, from Amy Slate's Amoray Dive Resort in Key Largo, which provides accommodations in addition to classes and trips, to Sea-Clusive Charters in Key West, which offers multi-day diving excursions to the Dry Tortugas.

Typically, reservations are required—or at least recommended—for all snorkeling and diving trips in Miami and the Florida Keys, and most of the time, operators include necessary equipment, such as tanks, weights, and snorkels, within their quoted prices. For more information about area wrecks and reefs, consult the **Florida Keys National Marine Sanctuary** (305/852-7717 or 305/292-0311, www.floridakeys.noaa.gov), and if you're interested in helping to preserve and protect the living coral reef ecosystems in Florida and elsewhere in the world, contact the **Reef Relief Environmental Center** (631 Greene St., Key West, 305/294-3100, www.reefrelief.org). Lastly, in the case of diving emergencies, especially as they relate to decompression illness (i.e., the bends), phone 800/662-3637 to reach the 24-hour hotline at **Mercy Hospital** (3663 S. Miami Ave., Miami, 305/854-4400, www.mercymiami.org).

GOLF

Although southern Florida is a recreationist's paradise, golf is less prevalent here than water-related activities like fishing and diving. Nevertheless, you'll find several golf courses in the region, including the **Biltmore Golf Course,** a well-landscaped, 18-hole course that surrounds the legendary Biltmore Hotel in the Miami area. Even the Florida Keys have a few

THE SHIPWRECK TRAIL

While many snorkelers and scuba divers primarily come to the Florida Keys to explore the vibrant living coral reefs that comprise the 220-mile-long Florida Keys National Marine Sanctuary, others are more interested in the historical resources that lie beneath the surface – namely the shipwrecks that pepper these offshore waters. Although some of these underwater vessels, such as the 510-foot **USS Spiegel Grove** near Key Largo, were intentionally sunk to create artificial reefs, several were actually doomed by the treacherous coral reefs that lure so many underwater enthusiasts today. Signifying the European Colonial, American, and Modern periods of Keys maritime history, nine of these shipwrecks – intentional and unintentional alike – now constitute the official Shipwreck Trail.

- *City of Washington:* Built in 1877 and now lying in 25 feet of water near Elbow Reef, this steel hull vessel was the first ship to assist the USS *Maine* following the explosion in Havana Harbor.

- *Benwood:* Constructed in England in 1910 and sunk in 1942, this ship now lies between French Reef and Dixie Shoals, in water that ranges in depth from 25 to 45 feet.

- *Duane:* Built in 1936 and now lying in 120 feet of water south of Molasses Reef, this U.S. Coast Guard cutter was formerly used in World War II, eventually decommissioned in 1985, and purposely sunk two years later as an artificial reef.

- *Eagle:* Constructed in Holland in 1962, this 287-foot freighter was donated by the Eagle Tire Company as an artificial reef in 1985 and now lies on her starboard side in 110 feet of water southeast of Lower Matecumbe Key.

- *San Pedro:* This 287-ton, Dutch-built Spanish ship, which wrecked south of Indian Key during a 1733 hurricane, has undergone several salvaging attempts since its discovery in 1960 and now serves as the San Pedro Underwater Archaeological Preserve State Park.

- *Adelaide Baker:* Constructed in 1863, this three-masted, square-rigged ship wrecked in 1889 while toting a cargo of milled timber and now lies in 25 feet of water four miles south of Duck Key.

- *Thunderbolt:* Built in West Virginia in 1942 to lay defensive coastal mines, this 188-foot steel ship was intentionally sunk in 1986 and now lies, encrusted with coral and sponges, in 120 feet of water four miles south of Key Colony Beach.

- *North America:* Lying in 14 feet of water in the sand and grass flats north of Delta Shoals, this vessel is believed to be the *North America*, built in 1833 in Bath, Maine, and lost in 1842 while transporting dry goods and furniture.

- *Amesbury:* Originally constructed as a U.S. Naval Destroyer Escort in 1943 and locally known as "Alexander's Wreck," this vessel was being towed to deep water to be sunk when it grounded and broke up in a storm five miles west of Key West.

A spar buoy identifies each of these historic sites, which are all accessible via private boat or diving charter. Underwater conditions vary from site to site, meaning that you can expect both easy, shallow-water dives as well as deeper dives with swift currents. For more information about the conditions, features, and history of each site along the Shipwreck Trail, contact the **Florida Keys National Marine Sanctuary** (305/852-7717 or 305/292-0311, www.floridakeys.noaa.gov) or consult area diving operators, many of whom offer charters or private trips to these sites. To help protect these fragile structures – all of which are artificial reefs that now support tropical fish and other marine creatures – remember to control your buoyancy, avoid anchoring near the sites, and refrain from damaging or removing any and all artifacts that you see.

options, from the exclusive **Ocean Reef Club,** which features two championship 18-hole courses on the northern end of Key Largo, to the 200-acre **Key West Golf Club,** which offers an 18-hole public golf course on the gulf side of U.S. 1. Many of these courses also provide golf club rentals, so there's usually no need to lug your own equipment with you—which is good news for those traveling by plane, bus, or any method with luggage restrictions.

SPECTATOR SPORTS

If you favor spectator sports, then you can't go wrong in Miami, where you'll find an array of professional teams on display. From September to December, for instance, football fans can watch the **Miami Dolphins** take on other NFL teams at the Sun Life Stadium, while from late April to early October, baseball lovers can flock to the same stadium to cheer on the **Florida Marlins**—until, that is, the team's new ballpark is ready for its scheduled 2012 opening. From October to April, basketball fans can catch the **Miami Heat** at the AmericanAirlines Arena, and even hockey fans will be happy in Miami, where the **Florida Panthers** also play between October and April at the BankAtlantic Center.

Entertainment and Events

NIGHTLIFE

While outdoor diversions may reign supreme in southern Florida, residents here certainly know how to celebrate the nighttime, too, especially in Miami and Key West. Miami's South Beach, for instance, a neighborhood favored during the daytime for its art deco–style buildings, comes alive with neon at night, when beautiful people flock to the area's trendy bars, hot dance clubs, and outlandish cabaret shows. From Key Largo to Geiger Key, you'll also find plenty of waterfront bars that feature drink specials and live music, but of course, it's Key West that houses a treasure trove of nightlife options, including hotel lounges, piano bars, and other watering holes that offer nightly entertainment. Here, after all, is where residents and tourists alike engage in the "Duval crawl," an attempt to stop by every bar along Old Town's main drag, from the predominantly gay Aqua Nightclub to the clothing-optional Garden of Eden to the lively Sloppy Joe's Bar.

INDIAN GAMING

Unlike other parts of Florida, the stretch between Miami and Key West offers few options for gamblers. One such option is the **Miccosukee Resort & Gaming,** a casino resort that lies west of Miami and is operated by the Miccosukee Tribe of Indians of Florida, a tribe that separated from the native Seminole Indians in the 1950s and gained federal recognition in 1962.

FESTIVALS AND EVENTS

Given the favorable climate, cultural diversity, and carefree vibe of southern Florida, it's no wonder that the region hosts numerous festivals and events throughout the year. In Miami, for instance, you'll learn firsthand about the varied cultures that shaped the city by attending such engaging events as the **Miami Gay & Lesbian Film Festival** in late April; Coconut Grove's **Miami/Bahamas Goombay Festival** in early June; and **Calle Ocho,** which usually occurs in mid-March and serves as one of the largest Hispanic block parties in the country. The Everglades, meanwhile, have their own curious history, informed by the Indian tribes that have called this mysterious region home. At the **Miccosukee Indian Arts Festival** in late December, for example, visitors can watch Native American dances and browse genuine arts and crafts in the Miccosukee Indian Village.

Naturally, the fun-loving Florida Keys offer their own share of annual festivals and events. In the Upper Keys, for instance, history is

ANNUAL ART CELEBRATIONS

Southern Florida hosts a number of annual cultural events that appeal to art and architecture aficionados. Every January, the **Art Deco Weekend Festival** lures visitors to South Beach's Art Deco Historic District, while the **Key West Craft Show** attracts over 100 skilled artists to Key West's Old Town. For a more unusual experience, consider visiting during **Sculpture Key West,** an annual wintertime exhibition of contemporary outdoor sculpture throughout the city.

In early February, art lovers venture south to the **Pigeon Key Art Festival,** an annual event featuring live music, art raffles, and the artwork of over 80 fine artists from around the country. Later in the month, the **Coconut Grove Arts Festival** lures even more paintings, jewelry, photography, and glass sculptures to the Miami area, while the **Old Island Days Art Festival** celebrates various art forms in Key West's Old Town.

Early December brings two more art festivals to this vibrant region: **Art Basel Miami Beach,** an enormous show featuring an exclusive selection of more than 250 art galleries from North America, Latin America, Europe, Asia, and Africa, and the **Big Pine and the Lower Keys Island Art Festival,** a smaller art and music event ideal for families. Typically from late December to early January, the **Miccosukee Indian Arts Festival** welcomes visitors to the Miccosukee Indian Village, where you can watch Native American dances and browse genuine arts and crafts. At multiple times from late December to mid-March, those interested in Key West's unique architecture can take a **Key West House and Garden Tour,** sponsored by the Old Island Restoration Foundation.

honored with zany happenings like the **Key Largo Conch Republic Days,** a late April event that honors the 1982 ceremonial secession of the Florida Keys from the United States. The Middle and Lower Keys, meanwhile, celebrate the great outdoors with the **Battle in the Bay Dragon Boat Festival** near Sombrero Beach in early or mid-May, the **Underwater Music Festival** near Looe Key Reef in early or mid-July, and the **Florida Keys Birding and Wildlife Festival,** which typically occurs in late September and features field trips throughout the region. As with other cultural offerings, Key West hosts the lion's share of annual celebrations, including the **Conch Republic Independence Celebration** in late April; **Hemingway Days,** which typically happens in late July and celebrates the life of Key West's most famous former resident; and **Fantasy Fest,** a rowdy late October event that features colorful parades, outrageous parties, and drag queens galore.

Accommodations and Food

ACCOMMODATIONS

Southern Florida contains a wide array of accommodations, from luxurious resorts to primitive campgrounds. Naturally, where you plan to stay depends on your interests, budget, and ultimate destination. Though spontaneity can be fun on a vacation, be aware that you might have to make reservations far in advance of your trip. Inns, cottages, and campgrounds can fill up quickly, especially during the peak winter season, from late December through April.

While this region offers a variety of unique resorts and inns, you'll also find plenty of major hotel and motel chains, from **Holiday Inn** (www.holidayinn.com) to **Travelodge** (www.travelodge.com). If you prefer staying in such a tried-and-true establishment, pick

© DANIEL MARTONE

Key Largo's Holiday Inn

often make up for that with personal service. The Sea Dell Motel in Marathon is a case in point. Situated amid palm trees and lush foliage, this family-friendly motel features affordable rooms, a heated pool, picnic and barbecue areas, high-speed Internet access, and proximity to some of the Middle Keys' most popular attractions.

Inns and Resorts

Southern Florida features some rather unique inns, bed-and-breakfasts, and resorts, especially in the Florida Keys. Perhaps it's no surprise that Key West possesses the lion's share of such one-of-a-kind lodgings, from The Mermaid & The Alligator Bed & Breakfast, an intimate inn situated within a lush tropical setting, to the Ocean Key Resort & Spa, which features beautifully furnished suites, fine dining, a fantastic spa, and proximity to a marina. Of course, the rest of the Florida Keys offer similarly enticing accommodations, and if you plan to stay in the Miami area—even for a night—you can't go wrong with the Biltmore Hotel in Coral Gables, a historic, 150-acre resort that features 275 sumptuous rooms and suites, a championship golf course, an amazing spa and fitness center, 10 tennis courts, a world-famous pool area, and several celebrated restaurants.

Cabins and Cottages

To experience the unique beauty and atmosphere of southern Florida, you should consider staying in a rustic cabin or charming cottage. At the Miami Everglades Campground, for instance, you can choose from among several different cabins and lodges, which can also be rented by the week or month. Naturally, you'll find even more cabins in the Florida Keys, including three stilted duplexes overlooking the bay at Bahia Honda State Park near Big Pine Key. In addition, the Florida Keys provide a wide array of cottages, from beachfront bungalows at Rock Reef Resort in Key Largo to stilted, two-bedroom accommodations at Conch Key Cottages on Walker's Island in the Middle Keys.

up a copy of the chain's national directory or consult its official website to find current locations, rates, and amenities. For more information about southern Florida's accommodations, consult organizations like **Miami Beach 411** (1521 Alton Rd., Ste. 233, Miami Beach, FL 33139, 305/754-2206, www.miamibeach411.com), the **Key West Innkeepers Association (KWIA)** (316A Simonton St., Key West, FL 33040, 305/295-1334 or 800/492-1911, www.keywestinns.com), or **The Lodging Association of the Florida Keys and Key West** (3152 Northside Dr., Ste. 101, Key West, FL 33040, 305/296-4959, www.keyslodging.org).

Independent Hotels and Motels

Despite the presence of various corporate-owned resorts and hotel chains, southern Florida offers a variety of independently operated lodgings, especially in the Florida Keys. While such places may not provide all the amenities that the more luxurious resorts do—such as continental breakfasts and spa services—they

© LAURA MARTONE

Peace and quiet reign at Conch Key Cottages in the Middle Keys.

Camping

For budget-conscious families or outdoor enthusiasts, southern Florida provides several camping options. At Collier-Seminole State Park, for instance, you'll find a 120-site, pet-friendly campground as well as primitive camping for hikers and canoeists. While the Everglades offer other options as well, you'll find even more RV parks and campgrounds in the region between Key Largo and the Dry Tortugas. Consult the **Florida Association of RV Parks and Campgrounds (FARVC)** (1340 Vickers Rd., Tallahassee, FL 32303, 850/562-7151, www.campflorida.com) for more information, and contact **ReserveAmerica** (800/326-3521, www.reserveamerica.com) to reserve a spot at one of southern Florida's state park campgrounds.

FOOD AND DRINK

Eating and drinking are popular pastimes in southern Florida, and luckily for visitors, there are a lot of choices available.

Regional Cuisine

Given the varied cultural influences in southern Florida, you'll find that the cuisine ranges from Creole dishes in Miami's Little Haiti to *cubanos* (Cuban sandwiches) in Little Havana to seafood galore in the Florida Keys. In fact, depending on the season, you're likely to spot fried catfish, grilled snapper or grouper, Caribbean-style mahimahi, gulf and rock shrimp, stone crab claws, and Florida lobster in the assorted seafood restaurants between Key Largo and Key West. Throughout the year, you'll be able to sample local delicacies like conch fritters, conch chowder, and key lime pie, and of course, given that it's the South, you'll often see grits and hush puppies on the menu, too. In the region's finer restaurants, you'll also encounter "Floribbean" cuisine, which consists of fresh Florida produce and seafood, with American, European, Caribbean, and Latin American influences. For more information about available eateries between Miami and Key West, consult the **Miami DiningGuide** (http://miami.diningguide.com) and the **Florida Keys Dining Guide** (www.keysdining.com).

Breweries and Wineries

Although you won't find too many microbreweries and wineries in southern Florida, Key West presents a couple of notable options. Home to the Southernmost Brewery, the only brewery in the Florida Keys, Kelly's Caribbean Bar, Grill & Brewery features such local favorites as Havana Red Ale, Key West Golden Ale, and Southern Clipper Wheat Beer. Meanwhile, The Key West Winery prepares unusual tropical wines, enhanced by flavors like key lime, mango, coconut, tangerine, pineapple, tomato, jalapeño, and much more.

Groceries and Specialty Stores

If you choose to stay in self-sufficient lodgings, such as a cottage with a well-equipped kitchen, then you'll be happy to know that there are numerous groceries throughout southern Florida, including several branches of **Publix** (800/242-1227, www.publix.com), each of which typically

CLASSIC KEY LIME PIE

© DANIEL MARTONE

Of all the regional treats favored in the Florida Keys, perhaps none is as widely known – or as universally celebrated – as key lime pie. While you'll encounter a variety of styles down here – from the deep-fried, cinnamon-encrusted version at the Island Fish Co. Restaurant & Tiki Bar in Marathon to the frozen, dark chocolate–covered pie-on-a-stick at the Blond Giraffe Key Lime Pie Factory in Key West – most gourmands seek the classic recipe, a creamy, tangy, sweet concoction on a graham cracker crust, the kind you'll find at Mrs. Mac's Kitchen in Key Largo.

If you simply can't wait to taste this treat on your next trip to the Florida Keys, never fear. With little fuss, you can easily make your own classic key lime pie, using this simple recipe.

CRUST INGREDIENTS
1½ cups crushed graham crackers
3 tbsp. sugar
6 tbsp. salted butter, melted

FILLING INGREDIENTS
4 large egg yolks
1 14-oz. can sweetened, condensed milk
½ cup freshly squeezed key lime juice (or bottled, if necessary)

INSTRUCTIONS
- Preheat the oven to 350°F.

- Combine the graham cracker crumbs, sugar, and melted butter in a medium-sized bowl.

- Press the mixture evenly into the bottom and sides of a nine-inch pie pan.

- Bake the pie shell at 350°F for 10-15 minutes, or until slightly brown.

- Place the pie shell on a wire rack to cool.

- Beat the egg yolks with an electric mixer until the color turns a pale yellow.

- Add the condensed milk and mix on low speed.

- Fold in the lime juice.

- Pour the mixture into the pie shell and bake at 350°F for 10-12 minutes.

- Once cooled, refrigerate the pie for at least six hours.

- When you're ready to serve, garnish the pie with real whipped cream and lime wedges.

features a pharmacy, a bakery, a deli, fresh sushi and produce, meat and seafood departments, wine and beer, as well as other services, such as automated teller machines (ATMs). Naturally, you'll also find specialty stores throughout this region. In Key West, for instance, there are several locations of the **Blond Giraffe Key Lime Pie Factory** (www.blondgiraffe. com), which specializes in everything from key lime juice to key lime meringue pie. In the Lower Keys, you'll even find a local coffee producer, the highly touted **Baby's Coffee** in the Saddlebunch Keys (800/523-2326, www.baby-scoffee.com), which serves many area establishments with flavored, specialty, Hawaiian, and locally inspired roasts.

Tips for Travelers

FOREIGN TRAVELERS

International travelers should understand current American policies before heading here.

Passports and Visas

While international travelers are required to show a valid passport upon entering the United States, most citizens from Canada and the 36 countries that are part of the **Visa Waiver Program (VWP)**—including France, Italy, Germany, Australia, New Zealand, Japan, and the United Kingdom—are allowed to travel to Florida without a visa. They will, however, still need to apply to the **Electronic System for Travel Authorization (ESTA).** All other temporary international travelers are required to secure a nonimmigrant visa before entering Florida. For more information, consult the **U.S. Department of State's Bureau of Consular Affairs** (202/663-1225, www.travel. state.gov).

Customs

Upon entering Florida, international travelers must declare any dollar amount over $10,000 as well as the value of any articles that will remain in the country, including gifts. A duty will be assessed for all imported goods; visitors are usually granted a $100 exemption. Illegal drugs, Cuban cigars, obscene items, toxic substances, and prescription drugs (without a prescription) are generally prohibited. In order to protect American agriculture, customs officials will confiscate certain produce, plants, seeds, nuts, meat, and other potentially dangerous biological products. For more information, consult the **U.S. Customs and Border Protection** (703/526-4200, www.cbp.gov).

Embassies and Consulates

While the embassies for most countries are located in Washington, D.C., some nations have consular offices in Miami. Such helpful European resources include the **Austrian Consulate Miami** (2445 Hollywood Blvd., Hollywood, 954/925-1100, www.austrian-consulatemiami.com, 9 A.M.–5 P.M. Mon.–Fri.), the **British Consulate-General Miami** (1001 Brickell Bay Dr., Ste. 2800, Miami, 305/374-3500, www.ukinusa.fco. gov.uk, 8:30 A.M.–4:30 P.M. Mon.–Fri.), the **Consulate General of the Federal Republic of Germany** (100 N. Biscayne Blvd., Ste. 2200, Miami, 305/358-0290, www.germany.info, 8:30 A.M.–4:30 P.M. Mon.–Thurs., 8:30 A.M.–2 P.M. Fri.), and the **Italian Consulate General Miami** (4000 Ponce de León Blvd., Ste. 590, Coral Gables, 305/374-6322, www.consmiami.esteri.it, 9 A.M.–noon Mon.–Tues. and Thurs.–Fri., 9 A.M.–noon and 3–5:30 P.M. Wed.).

Other helpful consular offices include the **Consulate General of Canada** (200 S. Biscayne Blvd., Ste. 1600, Miami, 305/579-1600, www.miami.gc.ca or www.canadainter-national.gc.ca, 8:30 A.M.–4 P.M. Mon.–Fri.), the **Consulate General of Costa Rica** (2730 SW 3rd Ave., Ste. 401, Miami, 305/871-7485, www. costarica-embassy.org, 9 A.M.–4 P.M. Mon.–Fri.), the **Consulate General of Mexico** (5975

SW 72nd St., Miami, 786/268-4900, www.sre. gob.mx/miami, 8 A.M.–6 P.M. Mon.–Fri.), and the **Consulate-General of Japan in Miami** (80 SW 8th St., Ste. 3200, Miami, 305/530-9090, www.miami.us.emb-japan.go.jp, 9 A.M.–noon and 1:30–5 P.M. Mon.–Fri.).

OPPORTUNITIES FOR STUDY AND EMPLOYMENT

With several colleges and businesses in southern Florida, there are plenty of educational and work-related opportunities for residents and travelers. If you're interested in such a long-term stay, your best bet would be to research the schools and companies that interest you, consider details like transportation and accommodations, and, for foreign travelers, look into U.S. visa policies *before* making travel or relocation plans. Of course, some facilities, such as the **Dolphin Research Center** (58901 Overseas Hwy., Grassy Key, 305/289-1121, www.dolphins.org, 9 A.M.–4:30 P.M. daily), offer short-term educational opportunities, such as trainer-for-a-day programs ($650 pp), that you might find enriching—without having to uproot your entire life.

VOLUNTEER VACATIONS

Sometimes, being a tourist isn't enough. If you want to explore southern Florida *and* lend a helping hand, then perhaps a volunteer vacation is right up your alley. National and state parks can especially use some extra assistance, and working in such diverse environments can be a truly rewarding experience. For more information about volunteering in Florida's national parks, contact the **National Park Service** (www.nps.gov/volunteer). For more information about volunteer opportunities at southern Florida's state parks, contact the **Florida State Parks Information Center** (3900 Commonwealth Blvd., Tallahassee, FL 32399, 850/245-2157, www.floridastateparks. org/getinvolved).

Of course, parks aren't the only places that need help. **Theater of the Sea** in Islamorada (305/664-2431, www.theaterofthesea.com), for instance, invites volunteer interns to assist the animal care staff in feeding and attending to the dolphins, sea lions, sea turtles, and other marine creatures on the premises during the spring, summer, and fall months. Curiously, other places, such as the nonprofit **Florida Keys Wild Bird Center** in Tavernier (305/852-4486, www.fkwbc.org), are entirely operated by volunteers.

ACCESS FOR TRAVELERS WITH DISABILITIES

Southern Florida offers limited accessibility for those with disabilities. Major store and hotel chains, such as Publix and Holiday Inn, are often wheelchair-accessible, as are attractions like the snorkeling excursions in John Pennekamp Coral Reef State Park in Key Largo and the Mel Fisher Maritime Museum in Key West.

As with most federal lands, Everglades National Park, which is open 24 hours daily, provides wheelchair-accessible visitor centers, featuring designated parking spaces, curb ramps, and automatic doors. In addition, vision-impaired and hearing-impaired visitors can utilize audio recordings, Braille signage, and assistive listening devices (ALDs) for use in the park's interpretive programs. Also, the **National Park Service** (www.nps.gov/fees_passes.htm) offers a special lifetime pass (free) for U.S. citizens and permanent residents with permanent disabilities, allowing them free access to any federal recreation site that charges an entrance fee, including Everglades National Park and Dry Tortugas National Park.

Nevertheless, plenty of establishments, such as independently owned inns and cottages in the Florida Keys, cannot accommodate wheelchairs. So, when in doubt about the possibility of access, simply call the establishment in question.

TRAVELING WITH CHILDREN

With its multitude of beaches, state parks, museums, boat tours, and other amusements, southern Florida is clearly a kid-friendly place. If you're traveling here with children, you'll surely find something for them to do. Just remember to supervise them at all times, both to keep them safe from harm and to minimize the possibility of disturbing others. Be advised, too, that while plenty of hotels and resorts welcome children, some lodgings, such as the Azul del Mar in Key Largo, are adults-only establishments.

TRAVELING WITH PETS

Although pets aren't allowed on most of southern Florida's beaches and within many hotels, restaurants, and stores, several places do welcome them, including state park campgrounds. In locations where dogs, cats, and other pets are allowed, it's crucial that you understand and follow any relevant rules. Typically, you are asked to keep your pets on a leash at all times, walk them in designated areas, control their behavior so as not to disturb or endanger others, and always pick up after them. Barking or aggressive dogs are usually forbidden everywhere. When in doubt, call ahead to verify the pet policies of a particular park, attraction, or establishment.

WOMEN TRAVELING ALONE

While it's admirable for an independent woman to explore the world on her own, it's important to take precautions, especially in urban centers like Miami and Key West. Although southern Florida is a relatively safe place, there are still too many things that can go wrong—on the road, in a campground, even in a crowd.

If you must venture out alone, tell someone back home about your intended travel plans, stick to daytime driving, and stay close to busy attractions, streets, and campgrounds. Try to stow your money, credit cards, and identification close to your person, as big purses make easy targets. If you feel that someone is stalking you, find a public place (such as a store or tourism bureau), and don't hesitate to alert the police. In addition, you should keep the doors to your lodging and vehicle locked at all times.

Before heading out on your trip, you should invest in a canister of pepper spray as well as a cell phone, which can be useful in an emergency. Just remember that cellular reception is limited in the region's more remote areas, such

© LAURA MARTONE

Pets are not allowed on public beaches in the Keys.

as the backcountry of the Everglades and the Florida Keys.

SENIOR TRAVELERS

Southern Florida is an exceptionally helpful place, so senior travelers should have little trouble finding assistance here. For help with directions, there are several visitor centers and tourism bureaus throughout the region, not to mention plenty of locals able to point you in the right direction. In addition, many attractions offer discounts to senior travelers. The **National Park Service** (www.nps.gov/fees_passes.htm) even offers a special lifetime pass ($10) for U.S. citizens and permanent residents aged 62 or older, allowing them free access to any federal recreation site that charges an entrance fee, including Everglades National Park and Dry Tortugas National Park.

GAY AND LESBIAN TRAVELERS

Parts of southern Florida, namely South Beach and Key West, are openly friendly to gay and lesbian travelers. Besides annual events like Pridefest and Fantasy Fest, Key West even has exclusively gay and/or lesbian accommodations and a variety of gay bars. For more information about gay-related events and establishments in Key West, contact the **Key West Business Guild** (513 Truman Ave., Key West, FL 33040, 305/294-4603, www.gaykeywestfl.com). Those traveling to Miami can consult www.miamigaytravel.com.

CONDUCT AND CUSTOMS

Florida is similar to other Southern states in temperament and traditions. While a major city like Miami might not follow the general rule, most areas of southern Florida, especially the Florida Keys, have a laid-back, friendly vibe. Many residents seem to embrace the value of having a good time while treating others with respect, though it's good to remember that a lot of the locals weren't necessarily born here. In fact, plenty of them have escaped colder climates in New England and the Midwest, giving them a sense of appreciation for the benefits of living in a bountiful, comfortable landscape like southern Florida.

Given the region's multiethnic history, reliance on tourism, and proximity to Cuba, foreigners and tourists are generally welcome here. Overall, the residents are helpful, hospitable, and gregarious. So, while in Florida, do as the natives do. Be kind and considerate, ask for help when you need it, thank others for their time, and, as a courtesy, ask permission before taking a photo.

WHAT TO TAKE

Foreign travelers will need passports, adapter plugs, and current converters. All adults should have **proper identification,** which you'll need to drive a rental car, rent certain equipment, and, of course, drink in a Key West bar.

Although you should pack light, be sure to include a swimsuit, a hat, beach shoes, an umbrella, and a lightweight jacket, just in case the weather turns chilly. Attire in the Keys is **casual,** even in upscale restaurants, so there's no need to bring fancy or formal outfits.

Sunscreen and toiletries are available throughout Miami and the Keys, but if your plans include activities like golfing and birdwatching, you might want to bring your **favorite clubs** and **binoculars.** Kayaks, bicycles, boats, and other outdoor gear are easy enough to rent once you get here.

Health and Safety

Despite the best-laid plans, trouble can occur at any time. Before hitting the road or boarding a bus, plane, boat, or train, it's critical that you pack a well-stocked first-aid kit and prepare yourself for the common pitfalls of traveling in southern Florida.

HEALTH RISKS

Given that outdoor diversions reign in Miami, the Everglades, and the Florida Keys, most of the possible health risks that you may face will probably involve the great outdoors.

Contaminated Water

Most of the water you'll encounter in southern Florida will be salt water in the ocean or brackish water in the backcountry, neither of which you should ever drink, due to the high probability of dehydration. Nevertheless, you may encounter fresh water in the Everglades and a few spots in the Florida Keys. At such times, the water may look inviting, but don't take a chance. Many of Florida's inland bodies of water may be tainted with *Giardia lamblia,* a nasty little parasite that is most commonly transmitted through mammal feces. The resulting illness, **giardiasis,** can result in severe stomach cramps, vomiting, and diarrhea. While Halizone tablets, bleach, and other chemical purifiers may be effective against such organisms, your best bet will be to use an adequate water filter (which filters down to 0.4 micron or less) or boil the water for at least five minutes.

Insects

With the prevalence of marshes and beaches in southern Florida, you'll find a wide array of insects in this region, from harmless ones like dragonflies to more bothersome critters. Perhaps the biggest concerns are **mosquitoes** and **fire ants,** whose stings can cause itchy red welts, or worse.

Mosquitoes are typically more prevalent during the wet season (May.–Oct.), especially during the summer months, when the humidity is at its worst. To protect against these relentless creatures, you should use a combination of defenses, including light-colored clothing, long-sleeved shirts, long pants, closed shoes, scent-free deodorant, and insect repellents containing DEET. In addition, you should avoid grassy areas and shady places. Instead, seek open, breezy locales, especially out on the water, and avoid peak hours for mosquito activity, namely sunrise and sunset. Also, try to open and close your car doors quickly, and keep your car windows rolled up, as there's little worse than being stuck in a vehicle with a roving, bloodthirsty mosquito.

Of course, if you are stung by a mosquito, you should be fine—unless you have an unforeseen allergy or the mosquito is a carrier for a disease like the West Nile virus. Beyond cleaning the affected area and treating it with calamine lotion, hydrocortisone cream, or aloe vera gel, all you can do is take some anti-inflammatory or antihistamine medication for the pain and swelling and wait for the skin to heal.

Fire ants, meanwhile, are large, aggressive red ants prevalent in tropical areas, such as southern Florida. Often nesting in moist soil near riverbanks, ponds, highways, and watered lawns, these ants are capable of building large, dome-shaped mounds. They are also inclined to inflict painful stings, whose aftereffects can be deadly to small animals and sensitive humans. To protect yourself and your pets, try to avoid fire ant colonies. If, however, you are stung by an ant—or several—avoid scratching the affected area and instead treat any bumps with a hydrocortisone cream or aloe vera gel. In addition, you can take an antihistamine medication to reduce the itching. Individuals who experience severe reactions, such as chest pain, nausea, sweating, loss of breath, serious swelling, and slurred speech, should consult a doctor or hospital immediately upon contact.

Plants

While hiking amid southern Florida's forests, marshes, and beaches, be careful where you step. It's easier than you think to trip on a root or other obstruction. In addition, unless you're certain that you've found a patch of recognizable fruit, you should refrain from digesting any tempting berries, flowers, plants, and the like without first consulting local residents or expert field guides.

Wild Animals

Since much of southern Florida comprises undeveloped marshes and forests, not to mention the surrounding waters, you're bound to encounter wild animals at times. While many of these, such as the iguanas and roosters that roam the streets of Key West, are fairly harmless, more dangerous creatures, such as alligators and Florida panthers, live here, too. To avoid perilous encounters with such animals, don't venture into places like the Everglades by yourself and try to observe all wildlife from a distance. In addition, although it should go without saying, you should never taunt, disturb, or feed any of the wildlife that you see.

Heatstroke

Hot, sunny days are common in southern Florida, and it's crucial that you prepare for them. Although sunscreen will help to prevent sunburn (which, if experienced often, can cause long-term problems for your skin), you must apply it frequently and liberally. Prolonged sun exposure, high temperatures, and little water consumption can also cause dehydration, which can lead to heat exhaustion—a harmful condition whereby your internal cooling system begins to shut down. Symptoms may include clammy skin, weakness, vomiting, and abnormal body temperature. In such instances, you must lie down in the shade, remove restrictive clothing, and drink some water.

If you do not treat heat exhaustion promptly, your condition can worsen quickly, leading to heatstroke (or sunstroke)—a dangerous condition whereby your internal body temperature starts to rise to a potentially fatal level.

© DANIEL MARTONE

An American alligator keeps a wary eye on tourists.

Symptoms can include dizziness, vomiting, diarrhea, abnormal breathing and blood pressure, cessation of sweating, headache, and confusion. If any of these occur, you must be taken to a hospital as soon as possible. In the meantime, your companions should move you into the shade; remove your clothing; lower your body temperature with cool water, damp sheets, or fans; and try to give you some water to drink, if you're able.

Hurricanes

One of the biggest concerns for travelers to southern Florida is, of course, the possibility of facing a hurricane, especially in an isolated place like the Florida Keys. Generally, the Atlantic hurricane season runs from June through November, though hurricanes have certainly occurred beyond this time frame. The best advice is to stock up on extra water, flashlights, batteries, and other supplies during the season, develop a possible exit strategy, and keep apprised of the weather at all times. Although most radio and television stations provide weather updates, the **National Weather Service** (1315 White St., Key West, 305/295-1316, www.srh.noaa.gov/key) also offers a weather hotline (305/294-7380), where you'll hear recorded forecasts, including information about tropical storms and hurricanes.

MEDICAL SERVICES

While southern Florida might feel a bit isolated at times, especially deep in the Everglades and down in the Florida Keys, expert medical services are never too far away. So, although you can utilize free services like **MD Travel Health** (www.mdtravelhealth.com) to learn about infectious diseases and illness prevention in the United States, it's good to know that in-person care is available throughout southern Florida.

Emergency Care

All of Florida is tied into the **911** emergency system. Dial 911 free from any telephone (including pay phones) to reach an operator who can quickly dispatch local police, fire, or ambulance services. While this service also works from cellular phones, be aware that you may find it difficult to make calls from the Everglades, Florida Keys backcountry, or offshore waters, where reliable cellular service isn't always guaranteed.

Hospitals and Pharmacies

If you experience an illness or injury while traveling through southern Florida, rest assured that, as with other U.S. states, hospitals abound even in the Florida Keys. Some of these area hospitals include **Mercy Hospital** (3663 S. Miami Ave., Miami, 305/854-4400, www.mercymiami.org), **Mariners Hospital** (91500 Overseas Hwy., Tavernier, 305/434-3000, www.baptisthealth.net), **Fishermen's Hospital** (3301 Overseas Hwy., Marathon, 305/743-5533, www.fishermenshospital.com), and the **Lower Keys Medical Center** (5900 College Rd., Key West, 305/294-5531, www.lkmc.com). Just be advised that most medical facilities will require you to have insurance or make a partial payment before admitting you for treatment or dispensing medication.

If you need to fill a prescription, you can do so at various pharmacies throughout southern Florida. Besides pharmacies like **Walgreens** (800/925-4733, www.walgreens.com), you'll find that several area grocery stores, such as **Winn-Dixie** (866/946-6349, www.winndixie.com) and **Publix** (800/242-1227, www.publix.com), have on-site pharmacies, too. If you're a foreign visitor with medical concerns, feel free to take advantage of the region's 24-hour, multilingual tourist assistance by phoning 800/771-5397.

Insurance

Although you might be the sort of traveler who likes to live dangerously, insurance is highly recommended while traveling in southern Florida. Whether you're a U.S. citizen driving your own car or an international traveler in a rented RV, you should invest in medical, travel, and automotive insurance before embarking upon your trip—to protect yourself as well as your assets. Research your insurance options and choose the policies that best suit your

HURRICANE CHECKLIST

Some out-of-towners are apprehensive about visiting the Florida Keys during the Atlantic hurricane season, which usually runs from June 1 to November 30. The truth is, however, that hurricanes are infrequent in this region, and many of the most popular events, such as Hemingway Days and Fantasy Fest, occur during this half of the year. Nevertheless, it's always a good idea to be prepared for the worst. So, if you do plan to visit the Florida Keys during hurricane season – whether for a quick getaway or an extended stay – keep apprised of weather updates and be prepared to evacuate if necessary.

In addition, you should stock up on certain essentials in advance, as you'll surely face long lines and depleted supplies once the storm threatens. Listed here are some suggested items, which will come in handy whether you're forced to stay through the storm or you find yourself stuck in an evacuation route. Of course, this isn't an exhaustive list, so be sure to set aside whatever else you might need, including photo albums, important papers, pet supplies, asthma inhalers, or other key items.

FOOD SUPPLIES

In general, you should have a two-week supply of nonperishable foods, especially low-salt and low-fat items that will minimize your thirst. Necessary goods, some of which must be purchased just before the storm, include:

- drinking water (one gallon per person daily) and ice

- nonrefrigerated juice and milk boxes

- canned and powdered milk

- powdered or canned beverages (coffee, fruit juice, etc.)

- prepared foods (canned soups, corned beef hash, tuna, etc.)

- canned fruit and vegetables

- dried fruit

- snacks (crackers, cookies, nuts, etc.)

- snack spreads (peanut butter, fruit preserves, etc.)

- raw vegetables

- sugar, salt, and pepper

- bread and cereals

- dry and canned pet food if necessary

KITCHEN SUPPLIES

The following items will be especially handy if you have to evacuate to a strange place, such as an ill-equipped motel:

- bottle opener

- manual can opener

- pocketknife

- matches in a plastic bag

- camp stove and canned cooking fuel

- ice chest or cooler

- paper plates and napkins

- plastic cups and utensils

HARDWARE

Most of the following items will only be necessary if you live in the Florida Keys year-round or stay here for extended periods of time:

- hammer and nails

- screwdrivers and screws

- power screwdriver

- shovel and pickax

- sheets of exterior plywood to board up windows

- plastic sheeting to cover furniture

- rope and duct tape

- sturdy working gloves

- canvas tarps

MEDICAL NEEDS AND TOILETRIES

Given that drugstores will be mobbed just before a storm and closed for days afterward, it's always advisable to collect the following items ahead of time, along with a two-week supply of prescription drugs:

- first-aid kit and first-aid handbook
- over-the-counter cold and allergy medicine
- children's medicines if necessary
- aspirin
- diarrhea and constipation medication
- insect repellent sprays and candles
- insect bite lotion
- bandages, sterile rolls, and adhesive tape
- cotton-tipped swabs
- antiseptic and disinfectant
- tweezers and needles
- plastic bags and jugs to store extra ice and water
- water filter and purification tablets
- Medic Alert tags
- soap and shampoo
- deodorant
- sunscreen
- feminine hygiene products
- emergency toilet (small, lidded garbage can with disinfectant, deodorizer, and plastic bags as liners)

BABY NEEDS

Obviously, the following items will only apply to those with children:

- disposable diapers
- baby wipes
- diaper-rash ointment or petroleum jelly
- baby cold and pain medication
- medicine dropper
- extra formula and baby food

HURRICANE KIT

Typically, it's a good idea to assemble this kit as soon as possible and store it in a cool, dry place. Be sure, too, to refresh the stock when necessary. Important items include:

- flashlights
- extra bulbs and batteries
- battery-operated radio or television
- battery-operated lanterns
- battery-operated clock
- working fire extinguishers
- waterproof matches
- plastic garbage bags
- scissors
- toilet paper
- rain gear and extra clothes
- swamp boots
- inexpensive, rabbit ears–style television antenna
- area maps
- list of emergency and nonemergency phone numbers
- copies of insurance policies

needs and budget. For travel insurance (which should include medical coverage), consider **SafeMex Travel Insurance & Assistance** (www.safemex.com).

CRIME AND POLICE

Despite the crime-ridden reputation of Miami, most of southern Florida is a relatively safe, laid-back place. People here are, for the most part, friendly and helpful. Still, whether you're visiting Miami's South Beach, Everglades City, Big Pine Key, or Key West, it's important to take precautions.

Never leave valuables in plain view on a car seat; secure them in the trunk, where they're less tempting to thieves. Similarly, in case of an accident on the highway, do not abandon your vehicle, as this might also invite thieves. When sightseeing, keep your money, credit cards, identification, and other important items hidden on your person; purses and backpacks are much easier to steal. Bicycles should be secured properly whenever they're left unattended, and just to be on the safe side, lock your hotel and car doors at all times.

Although the Florida Keys are definitely safer than most urban areas in the United States, it's still prudent to be aware of your surroundings. For instance, you should always stay alert when walking alone at night, especially on poorly lit, residential streets in Key West. As in other tourist hot spots in America, muggings have been known to happen here.

If you're traveling via RV, do not boondock alone in an isolated place. Try to stay in an RV park, a campground, or, at the very least, a well-lit parking lot. When venturing into the Everglades, for instance, try to camp with others. If you do find yourself in trouble, don't hesitate to find a phone and dial **911.** Of course, the time it takes police and emergency vehicles to reach you will depend upon your location.

While in the Keys, if you witness a crime of any kind, feel free to contact **Crime Stoppers of the Keys** (800/346-8477, www.tipsubmit. com) to offer an anonymous tip. Likewise, you can always consult the **Monroe County Sheriff's Office** (305/853-3211 or 305/292-7000, www.keysso.net).

Information and Services

Although southern Florida—especially the Everglades and the Florida Keys—often feels isolated from the rest of the country, you're not as secluded as you might think. In fact, you'll find plenty of necessary resources here, from helpful chambers of commerce to well-stocked post offices.

MAPS AND TOURIST INFORMATION

For general information on traveling in southern Florida, your best source is the state-run **Visit Florida** (850/488-5607 or 866/972-5280, www.visitflorida.com). Your call will be answered by a live person who can send you brochures and field your questions about festivals, activities, lodgings, and more. You may find it even more convenient to surf the website, which offers a comprehensive database of communities, accommodations, activities, golf courses, beaches, parks, attractions, shops, events, restaurants, and other aspects of southern Florida. You'll even find free maps and the latest deals here. Just be aware that some of the information can be out-of-date, so always call ahead when making travel plans.

Suggested Maps

In a state known for its tourism industry, you'll find no shortage of helpful maps, including Florida's official transportation map (www.thefloridamap.com). For more detailed information, you should consider purchasing a map from **AAA** (800/564-6222, www.aaa. com), which offers both a Florida state map ($4.95 nonmembers, members free) and a

Miami/Miami Beach map ($4.95 nonmembers, members free) that features smaller maps of Key West and the Florida Keys. **Rand McNally** (800/678-7263, www.randmcnally. com) also produces several helpful maps, including a folded Florida map ($4.95) and an EasyFinder Map to Miami ($7.95).

For more detail, **DeLorme** (800/642-0970, www.delorme.com) produces the *Florida Atlas & Gazetteer,* which divides the state into 102 large-scale maps, complete with GPS coordinates. Though the 15-inch-long format is unwieldy for hikers, it's a great resource for planning your trip; it even identifies historic sites, state parks, public beaches, and other points of interest throughout southern Florida. You can find it at many regional bookstores and gas stations for $19.95.

If you'll be exploring the backcountry, you should order an official topographical (topo) map produced by the **U.S. Geological Survey** (888/275-8747, www.usgs.gov). Florida's national parks have topo maps for sale at their visitor centers or ranger stations. Anglers will especially appreciate topo maps as well as nautical charts, such as those produced by **US Chart Services, Inc.** (930 SW 4th St., Fort Lauderdale, 954/524-6566, www.uschartservices.com). These free, full-color reproductions of official **National Oceanic and Atmospheric Administration (NOAA)** (800/638-8972, www.noaa.gov) charts of the Florida Keys are available at many local marine businesses.

Tourism Bureaus and Visitor Centers

In addition to **Visit Florida** (850/488-5607 or 866/972-5280, www.visitflorida.com), you'll find several helpful convention and visitors bureaus (CVBs) or chambers of commerce in southern Florida. To reach local tourism offices, consult the **Florida Association of Convention and Visitor Bureaus** (www. facvb.org) or simply contact the tourism bureaus directly.

On the Florida mainland, the **Naples, Marco Island, Everglades Convention & Visitors Bureau** (2800 Horseshoe Dr., Naples, FL 34104, 239/225-1013 or 800/688-3600, www. paradisecoast.com, 9 A.M.–5 P.M. Mon.–Fri.), the **Everglades Area Chamber of Commerce** (P.O. Box 130, Everglades City, FL 34139, 239/695-3172, www.evergladeschamber.net, 9 A.M.–4 P.M. daily), and the **Greater Miami Convention & Visitors Bureau (GMCVB)** (701 Brickell Ave., Ste. 2700, Miami, FL 33131, 305/539-3000 or 800/933-8448, www.miamiandbeaches.com, 8:30 A.M.–5 P.M. Mon.–Fri.) are all helpful resources.

For information about the Florida Keys, contact the **Monroe County Tourist Development Council** (1201 White St., Ste. 102, Key West, FL 33040, 305/296-1552 or 800/352-5397, www.fla-keys.com, 9 A.M.–5 P.M. Mon.–Fri.). To learn more about the Upper Keys, consult the **Key Largo Chamber of Commerce and Florida Keys Visitor Center** (106000 Overseas Hwy., Key Largo, FL 33037, 305/451-4747 or 800/822-1088, www.keylargo.org or www. keylargochamber.org, 9 A.M.–6 P.M. daily) or the **Islamorada Chamber of Commerce and Visitors Center** (P.O. Box 915, Islamorada, FL 33036, 305/664-4503 or 800/322-5397, www. islamoradachamber.com, 9 A.M.–5 P.M. Mon.–Fri., 9 A.M.–4 P.M. Sat., 9 A.M.–3 P.M. Sun.) on the bay side of Upper Matecumbe Key, near mile marker 83.2. For information about the Middle Keys, contact the **Greater Marathon Chamber of Commerce and Visitors Center** (12222 Overseas Hwy., Marathon, FL 33050, 305/743-5417 or 800/262-7284, www.floridakeysmarathon.com, 9 A.M.–5 P.M. daily). To learn more about the Lower Keys and Key West, consult the **Lower Keys Chamber of Commerce** (31020 Overseas Hwy., Big Pine Key, FL 33043, 305/872-2411 or 800/872-3722, www.lowerkeyschamber.com, 9 A.M.–5 P.M. Mon.–Fri., 9 A.M.–3 P.M. Sat.) or the **Key West Chamber of Commerce** (510 Greene St., 1st Fl., Key West, FL 33040, 305/294-2587, www. keywestchamber.org, 8 A.M.–6:30 P.M. daily).

COMMUNICATIONS AND MEDIA
Postal and Shipping Services

In southern Florida, a post office is never

terribly far away, especially via car, so it's easy to purchase stamps, receive mail (via "General Delivery" for temporary visitors), and send letters and packages all around the world. To locate a post office in Miami, the Everglades, and the Florida Keys, consult the **United States Postal Service** (800/275-8777, www.usps.com) or refer to the destination chapters in this guide.

If you need to send a package quickly (and cost isn't an issue), you'll also find plenty of shipping stores throughout southern Florida, including **The UPS Store** (99611 Overseas Hwy., Key Largo, 305/453-4877). For more information about shipping locations and services, contact **The UPS Store** (www.theupsstore.com) or **PostNet** (www.postnet.com).

Phones and Internet Access

Public pay phones can be found throughout southern Florida—at airports, gas stations, stores, bars, restaurants, hotels, and so forth. To place a call, listen for a dial tone, deposit the necessary coins, and dial the desired number (including 1 and the area code, if you're making a long-distance call). In the case of an emergency, you can dial 911 at no charge. For international calls, it's probably best to use a prepaid phone card, which you can often purchase in gas stations or convenience stores. To figure out the correct international calling code, visit www.countrycodes.com.

Nowadays, a cell phone is a necessary tool for travelers. It can make it easier to get roadside assistance, call an establishment for directions, and seek help in an emergency situation. Just be advised that cellular reception might be unreliable when you're traveling in the backcountry or in offshore waters.

As for the Internet, it's hard to imagine the days when travel was possible without it. With the help of a computer and a modem, you can research the Everglades' native flora, book a fishing charter, monitor the day's weather, view the menu of a Key West restaurant, and perform a host of other duties. Access to your own laptop can make such tasks even more convenient, especially since several of Florida's hotels, restaurants, and other establishments offer wireless

Internet access nowadays. Internet cafés also make it difficult to stay out of touch for long—especially down in Key West. Just remember that not all websites are updated regularly. Consult local residents or contact businesses directly before making any firm travel plans.

Publications and TV/Radio

You'll find publications throughout southern Florida, including daily newspapers like the *Miami Herald* (www.miamiherald.com), the *Florida Keys Keynoter* (www.keysnet.com), and the *Key West Citizen* (www.keysnews.com), plus monthly magazines, such as *Florida Monthly* (www.floridamagazine.com), *Florida Travel + Life* (www.floridatravellife.com), and *Time Out Magazine* (www.thekeyshookup.com). Such periodicals are terrific sources of information for festivals, restaurants, sporting events, outdoor activities, and other diversions.

Local television and radio stations, such as Key West's popular **US-1 Radio** (104.1 FM, http://us1radio.com), are also excellent sources for regional information, including up-to-the-minute weather details during hurricane season. Pick up a newspaper in your area for a list of channels.

MONEY
Currency and Credit Cards

Bank debit cards and major credit cards (like Visa and MasterCard) are accepted throughout southern Florida, even in the smallest towns. In addition, automated teller machines (ATMs) have become more prevalent, allowing travelers to withdraw cash whenever they need it. If you're uncomfortable using ATMs, you're sure to find a bank open during regular business hours (9 A.M.–4 P.M. daily) and sometimes on the weekend. That said, you'll need cash at self-registration campgrounds, and many independent motels, eateries, and stores will accept only cash or traveler's checks. As any wise traveler knows, you should never rely exclusively on plastic.

Foreign currency can be exchanged at all branches of the **First State Bank of the**

Florida Keys (www.keysbank.com) branches. For up-to-date exchange rates, consult www.xe.com.

Banks and ATMs

Throughout southern Florida, you'll find numerous automated teller machines (ATMs) at restaurants, stores, and other establishments, offering convenient access to your money. In addition, most regional banks provide access to ATMs inside and outside their branches. In Miami, there are several different banks available, including the **First Bank of Miami** (800/831-5763, www.firstbankmiami.com), which offers five branches in the Miami area. **TIB Bank** (800/233-6330, www.tibbank.com), meanwhile, has branches throughout southern Florida, including two in Naples, two in Homestead, and several in the Upper, Middle, and Lower Florida Keys. Also in the Florida Keys, you'll encounter several branches of the **First State Bank of the Florida Keys** (www.keysbank.com), from Key Largo to Key West.

Sales Tax

In southern Florida, most goods and services, save for perhaps movie tickets, often cost more than their listed price. That's due, of course, to state taxes—specifically, the 6 percent sales tax on taxable retail items and services, such as clothing and sightseeing tours.

Tipping

Although the amount of a gratuity depends on the level of service received, general tipping guidelines exist in Florida (and throughout the United States). Typically, restaurant servers should receive 15–20 percent of the entire bill, while pizza delivery drivers should receive at least 10 percent. In addition, taxi and limousine drivers should receive at least 15 percent of the entire fare, while valets, porters, and skycaps should expect around $2 per vehicle or piece of luggage. The housekeeping staff members of your hotel, inn, or resort also deserve a tip; a generally accepted amount is $2 per night.

Remember that tour guides, fishing guides, boat captains, and other excursion operators

© LAURA MARTONE

TIB Bank branches can be found throughout the Keys.

should be tipped as well. In fact, no matter how much such tours or trips cost, the gratuity is never included in the quoted price. Of course, how much you choose to tip is entirely up to you. While the exact amount of a tip will depend on the cost, length, and nature of the trip in question—not to mention your satisfaction with the services received—it's generally accepted to tip between 10 and 20 percent of the overall cost of the trip. If a guide or operator makes an exceptional effort, such as unexpectedly extending the length of a trip, then it's highly recommended that you increase the size of your tip accordingly. Tipping badly in a close-knit place like the Florida Keys can harm your reputation among other guides and operators, while tipping well could ensure even better service the next time.

WEIGHTS AND MEASURES
Electricity
In southern Florida, most standard electrical outlets operate at 120 volts. So, if you're coming from Europe, Asia, or a country that operates at 220–240 volts, you'll need to bring an adapter in order to use your hair dryer, laptop, or other small appliance. Outlets here vary between the two-pronged and three-pronged variety, for which you might also need an adapter—easily purchased in any decent hardware or building supply store. In fact, you'll find several **Home Depot** (www.homedepot. com) stores in the Miami area, including one just north of the Florida Keys (13895 SW 288th St., Homestead, 786/243-1969, 6 A.M.– 10 P.M. Mon.–Sat., 8 A.M.–8 P.M. Sun.).

Time Zone
Miami, the Everglades, and the Florida Keys are all located in the eastern standard time (EST) zone. Florida also observes daylight saving time. So, adjust your watches and alarm clocks accordingly.

RESOURCES

Glossary

These regional terms and abbreviations will help you navigate Miami, the Everglades, and the Florida Keys – and perhaps better understand the region's unique people, culture, and ecology:

airboat a small, open boat driven by a caged, rear-mounted airplane propeller and capable of traveling at relatively high speeds through marshes and shallow water; also called a swamp boat

Alligator Alley a nickname for the stretch of I-75 that runs from Naples, through the Everglades, to Fort Lauderdale; also called Everglades Parkway

backcountry areas within the Everglades and the Florida Keys that consist of shallow water and islands close to shore, ideal for fishing and kayaking

bight a body of water bounded by a bend in the shore

bougainvillea a tropical vine that flourishes throughout the Florida Keys, usually ablaze with colorful white, fuchsia, or vermilion flowers; also known as paper flowers

brackish water a mixture of fresh and salt water

BS a commonly used abbreviation for addresses on the bay side of U.S. 1 in the Florida Keys

cafecito Cuban coffee without milk

chum a foul mixture of fish blood and diced fish parts, usually tossed into open water to lure fish to the area

coastal prairie a region of vegetation that lies between the tidal mud flats of Florida Bay and dry land

coconut telegraph the laid-back, word-of-mouth method by which news travels in the Florida Keys

conch a multipurpose term used to describe a marine gastropod, a Bahamian immigrant, or a native inhabitant of the Florida Keys

conch fritter a fried ball made with spices and ground conch meat, popular as an appetizer in the Florida Keys

Conch Republic a micronation declared as a protest secession of the Florida Keys from the United States in April 1982

cortadito Cuban coffee with steamed milk

C.R. a commonly used abbreviation for a county road

cracker a term that refers to the state's early settlers, who cracked long whips to herd cattle and oxen; now, informally used to designate a native-born Floridian

Creole a language infused with French, African, Arabic, Spanish, and Portuguese, often heard in Miami's Little Haiti

cubano a flattened, grilled sandwich made with sliced ham, slow-roasted pork, Swiss cheese, and pickles, popularized by Cuban immigrants who settled in Miami in the early 1900s

cypress dome a dense cluster of cypress trees in water-filled depressions, found in the Everglades and Big Cypress National Preserve

Duval crawl the local expression for stopping by each bar along Key West's Duval Street, which stretches from the Atlantic Ocean to the Gulf of Mexico

epiphyte a plant, such as an orchid, moss, or fern, that grows on the branches, trunks, and leaves of trees and derives its water and nutrients from the air

estuary a partially enclosed body of water along the coast, where the fresh water from a river mixes with the salt water of the ocean

eyebrow house a type of Key West domicile that has an overhanging porch roof, which conceals the upper front windows

fire ants large, aggressive red ants, prevalent in tropical areas, capable of building large mounds, and inclined to inflict painful stings

fishing guide a person who is knowledgeable enough to lead a hired charter and teach the passengers how to catch fish in a given region

flats shallow-water areas that compose most of the backcountry in the Everglades and the Florida Keys, often covered by sand, rocks, or grass

"Floribbean" cuisine Florida's hybrid cuisine, consisting of fresh Florida produce and seafood, with American, European, Caribbean, and Latin American influences

Florida fighting conch a feisty mollusk found in the southeastern United States, known for its tendency to fight with potential collectors and predators

Florida lobster a warm-water crustacean that, unlike its New England counterpart, has no claws; also called a rock lobster or spiny lobster

gingerbread architecture an elaborate Victorian-era style of construction, prevalent throughout Key West

Gold Coast the area that extends from Fort Lauderdale to Miami, popular among movie stars, musicians, and other wealthy celebrities

goombay a form of calypso music and dancing popular in the Bahamas; also refers to a type of Bahamian drum, held between the legs and played with the hands or sticks

grass flats shallow-water areas covered in grass

grits dried, ground corn kernels, typically boiled and served with a Southern-style breakfast

grouper a firm white fish, popular in the Florida Keys

Gulf Stream a swift, warm ocean current that originates off the coast of southern Florida in the Gulf of Mexico and continues along the East Coast toward the North Atlantic Current

gumbo limbo a fast-growing, salt-tolerant tropical tree, which flourishes in the Everglades and has featherlike leaves and a shiny red exfoliating bark; also called the tourist tree for its resemblance to a sunburn

hardwood hammock a dense growth of trees on a slightly elevated area above a marshy region, present in the Everglades and the Florida Keys

hush puppy a crunchy, cornmeal fritter popular in the South and typically served with fried seafood

Intracoastal Waterway (ICW) a 3,000-mile-long waterway, partly natural and partly artificial, along the Atlantic and Gulf Coasts of America, meant to protect small boats from the dangers of the open sea

island time the perception of a slower, more relaxed way of life on islands like Key West

key a low, offshore island composed of sand or coral, the name of which is derived from the Spanish word *cayo*, meaning "little island"

mahimahi a sweet, lean fish also known as a dorado or dolphinfish

manatee the endangered state marine mammal, a giant yet gentle vegetarian preferring warm waters; also called a sea cow

mangrove swamp a coastal marine swamp prevalent in southern Florida and dominated by tight thickets of red, black, and white mangrove trees

marsh a flat, flooded, treeless area in the Everglades, containing plants such as sawgrass and cattails

MM the abbreviation for "mile marker," how most Floridians designate addresses along U.S. 1 in the Florida Keys

no-see-um a tiny biting gnat that thrives in coastal areas, especially in the summer; also known as a punkie

Old Florida a term used to describe Florida prior to theme parks and other commercial developments; now refers to the state parks, sleepy villages, and vast wildlands that still exist

OS a commonly used abbreviation for addresses on the ocean side of U.S. 1 in the Florida Keys

Overseas Highway the popular term for the stretch of U.S. 1 that links many of the keys between Key Largo and Key West

patch reef an isolated coral formation closer to the coast than the main offshore reef and usually filled with fish

pineland a type of terrain in the Everglades that contains slash pine forest, saw palmettos, and a wide array of tropical plant varieties

red tide a periodic massive bloom of toxin-producing marine algae, which causes Gulf waters to appear brownish-red, suffocates fish, contaminates shellfish, and affects the respiration of susceptible individuals

riptide a potentially life-threatening tide that opposes other tides, causing a violent disturbance in the ocean

sandspur the seed of the sandspur plant, prevalent in grassy or sandy areas and resembling a little spiked ball; also called a sandbur

sawgrass any of several sedges that have spiny, serrated leaf blades and are prevalent in the Everglades

saw palmetto a hardy fan palm that has spiny leafstalks and can grow in large clumps, present in places as varied as hammocks and coastal sand dunes

sea grape a native, salt-tolerant plant that grows on Florida's beaches and helps to stabilize sand dunes

sea oat a wispy, salt-tolerant plant found along the Atlantic and Gulf Coasts, where it helps to protect the state's beach dunes from erosion

skunked an unfortunate condition whereby one returns to the dock after a fishing trip, without having caught any fish

slough a channel of slow-moving water in a marshland

snook a tropical inshore fish found in the Florida Keys and notoriously difficult to catch

snowbird anyone who vacations or lives in Florida during the winter months, usually from November to April, to escape the cold and snow in other parts of the country

Snuba an underwater breathing system, patented by Snuba International, that combines features of snorkeling and scuba diving

Spanglish a mix of Spanish and English, spoken by many Miami residents

Spanish moss a specific epiphyte that resembles a grayish, lacy cluster and typically hangs from oak trees

S.R. a commonly used abbreviation for a state road

stingray shuffle the method by which people shift their feet as they venture into Gulf waters to avoid inadvertently stepping on a camouflaged stingray

Tamiami Trail the alternative name for U.S. 41, which connects Tampa to Miami and traverses the Everglades

trolling a type of fishing by which baited lines or lures are towed slowly through the water behind the boat

Turtle Walk a state-organized nighttime event, usually held in June or July, when the public can view sea turtles nesting and hatching on Florida's shores

watershed a region drained by a river, a river system, or another body of water

wetland a lowland area saturated by surface or ground water, with vegetation adapted to such conditions, prevalent throughout the Everglades

Suggested Reading

While not an exhaustive list of titles, the following books will shed some light on the singular geography, history, culture, and offerings of Miami, the Everglades, and the Florida Keys. Peruse them before your trip, and bring a few along for the ride.

CUISINE

Whether you plan to dine out for every meal or rent a place with a kitchen, you'll find a handful of books dedicated to this region's unique cuisine.

Gassenheimer, Linda. *Keys Cuisine: Flavors of the Florida Keys.* New York: Grove/Atlantic, Inc., 1991. From conch fritters to key lime cheesecake, this cookbook contains many of the classic recipes popularized in the Florida Keys—some of which might be challenging to re-create without access to regional ingredients.

Herbenick, Fran. *Appetizing Appetizers from The Florida Keys.* Bloomington, IN: AuthorHouse, 2008. Compiled by a longtime resident of the Florida Keys, this collection features many of the treats found in this flavorful region, from crab fritters to Blackbeard's clam pie.

Raichlen, Steven. *Miami Spice: The New Florida Cuisine.* New York: Workman Publishing Company, Inc., 1993. Penned by a cooking teacher and cookbook author, this collection of lively recipes illustrates the Cuban, Caribbean, and Latin American influences on Miami's culinary arts.

Shearer, Victoria. *The Florida Keys Cookbook: Recipes and Foodways of Paradise.* Guilford, CT: The Globe Pequot Press, Inc., 2005. Written by an experienced travel and food journalist, this multicultural cookbook presents more than 175 regional recipes, from wasabi grilled grouper to Bahamian bread pudding.

Voltz, Jeanne, and Caroline Stuart. *The Florida Cookbook: From Gulf Coast Gumbo to Key Lime Pie.* New York: Knopf, 1996. Dividing the Sunshine State into six distinct regions, this collection includes southern Florida recipes like frog legs and conch salad.

FICTION AND PROSE

Fictional tales, personal essays, and travel memoirs—though no substitute for practical guidebooks—can definitely give travelers a tantalizing sense of the cultural and natural diversity of Miami, the Everglades, and the Florida Keys.

Cerulean, Susan, ed. *The Book of the Everglades.* Minneapolis: Milkweed Editions, 2002. Separating the Everglades into five regions, this lively anthology presents environmental, historical, and human-interest essays from a variety of authors, including Carl Hiaasen and Susan Orlean.

Corcoran, Tom. *The Mango Opera.* New York: St. Martin's Press, 1998. The first in a series of Key West–based mysteries, featuring photographer-turned-detective Alex Rutledge. Other titles in the series include *Gumbo Limbo, Bone Island Mambo, Octopus Alibi, Air Dance Iguana,* and *Hawk Channel Chase.*

Hall, Barbara D., and Jon C. Hall. *Shoestring: An Adventure in the Florida Keys.* Bloomington, IN: AuthorHouse, 2008. After his conniving wife bankrupts him, a troubled lawyer takes his sailboat on an unforgettable voyage to Key West, in the company of a cormorant named Shoestring—and with his wife's real husband in hot pursuit.

Hemingway, Ernest. *To Have and Have Not.* New York: Scribner, 1999. Originally published in 1937, this novel, which was partially inspired by the eccentric people Hemingway met in Key West, focuses on a fishing boat captain who runs contraband between

Cuba and Florida. Other books written during Hemingway's prolific Key West period include *A Farewell to Arms* (1929), *Death in the Afternoon* (1932), *Winner Take Nothing* (1933), *Green Hills of Africa* (1935), and *For Whom the Bell Tolls* (1940).

Hersey, John. *Key West Tales: Stories.* New York: Vintage, 1996. Published posthumously, these short stories offer a snapshot of ordinary Key West residents facing momentous events in their lives.

Hiaasen, Carl. *Tourist Season.* New York: G. P. Putnam's Sons, 1986. This madcap Miami mystery is one of several Florida-based capers written by popular *Miami Herald* columnist Carl Hiaasen, whose extensive bibliography includes *Native Tongue* (1991), which takes place in Key Largo, and *Nature Girl* (2005), a romp through the Everglades.

Katzenbach, John. *In the Heat of the Summer.* New York: Ballantine Books, 1982. Adapted for the screen as *The Mean Season,* this debut novel by a *Miami Herald* crime reporter features a dangerous cat-and-mouse game between a clever serial killer who is terrorizing Miami and the journalist who has captured his attention.

McDonald, Tracy. *Get Slick.* St. Augustine, FL: BluewaterPress, 2007. In this novel, a Key West developer faces a cast of quirky characters, from hippies to homeless people.

Molloy, Johnny. *Hiking the Florida Trail: 1,100 Miles, 78 Days, Two Pairs of Boots, and One Heck of an Adventure.* Gainesville, FL: University Press of Florida, 2008. During this incredible three-month-long journey, a veteran hiker experiences Big Cypress National Preserve firsthand.

Murphy, George, ed. *The Key West Reader: The Best of Key West's Writers, 1830–1990.* Key West: Tortugas, Ltd., 1989. This impressive collection features the work of some of Key West's most celebrated writers, from Ernest Hemingway to Hunter S. Thompson.

Murrell, Muriel V. *Miami: A Backward Glance.* Sarasota, FL: Pineapple Press, Inc., 2003. In this engrossing memoir, the author shares vignettes about her life in Miami, from the glitzy 1920s through the postwar 1950s.

Newhagen, Jane Louise. *Sand Dollar: A Tale of Old Key West.* Parker, CO: Outskirts Press, 2007. In this historical novel, a young woman must deal with the realities of married life in 19th-century Key West.

Orlean, Susan. *The Orchid Thief: A True Story of Beauty and Obsession.* New York: Random House, Inc., 1998. This quirky tale of orchid fanatics in the Fakahatchee Swamp inspired the film *Adaptation.*

Willeford, Charles. *Miami Blues.* New York: Ballantine Books, 1984. In the first of Willeford's well-known crime series, Hoke Moseley, a chronically depressed, unorthodox homicide detective, must pursue an ex-convict who has recently relocated to Miami and stolen Moseley's gun and badge.

GEOGRAPHY AND ECOLOGY

Several books aim to familiarize visitors with southern Florida's unique flora, fauna, and topography.

Alden, Peter, Rick Cech, and Gil Nelson. *National Audubon Society Field Guide to Florida.* New York: Knopf, 1998. This comprehensive guide unravels the state's natural history, teaches visitors how to identify varied habitats and organisms, and explores some of Florida's finest parks and preserves.

Alderson, Doug. *Encounters with Florida's Endangered Wildlife.* Gainesville, FL: University Press of Florida, 2010. Blending adventure with cultural and natural history, this book features the state's rare, threatened, and endangered wildlife, from panthers to manatees.

Bartlett, Richard D., and Patricia P. Bartlett. *Florida's Snakes: A Guide to Their Identification and Habits.* Gainesville, FL: University Press of Florida, 2003. A color photograph accompanies the description of each snake in this guide, which covers more than 85 species and subspecies.

Daniels, Jaret C. *Butterflies of Florida.* Cambridge, MN: Adventure Publications, Inc., 2003. Containing large color photographs, this easy-to-use field guide helps travelers identify butterflies in the wild.

Hammer, Roger L. *Everglades Wildflowers: A Field Guide to Wildflowers of the Historic Everglades, Including Big Cypress, Corkscrew, and Fakahatchee Swamps.* Guilford, CT: The Globe Pequot Press, Inc., 2002. This guide offers detailed plant descriptions, drawings, and photographs of roughly 300 common wildflowers in this fertile region.

Hammer, Roger L. *Florida Keys Wildflowers: A Guide to the Common Wildflowers of the Florida Keys.* Guilford, CT: The Globe Pequot Press, Inc., 2004. Featuring hundreds of color photographs, this guide provides detailed plant descriptions for botanists and amateurs alike.

Kaplan, Eugene H. *Peterson Field Guide to Coral Reefs: Caribbean and Florida.* New York: Houghton Mifflin Company, 1982. Visitors can use this guide to identify the fishes, sponges, mollusks, and corals of southern Florida.

Landau, Matthew, and Larry Gates. *Eco-Touring the Florida Keys.* Flagstaff, AZ: Best Publishing Company, 2005. This guide offers travelers an introduction to the ecosystems, plants, and marine mammals that define the Florida Keys.

Levin, Ted. *Liquid Land: A Journey Through the Florida Everglades.* Athens, GA: The University of Georgia Press, 2004. Based on extensive research, this book recounts the negative impacts of draining the Everglades and describes the controversial restoration plan that could revitalize these fragile wetlands.

Lodge, Thomas E. *The Everglades Handbook: Understanding the Ecosystem.* Boca Raton, FL: CRC Press LLC, 2005. This book provides a comprehensive understanding of the Everglades, including the history of human influence.

Myers, Ronald L., ed., and John J. Ewel, ed. *Ecosystems of Florida.* Orlando, FL: University of Central Florida Press, 1990. This book offers a comprehensive examination of Florida's habitats, from pine flatwoods to salt marshes to coral reefs.

Nellis, David W. *Poisonous Plants and Animals of Florida and the Caribbean.* Sarasota, FL: Pineapple Press, Inc., 1997. Filled with illustrated information about poisonous organisms, toxins, symptoms, and treatments, this guide is essential for any outdoor enthusiast.

Nelson, Gil. *The Ferns of Florida: A Reference and Field Guide.* Sarasota, FL: Pineapple Press, Inc., 2000. Filled with photos, this guide identifies the state's varied ferns.

Nelson, Gil. *The Shrubs & Woody Vines of Florida: A Reference and Field Guide.* Sarasota, FL: Pineapple Press, Inc., 1996. Containing numerous photos and drawings, this guide enables travelers to identify more than 550 woody vines and shrubs.

Nelson, Gil. *The Trees of Florida: A Reference and Field Guide.* Sarasota, FL: Pineapple Press, Inc., 1994. Packed with photos and drawings, this comprehensive guide features a variety of native and exotic trees.

Renz, Mark. *Fossiling in Florida: A Guide for Diggers and Divers.* Gainesville, FL: University Press of Florida, 1999. This book offers help in finding, identifying, and preserving fossils.

Ripple, Jeff. *The Florida Keys: The Natural Wonders of an Island Paradise.* Stillwater, MN: Voyageur Press, Inc., 1995. With this gorgeous book, travelers can learn about the island chain's natural history, from its formation as a living coral reef to the ways in which climate, storms, ocean currents, and other factors have shaped the Keys and their inhabitants.

Taylor, Walter Kingsley. *A Guide to Florida Grasses.* Gainesville, FL: University Press of Florida, 2009. With over 500 color images, this guide will assist hikers, plant enthusiasts, and professional botanists in identifying the varied grasses of the Sunshine State.

Tekiela, Stan. *Birds of Florida Field Guide.* Cambridge, MN: Adventure Publications, Inc., 2005. Birding enthusiasts will find this easy-to-use guide helpful for exploring the Sunshine State.

Winsberg, Morton D. *Florida Weather.* Gainesville, FL: University Press of Florida, 2003. This book explains the forces that control the state's climate and offers advice for dealing with seasonal hazards.

Witherington, Blair, and Dawn Witherington. *Florida's Living Beaches: A Guide for the Curious Beachcomber.* Sarasota, FL: Pineapple Press, Inc., 2007. Focusing on the natural history of Florida's beaches, this guide features a variety of animals, plants, minerals, and manmade objects.

Witherington, Blair, and Dawn Witherington. *Florida's Seashells: A Beachcomber's Guide.* Sarasota, FL: Pineapple Press, Inc., 2007. Color photographs and clear descriptions help beachcombers to identify 252 different seashells.

HISTORY AND CULTURE

History buffs, amateur sociologists, and curiosity seekers will find a varied selection of books about southern Florida's intriguing past—and the people that have made Miami, the Everglades, and the Florida Keys what they are today.

Biondi, Joann. *Miami Beach Memories: A Nostalgic Chronicle of Days Gone By.* Guilford, CT: The Globe Pequot Press, Inc., 2006. Enhanced by hundreds of archival photographs, this oral history features the memories of criminals, taxi drivers, strippers, actors, and others who experienced this colorful area between the 1920s and 1960s.

Born, George Walter. *Historic Florida Keys: An Illustrated History of Key West & the Keys.* San Antonio: Lammert Publications, Inc., 2003. Written by a Key West–based preservationist, this book celebrates over 500 years of Florida Keys history.

Bramson, Seth H. *Miami: The Magic City.* Charleston, SC: Arcadia Publishing, 2007. Written by a Miami native and respected historian, this book celebrates the colorful history of southern Florida's megalopolis.

Burke, J. Wills. *The Streets of Key West: A History Through Street Names.* Sarasota, FL: Pineapple Press, Inc., 2004. In this unique take on Key West's history, the author explores the people whose names now grace the city grid, from Truman to Whitehead.

Caemmerer, Alex. *The Houses of Key West.* Sarasota, FL: Pineapple Press, Inc., 1992. This full-color, photographic survey of Key West's architectural treasures celebrates the city's varied building styles, from eyebrow houses to Conch Victorians.

Carter, W. Hodding. *Stolen Water: Saving the Everglades from Its Friends, Foes, and Florida.* New York: Simon & Schuster, Inc., 2004. In this exploration of the Everglades and its complicated existence, the author includes encounters with native flora and fauna—plus naturalists, farmers, politicians, and swamp inhabitants.

Cox, Christopher. *A Key West Companion.* New York: St. Martin's Press, 1983. Numerous photographs and several essays illustrate this curious history of the Conch Republic.

Douglas, Marjory Stoneman. *The Everglades: River of Grass.* Sarasota, FL: Pineapple Press, Inc., 1997. Originally published in 1947, this book helped to draw much-needed public attention to the area's rich flora, fauna, and history and to muster support for the creation of Everglades National Park.

Frawley-Holler, Janis. *Key West Gardens and Their Stories.* Sarasota, FL: Pineapple Press, Inc., 2000. Full of color photographs, this book explores the history and features of Key West's lovely gardens.

Fuson, Robert H. *Juan Ponce de León and the Spanish Discovery of Puerto Rico and Florida.* Blacksburg, VA: The McDonald & Woodward Publishing Company, 2000. Filled with critical documents, original maps, and historical illustrations, this extensive biography chronicles the life of the infamous Spanish explorer, who might have been the first Spaniard to set foot on Floridian soil.

Grunwald, Michael. *The Swamp: The Everglades, Florida, and the Politics of Paradise.* New York: Simon & Schuster, Inc., 2006. Written by an award-winning *Washington Post* reporter, this well-researched book explores the modern history of the Everglades, from drainage attempts to restoration.

Gutelius, Scott, Marshall Stone, and Marcus Varner. *True Secrets of Key West Revealed!* Key West: Eden Entertainment Limited, Inc., 2003. Intended for trivia lovers, this reference guide offers bizarre facts such as pirate rules, building oddities, and questions that visitors should never ask.

Hiaasen, Carl, and Diane Stevenson, ed. *Kick Ass.* New York: Penguin Putnam, Inc., 1999.

Hiaasen's first collection of selected *Miami Herald* columns about development, corruption, and other facets of southern Florida.

Hiaasen, Carl, and Diane Stevenson, ed. *Paradise Screwed.* New York: Penguin Putnam, Inc., 2001. Hiaasen's second collection of selected *Miami Herald* columns about life in southern Florida, spanning 15 years.

Homan, Lynn M., and Thomas Reilly. *Key West and the Florida Keys.* Mount Pleasant, SC: Arcadia Publishing, 2006. A collection of historic postcards that illuminate the intriguing history of the Florida Keys.

Jinbo, Susan. *Diary of a Key West Innkeeper.* Key West: Phantom Press, 2007. The zany adventures of a Chicago couple who moved to Key West, purchased a guesthouse, and eventually opted for a quieter life.

King, Gregory W. *The Conch That Roared.* Lexington, KY: Weston & Wright Publishing Co., 2003. This spirited book chronicles the bizarre, true story of Key West's 1982 secession from the United States and the subsequent formation of the Conch Republic.

Linsley, Leslie. *Key West: A Tropical Lifestyle.* New York: The Monacelli Press, 2007. Filled with full-color photographs and anecdotes about homeowners, designers, and architects, this book illustrates the unique character of several Key West residences.

McCally, David. *The Everglades: An Environmental History.* Gainesville, FL: University Press of Florida, 2000. In exploring the formation, development, and history of the Everglades, the author crafts an argument for abandoning agriculture in order to save this fragile ecosystem.

McIver, Stuart B. *Hemingway's Key West.* Sarasota, FL: Pineapple Press, Inc., 2002. For Hemingway fans, this book offers intriguing biographical information about one of Key

West's most famous residents, plus a two-hour walking tour of the city.

Muir, Helen. *Miami, U.S.A.* Gainesville, FL: University Press of Florida, 2000. Written by an environmental journalist, this book chronicles the last four decades of this unique city, a mixture of refugees, retirees, and corporations.

Ogle, Maureen. *Key West: History of an Island of Dreams.* Gainesville, FL: University Press of Florida, 2006. This well-researched book covers the colorful, controversial history of the place formerly known as Bone Key—from its 19th-century days as a pirate haven to its modern incarnation as a tourist hot spot.

Oppel, Frank, ed. *Tales of Old Florida.* Secaucus, NJ: Book Sales, Inc., 1987. A collection of essays from 1870 to 1911, including stories about boat rides through the Everglades and John James Audubon's birding adventures in the Florida Keys.

Posner, Gerald. *Miami Babylon: Crime, Wealth, and Power—A Dispatch from the Beach.* New York: Simon & Schuster, Inc., 2009. Penned by an investigative journalist, this fresh, forceful narrative shows how Miami Beach evolved from a quiet resort into the convergence of crime, finance, politics, and hedonism.

Raymer, Dorothy, and Tom Corcoran, ed. *Key West Collection.* Key West: The Ketch & Yawl Press, 1999. Highlighted with photographs by the mystery writer Tom Corcoran, this colorful collection features three decades' worth of newspaper articles by Raymer, a columnist of *The Key West Citizen* from the late 1940s to the early 1980s.

Reid, Thomas. *America's Fortress: A History of Fort Jefferson, Dry Tortugas, Florida.* Gainesville, FL: University Press of Florida, 2006. A compelling narrative about the history of the "American Gibraltar," once the most heavily armed coastal defense fort in the United States.

Shell-Weiss, Melanie. *Coming to Miami: A Social History.* Gainesville, FL: University Press of Florida, 2009. Extensively researched, this book explores the groups that this multicultural city comprises, from Jewish pioneers to Bahamian immigrants to Cuban exiles.

Shultz, Christopher, and David Sloan. *Key West 101: Discovering Paradise.* Key West: Phantom Press, 2005. This humorous book describes plenty of intriguing facets about Key West, from drag queens to the coconut telegraph.

Shultz, Christopher, and David Sloan. *Quit Your Job and Move to Key West: The Complete Guide.* Key West: Phantom Press, 2005. An amusing look at life in Key West, with advice for relocating to this crazy town.

Sloan, David L. *Ghosts of Key West.* Key West: Phantom Press, 1998. Written by the founder of Key West Ghost Tours, this book contains 13 chilling stories about the spirits that supposedly haunt the Southernmost City.

Standiford, Les. *Last Train to Paradise: Henry Flagler and the Spectacular Rise and Fall of the Railroad That Crossed an Ocean.* New York: Three Rivers Press, 2002. The incredible, ill-fated history of Flagler's efforts to connect the Florida Keys to the mainland.

Suib, Michael, and Nancy Butler-Ross, ed. *Confessions of a Key West Cabby.* Key West: SeaStory Press, 2003. In this entertaining compilation, a taxi driver shares his quirky columns from *The Key West Citizen* and *The Miami Herald.*

Viele, John. *The Florida Keys: A History of the Pioneers.* Sarasota, FL: Pineapple Press, Inc., 1996. Though slightly outdated, this loving account offers a glimpse into the curious history of these legendary islands.

PARKS AND RECREATION

Outdoor enthusiasts will find several books geared toward exploring and camping amid the beaches, swamps, rivers, and islands of Miami, the Everglades, and the Florida Keys.

Burnham, Bill, and Mary Burnham. *Florida Keys Paddling Atlas.* Guilford, CT: The Globe Pequot Press, Inc., 2007. From Key Largo to Key West, this detailed color atlas provides helpful information for kayakers and other shallow-water explorers.

Clement, Skip, and Andrew Derr. *Fly Fishing the Florida Keys: The Guides' Guide.* Portland, OR: Frank Amato Publications, Inc., 2005. Beyond colorful maps and hundreds of images, this how-to guide offers plenty of helpful information, from fly-fishing techniques to game fish descriptions.

Conway, David. *Fishing Key West and the Lower Keys.* Gainesville, FL: University Press of Florida, 2009. Filled with local knowledge, tips, and techniques, this guide will help even first-time anglers navigate these bountiful waters.

Friend, Sandra. *50 Hikes in South Florida: Walks, Hikes, and Backpacking Trips in the Southern Florida Peninsula.* Woodstock, VT: The Countryman Press, 2003. This guide features hikes throughout southern Florida, including the Everglades and the Florida Keys.

Hammer, Roger L. *A FalconGuide to Everglades National Park and the Surrounding Area.* Guilford, CT: The Globe Pequot Press, Inc., 2005. Containing historical facts, detailed maps, trail descriptions, and other useful information, this guide helps hikers, bikers, kayakers, canoeists, and wildlife lovers explore this remarkable region.

Harrigan, William. *Lonely Planet Diving & Snorkeling Florida Keys.* Footscray, Victoria, Australia: Lonely Planet Publications, 2006. Filled with maps and color images, this guide offers detailed diving information about 64 underwater sites, including shipwrecks and coral reefs.

Jewell, Susan D. *Exploring Wild South Florida: A Guide to Finding the Natural Areas and Wildlife of the Southern Peninsula and the Florida Keys.* Sarasota, FL: Pineapple Press, Inc., 2002. This comprehensive guidebook contains information about southern Florida's habitats, wildlife, parks, and recreational opportunities.

Keogh, Bill. *Florida Keys Paddling Guide: From Key Largo to Key West.* Woodstock, VT: The Countryman Press, 2004. Written by the owner of Big Pine Kayak Adventures, this guide offers route suggestions through this paddler's paradise, plus safety tips and information about regional wildlife and habitats.

Molloy, Johnny. *A Paddler's Guide to Everglades National Park.* Gainesville, FL: University Press of Florida, 2009. Filled with detailed maps and information about campsites, dangerous routes, wind challenges, and packing requirements, this guide reveals the pleasures and pitfalls of canoeing and kayaking through the Everglades.

Moore, Marilyn. *Moon Florida Camping: The Complete Guide to Tent and RV Camping.* Emeryville, CA: Avalon Travel Publishing, 2007. This comprehensive campground directory also contains advice on hiking trails, fishing spots, and other nearby attractions.

O'Keefe, Timothy. *Hiking South Florida and the Keys: A Guide to 39 Great Walking and Hiking Adventures.* Guilford, CT: The Globe Pequot Press, Inc., 2009. Containing detailed information about a wide range of hikes, this user-friendly guide includes excursions through Everglades National Park, Big Cypress National Preserve, John Pennekamp Coral Reef State Park, and the National Key Deer Refuge.

Patton, Kathleen. *Kayaking the Keys: 50 Great Paddling Adventures in Florida's Southernmost Archipelago.* Gainesville, FL: University Press of Florida, 2002. Packed with detailed maps and concise descriptions, this guide features a range of trips, from short paddles to overnight excursions.

Ripple, Jeff. *Day Paddling Florida's 10,000 Islands and Big Cypress Swamp.* Woodstock, VT: The Countryman Press, 2004. In addition to featuring trips for canoeists and kayakers, this guide includes information about equipment, outfitters, low-impact paddling, and the area's history and ecology.

Strutin, Michal. *Florida State Parks: A Complete Recreation Guide.* Seattle: The Mountaineers Books, 2000. Featuring Florida's entire state park system, this illustrated guide covers a wide array of activities, from canoeing in Fakahatchee Strand State Preserve to snorkeling in John Pennekamp Coral Reef State Park.

Valentine, James, and D. Bruce Means. *Florida Magnificent Wilderness: State Lands, Parks, and Natural Areas.* Sarasota, FL: Pineapple Press, Inc., 2006. Divided into six sections and filled with full-color images, this book provides a stunning journey through Florida's most precious wild areas.

Young, Claiborne S., and Morgan Stinemetz. *Cruising the Florida Keys.* Gretna, LA: Pelican Publishing Company, 2006. Offering reliable advice about traveling from the Port of Miami to the Dry Tortugas, this updated edition includes information about marinas, anchorages, restaurants, attractions, and other facilities.

REGIONAL TRAVEL

Mainstream travel guides typically offer details about southern Florida's towns, attractions, restaurants, and shops.

Goodwin-Nguyen, Sarah. *Key West: A Guide to Florida's Southernmost City.* New York: Channel Lake, Inc., 2009. This recently revised guide contains information about the city's beaches, restaurants, hotels, and attractions.

Muirhead, Marsh. *Key West Explained: A Guide for the Traveler.* Bemidji, MN: The Island Journal Press, 2008. This guidebook offers a little of everything, from historical facts to romantic tips to details about transportation, hotels, restaurants, and bars.

Reiley, Laura. *Moon Florida Gulf Coast.* Berkeley, CA: Avalon Travel, 2008. Among other Gulf Coast destinations, this guidebook includes information about Everglades City and its environs.

Williams, Joy. *The Florida Keys: A History & Guide.* New York: Random House, Inc., 2003. Illustrated by Robert Carawan and written by a part-time resident of Key West, this guide provides details about the Upper, Middle, and Lower Keys, including little-known spots.

Suggested Viewing

Southern Florida has long been a favorite spot for filmmakers. While sultry Miami has received most of the screen time—especially in television shows such as *Flipper* (1964–1967), *Miami Vice* (1984–1990), *CSI: Miami* (2002–present), *Dexter* (2006–present), and *Burn Notice* (2007–present)—places like the Everglades and Key West have also served as unique cinematic backdrops. Before traveling to southern Florida, take the time to view some of these selected films and experience the way others have interpreted this intriguing region.

Adaptation (2002). Written by Charlie Kaufman. Directed by Spike Jonze. Starring Nicolas Cage, Meryl Streep, Chris Cooper, and Tilda Swinton. Inspired by Susan Orlean's book *The Orchid Thief,* this award-winning film features a troubled screenwriter, a curious journalist, and an eccentric plant dealer in Florida's Fakahatchee Strand State Preserve.

Any Given Sunday (1999). Written by John Logan and Oliver Stone. Directed by Oliver Stone. Starring Al Pacino, Cameron Diaz, Dennis Quaid, Jamie Foxx, and James Woods. Filmed throughout Miami, this sports drama offers a behind-the-scenes look at the struggles between an aging coach, a quarterback legend, an arrogant rookie, and the young female owner of a professional Miami football team.

The Bellboy (1960). Written and directed by Jerry Lewis. Starring Jerry Lewis. In this madcap comedy, a mute, clumsy bellboy causes one mishap after another at the luxurious Fontainebleau Hotel in Miami Beach.

The Birdcage (1996). Written by Elaine May. Directed by Mike Nichols. Starring Robin Williams, Nathan Lane, Gene Hackman, Dianne Wiest, and Calista Flockhart. Based on the French comedy *La Cage Aux Folles,* this version features a gay cabaret owner in Miami's South Beach, who, with his drag queen companion, must feign heterosexuality in order to meet his son's future in-laws.

Clambake (1967). Written by Arthur Browne Jr. Directed by Arthur H. Nadel. Starring Elvis Presley and Shelley Fabares. In this musical comedy, shot throughout Miami, the Everglades, and the Florida Keys, the heir to an oil fortune trades places with a water-ski instructor at a Florida hotel in order to meet a girl who likes him for more than his father's wealth.

CrissCross (1992). Written by Scott Sommer. Directed by Chris Menges. Starring Goldie Hawn, Arliss Howard, David Arnott, James Gammon, and Keith Carradine. Filmed at Eden House and throughout Key West, this 1960s-era drama focuses on a young boy's efforts to stop his mother from stripping at a local topless bar.

Flipper (1963). Written by Arthur Weiss. Directed by James B. Clark. Starring Chuck Connors, Luke Halpin, and Kathleen Maguire. After enduring the ill effects of a red tide and a hurricane in the Florida Keys, a young boy finds an injured dolphin, nurses him back to health, and tries to convince his parents to let Flipper stay. This movie was partially filmed on Grassy Key, using several dolphins from the Dolphin Research Center.

Key Largo (1948). Written by Richard Brooks and John Huston. Directed by John Huston. Starring Humphrey Bogart, Edward G. Robinson, Lauren Bacall, Lionel Barrymore, and Claire Trevor. To honor the memory of a fallen friend, a former soldier travels to a run-down Key Largo hotel, where he's forced to confront a mob of gangsters during a hurricane.

Licence to Kill (1989). Written by Michael G. Wilson and Richard Maibaum. Directed by John Glen. Starring Timothy Dalton, Carey Lowell, Robert Davi, and Talisa Soto. After attending his friend's wedding in the Florida Keys, James Bond must go rogue in order to pursue a malevolent drug lord. Several key locales appear in this film, including the Ernest Hemingway Home, the Key West Lighthouse, and the Overseas Highway.

The Mean Season (1985). Written by Leon Piedmont. Directed by Phillip Borsos. Starring Kurt Russell, Mariel Hemingway, and Richard Jordan. In this taut thriller, inspired by John Katzenbach's debut novel *In the Heat of the Summer* and partially filmed in Everglades National Park, a serial killer lures a Miami reporter into a twisted game of cat-and-mouse.

Miami Blues (1990). Written and directed by George Armitage. Starring Alec Baldwin, Fred Ward, and Jennifer Jason Leigh. In this film, based on a detective novel by Charles Willeford, a released prisoner decides to start over in Miami, where he begins a violent one-man crime wave.

Miami Vice (2006). Written and directed by Michael Mann. Starring Colin Farrell, Jamie Foxx, and Naomie Harris. Inspired by the popular 1980s television series, this updated version features the romantic and professional complications of two Miami vice detectives, Crockett and Tubbs, while undercover as off-shore boat racers and outlaw smugglers.

Reap the Wild Wind (1942). Written by Alan Le May, Charles Bennett, and Jesse Lasky Jr. Directed by Cecil B. DeMille. Starring John Wayne, Ray Milland, Paulette Goddard, and Raymond Massey. Two ship salvage companies dispute ownership of the vessels that wreck upon the shoals of Key West in the 1840s.

Running Scared (1986). Written by Gary De-Vore and Jimmy Huston. Directed by Peter Hyams. Starring Gregory Hines, Billy Crystal, Steven Bauer, Jimmy Smits, Joe Pantoliano, Dan Hedaya, and Darlanne Fluegel. After vacationing in Key West, two streetwise Chicago cops return to the Windy City to battle a drug kingpin before retiring to the Florida Keys.

Scarface (1983). Written by Oliver Stone. Directed by Brian de Palma. Starring Al Pacino, Steven Bauer, Michelle Pfeiffer, and Mary Elizabeth Mastrantonio. In this violent remake of the 1932 classic, a Cuban refugee builds a powerful drug empire in modern-day Miami, only to let arrogance and paranoia cause his downfall.

True Lies (1994). Written and directed by James Cameron. Starring Arnold Schwarzenegger, Jamie Lee Curtis, Tom Arnold, Tia Carrere, and Eliza Dushku. In this big-budget remake of a French film, a secret agent must travel to the Florida Keys to stop a terrorist and save his marriage. The film's climax takes place on Florida's Seven Mile Bridge.

Internet Resources

CUISINE AND TRAVEL

Everglades Area
Chamber of Commerce
www.evergladeschamber.net
Use this website to find information about airboat tours, fishing guides, campgrounds, attractions, restaurants, gas stations, and other businesses in the Everglades.

The Florida Keys
www.floridakeys.com
This helpful website offers lodging, dining, and activity advice for those traveling to Key Largo, Islamorada, Marathon, Big Pine Key, and Key West.

Florida Keys Dining Guide
www.keysdining.com
This directory contains a wealth of bar and restaurant information for Key Largo, Islamorada, Marathon, and Key West, towns that especially favor conch, key lime pie, and seasonal seafood like stone crab claws, Florida lobster, and various fish.

The Florida Keys & Key West
www.fla-keys.com
Serving as the official website for the Monroe County Tourist Development Council, this portal provides information about the region's accommodations, restaurants, attractions, events, and recreational opportunities, plus interactive maps and advice about weather, hurricanes, weddings, and traveling with disabilities.

Florida Keys Treasures
www.floridakeystreasures.com
In addition to tourism information about the varied regions that compose the Florida Keys, you'll find regional recipes for treats like alligator tacos and key lime pie.

Florida Monthly
www.floridamagazine.com
The official website of *Florida Monthly* magazine contains plenty of information regarding the state's restaurants, festivals, and other facets.

Florida Travel + Life
www.floridatravellife.com
Here, you can check out the latest issue of *Florida Travel + Life* and even purchase past issues.

Gay Key West
www.gaykeywestfl.com
Operated by the Key West Business Guild, this website supports gay-friendly accommodations, events, and businesses.

Greater Marathon
Chamber of Commerce
www.floridakeysmarathon.com
Visitors can use this website to look up places to stay, eat, shop, and explore on the islands that Marathon comprises.

Greater Miami
Convention & Visitors Bureau
www.miamiandbeaches.com
This website features a wealth of information about accommodations, attractions, events, dining options, and special offers in the Miami area.

Islamorada Chamber of Commerce
www.islamoradachamber.com
Visitors will find listings of events, shops, restaurants, activities, accommodations, and water sports that pertain to the "sportfishing capital of the world."

Key Largo Chamber of Commerce
www.keylargo.org
Visitors can check this website for lodging, dining, shopping, and activity suggestions in the Key Largo area.

Key West Chamber of Commerce
www.keywestchamber.org
Here, travelers will find information about accommodations, restaurants, activities, events, and festivals in Key West.

Lower Keys Chamber of Commerce
www.lowerkeyschamber.com
This website provides information about activities, events, restaurants, and accommodations on and around Big Pine Key.

Visit Florida
www.visitflorida.com
You'll find a wealth of dining, lodging, and recreational information through this website, the official source for travel planning in the Sunshine State.

GENERAL INFORMATION
MyFlorida.com
www.myflorida.com
Through Florida's official website, you can look up state government agencies, research attractions and professional sports, locate highway construction, check campground availability, purchase fishing and hunting licenses, and even learn more about the state's landmarks and history.

U.S. Department of State
www.travel.state.gov
U.S. citizens can use this website to travel safely, via cruise or flight, to other countries, while international travelers will find guidelines for flying into and out of Florida.

HISTORY AND CULTURE
Division of Historical Resources
www.flheritage.com
History buffs will find information about the state's archaeological sites, historical markers, and past events.

Miccosukee Seminole Nation
www.miccosukeeseminolenation.com
This website offers historical information about the Miccosukee Seminole Indians, who now dwell in the Florida Everglades and operate one of the area's few casino resorts.

University Press of Florida
www.upf.com
Peruse this website for a wealth of Florida-related books—from biographies to field guides—that shed light on the state's history and culture.

PARKS AND RECREATION
Florida Department of Environmental Protection
www.dep.state.fl.us
The official DEP website includes information about Florida's state parks and trails system.

Florida Fish and Wildlife Conservation Commission
www.myfwc.com
Boaters, anglers, and hunters can find a slew of helpful information—from safety tips to wildlife facts to necessary regulations—on this comprehensive website.

Florida Keys Boating
www.floridakeysboating.com
This directory features a wide array of information for those interested in boating, fishing, diving, sailing, and other water sports in the Florida Keys.

The Florida Keys Fishing Directory
www.fishfloridakeys.com
This directory will assist anglers in finding fishing guides, charters, and boat rentals throughout the Florida Keys; included here are articles about specific fish, a fishing calendar, and information regarding weather, tides, lodging, and dining.

Florida Keys National Marine Sanctuary
www.floridakeys.noaa.gov
Snorkelers and scuba divers will find helpful information about the underwater features that compose this sanctuary, from the waters beside Biscayne National Park to the area around the Dry Tortugas.

Florida Sportsman Magazine
www.floridasportsman.com
Check this website for local fishing reports in the waters around Miami, the Everglades, and the Florida Keys.

Florida State Parks
www.floridastateparks.org
From this recreational portal, you'll learn everything you need to know about hiking, biking, boating, fishing, snorkeling, camping, horseback riding, and other activities in Florida's state parks and preserves. Also included here are maps, directions, and information regarding lodging, visitor centers, ecology, and history.

GORP
www.gorp.com
An in-depth portal for adventure travel and outdoor recreation, this website is an invaluable resource for information about campgrounds, national parks, recreational activities, and outdoor gear. You'll find plenty of Florida-related content here, including a Key West Weekender Guide.

National Park Service
www.nps.gov
The National Park Service provides detailed maps, brochures, and contact information for each of its nearly 400 parks, monuments, recreation areas, trails, and other natural and cultural sites throughout the United States. Use the state-by-state search function to learn more about southern Florida's protected places, including Biscayne National Park, Big Cypress National Preserve, Everglades National Park, and Dry Tortugas National Park.

Save-A-Turtle
www.save-a-turtle.org
This nonprofit organization educates the public about preserving rare and endangered marine turtles in the Florida Keys.

Save the Manatee Club
www.savethemanatee.org
This nonprofit organization teaches residents and visitors ways to protect the endangered manatee, the state's official marine mammal.

U.S. Coast Guard's Boating Safety Division
www.uscgboating.org
Use this comprehensive website to prevent accidents and fatalities while boating in southern Florida.

U.S. Fish & Wildlife Service
www.fws.gov
Here, you can find useful information about southern Florida's endangered species, such as the Florida panther and West Indian manatee, as well as details regarding wildlife refuges like the Crocodile Lake National Wildlife Refuge and National Key Deer Refuge, both in the Florida Keys.

Index

List of Maps

Acknowledgments

While it seems impossible to thank all of the people who contributed to this guide, I promise to give it a try.

Between family vacations as a child and more recent travels with my husband, Daniel, I've ventured to southern Florida many times over the years. During every stay, Dan and I have encountered plenty of friendly, helpful residents, usually willing to point us in the right direction—for the best key lime pie, the least crowded beach, or whatever else we sought at the time. So, thanks to everyone who's made each of our trips to Miami, the Everglades, and the Florida Keys a rejuvenating experience.

Of course, there are several folks to whom I'm particularly grateful. First, I offer a special thanks to the many hotel and resort owners, restaurant managers, park rangers, adventure outfitters, and tourism officials—especially Christina Baez—who made the job of compiling this guide a little easier. Thanks, too, to those who provided a few extra photographs for this book, and to the patient editors of Avalon Travel who offered valuable assistance during the preparation of this guide.

In addition, I'd like to thank my friends and family, all of whom have supported me during each of my frenzied writing projects. Most of all, I'm grateful to my husband, who supported me at each and every turn, even providing many of the images in this guide. As I often say, he's the best traveling companion a girl could ask for.

Lastly, I thank you, the reader. May your next trip to southern Florida, especially the Florida Keys, be as memorable as ours have been.

www.moon.com

DESTINATIONS | ACTIVITIES | BLOGS | MAPS | BOOKS

MOON.COM is ready to help plan your next trip! Filled with fresh trip ideas and strategies, author interviews, informative travel blogs, a detailed map library, and descriptions of all the Moon guidebooks, Moon.com is all you need to get out and explore the world—or even places in your own backyard. While at Moon.com, sign up for our monthly e-newsletter for updates on new releases, travel tips, and expert advice from our on-the-go Moon authors. As always, when you travel with Moon, expect an experience that is uncommon and truly unique.

MOON IS ON FACEBOOK—BECOME A FAN!
JOIN THE MOON PHOTO GROUP ON FLICKR

MAP SYMBOLS

Expressway	Highlight	Airfield	Golf Course
Primary Road	City/Town	Airport	Parking Area
Secondary Road	State Capital	Mountain	Archaeological Site
Unpaved Road	National Capital	Unique Natural Feature	Church
Trail	Point of Interest	Waterfall	Gas Station
Ferry	Accommodation	Park	Glacier
Railroad	Restaurant/Bar	Trailhead	Mangrove
Pedestrian Walkway	Other Location	Skiing Area	Reef
Stairs	Campground		Swamp

CONVERSION TABLES

°C = (°F − 32) / 1.8
°F = (°C x 1.8) + 32
1 inch = 2.54 centimeters (cm)
1 foot = 0.304 meters (m)
1 yard = 0.914 meters
1 mile = 1.6093 kilometers (km)
1 km = 0.6214 miles
1 fathom = 1.8288 m
1 chain = 20.1168 m
1 furlong = 201.168 m
1 acre = 0.4047 hectares
1 sq km = 100 hectares
1 sq mile = 2.59 square km
1 ounce = 28.35 grams
1 pound = 0.4536 kilograms
1 short ton = 0.90718 metric ton
1 short ton = 2,000 pounds
1 long ton = 1.016 metric tons
1 long ton = 2,240 pounds
1 metric ton = 1,000 kilograms
1 quart = 0.94635 liters
1 US gallon = 3.7854 liters
1 Imperial gallon = 4.5459 liters
1 nautical mile = 1.852 km

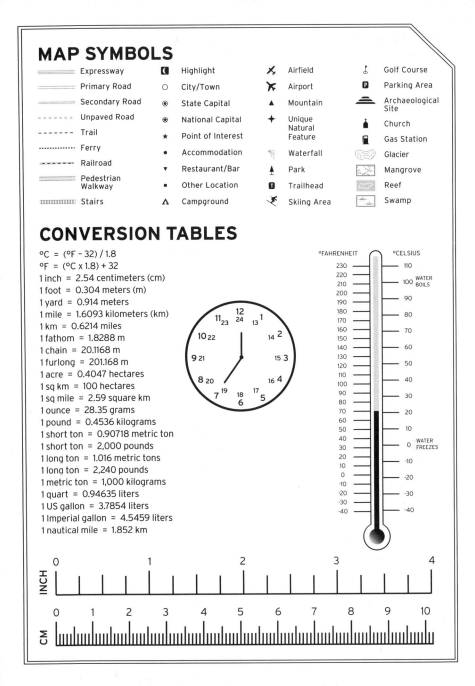

MOON FLORIDA KEYS

Avalon Travel
a member of the Perseus Books Group
1700 Fourth Street
Berkeley, CA 94710, USA
www.moon.com

Editor and Series Manager: Kathryn Ettinger
Copy Editor: Deana Shields
Graphics Coordinator: Darren Alessi
Production Coordinator: Darren Alessi
Cover Designer: Darren Alessi
Map Editor: Albert Angulo
Cartographers: Albert Angulo, Kat Bennett,
  Mike Morgenfeld
Indexer: Greg Jewett

ISBN: 978-1-59880-676-2
ISSN: 2158-1304

Printing History
1st Edition – January 2011
5 4 3 2 1

Text © 2011 by Laura Martone.
Maps © 2011 by Avalon Travel.
All rights reserved.

Some photos and illustrations are used by permission and are the property of the original copyright owners.

Front cover photo: Florida Everglades
  © PentaPictures / Alamy
Title page photo: © Daniel Martone
Interior color photos: Pages 4-5 © Daniel Martone; page 6 (inset) © Laura Martone, (bottom) © Daniel Martone; page 7 (top left) © Laura Martone, (top right) Courtesy of Greater Miami Convention & Visitors Bureau/www.gmcvb.com, (bottom left) © Daniel Martone, (bottom right) © Bob Care/Florida Keys News Bureau; pages 8, 10 © Daniel Martone; page 11 © Andy Newman/Florida Keys News Bureau/HO; page 12 Courtesy of Greater Miami Convention & Visitors Bureau/www.gmcvb.com; pages 14-15 © Daniel Martone; page 17 © Daniel Martone; page 18 © Laura Martone; page 19 © Daniel Martone; page 20 © Stephen Frink/Florida Keys News Bureau; page 21 © Daniel Martone; page 22 © Laura Martone; page 23 (top) © Daniel Martone, (bottom) © Laura Martone; page 24 © Haig Jacobs/Florida Keys News Bureau/HO

Printed in Canada by Friesens

KEEPING CURRENT

If you have a favorite gem you'd like to see included in the next edition, or see anything that needs updating, clarification, or correction, please drop us a line. Send your comments via email to feedback@moon.com, or use the address above.